READINGS IN MEDICAL SOCIOLOGY

DUANE A. MATCHA

Siena College

ALLYN AND BACON

Boston • London • Toronto • Sydney • Tokyo • Singapore

Senior Series Editor: Sarah L. Kelbaugh
Editor-in-Chief, Social Sciences: Karen Hanson
Series Editorial Assistant: Lori Flickinger
Marketing Manager: Jude Hall
Production Editor: Christopher H. Rawlings
Editorial-Production Service: Omegatype Typography, Inc.
Composition and Prepress Buyer: Linda Cox
Manufacturing Buyer: Julie McNeill
Cover Administrator: Jenny Hart
Electronic Composition: Omegatype Typography, Inc.

Library of Congress Cataloging-in-Publication Data

Readings in medical sociology / edited by Duane A. Matcha.
    p. cm.
    Issued to accompany: Medical sociology / Duane A. Matcha. 2000.
    Includes bibliographical references.
    ISBN 0-205-30861-9 (alk. paper)
    1. Social medicine.   2. Social medicine—Cross-cultural studies.   I. Matcha, Duane A. II. Matcha, Duane A. Medical sociology.

RA418.R373   2001
306.4'61—dc21

                                         00-038103

Printed in the United States of America

10 9 8 7 6 5 4 3 2 1   05 04 03 02 01 00

Credits appear on pages 467–468, which constitute an extension of the copyright page.

To Lisa and Annie,
two beautiful daughters who
far too quickly have grown
into young women

CONTENTS

Five years ago I began writing a textbook that addresses the cross-cultural breadth of medical sociology. After its publication in the summer of 1999, I began work on this supplementary reader, which, like the textbook, offers a cross-cultural perspective on medical sociology. Given the increased interest in the internationalization of health care, I believe that this reader is especially germane for a number of reasons.

First, advances continue to be made in medical technology. Biotechnology is revolutionizing not only how medicine is delivered but also what treatments patients receive. Much medical technology, however, is available only to individuals, corporations, or countries with the financial means necessary to purchase its ability to diagnose and heal. Thus, access to many of the life-extending and life-enhancing benefits that medical technology provides is generally limited, regardless of country. As a result, health inequalities persist not only within countries but among countries as well. The health of the global community remains divided between rich and poor, developed and developing nations. Health differences also exist between similar nations, such as the United States and other Organization for Economic Cooperation and Development (OECD) members. The United States spends a greater percentage of GDP on health care than do other industrialized nations but experiences poorer health outcomes in, for example, life expectancy and infant mortality. We also know that, regardless of the health care system, the development, purchase, and application of medical technologies significantly increase the cost of health care. The growth in medical technology during the last two decades of the twentieth century offers little reason to expect any slowdown in cost increases in the twenty-first century. The result will be an ever-growing proportion of GDPs being spent to purchase sophisticated medical technology that will not be applied equally among available populations. This increasing reliance on medical technology also raises bioethical questions about the boundaries of control: When is life-and-death decision making transferred from the patient to others (humans or machines)?

Second, many societies continue to experience a demographic transition that is resulting in an increasingly aged population. The populations of developing nations will slowly grow older, but many developed nations will face populations in which one out of every four or five citizens is over 65. An important question in the twenty-first century will be how health care systems will allocate funding for services to this segment of the population. Bearing on this point is the impact of medical technology on aging populations. Consider bioethical issues such as these: Who should have access to medical technology? When should the use of medical technology to extend or enhance life be discontinued? What is the relationship between the use of medical technology to extend or enhance life and the willingness of society to pay for such services? Answers to those questions are closely related to issues such as who will make such decisions and how are these decision-makers selected. Do these decision-makers represent the best interests of an aging population, the medical profession, funding agencies, the larger society?

Third, many developed nations are becoming increasingly culturally diverse. Although the emergence of multiple ethnic and racial groups enhances opportunities for the appreciation of cultural diversity, segments of all populations will continue to experience differential access to health care and thus different health outcomes. Consider, for example, a recent analysis of health care access in the United States on the basis of race and Hispanic origin. According to Kass, Weinick, and Monheit (1999), some one-third of Hispanics lack health insurance, compared with 22.9 percent of blacks and 13.1 percent of whites. More specifically, Hispanic males (37.2 percent) are most likely to be uninsured, and white females (11.9 percent) are most likely to be insured. In fact, females are more likely than males to be insured, regardless of race or Hispanic origin. These differences impact on the health status of these populations. Not surprisingly, Hispanics are most likely to identify their health status as fair or poor, with black Americans close behind; and white Americans are the least likely to consider their health status as fair or poor.

In the twenty-first century, it will become increasingly important to address the impact of technological and other changes on individual societies and on the larger social community. It is within this context that I developed this medical sociology reader. Although the work as a whole reflects a standard medical sociology format, each chapter contains three articles that present an American, a developed world (OECD classification), and a developing world perspective. Many of the articles incorporate one or more of the following sociological variables: age, sex, race and ethnicity, and social class. The purpose of this organization is to introduce students to a knowledge base that reflects the international breadth of medical sociology.

The book is divided into four parts. Part One, "The Historical Construction of Medical Sociology," consists of an introductory chapter, a chapter on the history of medicine, and a chapter on epidemiology. The four chapters in Part Two, "Health and Illness Behavior," cover health behavior, illness behavior, the sick role, and mental illness. The three chapters in Part Three, "Health Care Providers," cover physicians, nurses, and alternative medicine. The final part, "The Organization and Delivery of Health Care," covers hospitals, the financing of health care, and comparative health care systems, and it concludes with a chapter on the future of medical sociology.

These are exciting times for medical sociology. Regardless of one's area of interest, there is a wealth of opportunities (see, for example, the "Extra Issue" of the *Journal of Health and Social Behavior,* 1995), and access to the "electronic highway" is greatly expanding knowledge of health and illness within a social context. Such growth is not confined to the United States and other countries of the developed world. Rather, the sharing of information has become an increasingly global phenomenon. As a result, the twenty-first century will provide ample opportunities for medical sociologists to demonstrate their knowledge and skills.

ACKNOWLEDGMENTS

Many people aided in the development of this reader. Sarah Kelbaugh at Allyn and Bacon was particularly helpful throughout the process. The librarians at Siena College, as always, were superb (even though they were in the middle of a move to a new library).

Faculty or students who have any comments about this reader are welcome to contact me at *<matcha@siena.edu>*.

REFERENCES_____

Extra Issue. 1995. Forty Years of Medical Sociology: The State of the Art and Directions for the Future. *Journal of Health and Social Behavior.*

Kass, B. L., R. M. Weinick, and A. C. Monheit. 1999. Racial and Ethnic Differences in Health, 1996. MEPS *Chartbook No. 2.* AHCPR Pub. No. 99-0001. Rockville (MD): Agency for Health Care Policy and Research.

Matcha, Duane A. 2000. *Medical Sociology.* Boston: Allyn & Bacon.

PART ONE

THE HISTORICAL CONSTRUCTION OF MEDICAL SOCIOLOGY

CHAPTER 1

INTRODUCTION
A COMPARATIVE APPROACH

Chapter 1 is an introduction to medical sociology in the United States, Europe, and the developing world. As such, the chapter illustrates the objective of a comparative approach. Although all three articles examine the development of medical sociology, they do so relative to different population groups. The first two articles provide broad overviews regarding the development of medical sociology in the United States and Europe, and the third article addresses the paucity of medical sociology within the developing world. Although these articles examine the differential development of medical sociology worldwide, common threads link the material.

In the first article, David Mechanic provides an overview of medical sociology in the United States. He takes us beyond a historical analysis, however, as he examines concepts central to the development of medical sociology in the United States. Mechanic also examines some of the problems experienced by medical sociology in relation to economics and other disciplines as it attempts to reposition itself as a major player in the ever-changing field of health policy analysis. Finally, given the ongoing changes within the American health care system, Mechanic explores what medical sociology can offer the American health care community. He identifies issues that are core not only to medical sociology but also to sociology in general. For instance, he argues for greater study of institutional structures within the health care community and greater study of the relationship of those structures with the changing demographics within American society.

The second article is by Margot Jefferys, a pioneer in the development of medical sociology in Great Britain. Like Mechanic in the first article, Jefferys takes us beyond the historical and provides the social context within which medical sociology emerged in Great Britain. She identifies a number of changes that occurred in Western Europe after World War II that are of particular relevance to the emergence of medical sociology in Western Europe. For instance, reductions in the fertility and mortality rates altered the age structure of European nations. The result was a demographic shift toward increasingly older populations throughout the second half of the twentieth century. At the same time, nations were experiencing increased rates of mental health problems as a result of changes in their social and economic structures. Also, changes in cultural patterns, institutional structures, the provision of health care, and the physician/patient relationship all provided impetus to the emergence of medical sociology. Jefferys's discussions of medical optimism and the role of the state are particularly significant, for they offer a countervailing argument to the American view of the relationship between the state and its citizens relative to health care coverage.

The last article, by Eugene B. Gallagher, offers a view of medical sociology from a slightly different perspective. This article is actually an introductory piece for a 1989 special issue of the *Journal of Health and Social Behavior.* In it, Gallagher provides an overview and analysis of the articles located in the journal. Organizing the articles into cognate areas such as social factors in disease, and the organization of health services, Gallagher offers a snapshot of the relationship between medical sociology and the developing world. In that snapshot he identifies lack of concern with the developing world as well as rising expectations about health and health care among those living in the developing world as areas of importance to medical sociology. Though dated, this article forces us to examine some fundamentals of medical sociology. For example, are current research methodologies appropriate for the study of the third world? What are the differences between medical sociologists and medical anthropologists? These questions take us back to Mechanic as he questions the future role of medical sociology and its importance for health policy issues and to Jefferys and her discussion of the role of the state.

If the purpose of an introductory chapter is to whet the appetite of the reader, then these three articles make a compelling argument for a cross-cultural approach to medical sociology. On the one hand they all address the importance of medical sociology today and in the future. On the other hand, they also identify the intellectual challenges of medical sociology in the United States and throughout the world. Such recognition is helpful as the directions and future opportunities of medical sociology in the United States, in other nations of the developed world, and in the rapidly emerging developing countries of the world are located

AMERICAN PERSPECTIVE

SOCIAL RESEARCH IN HEALTH AND THE AMERICAN SOCIOPOLITICAL CONTEXT: THE CHANGING FORTUNES OF MEDICAL SOCIOLOGY

DAVID MECHANIC

The roots of important ideas in medical sociology can be traced back for centuries, but the discipline itself is a relatively contemporary one [1, 2] reflecting both core ideas in the parent discipline of sociology and the optimistic ideologies arising in the aftermath of World War II in relation to reconstruction and a desire for greater social equality. Thus, it should be no surprise to any thoughtful person that the fortunes of medical sociology, like other disciplines with public policy relevance, are tied intimately to prevailing values, attitudes and political dynamics. Medical sociology, as a field of sociology, emerged earlier than many of its sister health services sub-disciplines in economics, politics, geography, and the like. In the United States, where early development of medical sociology flourished, the National Institute of Mental Health, committed to a broad public health perspective in relation to mental health issues, supported training and research opportunities. This support greatly assisted the development of medical sociology, although much of its early focus was on mental health in contrast to general health issues. Although there was no single theory that informed medical sociological efforts, there were powerful conceptual frameworks that stimulated many early initiatives.

One dominant framework was based on the conception that disease and disability were in major ways products of material conditions of living, the social stratification of societies, and social inequalities among the varying strata. It was widely appreciated that life chances were highly contingent on one's social location at birth and the manner in which these social facts affected subsequent life trajectories. Even in areas where biological factors were seen as major causative influences, research in medical sociology sought to document broad and pervasive social influences. A classic study by Hollingshead and Redlich [3] gave impetus to such work in mental health in the 1950s and 1960s by demonstrating the importance of social class in the prevalence of treated mental illness, in the availability of treatment, in pathways into care, and in the types and continuity of care provided. Since that time, research in both psychiatric and social epidemiology has grown enormously, but most of these efforts are more narrowly framed than in earlier periods and are less focused on issues of social stratification and their implications for equitable care.

In the early years, the sick role was a powerful organizing concept, greatly influenced by Talcott Parsons' theoretical discussion in his book on *The Social System* [4]. Of particular importance was the hypothesis that the sick role served as a mode of tension-reduction and maintenance of social systems, and many of the early studies in this tradition sought to explore how the management of sickness by social groups as well as by individuals could serve societal as well as individual need. The classic study by Mark Field [5] on the manipulation of the sick role in the Soviet Union in the post-World War II years by both patients and government authorities was exemplary of this type of investigation. The study of sick-role behavior, and illness behavior more generally, also helped elucidate the complexity of illness presentation and treatment response, and contributed importantly to understanding the challenges in primary care and how effective care could be strengthened.

The study of illness behavior has become somewhat of a growth industry [6] but most current work neglects the structural implications related to how people define and respond to illness and how practitioners diagnose and manage such responses. Researchers from clinical disciplines, in particular, have stripped the concept of its social connections, and have used it, perhaps unwittingly, to further medicalize behavior. It is not uncommon for clinicians to seek to define 'abnormal' illness behavior [7], and to develop more refined diagnostic instruments of illness behavior to sort patients. Having been active in developing the original concept as an

approach to understanding variations of behavior in relation to adaptive needs and to the pressures of social and environmental contingencies, I have been surprised by requests from clinicians who seek from me a definition of diagnostic criteria or a formal system for classification of such behaviors. These requests reflect the medical perspective which seeks to classify syndromes for remedial intervention rather than to try and understand how variations in behavior come about [8]. In psychiatry, there is increasing emphasis on the measurement of somatization as a disorder [9] in contrast to studying these expressions as idioms of distress. While some investigators of illness presentations, such as Kleinman [10, 11] and Waitzkin [12], continue to seek their roots in social arrangements and explore the implications of illness behavior for the appropriate social role of clinicians, much of the work has become highly descriptive and separated from meaningful theoretical structures.

A third organizing principle of great importance in the early development of the discipline was that structures mattered, and that they could shape self-conceptions and meanings as well as behavior. Two important studies of mental hospitals by Stanton and Schwartz [13] and by Goffman [14] did much to encourage awareness of the importance of social arrangements for patient outcomes. Stanton and Schwartz directed attention to how the structure of professional relationships affected patient welfare. Goffman, in his theory of total institutions, suggested how the exercise of bureaucratic controls could restrict personal options so as to reshape self-identity. Although most public attention focussed on Goffman's substantive observations of the mental hospital, and their accuracy and generalizability, his more lasting contribution has been his powerful conceptualization of the potential ways in which total institutions affect self-conceptions and the extent to which institutions can be shaped to achieve varying social objectives.

In the areas noted, as well as many others defining the substance of medical sociology, there have been major advances in specifying research questions and research design, in sampling and measurement, and in analytic approaches. Often, however, the major integrating ideas that informed major perspectives are lost or ignored. Aspects of the larger conceptualizations most easily amenable to rigorous measurement and quantitative analysis were most likely to be retained, often divorced from their theoretical roots. As the decades went by, medical sociologists seemed less likely to ask the big questions, and when they did they were likely to be ignored not only by the larger public but also by their own colleagues. Those with sophisticated technical skills increasingly compete with others in related disciplines in health services research, social epidemiology, and public health for new research positions and opportunities, and often the outcomes of their research efforts are indistinguishable.

In a recent essay on policy and the politics of research in the United States, Daniel Fox [15] suggested that research on health affairs encompassed three competing normative frameworks: collective welfare, social conflict, and economizing. Researchers in the collective welfare framework see health as a social utility to be maximized and this perspective characterizes many who view health care from a planning framework. The social conflict perspective views health care outcomes emerging through the struggle among social classes and particularly appeals to those with Marxist sympathies. The economizing framework, in contrast, views the health care sector as a market governed by economic incentives and disincentives but influenced as well by professional and organizational behavior. Those operating within this framework seek to identify how to achieve improved efficiency, and are particularly sensitive to economic constraints. These descriptions, of course, are something of a caricature of complex points of view as Fox recognized, but his intent was to emphasize the extent to which research interests have shifted almost exclusively to an economizing perspective.

Medical sociology, which held a strong place among the disciplines in the 1950s and 1960s, lost ground relative to economics, particularly in the 1980s [2]. As the costs of medical care escalated in the United States following the implementation of Medicare and Medicaid, government increasingly turned away from issues of access and equity, areas of traditional concern to sociologists, toward a focus on cost-containment strategies. Beyond their professional interest in issues of cost-containment, economists share a powerful conception of supply and demand and of rational choice which, while often deficient in explanation, helps define a common core of interests and approaches. The health care system has become extraordinarily complex, and funders seeking solutions to immediate technical problems, most typically related to cost and other economic issues, prefer that researchers tackle delimited research problems amenable to sophisticated quantitative methods and modeling approaches. Consistent with pragmatic politics and financial constraints, they have less patience with researchers focused on humanistic issues or questions of social justice. Nor do they particularly like to hear that the problems of health, and those affecting disenfranchised groups such as the poor, the homeless, the uninsured and people with disabilities, are more due to our politics and social arrangements than the personal characteristics of those most affected. It is not that they lack sympathy with the plight of these groups but more that they see little room to maneuver within the constraints they view as relatively fixed. Suggestions falling outside these constraints, thus, seem likely to yield little payoff in investments of limited research dollars. Funding has been reasonably ample for those willing to address technical issues or to do their research within narrowly constrained objectives. But these parameters fit rather poorly the major perspectives and value preferences of many researchers who study social science issues in medicine.

In the 1980s, many of the optimistic assumptions that characterized post–World War II efforts and the social programs of the 1960s changed radically. There is now great skepticism about the potential of social reform and the value of social planning. Opinion makers and the population as a whole have less trust and faith in political leaders, experts, and the capacities of government bureaucracies. The view that markets provide the best signals of needs and wishes has gained wide currency even when applied to arenas like health that depart markedly from market assumptions [16]. And the types of individualism and promotion of self-interest consistent with these assumptions have gained a foothold sufficiently strong to undermine seriously the value of social action that extends beyond immediate interests. There is a debasement of cooperative values and instincts that have numerous ramifications, many neither obvious nor particularly political in any partisan sense.

In the United States, the destruction of the social bases of health insurance is perhaps the most serious consequence of these trends. The development of third party health insurance historically was a conservative response to the threat of a governmental system of health insurance [17] but nevertheless it sought to define community responsibility for sharing protection across wide sections of the population [18]. The concept of 'community rating' was social not only in that it involved sharing the risk of the costs of serious illness but it also reflected the value that those more vulnerable should pay no higher premium than others. Insurance, thus, was in a significant sense a community affair. The introduction of the idea of competitor encouraged insurers to segment markets, to use the lingo of the economic discipline, seeking to selectively enroll persons of low risk. It became increasingly difficult for small employers and the most vulnerable and needy persons to acquire insurance, contributing to the large ranks of uninsured persons. The motivation to avoid risk is now so dominant among insurers that persons who need protection the most face the largest barriers in acquiring health insurance.

The individualistic ethic, pervasive in so much of American life, also affects how broad health issues are seen. Much of the focus in public health is on seeking solutions to major health risks by urging individual responsibility and personal health action as compared with social and environmental remedies that address key health risks at their source. Unrealistic expectations about the potential of individual health decisions to determine future health are pervasive. The issue is not that it is unconstructive to urge people to refrain from smoking, substance abuse, poor nutrition habits and inactivity; these are clearly worthwhile endeavors. But there is a naïve conviction of the ease with which such changes are accomplished, even to the point of advocating financial penalties in the form of higher health insurance premiums for those who fail to conform. In contrast, there is little appreciation of the extent to which life imperatives and social opportunities and constraints either enhance or inhibit harmful personal behaviors [19]. Relative to personal behavior change, such alternatives as the improvement of living conditions, the development of new technologies, regulatory incentives, and environmental modifications receive little emphasis.

This is not to suggest, however, that there has been no progress at the social level. In many areas of concern to health, affected groups have organized to socially reconstruct expert conceptions, and those of the public, of their particular dilemmas. Perhaps most dramatic, symbolized by the passage of the Americans with Disabilities Act of 1989, has been the success of persons with disabilities in conveying politically that the loss of function connected with their impairments is as much a product of social barriers and restricted opportunities as it is due to inherent limitations. Families of the mentally ill, angry at facile psychodynamic theorizing by professionals blaming them for contributing to the disabilities of their family members, have organized nationally and are significantly altering the ways professionals relate to families. Mothers Against Drunk Driving (MADD) has put notable pressure on local law enforcement agencies to enforce existing statutes and have helped redefine public conceptions of the priority of this problem. Various groups have successfully lobbied to change the regulations affecting smoking in public places, and have contributed to a significant change in social norms. Major social movements, such as those for women's liberation and gay rights, have significantly contributed to reconceptualizing the nature of barriers these groups face from ones primarily defined as personal and health problems to issues of discrimination and blocked opportunities. All of the above represent social movements, and not social science, but in each case advocates could helpfully draw on important social science literature that provided helpful conceptualizations and facts vital to their missions.

THE ROLE OF SOCIAL SCIENCE

Research addressing broad societal issues, in contrast to delimited technical questions, rarely results in immediate applications or social change, and it would be naïve to expect otherwise [20]. The broader the issue, the more stake various groups have in its resolution, and political, in contrast to technical, considerations are likely to prevail. Research is a form of currency as varying interests negotiate a political resolution, but research is almost never definitive enough to resolve major issues on which strong political interests disagree. Taking a longer perspective, however, gives research a more important role than is immediately apparent.

A major function of social research is to develop the concepts and perspectives that shape how people come to conceptualize their worlds. Many of the social movements noted earlier where major changes occurred in how social problems were socially constructed, depended on frameworks and concepts of earlier social science efforts. These ideas filter into public consciousness indirectly by influencing the education of opinion makers and through them the public media and the political process. By the time these ideas became widely accepted they were seen as part of the cultural context, 'common sense' in the layperson's vernacular. But the 'common sense' of one era is quite different from another, and prevailing cultural perspectives tell us relatively little about the past or the future.

As a participant in medical sociology for more than 3 decades, I'm impressed with the extent to which research ideas, seen as quite foreign in the late 1950s, have been absorbed into the mainstream. Those who wish to emphasize the importance of research for social policy like to point to recent applications such as the use of Diagnostic Related Groups (DRGs) under Medicare or the current implementation of a relative-value fee schedule based on resource inputs [15]. These are highly complex payment systems affecting many billions of dollars of expenditures. But however important these innovations, they represent technical solutions to administrative challenges and are unlikely to stimulate new ways of approaching basic problems. In contrast, varying ideas about how medical care might be differently structured have concerned medical sociologists for decades. While most of us have a strong sense of the intractability of the medical care system, it is surprising how much of our thinking has come into the mainstream. Concerns of sociologists, once thought rather esoteric, such as patient's rights, choices in pregnancy and childbirth as well as in other types of care, the right to receive appropriate information about one's treatment, the misuses of medicine for social control, the misuses of technology, the importance of primary care and many others are now commonplace issues. Social scientists did much of the early work on how organization of care and payment arrangements affected access, utilization and outcomes, and on the development of group practice and HMOs. With HMOs now a major medical care alternative, it is easy to forget how recently they were thought of as 'medical soviets' or worse. When I began teaching about medical care there was a widespread conception that physicians had special expertise, indeed almost a monopoly, on matters of medical finance and organization. This would hardly be a respectable belief today.

There is little doubt that the questions researchers ask, and the way they conceptualize them, structure the types of answers that are possible. The types of questions that medical sociologists ask about social arrangements and the disadvantaged lost much of their appeal during the 1980s when the United States turned away from addressing issues of equity, a path followed by other Western countries as well, as they emulated the efficiency goals that were so much a part of the American health care rhetoric. In fact, while the rhetoric was about competition, the United States built the most elaborate health regulatory structure seen anywhere in the world. Such regulation in conjunction with the mirage of a free private marketplace, results in an extraordinarily wasteful administrative burden. There was a time when sociological studies that revealed the extraordinary gaps between statements of goals and organization and everyday realities were respectable and thought to be informative. By the 1980s there was little interest in research that revealed the emperor unclothed. As one high-ranking research administrator told me, "We can't learn anything useful from that kind of work." Such work however persists in altered forms, and has more recently been taken up in a variety of disciplines as the study of implementation processes [21, 22].

In the last two decades research within the economizing perspective has been dominant and pervasive, and so taken for granted that its assumptions are hardly seen as worthy of discussion. More recently, efforts to challenge these assumptions, as in the recent growth of behavioral and social economies [23], has gained ground, but has hardly impacted the mainstream of current health research. Thus, it is useful to more specifically examine some assumptions now dominating the medical care arena. In doing so, I pick for illustration perhaps the single most important social science study in the health field—the RAND Health Insurance Experiment (HIE). This randomized controlled study of varying co-insurance arrangements was carried out by an outstanding group of investigators who in the process have made important contributions to our knowledge.

At the time the RAND study was funded in 1973, national health insurance in the United States appeared imminent. The Congress was discussing a variety of proposals that would affect supply of services as well as demand. A decision not to fund the HIE, made in the Department of Health, Education and Welfare (now Health and Human Services), was overruled by the White House allegedly as part of an effort to delay a decision about national health insurance. The RAND researchers were explicit that the HIE had limited goals [24], and was not relevant to evaluating alternative proposals then being considered, but this distinction was not widely understood. Although it was clear that the HIE would provide valuable information, the design of the experiment greatly restricted the usefulness of the findings for predicting effects if a universal national system was put in place. It was apparent from the start that unlike a system of universal entitlements whose incentives would affect how health providers would respond, the complicated experimental variations affecting only a very small proportion of the populations in the communities studied would be unlikely to have significant, if any, impact on provider behavior. The study was focused on co-insurance effects in the care system as it existed, and could say little about how national changes might affect how health institutions and professionals organized and provided their services. In contrast, a major rationale for national health insurance is its opportunity to restructure how services are organized and provided.

Many important findings resulted from the HIE, but the single result that received largest attention, and has been repeatedly cited in academic journals, the policy literature and in the mass media, was that cost-sharing significantly reduced the demand for ambulatory medical care [25]. Further analyses suggested that the effects of cost-sharing on gross and not particularly sensitive measures of health status were minimal except among the poor who exhibited disadvantageous outcomes in the areas of blood pressure control and vision correction [26]. But, overall, these results supported the view that cost-sharing could lead to substantially reduced expenditure without major alterations in the public's health. Thus, the findings were commonly used to justify substantial increases in cost-sharing introduced in the 1980s, and were seen as vindication for those who advocated a market approach to health care.

Underlying the discussion of cost-sharing was an assumption made by many economists that consumers can make effective decisions about when they truly need medical care. The view was that cost-sharing made people more attentive decision-makers, thus reducing trivial and inappropriate requests for care. RAND analyses, however, which received far less attention and still are not widely known, showed that while copayment reduced the demand for medical care, it did not do so in a particularly discriminating way, reducing requests for care that would be appropriate and efficacious as much as care of little value [27]. In essence, the RAND analyses show that cost-sharing is a barrier to care that blocks access, irrespective of need or benefit, hardly a strong supporting argument for introducing strong market incentives into patients' health choices. It is testimony to the power of the economizing perspective that this result has been almost totally ignored.

THE FUTURE ROLE OF MEDICAL SOCIOLOGY

Focus on cost controls is unlikely to abate in western nations as increased knowledge and technology, growth of elderly populations, and public expectations will all contribute to escalating demands for services. It seems clear that a narrow perspective, unreceptive to consideration of significant structural changes, is likely to leave American health care in deep trouble.

Social science researchers have many roles in our current health system which will, no doubt, continue to develop [2]. They design and carry out many of the major national surveys that allow us to monitor changes in the health, utilization of services, and gaps in care. Working in collaboration with epidemiologists and researchers in medicine and public health, they seek to identify risk factors for varying diseases, preventive health behavior in-

itiatives, and effective ways of organizing services. They will continue to evaluate the implementation of health programs and the extent to which they meet defined objectives. These are all highly important and valued activities, but as we look toward the future it is important to also revitalize the role of critical scholarship in our efforts.

Health care as an institutional sector is greatly buffeted by the numerous economic and political forces that have a stake in the emerging structure. Health care is big business, and consumes an increasing proportion of gross domestic products throughout the world. The size and complexity of these highly dynamic health systems, subject both to rapid technological and economic changes, focuses attention on immediate administrative and managerial issues and away from basic questions of purpose and responsibility. There is little financial support for critical scholarship on these larger purposes, but these require attention nevertheless. The traditional role of medical sociology as a critical discipline that measures performance not only in terms of day-to-day objectives but in relation to deeper values needs revival. By critical I do not mean a debunking stance, an orientation sometimes attributed to the discipline [28]. In contrast, I refer to deeper scholarship that examines the direction and performance of health care institutions, and professional practices, in relation to our values, aspirations and ethical standards. Such scholarship must be technically proficient but also informed by historical perspective and interdisciplinary expertise.

While it may seem tangential to the current ideological trajectory, it is imperative to examine deeply the role of health institutions in modern societies with their changing demographics, household structures, economic processes and growing interdependence. How do changing community structures, religious institutions and transformations of communication and mass media affect the appropriate place of the health care sector and its roles in support and restoration as well as cure? How responsive are health institutions to the new types of health challenges and needs characteristic of modern societies? Given the aging of populations, and changing patterns of disease, what are the appropriate emphases on prevention, rehabilitation, maintenance, and caring relative to more acute care orientations? And how might health care institutions more appropriately address the roles of race, class, ethnicity, gender and age as major determinants of health status and outcomes?

It has been argued that the health care sectors in western countries redirected their attention to chronic disease as much as a half century ago, as configurations of illness changed with the reduction of common deadly infectious diseases [29]. While there has been much attention given to cancer, heart disease, and other chronic disease, the fundamental approach to prevention and care did not radically change, continuing to focus on intensity of service during the acute episode with relatively little in the way of prevention before the fact or rehabilitation and prevention of secondary disabilities. Risks of traditional illnesses among the young are now small, but the 'new morbidity' characterized by social pathologies related to risk-taking, violence and social disruption takes a large toll. Increasingly, we have a bimodal medical care challenge: 'new morbidities' predominate among the young; and irreversible chronic disease among the elderly. Since traditional medical care presently offers relatively little in dealing with social morbidities, health care systems have become predominantly highly technologically oriented elder care systems. But while elder care is basically a longitudinal care challenge of enhancing function and quality of life, most medical care remains focussed on the acute episode rather than on comprehensive longitudinal management.

Many agree that we require new approaches to the population's health, strategies that come to terms with personal, social and environmental risks and that fit the concept of chronic diseases as long-term developmental processes. Increasingly, we learn that aging and chronic disease are relatively independent processes, and that we often mistakenly attribute to aging deterioration associated with specific disease processes. Healthy aging requires intervention early in the processes of disease devel-

opment and subsequently throughout the life course. Once irreversible illness occurs, the challenge is to maintain function and independence responsive to people's goals and aspirations and not to medical imperatives. Increasingly we learn that the priorities of patients are quite different than those physicians believe them to be [30, 31].

Strong technological imperatives persist in medical care, even when the technical modalities have been demonstrated to be ineffective relative to more conservative care [32]. Whether this primarily results from the aggressive marketing of the medical care industries and motives of practitioners and institutions to maximize income and profits as some contend [12], or from the decision-making logic that physicians follow in taking care of patients, remains unclear. Certainly, all of these influences are important to some degree. There is need to explore thoroughly how these priorities might be altered and how to develop incentives consistent with broader social objectives that are not easily subverted.

Some would think it naïve to respond to the resistance to change in medical institutions by advocating more education given our awareness of the powerful economic and professional forces that keep medical care on its present trajectory. But the fact is that the technical imperative is sustained as much by public opinion and demands as it is by corporate and professional control. Surveys suggest persistent support among the public for technical innovation and application in medical care, and physicians often feel significant pressure from their patients to use these technologies and spare no efforts. This is reinforced by the manner in which the mass media report on new technical developments treating as major news promising indications from new experimental ventures. It is likely that those who follow these developments most closely and demand the newest technologies are those most educated. Thus, it seems clear that the issue is not only education but also the assumptions with which we approach issues of health and disease.

Education is, however, the single most important marker of the health of populations in both the developed and developing countries [33, 34]. Measures of education clearly represent a complex configuration of influences, and are closely tied to economic security, occupational status, styles of living, access to services, levels of knowledge, self-efficacy and self-esteem, and coping capacities [35]. Over the long run, changing health care assumptions involves changing culture itself, and improved education and consumer sophistication are crucial elements. The major impact of education may only be evident in the long course, but changing culture is a long-range endeavour, not susceptible to any quick fix.

Credible opinion leaders are necessary in any major educational efforts, and it is inevitable that physicians and other health professionals will retain the confidence of much of the public in matters of health. The study of professional socialization, and particularly medical education, was one of the areas of major focus in the early years of medical sociology and this initial interest needs some revival [36]. Changing the culture of medical care will require fundamental modifications in how health professionals approach their responsibilities, and the extent to which they feel responsible for the caring as well as the curing aspects of their roles. Sociological studies have repeatedly noted how the structure of the educational process, and the social system of the medical school, impeded communication and understanding between students and their educational mentors [37]. Students typically enter medical education with humane and caring motives, but increasingly become cynical as they confront the demands of their training programs. In the United States, and elsewhere I suspect, there is deep dissatisfaction with medical education among deans, faculty and students. The public, also, commonly complains of the lack of a caring attitude. Correcting failures in medical care processes depends more on structural arrangements than on teaching the values of caring more effectively. Developing the appropriate structures, however, depends critically on the attitudes of physicians and their sympathies for

the priorities and commitments these structures represent.

In the context of the dominant economizing perspective, medical sociology and the questions it typically addresses, sits on the periphery of policymakers' concerns. Yet the challenges we face in both the short and long term make it obvious that if we did not have a sociology of medicine and health, we would have to develop one. Despite our affluence, inequalities in health care are growing, and some disadvantaged groups are losing ground even in an absolute sense [38]. A significant proportion of the American population is uninsured or underinsured and economic jockeying among insurers and providers has demolished the concept of health as a community responsibility. We lack a viable approach in the United States for developing an appropriate longterm care structure or financing it [39]. Care for the chronically ill, and particularly such stigmatized groups as the mentally ill, substance abusers, and people with disabilities and AIDS, is highly fragmented. Strategies for prevention and to address the 'new morbidity' are underdeveloped and have low priority. Our medical practices are wasteful and administratively burdensome.

We should have no illusions. Medical care is a very large business that touches the interests of large segments of our population who depend on the sector for their livelihoods and economic survival. Even the most obvious needs, such as closing ineffective and outmoded institutions, meet protracted resistance from unions and communities. Much of the public still feels well served by existing medical institutions, which makes the challenge of responding to those whose needs are poorly addressed or not at all even more difficult. Medicine is now such a large part of interdependent economies that changes in medicine have important ramifications throughout societies. Despite these obstacles, we do a great service by reiterating our goals and the gaps between rhetoric and reality, eliciting the facts and reporting them as honestly as we can, and offering constructive directions for improved and more effective health services.

REFERENCES

1. Bloom S. W. Institutional trends in medical sociology. *J. Hlth Soc. Behav.* **27,** 265–276, 1986.
2. Mechanic D. The role of sociology in health affairs. *Hlth Aff.* **9,** 85–97, 1990.
3. Hollingshead A. and Redlich F. C. *Social Class and Mental Illness: A Community Study.* Wiley, New York, 1958.
4. Parsons T. *The Social System.* Free Press, New York, 1951.
5. Field M. *Doctor and Patient in Soviet Russia.* Harvard University Press, Cambridge, 1957.
6. McHugh S. and Vallis T. M. (Eds) *Illness Behavior: A Multidisciplinary Model.* Plenum, New York, 1986.
7. Pilowsky I. A general classification of abnormal illness behavior. *Br. J. Med. Psychol.* **51,** 131–137, 1978.
8. Mechanic D. *Medical Sociology,* 2nd ed., pp. 95–117. Free Press, New York, 1978.
9. Smith G. R. Jr. *Somatization Disorder in the Medical Setting.* National Institute of Mental Health, Rockville, MD, 1990.
10. Kleinman A. *Social Origins of Distress and Disease: Depression, Neurasthenia and Pain in Modern China.* Yale, New Haven, 1986.
11. Kleinman A. *The Illness Narratives: Suffering, Healing and the Human Condition.* Basic Books, New York, 1988.
12. Waitzkin H. and Britt T. Changing the structure of medical discourse: Implications of cross-national comparisons. *J. Hlth Soc. Behav.* **30,** 436–449, 1989.
13. Stanton A. H. and Schwartz M. S. *The Mental Hospital: A Study of Institutional Participation in Psychiatric Illness and Treatment.* Basic Books, New York, 1954.
14. Goffman E. *Asylums: Essays on the Social Situation of Mental Patients and Other Inmates.* Doubleday–Anchor, Garden City, NY, 1961.
15. Fox D. Health policy and the politics of research in the United States. *J. Polit. Pol. Law* **15,** 481–499, 1990.
16. Mechanic D. The medical marketplace and its delivery failures. In *Public Interest Law: An Economic and Institutional Analysis* (Edited by Weisbrod B. in collaboration with Handler J. F. and Komesar N. K.), pp. 350–374. University of California Press, 1978.
17. Starr P. *The Social Transformation of American Medicine.* Basic Books, New York, 1982.
18. Somers H. M. and Somers A. R. *Doctors, Patients, and Health Insurance.* B. Institution. Washington, DC, 1961.
19. Mechanic D. Promoting health. *Society* **27,** 16–22, 1990.
20. Mechanic D. Prospects and problems in health services research. *Milb. Mem. Fund Q.* **56,** 127–139, 1978.
21. Pressman J. L. and Wildavsky A. *Implementation.* University of California Press, Berkeley, 1973.
22. Nakamura R. and Smallwood F. *The Politics of Policy Implementation.* St. Martin's Press, New York, 1980.
23. Etzioni A. *The Moral Dimension: Toward a New Economics.* Free Press, New York, 1988.
24. Newhouse J. A design for a health insurance experiment. *Inquiry* **11,** 5–27, 1974.
25. Newhouse J. *et al.* Some interim results from a controlled trial of cost-sharing in health insurance. *N. Engl. J. Med.* **305,** 1501–1507, 1981.
26. Brook R. H. *et al.* Does free care improve adults' health? Results from a randomized controlled trial. *N. Engl. J. Med.* **309,** 1426–1434, 1983.
27. Lohr K. N. *et al.* Use of medical care in the RAND health insurance experiment: diagnosis- and service-specific analyses in a randomized controlled trial. R-3469-HHS. RAND Corporation, Santa Monica, CA, 1986.
28. Petersdorf R. G. and Feinstein A. R. An informal appraisal of the current status of medical sociology. In *The Role of Social Science for Medicine* (Edited by Eisenberg L. and Kleinman A.), Reidel, Dordrecht, 1981.
29. Fox D. *Health Policies, Health Politics: The British and American Experience, 1911–1965.* Princeton University Press, Princeton, NJ, 1986.
30. Wennberg J. Outcomes research, cost containment, and the fear of health care rationing. *N. Engl. J. Med.* **323,** 1202–1204, 1990.
31. Eraker S. A. and Politser P. How decisions are reached: physician and patient. *Ann. Int. Med.* **97,** 262–268, 1982.
32. Mechanic D. *Painful Choices.* Transaction Press, New Brunswick, NJ, 1990.
33. Bunker J., Gomby D. S., and Kehrer B. H. (Eds) *Pathways to Health: The Role of Social Factors.* Henry J. Kaiser Family Foundation, Menlo Park, CA, 1989.
34. Caldwell J. C. Routes to low mortality in poor countries. *Pop. Dev. Rev.* **12,** 171–220, 1986.
35. Mechanic D. Socioeconomic status and health: an examination of underlying processes. In *Pathways to Health: The Role of Social Factors* (Edited by Bunker J. P., Gomby D. S., and Kehrer B. H.), pp. 9–26. Henry J. Kaiser Family Foundation, Menlo Park, CA, 1989.
36. Light D. Medical and nursing education: surface behavior and deep structure. In *Handbook of Health, Health Care and the Health Professions* (Edited by Mechanic D.), pp. 455–478. Free Press, New York, 1983.

37. See as an example, Bloom S. The medical school as a social system: a case study of faculty–student relations. *Milb. Mem. Fund Q.* **49,** entire issue (part II), 1971.

38. National Center for Health Statistics. Advance report of final mortality statistics, 1988. *Monthly Vital Statistics Report* **39,** no. 7, suppl, 1990.

39. Pepper Commission. *A Call for Action: U.S. Bipartisan Commission on Comprehensive Health Care.* U.S. Govt. Printing Office, Washington, DC, 1990.

DEVELOPED WORLD PERSPECTIVE

THE DEVELOPMENT OF MEDICAL SOCIOLOGY IN THEORY AND PRACTICE IN WESTERN EUROPE 1950–1990

MARGOT JEFFERYS

There are many ways in which the development of medical sociology in Western Europe in the second half of the twentieth century can be reviewed. For example, it would be possible and profitable to examine the fluctuating strengths of the various theoretical approaches to the subject during the period. Its achievements and failures judged by different criteria could be highlighted. The reasons for the shifts in concern from the micro to the macrosociological level and back again could be explored. The disciplinary and institutional relationships of the sociology of medicine or health to other social and behavioural sciences (for example, to anthropology, in all its different forms, to psychology and to economics) could be considered. Each and every one of these approaches would be worthy of consideration when the history of medical sociology in Europe during the past 50 years comes to be written by a historian of the future as indeed it should be. My own approach to the topic, in which I stress the importance of the sociopolitical and health context within which the discipline grew and the significance of institutional provisions for the subject within academia and medical institutions, is a personal choice. It is prompted by my own experience as one of an initially small group of social scientists who became involved, almost accidentally, in the development of the discipline in the early post-

war years and was privileged to remain active in the field for over 40 years.

THE SOCIOMEDICAL CONTEXT

During the first half of the twentieth century, there had been a steady reduction in mortality rates of infants, children and young adults across Europe and a consequent increase in longevity. After a short-lived post-war "baby boom", birth rates continued their secular, long drawn-out decline. The decline undoubtedly reflected the increasing capacity (with the advent of the contraceptive pill) and desire of couples to limit the number of their offspring in order to secure for themselves and their children a higher standard of living.

Until the Second World War, the decline in mortality was due, in the main, to better nutrition, improved housing standards and personal hygiene. Prophylactic and secondary prevention measures applied by public health authorities probably played some part in reducing both mortality and chronic incapacity from diseases such as tuberculosis and, during the war years, from diphtheria. Advances in clinical medicine, based on biocellular research, pharmacological innovation and improved surgical techniques, had played little part in changing the health profile of nations in the first half of the century. Their promise, however, was there with the discovery and use of penicillin and antibiotic drug preparations in the mid-century which were beginning to have an effect on previously often lethal bacterial infections.

The result of these changes in fertility and mortality was to alter the age structure of populations significantly and, consequently, their health profiles. In short, by the mid-1950s it was becoming clear to epidemiologists that the major health problems of the second half of the century would be those of diseases most commonly experienced by middle-aged or elderly people—the so-called degenerative diseases—not those infectious diseases affecting mainly children and young adults. The prevailing medical dictum, however, was still that diseases of this kind—the cancers and heart conditions which were major causes of death, the musculoskeletal conditions which disabled permanently and the severe psychiatric disorders—were facets of old age itself. They were seen as essentially chronic, largely incurable and involving the medical profession primarily as controllers, not therapists. Nevertheless, such was the euphoria which accompanied some of the medical innovations of the period that doctors, although their healing powers were discounted, were seen as the appropriate profession to lead those whose main concern was primarily the social care of the dependent elderly or chronically disabled individuals. It was also popular perceptions of the medical profession's omnipotence which had enabled it to wrest the management of normal childbirth from the midwives, resulting, therefore, in a gender shift in power.

Another feature of the post–Second World War decades was the increasing prominence of mental health problems. As advances in medical technology appeared to be making a contribution to the problems of somatic disorders, the social and economic toll paid by individual sufferers, their significant associates and society at large from major and minor mental disorders became more apparent. The success of pharmacological advances in making inroads into the treatment of somatic

diseases brought about a degree of therapeutic optimism, if not euphoria, about the possibility of dealing with mental disorders of all kinds from mild anxieties to major psychoses through similar forms of treatment. The consequent medicalization of mental disorders and various forms of aberrant behaviour was a major feature of the 1950s and 1960s and had a profound influence on the development of medical sociology. So too did the growing tendency to attribute forms of deviant social behaviour to pathological processes which were more likely to yield to medical intervention, including pharmacological administrative measures rather than other forms of social control.

This changing health profile and related demographic population structure was accompanied by what, in retrospect, can be seen to be relatively profound changes in old established cultural patterns, social customs and expectations governing the relationships between those belonging to the different, hitherto highly stratified, social divisions of society. Gathering momentum in the 1960s, traditional time-honoured assumptions about the proper behaviours of the sexes, of the generations and of the social classes towards one another began to be questioned. The capacity of traditional authority structures, including the health care order, which had controlled the conduct of individuals within the basic social institutions of society, that is, within the family, the school, the university, the work-place and the church, began to break down. Older religious and secular sanctions were increasingly challenged. All this was occurring in an international and politically fraught confrontational situation—Cold War—where the stakes seemed to be nothing less than the annihilation or survival of the human species through the use of nuclear power.

HEALTH CARE PROVISION

The immediate post-war years saw an acceleration in the already established trend for national states to intervene, directly or indirectly, to facilitate and regulate access to medical care and to exercise surveillance over the health of their citizens, in particular the young. There was widespread popular as well as professional optimism that, given political commitment to health care and, consequently, the right kind of institutional arrangements for its delivery, age-old problems of ill-health and premature mortality could be solved.

In Western Europe, however, this therapeutic optimism was held in check by political difficulties involved in shifting established institutional arrangements affecting access and methods of training, regulating and paying health professionals. As a consequence, health care structures in the different countries of Western Europe continued to differ to some extent. The differences mostly reflected the relative power and interests of the dominant health profession, medicine. Embedded popular cultural beliefs and preferences concerning health and illness may also have played a part in preventing uniformity.

Whatever the arrangements, however, every national state experienced common dilemmas. These included how to contain the increasing cost of health care, particularly that part falling on the state directly, how to cater for the changing health needs occasioned by the survival of more and more people into old age and chronic incapacity, how to cope with growing expectations of health care to solve existential problems of existence as well as of somatic illness, how far to extend or reduce family and kin responsibility for the health and welfare costs of dependents, whether young, old or middle-aged, and how to redistribute scarce health resources so as to cover under-served geographical areas or deprived, disadvantaged social groups.

In every country, what was at stake was the power which the dominant professional group—the doctors—could or should exercise in decision making. In particular, the state, purporting to represent the interests of the population as expressed in the political process and given the salience of health for the economy, was everywhere engaged in power struggles with the medical profession. The former sought to restrict the latter's economic rewards and

its power to control the health care enterprise in order to provide a viable, efficient service at not too high a cost to the tax or premium insurance payer. Yet, the state also had a vested interest in ensuring that medicine remain a competent and acceptable instrument for maintaining social control and social cohesion. Managing the tension between these 2, potentially conflicting, objectives required political astuteness, especially when the clients or users of health services became more sophisticated and less subservient to the state itself as well as to paternalistic doctors. The study of the consequent complex power relationships was to become grist to a refurbished sociological mill.

SOCIOLOGICAL CONCERNS WITH HEALTH AND HEALTH CARE

Starting in the 1950s and gathering pace in the following decades, a significant growth occurred in the numbers of social scientists paying serious intellectual attention to the social significance of the varied health trajectories and experiences of individuals on the one hand and, on the other, to the social relationships generated around the societal arrangements designed to intervene to modify health statuses.

Sociological interest in the influence of social status and culture on the health of individuals was, of course, not an entirely new phenomenon in the 1950s. Durkheim's[1] classic study had earlier related the incidence of suicide to social cohesiveness and social demographers and reformers in Britain and elsewhere had drawn attention to the effect of various forms of social deprivation on the mortality rates experienced by different social class groups.

All the same, mainstream classical sociology within the Marxist, Weberian and Durkheimian traditions had paid little attention to health and to societal responses to ill-health as a salient institutional feature of contemporary societies affecting their stability or instability.

Talcott Parsons'[2] work in America in the 1940s and 1950s began to change all that. In Europe, the initial response to his ideas was somewhat muted. It was in the 1960s rather than earlier that sociologists in Western Europe began to consider seriously the social-control functions of national health care systems and how these were manifested in the authority invested in physicians and the institutions—such as hospitals and doctors' surgeries or offices—within which they worked. In Europe in the 1950s and 1960s, alternative, neo-Marxist inspired theoretical ideas competed with those of Parsons'[2] structural functionalism for the allegiance of those social scientists attracted to the study of health and health care systems. More recently and in something of a backlash against crude Marxist-inspired theories, Foucault's[3] theoretical perspectives have found increasing support.

At the same time—at least in Britain—social scientists with eclectic backgrounds nurtured in pragmatic approaches to social issues and informed by a mixture of social science disciplines, including political and economic theory and social psychology, were increasingly turning their attention to the social policy of the Welfare State. Some examined such questions as the relationships of the individual to the state and the social consequences of the state's intervention in market economies. Others tried to understand the factors governing the relationships between employers and employees in industry and between professionals and clients in service provision.

The turbulence in Western societies as a whole and in their constituent parts inevitably affected the preoccupations of those who intended to use the intellectual discipline of sociology to understand better the social processes of the contemporary world, including those generated in health care. Moreover, the global dilemmas drew into the academic net many young people who not only wanted to understand that world but to change the social order. They intended to use their disciplinary analytical skills and knowledge to help to alter the existing balances of power, in favour of those they considered disadvantaged and/or deprived as against

those who, conventionally, were endowed with the power of status and position.

A particularly important manifestation of revolt against the existing social order within the health as well as more general social context was the new feminism which took root in the 1960s and began to exercise great influence over existing patterns of professional and patient behaviour. It also began successfully to challenge the hitherto gender-blind sociological enterprise, regardless of whether this was driven by theoretical or policy considerations.[4]

For all these reasons, health and health care for the first time on a significant scale began to interest theoretical sociologists, social policy analysts and radical activists whose primary interest was to engineer change in major societal institutions. It was not surprising, therefore, that there was very little coherence in the emergent discipline of medical sociology. Attempts to impose one dominant strand or orthodoxy in the burgeoning field of sociology concerned with health and medicine failed. The sociology *of* medicine is itself eclectic, using a wide variety of theoretical and methodological frameworks. It co-exists, whether some of its proponents like it or not, with a pragmatic sociology *in* medicine.

THE SYMBIOTIC RELATIONSHIP BETWEEN SOCIOLOGIES IN AND OF MEDICINE

What follows is written from a British perspective and is based largely on personal experiences in that context. It may be less true of developments in other parts of Western Europe, where physicians were often in the forefront of the development of medical sociology and were perhaps less inclined to belittle the academic discipline of sociology than their British counterparts.

The relationship which existed in different forms during the last half century between those whose main objective was to develop an academic, intellectual discipline—the sociology *of* medicine—and those who interpreted their primary task as throwing light on problematic issues arising in the planning or operation of health care was problematic. In latter years, the former have increasingly sought to designate their field of study the sociology of *health* instead of the sociology of *medicine*. This is not only motivated by a desire to broaden the field to include phenomena which fall outside the purview of the orthodox medical profession and the institutions which it dominates; it is at least partially due to concern to emphasize even more strongly their disciplinary independence from the multitheoretical and pragmatic models used by practitioners of medicine.

Sociologists *in* medicine, however, whatever their aspirations, have been constrained by the need to accept that their bread and butter depends primarily upon throwing light on contemporary health or health care issues which are seen by research-funding organizations as requiring examination. In turn, these organizations themselves rely for advice on established authority on what to fund, that is, on the state, the super-state (i.e., the European Union), and the major health profession.

Throughout the period, exponents of the 2 sociological approaches to medicine were broadly distinguished not only by their focus but also by their institutional base. In general, the sociologists *of* medicine were located in university departments of sociology. The sociologists *in* medicine, on the other hand, were to be found in medical faculty departments or associated clinical or public health settings.

The institutional base in turn dictated the nature of the teaching as well as the research commitment. The sociologists *of* medicine were, in the main, in tenured posts. Their major commitment was to teach their subject to those opting to study sociology as an academic discipline. They had obligations to participate in the introductory teaching of general sociology as well as the opportunity to teach their own specialized subject to more advanced undergraduates as well as postgraduates (at least in more recent years). Such academic commitments were likely to encourage close contact with fellow sociologists and a knowledge of advances in the general field of sociology.

By contrast, the sociologists *in* medicine were, in the main, located in medically led departments or research units. They were generally employed on short-term contracts to work on particular research projects, which, most commonly, were directed by a medical doctor. Frequently, they would be asked to give lectures on some social aspect of medical care to skeptical and usually reluctant medical students or young doctors in a clinic or public health–based specialty. The time and opportunity for them to read more widely in general sociology were limited. Within their medically oriented work units, they were likely to be isolated. They could be the butt of jokes from members of the dominant culture which was apt to belittle their potential contribution if not to ridicule their subject. From the contrasts drawn here, it might be concluded that the sociologists *in* medicine were in much less favourable circumstances than the sociologists *of* medicine. In truth, however, the latter were often likely to envy the former at least for some things. The health care industry and its professional educational schools, despite their ambivalence towards the social sciences, were absorbing and giving some longer term career prospects to a steadily increasing number of social scientists. Moreover, there were psychic rewards as well as financial security to be had from close association with a profession with much higher status ratings than had academic sociology. Some welcomed the patronage.

In short, throughout the period, there were conflicts between sociologists *of* and sociologists *in* medicine, which arose from their differences in their institutional bases and in the related foci of their intellectual pursuits. However, the extent of the conflicts should not be exaggerated; nor were their effects all negative. Indeed, it can be argued that the result of conflict was not necessarily loss for either side and certainly not for the health of the discipline as a whole and of its proponents. It is true that, on both sides, prejudices were expressed often in terms which suggested the rigidities of thought processes, more usually associated with religious fundamentalism. The theorists accused the pragmatists of crimes such as mindless positivism, doctor sycophancy, triviality and opportunism. The pragmatists accused the theorists of self-indulgence, arrogance, ignoring the concerns of others about proof or generalizability and disinterest in righting the wrongs of a grossly inequitable distribution of resources to and within the health care system. From both sides, there were accusations of fallacies in reasoning arising from methodological inadequacy.

Nevertheless, the divisions which have and continue to exist have not led to serious destructive schisms. There is a high degree of collegiate cohesion despite the differences of approach and interpretive mode among sociologists who see some aspect of health or health-related activities at the micro- or macrolevel of analysis as their major field of research. This cohesion is due to the fact that, in practice, the various theoretical and pragmatic approaches have benefited from each other in ways they may not always be ready to recognize and openly acknowledge.

In particular, there have been at least 2 positive outcomes of an essentially symbiotic, mutually supportive relationship. First, the presence of sociologists within medically dominated institutions—the medical schools, hospitals and clinics—and the normalization and legitimacy of that presence as contributing to the overall objectives of those institutions, has undoubtedly benefited sociologists *of* as well as sociologists *in* medicine. It has done this because it has helped to break down the closely guarded, impregnable bastions of medical exclusivity. There has been a tendency for physicians to feel they possess their patients, particularly if they happen to be admitted to hospital. The activities that take place within these medical complexes are now more visible and, hence, open to examination and analyses in terms other than those chosen or dictated by the medical profession itself. Research resources and personnel have continued to expand and permit work across a wide spectrum of subjects.

Second, the vitality of the iconoclasm of the theory-building sociologists has acted as a spur to the sociologists whose close proximity to researchers from disciplines other than their own can expose them to a form of co-optation in which their own distinct disciplinary contribution could be drowned.

SOME CONCLUDING COMMENTS

To conclude on a personal note. The emphasis placed on internal divisions in British medical sociology undoubtedly reflects my personal experience as an actor during the period under review. As such, however, it may have documentary value for the future historian who comes to write a balanced assessment of the twentieth-century disciplinary developments in the sociology of medicine and health in Europe.

REFERENCES

1. Durkheim E. *Suicide: A study in sociology.* New York: Free Press, 1951 (originally published in 1897).
2. Parsons T. *The social system.* Glencoe, IL: Free Press, 1951.
3. Foucault M. *The birth of the clinic.* New York: Vintage, 1975 (original 1963).

4. Oakley A, Rigby AS, Hickey D. Women and children last? Class, health and the role of maternal and child health services. *Eur J Public Hlth* 1993, 3: 220–6.

DEVELOPING WORLD PERSPECTIVE

SOCIOLOGICAL STUDIES OF THIRD WORLD HEALTH AND HEALTH CARE: INTRODUCTION

EUGENE B. GALLAGHER

The purpose of this special issue is to exhibit the current work of sociologists on health and health care in Third World societies. This work—a broad sphere of activity—is intended to show the relevance of sociological approaches to the assessment and amelioration of health problems and to show also that greater acuity of sociological understanding can come from the study of health and illness in Third World settings.

As a concept and an empirical reality, "Third World" made its debut in the 1950's. Its signification has enlarged greatly since then. The national leaders who fashioned the goal of political, cultural, and economic independence from East and West for a "non-aligned" third world were Nasser of Egypt, Nkrumah of Ghana, Sukarno of Indonesia, and Tito of Yugoslavia (the Third World did not at first include Latin America). Its early social-science articulators were Peter Worsley (1964) and Irving Louis Horowitz (1966). The sweep of the category can be seen from the fact that, taken in its original form and without refinement, it now stretches, at the extreme of underdevelopment, from Haiti, Nepal, and Bangladesh, all the way to Taiwan and South Korea at the higher end of wealth and industrial productivity, with scores of nations between. Not only economic development but also cultural indices such as literacy enter into the contemporary heterogeneity of the Third World.

The focus of thinking and research about the Third World has expanded beyond political and ideological slogans, to embrace attention to empirical indicators of industrialization and development. The indicators published annually since 1978 by the World Bank in the World Development Report (with *World Development Report 1989* as the most

recent report in the series) have an influential audience of academics and policymakers. These indicators include categories familiar to economists such as gross national product, earnings and output from manufacturing, and energy production and consumption. Medical sociologists will no doubt be more interested in the indices that deal with health status and health resources. Thus, for 128 nations with populations over one million (thus excluding many small island-nations), the Report presents figures on birth, fertility, and mortality—with separate rates on infant and child mortality, and on the ratio of physicians and nursing personnel to the population (World Bank 1989).

Except for concern with the related issue of population growth, the developed world has paid little attention to health conditions and resources in the Third World. Najman recently wrote: "For people living in the developed countries there may be a reluctance to become greatly concerned with the health and health care needs of those living in the developing countries" (Najman 1989). More widely recognized are the economic, ethnic, religious, and political problems—and more recently, rampant environmental degradation—in Third World countries, which loom as major obstacles to global comity and security. Folded within these issues of macrosocial scale, however, are the health problems—the needs and hopes of individuals for better living and working conditions, for protection from disease, and for health care when ill. Even in the most impoverished Third World societies, and those that cling most rigidly to traditional orthodoxies, popular aspirations include rising expectations for health and health care. Berger speaks of the expectation of being delivered from "hunger, disease, and early death" as an aspect of modernization, and Elling notes that "adequate health and health care have come to be more and more regarded as fundamental and universal rights" (Berger et al. 1973; Elling 1980).

The articles presented here depict several aspects of sociological concern with Third World health and health care. We think of the Third World as geographically vast and diverse in the ways mentioned above; a single journal issue can go only so far in reflecting its diverseness. Even within this miniature frame, the intent has been less to convey a representative picture of current work than to select studies that hold special appeal in their data or those that use their Third World setting to test and sharpen our understanding of concepts and issues in medical sociology.

CLASSIFICATION OF THE STUDIES

It is not my intention here to critically discuss the articles but to offer, as it were, a guided tour of them within an interpretive framework—a tour which will, I hope, whet the reader's appetite to savor and digest the articles themselves.

The nine studies in this issue have been located within a set of four analytic categories commonly employed in medical sociology: (1) social factors in disease, (2) utilization of health services, (3) provider–patient relationships (including the doctor–patient relationship), and (4) organization of health services. There are of course other, more differentiated ways of classifying the contents of medical sociology but the foregoing reflect the perspectives of current textbooks as well as the ways in which many research studies in medical sociology journals commonly identify their foci.

SOCIAL FACTORS IN DISEASE

"Disease" in Category 1 refers to any negative health condition, without precise stipulation in the medical sense of disease, and without regard to sociologically nuanced contrasts between "disease"

and "illness." Three studies fall primarily in this category: those by Hunt (set in Africa), Gallin (Taiwan), and Andes (Peru). Hunt's disease is AIDS, Gallin's is poor mental health, and Andes' is infant mortality.

Hunt notes that AIDS in Africa has a different ecology and sex distribution (approximately 1:1) from its patterns in developed societies. It differs from AIDS in the United States because it is not linked to homosexual sexual contact or to intravenous drug use. A different epidemiology suggests a different social causation. Hunt traces the difference to a socioeconomic factor—the decline of African agriculture and the consequent job-seeking migration of African males and their lengthy separation from family settings. He carries the economic explanation further, to macrosocial theories of dependency and underdevelopment, applied to Africa.

In her ethnographic study of Taiwanese village women, Gallin finds that their morale, along with their physical health, is strong despite the long hours and stressful conditions of factory work and their many family duties. The task which Gallin sets for herself is not to determine the social causes of pathology but rather to determine why women remain healthy in the face of adversity—that is, to establish the social causes of resistance. Like Hunt, she employs a generalized macrosystem explanation. However, Taiwan is differently situated in the world economic system from African societies: the drive to manufacture goods for export from Taiwan has created a strong demand for female as well as male labor, and there is no appreciable male labor migration. Instead of weakening the family, the export-oriented economy has maintained it, even in the face of many other social changes. Schooled in traditional Chinese family values, the women accept their demanding lot with stoic affirmation.

Andes' study compares two towns in Peru that have many similarities yet differ markedly in their infant mortality rates. The town with the higher infant mortality rate is the "company town" of a multinational mining and refining corporation. The town with the lower infant mortality rate has a diversified economy based in fishing, agriculture, manufacturing, and tourism. Andes couches her explanation for the difference partly on a macrolevel argument concerning foreign monopolistic domination of the local economy for the town with the higher rate. However, she also emphasizes other points of contrast between the two towns. The town with the higher rate also has more unemployment and very little employment opportunity for women; further and more proximate to direct causes of infant mortality, it lacks a potable water supply, and the copper refining process releases noxious materials into air and water. Andes' analysis leads her to discount the importance of medical care facilities in comparison with environmental factors, and to invoke community-structure elements such as female employment in accounting for infant mortality.

UTILIZATION OF HEALTH SERVICES

The studies of Fosu (Ghana), Subedi (Nepal), and Glik and her associates (Guinea) lie within Category 2, dealing generally with the utilization of health services—questions such as medical consumer preferences for alternative kinds of services, access to services, the availability and distribution of resources, and social policy issues relative to these questions.

It is in regard to utilization of health services that sociologists might expect to find the greatest differences between the Third World and the industrial societies. Although situations of choice arise between traditional and modern alternatives in almost all societies, the choice falls on the side of tradition more frequently in Third World societies than in developed societies. Systems of traditional healing, with their associated practitioners and techniques, remain more important in Third World societies than in industrial societies. Yet modern scientific medicine has also come to be widely practiced in Third World societies. The anthropologist Charles Leslie believes that medical sociology has acquired a "modern medicine" bias that rele-

gates traditional medical systems to the status of fringe medicine (Leslie 1980) and largely ignores them. However, in defense of sociology, it might be argued that anthropologists have shown less interest in assessing the actual distribution of medical resources and in understanding which factors impel patients to seek one kind of resource rather than another. Medical sociologists are better suited for this work. Anthropologists have been mainly interested in refining the logic of traditional medical belief systems and determining their relation to overarching culture themes.

Although the Fosu and Subedi studies might be faulted by anthropologists for insufficient analysis of the belief content and the techniques of folk/traditional medicine in Ghana and Nepal, these sociological researches do investigate, within their respective survey samples and geographic areas, the utilization of traditional healing practitioners. Both studies also raise the question of the relationship between utilization of traditional resources and modern resources. Subedi sees the resort to traditional resources primarily as a diverting factor that delays patients from obtaining presumably more effective attention and treatment at the hands of modern personnel; in contrast, Fosu uses his findings to explore the question whether the relationship of traditional to modern can be seen as complementary rather than competitive. Both studies find in fact only a modest degree of resort to traditional medicine, perhaps because they were conducted in the capital cities of Accra and Katmandu; nevertheless, even that modest degree shows that traditional medicine is by no means confined to the rural areas. Information from studies such as these can inform the deliberations of national health policymakers concerning the scope that should be accorded to traditional personnel and resources within the evolution of national systems of health care.

Glik's study probes the use of an antimalarial drug—chloroquine—by mothers in rural and urban areas of Guinea, where malaria is endemic. Current professional thinking recommends the use of the drug whenever a child is feverish—on the presumption of malaria and in view of the drug's effectiveness and safety; it is also recommended during pregnancy on a purely prophylactic basis. Glik's research problem is to assess the causal role of various factors—categorized as individual, sociocultural, and structural—that are associated with the use of the drug. She found that urban mothers, more than rural, used the drug for their children, and that among nonusers' lack of access to health services was an important barrier. She also found that many mothers did not understand or accept the principle of prompt presumptive treatment for their children, and that they declined to use the drug themselves during pregnancy because they feared it would lead to miscarriage.

Readers familiar with the conceptual models that have propelled health utilization research in the United States—especially the models of Rosenstock (1966), Suchman (1967), and Anderson (1968)—will find the work by Fosu, Subedi, and Glik strongly flavored by these models. They used survey research, their questions being adapted to local respondents and situations. Leslie, from his anthropological perspective, is openly skeptical about the validity and value of surveys in developing societies because "they assume modes of thought that are alien to members of these societies" (1980, p. 194). It is difficult to weigh this criticism; a genuine refutation of it would require the comparison of results obtained by surveys with results obtained by other methods such as health diaries of utilization behavior or direct observation of help-seeking behavior. Lacking such evidence, it can at least be said that Third World studies which use concepts and variables previously formulated and tested are moving in the direction of cumulative knowledge-building.

PROVIDER–PATIENT RELATIONSHIPS

Waitzkin and Britt's study of medical discourse, with case-examples from Cuba, is the only study that falls within Category 3. (Readers might argue that it also falls in Category 4, the organization of health services, because it depicts the close working relationship between medical resources and social services.) The provider who receives the most attention is the physician, but it is essential to the picture that Waitzkin and Britt present that the Cuban physician has at his/her disposal other, community-based types of manpower to whom the patient can be referred.

Waitzkin and Britt believe that doctors in developed societies "marginalize" many of the problems that patients might, in a freer and more supportive communication situation, bring into the encounter—problems at work, family strains, and self-damaging behaviors. Such problems may or may not have somatic causes and manifestations. Doctors discourage such complaints because they cannot be diagnostically formulated according to biomedicine or because they call for resources that run beyond the doctor's control. Waitzkin and Britt believe that in Cuba, more than in capitalist societies and more than in other socialist societies, the communication situation is better for the patient. Their case examples show how paramedical personnel and community workers can be brought to the aid of patients, often with positive result. Waitzkin and Britt caution that these resources and communication patterns have become woven into the texture of Cuban society as the product of revolutionary change; non-revolutionary societies such as the United States can, however, effect medical changes in the same direction, they believe. Waitzkin and Britt also point out that Cuba is a relatively poor Third World society that has, with social reorganization but without massive investment of resources, considerably improved its health status.

ORGANIZATION OF HEALTH SERVICES

Category 4 is represented by the Quah and Cho studies. Quah's sociohistorical examination of the medical profession in Singapore and Cho's analysis of the emergence of government-based medical insurance in South Korea share a focus on the structure where medical problems are dealt with and how it has changed over time. Analyzing social contexts and structures, these studies are somewhat removed from the immediacy of providers and patients. In common with other studies of their genre and in contrast to studies of the social causes of disease and of utilization behavior, the Quah and Cho work stands closer to the macro-level preoccupations of history, political science, and economics, and more distant from those of psychology.

Quah applies analytic theory on the professions, in the mode of Freidson (1986), Johnson (1973), and Ritzer (1975), to the Singaporean medical profession. This leads her to doubt that any additional concepts are necessary to comprehend the nature of organized medicine in Singapore, and by extension, in other Third World societies. She does, however, believe that the early formulation of the profession and of medical training facilities under British control contributed to the present situation, in which by comparison to medicine in the United States, Singaporean medicine is more tightly under governmental control. She also finds that medicine as an occupation enjoys very high social prestige; her study thus adds another voice to the growing cross-national chorus that proclaims the high prestige of medicine. Such findings should not be dismissed simply because they repeat familiar facts; the public valuation of medicine and other occupations must be assessed in Third World societies as it has been in our own.

Cho's study of medical insurance in South Korea analyzes the sociopolitical dynamics of reluctant governmental response to restive demands by the labor stratum for greater rewards and for recognition of its role in pushing the economy forward. Her language and concepts draw on well-known theoretical positions in sociology, especially neo-Marxism and functionalism, and her arguments move within a macro-frame.

Within a strongly capitalist economy, the emergence of nationally sponsored social and medical security funds can be seen as a vital step in societal development. Just as the socialist Third World societies have spawned civil-servant medical cadres and

have made medical care a citizen's right (socialist medical systems are briefly compared by Waitzkin and Britt, as noted above), the capitalist societies have, with somewhat less uniformity, evolved schemes of public and private insurance payment that reimburse physicians and other health care providers without controlling them.

It is against this backdrop that Cho's study takes it place. She adopts a neo-Marxist, conflict theory stance that explores the power relationships between the South Korean government, the entrepreneurial class, and the industrial workforce. Yet a functionalist accent can also be detected in her analysis, where she holds that the increasingly skilled and specialized nature of the Korean labor force makes labor a more valuable factor in production and accordingly a more vital element, requiring security and protection such as health insurance gives, in the social structure. Further, her view that health insurance was a forced concession by the government to reduce class conflict can also be seen, from a functionalist perspective, as an adjustment—perhaps a late adjustment but not irreparably late—that maintained the cohesion and productivity of South Korean society.

IN CONCLUSION: SOCIOLOGICAL QUESTIONS ABOUT "HEALTH FOR ALL"

Although it might be possible to set out a logical, comprehensive research agenda for the medical sociology of the Third World, the work that actually gets carried out reflects a varied set of individual and group interests, blended with current priorities of foundations and international agencies such as the World Bank and WHO. The reader who examines the sponsorship, funding, and intellectual initiatives behind the research embodied in the articles of this special issue will find a variety of resources and motivations in play.

Just because sociologists can, through their research tools and distinctive perspective, make useful contributions to knowledge and planning concerning health in the Third World, it becomes especially important to reinvigorate, as it were, the sociological matrix of such work and to strengthen its articulation with core sociological concepts. If applied work can be likened to the branches—the most public parts—of the tree, then the supporting roots need tending and nurture from time to time. Applied work often makes openings to unsuspected empirical worlds and to social changes that stimulate sociological conceptualization. All too often, however, unreflective, mechanical applied work takes more from sociology than it gives back, and the roots then languish.

It is with this precept in mind that I will identify two topics that require closer sociological analysis than they have received, relating them to ideas and findings of articles in this issue.

The first issue concerns health manpower, especially the role of the physician, in relation to Third World health priorities. The second is the place of traditional health personnel and practices within the general development of national health resources.

These issues have high sociological valence within the program of "Health for All by the Year 2000." As promulgated by WHO at Alma Ata in 1978, Health for All puts forth a set of priorities that have received widespread discussion and broad, though not universal, endorsement from health officials, planners, and professionals (Mahler 1988; World Health Organization 1978). As a medical–social vision and ideology, Health for All lays out goals and implementing steps for improving health in the Third World. It emphasizes national and local self-reliance—mobilizing effort and involvement at the community level, and holding fast against what the WHO leadership sees as an overdependence upon expensive hospital-based technology and medical specialization that is enveloping the industrial societies. Health for All emphasizes environmental health, especially potable water and basic sanitation—woefully lacking in many Third World societies. Within the sphere of more definitively medical measures, it emphasizes immunization against the common and widespread infectious diseases of childhood, as well as maternal and child health. Within the still narrower sphere of clinical care of sick or symptomatic individuals, the emphasis falls upon community-based primary care, in contrast to hospital-based specialist care. Primary care receives priority because it matches medical resources with the prevailing medical needs of Third World populations. Many Third World societies have high birth rates, a mean population age under twenty, and a heavy burden of infectious diseases such as malaria, schistosomiasis, and chlamydia trachoma. Under such circumstances, according to the Health for All manifesto, sophisticated medical care is less needed than relatively simple medical measures such as antibiotics and, for infected children, oral rehydration. Further, in this view, there are too few physicians in most Third World societies to have much impact and, in any event, the relatively small supply of physicians is highly concentrated on the largest cities, catering to a wealthy clientele.

While there can be little dispute with the foregoing view that the medical profession in many Third World societies is a virtually useless appendage to the body politic, the Health for All formula also seems deficient and non-strategic for failing to project, even at the ideal level, a view of how physicians can work within their accustomed framework of technical skill and clinical concern for the individual patient, and still function to the benefit of the community. The Waitzkin-Britt picture of the Cuban physician shows him (or her) as communicatively and administratively adept, functioning with the traditional physicianly authority but also, and less traditionally, with considerable social resources at his (or her) disposal. In a sharply contrasting, economically laissez-faire society, the Saudi physician Sebai nevertheless strikes a similar note by appealing to the leadership component of the medical role. Sebai urges Third World physicians to become health educators to promote the health of individuals with a community context (Sebai 1981).

Given the high regard for technical clinical skill that is imparted through medical education worldwide, it is not clear that Third World physicians can be persuaded to become health educators or coordinators for social resources, however necessary those functions may be. Even so, the Health for All agenda can shift to another priority, namely, the radical reform of medical education to produce physicians who are more strongly oriented toward goals of community health and less concerned with technical skill (given the intensely technical focus of contemporary medical education, even orienting the student to the "whole patient" would be a major reform). With that shift, however, it may begin to appear that the Health for All agenda, taken literally, is an uncompromisingly utopian statement of how health affairs should move in the Third World—rather than a negotiable position that could have realistic impact on evolving trends.

It would be an ambitious but sociologically valuable undertaking to analyze the goals and program of Health for All, treating it first of all as a document to be situated in the context of its social time and place, then looking at its audiences and its impact in relation to health needs and services in the Third World. I have drawn attention to the blind spot in Health for All regarding the role and use of physicians not only because of its intrinsic importance but because medical sociologists in developed societies, especially the United States, have an intellectual stock in analyzing health manpower configurations, especially in health care systems that are centrally driven by the medical profession, in the "professional dominance" mode (Freidson 1970a, b). It is also true that this cadre of medical sociologists is familiar with, and not hesitant to point out, the potential public disadvantages of physician-dominated health care. Many would be prepared to seek out the possible advantages of a low-physician-impact system such as Health for All seems to envision.

If the Health for All agenda is definite in assigning little importance to clinical medicine in health development, it is, in contrast, vague in regard to the role of indigenous practitioners and traditional medicine in health development. The

articles in this issue that deal with this topic, those by Fosu and Subedi, are primarily concerned with utilization and not with the policy issue of how much traditional medicine should be available, on what terms, and in what kind of relationship to modern medicine; but utilization studies are of course quite important, especially as they explore the value and functions of traditional medicine for patients.

At the risk of oversimplifying, it might be said that the Health for All program is firmly in favor of modern medicine, that is, procedures and interventions that are grounded in modern science, though shrinking back from its "excesses." This reluctance seems to arise not because modern medicine is viewed as ineffective (though of course the "excesses" are sometimes ineffective or even harmful) but because it is expensive and consequently available only to elites. In contrast, traditional medicine is often more accessible to the average person (though sometimes it can also be expensive and inconvenient to obtain). On the surface, the exploitation of traditional medicine would seem to be consonant with Health for All's objective of using available resources and community empowerment by action for health. The vague and ambivalent position of Health for All in regard to traditional medicine stems more largely, I believe, because of doubts concerning its interventive effectiveness—and its safety as practiced by traditionally trained practitioners. The same attitude applies at other points in health care systems, e.g., the reluctance of health insurance plans in industrial societies to cover "alternative" medicine and the characteristic unwillingness of nascent health insurance schemes in Third World societies (such as South Korea in Cho's sociohistorical analysis) to include traditional medicine in its covered services.

If this argument makes a reasonable statement, it provides a link between what medical sociologists study in developed societies and what is emerging in the Third World. Problems of major illness or life-and-death consume so many resources that only the privileged, the well-insured, and the rich can afford them. Scarcity looms and socially abhorrent inequity ensues—then attention gets directed to what people can do for themselves. However, self-help, indigenous resources (such as traditional medicine), and prevention only postpone for a time the onset of major chronic diseases, and then what people can do for themselves seems not enough as the chronic diseases become more severe. Pressure redoubles for broad access to modern medicine. Of course the societies of the Third World, varied as they are, are not destined to repeat the dilemmas and the mistakes of the industrial societies. Perhaps "we" will have much to learn from "them." In any event, the scene presents opportunities and compelling challenges for medical sociology.

REFERENCES

Andersen, Ronald M. 1968. *A Behavioral Model of Families' Use of Health Services.* Chicago: Center for Health Administration Studies Research Series, No. 25.

Berger, Peter L., Brigette Berger, and Hansfried Kellner. 1973. *The Homeless Mind—Modernization and Consciousness.* New York: Random House.

Elling, Ray H. 1980. *Cross-National Study of Health Systems—Political Economics and Health Care.* New Brunswick, NJ: Transaction Books.

Freidson, Eliot. 1970a. *Professional Dominance: The Social Structure of Medicine.* New York: Atherson.

———. 1970b. *Profession of Medicine.* New York: Dodd, Mead.

———. 1986. *Professional Powers.* Chicago: University of Chicago Press.

Horowitz, Irving Louis. 1966. *The Three Worlds of Development.* New York: Oxford University Press.

Johnson, Terence. 1973. "Imperialism and the Professions." Pp. 281–310 in *Professionalization and Social Change,* edited by Paul Halmos. Keele: University of Keele.

Leslie, Charles. 1980. "Medical Pluralism in World Perspective." *Social Science and Medicine* 14B:191–95.

Mahler, Halfdan. 1988. "Present Status of WHO's Initiative, 'Health for All by the Year 2000'." *Annual Review of Public Health* 9:71–97.

Najman, Jackob M. 1989. "Health Care in Developing Countries." Chapter 16 (pp. 332–46) in *Handbook of Medical Sociology* (Fourth Edition), edited by Howard E. Freeman and Sol Levine. Englewood Cliffs, NJ: Prentice Hall.

Ritzer, George. 1975. "Professionalization, Bureaucratization, and Rationalization: The Views of Max Weber." *Social Forces* 53:627–34.

Rosenstock, Irwin M. 1966. "Why People Use Health Services." *Milbank Memorial Fund Quarterly* (Part 2) 44:94–124.

Sebai, Zohair. 1981. *The Health of the Family in a Changing Arabia: A Case Study in Primary Health Care.* Jeddah, Saudi Arabia: Tihama Press.

Suchman, Edward A. 1967. "Preventive Health Behavior: A Model for Research in Community Health." *Journal of Health and Social Behavior* 8:197–209.

World Bank. 1989. *World Development Report 1989.* New York: Oxford University Press.

World Health Organization. 1978. *Alma-Ata 1978: Primary Health Care.* Geneva: WHO "Health for All" Series, No. 1.

Worsley, Peter. 1964. *The Third World.* Chicago: University of Chicago Press.

CHAPTER 2

THE HISTORY OF MEDICINE

The articles in Chapter 2 cover three distinct historical periods in the development of modern medicine. Although these periods represent only a partial listing of the specific historical junctures within the development of modern medicine, they illustrate the importance of a historical perspective to sociological analysis (see also McKeown, 1970). Consider the following statement by C. Wright Mills written some four decades ago. His points are as significant today as they were then.

> *In our time problems of the Western societies are almost inevitably problems of the world. It is perhaps one defining characteristic of our period that it is one in which for the first time the varieties of social worlds it contains are in serious, rapid, and obvious interplay. The study of our period must be a comparative examination of these worlds, and of their interactions. Perhaps that is why what was once the anthropologist's exotic preserve, has become the world's "underdeveloped countries," which economists no less than political scientists and sociologists regularly include among their objects of study. That is why some of the very best sociology being done today is work on world areas and regions. (Mills, 1959, p. 150)*

The articles in Chapter 2 illustrate the importance of a cross-cultural perspective of medical sociology and are connected by their effort to provide a social context for the development of what is now considered "modern" medicine.

Although the articles in this chapter begin with the American perspective, historically this chapter begins with Bruce Lawrence Ralston's "I Swear by Imhotep the Physician." In this article, Ralston, as have others (Pickett, 1992), identifies Imhotep as the true "father of medicine," not the fabled Hippocrates. Although Hippocrates is significant within the development of "Western" medicine, his role has been idealized beyond its actual impact because of what was *not* known about Imhotep. Archaeological digs, however, have located the work of Imhotep antedating Hippocrates by more than a millennium, thus establishing the foundation of "Western" medicine not in Greece but in Egypt. As the life and work of Imhotep continues to be unearthed, his significance to medicine will only increase. As Ralston points out, his importance was well understood by the Greeks who traveled to Egypt to study his approach to medicine.

Moving forward, Vern L. Bullough's article on status and medieval medicine offers insight into the development of medicine at a particularly difficult historical period. The article offers a glimpse into the relationship between the practice of medicine and the resultant social status of the practitioners. Bullough also discusses the relationship between the social status of the physician and the treatment that patients received.

What is known about medicine in the Middle Ages is that medical advances were extremely limited because of religious controls. Medicine was considered an intellectual endeavor to be pursued by clerics. As a result, those physicians who practiced medicine did not engage in manual labor in the pursuit of their profession. Instead, they relegated manual labor to surgeons, who then attempted to claim equal status with physicians by relegating their manual labor to barber surgeons. Throughout all of this "professionalization" of medicine, physicians rarely treated the majority of citizens. Like Ralston, Bullough addresses the evolutionary progression of the physician within an evolving universe of medicine and its practitioners.

The first article in this chapter, by John Duffy, examines the development of medicine (public health) in the United States. Beginning with the colonial period and moving forward to the present, Duffy provides a solidly realistic portrayal of life, health, and death in a developing (preindustrial and industrial) America. He addresses differences between urban and rural health as well as differences in health outcomes by social class and race. Thus, throughout the article, the impact of these socio-logical variables is expressed in the changing nature of American society and its health. As Duffy points out, the history of medicine in the United States is rife with problems such as the continuing maldistribution of physicians. Duffy also discusses the increasing role of government in the American health care community. This point is particularly interesting, for the role of government is another common theme (though somewhat less specific) in the other articles in this chapter.

REFERENCES

McKeown, Thomas. 1970. A Sociological Approach to the History of Medicine. *Medical History,* vol. 14, pp. 342–451.

Mills, C. Wright. 1959. *The Sociological Imagination.* New York: Oxford University Press.

Pickett, Anthony Carl. 1992. The Oath of Imhotep: In Recognition of African Contributions to Western Medicine. *Journal of the National Medical Association,* vol. 84, no. 7, pp. 636–637.

AMERICAN PERSPECTIVE

THE COMMUNITY'S HEALTH

JOHN DUFFY

From earliest colonial days American communities have taken measures to promote the health of their citizens. For the first three centuries health laws fell into three main categories: sanitation, quarantine, and the regulation of food supplies and markets. The motive for sanitary laws was a mixture of esthetics and a wish to promote health. It had become evident early in history that dirt and crowding were conducive to sickness, and it was even more clear that the presence of garbage, dead animals, and overflowing privies were offensive to the senses. In the second category were the quarantine laws. Until the bacteriological revolution in the late nineteenth century, pestilences were strange and unaccountable phenomena. A number of theories were posited to explain them, but the public was convinced that epidemics spread from person to person, and that disease could be kept out through quarantine laws or avoided by isolating the sick.

Consequently, beginning in the late seventeenth century, colonial legislatures enacted a series of quarantine measures. The third category of health laws, those relating to the food supply, included town ordinances prohibiting the sale of "blowne" meat or putrid fish, regulating the price and weight of loaves of bread, and measures to keep the public markets in a sanitary condition.

Fortunately towns and cities in the colonial period were never as crowded and dirty as their European counterparts, and as a result the colonies enjoyed relatively good health. The immediate post-Revolutionary years saw a rapid increase in urban population and an even greater increase in sanitary problems. More important in terms of public health was the series of devastating yellow fever outbreaks that occurred in every American port from New England to Georgia during the years from 1793 to 1806. These repeated attacks led to the formation of the first temporary boards of health and the appointment of the first permanent health officers. The latter consisted usually of a health (quarantine) officer of the port and a port physician. In addition to the usual quarantine and sanitary measures, civic officials, reflecting the paternalism of colonial days, went to great lengths to provide medical care for the sick and food and shelter for their families. Once yellow fever was no longer a threat, the health boards ceased to exist, most of the laws fell into abeyance, and the two health offices became political plums. In the South, where the yellow fever attacks intensified, the port health officers were under constant pressure to minimize any restrictions on shipping.[1]

The rise of the industrial revolution in the early nineteenth century brought with it the concept of rugged individualism, one that emphasized a minimum role for government. In America its effects were exaggerated by the rise of Jacksonian democracy with its anti-intellectual and antimonopolistic spirit. The industrial revolution also brought large numbers of rural Americans and immigrants into towns and cities ill-prepared to handle the influx. Jammed into old and dilapidated housing and forced to rely on shallow water wells or hydrants located a block or two away, these poorly paid workers, living in incredibly brutal conditions, became a class apart from the middle and upper groups. Conscious of their own rectitude, the latter blamed the high morbidity and mortality rates among the poor upon their intemperance and filthy living conditions.

Little was done about the deplorable state of the city slums except on the occasional appearance of a deadly epidemic disorder. Two major Asiatic cholera outbreaks swept through the United States, one in 1832–33 and the second in 1849–50. In each case civic officials reacted by appointing temporary boards of health and instituting large-scale programs to cleanse their cities and eliminate the worst sanitary abuses. Once the danger was past, the abuses quickly reappeared. The second cholera epidemic, which coincided with the beginning of the sanitary movement, did provide the sanitary reformers with ammunition, and for the rest of the century the threat of cholera continued to give an impetus to sanitary reform.[2]

The first step to improve health conditions was to determine the level of health in the community, and this required the collection of vital statistics. A group of New Yorkers in 1836 took the initiative by founding the New York Statistical Society. The society survived only briefly, but its work was picked up by Lemual Shattuck, Dr. Edward Jarvis, and other Boston reformers. They organized the American Statistical Society, and Jarvis and Shattuck then joined forces to pressure the state legislature into passing the Massachusetts Registration Act of 1842. The law established a system for registering vital statistics, and Shattuck played a major role in shaping both the law and the resulting system. Shattuck's method for collecting vital statistics in Massachusetts set the pattern for registration systems in other states.[3]

By the mid-nineteenth century a number of American physicians—men such as Jarvis of Massachusetts, John H. Griscom and Elisha Harris of New York, Edwin M. Snow of Rhode Island, and Edward Barton and J. C. Simonds of New Orleans—were beginning to call attention to the deplorable living conditions of the workers and the desperate need for sanitary reform. Along with cholera, a series of major yellow fever epidemics in the 1850s had ravaged the southern port cities and threatened the entire East Coast. The ever-present danger of these diseases induced another of the sanitarians, Dr. Wilson Jewell of Philadelphia, to call for a national sanitary convention in 1857. The original purpose of the meetings was to standardize the quarantine laws, but in the successive meetings it became clear that the majority of delegates were convinced that the best defense against epidemic diseases was an effective sanitary program. The outbreak of the Civil War in 1861 ended these national meetings and temporarily delayed the movement for reform.[4]

The enormous amount of sickness among both Northern and Southern troops and the success achieved in reducing this sickness through enforc- ing sanitary regulations in army camps gave re- newed strength to the sanitary movement. A major agency promoting camp sanitation during the war was the United States Sanitary Commission, a group of civilian reformers who aided the Union army in many ways, but whose most lasting contri- bution was to help spread the doctrine of commu- nity sanitation and personal hygiene.

By the 1870s the sanitary movement in Amer- ica was in full swing. New York City in 1866 had created the first permanent board of health and in so doing provided a model for several other major cities. In 1872 the American Public Health Associ- ation came into existence, foreshadowing the es- tablishment of public health as a discipline of its own. In response to a series of yellow fever epi- demics and the threat of cholera the first national quarantine law was passed in 1878. This same year a major yellow fever outbreak that spread far up the Mississippi Valley prompted Congress to establish the first National Board of Health. Organized in the spring of 1879, the board was essentially a quaran- tine agency, although its members envisioned a wider purpose. Unfortunately it fell afoul of state and local health officials who were jealous of its authority, and of the United States Marine Hospital Service, whose officials also saw the National Board as a potential threat. Moreover the idea of the federal government dabbling in social concerns was counter to the spirit of the day. The result was that the board, although officially in existence until 1893, ran out of funds in 1883 and to all intents and purposes disappeared.[5]

At the state and local level the sanitary reform- ers were making steady progress. Louisiana had es- tablished the first state board of health in 1855, although it was essentially a health board for the city of New Orleans. In 1869 Massachusetts took the lead in establishing an effective board of health with statewide authority.[6] Most of the remaining states quickly followed suit. The majority of state health boards functioned primarily in an advisory capacity, since they had virtually no funding and

very little authority. Most state boards accom- plished little, but in a few states, where the health commissioner or president of the board was a strong individual, considerable progress was made in establishing public health programs at the city or town level. By the 1880s health officials were be- ginning to widen their concerns to include urban housing, air pollution, the health of infants and schoolchildren, and vital statistics. The first chemi- cal laboratories appeared to test food and water, and health inspectors began checking on tenement housing, privies, plumbing, food-processing plants, and other possible sources of disease.

This cheerful picture of steady progress in community health had little to do with life in the United States in the nineteenth century. The rapid growth of urban areas had as its corollary a compa- rable increase in human misery. The well-to-do generally moved out of their old homes to new ones on the outskirts of the city, leaving their former residences to be occupied by an influx of workers seeking employment. As these houses overflowed, newcomers were forced to move into barns, stables, old factory buildings, and any other available type of shelter. In the second half of the century entrepreneurs began building multistory tenements, most of which had neither water nor any other amenities, and in which windows and ventilation were sadly deficient. It is a commentary on such conditions that New York, a relatively pro- gressive city, passed a law in 1887 requiring new tenements to have one water closet or privy for ev- ery fifteen persons.[7]

There is scarcely an American city without its horror stories describing the squalid circumstances in which a good share of its inhabitants lived. In one small area of Chicago in the 1890s there were 811 sleeping rooms without outside windows and less than 3 percent of families had their own bath- rooms. The *Weekly Medical Review* reported that the industrial workers were compelled to live in tainted tenements or "low fetid hovels, amidst pov- erty, hunger and dirt," where "in foulness, want and crime, crowded humanity suffers, and sickens, and perishes."[8] Dr. Joseph Jones, president of the Louisiana State Board of Health, declared in 1881: "One third of those dying in New Orleans die in poverty, and are buried at the public expense. One sixth of those who die in New Orleans, perish in silence and misery, with no kind companion, no efficient medicine, and no generous physician."[9] New Orleans at this date had no sewerage, a completely inadequate water system, and an inefficient city government.

New York City, which had one of the best municipal health departments, had only limited success in dealing with the health and social problems of its residents. Its teeming tenements produced so much garbage and human wastes that even under the best of conditions horses and wagons would have had difficulty removing them. The situation was compounded by the inefficiency and corruption that pervaded virtually all city governments. Street cleaning and the removal of the contents of privies was still a lucrative form of political patronage in American cities; the result was that in New York and elsewhere the streets and gutters were constantly filled with piles of garbage, dead animals, and the overflow from privies. To add to the distinctive urban atmosphere, dairy barns and stables accumulated huge manure piles, slaughterers let blood drain into the gutters and dumped offal outside their doors, and a host of other so-called "nuisance" industries befouled the atmosphere and created breeding grounds for a myriad of flies.

Nearly all early health leaders remarked on the enormous mortality among infants and children. Their comments were understandable, since the first few decades of the nineteenth century witnessed a steady rise in general urban mortality and an even greater rise in that of children under five years of age. The Boston City Registrar in 1865 compared the number of deaths of children below the age of five to deaths from all age groups and found that the percentage of children's deaths had shown a steady increase, rising from 23.0 percent in the years 1820–24 to a peak of 46.6 percent in 1855–59. Granting questions as to the accuracy of these statistics, infant mortality was on the rise in all major cities during these years and remained a major problem throughout the nineteenth century. The vital registrar of New York City, where the infant mortality rate was at least as high, in 1879 found it "gratifying, if not entirely satisfactory" that infant mortality had not risen significantly since the establishment of the Board of Health in 1866.[10]

Nothing indicates human degradation and the wastage of infant life better than the large numbers of foundlings picked off the street of major cities. Foundlings in New York City were cared for by the female inmates of the almshouses and few lived beyond a year. In 1866 a special hospital was built for foundlings, but the infant mortality rate continued to average around 60 percent. In 1897 when the hospital was under attack, the Commissioner of Charities blandly stated that the 96 percent mortality rate was "not as bad as it looks," since many children were sick on arrival and others had been sent there to spare the parents the cost of a funeral. He further explained that limited funds compelled the institution to use women from the workhouse who mistreated the babies.[11]

In rural areas and small towns, health conditions were better for the lower income groups than in the cities. The environment could absorb the limited quantities of garbage and wastes, the water supply was usually safer, fresh air and sunshine were plentiful, and the food supply was generally— although not always—better. In the South, for example, the one-crop system tended to discourage the establishment of vegetable gardens, and tenant and small farmers who did raise chickens and vegetables often sold them for cash. While escaping some of the endemic disorders of the cities— smallpox, measles, mumps, scarlet fever, diphtheria, whooping cough, typhoid and other enteric infections—rural areas were subject to fatal and debilitating forms of malaria.

Scarcely any section of America avoided malaria at some time in its history, and the disease moved westward with the frontier all the way to California. In 1874 the New Jersey State Health

Commissioner declared that malaria was the state's principal medical problem, and it was 1890 before northern Illinois was free of the fever. Even New York City was recording almost 100 deaths annually from malaria as late as 1900, although the disease was usually contracted outside the city.[12] A number of states began antimosquito programs in the early years of the twentieth century, but it was not until the New Deal brought better housing, screening, improved medical care, and a higher standard of living in the 1930s that any real progress was made. The massing of troops in the southern army camps in World War II forced the federal government to take decisive action against the threat of malaria. One of the most successful government agencies, the Atlantic-based Office for Malaria Control in War Areas, was largely responsible for the virtual elimination of malaria from the United States. At the end of the war, this agency was transformed into the present Centers for Disease Control.

By 1900 the two great dramatic pestilences that had aroused the most attention, yellow fever and cholera, were no longer a serious threat. One last outbreak of yellow fever occurred in New Orleans in 1905, but by this date the work of Walter Reed and his associates of the United States Marine Hospital Service had demonstrated the *Aedes aegypti* as the vector of the disease, and a massive campaign against mosquitoes soon ended the epidemic. The significance of these two disorders arises from the general fear they aroused. Their successive outbreaks supplied the impetus to the call for the National Sanitary Conventions in the 1850s, the establishment of the New York Metropolitan Board of Health, the first national quarantine law, and the National Board of Health. As late as 1892 the threat of cholera impelled the New York City Council to establish the city's first diagnostic laboratory.[13]

While these more dramatic pestilences drew most attention, a number of endemic disorders brought far more sickness and death. The leading cause of death was pulmonary tuberculosis. Known as consumption, its diagnosis was tantamount to a death sentence, and it was assumed that the only hope was to move to another climate. Koch's discovery of the bacillus in 1882 opened the way for treatment in the twentieth century, but as late as 1930 it was still a serious problem. Smallpox, which had been reduced to minor proportions in the early nineteenth century, began to flare up as the dreadful epidemics of earlier years faded from public memory and people grew careless about vaccination. Renewed drives for vaccination gradually brought it under control by the early twentieth century. In 1959 the World Health Organization began a drive to eliminate smallpox on a worldwide basis. Within approximately twenty years the program had succeeded, one of the great medical triumphs of this century.

Throughout the nineteenth century, diphtheria, scarlet fever, measles, and whooping cough constantly winnowed the ranks of infants and children. The most fatal disorder, diphtheria, showed a rising incidence in the latter part of the century. Fortunately, just as it reached a peak in the 1890s, advances in bacteriology made it possible to diagnose, treat, and finally prevent this fearful children's disease.

Although health conditions for all Americans left much to be desired, for African Americans and other minority groups the situation was far worse. As of 1900 life expectancy at birth for whites was 47.3 years, for nonwhites the figure was 33.0.[14] Some Native Americans were still fighting a hopeless battle to maintain their way of life, and the tribes who had given up the struggle found themselves in a netherland. The old values were gone, but they could not accept those of the whites; hence they eked out a bare living on reservations, beset by disease and alcohol abuse. The case of the blacks was little better. Free blacks in the antebellum area tended to be the lowest of economic classes, and as such were most subject to malnutrition and received the least medical care. The health of slaves in this era depended largely upon the beneficence and intelligence of their masters, but it is a reasonable assumption that it was below that of whites.[15]

The freedom blacks gained by the Civil War brought little if any improvement in their collective health, since any benefits were minimized for most of them by their economic dependence. Without capital or resources and with few skills, the majority were forced into economic peonage, either as free laborers or through the sharecropping system. Whereas most planters had felt some responsibility for the health and welfare of their slaves, they quickly shucked off this responsibility with emancipation. Many former slaves fled to towns and cities, where they encountered the endemic urban contagions and found their economic situation little better.

In the northern cities discrimination forced blacks into the lowest-paying jobs and compelled them to live in the worst slums. While some were able to fight their way out of the poverty cycle, the majority shared the abject misery of the poorest whites. Their economic condition was faithfully reflected in the vital statistics—everywhere their morbidity and mortality rates were far in excess of that of the general population.

Offsetting this grim picture of life in the last two decades of the nineteenth century, these same years saw the professionalization and institutionalization of public health. The American Public Health Association was organized in 1872, and the next thirty years witnessed the appearance of state and local health boards. In this period, too, the bacteriological revolution radically changed both medicine and public health. By the 1890s public health departments were establishing laboratories for diagnostic purposes and were beginning to make vaccines. They were also strengthening many of their existing programs and broadening their activities to include maternal and child health care, diagnostic services for physicians, dispensaries and clinics for the poor, and environmental concerns, and they were beginning to take an interest in occupational health. Health education, too, was becoming a significant part of public health work. The moves into new areas were helped by advances in technology and engineering that enabled health departments to

spin off to separate government agencies functions such as garbage collection, water supplies, sewerage, and street cleaning, with health officials maintaining only minimal supervision.

One of the most important of the new fields was health education. Whereas health officials had formally campaigned for sanitary measures to prevent foul miasmas, they now concentrated on educational programs to eliminate pathogenic organisms. Stimulated by a drive against pulmonary tuberculosis, campaigns were organized against the common drinking cup and spitting in public. People were urged to cover their mouths when coughing and to eliminate flies and other insects capable of carrying disease. Health educators taught schoolchildren to brush their teeth and wash their hands and faces, and they emphasized the need for personal hygiene.

Until the twentieth century, public health was essentially an urban phenomenon, but the entrance of the automobile helped inaugurate a new era for rural health. Yet it was the railways that first brought health education to small towns and rural communities. The idea of using a train for health education purposes was first conceived by Dr. Oscar Dowling, president of the Louisiana State Board of Health. In 1910 he secured two cars from a local railway, one as an exhibit and demonstration car and the other to accommodate staff workers, and sent the train on an eight-month tour of the state. At the end of this time he reported that every town of 250 or more inhabitants had been visited.[16] The health train's success prompted a number of other states to follow suit.

Dr. Dowling's health-train tour coincided with the emergence of the first county health departments. The movement for rural public health grew out of the Rockefeller Sanitary Commission's efforts to eliminate hookworm in the South and was given further stimulus in 1914 by the Public Health Service's interest in pellagra and typhoid. As towns and cities began providing safe water, typhoid was becoming largely a rural problem. Both the commission and the health service recognized that any permanent solutions to the health problems in rural areas required the establishment of local health units. In the same decade, 1910–20, the National Tuberculosis Association, the Red Cross, and the United States Children's Bureau began sending public health nurses into rural areas and sponsoring a variety of health programs. Subsequently other foundations and agencies entered the picture. The number of county health units grew slowly, however, until the New Deal and World War II gave a sharp impetus to the rural health movement.

Although lay people had taken a major role in the British and Continental sanitary movements, in America nearly all of the early leaders had been physicians. The successes gained in the second half of the century, however, had been made possible by the appearance of sanitary associations consisting of business and professional men and middle- and upper-class women. New Orleans depended on trade and commerce, and intelligent businesspersons in the 1880s and 1890s realized that the city's reputation for disease and pestilence was scarcely conducive to encouraging the influx of new capital or business enterprises. In consequence the more enlightened of them began to support the local sanitary association, pushed for expensive water and sewer systems, and generally advocated public health measures. In Memphis, which was devastated by the 1878 yellow fever epidemic and where conditions may have been even worse than in New Orleans, the business community initiated a complete overhaul of the municipal government and instituted major public health reforms.[17] Enlightened self-interest did not characterize all of the business community, but individual members contributed to the health reform movement throughout the country.

While individual physicians had led the public health movement, organized medicine played only a minor part. The leadership of the AMA supported many of the reforms, but the association itself had little political influence until its reorganization in the early years of the twentieth century. As indicated earlier, the reorganized AMA and its constituent societies strongly supported public health

legislation so long as it did not interfere with private practice. For example, they cooperated with school medical inspection up to a point. When school nurses and medical inspectors began uncovering an alarming number of medical problems among poor children, health departments began setting up clinics to provide free health services. The medical profession, determined to keep the private fee-for-service system, reacted strongly and succeeded in closing most of these clinics. At the same time these physicians were equally successful in closing the many public dispensaries providing virtually free care to the lower income groups. In the case of the dispensaries, the changing nature of medicine would probably have brought their demise in any case.[18]

Since public health budgets depend upon politics, public health officials out of necessity cannot afford to offend any significant pressure group; hence, as the political power of the medical profession grew, health departments withdrew from the health care area and concentrated on such matters as health education, environmental conditions, inspection of food and water supplies, limited maternal and child programs, medical inspection of children, vaccination programs, and limited screening for diseases.

The federal government, which spent millions of dollars on diseases of farm animals, birds, and plants in the nineteenth century, spent almost nothing on the health of its citizens. The sum total of its contributions were the United States Marine Hospital Service, founded in 1798 to provide for sick seamen, the short-lived National Board of Health, and a weak national quarantine law. The first decade of the twentieth century saw the founding of the Hygienic Laboratory in 1901, the forerunner of the National Institutes of Health, and the passage of the Pure Food and Drug Law of 1906. The next federal action came in 1912 with the creation of the United States Children's Bureau and the transformation of the Marine Hospital Service into the Public Health Service. In this transformation, the Public Health Service was given responsibility for research and investigation of communicable diseases. World War I drew attention to venereal diseases, and a Federal Division of Venereal Diseases was established to assist cities and states in dealing with these infections. The first significant move by the federal government into the health care field came with the Sheppard–Towner Act of 1921. This measure broke new ground by providing grants-in-aid to states instituting maternal and child care programs. In part due to bitter opposition from the AMA, the program was allowed to lapse in 1929.[19]

The New Deal marked the first substantial efforts by the national government to enter the health care area. Almost every New Deal agency, temporary or permanent, made some contributions to health. As early as June 1933 the Federal Emergency Relief Administration authorized the use of its funds for medical care, nursing, and emergency dental work; Civilian Conservation Corps workers received medical care; the Civil Works Administration promoted rural sanitation and helped to control malaria and other diseases; and both the Works Progress Administration and the Public Works Administration built hospitals, health centers, and sewerage plants and contributed to other public health projects. In 1935 Titles V and VI of the Social Security Act authorized the use of federal funds for crippled children, maternal and child care, and the promotion of state and local public health agencies. As health sociologist Roy Lubove has pointed out, the Social Security Act is of special significance, since it established a permanent machinery for distributing federal funds for health purposes and recognized special needs in allocating these funds.[20]

The appropriation for health under the Social Security Administration grew rapidly in the late 1930s, aided by the results of a National Health Survey undertaken in 1935–36. This survey confirmed what earlier ones had shown, that the lowest economic groups suffered the greatest amount of sickness and disability and received the least medical care. Parenthetically, we might note that if all the money spent on rediscovering this fact in the past fifty years had been used for health care, it is quite possible that we would have fewer health problems today. Whatever the case, the survey showed that the average expenditure by states for public health amounted to only eleven cents per capita, and that municipal expenditures were not much higher. The bleak picture presented by this report provided further ammunition for reformers who had already made American health problems a significant political issue. In 1939 the Wagner Bill to establish a national health program was introduced into Congress. President Roosevelt's preoccupation with the war, the opposition of organized medicine, and other factors prevented its passage.

The decade of the 1940s saw limited progress in public health, although general health conditions improved steadily, largely as a result of the wartime and postwar prosperity. The billions of dollars spent on military camps and industries in the South raised the economic standard and health level of the entire region. Efforts to promote a national heath program proved abortive, and the only significant steps by the federal government were the Hill–Burton Act of 1946 to promote the construction of hospitals and to start pouring funds into medical research. The tremendous expansion of the armed forces, however, meant that millions of Americans received medical and dental care—for many of them a relatively new experience. In addition, as veterans they were henceforth eligible for health benefits.

The 1950s saw the federal government support the construction of medical and public health schools, appropriate large sums for health research, and in 1953 establish a Department of Health, Education and Welfare. In these years federal spending for health-related services rose dramatically. As of 1960 annual federal expenditures amounted to almost three billion dollars, and by 1970 the figure had risen to approximately twenty billion. The purpose of the Hill–Burton Act was to facilitate the construction of hospitals in rural areas, but Congress steadily broadened the original act. States seeking funds were required to develop statewide hospital plans, but these plans proved meaningless. While the Hill–Burton Act did achieve some success in promoting hospitals in rural areas, the act failed woefully when it decentralized hospital policy and placed it in the hands of local and state leaders, which resulted in the continuing duplication of hospital facilities. Moreover, in response to public demand, Congress continued to enact more patchwork legislation relating to health, adding to the multiplicity of federal agencies involved in some aspect or aspects of health. By 1970 federal health programs were spread over 221 agencies or departments.[21]

The fight for direct health care remained in abeyance during the Republican years, 1952–60, and was not revived until the 1960s. The opening wedge was a bill to provide medical care for the aged—a group whose emotional appeal, while not quite on par with motherhood, was still high—and, what was possibly more important, a group whose numbers and voting power were increasing. The first success came in 1962 with the passage of the Kerr–Mills Bill, which provided medical care for a limited group of the aged sick. The fight to extend these benefits culminated in the Medicare and Medicaid amendments to the Social Security laws in 1965. Essentially these amendments provided low-cost government subsidized medical insurance for Social Security recipients. In an interesting switch, the AMA and its allies sought to expand the benefits of the Medicare and Medicaid bill in hopes of killing it, while the liberals sought to minimize them in order to guarantee passage of the bill. The result was a far more generous program than the sponsors of the bill had envisioned. The past twenty-five years have seen Medicare and Medicaid steadily broadened to cover more individuals and provide greater benefits. By 1986 Medicare was providing coverage for over twenty-eight million Americans. In the process its budget grew from $4.7 billion in 1967 to $64.6 billion in 1984 and it still continues to grow.[22]

The concept of medical insurance in America dates back to the contract practice of medicine in the nineteenth century, but its present form is of more recent origin. In 1929 a group of teachers in Dallas, Texas, contracted with Baylor University Hospital to provide service benefits at a fixed fee per semester. The idea was picked up by the American Hospital Association in the early 1930s and led directly to the Blue Cross (hospital) and Blue Shield (medical and surgical) programs. As unions and corporations began negotiating health benefits, private corporations moved into the health insurance business. In the succeeding years voluntary health insurance experienced an explosive growth, encouraged in part by the medical profession's acceptance of it.

Growing alongside health insurance came another form of medical care somewhat akin to the former contract practice, the prepaid group practice. Two of the most successful of these are the Kaiser Foundation Health Plan organized in California in 1942 and the Health Insurance Plan of Greater New York dating back to 1947. By 1960 each of these plans was providing complete medical care to over half a million subscribers. Physicians participating in these early health maintenance organizations (HMOs) were subject to considerable pressure from the AMA and local medical societies, but the steady growth of HMOs has forced the medical profession to accept them.[23] Today they supply health care to over thirty million Americans.

A major factor in the rise of HMOs has been the impact of business corporations. The enactment of the Coal Mine Health and Safety Act of 1969 and the more comprehensive Occupational Health and Safety Act of 1970 made companies liable for the health of their employees and led them into health planning. Unions had long been pressing for health benefits, and by 1984 industry was providing health care coverage for about forty million Americans. As the cost of health care to industry escalated, corporations began turning first to HMOs as a method of restructuring and rationalizing health care. In more recent years, as a result of their studies of the entire health care system, a number of industrial leaders appear to be moving toward a comprehensive system of health insurance at the state or national level.[24]

The momentum developing in the 1960s may well have led to a national health insurance program in the 1970s had it not been for an economic recession and the Watergate scandal leading to the resignation of President Nixon. The rapidly increasing cost of medical care in the 1980s, however, once again brought national health insurance to the fore as a means for bringing health expenditures under control. In 1989 Walter B. Maher, director of employee benefits for Chrysler Corporation, described the United States health care system as "broke, both literally and figuratively." Adding that health costs had become a major competitive problem for American businesses, he declared the time is right for a fundamental change. Echoing his views, Jack Shelton, manager of employee insurance for the Ford Motor Company, declared that the problem was too large to be handled at the company level and there "needs to be some national strategy to respond to it."[25]

American medical care today is provided by or paid for through a variety of methods and agencies—Blue Cross and Blue Shield, commercial insurance, government-subsidized health insurance, and various forms of group practice. In addition, the government provides direct medical care to millions of individuals through the armed forces, the Veterans Administration, the Public Health Service, Indian Health Service, and a range of other agencies. Through outright grants and matching funds the federal government also subsidizes medical care for millions of other Americans.

Every major city has at least one municipal hospital and various clinics, dispensaries, and health care centers offering outpatient and inpatient services to those who cannot afford private medicine. In addition, state and county agencies supplement these services with a number of medical institutions and programs. Paralleling the state and government services are those offered by voluntary associations that concentrate upon specific medical problems or problem areas such as cancer and mental health. While voluntary groups tend to place their major efforts upon health education and raising funds for research, they also provide some diagnostic and treatment facilities.

The effect of government participation in health care has been to make medical service available to many individuals who formerly seldom visited a physician except in dire emergencies. Medicare and Medicaid have been of great help to the aged, but Medicare, although intended originally to help aged workers, has become a major benefit for senior members of the middle class, while Medicaid, a joint federal–state program intended to provide coverage for the poor, has been under-funded and supplies only second-class medical care. Moreover, some thirty-five million or more individuals in the lower income brackets ineligible for Medicare are neither covered by employer insurance nor able to afford personal health insurance. Hence any type of serious illness or injury becomes both a personal and economic catastrophe.

Aside from excessive duplication, the health care system has led to a maldistribution of physicians. For both financial and professional reasons, physicians tend to avoid urban ghettos and rural areas. In an effort to deal with this problem, beginning in the 1960s the federal government offered scholarship loans to medical students with the proviso that most of the loan would be canceled if the recipient practiced in an underserved area for a limited time. Another program, the National Health Services Corps, offered physicians a choice of military service or practicing in an area short of physicians. Individual states, too, subsidize medical students on a similar basis. Programs such as these are of help, but the same factors that draw physicians into affluent urban and suburban centers still operate once these physicians have served their time. The best program developed so far is the Area Health Education Centers. These centers are designed to attract young physicians into areas where they are needed and at the same time providing continuing education for local health professionals.[26]

With business leaders, unions, and large segments of the public beginning to demand some type of comprehensive medical program, what can Americans expect for the future? Unlike the older Western countries, philanthropy and volunteerism are firmly embedded in the American tradition, and the association of the word "socialist" with the British national health program makes it unlikely that it would appeal to Americans. All efforts in the past to provide some form of federal health insurance have included the principle of decentralization and minimum federal interference. Unfortunately there is need to restructure medical services, and health insurance in itself cannot do so; in fact, it may merely compound the problems.

The Canadian medical system has been the subject of considerable discussion in recent medical and lay publications. Whatever the advantages or disadvantages of the British and Canadian systems, both of them provide the average citizen with at least as good care as he or she receives in the United States and at a lower cost. A possible harbinger of the future is the recently adopted Massachusetts universal health insurance plan, which in effect requires employers to offer health insurance to all full-time employees and sets up a state fund financed by a payroll tax to enable the unemployed to buy insurance. Among the proposed health plans currently under construction is one to extend the Massachusetts program to the national level.

Whether or not the United States adopts some type of comprehensive medical care system, group practice is here to stay, and the traditional fee-for-service system is obviously coming under constraints. The development of Peer Review Organizations (PROS), designed to prevent questionable hospital admissions, and Diagnosis Related Groups (DRGs), intended to serve as check on the expanding costs of Medicare, are indicative of the trend toward government regulation of medicine. In addition, government and private insurance companies are beginning to place limits on fees or at least are requiring physicians to justify them.

No one can predict what the future holds, but the present trend is clearly toward more government involvement in medical care. While many physicians still feel that medical care is a privilege, public opinion is beginning to consider it a right. Congress seldom provides leadership, but it does respond to public pressure. A national health law of some type seems almost inevitable; whether or not it is a sound one will depend on the willingness of the medical profession to face up to social and political realities and assist in writing a good measure.

NOTES

1. For a more detailed account of public health in this period, see Duffy, *The Sanitarians,* chapters 1–3.

2. Ibid., chapters 4–7.

3. James H. Cassedy, *American Medicine and Statistical Thinking, 1800–1860* (Cambridge, Mass., 1984), 194–99.

4. Cavins, "National Quarantine and Sanitary Conventions," 404–26.

5. Peter W. Brutton, "The National Board of Health" (Ph.D. diss., University of Maryland, 1974), 54ff.

6. For an account of early public health in these two states, see Gordon E. Gillson, *Louisiana State Board of Health: The Formative Years* (n.d., n.p.), and Barbara G. Rosenkrantz, *Public Health and the State: Changing Views in Massachusetts, 1842–1936* (Cambridge, Mass., 1972).

7. Duffy, *A History of Public Health in New York City, 1866–1966,* chapter 6 and pp. 220–35; Duffy, *The Sanitarians,* 178.

8. Bonner, *Medicine in Chicago,* 20–21; *Annual Report of the Louisiana State Board of Health, 1881* (New Orleans, 1882), 242–44.

9. Duffy, *Matas History of Medicine in Louisiana,* 2: 465–66.

10. Richard R. Meckel, *Save the Babies: American Public Health Reform and the Prevention of Infant Mortality, 1850–1929* (Baltimore, 1990), 29, 38.

11. Duffy, *History of Public Health in New York City, 1866–1966,* 208–11.

12. Stuart Galishoff, *Safeguarding the Public Health: Newark, 1895–1918* (Westport, Conn., 1975), 70; Duffy, *History of Public Health in New York City, 1866–1966,* 163.

13. Duffy, *History of Public Health in New York City, 1866–1966,* 94–95.

14. U.S. Department of Commerce, *Historical Statistics of the United States: Colonial Times to 1957, A Statistical*

Abstract Supplement (U.S. Government Printing Office, Washington, 1960), 25.

15. Todd L. Savitt, *Medicine and Slavery: The Diseases and Health Care of Blacks in Virginia* (Urbana, 1978); John Duffy, "Slavery and Slave Health in Louisiana," *Bulletin of the Tulane University Medical Faculty* 26 (1967):1–6.

16. Gordon E. Gillson, *Louisiana State Board of Health: The Progressive Years* (Baton Rouge, 1976), 216–22.

17. John H. Ellis, "Businessmen and Public Health in the Urban South during the Nineteenth Century, New Orleans, Memphis, and Atlanta," *Bull. Hist. Med.* 44 (1970):197–212.

18. John Duffy, "The American Medical Profession and Public Health: From Support to Ambivalence," *Bull. Hist. Med.* 53 (1979):8–9.

19. Duffy, *The Sanitarians,* 247–49.

20. Roy Lubove, "The New Deal and National Health," *Current History* 45 (August 1963):77–86.

21. Stevens, *American Medicine and the Public Interest,* 500–503, 509–13; Daniel M. Fox, *Health Policies: Health*

Politics: The British and American Experience, 1911–1965 (Princeton, 1986), 130ff.

22. David Blumenthal, Mark Schlesinger, and Pamela D. Drumheller, eds., *Renewing the Promise: Medicare and Its Reform* (New York, 1988), 15–16.

23. Cecil G. Sheps and Daniel L. Drosness, "Medical Progress, Prepayment for Medical Care," *New England Journal of Medicine* 264 (1961):390–96, 444–48, 494–99.

24. Betty Leyerle, *Moving and Shaking American Medicine: The Structure of a Socioeconomic Transformation* (Westport, Conn., 1984), 8–9, 79, 137.

25. *Wall Street Journal,* April 3, 1989.

26. Fitzhugh Mullan, "The National Health Service Corps and Health Personnel Innovations," in *Reforming Medicine: Lessons of the Last Quarter Century,* ed. Victor and Ruth Sidel (New York, 1984), 184–85.

DEVELOPED WORLD PERSPECTIVE

STATUS AND MEDIEVAL MEDICINE

VERN L. BULLOUGH

It has often been pointed out by scholars of medieval science that, after the middle of the fourteenth century, there seems to have been a shift in the balance of interests towards a concentration on methodology.[1] While the scientist was still active, his time was more often spent in linguistic and logical analysis of problems and statements, and quite frequently the original problem was lost in the subtlety of analysis.[2] While this, like any generalization, can be challenged,[3] there seems to be a great deal of truth in it. In attempting to explain why this might be the case, the writer has been struck by the importance of status concepts in the development of ancient and medieval science, especially of medicine.

Science seemingly has developed best when the speculative reasoning of the philosopher, scientist, or mathematician is in closest touch with the manual skill of the craftsman.[4] While this might not be so important in modern science when sci-

ence has become the parent of technology, it was probably the most important factor in ancient and medieval science when technology was the parent of science.[5] If such a generalization is valid for earlier scientific investigation then science would either be encouraged or handicapped by the class "status" recognition given to those who performed manual labor in society, or who in effect had the necessary manual and/or technical skills.

Generally manual work in classical times was the lot of slaves, and any free man who tried his hand at it, even in the most casual way, lost status.[6] In view of the long series of Greco-Roman medical writings, military devices, treatises on building, engineering, agriculture, and other branches of applied mechanics, it appears that the separation of the manual from the theoretical was never drawn very rigidly.[7] Still many scholars have emphasized that the Greeks and Romans were not particularly superior in technology to more ancient empires, but were probably inferior.[8] The curve of technological development began to rise again in the medieval period, influenced in part by Islamic and Byzantine concepts and ideas,[9] but also by certain internal developments in medieval society. Professor Lynn White, Jr., has pointed out to American scholars the mushrooming developments of the medieval period.[10] In accounting for this, Professor White has emphasized at least two points. First, medieval labor was free, that is, it was done by free men, and this tended to emancipate technology from the restrictions of slavery.[11] Second, the Christian ascetic ideal as influenced by St. Benedict and others emphasized manual labor, thereby making invention and experimentation respectable.[12] The dual concepts of monasticism that "to labor is to pray" and that intellectual labor, as well as manual labor, were both suitable activity for monks led to the great outpouring of technological ideas which reached fruition in the middle ages: the water wheel, windmills, counterweight artillery, mechanical clocks, gunpowder, and so forth.[13]

It would seem natural to assume that the rate of increase of scientific and technological developments would increase when intellectual labor became institutionalized in the universities. This in fact did happen in the twelfth and thirteenth centuries, but once the newly developing universities were established the rate ceased to increase, or at least the rate of contributions of the university-trained scholars did. The great age of the University of Montpellier as a medical school was in the thirteenth century. Much the same can be said of Paris and Bologna. After this they declined. Why the drop in the fourteenth century? Certainly the political, religious, and social unrest of the period plus the inertia caused by the plague are important, but more important at least in medicine was the status conflict within the profession—a conflict which led to the fragmentation of the medical profession.

In the earlier medieval period there had been no separation of medicine from surgery. The general practitioners, usually called *medici,* were drawn both from the clergy and from the laity. If they were monks or clerics they had probably acquired their medical knowledge, at least in part, through their liberal arts training. If lay practitioners, they had probably acquired it almost entirely through empirical means.[14] Such methods were in keeping with the concepts of education then existing: practical (for the nobles), speculative (for the clerics), and technical (for the *laboratores*). Education was not particularly institutionalized, so no hard or fast line could be drawn. As the scholarly curriculum came to be established toward the end of the tenth century, there appeared to be some sort of distinction developing.[15]

When universities developed in the twelfth century, they became for the most part the home of the speculative studies. These were not especially technical nor practical, but they were vocational in that they tended to fit the student for the task he was to perform. The seven liberal arts were not the end of the educated man, but rather a basis for advanced studies in the higher faculties: theology, canon law, civil law, and medicine. These were conceived of as speculative disciplines but with practical application. The theologian's duty was to define the dogma of the church, to distinguish heresy, to reconcile or disprove knowledge dangerous to the church. The canon lawyer was to organize, codify, and administer within the church, an intensely practical job as indicated by the increasing number of lawyer popes. The civil lawyer was to do much the same thing for the state, although at times there was a conflict between his obligation to the state and his duty to the church. This conflict resulted in forbidding the University of Paris, possibly the greatest of medieval universities, to offer civil law. The physician was to speculate on the causes of illness, erect medical systems, and heal and cure the sick. Medicine lacked the intellectual prestige of theology, or the opportunities for advancement found in law, but it was an aristocratic profession nonetheless.[16] In order for medicine to live up to its speculative status which it had newly won, the physician would be extremely loath to use manual techniques. If he did, he might lose status *vis-à-vis* the other groups. This status consciousness was reinforced by the medieval practice of regarding all students as clerics by the very nature of their studies. That is, university education was for the speculative, hence those going through the educational process were *ipso facto* clergy, even though of minor orders.[17]

If the above thesis is correct, then medieval attitudes, once medicine was institutionalized, would tend to create a gulf between the speculative practitioner, the physician, and the manual one, the surgeon. The physician, in attempting to make his profession as equally cerebral and speculative as the lawyer or theologian, avoided a loss of status which might have come from the use of manual techniques. In fact all manual performances connected with the treatment of the sick came to be looked upon as unworthy of the physician, as *infra dignitatem.* This would leave a void, one filled by the emerging surgeons. But unfortunately the physician's attitude had repercussions. Surgeons were unwilling to be consigned to the class of manual practitioners. They attempted to claim equal status with the physicians by imitating the attitudes and outlook of their rivals and by doing as little manual work as possible. Such a conflict led to the neglect of many aspects of medicine and the emergence of other groups, barbers, barber-surgeons, apothecaries, and others, to fill them. The physicians, cut off to some extent from the actual contacts with the anatomical knowledge available to the surgeon, attempted to build up a natural philosophy of medicine; the surgeon, attempting to rival the physicians, increasingly neglected some of the more important aspects of surgery in order to concentrate on the theoretical aspects which would give them greater status; but unfortunately they lacked the learned tradition which would make this entirely intelligible to them; the barbers, content to be empirical practitioners, were not so well versed in the theoretical aspects of medicine, while the apothecary became an increasingly narrow spe-

cialty. Enough for generalizations, how does the theory hold up in practice?

Medicine first emerged as a university course in the twelfth and thirteenth centuries at Bologna, Montpellier, and Paris, although an earlier famous school had existed at Salerno.[18] Salerno, however, was not technically a university until late in the Middle Ages, when it had been eclipsed in reputation by the other schools. Salerno is important, however, because it was here that Arabic, and Arabic–Greek medical writings were first translated into Latin and various empirical traditional ideas were put to paper. With the appearance of the university the term physician, *i.e.,* the university-educated medical practitioner, entered common usage. As a member of a newly developing profession, the physician was extremely conscious of his status, and soon attempted to bring the other developing medical practitioners under his control. He did this by attempting to establish standards, but the standards were set rather arbitrarily by himself. In so doing he violated the drive for status of the other medical groups, thus causing further confusion in the medical profession.

In 1271 the physicians of the medical university at Paris reproached another developing group, the surgeons, for trying to exceed the limits of their "trade."[19] The use of the word trade was, very probably, in the nature of an attempt by the physicians to lower the status of the surgeons whose training was usually by apprenticeship. The surgeons, however, attempting to achieve status equal to the physicians, were unwilling to abide by the pretensions of their rivals. In an attempt to develop their "profession" (the term they preferred to use) the surgeons adopted or imitated the symbols and paraphernalia of the physicians such as the long robe, Latin books, the collegiate organizations, and so forth.[20] But in challenging the status of the physicians, the surgeons neglected their role in society which was soon claimed by another group of medical practitioners, the barbers or barber-surgeons, first mentioned in France in 1301.[21]

This conflict in role again came from the medieval idea that status depended on whether one's job was manual or not, so that the surgeons in order to raise their status would have to make their occupation more speculative and less manual. This the surgeons attempted to do by distinguishing between "worthy" and "unworthy" operations. This was much harder to do in practice than in theory and the surgeons soon found they were working themselves out of a job, since the barbers were taking over all surgery. In 1372 a royal decree restricted the barbers to preparing and administering plasters, ointments, and other medicines convenient and necessary to heal clous, bosses, apostumes (boils, tumors, and bruises) and all open wounds. This was more than the surgeons wanted the barbers to do, but the king refused to restrict the barbers further, because the surgeons regarded themselves as men of such great estate they did not treat poor people. Hence, to limit the barbers further would be prejudicial to the public interests.[22] In other words, in their search for status the surgeons nearly lost control of their trade.

In addition to the surgeons and barbers, another group, the apothecaries, also complicated the medical picture. The physician argued, somewhat successfully, that all medicine should be under him in order to preserve ethical standards.[23] While he himself might not deign to do surgery or have anything to do with surgery, the physician had to rely on drugs and concoctions to cure his patients. His livelihood depended in part upon the apothecary so that he was willing to fight hard to keep the apothecary under his control. A logical way of doing so would have been to combine the apothecary and physician in the same person, a development that did occur to some extent in England at a later date. This, however, would lower the status of the physician by changing his occupation from a speculative one to a manual one, *i.e.,* preparing medicines. The apothecary had developed from the herbalist and spicer, merchants or traders, and were already members of the *laboratores,* although some man-

aged to raise themselves to positions of power in the cities. Rather than weakening his own status by such an alliance, or allowing the apothecaries to extend themselves, the physician appealed to king or pope for control over the apothecaries. In the thirteenth century the apothecaries and herbalists were censured by the medical faculty of Paris for expanding their practice to the point where it infringed on the rights and duties of the physicians.[24] Effective control over the apothecaries was not achieved until the king intervened to grant the medical university in Paris control over the apothecaries, including the right of inspection.[25] The university was quick to prosecute any individual for violating its regulations.

But, while the physicians might get royal backing for their control over the apothecaries, it was a more difficult matter to bring the surgeons or barbers under control. The physicians especially resented the pretensions of the surgeons to a higher status. Unwilling to enter the surgical profession themselves, they instead hit upon a substitute. To counter the pretensions of the surgeons and to strengthen the barbers as well as themselves, the medical faculty of the university aided the barbers. By so doing they made the barbers dependent upon them, and at the same time weakened the power of the surgeons. At the same time they could keep their status since they still refused to practice manual medicine. Parisian barbers received training in anatomy at least from the beginning of the fifteenth century, and probably much earlier from the faculty of medicine at Paris.[26] At the same time the barbers were given theoretical instruction in surgery through lectures on the subject from the works of such men as Guy de Chauliac, first in Latin, then in French.[27] This gave the barbers a better chance to compete with the surgeons, and since they were not so concerned with the status symbols as the surgeons, they were more willing to subject themselves to the faculty.

In attempting to make good their claims to jurisdiction over all medicine, the physicians of the university met with considerable opposition from the populace. The non–university-trained people were for the most part the only doctors the general public had any contact with, since most physicians restricted themselves to treating the upper classes. Attempted regulation by the physicians might lead to higher prices and even less accessibility. In one of the most famous cases of attempted regulation, that of Jacoba Felicie de Almania, in 1322, one of the main points in the testimony of her defense witnesses was that she, unlike the physicians, refused to take any fee until her patients were cured.[28] When royal regulation was not sufficient to bring various practitioners under their control, the physicians turned to the popes for support, making their control a matter of moral welfare, by alleging that their rivals caused many deaths.[29]

While the above hypothesis can be documented for Paris, how valid is it elsewhere? Here, considerable qualification must be made. That is, the university physician made up only a small minority of the people practicing medicine so that he was usually only present in the more important cities or university towns. Most of the people in the middle ages were treated by the barber-surgeons or by plain simple housewife remedies, and never saw a university-trained man. With this qualification it appears that the generalization can have some validity. For Montpellier somewhat the same result can be found.[30] In England the universities were much weaker, but near the end of the fourteenth century they, too, began to act.[31] Royal regulation did not appear until the fifteenth century, when the practice of medicine was restricted to university graduates,[32] although there were some provisions for surgeons to practice their art in a subordinate status.[33]

In Germany the universities were slower to develop so that regulation also appears later. However, the same general trend is evident. At Colmar, regulation of the apothecaries by the physicians is apparent in the fourteenth century. Apothecaries were allowed to sell drugs only on prescription of a physician, and the physicians were also allowed to inspect the shops of apothecaries.[34] In Vienna no regulations are extant from the fourteenth century, but those of the fifteenth century were drawn on much the same lines as earlier ones at Paris; that is, the medical faculty of the university had control over the auxiliary medical practitioners.[35]

In Italy such dichotomy of medical practice is much more difficult to demonstrate, perhaps because, in Italy, the city movement was more developed and the prejudice against manual labor might have been less, or because, by the accident of educational development, surgeons from the first were included within the universities at Bologna and Salerno. At any rate the generalization does not quite hold so well here, but even in Italy the physician achieved much more prestige.

Whether detailed documentation can always be given, however, is rather unimportant, for it is still a fact that medicine and surgery became separated during the later medieval period. While there might be various explanations for this separation, it is due, perhaps mainly, to the attitudes of the medieval people themselves, and can best be explained in sociological terms. Part of the separation might have been beneficial, but the total effect of the separation was not. All the divisions within medicine have to share some of the blame, but perhaps the separation really demonstrates how much medical attitudes are part of the general cultural setting. The long separation of surgery and medicine also indicates how cultural ideals of the past continued to exert the prestige of tradition on the development of medicine for a long time thereafter. If a comparison of medicine and science can be made, it is also apparent why later medieval science became somewhat overly concerned with methodology; it had in effect lost its contact with technology.

NOTES

1. A. C. Crombie, *Robert Crossesteste and the Origins of Experimental Sciences* (Oxford: Clarendon Press, 1953), p. 295; Lynn Thorndike, *A History of Magic and Experimental Science,* II, 883, 969; George Sarton, *Introduction to*

the History of Science (Baltimore: Williams & Wilkins for the Carnegie Institution of Washington, 1948), III, passim.

2. James A. Weisheipl, O. P., *The Development of Physical Theory in the Middle Ages* (New York: Sheed and Ward, 1959), p. 63.

3. Lynn Thorndike, *op. cit.,* IV, 612–13, felt that perhaps his earlier statement had been too strong.

4. A. C. Crombie, *Augustine to Galileo: The History of Science A.D. 400–1650* (Cambridge, Mass.: Harvard U. Press, 1953), p. 143.

5. Charles Singer, "Epilogue," in Charles Singer, E. J. Holmyard, A. R. Hall, Trevor I. Williams, *et al., A History of Technology* (New York: Oxford U. Press, 1956), II, 774.

6. Lynn White Jr., "Dynamo and Virgin Reconsidered," *The American Scholar* (Spring, 1958), p. 187.

7. Crombie, *Augustine to Galileo,* p. 143.

8. Singer, *op. cit.,* II, 754–55. Professor Lynn White Jr. indicated his disagreement with Singer on this point in a personal note to me.

9. Other sources have also been put forth. See for example the brief summation by Lynn White, Jr., "Tibet, India, and Malaya as Sources of Western Medieval Technology," *American Historical Review,* 65 (1960), 515–26.

10. Lynn White Jr., "Technology and Investigation in the Middle Ages," *Speculum,* 15 (1940), 141–59.

11. White, "Dynamo and Virgin," *op. cit.,* p. 187.

12. *Ibid.*, p. 188.

13. *Ibid.*, p. 191.

14. Loren C. MacKinney, *Early Medieval Medicine* (Baltimore: The Hideyo Noguchi Lectures, Johns Hopkins Press, 1937). See also his "Medical Education in the Middle Ages," *Journal of World History,* 2 (1955), 835–51.

15. MacKinney, *Early Medieval Medicine*, p. 131; Ernest Wickersheim, "L'evolution de la profession medicale au cours du moyen age," extrat du *Scalpet,* Nos. 42-43-44 (1924), p. 71.

16. See for example Hastings Rashdall, *The Universities of Europe in the Middle Ages* (New Edition edited by F. M. Powicke and A. B. Emden, 3 vols., Oxford: Clarendon Press, 1936), and Charles Homer Haskins, *The Rise of Universities* (New York: Henry Holt & Co., 1923).

17. This led to some church regulation of medical practice including prohibitions against the practice of medicine by regular clergy. Most such prohibitions were applied also to law so that the purpose might have been that of preventing outside interests of any kind from intruding within the walls of the monastery. One of the earliest of such prohibitions was in 1131 at the Council of Rheims under Innocent II where *"Ne monachia aut regulares canonici leges aut mediciniam cause lucri discant."* See J. D. Mansi, *et al.*, *Sacrorum con-*

ciliorum nova et amplissima collection (new edition: Florence and Venice, 1759–98), XXI, col. 459. Such prohibitions were restated at the second Lateran (1139, Innocent II), the Council of Montpellier (1162, Alexander III), the Council of Tours (1163, Alexander III), Second Council of Montpellier (1195, Celestine III), Council of Paris (1212, Innocent III). See *Ibid.*, XXI, cols. 528, 1160, 1179; XXII cols. 831, 1160. The repetitions indicate that it was difficult to enforce or in fact often ignored. At the fourth Lateran (1215, Innocent III), a specific prohibition was made against the practice of surgery by clergy; *Ibid.*, XXII 1006–1007. This prohibition was to apply to both secular and regular clergy. Again as late as the end of the thirteenth century, at the diocesan synod of Würzburg (1298, Boniface VIII), the prohibition was being repeated; *Ibid.*, XXIV, col. 1190. This prohibition against surgery is not especially an attempt to prevent the practice of surgery but rather, at least in my opinion, an attempt of the emerging university faculties to achieve a higher status for their profession. Some support for this argument can be given by the fact that the faculty of the University of Paris prohibited its bachelors from practicing manual surgery. See [Jean-Bapt'. Louis Chomel], *Essai historique sur la médecine en France* (Paris Lottin l'Aîné, 1762), p. 150. This prohibition prevailed into the fifteenth century when a surgeon who wished to become a physician was not allowed to do so until he swore that he would no longer practice manual surgery. See *Commentaire de la faculté de médecine de l'université de Paris,* ed. with an introduction by Ernest Wickersheimer ("Collection de documents inédits sur l'histoire de France," Paris: Imprimerie Nationale, 1915), p. 47. Henceforth *Commentaires.* In Italy also the decree was not observed even by the universities, *infra.*

18. For an account of the development of these schools see Paul Oskar Kristeller, "The School of Salerno," *Bulletin of the History of Medicine* (henceforth *BHM*), XVII (1945), 138–94; Vern L. Bullough, "The Development of the Medical University at Montpellier to the End of the Fourteenth Century," *BHM*, XXX (1956), 508–43; Bullough, "The Medieval Medical University at Paris," *BHM*, XXXI (1957), 197–211; and Bullough, "Medieval Bologna and the Development of Medical Education," *BHM*, XXXIII (1958), 201–15.

19. *Chartularium Universitatis Parisiensis,* ed. and annotated by Henry Denifle and Aemelio Chatelain (Paris, Fratrum Delalain, 1889–1897), I, No. 434, 489. Henceforth abbreviated as *Chart. Univ. Paris.*

20. For a more detailed account of the development of the medical guilds at Paris, see my "The Development of the Medical Guilds at Paris," *Medievalia et Humanistica,* XI (1958), 33–40.

21. Rene de Lespinasse (ed.), *Les métiers et corporations de la ville de Paris* ("Histoire générale de Paris," Paris: Imprimerie Nationale, 1886–97), III, 628.

22. *Ordonnances de rois de France,* edited by Eusèbe Jacob de Lauriére, Denis Francois Secousse, *et al.* (Paris: 1723–1849), V, 530–31; henceforth abbreviated *Ordonnances.*

23. In this claim the physicians might have some justification because medical ethics probably reached a new high in the fourteenth century. See Mary Catherine Welborn, "The Long Tradition: A Study in Fourteenth-Century Medical Deontology," in James L. Cate and E. N. Anderson (eds.), *Medieval and Historiographical Essays in Honor of James Westfall Thompson* (Chicago: The University of Chicago Press, 1938), pp. 344–57.

24. *Chart. Univ. Paris,* I, No. 434, 489.

25. *Ordonnances,* II, 532–35, and Lespinesse, *op. cit.,* I, 504–05.

26. *Commentaires,* p. XXXV.

27. *Ibid.,* 353.

28. *Chart. Univ. Paris,* II; Nos. 811–16, 255–67. For an account of these struggles see Pearl Kibre, "The Faculty of Medicine at Paris, Charlatanism, and Unlicensed Medical Practices in the Later Middle Ages," *BHM,* XXVII (1935).

29. *Chart. Univ. Paris,* I, No. 844, 285–86, No. 900, 336–37, No. 1138, 602–03, III, No. 1197, 7–8.

30. Cartulaire de L'université de Montpellier, published under the auspices of the Conseil Générale des Facultes de Montpellier (Montpellier: Richard Frères, 1890), I (Period 1181–1499), No. 2, 180–83, No. 4, 186, No. 14, 202–03, No. 35, 236–38, No. 68, 344, par. 12, No. 127, 476, No. 162, 569–71, No. 194, 682–83.

31. Henry Anstey (ed.), *Municimente academico or Documents Illustrative of Academical Life* (Rolls Series, London: Longmans Green, Reader and Dyer, 1868), I, 236–37.

32. *Rotuli parliamentorium; ut et petitiones et placita in parliamente* (London, 1767–77), IV, 130, 158.

33. *Ibid.,* IV, 130.

34. Karl Baas, "Studien sur Gaschichte des Mittelalterlichen Medizinalwesens in Colmar," *Zeitschrift für die Geshcichte des Oberrheins,* 61 (1907), 217–46.

35. Leopold Senfelder, "Oeffentliche Gesundheispflege und Heilqunde," *Gescheichte der Stadt Viens,* ed. Albert Starzer (Vienna: Adolf Holzhausen, 1905), II, Pt. II, 1040–44.

DEVELOPING WORLD PERSPECTIVE

I SWEAR BY IMHOTEP THE PHYSICIAN

BRUCE LAWRENCE RALSTON

It has been traditional for fledgling physicians to take the Hippocratic Oath on completion of their university training and at the beginning of their medical careers. This code has remained an important canon of medical ethics for over 2,000 years. The oath itself is an unusual and unique document in that it is not consistent with true Hippocratic ideals, and probably represents a guild oath of hereditary priests and practitioners known as Aesculapiads. It is most compatible with the teachings of the Pythagorean school which flourished over a generation after Hippocrates' death, circa 375 B.C.[1]

Among the interesting features of the oath are the opening words "I swear by Apollo the physician, and Aesculapius, and Hygeia, and Panacea...." This unabashed fealty to pagan gods is wholly un-Hippocratic, and its twentieth century perpetuation invites thoughtful consideration.

GREEK PANTHEON

Apollo, son of Zeus, and one of the leading Olympian deities, was a many-faceted god. With respect to his role in medicine, he was responsible for bringing and averting disease.[2] He was physician to the other gods, healing with the peony root. It is not certain that healing was part of his early cult.

The first reference to Aesculapius is in the *Iliad,*[3] written about 800 B.C. and referring to the period of the Trojan War, about 1200 B.C. He is a human being, a "clever leech," a minor chieftain from Thessaly. His two sons, Machaon and Podalirius, were physicians in this war, one being the prototype physician and the other the prototype surgeon. Over the following centuries, Aesculapius was ranked as a local hero, then worshiped as an earth spirit by his descendants. His most ancient shrine was in Trikke in Thessaly; the serpent was his symbol and he acquired an oracle. As his cult spread southward, it came into conflict with that of Apollo, based at Delphi. About 600 B.C., a political union was effected between the two, centered in Epidaurus. Aesculapius became the active healing god, the son of Apollo, his mentor.[4] At this time, a series of birth legends originated to sanctify this event. The nymph Koronis, pregnant by Apollo, is killed by him for infidelity. The child, delivered by cesarean section by Apollo, is reared by the centaur Chiron who teaches him medical skills. He becomes so expert that Pluto accuses him of depopulating Hades, and angry Zeus slays him with a thunderbolt. Sorrowing Apollo then has Zeus make him an immortal god among the stars.

Aesculapius, having passed through the stages of local hero, demigod, and finally, the specific god of medicine, had temples erected to him throughout Greece and the later Roman world. These aesculapia or healing temples were essentially sanitoria where therapy was carried out by "incubation" through sleep and revealed dreams. Hygeia joined the cult at a later date, assisting with the sacred serpents. Panacea, his other daughter, assisted with the treatments. These temples also served as a repository of medical knowledge. Hippocrates, and also Aristotle, came from such an aesculapiad, or priestly family, of the Coan school.

We are known as the "Sons of Aesculapius," and he is our tutelary "deity," emblematic of the medical profession. He is commonly represented as an older man, with a beard, sitting or standing, usually holding the staff with a serpent coiled about it. This has been adopted, along with the caduceus, as a symbol of the profession.

Since past is but prologue, we shall now go back in time about twice the period between us and Hippocrates, to examine the spoor of another contender for our paternity.

IMHOTEP

Fifteen hundred years anterior to Aesculapius and almost 5,000 years ago lived an individual who has been described by Breasted[5] as "the first outstanding individual in history." Imhotep, whose name means "he who comes in peace," lived at a time in Egyptian history comparable to the Periclean age and the Renaissance. These periods, characterized by sharp intellectual and social ferment after a period of slow development or inactivity, permitted the emergence of gifted individuals.

Although he was ultimately deified as the god of medicine, his contributions in other areas are equally important considerations in evaluating the capabilities of the man, and, at this distance in time, his reality.

1. As chief architect under King Zoser of the third dynasty, he designed and built the Step Pyramid, the first of the pyramids, also the world's first large stone structure, and the direct prototype of the Great Pyramid of Cheops.[6]
2. This pyramid was surrounded by a funerary complex built of stone, and has never been duplicated in Egypt or elsewhere. Two hundred years before Athens and Corinth, he had perfected basic architectural forms such as fluted columns with astragal bases, flowered capitals, portals, ornamented friezes, and pillared halls. From this complex was recovered the seated figure of Zoser, the earliest known life-size figure of stone.[7] He was also responsible for the construction of other stone buildings, among these the early temple of Edfu.
3. He was a sage, scribe, and philosopher, the author of a book of maxims that has now perished, but was quoted by his descendants for at least 15 centuries.[5]

4. As grand vizier, equivalent to prime minister, he held the most responsible position in the kingdom after that of the pharaoh.

5. He was an astronomer, referred to in the Hermetic literature and associated with the god Thoth.

6. Also, he was the first high priest of Heliopolis, the most important priesthood in Egypt at that time, as well as chief lector priest concerned with ceremonies for the dead.

Some facts are known about Imhotep's life. His mother was Kreduonk, and his father, Kanifer, was also an architect. He began work for Zoser as a young man. His titles indicate that he was not of royal blood but was, rather, a self-made man. The king allowed him an almost unheard-of favor by permitting his name to appear on a royal statue. There is no information as to his longevity or his death. Almost certainly, he is buried in a tomb close to that of his king, Zoser, at Sakarra, this being the custom at the time.[8]

In 1957, Prof. W. B. Emery was excavating the archaic first and third dynasty cemeteries in North Sakarra dating from about 2800 B.C. Test pits disclosed ibis mummies. These birds are sacred to the god Thoth, who is also associated with Imhotep in the Egyptian pantheon. In 1964 Emery found that in Ptolemaic times, 200 B.C., the ground had been flattened to form a wide platform for a large temple. Thirty-five feet beneath it was a fantastic catacomb with over 1 million ibis mummies. One of Imhotep's titles was "first chief one of the ibis." Also found were relics of prayers, dreams, priestly interpretations, and votive models of parts of the body that had been cured. Emery felt that this composite represented the remains of a monumental shrine which had been built and rebuilt by the Egyptians of the Ptolemaic age to their god Imhotep, and to which they had brought their offerings, including the ibis birds. He felt that this temple was built over the tomb of Imhotep, which must be in the vicinity.[9]

Emery dug for seven years and died during excavations in 1971. At the time of his death he was confident that he was very close to Imhotep's tomb.[10]

In the view of William Osler, M.D., Imhotep was "the first physician to emerge from the mists of antiquity,"[11] and to Breasted[12] he was the earliest known physician in history and, as such, he was medical advisor to the pharaoh. The Edwin Smith Surgical Payyrus, the earliest known scientific treatise, has been dated paleographically to the same period, and Breasted speculates on whether or not Imhotep may have been its author. The books he is known to have written have been lost.

Following his death, Imhotep was venerated as a hero, and about the time of the New Kingdom, circa 1580 B.C., was elevated to the status of demigod. In this role he has been represented in numerous bronze statuettes, appearing as a young man, usually seated, wearing a cap and reading intently from the equivalent of a book, a roll of papyrus. He was elevated to full divinity about the time of the Persian period, 525 B.C., now being portrayed as carrying the uas scepter and the ankh sign. On the monuments, he is now referred to as "son of Ptah," the patron god of Memphis, and his cohort Sekmet, replacing their son Nefertum. At a later time he rose to become the dominant god of Memphis. During the Ptolemaic period he was referred to by the Greeks as Imouthes and identified fully with their Asklepios, later the Aesculapius of the Romans.

There is now evidence that this deification began at a considerably earlier period. In a papyrus written in 2 A.D. there is a statement that Mycerinus, fourth dynasty pharaoh, established temples and monuments for Imhotep, son of Ptah.[6] If the papyrus is to be trusted, then Imhotep was deified as early as 100 years after his death. Numerous sanitoria or "houses of life" sprang up, which were resorted to by sick and afflicted patients, coming from great distances. Of these, the largest was at Memphis, the metropolis in which Imhotep was especially venerated, and which was very close to Naucratis, city of the Greeks. Several of the sanitoria are still in existence, the most important being on the island of Philae and at Deir el-Bahri.

PAST IS PROLOGUE

Granted the temporal precedence of Egyptian medical knowledge, was there, in fact, any direct influence on developing Greek medical practice? Considerably earlier than the New Kingdom, a steady stream of Greek visitors descended on Egypt.[13] It may be recalled that after the fall of Troy, Menalaus and Helen visited Egypt and brought back gifts and medicines.[14] About 600 B.C. the Greeks were given their own entrepot city, Naucratis, on a Nilotic branch in the delta, and were the only ones accorded this privilege.[15]

Many of the most important pre-Socratic and Socratic Greek scientists and philosophers studied in Egypt.[16] They represented all schools. Thales of Miletus is the earliest known, circa 575 B.C., and came away with the principles of geometry.[17] Solon of Athens and Pythagoras of Croton preceded Hippocrates. It was from Pythagoras that Hippocrates derived his concept of "critical days." Democritus of Abdera spent five years in Egypt and, according to Strabo,[18] Plato, and the astronomer Eudoxis, spent up to 13 years in Egypt, establishing a school there.

Herodotus, the historian, visited Egypt about 450 B.C., and described a highly advanced state of medical specialization. He also stated that almost all the names of the gods and their cults came into Greece from Egypt.[19]

Almost nothing is known about the life of Hippocrates, except that he was born in Cos, died in Larissa, and traveled widely. Some writers feel that he visited Egypt, as did his contemporaries, Democritus and Plato.[20] Many of his case reports are from Adbera where he spent considerable time with his lifelong friend, Democritus, who, besides atoms, wrote on anatomy, epidemics, prognostics, and diet.

INCUBATION SLEEP

The therapeutic ritual associated with incubation sleep provides a very good index of continuity in practice. In Egypt, dreams were regarded with re-ligious reverence. The power to dream and cause others to dream was encouraged, and sleeping in temples to obtain a remedy during sleep (incubation) was common. In the vision, the god appeared, addressed the suppliant by name, cured him, or told him to find his cure in a sealed naos or box in the morning, which he would copy and replace. The instructions were in direct language and required no official interpreters during the pharaonic period.[4]

Incubation sleep was carried out in the temple of Ptah at Memphis from the earliest times. In this capacity he was known as Ptah–Sotmu, meaning Ptah "who hears." It was at Memphis, the largest city of the ancient world at that time, that Imhotep became ascendant, a short distance from the Greek city of Naucratis. As far south as Nubia, incubation sleep had been practiced over the centuries, and also in the temple of Thoth, who was related to Imhotep, particularly from the eighteenth dynasty onward.

The incubation ceremonies were usually followed by gifts, particularly votive, of the parts of the body cured.

These ceremonies were transferred "en bloc" to the aesculapia in Greece where they spread rapidly after the deification of Aesculapius by union with Apollo in the fifth century B.C. Similar votive offerings are to be found in the Greek temples.

In the third century B.C., Ptolemy I had established in Egypt a new god, Serapis, to satisfy both his Greek and Egyptian subjects. Serapis was a strong healing deity. The old Egyptian ritual was superseded by compulsory priestly interpretation of dreams, a practice that led to many abuses. This cult ultimately spread to mainland Greece as a strong rival to Aesculapius.

There are many other examples of filiation between ancient Egyptian and pre-Alexandrian Greek medicine. These include certain unusual marker medications such as women's urine, quills, and fried mice; the use by the Greeks of numerous Egyptian names of drugs, illnesses, and anatomy; the identical ways of handling clavicular fractures and jaw dislocation in the Edwin Smith papyrus and the Hippocratic texts; and the similarity of unusual diagnostic tests.[13]

PARALLEL LIVES

Plutarch, who also visited Egypt, narrated in a series of books the accounts of one Greek and one Roman, followed by a comparison of each pair, the so-called *parallel lives.* So may Aesculapius and Imhotep be regarded. They both came from humble beginnings, practiced as physicians, and after their deaths became demigods and ultimately fully deified, one the son of Apollo and the other of Ptah. Both were responsible for the establishment of ongoing medical facilities in which patients were treated, in a remarkably similar manner, and knowledge accumulated.

Aesculapius has been chosen as the tutelary deity of medicine, not because of any particular accomplishment, but because he represented the most remote point in time from which we could evolve an ongoing medical tradition. Yet Homer, who introduced Aesculapius to the world, can describe him only as a blameless leech; conversely, he depicts contemporary Egypt as teeming with medicines, the land where the physician is skillful beyond all men. Classical writers, such as Herodotus and Diodorus, could elaborate in part, but the door to our pre-classical past remained closed until the hieroglyphs were deciphered in 1822. By that time, Greek mythology had become so involved with our history of medicine that a proper balance could not be restored.

We now know that over one and one-half millennia before Aesculapius there lived a man of universal talent, a gifted administrator, architect, engineer, wise man, philosopher, astronomer, and high priest, inter alia. It was for none of these that he was deified, but for his role as a physician. He was known to have written books, and is usually portrayed reading or writing in one. His professional career coincides so closely in time with the remarkable Edwin Smith papyrus that he is considered its possible author.

It has been possible to trace the transfer of Egyptian medical traditions to the aesculapiad school in Greece. The surprising cultural diffusion was made possible by Greek philosophers and scientists who in large numbers visited and studied in Egypt, including close associates of Hippocrates and, possibly, Hippocrates himself.

COMMENT

The scholastic bones may also be fleshed out, because the very buildings that Imhotep built are still standing as are statue fragments with his name on them. Scholars are in active pursuit of his actual tomb, possibly even his physical remains.

Ancient Egypt, after its second millennium, began to show sclerosis and regressed under a deathless priestly embrace. This in no way detracts from its brilliant beginnings when future western civilization was barbaric.

Returning to our Hippocratic Oath of allegiance. It is inadvisable to swear, particularly to pagan gods; but if one must swear, why not to Imhotep?

REFERENCES

1. Richards, D. W.: Hippocrates of Ostia, *J.A.M.A.* **204:** 115 (1968).
2. Garrison, F.: *An Introduction to the History of Medicine,* 2nd ed., Philadelphia and London, W. B. Saunders, 1921, p. 75.
3. Homer: *The Iliad,* translated by R. Fitzgerald, New York City, Doubleday and Company, 1974, pp. 59, 95, 267.
4. Jayne, W. A.: *The Healing Gods of Ancient Civilizations,* New Haven, Connecticut, Yale University Press, 1925, pp. 29, 74.
5. Breasted, J. H.: *The Dawn of Conscience,* New York City, Charles Scribner's Sons, 1961, pp. 141, 163.
6. Hurry, J. B.: *Imhotep,* Oxford University Press, Humphrey Milford, 1926, p. 6.

7. Bratton, F. G.: *A History of Egyptian Archeology,* London, Robert Hale, 1967, pp. 21, 97.

8. Fakhry, A.: *The Pyramids,* Chicago and London, The University of Chicago Press, 1969, p. 24.

9. Mertz, B.: *Red Land, Black Land,* London, Hodder and Stoughton, 1967, pp. 188, 250.

10. Friendly, A.: Search for tomb in Egypt uncovers vast animal cult, *Smithsonian* **4:** 66 (1973).

11. Cushing, H.: *The Life of Sir William Osler,* London, Oxford University Press, 1940, p. 1042.

12. Breasted, J. H.: *The Edwin Smith Surgical Papyrus,* Chicago, The University of Chicago Press, 1930, pp. 3, 9.

13. Ghalioungui, P.: *Magic and Medical Science in Ancient Egypt,* London, Hodder and Stoughton, 1963, pp. 107, 164.

14. Homer: *The Odyssey,* translated by R. Fitzgerald, Garden City, New York, Doubleday and Company, 1961, pp. 61, 64.

15. Edwards, A. E.: *Egypt and Its Monuments,* New York City, Harper and Brothers, 1891, p. 26.

16. *Diodorus of Sicily,* translated by C. H. Oldfather, Cambridge, Harvard University Press, Loeb Classical Library, 1968, vol. 1, pp. 96, 327.

17. Farrington, B.: *Greek Science* (I), Harmondsworth, Middlesex, Penguin Books, 1949, p. 31.

18. *The Geography of Strabo,* translated by H. L. Jones, Cambridge, Harvard University Press, Loeb Classical Library, 1967, vol. 17, p. 29.

19. *The Egypt of Herodotus,* translated by G. Rawlinson, London, Martin Hopkinson and Company, vol. 2, pp. 29, 44.

20. Petersen, W. F.: *Hippocratic Wisdom,* Springfield, Illinois, Charles C. Thomas, 1946, pp. 172, 226.

CHAPTER 3

EPIDEMIOLOGY

This chapter will acquaint the reader with a number of epidemiological concepts relevant to medical sociology. It is important, however, to first define epidemiology. In a medical sociology text (Matcha, 2000, p. 96) I defined it as "the study of how disease is distributed within populations." Epidemiologists are interested in patterns of disease and the outcomes—that is, morbidity and mortality—of disease. The distribution patterns reflect the political and economic frameworks (or the lack thereof) that construct opportunities that differentially influence health outcomes among populations. The reader is encouraged to critically examine the role of the state and its economic structure relative to such differential health outcomes within all three of the articles in this chapter.

In the first article, William G. Rothstein examines a multiplicity of concepts, such as morbidity rates, mortality rates, and life expectancy, relative to the development of the United States. With the occurrence of broad social forces such as urbanization and industrialization throughout the 1800s, life chances for an increasing number of Americans declined. Throughout the twentieth century, however, Americans experienced a rapid expansion of life expectancy and a concomitant decline in morbidity. As Rothstein points out, however, these changes are attributable not to advances in medicine or medical technology but to improving standards of living and public health measures for increasingly larger segments of the population. Nevertheless, such health improvements continue to be identified as occurring differentially throughout society—that is, examining health improve-

ments on the basis of sex, social class, and race and ethnicity demonstrates ongoing social inequality between population categories.

In the second article, Donald Cameron and Ian G. Jones provide a historical overview of John Snow and his efforts to explain the outbreaks of cholera in mid-nineteenth-century England. In addition, Cameron and Jones suggest that Snow believed that to fully understand epidemiology required knowledge of the entire community. For example, Snow argued that the lack of spread of cholera was related to implementation of public health measures. Furthermore, he suggested that social class was related to whether such measures were applied. Cameron and Jones also discuss the work of Snow relative to the spread of cholera among coal miners. The authors also point out that Snow recognized the importance of statistical analysis as supportive evidence for his theory, rather than using statistical measures to create a theory.

The final article, by Mary T. Bassett and Marvellous Mhloyi also illustrates the relationship between social conditions and disease patterns among specific population groups. The authors examine how social conditions have influenced the AIDS epidemic within many African countries in general and Zimbabwe in particular. Some of the reasons they discuss for the transmission of AIDS include a transitory labor market, increasing levels of urbanization, poverty, and the loss of land. Furthermore, they argue that family structure and sexual relations in Zimbabwe have been impacted by a history of paternalism and colonialism.

Given the interconnection of variables such as morbidity, life expectancy, and age and sex, these three articles nicely demonstrate the cross-cultural importance of medical sociology. In an effort to further understanding of these concepts, the reader is encouraged to locate mortality rates, infant mortality rates, and the life expectancy of men and women in a variety of countries. Also, what is the historical context in which the political and economic institutions developed in each of these countries? What is the economic level of development for each country (i.e., developing, developed)? This exercise is even more revealing when combined with health care financing (see Chapter 12).

REFERENCE

Matcha, Duane A. 2000. *Medical Sociology.* Boston, MA: Allyn & Bacon.

AMERICAN PERSPECTIVE

TRENDS IN MORTALITY IN THE TWENTIETH CENTURY

WILLIAM G. ROTHSTEIN

This article examines one of the most remarkable transformations in the history of mankind. The twentieth century has witnessed the greatest and most rapid changes in both death rates and causes of death in recorded history. At the beginning of the century, infectious diseases were the paramount cause of death in all societies, killing millions of infants, children, and young adults. After 1900 death rates from these diseases declined rapidly in advanced countries, enabling many more people to live to old age. The increasing number of the elderly died from chronic and degenerative diseases, especially heart disease, cancer, and stroke. In recent decades, death rates from heart disease and stroke have declined, while those from cancer have not. The reasons for these trends have been the subject of continuing conjecture and debate.

DISEASES IN HUMAN HISTORY

Infectious diseases first became common thousands of years ago when human beings settled in villages to farm the land, tend domestic animals, and trade with residents of other villages. When those events occurred, enough people had contact with each other to enable the microorganisms that cause diseases to find a continuing reservoir of uninfected individuals and thereby survive indefinitely. In earlier hunting and gathering societies, the populations were so small than any pathogenic microorganisms soon ran out of uninfected individuals and died out. From the onset of village societies until early in the twentieth century, human beings fell victim to a growing number of infectious diseases, which became the major cause of death in all societies. Most of the victims of these diseases were children and young adults.[1]

The situation worsened when international and intercontinental travel dispersed diseases around the world, beginning in the late fifteenth century. The early European explorers spread tuberculosis, smallpox, measles, scarlet fever, and other infectious diseases to the Americas, the Pacific Islands, and other parts of the world that had never known them. They returned to Europe bringing yellow fever, cholera, and other infectious diseases from

Africa and Asia. International travel also spread previously regional epidemics around the world as infected travelers unknowingly brought the diseases to different countries and continents.

Urbanization and industrialization in the eighteenth and nineteenth centuries forced the laboring classes of western nations to live in unsanitary housing, drink polluted water and milk, suffer diseases caused by unhygienic methods of sewage disposal, and eat a less nutritious diet than was available in many rural areas. Children suffered most from this unhealthy environment. In some American and European cities in the nineteenth century, one out of every four infants died before their first birthday.

Three fundamental changes were necessary to improve the health of the population. One was a higher standard of living to strengthen resistance to disease. This required better food, housing, and clothing, healthier home and work environments, lower birth rates, and a level of education that would enable people to understand and adopt the growing scientific knowledge about health care. The second change was improved public health measures by government to prevent diseases from infecting people. The third was effective clinical medicine, for the treatment of individual patients.

Perhaps the best available historical evidence concerning a society's standard of living is the height of its children and adults. A slow rate of growth during childhood and a short ultimate height that continues for decades in a society is clear evidence of a low standard of living. A study of the heights of British boys, adolescents, and military recruits found a slow but steady increase in the heights of those born from about 1750 to about 1840, a decline in their heights to the 1870s, a gradual return to early nineteenth-century heights by the end of the century, and a rapid increase in heights in the twentieth century. The study also found much taller heights among the children of the wealthy than other children before the twentieth century, indicating that heights throughout the period were strongly affected by the standard of living. Less comprehensive data showed that American men were one to two inches taller than the British (and other European) men throughout this period, but experienced the same growth trends as British men.[2]

These trends suggest that industrialization and urbanization had a deleterious effect on human health during the middle of the nineteenth century. Industrialization and world trade also lowered the standard of living of many rural people, whose cottage industry and small-scale farming could not compete with goods produced on a large-scale elsewhere. A lower birth rate at the end of the nineteenth century and greater national wealth in the twentieth century increased the overall standard of living.[3]

Public health and clinical medicine advanced in the late nineteenth century due to better microscopes and related technologies that enabled scientists to explore the world invisible to the naked eye. During and after the 1870s, the disease-causing roles of many bacteria and other parasites were discovered. Government officials soon developed public health programs to keep bacteria from infecting human beings. Sewerage systems prevented sewage from contaminating water supplies and coming into contact with human beings, water supplies were chemically purified to destroy bacteria, milk and foods were made to conform to standards of bacteriological cleanliness, vectors of infectious diseases like mosquitoes and rodents were controlled, and housing standards were gradually raised.

The first effective clinical treatments for many diseases were developed about the same time. Surgery was revolutionized in the 1880s after it was discovered that antiseptic procedures and sterilization prevented the wounds from becoming infected. Diphtheria antitoxin, discovered in 1894, was the first effective treatment for a major infectious disease. In the ensuing decades, treatments were developed for diabetes, pellagra, and pernicious anemia. The most revolutionary improvements occurred in the late 1930s with the discovery of sulfa drugs, the first general antibiotics. Penicillin, streptomycin, and other antibiotics followed in the 1940s.

Vaccines to immunize individuals against infectious diseases were also developed. Smallpox vaccination was developed in the late 1790s, but it remained unique until well into the twentieth century, when vaccines were developed for infectious diseases like diphtheria, tetanus, polio, rubella, and measles.

As fewer individuals died in childbirth and early adulthood from infectious diseases, they lived to older ages and contracted diseases related to the aging process, such as heart disease, cancer, diseases of the blood vessels, and diseases of individual organs like diabetes, emphysema, or kidney disease. These chronic and degenerative diseases have become the major causes of death in advanced societies. The change in causes of death from infectious diseases to chronic and degenerative diseases, often called an "epidemiological revolution," has had a momentous effect on our society. The remainder of this article will examine the nature of these changes.

BASIC CONCEPTS

Two kinds of statistics are used to describe the state of health in a population. One concerns deaths or *mortality*. The other concerns illness or *morbidity*. Historical data on mortality are the most frequently used measures of trends in the health of the population because all deaths and their causes have been reported to local or state government agencies for many years. Reliable historical data on morbidity exist for only a small number of diseases, mostly communicable diseases, that must be reported to the government. Morbidity data also pose problems because illnesses vary in the degree and permanence of the disability they produce. The health impact of a common cold, a heart attack, and diabetes vary so greatly that it makes little sense to group them together in a single category.

In examining mortality trends in a population, we use death *rates* rather than numbers of deaths.

The number of deaths are unsatisfactory because they increase or decrease with changes in the size of the population regardless of any change in its health status. Death rates enable us to compare populations of different sizes.

A mortality rate is a fraction in which the numerator consists of the number of persons who have had the experience in question (in this case, death) and the denominator includes all those who could have had that experience (the population). The formula for the *crude death rate* is the number of deaths in a population during a time period divided by the average population during the time period. The population in question may be the population of a nation, the population of a particular state or city, or the number of persons in a particular group, such as women aged 35–44. The time period is usually a specific year, but it can be a month or any other time period of interest.

Death rates always equal 1 or are less than 1, because the numerator (the number of people who died) can never be larger than the denominator (the population). This entangles us in decimal places. To eliminate this nuisance, we usually list death rates per 1,000 persons. For example, if 60 people in a community of 2,000 persons died in a given year, the crude death rate would be 60 divided by 2,000, which equals 0.03. This means that 3 of every 100 people in the community died in that year. We can change the statistic to the death rate per 1,000 by multiplying .03 by 1,000, which equals 30. This says that 30 out of every 1,000 people in the community died in that year. The first number (0.03) gives us the death rate per person; the second (30) gives us the death rate per 1,000 persons.

Death rates per 1,000 persons are useful for examining total deaths, but most individual diseases produce so few deaths that we use death rates per 100,000 persons to eliminate the decimal point. For example, if 800 persons in a population of 20,000,000 died of a particular disease in a given year, the crude death rate equals 800 divided by 20,000,000, or .00004. If we multiply .00004 by 100,000, we get a death rate of 4 per 100,000.

Death rates can be very deceptive because of these arithmetic manipulations. It is easy to forget that the 4 in the above example represents 4 deaths from that disease per 100,000 persons in a given year. In a city of one million persons, only 40 would die from that disease in a year. Such statistics become even more misleading when people speak of changes like a doubling of the death rate. If the death rate just cited doubled in a year, which sounds quite alarming, the number of deaths from that disease would rise from 4 per 100,000 persons to 8 per 100,000 persons, or from 40 deaths per year in the city of one million to 80 deaths per year. Very few people would notice such a change.

One way to assess changes in the health status of the population is to compare death rates at different times. Because crude death rates disregard changes in the age distribution of the population, they can be misleading when used in this way. An increase in the crude death rate over time may indicate only that there were more old people and fewer young people in the population at the end of the period, not that the population was less healthy.

In order to deal with changes in the age distribution of a population, epidemiologists use age-specific and age-adjusted death rates. *Age-specific* death rates are death rates for specific age groups in the population, such as persons 1–4 years of age or 65–74 years of age. By examining death rates for specific age groups, we need not be concerned about changes in the age distribution. *Age-adjusted* death rates adjust the death rate in a population so that the age distribution in every year studied corresponds to the age distribution that existed in a base year chosen for convenience (1940 in most U.S. government statistics). The population for every year except the base year is mathematically adjusted so that the percentage of the population in each age group is the same as in the base year. Although the resulting data do not describe the actual death rates in the population in any year except the base year, they permit comparisons between death rates in different years while holding constant the age distribution of the population.

In addition to total death rates, we are also interested in death rates from specific causes, such as cancer, AIDS, or accidents. Death rates from specific causes are subject to several problems that do not occur with overall death rates.

Information about causes of deaths are obtained from death certificates filled out at the time of death by the patient's physician, or in some cases a medical examiner or a coroner. The death certificate requires the physician to list both the "immediate" and "underlying" causes of death, which might be pneumonia and a stroke, respectively. The physician selects the specific causes of death from the current revision of the *International Classifications of Diseases.*

Several factors reduce the utility of time trends for causes of death for specific diseases. Many diseases, like heart attacks, cancer, stroke, and tuberculosis, are diagnosed differently now than they were early in the century, which makes it difficult to compare death rates at different periods. Physicians also tend to be more sensitive to diseases that are prevalent in the community. Early in the century, when heart disease was less prevalent than it is today, physicians often overlooked or misdiagnosed it. At the same time, they sometimes attributed deaths from other causes to tuberculosis, which was extremely common. Another problem, that has become more important in recent years, is that elderly people often have two or more serious diseases at the time of death, which makes it difficult to know the exact cause of death.

Nation-wide statistics on death rates were first gathered in the U.S. in 1900, but included only 10 states, the District of Columbia, and a number of cities in other states. This "Death Registration Area" was steadily expanded as more states gathered the necessary statistics until it covered the entire continental U.S. in 1933. Birth registration states (which are used to calculate infant mortality rates) were first listed in 1915 and did not include the entire continental U.S. until 1933 also. The original Death Registration Area consisted of the urbanized and older states, which had lower death rates then the non-reporting states, so that U.S. death rates before 1933 are very slightly lower than would have been the case had all states reported.[4]

THE DECLINE IN MORTALITY RATES

A remarkable decline in the crude death rate (Table 1) has occurred in the twentieth century. In 1900, there were 17.2 deaths for every 1,000 persons in the nation (for those states and cities in the Death Registration Area). In 1930, the rate dropped to 11.3 deaths per 1,000 persons, in 1960 to 9.5, and in 1991 to 8.6 deaths for every 1,000 persons. We may illustrate the significance of the decline in this way: In 1991, 2,169,000 persons died in the U.S.[5]; had the death rate of 1900 remained unchanged, 4,338,000 persons would have died in 1991. Thus, over 2 million lives were saved in 1991 compared to 1900 due to the decline in the death rate.

The decline was most rapid early in the century and has slowed in recent decades. Between 1900 and 1930 the death rate dropped by 5.9 deaths

per 1,000 persons, while between 1960 and 1991 the decline was only 0.9 deaths per 1,000 persons.

Table 1 also shows changes in age-specific death rates. Deaths throughout the century have been most likely to occur at the extremes of the life cycle—among the very young and the very old. This has been true from time immemorial. Death rates are high in the first year of life, but they drop very rapidly, so that the death rate over the entire life cycle reaches its nadir between 5 and 14. It rises slowly during early adulthood, and then ascends quite rapidly among the oldest age groups.

The greatest change in age-specific mortality rates in the twentieth century has been the decline in death rates among the young. In 1900, 162.4 of every 1,000 infants born alive died in the first year of life. This amounted to 1 out of every 6 infants, an appalling toll. The rate has declined steadily to 9.2 per 1,000 in 1991, or 1 out of every 109 infants. The significance of this change may be indicated thus: in 1991 there were 36,766 deaths in the first year of life.[6] Had the 1900 infant mortality rate remained unchanged, there would have been 649,000 deaths in the first year of life in 1991.

The death rate among children 1–4 years of age also plummeted from 19.8 per 1,000 in 1900 to only 0.5 per thousand in 1989. This age group, which had a higher than average death rate in 1900, now has the second lowest death rate among all age groups.

Looking at the table from a different perspective, in 1900 only one age group had a death rate of less than 5.9 deaths per 1,000: 5–14 years of age. In 1989, every age group from 1–4 years of age to 45–54 years of age bettered that statistic. Death has now become a rarity among children and young and middle-aged adults.

There have also been impressive declines in death rates among the elderly from 1900 to 1991, but they are less striking than the declines among the young. Among those age 65–74, the drop has been from 56.4 to 26.2 deaths per 1,000 persons. Among those 75–84, the drop has been from 123.3 to 58.9 deaths per 1,000 persons, and among those

TABLE 1 Crude and Age-Specific Death Rates, 1900–91 (deaths per 1,000 population)

AGE GROUP	1900	1930	1960	1991
All ages	17.2	11.3	9.5	8.6
Under 1 year	162.4	69.0	27.0	9.2
1–4	19.8	5.6	1.1	0.5
5–14	3.9	1.7	0.5	0.2
15–24	5.9	3.3	1.1	1.0
25–34	8.2	4.7	1.5	1.4
35–44	10.2	6.8	3.0	2.2
45–54	15.0	12.2	7.6	4.7
55–64	27.2	24.0	17.4	11.8
65–74	56.4	51.4	38.2	26.2
75–84	123.3	112.7	87.5	58.9
85 and over	260.9	228.0	198.6	151.1

Sources: 1900–60: U.S. Bureau of the Census, *Historical Statistics of the United States, Colonial Times to 1970* (Washington, DC: GPO, 1943), part 1, p. 60; 1991: unpublished data, National Center for Health Statistics.

85 and over, the drop has been from 260.9 to 151.1 deaths per 1,000 persons.

Another important factor affecting mortality rates is sex (Table 2). Throughout the century females have had lower death rates than males in all age groups. Among the very youngest, the sex difference has narrowed since 1900, so that female infants and young children now have only a slightly lower death rate than males. At the oldest ages, on the other hand, the sex difference has steadily widened, so that older women now have significantly lower death rates than older men.

Some may conclude that if fewer people are dying today, the American population should be growing at a faster rate than it did in 1900. Population growth depends on three factors: the number of deaths, the number of births, and the migration of people to and from America. Since 1900 both the birth and net migration rates have declined substantially, so that overall population growth has slowed substantially.[7]

INCREASES IN LIFE EXPECTANCY

To consider the effect of changes in death rates on the lifespan, Table 3 examines changes in life expectancy since 1900. *Life expectancy* tables show the average number of *remaining* years of life of a person of a given age. Life expectancy is not based on the actual experience of the people described, because that information will not be available until all of those persons have lived out their lives. Instead, it assumes that persons born now, for example, will have the same probability of being alive when they reach a given age that persons born that many years ago have of being alive now. Even though this is a poor assumption, it is the same throughout the table, so that the comparisons are useful even though the predictions will not be.

TABLE 2 Age-Specific Death Rates for Selected Age Groups by Sex, 1900–91 (deaths per 1,000 population)

AGE GROUP	1900	1930	1960	1991
Under 1 year				
Male	179.1	77.0	30.6	10.2
Female	145.4	60.7	23.2	8.0
1–4 years				
Male	20.5	6.0	1.2	0.5
Female	19.1	5.2	1.0	0.4
55–64 years				
Male	28.7	26.6	23.1	15.2
Female	25.8	21.2	12.0	8.7
65–74 years				
Male	59.3	55.8	49.1	34.4
Female	53.6	46.8	28.7	19.8
75–84 years				
Male	128.3	119.1	101.8	76.9
Female	118.8	106.6	76.3	48.0
85 years and over				
Male	268.8	236.7	211.9	178.0
Female	255.2	221.4	190.1	140.1

Sources: 1900–60: U.S. Bureau of the Census, *Historical Statistics of the United States, Colonial Times to 1970* (Washington, DC: GPO, 1943), part 1, pp. 61–62; 1991: unpublished data, National Center for Health Statistics.

TABLE 3 Remaining Year of Life Expectancy by Sex, 1900–89

	1900	1960	1970	1980	1989
At birth					
Male	46.3	66.6	67.1	70.0	71.8
Female	48.3	73.1	74.8	77.4	78.6
At age 40					
Male	—	31.4	31.5	33.6	34.8*
Female	—	36.6	37.6	39.8	40.2*
At age 65					
Male	11.5	12.8	13.1	14.1	15.2
Female	12.2	15.8	17.0	18.3	18.8

*1988

Sources: birth, age 65: National Center for Health Statistics, *Health United States, 1991* (Hyattsville, MD: Public Health Service, 1992), 140; age 40: U.S. Bureau of the Census, *Statistical Abstract of the United States: 1991* (Washington, DC: GPO, 1991), 73.

Table 3 shows that average life expectancy at birth has increased by about 25 years for men and 30 years for women from 1900 to 1989. Life expectancy at birth has increased so greatly because death rates drop sharply after the first year of life. If an infant survives the first year of life, the chances are very good that he or she will live another 60 years or more. Consequently every infant death that is prevented has a dramatic impact on total life expectancy.

The sex difference in life expectancy at birth has also grown. In 1900 the average female could expect to live 2 years more over her lifespan than the average male; by 1989 this difference had expanded to almost 7 years. Both social and biological factors contribute to this difference. With regard to social factors, men engage in many life-shortening behaviors to a greater extent than women: for example, they are more likely to smoke cigarettes (although the sex difference is narrowing), use beverage alcohol and drugs, commit suicide, and die of violence or injuries sustained at work or in other accidents. Biological factors are believed to have some involvement in women's lower rates of heart disease, stroke, and some other diseases.[8]

When we examine changes between 1900 and 1989 in the average number of years of life remaining at age 65, the increases are considerably smaller, especially for men. In 1900, a 65-year-old man could expect to live an average of 11.5 more years, to age 76.5, while a woman of the same age could expect to live an average of 12.2 more years, to age 77.2. In 1989, men 65 years of age lived an additional 3.7 years on the average (to age 80.2), while women 65 years of age lived an additional 6.6 years on the average (to age 83.8).

These data indicate clearly that a revolutionary decline has occurred in death rates, that this revolution has had its greatest impact on the young and least impact on the elderly, and that females have benefited more than males, especially among the elderly. We will now examine explanations for these remarkable changes.

THE DECLINE IN INFECTIOUS DISEASE DEATH RATES

In order to understand the reasons for the declining death rates of the U.S. population, and particularly the great reduction in death rates among the very young, we must examine the causes of death for the whole population and for individual age groups. These show clearly that a decrease in death rates from infectious diseases among the young has been responsible for most of the decline in mortality.

Table 4 shows the crude death rates per 100,000 population from 1900 to 1991 for the nine leading causes of death categories in 1900. Most categories contain more than one disease. Crude death rates, which are not adjusted for changes in the age composition of the population, are used because they were the only data available for the first half of the century.

In 1900, nine categories accounted for 63 percent of all deaths. Five of them, mostly infectious diseases, had their greatest impact on the young. Influenza and pneumonia were major causes of death among infants and very young children, as were gastritis and enteritis, which were caused by bacteria-laden milk, water, and food. The communicable diseases of childhood included diphtheria, measles, scarlet fever, and whooping cough. Tuberculosis was primarily a killer of adolescents and young adults, but it prevented millions from living into old age. Accidents, too, were major killers of the young.

Deaths from these diseases declined markedly from 1900 to 1950. Mortality rates from the infectious diseases in the group—influenza, pneumonia, tuberculosis, diphtheria, measles, scarlet fever, and whooping cough—dropped from 472 deaths per 100,000 persons in 1900 to 55 deaths per 100,000 persons in 1950. Gastritis and enteritis also declined greatly. By 1991 tuberculosis had practically disappeared (although it reappeared in the 1990s in AIDS patients), pneumonia and influenza have become diseases of the elderly rather than diseases of the young, and the other diseases that affect the

TABLE 4 Crude Death Rates by Cause, 1900–91, for Leading Causes of Death in 1900 (deaths per 100,000 population)

CAUSE	1900	1930	1950	1991
All causes	1791.1	1132.1	963.8	860.3
Influenza and pneumonia	202.2	102.5	31.3	30.9
Tuberculosis	194.4	71.1	22.5	0.7***
Gastritis and enteritis	142.7	26.0	5.1	**
Heart disease	137.4	216.7	356.8	285.9
Cerebrovascular disease	106.9	89.0	104.0	56.9
Nephritis, nephroses	88.7	91.0	18.7	8.5
Communicable diseases of childhood*	75.4	14.8	1.5	**
Accidents	72.3	79.8	60.6	35.4
Cancer	64.0	97.4	139.8	204.1

*Diphtheria, measles, scarlet fever, and whooping cough

**No longer listed

***1989

Sources: U.S. Bureau of the Census, *Historical Statistics of the United States, Colonial Times to 1970* (Washington, DC: GPO, 1975), part 1, p. 58; U.S. Bureau of the Census, *Statistical Abstract of the United States: 1958* (Washington, DC: GPO, 1958), 68; U.S. Bureau of the Census, *Statistical Abstract of the United States: 1960* (Washington, DC: GPO, 1960), 65; U.S. Bureau of the Census, *Statistical Abstract of the United States: 1991* (Washington, DC: GPO, 1991), 79; "Advance Report of Final Mortality Statistics," *Monthly Vital Statistics Report* 42 (31 August 1993), suppl. 1, p. 5.

young have become insignificant as causes of death.

These declines were due more to improvements in the standard of living and public health measures than to better medical treatment of the sick. Gastritis and enteritis were eliminated by measures such as pasteurization of milk and purification of water supplies. Death rates from tuberculosis, pneumonia, and communicable diseases of childhood experienced most of their decline long before effective treatments existed for them. Although public health measures like better housing and quarantine of the infected played a role, most of the decrease appears to have been due to a higher standard of living that strengthened the resistance of people to the diseases and enabled them to survive the diseases if they became ill.[9]

Public education was also important in this revolution. Until well into the twentieth century, millions of Americans drank from metal drinking cups kept next to fountains for all to use, did not sterilize bottles or take other measures necessary for hygienic feeding of infants, let their children sleep in the same bed and play with siblings with contagious diseases like diphtheria and scarlet fever, purchased unrefrigerated and bacteria-laden milk and meat, used polluted wells and water supplies without boiling the water, and took baths in bathtubs after others had used the same water. These and many other similar behaviors have disappeared because the public has been educated about personal hygiene.

One type of medical care that has been related to the decline in infectious diseases is vaccination. It is widely agreed that smallpox vaccination played a role in the decline of that disease, and some studies have found that diphtheria vaccine played a much greater role than diphtheria antitoxin in the decline of that disease. Vaccines for measles and polio are believed to have contributed to the decline in those diseases. Support for this view was shown by the rise in the measles case rate when federal support for measles immunization was reduced in the 1980s.

The decline in infectious diseases had important indirect health benefits as well. Nephritis and other kidney diseases are more likely to occur in adults who contracted scarlet fever or other streptococcal infections as children. As the incidence of streptococcal diseases has declined, so has the incidence of kidney diseases, which have dropped from a major cause of death in 1900 to a relatively minor one today.[10]

CHRONIC AND DEGENERATIVE DISEASES AS MAJOR CAUSES OF DEATH

As fewer younger persons died from infectious and bacterial diseases, they survived to old age and succumbed to chronic and degenerative diseases like heart disease, cancer, and cerebrovascular disease (stroke). Crude death rates from these three diseases combined increased from 308 per 100,000 in 1900 to 546 per 100,000 in 1991.

In describing recent trends in mortality we can avoid the problems created by changes in the age distribution of the population by using age-specific or age-adjusted death rates. For this reason we will limit the analyses to the years since 1950.

Table 5 lists the age-adjusted death rates (they standardize the age distribution of the population so that it is the same for every year in the table) between 1950 and 1991 for the nine leading causes of death categories in 1991. The nine categories together accounted for 80 percent of all deaths in 1991. Each category listed (except AIDS) includes a number of specific diseases. For example, within the heart disease category, the most common condition is ischemic (meaning deficient in blood) heart disease (often called coronary heart disease or heart attack), in which the blood supply to the heart muscle is interrupted, killing some heart muscles cells (called a myocardial infarction). Cancer encompasses hundreds of specific diseases

involving different organs and types of cell abnormalities. The most common cerebrovascular (meaning the blood vessels of the brain) disease is stroke, which is an interruption of the blood supply to the brain. Chronic obstructive pulmonary (pertaining to the lungs) disease includes emphysema, bronchitis, and asthma, all disorders affecting the supply of air to the lungs. Diabetes encompasses a number of conditions involving excessive urination, the most important of which is diabetes mellitus, a malfunctioning of the cells that produce insulin. The trends shown are for all diseases in each category; trends for specific diseases within a category can vary.

Table 5 shows that the age-adjusted death rate trends from 1950 to 1991 differ substantially by category. The death rate for heart disease has declined substantially, although it remains the major cause of death. A drop has also occurred in the mortality rate for cerebrovascular diseases and, to a lesser extent, from diabetes. Pneumonia and influenza have continued to decline as causes of death. The death rate from cancer, the second largest cause of death, has increased slightly, and that from chronic pulmonary diseases has shown an ominous rise.

Table 6 shows the age-specific death rates from heart disease from 1900 to 1991 for the age groups most affected by it. From 1900 to about 1950, overall heart disease death rates rose steadily for each age group (the rates for ischemic heart disease continued to rise until the late 1960s). The growing proportion of older persons could not be responsible for the increase in heart disease rates, because a larger proportion of people *within* each age group died of heart disease in 1950 than in 1900. It is now recognized that an epidemic of heart disease occurred in the first two-thirds of this century, and that it occurred in all advanced societies, not only the United States.[11] Then, beginning about 1950 for non-ischemic heart disease and in the late 1960s for the more prevalent ischemic heart disease, mortality rates declined steadily for all age groups. Currently heart disease death rates

TABLE 5   Age-Adjusted Death Rates by Cause, 1950–91, for Leading Causes of Death in 1991 (deaths per 100,000 population)

CAUSE	1950	1970	1991
All	840.5	714.3	513.7
Heart disease	307.2	253.6	148.2
Cancer	125.3	129.8	134.5
Accidents, including motor vehicle	57.5	53.7	31.0
Cerebrovascular diseases	88.6	66.3	26.8
Chronic obstructive pulmonary disease	4.4	13.2	20.1
Pneumonia and influenza	26.2	22.1	13.4
Diabetes mellitus	14.3	14.1	11.8
Suicides	11.0	11.8	11.4
Human immunodeficiency virus infection (AIDS)	—	—	11.3

Sources: 1950–70: National Center for Health Statistics, *Health, United States, 1991* (Hyattsville, MD: Public Health Service, 1992), 156; 1991: "Advance Report of Final Mortality Statistics," *Monthly Vital Statistics Report* 42 (31 August 1993), suppl. 1, p. 6.

for the 45–54-, 55–64-, and 65–74-year age groups are lower than they were in 1900, and those for the older age groups have declined significantly from their 1950s levels but remain higher than their 1900 levels. A similar trend has occurred in many other advanced nations, although the declines began a few years later in some of them.

Table 7 shows trends in age-specific death rates from 1950 to 1989 by sex for *ischemic* heart disease, the most common kind of heart disease. Three major patterns are evident. Ischemic heart

disease mortality rates for both sexes increased from 1950 to 1970 (they actually peaked in the late 1960s) and have declined subsequently. Men have much higher death rates from ischemic heart disease in each age group than do women. The decline in ischemic heart disease mortality rates has benefited women as much as men, even though it is much less prevalent among women.

Understanding these trends has been made more difficult by changes in the diagnosis of heart disease by physicians.[12] Heart disease has no ubiq-

TABLE 6   Age-Specific Death Rates from Heart Disease 1900–91 (deaths per 100,000 population)

AGE GROUP	1900	1930	1950	1970	1991
45–54 years	173.0	238.9	308.6	238.4	118.0
55–64	414.1	598.6	808.1	652.3	357.0
65–74 years	957.3	1493.9	1839.8	1558.2	872.0
75–84	1751.9	3476.7	4310.1	3683.8	2219.1
85 and over	2249.8	6680.9	9150.6	7891.3	6613.4

Sources: 1900, 1930: Forrest E. Linder and Robert D. Grove, *Vital Statistics Rates of the United States, 1900–1940* (Washington, DC: GPO, 1943), 253; 1950–70: National Center for Health Statistics, *Health, United States, 1991* (Hyattsville, MD: Public Health Service, 1992), 163; "Advance Report of Final Mortality Statistics," *Monthly Vital Statistics Report* 42 (31 August 1993), suppl. 1, p. 18.

TABLE 7 Age-Specific Death Rates from Ischemic Heart Disease by Sex, 1950–88 (deaths per 100,000 population)

AGE GROUP	1950	1970	1988
Male			
45–54 years	316.6	338.0	134.5
55–64	792.9	904.6	401.3
65 and over	2041.1	3022.5	—
65–74	—	2010.0	956.9
75–84	—	4222.7	2277.5
85 and over	—	7781.5	5236.2
Female			
45–54 years	76.0	84.0	36.8
55–64	275.0	299.1	147.1
65 and over	1334.0	2071.5	—
65–74	—	978.0	453.1
75–84	—	2866.3	1413.1
85 and over	—	6951.5	4374.2

Sources: 1950: U.S. Bureau of the Census, *Statistical Abstract of the United States: 1980* (Washington, DC: GPO, 1980), 80; 1970, 1988: U.S. Bureau of the Census, *Statistical Abstract of the United States: 1991* (Washington, DC: GPO, 1991), 83.

uitous signs or symptoms. Many people have heart attacks without realizing it. Physicians often have difficulty diagnosing heart disease, because routine and even sophisticated diagnostic tests can fail to reveal abnormalities. If physicians do not look carefully for heart disease, they can easily overlook it.

At the beginning of the century, when heart disease was uncommon, physicians overlooked it quite often. As it became more prevalent, physicians became sensitized to it and were more likely to recognize it as a cause of death. The development of the electrocardiograph also made more accurate diagnosis possible. Even after midcentury, however, physicians continued to misdiagnose heart disease. A study in one hospital found that deaths diagnosed as due to heart disease were understated (as measured by autopsy findings) in the 1960s and 1970s compared to the 1980s. These findings suggest that the increase in heart disease death rates between 1900 and midcentury was

smaller than the official statistics indicate and that the current decline may be greater.[13]

Regardless of diagnostic improvements, the overall trends are indisputable—heart disease mortality rates rose substantially early in the century and have declined in recent years. The trends occurred in many advanced nations with different systems of training physicians and different ways of recording vital statistics. Careful and thorough studies of trends in heart disease death rates in specific regions and cities in the U.S. and other nations covering a decade or more have shown conclusively that heart disease rates have declined in recent years.[14]

What factors caused the great increase in heart disease death rates from 1900 to midcentury and their subsequent decline? Several possible explanations can be easily dismissed. Both the upward and downward trends occurred so rapidly that they must have been caused by social and environmental changes, not changes in human biology. Both the rise and fall occurred in many advanced nations about the same time, so that they cannot be due to changes unique to American society. The trends occurred for both men and women, so that factors that would benefit one sex more than the other cannot be responsible.

The most frequently advanced reasons for the increase in heart disease death rates early in the century are based on the greater wealth of industrialized societies. Research has shown that "a diet excessive in calories, fat, and salt, sedentary habits, unrestrained weight gain, and cigarette smoking predispose to coronary heart disease."[15] It is claimed that early in the twentieth century higher standards of living enabled people to eat more meat and other fatty foods that occluded their arteries and made them overweight. Changing work and home activities and the use of automobiles and mass transportation resulted in less physical exertion and exercise. Cigarette smoking became popular. These and other changes also increased heart disease death rates indirectly by producing higher rates of hypertension, diabetes, and other conditions that made people more susceptible to heart disease.

The major issue in explaining the recent decline in heart disease death rates is whether it was caused by (1) preventive measures that reduced the incidence of fatal heart disease, or (2) better treatment of heart disease.[16] Are fewer people getting fatal heart disease or are people with heart disease receiving better treatment and so are less likely to die? The prevention theory attributes the decline to the same factors that are considered to have caused the rise in heart disease death rates: changes in diet, more exercise, cessation of smoking, reduced blood cholesterol levels, and, possibly, treatment of high blood pressure. The treatment theory points to pre-hospital life support systems and better hospital and continuing care of cardiac patients as enabling more heart disease patients to survive.

Studies of heart disease deaths in several American cities connect much of the decline in the heart disease mortality rate in recent years to a decline in out-of-hospital deaths.[17] This may indicate that fewer people were having heart attacks or that they were having milder heart attacks, supporting the prevention theory. A less likely but possible interpretation is that heart disease patients were receiving better care and so were less likely to have a fatal recurrence after leaving the hospital, supporting the treatment theory.

None of the explanations for the rise in heart disease mortality rates is entirely persuasive. Changes in diet and lifestyles that are supposed to have caused the increase in heart disease early in the century often did not occur until decades later. Cigarette smoking did not become popular until the 1920s and would not have had a measurable impact on heart disease death rates until the late 1930s. No evidence exists that physical activity decreased at the beginning of the century. The automobile was not widely used as a mode of transportation until the 1920s. Perhaps most puzzling is the fact that the increase occurred in many nations about the same time, but it has not been shown that

they all experienced appropriate changes in diet and lifestyle at the same time.

Explanations for the decline in heart disease mortality rates are equally problematic. The decline began before public health programs designed to discourage cigarette smoking and change lifestyles could have had an impact, and it also occurred in nations without such programs. The decline has taken place in nations that have taken little interest in pre-hospital resuscitation, intensive coronary care units, or other methods of care in widespread use in the United States. Even programs to lower mild or moderate hypertension, which reduce the risk of stroke, have not been clearly linked to a reduced risk of coronary heart disease. One review has concluded that "no one has yet established a convincing fit of trends for any risk factor with cardiovascular mortality trends.[18]

The trends for cerebrovascular disease are very similar to those for heart disease, as are the issues involving causes. For those reasons, they will not be discussed here.[19]

When we turn to cancer (Table 8), we find a disheartening picture. Overall cancer death rates for men aged 45 and over rose steadily from 1940 to 1970, while they declined for women over those years. From 1970 to 1988, cancer death rates declined for both men and women aged 35–44 and 45–54 (attributed to a decline in lung cancer death rates), but they have risen for all older groups of both sexes. Similar patterns have been found in other advanced nations, indicating that these patterns are international in scope.[20]

Trends in overall cancer mortality rates are difficult to interpret because they can change if the mix of types of cancers changes, even if the mortality rate of each type of cancer does not change. For example, if cancers with higher mortality rates become more prevalent relative to cancers with lower mortality rates, overall cancer mortality rates will increase, even though mortality rates from each individual type of cancer have not changed.

TABLE 8 Age-Specific Death Rates from Cancer by Sex, 1940–88 (deaths per 100,000 population)

AGE GROUP	1940	1950	1970	1988
Male				
35–44 years	—	—	53.0	39.7
45–54	135.3	156.2	183.5	166.3
55–64	352.2	413.1	511.8	526.7
65 and over	896.2	968.9	1221.2	1398.6
65–74 years	—	—	1006.8	1072.7
75–84	—	—	1588.3	1861.0
85 and over	—	—	1720.8	2527.9
Female				
35–44 years	—	—	65.6	48.5
45–54	204.1	194.0	181.5	154.9
55–64	384.1	368.2	343.2	376.6
65 and over	792.3	755.7	708.3	840.5
65–74 years	—	—	557.9	659.2
75–84	—	—	891.9	982.6
85 and over	—	—	1096.7	1292.8

Sources: 1940, 1950: U.S. Bureau of the Census, *Statistical Abstract of the United States: 1980* (Washington, DC: GPO, 1980), 80; 1970, 1988: U.S. Bureau of the Census, *Statistical Abstract of the United States: 1991* (Washington, DC: GPO, 1991), 84.

National data on the incidence of cancer (the number of new cases) are available for selected areas in the United States since 1973. They show a steady increase in the age-adjusted rates of new cases of cancer per 100,000 population from 319.8 in 1973 to 376.6 in 1989.[21] The increases have occurred for both men and women.

Significant sex differences exist in cancer mortality rates. In 1988, the overall cancer mortality rate per 100,000 was 215.5 for men and 180.0 for women. With the exception of breast cancer, men had higher mortality rates from every major cancer site. The most important of these sex differences was for lung cancer death rates.[22]

In terms of specific cancer sites, mortality rates from two major kinds of cancer have changed dramatically in most western countries in the last half-century. One is the increase in death rates from lung cancer. The age-adjusted mortality rate from cancer of the respiratory system per 100,000 population increased from 12.8 in 1950 to 28.4 in 1970 and 59.1 in 1991.[23] This is attributed to cigarette smoking, based on three kinds of evidence. One consists of studies showing a strong relationship between smoking and lung cancer in individuals: individuals who smoke more cigarettes or have smoked cigarettes for a longer period of time are more likely to contract lung cancer. The second is that lung cancer, which was a very rare form of cancer in the nineteenth century, became more prevalent about two decades after cigarette smoking became popular, which is about the time it takes for smoking to produce cancer.

The third type of evidence is based on the decline in the proportion of persons 18 years of age and over who smoke cigarettes, from 42 to 25 percent between 1965 and 1990. The reduction has occurred for both sexes and all age groups. Lung cancer mortality rates have declined recently among younger age groups, who would be the first to benefit because they have smoked for fewer years. The mortality rates per 100,000 population for cancers of the respiratory system for those 45–54 years of age increased from 22.9 in 1950 to 56.5 in 1980 and then declined to 46.9 in 1991. The comparable rates for those aged 65 to 74 increased from 69.3 in 1950 to 243.1 in 1980 and 300.0 in 1991.[24]

The other dramatic change in cancer mortality rates has been the striking decline in death rates from stomach cancer.[25] Before 1940 stomach cancer was a major cause of cancer mortality for both sexes and all age groups; today it is relatively uncommon. The decline has occurred in most western nations and Japan, although it has been greater and occurred earlier in the United States than most other nations. The most frequently proposed causal factors involve changes in diet, particularly the decline in the consumption of salted, smoked, and fried foods. Before the canning and freezing of vegetables and refrigeration of foods, human diet in Western countries included substantial amounts of salted vegetables, such as pickles and sauerkraut, and meats preserved with salts and nitrates, including sausages, ham, salami, and bologna. Canning, refrigeration, and freezing have reduced the need for these methods of preservation. However, no clear-cut evidence exists to support the diet theory, especially in terms of showing appropriate and timely changes in diet in all the nations that have experienced declines in stomach cancer rates.

As with heart disease, changing methods of diagnosis have affected cancer mortality rates. A British authority on lung cancer concluded that lung cancer death rates were understated early in the century because of the difficulty of diagnosing what was then a rare disease. He believes that lung cancer mortality rates for non-smokers today are probably the same as the overall population rates before smoking became widespread. Consequently he estimates that the rise in lung cancer death rates during the first quarter of the century in England and Wales was due almost entirely to more accurate diagnoses (primarily by the use of chest X-rays) rather than an actual increase in lung cancer mortality.[26]

Most cancer is considered to be environmental in origin. This is based on regional differences in specific types of cancers and on the evidence that people who move from one region to another contract different types of cancer than those who remain. As an example, Japanese women who emigrated to Hawaii have much lower rates of stomach cancer than their grandmothers but much higher rates of breast cancer.[27] The specific environmental factors involved are seldom well understood, however.

The inability to identify the causes of individual cancers and other chronic diseases is due to the complex nature of the diseases. These diseases take decades to develop, are produced by several factors operating simultaneously, and are retarded by still other factors. Researchers must therefore obtain data on many details of an individual's life over many years, which is rarely possible. Furthermore, mortality rates are low enough that it is necessary to study many thousands of people to obtain enough cases for a meaningful study. To avoid these problems, researchers usually study populations rather than individuals, by, for example, comparing the diet of a country or region with a low rate of stomach cancer to the diet of another country or region with a high rate. Because people within each country or region have different diets, the results are much less useful than if only individuals with specified diets were studied. This kind of research produces suggestive rather than definitive findings. Most knowledge about the environmental causes of cancer and heart disease is based on suggestive findings from a number of studies.

Because most cancers cannot be cured, research has focused on trends on the number of years that cancer patients live after diagnosis. The standard measure of cancer survival is the five-year survival rate, which is defined as the number of persons who are alive five years after they have been diagnosed as having cancer, divided by the number of persons diagnosed with the disease at the beginning of the period. Five-year survival rates for individual cancer sites vary widely, from about 10 percent for lung cancer and even less for a few other sites, to over 70 percent for bladder, breast, skin, and prostate cancers.[28]

A major concern is whether five-year survival rates have increased in recent years. A federal government study comparing five-year survival rates in 1950 with those in 1982 found real improvements in a few cancers, mostly rare ones, but only marginal improvement in the most frequent cancer sites. Five-year survival rates have a major methodological limitation. As physicians have become more aware of cancer and have better diagnostic devices, they look for it and diagnose it earlier than they did in the past. Thus patients are more likely to survive for five years because the disease was diagnosed in an earlier stage. For example, if a physician who is not alert to the possibility of cancer diagnoses a case of cancer in 1994, the patient will have survived for five years in 1999. If the physician had been more alert to the disease or had better diagnostic tools and diagnosed the same case a year earlier, in 1993, the patient would have reached the five-year mark a year earlier, in 1998, when the disease was less advanced. Earlier diagnosis will improve five-year survival rates regardless of changes in treatment. Earlier diagnosis is widely believed to be responsible for most of the modest improvements in five-year cancer survival rates.[29]

AIDS is the only major disease cause of death to claim most of its victims among the young. The first cases of human immunodeficiency virus infection were observed in the early 1980s, but no U.S. death rates existed until 1987, when an age-adjusted mortality rate of 5.5 per 100,000 population was recorded. In 1991, the age-adjusted mortality rate reached 11.3 per 100,000 population. AIDS deaths in 1991 were concentrated in the 25–44 year age group, with a mortality rate of 47.3 per 100,000 among men aged 25–44 and 6.4 per 100,000 among women aged 25–44. Deaths from AIDS constituted 18.6 percent of all deaths among men and 6.2 percent of all deaths among women in that age group.[30] The sex difference is expected to diminish in the future.

SOCIAL CLASS AND MORTALITY

For many centuries the rich have been known to have lower mortality rates than the poor. During most of recorded history, the differences have been attributed to the higher standard of living of the rich, their physical separation from the poor that protected them from contagious diseases, and their access to better public health measures, including sewage disposal and uncontaminated water. They received their medical care from better trained physicians, but until the twentieth century this was of little benefit because physicians could do little to prevent death or cure illness.

During the last years of the nineteenth century and the first decades of the twentieth century, im-

provements in medicine aroused the expectation that equalizing access to medical care would eliminate the differences in mortality rates between the rich and the poor. National governments improved access to health care for the poor, at first in Germany and later in other European nations. National health care programs did not develop in the United States because health care for the poor was a local and state government responsibility (as well as private charity). Local and state governments operated public hospitals and/or reimbursed physicians and voluntary hospitals for the care of charity patients. A few cities (most notably New York City) and states accepted their responsibilities conscientiously, but most were parsimonious in providing medical care to the poor. In 1965, with the enactment of Medicare and Medicaid, the federal government assumed substantial responsibility for the medical care of the poor. These programs improved the quality of health care provided to the poor but did not make it equal to the care given others.

As the poor obtained access to better health care in all countries, it was expected that mortality rates would become more equal among socioeconomic status (SES) groups. One possibility was a general narrowing of the differences in mortality rates for all SES groups. Another was a threshold effect, in which the rates for those above a certain SES level would become more similar, but the rates for the lowest SES groups would remain higher.

Data from the United States and England have shown that neither trend has occurred. The mortality rates of all SES groups have declined substantially, but the differences among them have increased. One British study placed men under age 65 in five occupational groups from high to low social status and found that the differences in mortality rates among the groups increased significantly between 1931 and 1981. A study of Americans 25 to 64 years of age found a greater difference in mortality rates between the lowest and highest educational groups and the lowest and highest income groups in 1986 than in 1960. These patterns held for white men, white women, black men, and black women. The same trends have also been found for the major diseases considered individually. For example, studies in several countries have found that the greatest decline in heart disease mortality rates has occurred in the higher educational and occupational groups.[31]

Several aspects of this phenomenon should be emphasized: (1) overall mortality rates for all SES groups have declined steadily over time so that members of all SES groups are living longer today; (2) the differences in mortality rates among SES groups in the U.S. exist for both men and women and for whites and blacks; (3) the differences in mortality rates among SES groups exist for all age groups and are not limited to the elderly or to infants; (4) the differences in mortality rates among SES groups exist for many individual diseases, including heart disease, cancer, and stroke; and (5) many SES factors operate together to cause the differences in mortality, including education, income, occupation, parent's SES (used as a measure of SES during a person's childhood), as well as other unknown factors.

The fundamental issue in mortality differences among SES groups is not the higher mortality rates of the lowest SES groups, for which many plausible explanations have been offered. The issue is the inability to explain the growing differences among the highest SES groups. Surely the second highest SES group, for example, has more than an adequate standard of living, benefits from public health measures, has ready access to high quality medical care, and possesses sufficient education and income to live healthy lifestyles. The differences between their death rates and those of the highest SES group should, therefore, be narrowing, but for unknown reasons they are widening.

SES differences in mortality provide an appropriate context to discuss racial differences in mortality rates. In 1991 white males had an age-adjusted mortality rate of 6.3 deaths per 1,000 population, while black males had a rate of 10.5 per 1,000 population. The corresponding figures for white and black females were 3.7 per 1,000 population and 5.8 per 1,000 population. Lower mortal-

ity rates for whites existed for all major disease categories except suicides. Socio-economic factors must be responsible for these differences, because no known biological factors can explain them. One study found that these so-called "racial" differences in mortality rates were due to differences in age, sex, marital status, family size, and family income between the white and black populations (married persons have lower mortality rates than unmarried ones and members of smaller families have lower mortality rates than members of large families).[32] Black–white differentials in mortality rates are manifestations of the broader SES and demographic differences that exist in our society.

CONCLUSION

In reflecting on trends in mortality rates during the twentieth century, no conclusion is more remarkable than the astonishing number of unanticipated and unexplained changes that have occurred. Death rates from infectious diseases, the major cause of death in the nineteenth century, declined much more spectacularly than any physician in 1900 would have dared to predict, but no explanations for the decline have received universal acceptance. Death rates from stroke and heart disease rose to epidemic proportions in the first half of the twentieth century. This led observers in the 1950s and 1960s to pontificate that increasing death rates from heart disease and stroke were the inevitable fate of mankind in a post-infectious disease era. Despite these claims, mortality rates from both diseases declined dramatically in recent decades. None of the proposed explanations for these rises and declines are supported by convincing evidence.

Other mortality trends have been less gratifying. Overall cancer death rates have remained stable in recent decades. Two favorable developments stand out: the recent decline in lung cancer rates among younger age groups, almost surely due to a decline in smoking, and the continuing decline in stomach cancer death rates, which has no accepted explanation. The lack of decline in death rates from other types of cancer is especially disappointing when we consider the billions of dollars that have been spent on cancer research. Other discouraging and unexplained trends include the widening differences in mortality rates among SES groups and the growing death rates from chronic obstructive pulmonary diseases, which occur after years of painful disability.

The trends in mortality rates are made more baffling by their multinational nature. Most advanced nations have experienced similar trends in death rates, but they differ in many factors that have been offered as explanations, including their social structures, cultures, diets, housing, industries, sources of energy, modes of transportation, occupations, pollutants, and geographic and physical environments.

When physicians are confronted with such inexplicable trends, they tend to explain them according to their cultural predispositions.[33] American physicians like to attribute the positive trends to medical interventions—new drugs, new types of surgery, new medical and surgical specialties, new health care procedures like intensive care units and helicopter evacuation teams, and new public health initiatives. They like to believe that the problem areas, like cancer, await the expenditure of more money on specialists, more money on research, more money on equipment, more money on treatment. British physicians, on the other hand, note that nations that have spent only a fraction of the money that Americans spend on health care have experienced the same positive and negative trends. They believe that more general social changes—in broad public health measures, in the standard of living, in lifestyles—are responsible.

Useful explanations of mortality trends can never be achieved by studying individual diseases as disconnected entities. The human being is an organism, which means that changes in one part of the organism affect the whole organism. To understand changes in the incidence of any particular disease, we must understand factors that affected the organism in the past or are affecting it currently. These include biological factors, like diseases that the person has contracted, and social factors, including the society and culture in which the person lives, as well as the interrelationship between the two.

NOTES

1. A. Cockburn, *The Evolution and Eradication of Infectious Diseases* (Baltimore: Johns Hopkins Press, 1963).

2. R. Floud, K. Wachter, and A. Gregory, *Height, Health and History: Nutritional Status in the United Kingdom, 1750–1980* (Cambridge, Eng.: Cambridge University Press, 1990); and R. W. Fogel, "The Conquest of High Mortality and Hunger in Europe and America: Timing and Mechanisms," in *Favorites of Fortune: Technology, Growth, and Economic Development since the Industrial Revolution,* ed. P. Hoginnet, D. S. Landes, and H. Rosovsky (Cambridge: Harvard University Press, 1991), 52–54.

3. J. R. Giles, L. A. Tilly, and D. Levine, eds., *The European Experience of Declining Fertility, 1850–1970: The Quiet Revolution* (Cambridge: Blackwell, 1992).

4. F. E. Linder and R. D. Grove, *Vital Statistics Rates in the United States, 1900–1940* (Washington, DC: GPO, 1943), 95–96 and passim.

5. "Advance Report of Final Mortality Statistics 1991," *Monthly Vital Statistics Report* 42 (31 August 1993), suppl. 2, p. 16.

6. Ibid., 16

7. See R. Daniels, *Coming to America: A History of Immigration and Ethnicity in American Life* (New York: HarperCollins, 1990).

8. I. Waldron, "Recent Trends in Sex Mortality Ratios for Adults in Developed Countries," *Social Science and Medicine* 36 (1993): 451–62; and L. M. Verbrugge, "The Twain Meet: Empirical Explanations for Sex Differences in Health and Mortality," *Journal of Health and Social Behavior* 30 (1989): 282–304.

9. For a discussion of the causes of the decline, see S. J. Kunitz, "Explanations and Ideologies of Mortality Patterns," *Population and Development Review* 13 (1987): 379–408, and articles in *Milbank Memorial Fund Quarterly* 55 (Summer 1977).

10. H. Hansen and M. Susser, "Historical Trends in Deaths from Chronic Kidney Disease in the United States and Britain," *American Journal of Epidemiology* 93 (1971): 413–24.

11. R. Doll, "Major Epidemics of the 20th Century: From Coronary Thrombosis to AIDS," *Journal of the Royal Statistical Society* A 150 (1987): 373–95; T. J. Thom, "International Mortality from Heart Disease: Rates and Trends,"

International Journal of Epidemiology 18 (1989), suppl. 1, pp. S20–S28.

12. L. H. Kuller, "Issues in Measuring Coronary Heart Disease Mortality and Morbidity," and R. B. Wallace, "How Do We Measure the Influence of Medical Care on the Decline of Coronary Heart Disease?" both in *Trends in Coronary Heart Disease Mortality: The Influence of Medical Care,* ed. M. W. Higgins and R. V. Luepker (New York: Oxford University Press, 1988), 44–53, 88–93.

13. W. E. Stehbens, "An Appraisal of the Epidemic Rise of Coronary Heart Disease and Its Decline," *Lancet* 1 (1987): 606–11; and B. Burnand and A. R. Feinstein, "The Role of Diagnostic Inconsistency in Changing Rates of Occurrence for Coronary Heart Disease," *Journal of Clinical Epidemiology* 45 (1992): 929–40.

14. See R. Beaglehole, "International Trends in Coronary Heart Disease Mortality, Morbidity, and Risk Factors," *Epidemiologic Reviews* 12 (1990): 1–15.

15. W. B. Kannel and T. J. Thom, "Declining Cardiovascular Mortality," *Circulation* 70 (1984): 332.

16. See T. J. Thom and W. B. Kannel, "Downward Trend in Cardiovascular Mortality," *Annual Review of Medicine* 32 (1981): 427–34; R. I. Levy, "The Decline in Cardiovascular Disease Mortality," *Annual Review of Public Health* 2 (1981): 49–70; L. Goldman and E. F. Cook, "The Decline in Ischemic Heart Disease Mortality Rates," *Annals of Internal Medicine* 101 (1984): 825–36; and Beagelhole, "International Trends."

17. L. H. Kuller et al., "Sudden Death and the Decline in Coronary Heart Disease Mortality," *Journal of Chronic Diseases* 39 (1986): 1001–19; and Beaglehole, "International Trends," 5.

18. Kannel and Thom, "Declining Cardiovascular Mortality," 335.

19. See B. Modan and D. K. Wagener, "Some Epidemiological Aspects of Stroke: Mortality/Morbidity Trends, Age, Sex, Race, Socioeconomic Status," *Stroke* 23 (1992): 1230–36; and J. P. Whisnant, "The Decline of Stroke," *Stroke* 15 (1984): 160–68.

20. R. Doll, "Are We Winning the Fight Against Cancer? An Epidemiological Assessment," *European Journal of Cancer* 26 (1990): 500–508; D. L. Davis et al., "International Trends in Cancer Mortality in France, West Germany, Italy, Japan, England and Wales, and the United States," *Annals of the New York Academy of Sciences* 609 (1990): 5–48.

21. Barry Miller et al., eds., *Cancer Statistics Review, 1937–1989* (Washington, DC: National Cancer Institute, 1992), part 2, p. 4.

22. U.S. Bureau of the Census, *Statistical Abstract of the United States: 1991* (Washington, DC: GPO, 1991), 84.

23. National Center for Health Statistics, *Health United States, 1991* (Hyattsville, MD: Public Health Service, 1992), 169; and "Advance Report of Final Mortality Statistics 1991," 18.

24. National Center for Health Statistics, *Health United States, 1991,* 203, 169; and "Advance Report of Final Mortality Statistics," 18.

25. See J. Higginson, C. S. Muir, and N. Munoz, *Human Cancer: Epidemiology and Environmental Causes* (Cambridge, Eng.: Cambridge University Press, 1992), 273–82; and C. P. Howson, T. Hiyama, and E. L. Wynder, "The Decline in Gastric Cancer: Epidemiology of an Unplanned Triumph," *Epidemiologic Reviews* 8 (1986): 1–27.

26. Doll, "Major Epidemics," 376–77.

27. Davis et al., "International Trends," 6.

28. National Center for Health Statistics, *Health United States, 1991,* 199.

29. U.S. General Accounting Office, *Cancer Patient Survival: What Progress Has Been Made?* (Washington, DC: GPO, 1987).

30. National Center for Health Statistics, *Health United States, 1991,* 156; and "Update: Mortality Attributable to HIV Infection/AIDS Among Persons Aged 25–44 Years—United States, 1990 and 1991," *Morbidity and Mortality Weekly Report* 42 (2 July 1993): 482.

31. R. G. Wilkinson, "Socio-economic Differences in Mortality," in *Class and Health: Research and Longitudinal Data,* ed. Wilkinson (London, Eng.: Tavistock, 1986), 2; G. Pappas et al., "The Increasing Disparity in Mortality Between Socioeconomic Groups in the United States, 1960 and 1986," *New England Journal of Medicine* 329 (1993): 103–9; C. C. Seltzer and S. Jablon, "Army Rank and Subsequent Mortality by Cause: 23-Year Follow-up," *American Journal of Epidemiology* 105 (1977): 559–66; Beaglehole, "International Trends," 4; and J. P. Bunker, D. S. Gomby, and B. H. Kehrer, eds., *Pathways to Health: The Role of Social Factors* (Menlo Park, CA: Henry J. Kaiser Family Foundation, 1989).

32. "Advance Report of Final Mortality Statistics 1991," 15; and R. G. Rogers, "Living and Dying in the U.S.A.: Sociodemographic Determinants of Death among Blacks and Whites," *Demography* 29 (1992): 287–303.

33. Cf. Kunitz, "Explanations and Ideologies."

JOHN SNOW, THE BROAD STREET PUMP AND MODERN EPIDEMIOLOGY

DONALD CAMERON AND IAN G. JONES

In a recent paper in this journal on the Broad Street Pump Dr. Smith makes a construction based on a theory which has nothing to do with the behaviour of the cholera vibrio or with the people involved.[1] It consists of assumptions about the number of persons at risk and about a constant infectivity of the water supply, and it assumes that water was the only medium for the transmission of the disease. These assumptions are purely speculative and are at variance with contemporary evidence.

Henry Whitehead, a friend and collaborator of John Snow, showed that infection from the Broad Street Pump after 2 September 1854 was most unlikely.[2] He himself drank from it at 11 P.M. on 3 September with no ill effects. Vehicles other than water were probably responsible for those infected after 2 September. In the same paper Whitehead shows that, although the removal of the pump handle did not abbreviate the epidemic, it prevented a recurrence. The father of the child whose excreta infected the Broad Street Pump well from 30 August to 2 September, took ill on 8 September, the day the handle was removed. He was ill and died in the same room as his daughter, and since his domestic cesspit leaked into the well it was presumably reinfected.

Whitehead's epidemiology made important contributions to the understanding of cholera and to the ultimate acceptance of Snow's theory.[3,4] Since Smith's paper seems in accord with modern epidemiology teaching and in disagreement with the work of Snow which is often claimed as an early example of that teaching, a reappraisal of Snow and of his relation to current work is long overdue.

John Snow, as nearly everyone agrees nowadays, was a genius in epidemiology. But not all are agreed wherein his genius lies. Opinion was different in his own day. The most powerful medical authorities were convinced that he was mistaken or that his reports wrongly interpreted the facts that his researches uncovered.

We wish to make a statement about Snow's achievement and show how modern epidemiologists have misunderstood his work and misinterpreted it as an early example of their own empiricist epidemiology.

Snow claimed no 'method' of epidemiology. Careful reading shows the way he worked and discloses the rich variety of skill and knowledge he introduced to his researches. He is clear that the way of life of the community, its economic system, its educational system, its culture, impresses itself on each of its members. He summarizes some of the ideas he developed thus: "…I enumerated various circumstances connected with the pathology of Cholera, and with its progress as an epidemic, which led me to the conclusion that it is propagated by the morbid poison which produces it being accidentally swallowed; and this morbid poison becomes multiplied and increased in quantity on the interior surface of the alimentary canal, and that it passes off in the ejections and dejections, to produce fresh cases of the disease in those who happen to take the morbid matter into the stomach. I explained what great facilities there are for the Cholera evacuations being accidentally swallowed in the crowded habitations of the poor, where the inmates cook, eat, live, and sleep in the same apartment, and pay little regard to washing the hands, since these evacuations are almost devoid of colour and odour, and are usually passed involuntarily in the latter stages of the disease. It is in the families of the poor that cholera is often observed to pass from one individual to another, while in cleanly dwellings, where the hand-basin and towel are in constant use, and where the rooms for cooking, eating and sleeping are distinct from each other, the communication of cholera from person to person is rarely observed. In the houses of the poor, also, the disease is hardly ever contracted by medical, clerical, and other visitors, who do not eat or drink in the sick-room, while it often fares differently with the social visitor, who comes either to see the patient or attend his funeral.

"The cholera has visited the mining districts of this country with unusual severity, in each of the epidemics we have had. The following is the explanation of this circumstance: the pits are without any privies, and the excrement of the workmen lies about almost everywhere, so that the hands are liable to be soiled with it. The pitmen remain under ground eight or nine hours at a time, and invariably take food down with them into the pits, which they eat with unwashed hands, and without knife and fork; therefore, as soon as a case of cholera occurs among any of the pitmen, the disease has unusual facilities of spreading in the way I have pointed out.

"In my former paper I also showed that the cholera evacuations have the property of communicating the disease after being mixed with the drinking-water of the people, and I related a number of instances in which sudden and severe outbreaks of the malady occurred in the epidemics of 1832 and 1849 among persons using the water of ditches and pump-wells contaminated with excrementitious matters. It is particularly to be remarked that, in those instances, there were one or two cases of cholera in the community whose evacuations polluted the water, just before the great outbreak. I also related a number of facts to show that cholera was communicated through the water supply to many districts of London, and to several other towns where the water was obtained from a river receiving the sewage of the town. This division of my views on cholera which refers to its communication through the medium of drinking water, has apparently obtained a greater amount of attention from the Profession, than my views respecting its more immediate communication by the cholera poison being swallowed without the water. While I speak on this division of the subject, however, I must beg the Society to bear in mind also the other part of my views, first alluded to, for I am well aware that the part which relates to polluted water will not of itself explain the whole progress of the diseases as an epidemic."[5]

Snow rejected the theory, prevalent in his time, that the infective material is a chemical substance which is not necessarily derived from another patient. He believed that it is a living cell: 'For the morbid matter of cholera having the property of reproducing its own kind, must necessarily have some sort of structure, most likely that of a cell. It is no objection to this view that the structure of the cholera poison cannot be recognized by the microscope, for the matter of smallpox and chancre can only be recognized by their effects, and not by their physical properties."[6]

The same biological arguments explain the incubation period: "The period which intervenes between the time when a morbid poison enters the system, and the commencement of the illness which follows, is called the period of incubation. It is, in reality, a period of reproduction, as regards the morbid matter; and the disease is due to the crop or progeny resulting from the small quantity of poison first introduced."[7]

It seems to us, that Snow here carried the germ theory of disease as far as anyone did before the advent of the science of bacteriology, at least as far as Henle and with more supporting evidence. The agent only remained to be visualized by Pacini in 1865 and cultivated on a plate by Koch in 1883.

Snow used statistics to help to confirm a theory he had already established, by providing supporting evidence he could not conveniently demonstrate in any other way. He did not use the statistics to provide the theory, as Farr had done in his demonstration of an association between the incidence of cholera and height above the Thames. Snow was not seeking associations but connecting causal chains. Humean notions of cause so beloved by modern epidemiologists never enter his thinking.

Snow brought all his biological, medical, and social knowledge into his enquiries and within medicine he deployed clinical, pathological, microscopical and chemical skills and knowledge and of course he expressed these skills logically and where appropriate with arithmetical analysis. He formed a theory about the communication of infectious diseases in general and cholera in particular and confirmed it by all means available to him including statistical analysis. His epidemiology was by no means one sided. He, a consistent materialist, made a concrete analysis of every situation and because of this formulated answers to the problem of the prevention of cholera and other gastrointestinal disease in his own day which would solve the very difficult problem of food poisoning in ours.

In Snow's day, of the important sanitarians, only Budd accepted his theory. However, the message which many people associated with him, that water was somehow involved, was so telling that it was acted on both by local and central authorities.

Simon and Farr prepared material for a report which Simon made to the General Board of Health in 1856 on the 1848–49 and the 1853–54 cholera outbreaks, which clearly implicated polluted water as supplied by the water companies in London. It does not mention Snow.

Frazer comments: "This statistical investigation, one of the most important of all the epidemiological investigations undertaken in this country, in conjunction with Snow's observations, conclusively proved that *materies morbi* containing the cholera infection could be carried in water."[8]

But Frazer is going too far. Simon and Farr merely showed an association with water. They were not concerned with *materies morbi* or with a cholera infection. These gentlemen believed that the culprit was an effluvium produced by rotting animal and vegetable matter, not necessarily specific to cholera but predisposing to it. As Snow has pointed out, you may blame water even if you think only an effluvium responsible, or if you think the effluvium is not specific but merely predisposes towards the disease. But he warns against ideas of predisposition: "I do not deny that the period of life, being ill or well nourished, and other evident conditions of the patient, influence his liability to certain epidemic diseases. The predisposition objected to above is that which is assumed, without any symptoms of its existence, merely from the fact of the patient taking the disease."[9] Here again we have Snow the materialist warning against a purely speculative notion.

The report then, did not prove the presence of *materies morbi*. Simon did not believe in them. He did not consider the material he was dealing with specific to any disease. Snow's statistics did not prove their presence. Nor could they. It was the whole concatenation of his evidence, including the statistics that proved the presence of the *materies morbi* and went a long way towards showing their nature as living, reproducing, cellular micro-organisms. The proof arose out of the public health practices which eliminated cholera from Britain in the next few decades.

In our day when the knowledge that much disease is caused by micro-organisms, is more than 100 years old and we have had time to reflect on it, John Snow's work is still misunderstood. For long he was forgotten. His *Dictionary of National Biography* entry by D'Arcy Power misrepresents his achievement and is inaccurate. Snow is mentioned in modern writing but this frequently misses the point that he was a rounded epidemiologist, unlike Farr who brought nothing to bear on the subject but statistics.

Modern awareness of Snow's work begins with the publication by the Commonwealth fund of "Snow on Cholera" in 1936. Its editor, Wade Hampton Frost, in a brief introduction sets out Snow's achievement admirably.[10] In 1955 in celebration of the centenary of Snow's main work on cholera in papers read to the Royal Society of Medicine, Mackintosh presents a view that suggests that statistical work on cholera was all that Snow ever did.[11] Hill gives a more comprehensive picture but exaggerates the importance of Snow's statistics.[12]

This is the beginning of a modern return to the attitude among the profession which Snow complained of finding in his contemporaries. Modern epidemiologists concentrate on the water transmission of cholera because that involves the use of statistics in a way they understand, reducing all determination to chance, and denying necessity.

Among Snow's views on cholera, the first 'division' as he calls it, depends on evidence which involves examining the physical, chemical, biological, sociological and political processes. All these present as underlying trends, outstanding single cases and other tendencies which in their totality point clearly to a theory of cause and mechanism of infection. Although this sort of evidence is not entirely ignored in modern textbooks, it is neglected and wherever possible presented as chance occurrence to be subjected to the appropriate statistical procedure in the future. These forms of reasoning however, and this necessity, do enter into the experience of the majority of practising epidemiologists in their day-to-day duties, tracing the causes of outbreaks of communicable disease, or of industrial injury or poisoning. In these circumstances epidemiologists make a judgment on all the evidence, whatever its nature. This may include statistical material and an assessment of probabilities but it is never entirely that, or even mainly that. In this respect epidemiology textbooks dealing with infectious diseases stand apart, for they present this subject extensively.

Macmahon and Pugh mention Snow no less than nine times[13] but they do not even attempt to discuss those non-arithmetical parts of his epidemiology which long predated his statistical studies. In their general treatment of epidemiology they allot only a few paragraphs to this important subject and their discussion is entirely inadequate. On Snow's work, they concentrate on his observation that water is the chief method of spread of cholera and present that as if it were his main theory. They present even this in a way that does not distinguish Snow's theory from those of his chief antagonists. At the beginning of their book Macmahon and

Pugh admit adherence to a Humean philosophy of cause. This does not absolve them from indicating that there are other modes of thinking in epidemiology and that they are represented in Snow's work.

Barker and Rose mention Snow twice. There is no mention of his theory. On the first occasion there is a gross inaccuracy: "Undeterred he removed the handle of the Broad Street Pump, and the number of new cases in the neighbourhood dropped impressively."[14] On the second they say, "Dr. John Snow showed that the outbreak of cholera around Broad Street in London resulted from the contamination of drinking water with excrement from cholera sufferers."[15] The pump handle was removed by, or on behalf of the local vestrymen, certainly not by John Snow, and both Snow and his contemporaries clearly state that the outbreak was declining anyway. As to the contamination of the well, Snow says: "Whether the impurities of the water were derived from the sewers, the drains, or the cesspools, of which latter there are a number in the neighbourhood, I cannot tell."[16] In fact it was Whitehead who discovered the source of the contamination. Snow deduced it from his theory. Again their general epidemiological discussion omits a proper treatment of the construction of theories of causation. All determination is reduced to chance.

Morris mentions Snow three times.[17] He too concerns himself solely with Snow's statistics on water supplies. Although his book does not, like the others, set itself out to be a systematic text on epidemiology it does aim at community medicine and at "students and practitioners of clinical and laboratory medicine." It too should, therefore, at least consider the rest of Snow on cholera and the more general epidemiological principles that that raises, and not confine itself as it does to a narrow empiricism.

The Lilienfelds have written a more comprehensive text.[18] They discuss Snow, but only his remarks on water supplies. Like the others, they do not discuss his earlier, non-statistical work. There is a systematic neglect of the evidence upon which Snow built his theory. Without that evidence and that theory it is very doubtful that he would ever have embarked upon his statistical studies. As we indicated at the beginning, Snow was aware of this neglect.

The Lilienfelds have this to say: "John Snow's achievement was based on his logical organization of observations, his recognition of a natural experiment, and his quantitative approach in analyzing the occurrence of a disease in a human population."[19] This effectively summarizes the opinions of most modern epidemiologists. They are so convinced that there is an epidemiological method and that it is essentially arithmetical, probabilistic and empiricist that they miss the point of John Snow's contribution to science. In doing so they trivialize it as they trivialize epidemiology.

John Snow's contribution was to evolve an elegant, internally and externally consistent theory which concerned the mechanisms and processes involved in every aspect of the subject he had chosen to study. In order to do this he did not restrict himself to any method. He used all skills available to himself and his colleagues. He published his theory, and practical suggestions for the prevention of cholera arising out of it, both internally in medical meetings and to the medical press, and to the public in the form of pamphlets and in reports addressed to the appropriate authority. This surely should be the objective of all epidemiological work.

REFERENCES

1. Smith C. E. The Broad Street Pump Revisited. *Int J Epidemiol* 1982: **11**:99–100.
2. Whitehead H. Remarks on the outbreak of cholera in Broad Street, Golden Square, London, in 1854. *Transactions of the Epidemiological Society of London* 1867: **3**:99–104.
3. Snow J. *On the mode of communication of cholera.* London, Churchill, 1849.
4. Snow J. *On the mode of communication of cholera.* London, Churchill, 1855.
5. Snow J. Further remarks on the mode of communication of cholera: Including some comments on the recent reports of cholera by the General Board of Health. *Medical Times and Gazette* 1855: **2**:31–5, 84–8.
6. Snow J. *On the mode of communication of cholera.* London, Churchill, 1855, p 15.
7. Ibid p 15–16.
8. Frazer W. M. *History of English Public Health 1834–1939.* London, Baillere, Tindall & Cox, 1950, p 64–5.
9. Snow J. *On continuous molecular changes, more particularly in their relation to epidemic diseases.* London, Churchill, 1853, p 15.

10. Frost W. H. (ed). *Snow on cholera.* New York, The Commonwealth Fund, 1936, ix–xxi.
11. Mackintosh J. M. Snow—the man and his times. *Proceedings of the Royal Society of Medicine* 1955: **48**:1004–7.
12. Hill A. B. Snow—an appreciation. *Proceedings of the Royal Society of Medicine* 1955: **48**:1008–12.
13. Macmahon B, Pugh T. F. *Epidemiology: Principles and methods.* Boston, Little, Brown, 1970.
14. Barker D. J. P., Rose G. *Epidemiology in medical practice.* 2nd ed. Edinburgh, Churchill Livingstone, 1979, p 91.
15. Ibid p 125.
16. Snow J. *On the mode of communication of cholera.* London, Churchill, 1855, p 53.
17. Morris J. N. *Uses of epidemiology.* 3rd ed. Edinburgh, Churchill Livingstone, 1975.
18. Lilienfeld A. M., Lilienfeld D. E., *Foundations of epidemiology.* 2nd ed. New York, Oxford University Press, 1980.
19. Ibid p 37.

WOMEN AND AIDS IN ZIMBABWE: THE MAKING OF AN EPIDEMIC

MARY T. BASSETT AND MARVELLOUS MHLOYI

The AIDS epidemic in Africa, first reported in 1983 among patients from central Africa who sought medical care in European centers (1), has now reached major proportions. In some urban areas, the prevalence of infection by HIV, the human immunodeficiency virus, in the adult population is approaching 20 percent (2–4). The burden on health services is already being felt: in Ivory Coast, where the first person with AIDS was diagnosed as recently as 1985, over 40 percent of hospitalized patients in the capital city are seropositive (5). Popular concern about the disease reflects these figures. In Uganda, where the wasting syndrome "Slim Disease" was described in the early 1980s, a community-based survey found AIDS to be identified as the number one health problem. Affecting young people who have successfully survived the risks of death in early childhood, AIDS is causing deaths in an economically important age group (15 to 45 years) that was previously relatively protected from mortality. Perinatal transmission threatens hard-won gains in the reduction of infant mortality. Though dwarfed by the big killers—malnutrition and parasitic and bacterial infections—AIDS is having an important and still-evolving effect on health, and poses a substantial threat to present and future generations.

Efforts to halt the epidemic of AIDS in Africa will fall short if we fail to consider the diverse components, both social and biological, that contribute to its spread. Drawing on our joint experience as a clinician/epidemiologist and a social scientist in Zimbabwe, we will explore how current patterns of AIDS transmission in our country—and in Africa more generally—are driven by a combination of factors stemming from the intersection of traditional culture with our colonial legacy and

present-day political economy. In particular, we will examine how social conditions have shaped the course of AIDS through their effects on sexual relationships within and outside fast-changing family structures. By focusing on the particular situation of women in Zimbabwe, and by highlighting how the epidemic is perpetuated by patterns of trade, migrant labor, and sexually transmitted diseases, we hope to suggest a broader framework for comprehending and preventing AIDS in Africa.

UNDERSTANDING AIDS IN AFRICA: THE DIFFERING EXPLANATIONS

Early in the epidemic, investigators working in Africa noted that AIDS was occurring about as often in women as in men. This was in striking contrast to the pattern seen in North America and Europe (now called "Pattern 1"), where male predominance reflected the fact that the major risk group in these regions was homosexual men. The different epidemiological profile of AIDS in central and eastern Africa, however, supported the hypothesis that heterosexual intercourse was the major mechanism of transmission in these parts of Africa. Because of the subsequent large numbers of infected women, perinatal transmission also took on significant public health importance. It is generally estimated that these two mechanisms—heterosexual intercourse and perinatal transmission—account for 80 percent of AIDS cases in Africa. In Zimbabwe, where blood supplies have been screened for HIV-1 since 1985, the proportion attributable to these two routes of spread is certainly even higher. Blandly labeled "Pattern 2," this pattern of spread has been regarded as ominous and threatening ever since it was first described.

Since the initial studies of AIDS in Africa, our appreciation of the modes of transmission has expanded, but the basic framework remains unchanged: AIDS in Africa is a sexually transmitted disease with no special risk groups. In this article we suggest that an understanding of the full dimension of the AIDS outbreak in Africa, what Jonathan Mann (6) has described as the "third epidemic," requires that the discussion be broadened. We need to go beyond the supposedly neutral terms of "risk group" and "risk factor" to examine the social context in which the epidemic has taken hold and is spreading. Any epidemic sustains itself largely because of the social organization that supports its propagation, not simply because of the biological characteristics of the "causative agent." In the case of HIV, the single most important biological feature, from a public health point of view, is the long period (years) of asymptomatic infection during which transmission can occur. Although lethal, HIV is relatively noninfectious: who gets infected and who does not has more to do with socially determined behavior than with pathogenicity. Just as much as HIV is a requirement for the AIDS epidemic, so too are the social relations that mold, even determine, the setting of each individual's exposure and susceptibility to infection.

What is it about Africa that explains its particular mass pattern of disease? Behind the "how" of transmission lies a "why" which haunts the understanding of AIDS in Africa. Addressing these issues has important implications for control of the epidemic. In this article we focus on the more difficult question of "why," in part because we believe much of the "how" has already been explained. Our central thesis is that the stage on which this epidemic is unfolding has been set by the social realities of Africa: the migrant labor system, rapid urbanization, constant war with high levels of military mobilization, landlessness, and poverty.

In Africa, traditional cultures are filtered through the facts of colonization and the market economy, both of which have transformed traditional family roles. The history of social misery

and dispossession under colonialism has left its stamp on the facts of everyday life: how the family is organized, the role of women, and the role of men. In this sense, the traditional cultures of precolonial societies no longer exist. Instead, culture represents an adaptation of tradition to the changing society. In recent years, the world economic crisis has eroded many of the social gains of independent African countries. This, in broad strokes, is the setting in which the AIDS epidemic is occurring.

The heterosexual transmission of AIDS in Africa poses a frightening specter to the West. Although heterosexual transmission had been identified in North America prior to the description of AIDS in Africa (7), the number of such cases was small and, though growing, remains small. Western explanations for the heterosexual pattern in Africa have been marked by both media hysteria and scientific racism. Images of the dark continent, harboring dangerous diseases, inhabited by people whose social interactions are propelled by sexual frenzy, have long been engraved in the Western view of Africa. Eminent scientists proclaimed the origin of the epidemic to be Africa before data to substantiate their hypothesis were definitive (8). Work on genetic markers for susceptibility rapidly found its way into print (9). Even data on cranial capacities, a relic of eugenic science, were trotted out to explain African susceptibility (10).

This cultural assault, coupled with the fear of loss of needed foreign currency in tourist revenues and investment, was followed by an unfortunate delay in, and even suppression of, the African public health response to the AIDS outbreak. To admit the existence of the AIDS epidemic became tantamount to admitting the inferiority of African ways of life. This was particularly galling when it was clear that the vast majority of cases were initially diagnosed in the United States. The weight of numbers has now stripped away African preoccupation with the intrigues of international science. Researchers in Africa, in both the social and biological sciences, with the support of their governments, have turned their attention to the ways in which the epidemic can be slowed.

WOMEN AND AIDS IN AFRICA: REASONS FOR PARTICULAR CONCERN

In this article our focus is particularly on women. This emphasis derives from several concerns. First, women in Africa are being portrayed as the dangerous vector of the AIDS outbreak. For example, in terms of epidemiological investigations, this has meant an emphasis on study of female prostitutes to the exclusion of other women. The devastating level of infection documented in some groups of women who sell sexual services is wrongly interpreted to mean that without them, the epidemic would not be occurring. Usually, as Padian (11) has pointed out, all we know is that these women, infected by their clients, are experiencing the brunt of the epidemic. Usually, because we have not identified or studied the men who use prostitutes, we do not know the extent of HIV infection among this group of men. Although it is plausible that female prostitutes contribute to the spread of HIV, we do not know the extent to which the propagation of the epidemic depends on them.

If not depicted as a dangerous source of infection, women are of interest to those conducting AIDS research or designing interventions mainly when in their pregnant state. Numerous surveys record the prevalence of HIV infection among prenatal women. Information on the extent of infection in this group is important for charting the course of the epidemic. Still, the image of women becomes one of contaminated vessels bearing condemned babies. Because of the shorter natural history of infection in children, a woman may be identified as seropositive because of a sick child, before she herself shows signs of being ill. This reinforces the notion that the mother is solely responsible for the child's serostatus.

These negative portrayals alone are reason enough to examine the position of women in this epidemic. Dangerous precedents exist for the curtailment of women's rights in the face of outbreaks of other sexually transmitted diseases (12). But the position of women is important for still other reasons. The limited control that women have to determine their own lives forms parts of the social substrate of the current epidemic, as we will describe in more detail. The subordination of African women in patrilineal societies places them at a special disadvantage with regard to their ability or willingness to intervene and reduce their own risk of HIV infection. For many women, faced with divorce or dire poverty on the one hand and the risk of HIV infection on the other, the choice becomes one of "social death" or biological death. No one involved in caring for HIV-infected women in Zimbabwe, and presumably elsewhere, can fail to be struck by the limited options women have in negotiating their sexual relations.

Appreciation of these constraints should inform our efforts in developing intervention strategies. In many settings, women in the younger age groups are actually experiencing higher levels of infection than men. In Zaire, women have a higher prevalence of HIV infection until the age of 35 (13). In Ghana, among those diagnosed with AIDS, women outnumber men (14). Ghana's female predominance, Neequaque (14) suggests, may result from women returning home to Ghana when they are ill, after having engaged in sex work in neighboring Ivory Coast.

Unfolding behind these statistics are family tragedies with wrenching human dimensions:

- An elderly woman is carried into the clinic by her daughters. She is wasted by chronic diarrhea which, compounded with severe peripheral neuropathy, has left her unable to walk. She has been tested for HIV but has not been informed of her diagnosis. In privacy, she is told that she has AIDS and that her prognosis is poor. Does she want to go home or come into hospital? "I will go home," she says. Should we discuss the diagnosis with her children? "Are they in danger?" she asks. No.

Then she will keep it to herself. And her husband? Well, he comes around only now and then, and she is staying with her elder daughter. What does he do for a living? He is a long-distance truck driver. "He provided well for the family," she says, "driving up and down and bringing us money and bringing us AIDS." She thanks us for explaining what is happening to her and goes home.

- A young woman of 24, her pretty face scarred by a rash, comes to the clinic with her 1-year-old child, the third born. The child is well dressed, for clinic day. He clings to his mother. I pat his head and feel his neck: he has enlarged lymph nodes and looks small for his age. She asks, "Can I please have another HIV test?" Her husband sent her and the boy home to her parents when told of her HIV status. He will only take her back if the test is negative. He is not providing any support. No, he refused testing, saying he is fine. The first two children are fine, they have been kept by the paternal grandmother. She has not seen them in six months.

- A woman in her mid-30s, divorced and caring for her two children, frankly states that she supplements her income by having "friends." The children are brought in for testing: they are negative. They are living with their maternal grandparents, she supports them. Can she get her partners to use condoms? She has tried and they refuse. What arrangements can she make for the children if she gets sick? She shakes her head: "My children will suffer."

These cases illustrate that, in Africa, as everywhere, women are the caregivers. They take the larger responsibility for the maintenance of family health and care of the sick. Women are caring for the sick children, sick husbands, and sick relatives who have AIDS. Care for a sick child must carry on in the face of her own illness and an uncertain future for (usually) both parents (15). How can we support this role? Will traditional coping mechanisms within the extended family hold up?

In their role as caregivers and consumers of family planning techniques, women may be more accessible than men to health care providers. But as a locus of change in this epidemic, women may have the most limited options. Prescriptions to control the spread of AIDS must take into account these constraints and include efforts to increase women's options.

TRACING THE SPREAD OF AIDS IN AFRICA: THE ROLE OF TRADE, MIGRANT LABOR, AND URBANIZATION

The path of the AIDS epidemic among both women and men in Africa cannot be understood apart from the realities of commerce and civil strife. Data suggest that the epidemic first became established in the central African countries of Zaire, Rwanda, and Burundi. Early sporadic cases may have been identified as early as the 1960s in Zaire (16), with the epidemic form beginning to appear in the mid-1970s. AIDS was next identified in Uganda, to the east, and in Zambia, to the south. Following the routes of trade and population movement, the epidemic soon spread even further east, to Kenya and Tanzania, and also further south, to Zimbabwe and Malawi. Together, these countries form the large hinterland of South Africa's labor reserve. That infection travels in the wake of trade is shown by the experience of the small town of Kasensero in southern Uganda, located along the truck route to the capital of Kampala. Recent reports suggest that up to half of all deaths in this town are attributable to AIDS (17). Undoubtedly the tremendous social disruptions experienced during Uganda's recent war-torn years have also contributed to the spread of the virus.

Within Zimbabwe, data support a north-to-south spread. In 1985, for example, 3 percent of blood donors in the northern city of Harare were seropositive, compared with 0.05 percent in the city of Bulwayo, to the south. South Africa, the southern tip of the continent, continues to report low rates of infection (below 5 percent), but the doubling time of the incidence of infection is six month (18). While no evidence of HIV seropositivity was found in 1987 among attenders at a South African clinic for the treatment of sexually transmitted diseases (STDs), by 1988 the prevalence rate had risen to 1.1 percent among women and to 0.6 percent among men (19).

The populous west coast of Africa, belonging to a different axis of trade and commerce connections than east–central Africa, has been affected by AIDS more recently. For example, Nigeria— where one in five Africans live—has relatively few cases of AIDS. But seroprevalence data suggest that the virus is present in the Nigerian population: one survey found that about 1 percent of prostitutes were infected (20). In addition, the identification of a second human immunodeficiency virus (NIV-2) in Senegal in 1985 adds another dimension to the epidemic in west Africa.

In all, 43 of Africa's 50 countries have reported cases of AIDS to the World Health Organization. Some 80 percent of these cases have occurred in nine nations at the center of the epidemic; these countries account for about one-sixth of Africa's population (21). But it would be shortsighted to describe the epidemic as geographically limited. Once HIV is present in a population, the incidence of infection can undergo exponential spread. In Zimbabwe, blood donor data suggest a rapid rise in HIV infection in recent years. In 1985, an average of 2.3 percent of donations tested positive on a single ELISA (enzyme-linked immunosorbent assay), but the figure in some urban areas five years later exceeds 15 percent. In Ivory Coast, the prevalence rose from 1 to 4 percent in two years (22); among prenatal women in Lilongwe, Malawi, it rose from 3 percent in 1986 to 18 percent in 1989 (23); in Bangui, Central African Republic, it rose from 2 percent in 1985 to 7 percent in 1989 (24). In the absence of aggressive intervention efforts, rapid spread of the virus seems likely.

Researchers often remark that HIV infection seems to be an urban rather than a rural problem (25). Much of Africa's population presumably should be protected, since the majority (from 60 to 90 percent) still is rural. But data suggest that significant rates of infection nonetheless are occurring in rural areas: 12 percent in a community sample in rural Uganda (26), 4.9 percent in a sample including prenatal women and donors from rural Tanzania (27), and 3.2 percent among hospital patients in rural Zimbabwe (28). Sparing of these regions seems a function more of the level of technological development (roads, bus transport, etc.) than of any "cultural barriers" to infection due to the strength of "traditional" values in rural areas. Undisrupted traditional culture simply no longer exists, particularly in regions where migrant labor was forcibly introduced at the turn of the century. At present, rates of urban migration in Africa are the highest in the world. In Zimbabwe, which has a good infrastructure and where movement between town and rural areas is frequent, many researchers do not expect the rural–urban gradient to be sustained. The history of Zimbabwe serves as an example of the role of recent colonial history, particularly in the settler colonies, in establishing the social context of the epidemic.

UNDERSTANDING THE EPIDEMIOLOGY OF AIDS IN ZIMBABWE: THE POLITICAL ECONOMY OF FAMILY STRUCTURES

Zimbabwe became independent in 1980 after a long and bitter war against the settler regime that left at least 20,000 dead (29). Its period of colonization lasted nearly a century. White "pioneers" in search of gold entered the territory from South Africa in the 1890s. The final uprising in opposition to the European incursion was defeated in 1897. When gold failed to materialize, the settlers turned to agriculture, and the expropriation of African lands rapidly followed. Land alienation served the dual function of expanding the commercial agricultural sector and creating a labor pool among the now landless peasants. The forced entry of African men into the cash economy was furthered by the introduction of a hut tax that required cash payment. By the 1930s, the law of the land decreed that whites—who comprised less than 5 percent of the population—own half of the land, while the original inhabitants—who comprised 95 percent of the population—be relegated to the remaining half. This "other half," then called the "Tribal Trust Lands" and now called the "communal areas" consisted of the least arable lands.

Prior to the colonial period, traditional Zimbabwean societies were patrilineal (30). Marriage was, and is today, accompanied by payment of a bride-price in compensation to the wife's family for loss of her labor and reproductive capacity, and also as a token of esteem and affection from one family to another. In Zimbabwe, the bride-price has taken on new economic meaning in a market economy. Payment is substantial and may take years to complete. In precolonial times, women returned to their natal family only if divorced. The commitment implicit in married life was not to male sexual fidelity, but to financial support of the wife and offspring (who became part of the male lineage). If wealth permitted, men could have more than one wife. These additional wives did not displace the older wives, who instead maintained their status as senior wives and also could share in the labor of more junior wives. Having multiple wives, however, is beyond the financial capability of most men: according to a 1982 study, under 5 percent of married women in Zimbabwe were in polygamous unions (31).

Patriarchal values parallel the patrilineal system of inheritance and dominated Zimbabwe's traditional societies. Women's entitlement was limited, but it was not nonexistent. For example, women were entitled to the earnings of their own handwork, to plots on which to grow family foods, and to certain gifts of motherhood (30). These limited protections were further curtailed during the colonial period, when European settler society introduced its own patriarchal values. Codification of European-identified "traditional" law reduced women to perpetual minority status in the guardianship of either their fathers or their husbands. Property rights were extremely limited, as were

rights even to their own children. Surveys in the early 1980s showed that about half of households in rural areas of Zimbabwe were de facto headed by women (32). But responsibility does not translate into control. Women did not become owners of either land or the products of their labor. While many of the legal barriers to women's equality were overturned in a series of laws passed after Zimbabwe's independence in 1980, decades of legally entrenched social inequality will take time to overcome.

Barriers to women's equality in Zimbabwe, however, stem not simply from patriarchal values but also from the land hunger created by European expropriation. Severe overcrowding in the most unproductive areas meant that women rarely were awarded land in their own right. As men left to work in the towns and on large-scale farms and mines, women and families were left behind to manage as subsistence farmers. Rural women's labor also increased, as it extended to tasks originally performed by men. A study of peasant woman's "typical" workday suggests that it extends from 4:30 A.M. until 9 P.M. In 1982, of an estimated 780,000 families in the peasant sector, nearly a third (235,000) operated on this split-family strategy (33).

As family separation became a feature of life, the rules of sexual relationships outside marriage also changed. Husbands formed other liaisons in town. These relationships might even supersede the rural wife, leading to divorce or a reduction in remittances. The impact on the rural families left behind could be catastrophic. Loss of cash income from the towns placed women-headed households at a far higher risk of having malnourished children; in one study, the risk was found to increase sixfold (34). The rural income might even be used to supplement urban expenses. Those men who could not afford to maintain urban wives opted for more casual arrangements. These multiple relationships, often referred to as modern-day versions of polygamy, actually differ considerably from the polygamous unions of Zimbabwe's traditional culture, described above.

In sharp contrast to the practice of polygamy in the precolonial era, the multiple relationships that arose in the urban setting of the colonial and postcolonial Zimbabwean society are not rare: they are practically universal. Obviously, this has required a change in where both women and men live, as well as in their patterns of sexual interaction. Although urban female migration initially was restricted both legally and by the lack of employment prospects, some women migrated to meet the demand for sexual services created by the artificial settlement of men without their families. An urban woman, particularly one divorced or unmarried, became synonymous with a prostitute. This stereotype is strong and has found its way into the AIDS control program. An early poster depicted a woman in a miniskirt and high-heeled boots, dragging on a cigarette, and the caption exhorted men to remain faithful to their families. (The poster concept, we are told, was developed by women!)

In Zimbabwe, as in other parts of Africa (35, 36), the exchange of sex for money or for other goods and services covers a broad range of arrangements. Many are not socially considered to be prostitution. Some of these women sell single sexual encounters. Probably more common are situations in which men pay for ongoing sexual and domestic services. These may range from sporadic payments to stable live-in partnerships. The definition of a prostitute therefore becomes somewhat arbitrary. Women who live apart or are divorced from their husbands may supplement their low incomes with gifts from male friends. Most would not enter into liaisons without financial compensation, and none would consider themselves prostitutes. In addition, some women who work as seasonal laborers support themselves off-season by selling sex. Others sell sex to meet a specific obligation, such as school fees. Younger women, even those of school age, may trade sex for the status of an older lover who can give them otherwise inaccessible goods or experiences (meals in hotels, riding in an expensive car, and so on). These men are popularly known as "sugar daddies." Finally, employed women may be forced to exchange sex for job security.

Popular belief holds that those patterns are well established in towns, but rural life also offers the opportunity for commercial sex. Rural "growth points" (rudimentary business centers), army camps, and similar locations provide the setting for such exchanges to occur. It is also widely believed that some urban women, particularly professional women, are both willing and have the opportunity to "balance the score" with their errant husbands. Whatever the extent of this practice, strong social sanctions exist against women engaging in extramarital sex. Although hardly any data exist on contemporary sexual relations in Zimbabwe, it seems safe to state that few women feel they are in the position to have sexual relations without some sort of benefit, whether social (including marriage) or material. For the vast majority of women, sexual relationships occur in the context of marriage (37, Table A.2.2, p. 65). By the age of 20 to 24 years, 75 percent of women in Zimbabwe have been married, in line with the traditionally sanctioned requirement that childbearing occur within marriage.

AIDS AND SEXUALLY TRANSMITTED DISEASES IN ZIMBABWE: AN IMPORTANT CONNECTION

The changing nature of marital and extramarital sexual relationships in Zimbabwe has profoundly influenced patterns of transmission of not only AIDS, but other STDs as well. The link between these STDs and AIDS is twofold. Serving as a marker of sexual activity outside the family unit, the presence of STDs indicates likely areas where AIDS may spread. In addition, data suggest that STDs may be a cofactor for HIV infection (15, 38), as discussed below.

At present, STDs are common in Zimbabwe. Last year, over 900,000 cases of STDs were treated nationwide (39). With the population estimated at 10 million (and assuming one case per person), this averages out to treatment of nearly one-quarter of the adult population! Popular ideas about STDs suggest that little stigma is attached to male infection. Having an STD is almost a rite of passage into manhood, proof of sexual activity: "A bull is not a bull without his scars." Consistent with both data and belief, a study on HIV infection among male factory workers found that a history of prior STD was common among both seropositive and seronegative men: 100 and 75 percent respectively (40). Other risk factors, now documented in numerous studies of AIDS in Africa, were also more common in the HIV-positive group, e.g., multiple partners, a history of payment for sex. What was unexpected was the high prevalence of high risk activities among the seronegative men: 40 percent reported an STD in the previous year, and the majority (67 percent) had paid money for sex. Seropositive men were more likely than seronegative men to report a history of genital ulcer. In the light of these data, one can hardly characterize the seronegative comparison group as "low risk."

Many investigators now believe that the enhanced risk of heterosexual transmission of AIDS in Africa may largely be explained by high rates of concurrent infection with another STD (15, 38, 41). Of particular concern is chancroid, an STD that is common in Africa but not in the West. In Zimbabwe, about half of genital ulcer disease is due to chancroid. The important role of such ulcers in HIV transmission is biologically plausible. Both disruption of the mucosal barrier and the presence of HIV-infected white blood cells would explain the increased likelihood of infection. In our clinic in Harare, where we have been seeing patients referred for HIV infection for a number of years, we found that among those couples in which the male partner was the index case, a history of genital ulcers was three times more likely among men in couples where HIV infection was concordant rather than discordant (15).

The focus on genital ulcers as an important cofactor for HIV transmission has both positive and negative features. While it offers new approaches for intervention programs, it also shifts emphasis from the broader social context of STD occurrence to more narrow medical concerns. Certainly any intervention that results in reduced rates of STDs, such as increasing public awareness about the availability of treatment for STDs, will also mean a diminution of HIV transmission. It is said that some women now inspect men for signs of genital ulcer before agreeing to have sex, a strategy that may be particularly useful for women engaged in commercial sex. The focus on genital ulcer also is appealing because it seems to eliminate all of the value-laden issues that accompany interpretation of other risk factors, such as multiple partners and prostitute contact. Zimbabwe's Ministry of Health has generated protocols for STD treatment, and the nation's independence made access to medical care effectively universal. Nonetheless, the number of cases of STDs in Zimbabwe increases yearly. To reduce the problem of HIV transmission to the problem of controlling genital ulcer is to search for a "technological fix" that fails to address the social factors that jointly underlie both problems.

As suggested by our work in Harare (15), it is against this background of high rates of STDs that AIDS transmission occurs, and in most cases it is the male partner who introduces HIV infection into the family unit. In our clinic, we ask married patients to bring their spouses. About half of the partners eventually appear for screening. The main reason that other partners do not come is because they live elsewhere, usually in the rural areas. Among the initial 75 couples, reported risk factors for AIDS were more prevalent among men than women, who universally denied having multiple partners. Only in two couples was the wife seropositive and the husband seronegative. In both cases, the wife had an identifiable risk factor (blood transfusion, first marriage to a partner who died of an AIDS-like illness). Although we do not know the duration or timing of infection in the couples we have studied, the paucity of female-positive/male-negative couples supports our impression that wives are most often placed at risk by their husbands. Moreover, because women in general are more likely to use health services than men, referral patterns seem unlikely to explain the small number of women as the index cases.

We are seeing more women now, usually referred because of HIV-related illness in a child. Often the mother has been tested without the involvement of the husband. Increasingly, the husband declines screening and sometimes rejects the mother and child. These are the realities of AIDS experienced by women in Zimbabwe.

AIDS PREVENTION IN AFRICA: PROSPECTS FOR THE FUTURE

We have discussed how sexual relationships in Zimbabwe and, by extension, other parts of sub-Saharan Africa are far more complex than the term "promiscuous" implies. To halt the current epidemic spread of AIDS, we will have to reckon with these patterns as we encourage changes in individual behavior—so far the only universally available "weapon" to combat this disease. The fact that historically produced social conditions have created situations that promote behavior which we now call "high risk" should not be taken to mean that this behavior is inevitable, or that only a complete social transformation will permit meaningful interventions to reduce transmission of HIV. Instead, our point is that the pattern of sexual relations, which places many people at risk for HIV infection, is not due to some "natural proclivity" of African men or to some inherent feature of "human nature," but is social in origin, and so can be changed. In Zimbabwe, the twin legacies of the patriarchy and colonialism seem the most important factors in shaping family structure, sexual relations, and the risk of HIV infection. If we do not take this into account, we cannot hope to develop specific and effective interventions to halt the spread of AIDS.

A first and urgent step in AIDS prevention is to ensure that people are provided with information and resources necessary to diminish their chance of being infected by HIV. As far as possible, the pub-

lic health campaign should be rooted in organizations that people know and trust. Schoepf and coauthors (42) report that in Zaire, people initially joked that AIDS was an "imaginary syndrome invented by Europeans to discourage African lovers." This attitude betrays a distrust of outside prescriptions for changes in sexual behavior, prescriptions that were initially seen as part of population control programs. Clinics, schools, and the radio are all natural places for information to be made available. In settings where the government is not trusted, other organizations become particularly important: the trade union movement, women's groups, grassroots organizations—all need to be convinced of the importance of adding AIDS prevention to their agenda.

The campaign should bring information about HIV transmission and prevention into everyday life in forms accessible to a population in which many people are illiterate and a biological understanding of disease is virtually absent. A series of articles on AIDS in Zimbabwe's national newspaper in 1987 was replete with such terms as "killer lymphocytes," "T4 cells," and the like, and required a university-level biology background. Decades of experience in health education can be brought to bear on developing methods of getting across information about AIDS in ways that are popular, nonjudgmental, and hopeful. For example, a leading musician here recently came out with a song about AIDS, as have musicians in Zaire, Uganda, Zambia, and elsewhere.

For most people, celibacy or a single lifetime partner are not realistic options. Efforts should therefore focus on reducing transmission. In practice this means limiting the number of partners and using condoms. Condoms cost only a few cents each, but providing them in adequate numbers to the sexually active population of the continent will still run into millions of dollars. Most African governments are facing cuts in social expenditures as a result of structural adjustment, and many cannot afford the cost of condoms or, indeed, the overall public health campaign. International aid will continue to be vital in AIDS control.

Adopting the use of condoms is more complicated than learning how to use them (42). While the distribution, and presumably use, of condoms appears to be increasing (43), a recent national survey of Zimbabwean men found that only 35 percent said they had ever used condoms (44). Most viewed condom use as appropriate for prostitutes, but not within marriages or other stable arrangements. As we have suggested, women are in a weak position to dictate how sex takes place. As seroprevalence increases and individuals are more likely to know personally someone with AIDS, more women may be willing to risk abuse or divorce to reduce their risk of infection. Further complicating matters is the fact that many women want to have children. Clearly acceptable alternatives to condoms need to be found that allow women to control use and possibly permit conception. Some possibilities have been outlined by Stein (45).

Unfortunately, we have little direct experience with such a broad public health program. So far, at-

tention in Zimbabwe has focused on individual counseling and case identification. Blood donors who test positive are not informed of a "problem" (unless they ask) and are permitted to continue to donate blood (which subsequently is discarded). Research activities have been subject to careful and lengthy scrutiny. Posters about AIDS on clinic walls are now three years old. The pace is picking up, but progress is slow. Reports from other centers (46, 47) support some optimism about people's ability to change high-risk behaviors.

We have had ample time to reflect on the social implications of the AIDS epidemic. We have agonized as we see patients who are infected and who had no knowledge of their risks. Fathers as well as mothers suffer when their children become sick or, though seemingly well, carry a death sentence in their small bodies. For all the hardships of womanhood in Africa, there is no doubt that children are universally cherished. To protect their future may be the strongest incentive in the campaign to reduce HIV transmission.

ACKNOWLEDGMENTS

Our thanks to Albie Sachs and Shiraz Ramji for helpful comments on earlier drafts of this article, and to Nancy Krieger for her active editorial assistance.

REFERENCES

1. Clumeck, N., et al. Acquired immunodeficiency syndrome in African patients. *N. Engl. J. Med.* 310:492–497, 1984.
2. Nationwide community based serological survey of human immunodeficiency virus type 1 (HIV-1) and other human retrovirus infections in a central African country. Rwandan HIV seroprevalence study group. *Lancet* 1:941–943, 1988.
3. Carswell, J. W. HIV infection in healthy persons in Uganda. *AIDS* 1:223–227, 1987.
4. Malbye, M., et al. Evidence for heterosexual transmission and clinical manifestations of human immunodeficiency virus infection and related conditions in Lusaka, Zambia, *Lancet* 2:1113–1115, 1986.
5. DeCock, K. M., et al. Rapid emergence of AIDS in Abidjan, Ivory Coast. *Lancet* 2:408–411, 1989.
6. Mann, J. M. Social, cultural and political aspects: An overview. *AIDS* 2 (Suppl.):S207–S208, 1988.
7. Harris, C., et al. Immunodeficiency in female sexual partners of men with the acquired immunodeficiency syndrome. *N. Engl. J. Med.* 308:1181–1184, 1983.
8. Sabatier, R. *Blaming Others: Prejudice, Race, and Worldwide AIDS.* The Panos Institute, Washington, D.C., 1988.
9. Eales, L. J., et al. Association of different allelic forms of group specific component with susceptibility to and clinical manifestations of human immunodeficiency virus. *Lancet* 2:277–283, 1987.
10. Rushton, J. P., and Bogaert, A. F. Population differences in susceptibility to AIDS: An evolutionary analysis. *Soc. Sci. Med.* 28:1211–1220, 1989.

11. Padian, N. Prostitute women and AIDS: Epidemiology. *AIDS* 2:413–419, 1989.

12. Schoepf, B. G. Methodology, Ethics, and Politics: AIDS Research in Africa for Whom? Unpublished manuscript.

13. Quinn, T., et al. AIDS in Africa: An epidemiological paradigm. *Science* 234:955–963, 1986.

14. Neequaque, A. R., Osei, L., and Mingle, A. A. Dynamics of HIV epidemic: The Ghanaian experience. In *The Global Impact of AIDS,* edited by A. Fleming and M. Carballo, pp. 9–15. Alan R. Liss, New York, 1988.

15. Latif, A. S., et al. Genital ulcers and transmission of HIV among couples in Zimbabwe. *AIDS* 3:519–523, 1989.

16. Sonnet, J., et al. Early AIDS cases originating in Zaire and Burundi (1962–1976). *Scand. J. Infect. Dis.* 19:511–517, 1987.

17. Hooper, E. AIDS in Uganda. *Afr. Aff.* 86:469–477, 1987.

18. Schapiro, M., Crookes, R. L., and O'Sullivan, E. Screening antenatal blood samples for anti-human immunodeficiency virus antibodies by a large pool enzyme-linked immunosorbent assay system: Results of an 18 month investigation. *S. Afr. J. Med.* 76:245–249, 1989.

19. *Annual Report of the Medical Research Council,* p. 17. South Africa, 1988.

20. Mohammed, F., et al. HIV infection in Nigeria [letter]. *AIDS* 2:61–62, 1988.

21. Chen, J., and Mann, J. M. Global patterns and prevalence of AIDS and HIV infection. *AIDS* 3 (Suppl. 1): S247–S252, 1989.

22. Mann, J. M. Global AIDS in the 1990s. Unpublished document. Global Program on AIDS/Dir/89.2. World Health Organization, Geneva, 1989.

23. Liomba, N. G., et al. Comparison of Age Distribution of Anti-HIV-1 and AntiHBc in an Urban Population from Malawi. Abstract No. W.G.027. Fifth International Conference on AIDS, Montreal, 1989.

24. Somse, P., et al. Les aspects épidémiologiques des affections liées aux VIH1 et 2 en République Centrafricaine. Abstract No. W.G.028. Fifth International Conference on AIDS, Montreal, 1989.

25. Turshen, M. *The Politics of Public Health,* pp. 219–241. Rutgers University Press, Rutgers, NJ., 1989.

26. Kenegeay-Kayondo, J. F., et al. Anti-HIV Seroprevalence in Adult Rural Populations in Uganda and Its Implication for Preventive Strategies. Abstract No. T.A.P.111. Fifth International Conference on AIDS, Montreal, 1989.

27. Dolmans, W. M. V., et al. Prevalence of HIV-1 antibody among groups of patients and healthy subjects from a rural and urban population in Mwanza region, Tanzania. *AIDS* 3:297–299, 1989.

28. Mertens, T., et al. Epidemiology of HIV and hepatitis B virus (HBV) in selected African and Asian populations. *Infections* 17:4–7, 1989.

29. Stoneman, C. *Zimbabwe's Inheritance.* St. Martin's Press, New York, 1982.

30. Batezat, E., and Mwalo, M. *Women in Zimbabwe,* pp. 9–12. Sapes Trust Jongwe Printers, Harare, Zimbabwe, 1989.

31. Central Statistical Office. *Report on Demographic Socio-economic Survey of the Communal Lands. Permanent Sample Survey Unit Programme* (ZNHSCP). Report No. 1 to 5. Zimbabwe, 1984/85.

32. Riddell, R. *Report of the Commission of Inquiry into Incomes, Price, and Conditions of Service.* Government of Zimbabwe, Harare, 1982.

33. Callear, D. *The Social and Cultural Factors Involved in Production by Small Farmers in Wedza Communal Area, Zimbabwe,* p. 22. Division for the Study of Development, UNESCO, Paris, 1982. [cited in reference 37].

34. Thiesen, R. J. *Agro-economic Factors Relating to the Health and Academic Achievement of Rural School Children.* Tribal Areas of Rhodesia Research Foundation, Salisbury [Harare], 1975. [cited in reference 37].

35. Day, S. Prostitute women and AIDS: Anthropology. *AIDS* 2:421–428, 1989.

36. Larson, A. Social context of human immunodeficiency virus transmission in Africa: Historical and cultural bases of east and central African sexual relations. *Rev. Infect. Dis.* 2:716–731, 1989.

37. UNICEF. *Children and Women in Zimbabwe: A Situation Analysis.* Government Printers, Harare, Zimbabwe, 1985.

38. Cameron, D. W., et al. Female to male transmission of human immunodeficiency virus type 1: Risk factors for seroconversion in men. *Lancet* 2:403–407, 1989.

39. Secretary for Health. *Annual Report, 1988.* Government Printers, Harare, Zimbabwe, 1989.

40. Bassett, M. T., et al. HIV infection in Urban Men in Zimbabwe. Abstract No. Th.C.581, Sixth International Conference on AIDS, San Francisco, 1990.

41. Kreiss, J. K., et al. AIDS virus infection in Nairobi prostitutes: Spread of the epidemic to East Africa. *N. Engl. J. Med.* 314:414–418, 1986.

42. Schoepf, B. G., et al. AIDS in society in Central Africa: A view from Zaire. In *AIDS in Africa,* pp. 211–235. The Edwin Mellon Press, Lewiston, N. Y., 1988.

43. Condom use on the increase. *The Herald* (Harare, Zimbabwe), September 6, 1989, p. 1.

44. Mbivzo, M., and Adamchak, D. J. Condom use and acceptance: A survey of male Zimbabweans. *Cent. Afr. J. Med.* 35:519–558, 1989.

45. Stein, Z. HIV prevention: The need for methods women can use. *Am. J. Public Health* 80:460–462, 1990.

46. Ngugi, E. N., Plummer, F. A., and Simonsen, J. N. Prevention of transmission of human immunodeficiency virus in Africa: Effectiveness of condom promotion and health education among prostitutes. *Lancet* 2:887–890, 1988.

47. Ngugi, E. N., and Plummer, F. A. Health outreach and control of HIV infection in Kenya. *J. Acquired Immunodeficiency Syndromes* 6:566–570, 1988.

PART TWO

HEALTH AND ILLNESS BEHAVIOR

CHAPTER 4

HEALTH BEHAVIOR

The articles in Part One examined historically broad areas of study associated with medical sociology. Part Two turns our attention to the variations of health and illness behavior that exist not only between, but also within, cultures. We begin with an examination of what people do to maintain their health. Health and health behavior are cultural constructs—that is, what constitutes health, and the methodologies and beliefs of maintaining it, may differ between as well as within cultures. The first two articles examine the Health Belief Model, one of the classic concepts in medical sociology.

In the first article, from an American perspective, Irwin M. Rosenstock provides insight into the origins of the Health Belief Model (HBM). Essentially, the HBM argues that "an individual's subjective evaluation of an illness situation, including the value placed on a particular outcome and the belief that a particular action will result in that outcome, becomes the key variable in the utilization of health services" (Loustaunau and Sobo, 1997, p. 87). Rosenstock provides the reader with insight into the dynamics of the HBM and into its historical and theoretical context. Although the article is relatively short, Rosenstock outlines the central components of the HBM (perceived susceptibility, perceived seriousness, perceived benefits, perceived barriers, and cues to action) and addresses the process through which they were developed.

Although considerable research of the Health Belief Model exists, it has been conducted primarily in the United States or other Western industrialized nations. The second article, by Stella R. Quah, is an effort to determine whether the HBM works in cultures outside the United States and Western Europe. Situated in Singapore, Quah examines the relationship between preventive health behavior (relative to cancer, heart disease, and tuberculosis) and respondents' knowledge of disease etiology and diagnosis, potential restrictions, its effect of preventive behavior on normal role behavior, and the extent to which respondents consider themselves vulnerable to the disease. Indicators of preventive health behavior included smoking, drinking, exercise, preventive actions, and medicines at home. According to Quah, the three ethnic groups that constitute Singapore (Chinese, Malay, and Indians) differ in health beliefs. Her findings support the position that ethnicity serves as a explanatory variable for preventive health behavior patterns, thus weakening the explanatory power of the HBM. Addressing the limitations of her research, Quah qualifies the differences between her research and that of Rosenstock. The HBM is helpful in understanding preventive health behavior, she feels, but the inclusion of variables that address ethnicity, gender, and religious affiliation is necessary.

The third article (from a developing country perspective) is not an application of the HBM, but it is nonetheless applicable to our understanding of health behavior. K. A. S. Wickrama and Pat M. Keith address differences in the utilization of health services by male- and female-headed households in Sri Lanka. Comparing rates in two communities in Sri Lanka, the authors found differences in health care utilization rates in male- and female-headed households. They also report that other sociodemographic characteristics such as age, marital status, and education influence health care utilization rates. The consequences of their findings are of particular importance, for female-headed households are expected to increase, thus potentially increasing health care utilization rates as well as pressure on the health care system within Sri Lanka.

REFERENCE

Loustaunau, Martha O., and Elisa J. Sobo. 1997. *The Cultural Context of Health, Illness, and Medicine.* Westport, CT: Bergin & Garvey.

AMERICAN PERSPECTIVE

HISTORICAL ORIGINS OF THE HEALTH BELIEF MODEL

IRWIN M. ROSENSTOCK

It is always difficult to trace the historical development of a theory that has been the subject of considerable direct study and has directly or indirectly spawned a good deal of additional research. This is certainly true of the Health Belief Model, perhaps even more than usual because the Model grew out of a set of independent, applied research problems with which a group of investigators in the Public Health Service were confronted between 1950 and 1960. Thus, the theory and development of the Model grew simultaneously with the solution of practical problems. Two classes of circumstances should be described which were largely responsible for the type of model that ultimately emerged. These concern the settings in which research was required and the training and background experiences of those who participated in the development of the Model.

HEALTH SETTINGS

During the early 1950s the Public Health Service was for the most part oriented toward the prevention, not the treatment, of disease. Medical care was largely beyond the pale of what was considered appropriate public health work, although there had been some notable historical exceptions. Thus, problems connected with patients' symptoms, their compliance with medical regimens, or with physician–patient communications were not a focus of public health concern. What was clearly evident at the time, however, was the widespread failure of people to accept disease preventives or screening tests for the early detection of asymptomatic disease; these included tests or prevention first for TB,[1] somewhat later for cervical cancer, dental disease and, still later, rheumatic fever, polio and influenza. It was also noted that the various preventive measures or tests were usually provided on a demonstration basis, free of charge, or at very low cost.

The foregoing factors to a large extent influenced the kind of theory that would have to be developed to explain preventive health behavior. Such a theory would have to deal with the behavior of individuals who were not currently suffering disabling disease. It would have to be oriented to the avoidance of disease. While it could not overlook the potential role of barriers to accepting health services, it would have to attempt to explain the behavior of people who were being charged little or nothing for the service.

THE RESEARCHERS

Those of us* who first worked on the several programmatic problems posed by the public health problems described earlier were all trained as social psychologists. As such, we had been influenced in considerable measure by the theories of Kurt Lewin. All of us exhibited a phenomenological orientation, that it is the world of the perceiver that determines what he will do and not the physical environment, except as the physical environment comes to be represented in the mind of the behaving individual. Finally, we early researchers had a strong philosophical commitment toward theory building and not merely solving practical problems one at a time. We were thus committed toward the gradual accretion of scientific information by building on the work of others.

It should also be noted that during the period of time discussed there were relatively few behavioral scientists engaged in full-time research on health problems. To be sure, there were some notable exceptions, but for the most part there was little information within health research itself to guide these investigators.

These factors almost foreordained that the early researchers concerned with the Health Belief Model would work cooperatively, build on each other's work, develop theory that would include a heavy component of motivation and the perceptual world of the behaving individual; and that the orientation of the work would be toward developing a theory not only useful in explaining a particular program problem, but also adaptable to other problems. Also, in the Lewinian tradition, the theory could be expected to focus on the current (ahistorical) dynamics confronting the behaving individual rather than on the historical perspective of his prior experiences. The investigators were of the opinion that it is the present state of affairs that determines actions, with history playing a role only insofar as it is represented in the present dynamics.

THE BELIEFS

The major outlines of what later came to be known as the Health Belief Model are understandable in the light of the historical perspective provided. The implicit conception following Lewin was of an individual existing in a life space composed of regions some of which were positively valued (positive valence), others of which were negatively valued (negative valence), and still others of which were relatively neutral. Diseases, if they were represented in the life space at all, would be regions of negative valence which could be expected to exert a force moving the person away from that region, unless doing so would require him to enter a region of even greater negative valence. One's daily activities were thus conceived of as a process of being pulled by positive forces and repelled by negative forces. The earliest characteristics of the Model, as they were translated from the foregoing abstraction, were that in order for an individual to take action to avoid a disease he would need to believe (1) that he was personally *susceptible* to it, (2) that the occurrence of the disease would have at least moderate *severity* on some component of his life, and (3) that taking a particular action would in fact be *beneficial* by reducing his susceptibility to the condition or, if the disease occurred, by reducing its severity, and that it would not entail overcoming important psychological *barriers* such as cost, convenience, pain, embarrassment. With respect to taking a test for the early detection of a disease, the same factors were deemed necessary, but in addition there was also the requirement that the individual believe he could have the disease even in the absence of symptoms.[1–3]

Perceived Susceptibility

Individuals were believed to vary widely in their acceptance of personal susceptibility to a condition. At one extreme might be the individual who denies any possibility of his contracting a given condition. In a more moderate position is the person who may admit to the "statistical" possibility of a disease occurrence, but a possibility that is not likely to happen. Finally, a person may express a feeling that he is in real danger of contracting the condition. In short, as it has been measured, susceptibility refers to the subjective risks of contracting a condition.

Perceived Seriousness

Convictions concerning the seriousness of a given health problem may also vary from person-to-person. The degree of seriousness may be judged both by the degree of emotional arousal created by the thought of a disease as well as by the kinds of difficulties the individual believes a given health condition will create for him.[4]

A person may, of course, see a health problem in terms of its medical or clinical consequence. He would thus be concerned with such questions as whether a disease could lead to his death, or reduce his physical or mental functioning for long periods of time, or disable him permanently. However, the perceived seriousness of a condition may, for a given individual, include such broader and more complex implications as the effects of the disease on his job, on his family life, and on his social relations. Thus, a person may not believe that tuberculosis is medically serious, but may nevertheless believe that its occurrence would be serious if it created important psychological and economic tensions within his family.

Perceived susceptibility and severity having a strong cognitive component are at least partly dependent on knowledge.

Perceived Benefits of Taking Action and Barriers to Taking Action

The acceptance of one's susceptibility to a disease that is also believed to be serious was thought to provide a force leading to action, but not defining the particular course of action that was likely to be taken.

The direction that the action takes was thought to be influenced by beliefs regarding the relative effectiveness of known available alternatives in reducing the disease threat to which the individual feels subjected. His behavior was thus thought to depend on how beneficial he believed the various alternatives would be in his case. Of course, there must be available to him at least one action that is subjectively possible. An alternative is likely to be seen as beneficial if it relates subjectively to the reduction of one's susceptibility to or seriousness of an illness. Again, the person's beliefs about the availability and effectiveness of various courses of action, and not the objective facts about the effectiveness of action, determine what course he will take. In turn, his beliefs in this area are undoubtedly influenced by the norms and pressures of his social groups. The literature on delay in seeking diagnosis for cancer symptoms[5,6] may reflect a conflict between (1) a strong feeling of *susceptibility* to what is regarded as a most *serious* disease and (2) a real conviction that there are no *efficacious methods* of prevention and/or control.

An individual may believe that a given action will be effective in reducing the threat of disease, but at the same time see that action itself as being inconvenient, expensive, unpleasant, painful or upsetting. These negative aspects of health action serve as *barriers* to action and arouse conflicting motives of avoidance. Several resolutions of the conflict were thought to be possible. If the readiness to act was high and the negative aspects were seen as relatively weak, the action in question was likely to be taken. If, on the other hand, the readiness to act was low while the potential negative aspects were seen as strong, the negative aspects functioned as barriers to prevent action.

Where the readiness to act was great and the barriers to action were also great, the conflict was thought to be more difficult to resolve. The individual was highly oriented toward acting to reduce the likelihood or impact of the perceived health danger. He was equally highly motivated to avoid action since he saw it as highly unpleasant or even painful.

Sometimes, alternative actions of nearly equal efficacy might be available. For example, the person who feels threatened by tuberculosis but fears the potential hazards of x-rays may choose to obtain a tuberculin test for initial screening.

But what can he do if the situation does not provide such alternative means to resolve his conflicts? Experimental evidence obtained outside the health area suggested that one of two reactions occur. First, the person might attempt to remove himself psychologically from the conflict situation by engaging in activities which did not really reduce the threat. Vacillating (without decision) between choices may be an example. Consider the individual who feels threatened by lung cancer, who believes quitting cigarette smoking will reduce the risk but for whom smoking serves important needs. He may constantly commit himself to give up smoking soon and thereby relieve, if only momentarily, the pressure imposed by the discrepancy between the barriers and the perceived benefits.

A second possible reaction was a marked increase in fear or anxiety.[7] If the anxiety or fear became strong enough, the individual might be rendered incapable of thinking objectively and behaving rationally about the problem. Even if he were subsequently offered a more effective means of handling the situation, he might not accept it, simply because he could no longer think constructively about the matter.

CUES TO ACTION

The variables which were originally described under the heading of perceived susceptibility and severity as well as the variables that defined perceived benefits and barriers to taking action, have all been subjected to research which will be reviewed in subsequent chapters. However, one additional variable was believed to be necessary to complete the model, but it has not been subjected to careful study.

A factor that serves as a cue, or a trigger, to appropriate action appeared to be necessary. The combined levels of susceptibility and severity provided the energy or force to act and the perception of benefits (less barriers) provided a preferred path of action. However, we believed the combination of these could reach quite considerable levels of intensity without resulting in overt action unless some instigating event occurred to set the process in motion. In the health area, such events or cues might be internal (e.g., perception of bodily states) or external (e.g., interpersonal interactions, the impact of media of communication, or receiving a postcard from the dentist).

The required intensity of a cue that was deemed sufficient to trigger behavior presumably varied with differences in the levels of susceptibility and severity. With relatively little acceptance of susceptibility to or severity of a disease, rather intense stimuli would be needed to trigger a response. On the other hand, with relatively high levels of perceived susceptibility and severity even slight stimuli may be adequate. For example, other things being equal, the person who barely accepts his susceptibility to tuberculosis will be unlikely to check upon his health until he experiences rather intense cues. On the other hand, the person who readily accepts his constant susceptibility to the disease may be spurred into action by the mere sight of a mobile x-ray unit or a relevant poster.

Unfortunately, the settings for most of the research on the Model have precluded obtaining an adequate measure of the role of cues. Since the kinds of cues that have been hypothesized may be quite fleeting and of little intrinsic significance (e.g., a casual view of a poster urging chest x-ray), they may easily be forgotten with the passage of time. An interview taken months or years later could not adequately identify the cues. Freidson had described the difficulties in attempting to assess interpersonal influences on cues.[8] Furthermore, respondents who have taken a recommended action in the past will probably be more likely to remember preceding events as relevant than will respondents who were exposed to the same event but never took the action. These problems make testing the role of cues most difficult in any retrospective setting. A prospective design, perhaps a panel study, will probably be required to assess properly how various stimuli serve as cues to trigger action in an individual who is psychologically ready to act.

OTHER VARIABLES

In addition to the foregoing set of variables, early abortive attempts were made to include as a motivational variable the concept of salience of health and illness for the individual. The attempts were abortive because no good operational measure of the concept of salience could be devised; we came to believe that the perception of susceptibility to and severity of a particular condition would itself be motivating. It will subsequently be seen that the concept of motivation was later reintroduced into the Model.[9]

Finally, our view of the role of demographic, sociopsychological, and structural variables was that they served to condition both individual perceptions and the perceived benefits of preventive actions, a view we have not subsequently modified. Figure 1 portrays the original Health Belief Model.

It should be noted explicitly that the Model had a clearcut avoidance orientation; diseases were regarded as negatively valent regions to be avoided. This is in contrast to the view that some particular state of health might possibly serve as a positively valent region that would pull a person toward it. It is still not known whether the improvement of health in an already healthy person does have some motivating force in influencing action. This grows out of the difficulty of giving positive health any operational meaning. Surely, the exer-

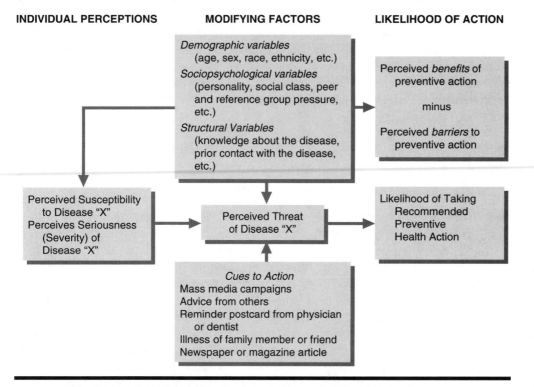

FIGURE 1   The "Health Belief Model" as Predictor of Preventive Health Behavior (after Becker et al.[9])

Source: From "A New Approach to Explaining Sick-Role Behavior in Low-Income Populations," by M. H. Becker, R. H. Drachman, and J. P. Kirscht, 1974, *American Journal of Public Health, 64*(3), pp. 205–216. Copyright © 1974 by APHA. Reprinted with permission.

cise and dietary mania observed over the last decade represent behaviors that could be regarded as striving toward improved health, but it is just as easy to explain them (insofar as they are health related at all) as behavior undertaken to avoid a deleterious situation. Again, there are individuals who exercise and engage in other actions having health implications but who do so for reasons quite unre-

lated to health, perhaps for aesthetic reasons or for the sheer exhilaration felt by many by the performance of physical work. Again, the question of whether the avoidance orientation in the Health Belief Model is adequate to account for the so-called positive health actions taken by people remains unresolved.

REFERENCES

1. Hochbaum G: *Public Participation in Medical Screening Programs: A Sociopsychological Study.* Public Health Serv. Publ, No. 572.
2. Rosenstock IM: What research in motivation suggests for public health, *Am J Public Health* 50:295–302, (Mar) 1960.
3. Rosenstock IM: Why people use health services. *Milbank Mem Fund Q* 44:94–127, (Jul) 1966.
4. Robbins P: Some explorations into the nature of anxieties relating to illness. United States Department of Health, Education, and Welfare, Public Health Service, *Genetic Psychol Monogr* 66:91–141, 1962.
5. Blackwell B: The literature of delay in seeking medical care for chronic illnesses. *Health Educ Monogr* 16:3–31, 1963.
6. Green L W, Roberts B J: The research literature on why women delay in seeking medical care for breast symptoms. *Health Educ Monogr* 2(2):129–177, (Sum) 1974.
7. Miller NE: Experimental studies of conflict. In Hunt, JMcV: *Personality and the Behavior Disorders.* New York, The Ronald Press, 431–465, 1944.
8. Freidson E: *Patients' Views of Medical Practice.* New York, Russell Sage Foundation, 1961.
9. Becker M H, Drachman R H, Kirscht J P: A new approach to explaining sick role behavior in low-income populations. *Am J Public Health* 64:205–216, 1974.

DEVELOPED WORLD PERSPECTIVE

THE HEALTH BELIEF MODEL AND PREVENTIVE HEALTH BEHAVIOUR IN SINGAPORE

STELLA R. QUAH

THE HEALTH BELIEF MODEL

The main characteristic of the Health Belief Model (HBM) is its emphasis on perception and motivation, thus reflecting the strong influence of Kurt Lewin's field theory [1,2]. Basically, the HBM put forth by Rosenstock [3] indicates that in order for an individual to take action (either to prevent or to cure a given disease), this person would have to (1) perceive the disease as having "at least moderate severity"; (2) perceive him/herself personally

susceptible, vulnerable or already affected by that disease; (3) believe that there are specific benefits in taking the given action, i.e. the disease will be effectively prevented or cured; and (4) the individual would have to perceive no major "barriers"—e.g. cost, convenience, pain, embarrassment—impeding his taking that action [4].

Although the HBM has been applied to the analysis of different types of health-related behaviour [5], in the study presented here the HBM is used for the analysis of *preventive* health behaviour.

In his application of the HBM Rosenstock followed the definition of preventive health behaviour originally suggested by Kasl and Cobb. The latter indicate that preventive health behaviour is the activity undertaken by persons who believe themselves healthy, for the purpose of preventing or detecting disease in an asymptomatic stage [6]. The same definition is followed in the present study.

The HBM has been tested empirically and corroborated in numerous instances. Yet, the overwhelming majority of these studies have been conducted on North American or European subpopulations, mainly in the United States [7,8]. Rosenstock's own studies are based on North American data. It is perhaps because of this that he emphasizes the economic differences or what he calls the "culture of poverty," and does not include any other sociostructural variables, with the exception of education. Put simply, not enough has been done to see whether the HBM "works" in other cultural settings. Considering that this framework is based on Lewin's field theory principles, and that Lewin himself acknowledged the importance of social factors in determining the needs of a person, the test of the HBM in different cultural settings can contribute significantly towards its refinement.

Indeed, for the analysis of preventive health behaviour in a Southeast Asian nation, it is imperative to take into consideration the influence of ethnic or cultural values and beliefs. The cultural differences among ethnic groups might prove crucial in the perception of seriousness and susceptibility to disease, as well as in the perception of social sanctions attached to a given disease [9]. The HBM overlooks this cultural dimension. Mechanic [10] hints to this weakness when he says that the "predictive power" of the HBM is "modest" because "environmental conditions" have been neglected by Rosenstock. Mechanic's "environmental conditions" are more structural (i.e. accessibility of services, transportation and other "organizational arrangements") than attitudinal. I consider attitudinal aspects, which usually have their roots in cultural and religious values, even more important than structural conditions, as potential explanatory factors of preventive health behaviour. Yet, despite these omissions, the HBM is used frequently in the study of health-related behaviour. Although Mechanic criticizes the overall weak predictive power of the HBM and some components of the HBM such as disease knowledge have been found to provide a very limited explanation of preventive health behaviour [11], other empirical studies cited by Rosenstock, Kasl and Cobb and Becker, among others, corroborate some of the HBM propositions, particularly the role of the variable vulnerability or susceptibility [12]. Therefore, the testing of the HBM outside the North American and European settings will add information on its explanatory power. The underlying assumption guiding this test is that the three main ethnic groups (Chinese, Malays and Indians) in Singapore differ in their respective health beliefs and values.

STUDY PROCEDURE

The empirical testing of the HBM was carried out by means of a survey design including personal interviews following a structured questionnaire. The population selected for the study was the total number of Singapore citizens aged 21 years and older. A sample of 1900 was drawn using a proportionate stratified random sampling with systematic selection. This sample size was determined by the criteria of 95% confidence level and + or − 3% confidence limits, in addition to the adjustment of the original sample of 890 needed, based on the estimated response rate, eligibility rate and coverage rate. A final sample of 1231 persons were successfully interviewed thus providing a 67% response rate from the adjusted sample.

The HBM as tested in this study, comprises one dependent variable, i.e. preventive health behaviour; and four independent variables: knowledge of disease etiology and prognosis, perceived social sanctions, perceived disruption of normal role activities, and perceived personal vulnerability. There are two intervening variables namely perceived benefits and perceived barriers to preventive action. All these seven variables are derived from the HBM presented by Rosenstock. In addition to these HBM factors, a set of variables tentatively labelled "antecedent" or background variables was also introduced in the analysis. These antecedent variables are ethnicity and religious affiliation, sex, social class (measured by a combined score of income, occupational prestige and level of formal education), age, exposure to mass media and future-orientation.

A brief summary of the respective operational definitions follows. The dependent variable, preventive health behaviour, required some specific focus for empirical measurement. Thus, three main diseases were used as the research focus, i.e. preventive health behaviour with regard to cancer, heart disease and tuberculosis. And, five activities served as indicators of such preventive health behaviour. These activities are smoking, drinking of alcoholic beverages, practice of regular exercise, taking general preventive actions, and keeping medicines at home. While the first three activities are, according to medical opinion, related to cancer, heart disease and tuberculosis, the latter two activities aim at other generalized preventive behaviour.

The individual's level of disease knowledge is represented by his/her answers to simple questions on the etiology (why does a person get cancer/tuberculosis/heart disease?) and prognosis (when you think about cancer/tuberculosis/heart disease, how serious do you think it is?) of the three diseases. These answers were classified into correct or incorrect following medical criteria [13]. The second independent variable, perception of social sanctions for a person with cancer, heart disease or tuberculosis, was measured by the subject's perception of the sick individual as personally responsible for contracting the disease. This perception of blame was measured individually for cancer, heart disease and tuberculosis.

The third independent variable, i.e. perceived threat of disruption of normal role activities caused

by the disease, was measured by questions on two activity areas. One was the perceived disruption of the person's job duties and the other was on his/her normal activities at home. The fourth independent variable, perceived personal vulnerability was measured by a five-point Likert scale, specially constructed for this purpose. It measured the respondent's level of agreement or disagreement with eight statements on his/her personal vulnerability to cancer, tuberculosis and heart disease.

As for the two intervening variables, perception of benefits and barriers to preventive action, they were measured as follows. For the perception of benefits, two steps were taken: the first was to detect the individual's awareness of at least one "effective" way of preventing each of the three diseases; the second step was to create a composite score of perception of benefits of preventive action, with the responses obtained in the first step. Data on the perception of barriers were obtained by questions on two aspects of accessibility to preventive services namely, whether the person had information on the existence of a preventive service, and if such services exist, how costly did he/she think they were.

The measurement of the antecedent variables presented relatively less problems than the measurement of the HBM variables. Ethnic affiliation was simply obtained by self-classification of the respondents. The majority of the population in Singapore falls into one of three main ethnic groups: Chinese, Malay and Indian. At the time of data collection their proportion in the population was 77.5, 13.3 and 7.0% respectively. A minority of the population is officially classified under "Others" and it comprised just about 2% of the total population. This study deals only with the three main ethnic groups. The same self-classification was used for religious affiliation. The individual's exposure to mass media was detected by means of questions on frequency of television viewing, listening to the radio and reading of newspapers. A related and more significant indicator in preventive health behaviour was also introduced: the individual's awareness of any of the health campaigns launched by the government during the twelve months preceding the interview. The person's future-orientation or attitudes towards control over his/her own life was measured by Rotter's locus of control scale [14].

A team of 21 specially trained interviewers conducted the personal interviews from the representative sample of Singapore citizens from April to September, 1977. Each respondent was contacted at his/her home by an interviewer of the same sex and ethnic group; and the interview was conducted in the language of choice of the respondent which included Malay, Tamil, English, Mandarin and several Chinese dialects. The average length of the interview was fifty minutes.

The data were analyzed at two levels. The first level comprised parametric and non-parametric measures of association. Those variables yielding significant associations were then included in the second level of analysis, i.e. regression and factor analyses. The SPSS [15] was used for all the statistical procedures. The factor analysis rotation chosen was direct oblimin rotation as it allows more flexibility than the other orthogonal rotation, given the latter's required assumption of independence among factors. Moreover, direct oblimin rotation provides two factor matrices, the primary *structure* matrix and the factor *pattern* matrix. The loadings in the factor pattern matrix represent the attempt to predict the value of one dependent variable from a number of independent variables clustered in a factor. The discussion of findings will be based on the factor pattern matrices. The complete factor pattern matrices for the three ethnic groups can be found in Appendix A and the list of the variables used in Appendix B. A summary of the main factor analysis findings is presented in Table 1.

THE INFLUENCE OF ETHNICITY

Ethnicity is used in this study as one of the angles from which preventive health behaviour and its association with a set of independent and intervening variables is analysed. But it is important to clarify first the significance of ethnicity at two levels. On the one hand, one must be assured that ethnicity, as an explanatory variable, is relevant to the study of health-related behaviour in general and preventive health behaviour in particular. On the other hand, it is important to establish the relevance of ethnicity in Singapore: i.e. whether other sociological studies have found important differences in behaviour among the three main ethnic groups discussed here, i.e. Chinese, Malays and Indians.

Ethnicity as an Explanatory Variable

The underlying assumption of the present analysis is that these three ethnic groups differ not only in terms of racial characteristics but also in terms of cultural values and beliefs. Hence the expected differences in their preventive health behaviour patterns. King's definition of ethnic group serves as one of the bases for these assumptions. King sees ethnic boundaries delimiting a cultural setting where people share "common backgrounds in language, customs, beliefs, habits and traditions, frequently in racial stock and country of origin" in addition to "a consciousness of kind" [16].

The relevant literature is abundant in studies linking ethnicity and health-related behaviour. Benjamin Paul, Lyle Saunders, Mark Zborowski and Margaret Mead [17–19] among others, reported empirical findings on the influence of ethnic values and beliefs on health behaviour. Paul pointed to the "cultural gap" as one of the main reasons for the failure of some prevention programmes. Polgar [20] agrees and asserts that by overlooking the importance of culture, public health planners follow four fallacies. These fallacies are (1) the fallacy of the empty vessels, i.e. assuming that the target population is void of health beliefs and customs; (2) the fallacy of the separate capsule, i.e. that health matters are treated by the target population as separate events, independent of other daily events and activities; (3) the fallacy of the single pyramid, i.e. assuming a simplistic communication system from leaders to grassroots;

TABLE 1   Factors with the Highest Contribution to the Variance of the Five Preventive Health Behaviours (Factor Pattern Matrix Coefficients)*

FACTORS[†]	KEEPING MEDICINES AT HOME	GENERAL PREVENTIVE HEALTH BEHAVIOUR	ABSTENTION FROM SMOKING	REGULAR EXERCISE	ABSTENTION FROM ALCOHOL
Chinese					
Knowledge of disease	0.335 (11.0%)	0.340 (11.6%)	0.044	0.122	0.028
Female PHB	0.126	−0.238 (6.0%)	0.549 (30.1%)	−0.206 (4.2%)	0.446 (19.9%)
Modernization	0.025	0.054	0.188	−0.254 (6.5%)	−0.122
Malay					
Knowledge of disease	0.242 (5.8%)	0.050	0.112	−0.122	0.010
Female vulnerab.	−0.018	0.097	−0.506 (25.6%)	−0.123	−0.123
General vulnerab.	0.033	−0.182	−0.027	0.221 (5.0%)	0.044
Indian					
Female PHB	0.549 (30.1%)	0.059	0.579 (33.5%)	−0.183	0.198
Perception of benefits	−0.128	0.648 (42.0%)	0.015	0.459 (21.0%)	0.015
Perc. Soc. Sanctions	−0.144	−0.156	0.166	0.246 (6.0%)	0.042

*Figures in parentheses are the square values of the factor pattern matrix coefficients. These square values represent the direct contribution of a given factor to the variance of the five PHB variables (cf. Nie *op. cit.*).

[†]Only factors with loadings higher than 0.200 are considered significant enough to be discussed.

and (4) the fallacy of the interchangeable faces which is the assumption of uniformity in people's behaviour and culture.

The wealth of relevant literature is however on responsive or illness behaviour rather than on *preventive* health behaviour [21]. Reviewing the work of Edward Suchman on health-related behaviour and ethnicity, Geertsen *et al.* [22] conclude that there is indeed an association between these two variables. More detailed data on this correlation is provided by Mechanic [23], Robertson and Hea-

garty [24] and Kosa and Zola [25]. In fact Mechanic concludes that "cultures are so recognizably different that variations in illness behaviour in different societies hardly need demonstration" [26]. But the point here is precisely that the focus is on *illness* behaviour. The work of Kleinman [27], for example, deals mostly with *patients* and *healers*. The impact of ethnicity on *preventive* health behaviour requires further analysis. The studies mentioned above give sufficient grounds to assume that ethnic differences also exist with regard to preventive health behaviour. And a few more specific studies reinforce this assumption, i.e. Anderson and Anderson's description of medical and food beliefs among Chinese fisherman [28]; Dunn's brief discussion on personal health behaviour among Malaysian Chinese [29]; references to body management among the Japanese by Caudell [30]; and the three papers on preventive medicine by Paul, Cassel and Khare in Landy's volume [31].

As for the relevance of ethnic differences in sociological studies conducted in Singapore, there is also abundant evidence. One may begin with official population statistics indicating differences among Singaporean Chinese, Singaporean Malays and Singaporean Indians (all of whom shall hereafter be referred to as simply Chinese, Malays, and Indians) along various dimensions such as fertility patterns, age at first marriage, divorce rates, morbidity, income distribution, occupational status and attainment of tertiary education, to mention but a few. Social scientists conducting empirical research in Singapore commonly include ethnicity among their main variables and actually report differences [32] among these three subpopulations in terms of aspects such as political attitudes, religious beliefs and utilization of curative health services. However, this study is the first large scale inquiry into *preventive* health behaviours *in Singapore*. The basic assumption that the three ethnic groups differ in their preventive health behaviour is partially supported by the figures in Table 2. With the exception of smoking, all the other four health behaviours analysed have significant associations with ethnicity. What follows is a discussion of each ethnic group separately, describing the preventive health behaviour patterns presented by the group and its respective deviations from the similarities with the HBM.

The Chinese

Do the Chinese show any tendency towards preventive health behaviour according to the expectations of the HBM? Basically, no. But some

important and interesting qualifications can be made based on the study findings. The average Chinese (just as the average Malay or Indian) does practice some form of preventive health behaviour (cf. Table 2), but his/her actions do not necessarily follow the set of motivational forces outlined by the HBM. This is illustrated by the five selected manifestations of preventive health behaviour, i.e. abstention from smoking, abstention from drinking alcohol, regular exercise, general disease preventing practices (i.e. general preventive health behaviour) and keeping medicines at home.

The factor analysis of all HBM variables and antecedent variables in the Chinese sample revealed eight factors. Six of them represent HBM variables namely, knowledge of disease etiology, perceived disruption of normal activities, perceived social sanctions, perceived personal vulnerability, perceived barriers to preventive action against cancer and heart disease, and perceived barriers to preventive action against tuberculosis. The other two factors represent antecedent variables. They are female preventive behaviour and modernization. Three of the eight factors are found to affect the five preventive behaviours among the Chinese, and only one of these factors is part of the HBM. The HBM factor is knowledge of disease etiology; the other two factors are female preventive behaviour and level of modernization. The respective figures on the highest factor loadings and the corresponding proportion of the dependent variable explained by each factor, are presented in Table 1.

The factor knowledge of disease etiology includes information on the etiology of cancer, heart disease and tuberculosis. This factor provides two interesting findings. It has a stronger effect than all other explanatory factors in the HBM, upon two types of activities, i.e. the practice of general preventive behaviour and keeping medicines at home. But it has practically no impact upon the person's decision to smoke, to drink alcohol or to practice regular exercise. Actually, the second finding is not as surprising as the first one. Other studies have demonstrated that knowledge is not a powerful mo-

TABLE 2 Preventive Health Behavior (PHB) Variables by Ethnic Group (in Percentages)*

PHB VARIABLES	CHINESE	MALAY	INDIAN	TOTAL SAMPLE	p <	GAMMA
Keeps medicines at home regularly						
Yes	50	62	56	52		
No	50	38	44	48		
Total	100	100	100	100	0.01	–0.183
(N)	(963)	(167)	(122)	(1252)		
General PHB: has done something to protect himself from falling ill						
Yes	44	74	45	48		
No	56	26	55	52		
Total	100	100	100	100	0.00001	–0.358
(N)	(975)	(167)	(125)	(1267)		
Smokes						
Yes	27	35	28	28		
No	73	65	72	72		
Total	100	100	100	100	NS	NS
(N)	(972)	(166)	(126)	(1264)		
Exercises regularly						
Yes	34	59	29	37		
No	66	41	71	63		
Total	100	100	100	100	0.00001	–0.268
(N)	(974)	(167)	(126)	(1267)		
Drinks alcoholic beverages						
Yes	35	5	36	31		
No	65	95	64	69		
Total	100	100	100	100	0.00001	–0.426
(N)	(971)	(166)	(124)	(1261)		

*Excluding respondents who did not answer the respective questions

NS—not statistically significant, i.e. $p > 0.05$

tivational trigger of preventive action [34]. Moreover, both activities represent a generalized tendency towards prevention and are not specifically addressed to either cancer, heart disease or tuberculosis.

Thus, although the proportion of variance explained by knowledge of disease etiology is modest, i.e. 11.0% of the variance of the variable "keeping medicines at home," and 11.6% in the variance of the variable "general preventive behaviour" its impact is nevertheless significant and interesting. Compared to those who do not know about disease etiology, Chinese who have correct knowledge on disease etiology show a stronger tendency to follow some daily activities which, in their view, protect them from falling ill. These activities are diversed, for example, taking regular meals, eating the "proper" food, and "getting enough rest after work." Similarly, these "knowledgeable" Chinese are more likely than their less informed counterparts, to keep medicines at home for eventualities; the medicines normally kept are both traditional (i.e. herbs, Chinese remedies) as well as non-traditional (i.e. "Western" over-the-counter drugs).

The factor "female preventive behaviour" represents only one antecedent variable, gender, which is not included in the classical HBM [35]. This factor is labelled "female" preventive behaviour because it is females who manifest a stronger inclination to practise the preventive behaviour under analysis. Compared to all the HBM factors, this one is a more powerful motivational factor for two of the specific preventive activities studied, that is, abstention from smoking and alcohol drinking. Female preventive behaviour explains 30.1% of the variance in smoking and 19.9% of the variance in alcohol drinking among the Chinese. In contrast, none of the HBM factors can explain individually more than 1% of the variance in either one of these two preventive behaviours. Hence their exclusion from Table 1.

This finding indicates that among the Chinese, females are clearly more inclined to abstain from smoking and drinking. Although previous observation of female behaviour in Singapore hinted to this tendency, the strength of this factor in motivating abstention from cigarettes and alcohol was unexpected. Both activities, but particularly abstaining from smoking, are very important preventive measures against all three diseases included in the analysis, i.e. cancer, heart disease and tuberculosis. Unfortunately, it is rather difficult to unravel the components of female preventive behaviour. Traditional sex-role stereotypes might provide some answers.

Sex-role stereotypes are culture-derived definitions of approved and appropriate behaviour for males as opposed to females [36]. Sex-role stereotypes are common features in every community and generally internalized by both males and females. In Singapore, sex-role stereotypes are reflected in the reasons given by female respondents for not smoking. Some responses were "it is not nice for a girl to smoke"; "not good for a girl's reputation"; or that they "never learnt how to smoke." These responses suggest that the perception of smoking as a "masculine" trait can still be found in Singapore despite the numerous economic and social signs of modernization.

Yet, sex-role stereotyping is not the only or even perhaps the most important explanation. The factor female preventive behaviour suggests the influence of other elements in addition to sex-role stereotypes. Indeed, data on the motivation for not smoking reveal a definitive tendency for females to avoid cigarettes in order to protect their health. The majority (66.1%) of respondents in the total sample of citizens who say that they do not smoke to prevent illness, are females. The same female majority appears given the same reason among the Chinese. Therefore, the avoidance of smoking among females cannot be interpreted solely as a traditional cultural value of appropriate female behaviour. It is clear that females tend to be more aware than males of the harmful effects of cigarette smoking and act accordingly. The sex-role values attached to abstention from smoking reinforce this preventive behaviour. The same combination of cultural values and actual awareness of ill effects apply to the female inclination to abstain from alcohol drinking.

The third main motivational factor found related to preventive health behaviour among the Chinese may be called modernization. This factor represents the combined effects of high level of education, young age, high exposure to mass media and awareness of public health campaigns. Modernization contributes to 6.5% of the variance in the practice of regular exercise among the Chinese. In other words, young, educated and well-informed Chinese are more likely to exercise regularly than their older, less educated and less informed counterparts. While the proportion of variance in exercise explained by modernization is rather small, none of the HBM variables contributes more than one per cent to the understanding of this preventive behaviour. The second important factor in this connection is female preventive behaviour. It explains 4.2% of the variance in exercise. Chinese females are less inclined to do regular exercise than Chinese males; but this difference in inclination between the sexes is minimized among educated, young, and well-read Chinese adults.

The overall picture of preventive health behaviour emerging from the Chinese data indicates that only one of the HBM variables namely, disease knowledge, has some impact upon one of the dimensions of preventive health behaviour. The two other factors related to smoking and alcohol drinking are "new." They have been labeled tentatively, female preventive behaviour and modernization, based on the nature of the variables that clustered in each of them.

The Malays

The main feature of the Malay pattern of preventive behaviour is that it differs significantly from the pattern found among the Chinese sample. Eleven factors were identified by the factor analysis of the Malay sample, eight of them representing HBM variables; two others representing new aspects of attitudes; and one representing an antecedent variable. The eight HBM factors are: knowledge of disease etiology, perceived social sanctions, perceived disruption of normal activities, general vulnerability, female vulnerability, and three factors on barriers to preventive action. Of the eleven factors, only three were outlined by the data as the main explanatory factors in preventive health behaviour among the Malays (see Table 1).

One of these three is the HBM factor knowledge of disease etiology. Malays who are more informed on the etiology of cancer, tuberculosis and heart disease, are more likely than other Malays to keep medicines at home for eventualities. However, disease knowledge is not a strong motivational factor as it only explains 5.8% of the variance in this practice of keeping medicines at home.

A rather interesting combination of perception of personal vulnerability and female inclination towards disease prevention, emerged from the Malay data as the main factor contributing to the variance in abstention from smoking. Indeed, 25.6% of the variance in abstention from smoking is explained by this combined factor which may be labelled "female perceived vulnerability to disease." No other factor contributes more than 3% of the variance in abstention from smoking, thus making female per-

ceived vulnerability the most important explanatory factor.

Comparing this finding with the Chinese data an important difference can be appreciated. Chinese females are more inclined than Chinese males to avoid smoking; they do so moved by their perception of what is proper feminine behaviour as well as by their general desire to protect their health. In contrast, the belief among Malay females is not only that it is improper for girls to smoke, but that there is a link between smoking and cancer and tuberculosis. More specifically, Malay females are less likely than Malay males to see themselves vulnerable to cancer and tuberculosis precisely because they avoid smoking. Smoking is more predominant among Malay males, who, in turn, manifest a higher perception of perceived vulnerability to these diseases.

The third significant HBM factor is perceived general vulnerability which represents the Malays' feelings of susceptibility to illness in general. This factor explains 5.0% of the variance in the practice of regular exercise. This proportion of explained variance is low but no other factor has a higher contribution. However, religion, a non-HBM variable which was not included in the factor analysis, plays an important part as will be seen later.

None of the HBM factors is significantly related to abstention from alcoholic drinks among the Malays. This is another unique feature of the Malay pattern of preventive health behaviour. The drinking of alcoholic beverages is prohibited among orthodox Muslims. The overwhelming majority of Malays in Singapore are Muslims[37] and religious and health beliefs are closely related among the Malays. This can also be seen in their general preventive behaviour which again is not explained by any of the HBM factors. When religion was introduced into the analysis [38], a significant association was found. A higher proportion of Muslims compared to people of other religions or agnostics, report following general preventive practices regularly to avoid falling sick. Similarly, the Muslims, more than others, are inclined to do regular physical exercise.

Further findings support the assertion that religion is an important influence in the Malay pattern of preventive health behaviour. Muslims are more inclined than Buddhists, Hindus, Christians or agnostics, to perceive social sanctions for cancer. Muslims also, together with Hindus, are more likely than believers or agnostics to perceive social sanctions for heart disease and tuberculosis. Similarly, Muslims have a higher tendency to see themselves personally vulnerable to disease in general than other believers and agnostics. In other words, religious beliefs may well constitute a distinguishing feature between Malays and other ethnic groups concerning preventive health behaviour. Among Malays, religion and cultural and social values are closely intertwined so that Islam becomes a way of life [39].

The Indians

The comparison between Malays and Chinese illustrates the main argument of this paper: preventive health behaviour patterns vary clearly in terms of ethnicity which involves both cultural as well as religious values. The data from the Indian population reinforce that argument. The factor analysis of the Indian sample revealed eleven factors, eight of which represent HBM variables. The HBM factors are knowledge of disease etiology (general), knowledge of cancer, perceived social sanctions, perceived disruption of normal role activities, perceived benefits of preventive action, perceived barriers to prevention of heart disease, perceived barriers to prevention of cancer and perceived barriers to prevention of tuberculosis. The other three factors are female preventive behaviour, level of information, and age. Only three of the eleven factors are significant. The pattern of preventive behaviour among the Indians is characterized by the influence of two HBM factors not active among Chinese or Malays, i.e. the perception of benefits of preventive action and perceived social sanctions, and a "new" (non-HBM) factor, female preventive behaviour, which was also found among the Chinese.

Three of the five preventive behaviours analysed are influenced by the factor female preventive behaviour, although not with the same intensity. These behaviours are keeping medicines at home, abstention from smoking and abstention from alcoholic drinks. Female preventive behaviour contributes to 33.5% of the variance in abstention from smoking, and 30.1% of the variance in keeping medicines at home. The influence of this factor upon abstention from alcohol is however, rather modest; it only contributes 3.9% of the variance in the latter. Basically, Indian females show a much higher tendency than Indian males to keep medicines at home for eventualities, to abstain from smoking and to avoid alcoholic drinks. Just as in the case of Chinese and Malay females, the evidence indicates that Indian females regard smoking as a "masculine" activity, traditionally disapproved for females. The same belief applies to alcohol consumption.

The factor perceived benefits is the most important in understanding general preventive health behaviour and exercise among Indians. The perception of benefits accounts for 42.0% of the variance in their general preventive practices and 21.0% of the variance in their practice of regular exercise. Perceiving the benefits of preventive action against cancer, heart disease and tuberculosis on the one hand, and being aware of personal vulnerability to tuberculosis on the other hand, are states that stimulate both general preventive practices and regular exercise among Indians. This motivation occurs equally for both males and females. Malays and Chinese on the contrary, show some male predominance on these two preventive activities. Finally, the practice of regular exercise is also stimulated, although to a lesser extent, by the perception of social sanctions, i.e. the feeling that an individual is personally responsible for the state of his/her health.

CONCLUSION

The preceding discussion has been aimed at supporting with empirical evidence the assumption that the explanatory power of the HBM weakens considerably when it is tested in different cultures and among different ethnic groups. The data presented highlight the core of the findings and corroborate this assumption. Further details on factor analysis matrices, correlation and regression coefficients are reported in the larger study [40]. While only the most relevant aspects of the ethnicity dimension in the larger study have been presented here, it is hoped that this summary has conveyed the two key findings.

These two findings are: (a) There is a common denominator in all three ethnic groups that distinguishes them as a whole from the North American populations used in previous tests of the HBM; as Southeast Asian groups, they all share similar sex-role values regarding what is appropriate behaviour for women as opposed to men. And, it happens that smoking and drinking alcohol fall into the category of social behaviour not acceptable for women. These sex-role values are the outcome of cultural and/or religious beliefs on the role of women in society. (b) At the same time, there are differences in preventive behaviour within these three ethnic groups despite the fact that they are citizens of the same nation and thus share a basic social, economic and political environment. Their respective cultural and religious beliefs and practices represent a significant determinant of the pattern of preventive health behaviour followed by each group. Their differences in this respect, help to substantiate the assumption that, while as ethnic groups, "they coexist peacefully within the same political unit,...they remain largely separate culturally" [41]. Correspondingly, the data do not back up the premise that the labels "Chinese," "Malay" and "Indian" are an artifice of politics and do not represent actual ethnic differences [42].

While the overall conclusion is that the HBM does not contribute significantly to the explanation of preventive health behaviour in Singapore, some qualifications must be made regarding the limitations of the study. Firstly, the present analysis deals with five specific preventive behaviours and three

diseases; thus the findings should be regarded as applicable only to those five behaviours and the three diseases. Secondly, there is the question of measurement. Rosenstock rightly points to the problem of comparability of findings indicating that "no two studies of the model's variables have used identical questions for determining the presence or absence of each belief" [43]. In this respect, the measurement of the HBM variables in this study is comparable, although not identical, to the questions used in the first five studies applying the HBM model as described by Rosenstock [44].

Thirdly, the type of research design used in any study tends to influence the nature of its findings. This study is based on a survey design. Rosenstock suggests the use of an experimental design, but very frequently unavoidable constraints impede the use of experimental or time series designs and make survey design a more feasible choice. Schelzel [45] for example, used a survey design in his test of the HBM among heart disease screening programme participants in Pennsylvania; his general finding coincides with that of this study namely, his data do not support the HBM. The limitations of the survey design in analysing attitude formation or the "genesis of beliefs" as Rosenstock puts it [46], must be acknowledged. Yet, Rosenstock [47] has pointed to a solution: introducing test variables such as intervening, extraneous, and antecedent variables into the survey design "enables one to exploit some of the virtues of the experimental design while avoiding the inappropriateness of experimentation for many sociological problems." The factor analysis technique applied in this study includes all these types of variables but, of course, it does not correspond entirely to an experimental design.

All things considered, the application of the HBM to the Singapore population has been theoretically useful. In all three samples, some of the basic HBM variables clustered in the expected fashion; the variables on knowledge of disease formed one factor among Chinese and Malays; the variables on perceived social sanctions for the three diseases also clustered in one factor in the three samples; and the same occurred with the variables on perception of disruption of normal activities caused by each disease. On the other hand, perceived personal vulnerability and the perception of both barriers to action and benefits of preventive action did not follow their assumed unidimensionality. Their splitting into various factors indicates the relevance of testing the HBM in the context of specific diseases and different ethnic groups. This problem is further discussed elsewhere [48]. In general, by analysing preventive health behaviour through the HBM "lens," it has been possible to detect behavioural patterns that could have remained hidden, for example, the ethnic differences in the salience of the various HBM factors. Their very deviation from the HBM has made these patterns more "visible." Using the HBM as an ideal type—in the Weberian sense—has helped to delineate differences and similarities between the Singapore sample and samples from other studies, as well as among the three ethnic groups in Singapore. Finally, the findings reported here lead me to recommend the inclusion of three variables in future applications of the HBM: these variables are ethnicity, gender and religious affiliation.

REFERENCES

1. Lewin K. *A Dynamic Theory of Personality,* McGraw-Hill, New York. 1935.
2. Lewin K. *Principles of Topological Psychology,* McGraw-Hill, New York. 1936.
3. Rosenstock, I. M. Why people use health services. *Milbank Meml. Fund Q.* **44,** 94–124, 1966. Rosenstock I. M. Prevention of illness and maintenance of health. In *Poverty and health. A Sociological Analysis* (edited by Kosa J., Antonovsky A., and Zola I. K.), pp. 168–170. Harvard University Press, Cambridge, MA, 1969.
4. Rosenstock I. M. The health belief model and preventive health behavior. In *The Health Belief Model and Personal Health Behavior* (Edited by Becker M. H.), pp. 42–50. Slack, Thorofare, NJ, 1974.
5. To illustrate with some of the most recent studies, one may refer to the following: Leavitt F. The health belief model and utilization of ambulatory care services. *Soc. Sci. Med.* **13A,** 105–112, 1979; Bloom Cerkoney K. A. and Hart L. K. The relationship between the health belief model and compliance of persons with diabetes mellitus. *Diabetes Care* **3,** 594–598, 1980; Stunkard A. J. Adherence to medical treatment: overview and lessons from behavioural weight control. *J. Psychosomatic. Res.* **25,** 187–197, 1981; King J. B. The impact of patients' perception of high blood pressure on attendance at screening. *Soc. Sci. Med.* **16,** 1079–1091, 1982; Ross D. J. and Guggenheim F. G. Compliance and the health belief model: a challenge for the liaison psychiatrist, *Gen. Hosp. Psychiat.* **5,** 31–35, 1983.
6. Kasl S. V. and Cobb S. Health behavior, illness behavior and sick-role behavior. *Archs Envir. Hlth* **12,** 246–266; 531–541, 1966. The quotation is from p. 248.
7. See for example, Green L. *Status Identity and Preventive Health Behavior.* Pacific Health Education Reports, 1, 130, 1970; Williams A. F. and Wechster H. Dimensions of preventive health behavior. *J. Consult. Clin. Psychol.* **40,** Suppl., 420, 1973; Coburn D. and Pope C. R. Socioeconomic status and preventive health behavior. *J. Hlth Soc. Behav.* **15,** 67–77, 1974. The two review studies by Marshall Becker i.e. Becker M. H. (Ed.) *The Health Belief Model and Personal Health Behavior.* Slack, Thorofare, NJ, 1974; and Becker M. H. Psychosocial aspects of health-related behavior. In *Handbook of Medical Sociology* (Edited by Freeman H. E., Levine S. and Reeder L. G.), 3rd edition, pp. 253–274. Prentice-Hall, Englewood Cliffs, NJ, 1979. And more recent studies such as Michielutte R. and Diseker R. A. Children's perception of cancer in comparison to other chronic illnesses. *J. Chron. Dis.* **35,** 843–852, 1982; Schlueter L. A. Knowledge and beliefs about breast cancer and breast self-examination among athletic and non-athletic women. *Nurs. Res.* **31,** 348–353, 1982; Roskies E. *et al.* Changing the coronary prone (Type A) behavior pattern in a nonclinical population. *J. Behav. Med.* **1,** 201–216, 1978; Stewart P. J. and Rosser W. W. The impact of routine advice on smoking cessation from family physicians. *CMA JL* **126,** 1051–1054, 1982; and King J. B. *op. cit.*
8. Only one of the studies cited by Becker M. H. *op. cit.,* 1979 was conducted outside continental United States, i.e. Suchman E. A. Preventive health behavior: a model for research on community health campaigns. *J. Hlth Soc. Behav.* **8,** 197–209, 1967.
9. The importance of culture in the study of health and disease is a universal premise. Among the most well-known and relevant studies are: Zborowski M. Cultural components in response to pain. *J. Soc. Issues* **8,** 16–30, 1952; Saunders L. *Cultural Differences in Medical Care.* Russell Sage, New York, 1954; Paul B. D. (Ed.) *Health Culture and Commu-*

nity. Russell Sage, New York, 1955; King S. H. *Perception of Illness and Medical Practice.* Russell Sage, New York, 1962; Polgar S. Health action in cross-cultural perspective. In *Handbook of Medical Sociology* (Edited by Freeman H. E., Levine S. and Reeder L. G.), 1st edition. Prentice-Hall, Englewood Cliffs, NJ, 1963; Leslie C. (Ed.) *Asian Medical Systems: A Comparative Study.* University of California Press, Berkeley, 1976; Sanborn K. O. and Katz M. M. Perception of symptom behavior across ethnic groups. In *Basic Problems in Cross-Cultural Psychology* (Edited by Poortinga Y. H.), pp. 236–240. IACCP, Amsterdam, 1977; Landy D. (Ed.) *Culture, Disease and Healing.* Macmillan, New York, 1977; Kleinman A., Kunstadter P., Alexander E. R. and Gale J. L. (Eds.) *Culture and Healing in Asian Societies.* Schenkman, Cambridge, MA, 1978; and Kleinman A. *Patients and Healers in the Context of Culture.* University of California Press, Berkeley, 1980.

10. Mechanic D. *The Growth of Bureaucratic Medicine. An Inquiry Into the Dynamics of Patient Behavior and the Organization of Medical Care.* Wiley, New York, 1976.

11. Coburn D. and Pope C. R. *op. cit.,* p. 76.

12. Haefner D. P. and Kirscht J. Motivational and behavioral effects of modifying health beliefs. *Publ. Hlth Rep.* **85,** 478–484, 1970; and Becker M. H. *op. cit.,* 1979.

13. Medical criteria was deemed the most objective point of reference to classify answers into correct and incorrect. This dichotomous classification of answers also facilitated the application of factor analysis.

14. Rotter J. B. Generalized expectancies for internal versus external control of reinforcement. *Psychol. Monogr.* **80,** 609, 1966.

15. Nie N. H. *SPSS,* 2nd edition. McGraw-Hill, New York, 1975.

16. See King S. H. *op. cit.,* p. 79.

17. See Paul B. D. *op. cit.;* Paul B. D. Anthropological perspectives on medicine and public health. *Annls Am. Acad. Polit. Soc. Sci.* **346,** 34–43, 1980; and Mead M. Understanding cultural patterns. *Nurs. Outlook* **4,** 260–262, 1956.

18. Saunders L. *op. cit.*

19. Zborowski M. *op. cit.*

20. Polgar S. *op. cit.*

21. See for example, Saunders L. *op. cit.;* Zborowski M. *op. cit.;* and Sanborn K. O. and Katz M. M. *op. cit.*

22. Geertsen R. *et al.* A reexamination of Suchman's views on social factors in health care utilization. *J. Hlth Soc. Behav.* **16,** 226–237, 1975.

23. Mechanic D. *Medical Sociology,* 2nd edition. Free Press, New York, 1978.

24. Robertson L. and Heagarty M. *Medical Sociology: A General Systems Approach,* Nelson Hall, New York, 1975.

25. Kosa J. and Zola I. K. *op. cit.*

26. Mechanic D. *op. cit.* p. 261, 1978.

27. Kleinman A. *op. cit.* 1980.

28. See Anderson E. N. and Anderson M. L. Folk dietetics in two Chinese communities and its implications for the study of Chinese medicine. In *Patients and Healers in the Context of Culture* (Edited by Kleinman A.), pp. 69–100. University of California Press, Berkeley, 1980.

29. Dunn F. (1978) Medical care in the Chinese communities of peninsular Malaysia. In *Patients and Healers in the Context of Culture* (Edited by Kleinman A.), pp. 143–172. University of California Press, Berkeley, 1980.

30. Caudell W. The cultural and interpersonal context of everyday health and illness in Japan and America. In *Asian Medical Systems: A Comparative Study* (Edited by Leslie C.), pp. 159–177. University of California Press, Berkeley, 1976.

31. Landy D. *op. cit.,* pp. 231–250.

32. See for example, Chen P. S. J. and Evers H. D. (Eds.) *Studies in ASEAN Sociology: Urban Society and Social Change.* Chopman Enterprises, Singapore, 1978; Bellington S. S. *Malaysia and Singapore. The Building of New States.* Cornell University Press, Ithaca, 1978; Ooi J. B. and Chiang H. D. (Eds.) *Modern Singapore.* Singapore University Press, Singapore 1969; Hassan R. *Families in Flats.* Singapore University Press, Singapore, 1977; Hassan R. *Singapore: Society in Transition.* Oxford University Press, Singapore, 1976; Clammer J. The institutionalization of ethnicity: the culture of ethnicity in Singapore. *Ethnic Racial Stud.* **5,** 127–139, 1982; Gwee A. L., Lee Y. K. and Tham N. B. A study of Chinese medical practice in Singapore. *Singapore Med. J.* **10,** 2–7, 1969.

33. Nie N. N. et al., *op. cit.*

34. See for example, Becker M. H. *op. cit.,* 1979; Kasl S. V. and Cobb S. *op. cit.;* Haefner D. P. *et al., op. cit.;* Graham S. Studies of behavioral change to enhance public health. *Am. J. Publ. Hlth* **63,** 327–334, 1973; Coburn D. and Pope C. R. *op. cit.*

35. See Refs [3–7].

36. See Guttentag M. and Bray H. *Undoing Sex-Role Stereotypes: Research and Resources for Educators.* McGraw-Hill, New York, 1976.

37. Ministry of Culture. *Singapore Facts and Pictures 1977,* p. 176. Publications Division, Ministry of Culture, 1977.

38. As a nominal variable, religion was not included in the factor analysis but was introduced at other stages of the data analysis.

39. See Colson A. C. The prevention of illness in a Malay village: An analysis of concept and behavior. Ph.D. dissertation, Stanford University, 1970; Tham S. C. *Malays and Modernization.* Singapore University Press, Singapore,

1977; Husin Ali S. *The Malays: Their Problems and Future.* Heinemann Asia, Singapore, 1981.
40. See Quah S. R. Preventive health behaviour in Singapore. Unpublished Ph.D. dissertation, University of Singapore, Singapore, 1980.
41. Clammer J. *op. cit.* 128.
42. Benjamin G. (1976) The cultural logic of Singapore's multiracialism. In *Families in Flats* (Edited by Hassan R.), pp. 115–133. Singapore University Press, Singapore, 1976.
43. Rosenstock I. M. *op. cit.* p. 45, 1969.

44. *Ibid.*, pp. 45–48.
45. Schelzel G. W. An application of the health belief model to a preventive health behavior among high risk heart disease screening program participants. Ph.D. dissertation, Pennsylvania State University, 1977.
46. Rosenstock I. M. *op. cit.* p. 45, 1969.
47. Rosenberg M. *The Logic of Survey Analysis,* p. 82. Basic Books, New York, 1968.
48. Quah S. R. *op. cit.*

APPENDIX A: FACTOR ANALYSIS MATRICES

TABLE A1 Factor Pattern Matrix of 32 Variables on Eight Factors for the Chinese Sample

	CHINESE FACTORS							
VARIABLES	1 Disease Knowledge	2 Female PHB	3 PDR	4 PSS	5 HD/CA Access	6 Modernization	7 TB Access	8 PPV
1. KEEPMED	0.335	0.126	−0.024	0.007	0.104	0.025	−0.100	0.047
2. GNALPHB	0.340	−0.238	−0.029	0.051	−0.156	0.054	0.025	−0.032
3. SMOKE	0.044	0.549	−0.004	−0.071	−0.074	0.188	0.072	−0.018
4. EXERCISE	0.122	−0.206	0.010	0.033	−0.134	−0.254	0.084	−0.002
5. DRINK	0.028	0.446	−0.023	−0.018	0.022	−0.122	0.025	−0.021
6. KOMS	0.720	0.133	−0.102	−0.043	−0.512	0.054	−0.067	0.058
7. CORHDETI	0.588	0.051	−0.016	−0.019	−0.171	−0.029	−0.057	0.050
8. CORCAETI	0.472	−0.011	−0.027	−0.087	−0.031	−0.062	0.040	0.045
9. CORTBETI	0.487	0.022	0.000	0.005	−0.088	−0.160	−0.080	0.056
24. BENSCORE	0.396	−0.018	−0.008	−0.067	−0.182	−0.162	−0.023	0.122
20. ALLSCORE	0.248	−0.001	−0.087	−0.115	0.047	−0.178	−0.119	0.058
32. SEX	0.046	0.804	0.012	−0.001	0.013	0.149	−0.035	0.056
13. TOTPDRHD	0.032	0.042	−0.826	0.018	0.052	0.010	−0.011	0.009
15. TOTPDRTB	−0.171	−0.108	−0.771	0.024	−0.047	0.021	0.072	−0.031
14. TOTPDRCA	0.085	0.101	−0.731	0.040	−0.004	0.050	−0.047	0.022
10. HDBLAME	0.120	0.041	0.027	0.778	−0.013	−0.049	0.002	−0.009
11. CANBLAME	−0.146	−0.132	−0.009	0.681	0.003	−0.019	0.037	−0.041
12. TBBLAME	0.057	0.072	0.000	0.670	−0.016	−0.028	−0.012	0.037
25. HDCOST	0.051	−0.029	−0.001	0.000	0.763	−0.023	0.177	0.078
28. HDTEST	−0.135	0.075	0.018	−0.010	0.724	0.041	−0.025	0.024
26. CANCOST	0.117	−0.163	0.024	−0.068	0.673	0.038	0.149	−0.091
29. CANTEST	−0.095	0.012	0.054	0.017	0.631	−0.027	−0.032	−0.022
21. EDULEVEL	0.091	0.044	−0.031	0.038	0.019	0.748	0.022	0.106
31. AGE	−0.048	−0.056	−0.014	0.008	−0.053	−0.671	0.025	0.015
23. MASSMEDIA	0.000	−0.141	−0.043	0.046	−0.076	0.540	0.032	0.132
22. CAMPAIGN	0.270	0.049	−0.029	0.104	−0.153	0.346	0.047	0.091
16. PPVGENERAL	−0.025	−0.029	0.017	0.030	0.007	0.176	0.102	0.013
27. TBCOST	0.058	0.056	−0.007	0.003	0.128	−0.127	0.818	−0.023
30. TRTEST	−0.128	0.179	0.077	−0.034	0.135	0.074	0.478	−0.034
17. PPVCANCER	0.084	−0.028	−0.010	0.111	0.025	0.017	−0.068	0.653
18. PPVHD	0.130	−0.063	−0.025	−0.123	0.002	0.029	0.003	0.441
19. PPVTB	−0.257	0.026	0.036	−0.019	−0.047	0.002	0.041	0.298

TABLE A2   Factor Pattern Matrix of 32 Variables on Eleven Factors for the Malay Sample

VARIABLES	1 Disease Knowledge	2 Drinking	3 PSS	4 Place Access	5 PDR	6 Female PPV	7 Modernization
1. KEEPMED	0.242	−0.115	−0.031	0.048	−0.003	−0.018	0.039
5. DRINK	0.010	0.540	0.085	0.049	−0.082	−0.123	−0.002
4. SMOKE	0.112	0.181	−0.093	−0.060	0.083	−0.506	0.032
2. GNALPHB	0.050	0.078	0.007	0.073	−0.015	0.097	0.117
3. EXERCISE	−0.122	−0.042	−0.070	−0.098	−0.017	−0.123	−0.182
6. KOMS	0.759	0.025	0.075	0.118	0.026	−0.099	−0.018
9. CORTBETI	0.593	0.162	−0.009	−0.026	0.112	0.059	−0.047
7. CORHDETI	0.489	−0.178	−0.053	−0.044	0.069	−0.085	−0.023
8. CORCAETI	0.423	−0.052	−0.141	−0.057	−0.057	−0.038	−0.084
24. BENSCORE	0.469	0.145	−0.039	−0.168	−0.040	−0.091	0.009
12. TBBLAME	−0.053	−0.006	0.858	0.067	0.013	−0.041	−0.042
11. CANBLAME	0.046	0.111	0.755	−0.083	0.113	−0.021	0.121
10. HDBLAME	0.120	0.007	0.741	0.018	−0.043	−0.107	−0.102
29. CANTEST	0.003	−0.041	0.057	0.771	−0.117	−0.104	−0.098
28. HDTEST	−0.003	0.048	0.068	0.631	−0.063	0.108	−0.121
30. TBTEST	−0.148	0.122	0.009	0.356	0.012	0.040	0.097
20. ALLSCORE	−0.040	−0.050	0.052	−0.308	−0.053	0.067	−0.274
13. TOTPDRHD	−0.111	−0.023	−0.030	0.039	1.021	−0.030	0.054
14. TOTPDRCA	−0.109	0.088	0.005	−0.178	0.608	−0.059	−0.115
15. TOTPDRTB	0.168	−0.176	0.119	0.041	0.529	0.051	0.025
32. SEX	0.190	−0.088	0.132	0.122	−0.130	0.668	0.187
19. PPVTB	−0.134	−0.101	−0.039	0.027	0.019	−0.503	0.131
17. PPVCANCER	0.114	0.029	−0.131	−0.219	0.066	−0.326	0.117
21. EDULEVEL	0.066	0.031	−0.028	0.061	0.088	−0.131	−0.803
31. AGE	0.056	0.198	−0.114	−0.032	0.036	0.413	−0.703
23. MASSMEDIA	0.115	0.111	0.030	−0.034	0.034	0.274	−0.566
22. CAMPAIGN	0.288	0.134	0.083	0.009	0.114	0.038	−0.350
27. TBCOST	−0.061	0.028	−0.059	−0.077	−0.043	−0.159	−0.116
18. PPVHD	0.058	−0.039	−0.093	−0.002	0.062	−0.071	−0.115
16. PPVGENERAL	−0.066	0.058	−0.009	−0.025	0.000	0.065	0.036
25. HDCOST	0.081	−0.065	−0.018	0.083	0.001	0.045	0.081
26. CANCOST	−0.012	−0.038	−0.064	0.118	0.018	0.030	0.009

TABLE A2 Continued

	MALAY FACTORS			
	8	9	10	11
VARIABLES	TBCOST Access	PHB General	PPV General	HD/CA Cost Access
1. KEEPMED	−0.112	0.055	0.033	0.121
5. DRINK	0.033	0.052	0.044	0.011
4. SMOKE	−0.094	0.000	−0.027	0.031
2. GNALPHB	0.003	−0.500	−0.182	0.076
3. EXERCISE	−0.044	0.081	0.221	−0.114
6. KOMS	0.010	0.008	−0.175	0.096
9. CORTBETI	−0.122	−0.050	−0.127	−0.217
7. CORHDETI	−0.021	−0.081	−0.124	0.097
8. CORCAETI	0.044	−0.020	0.073	−0.041
24. BENSCORE	−0.009	0.007	−0.017	0.097
12. TBBLAME	−0.103	−0.009	−0.027	0.020
11. CANBLAME	−0.055	0.058	−0.064	−0.080
10. HDBLAME	0.149	0.001	0.086	0.155
29. CANTEST	0.039	0.008	−0.072	−0.085
28. HDTEST	0.050	−0.028	−0.019	−0.254
30. TBTEST	0.247	−0.050	−0.013	0.127
20. ALLSCORE	0.120	0.088	−0.228	0.031
13. TOTPDRHD	0.037	0.102	−0.068	−0.074
14. TOTPDRCA	−0.067	−0.057	0.015	0.049
15. TOTPDRTB	0.090	−0.060	0.067	0.042
32. SEX	0.006	−0.116	0.022	0.168
19. PPVTB	0.088	0.031	0.198	−0.132
17. PPVCANCER	0.018	0.155	0.067	−0.023
21. EDULEVEL	−0.100	0.057	−0.101	0.043
31. AGE	0.164	−0.033	0.073	0.092
23. MASSMEDIA	0.042	0.197	0.069	0.033
22. CAMPAIGN	−0.178	0.032	0.074	0.066
27. TBCOST	0.827	−0.028	0.060	−0.293
18. PPVHD	0.114	0.043	−0.005	0.007
16. PPVGENERAL	0.052	−0.008	0.732	0.002
25. HDCOST	0.101	−0.029	0.062	−0.920
26. CANCOST	−0.126	0.026	−0.025	−0.729

TABLE A3   Factor Pattern Matrix of 32 Variables on Eleven Factors for the Indian Sample

VARIABLES	INDIAN FACTORS						
	1 Disease Knowledge	2 Female PHB	3 PSS	4 HD Access	5 PDR	6 Cancer Knowledge	7 Information
1. KEEPMED	0.019	0.549	−0.144	0.027	−0.000	−0.062	−0.033
4. SMOKE	−0.035	0.579	0.166	−0.001	−0.112	0.112	0.045
5. DRINK	−0.176	0.198	0.042	0.067	0.024	0.152	−0.031
2. GNALPHB	0.017	0.059	−0.156	0.000	−0.057	−0.074	−0.072
3. EXERCISE	−0.027	−0.183	0.246	−0.054	−0.059	−0.179	0.129
6. KOMS	0.627	0.116	0.008	0.133	−0.086	−0.310	0.118
9. CORTBETI	0.589	−0.091	−0.059	0.095	−0.094	0.112	0.055
17. PPVCANCER	0.358	0.087	0.261	0.036	−0.027	−0.089	0.062
22. CAMPAIGN	0.294	0.107	0.021	0.033	0.075	0.206	0.263
32. SEX	0.022	−0.803	0.047	0.047	0.042	0.072	−0.169
10. HDBLAME	−0.016	0.119	−0.767	−0.063	−0.096	0.031	0.164
12. TBBLAME	0.095	−0.042	−0.713	0.106	0.107	−0.035	−0.016
11. CANBLAME	−0.152	−0.152	−0.667	−0.030	−0.088	0.198	−0.161
28. HDTEST	0.130	0.059	0.057	0.987	−0.034	0.014	−0.020
25. HDCOST	−0.319	0.147	0.019	0.408	−0.013	0.296	0.237
13. TOTPDRTB	−0.132	0.004	−0.156	−0.072	−0.676	0.080	0.069
15. TOTPDRHD	0.051	0.076	0.097	0.055	−0.649	−0.070	0.011
14. TOTPDRCA	0.052	0.054	0.068	0.069	−0.601	−0.032	0.144
8. CORCAETI	−0.017	−0.079	−0.080	0.058	−0.021	0.666	−0.188
20. ALLSCORE	0.110	−0.038	0.098	0.041	0.092	−0.307	0.219
23. MASSMEDIA	−0.016	0.000	−0.131	0.005	−0.077	0.128	0.783
21: EDULEVEL	0.330	−0.004	0.104	−0.041	0.100	0.060	0.416
16. PPVGENERAL	−0.013	0.089	−0.019	0.004	−0.004	0.015	−0.291
27. TBCOST	0.040	0.040	0.093	0.005	0.146	−0.172	0.155
30. TBTEST	−0.002	−0.061	0.017	0.095	−0.011	−0.054	−0.274
24. BENSCORE	0.075	−0.003	0.129	0.016	0.055	−0.040	0.130
19. PPVTB	0.033	−0.204	0.042	0.130	−0.026	−0.034	0.031
26. CANCOST	0.053	−0.030	−0.091	0.035	0.090	0.046	0.071
29. CANTEST	0.135	−0.111	0.025	0.185	0.041	−0.104	−0.192
31. AGE	−0.146	−0.285	−0.015	−0.091	−0.036	−0.127	−0.130
7. CORHDETI	0.268	0.187	0.042	−0.084	−0.019	−0.269	0.097
18. PPVHD	0.236	0.089	−0.071	−0.012	0.054	−0.001	0.029

TABLE A3   Continued

	INDIAN FACTORS			
	8	*9*	*10*	*11*
VARIABLES	*TB Access*	*Benefits*	*Cancer Access*	*Age–Heart*
1. KEEPMED	−0.091	−0.028	−0.083	0.081
4. SMOKE	0.088	0.015	0.048	−0.120
5. DRINK	−0.013	0.015	0.186	−0.083
2. GNALPHB	0.063	0.648	−0.076	−0.018
3. EXERCISE	0.042	0.459	−0.080	−0.133
6. KOMS	0.000	0.028	0.110	0.029
9. CORTBETI	−0.036	−0.018	0.055	−0.069
17 PPVCANCER	−0.092	0.014	−0.100	0.068
22. CAMPAIGN	−0.049	0.199	−0.080	−0.081
32. SEX	0.016	0.185	−0.085	−0.036
10. HDBLAME	−0.008	−0.031	−0.027	0.105
12. TBBLAME	−0.072	0.119	−0.024	−0.008
13. CANBLAME	−0.100	0.040	0.198	−0.293
28. HDTEST	0.071	−0.054	0.029	0.039
25. HDCOST	0.114	−0.171	0.308	−0.001
13. TOTPDRTB	0.049	−0.127	0.047	−0.015
15. TOTPDRHD	0.080	−0.081	−0.013	−0.072
14. TOTPDRCA	−0.072	0.091	0.169	0.163
8. CORCAETI	0.083	0.088	−0.041	−0.005
20. ALLSCORE	0.273	0.119	0.130	−0.199
23. MASSMEDIA	−0.014	0.091	−0.089	−0.110
21. EDULEVEL	−0.072	−0.003	−0.089	−0.145
16. PPVGENERAL	0.045	0.027	−0.168	−0.077
27. TBCOST	0.851	0.008	0.159	0.050
30. TBTEST	0.717	0.101	−0.137	−0.086
24. BENSCORE	−0.114	0.405	−0.058	0.162
19. PPVTB	−0.001	−0.384	−0.088	−0.057
26. CANCOST	0.183	−0.030	0.883	0.092
29. CANTEST	−0.133	0.061	0.632	−0.040
31. AGE	−0.247	−0.020	−0.121	0.409
7. CORHDETI	−0.108	0.052	0.059	0.389
18. PPVHD	0.127	−0.110	−0.161	−0.316

APPENDIX B: LIST OF VARIABLES

TABLE B1 List of Main Variables by Code Name and Type

TYPE/CODE NAME	VARIABLE
Dependent variables	
KEEPMED	Keeping medicines at home
GNALPHB	General preventive health behaviour
EXERCISE	Regular exercise
SMOKE	Smoking
DRINK	Drinking alcoholic beverages
Independent variables	
KOMS	Knowledge overall mean score
CORHDETI	Knowledge of etiology of heart disease
CORCAETI	Knowledge of etiology of cancer
CORTBETI	Knowledge of etiology of tuberculosis
HDBLAME	Perception of social sanctions against those with heart disease
CANBLAME	Perception of social sanctions against those with cancer
TBBLAME	Perception of social sanctions against those with tuberculosis
TOTPDRHD	Perception of total disruption of normal role activities due to heart disease
TOTPDRCA	Perception of total disruption of normal role activities due to cancer
TOTPDRTB	Perception of total disruption of normal role activities due to tuberculosis
PPVGENERAL	Perceived personal vulnerability to disease in general
PPVCANCER	Perceived personal vulnerability to cancer
PPVHD	Perceived personal vulnerability to heart disease
PPVTB	Perceived personal vulnerability to tuberculosis
Intervening variables	
BENSCORE	Combined score of the perception of benefits of taking preventive action against heart disease, cancer and tuberculosis
HDCOST	Perception of cost of examination as a barrier to preventive medical check-ups for heart disease
CANCOST	Perception of cost of examination as a barrier to preventive medical check-ups for cancer
TBCOST	Perception of cost of examination as a barrier to preventive medical check-ups for tuberculosis
HDTEST	Information on preventive health services for heart disease
CANTEST	Information on preventive health services for cancer
TBTEST	Information on preventive health services for tuberculosis
Antecedent variables	
ALLSCORE	Total future-orientation score
EDULEVEL	Highest level of formal education attained
SES	Socio-economic status
CAMPAIGN	Awareness of health campaigns during past year
MASSMEDIA	Total mass media exposure score
AGE	Age
SEX	Sex

DEVELOPING WORLD PERSPECTIVE

USE AND EVALUATION OF HEALTHCARE SERVICES BY MALE- AND FEMALE-HEADED HOUSEHOLDS IN RURAL SRI LANKA

K. A. S. WICKRAMA AND PAT M. KEITH

There is growing concern about inequality in access to health services among various groups of people—by geographical location, between rural and urban areas, between old and young, and by gender. Among those who may be overlooked and who may be vulnerable to poorer health are families of female heads of households, and recent evidence indicates that the number of Third World households managed by women is increasing. The prevalence of these families varies from 10 percent in Nepal and Kuwait to over 40 percent in Panama and Botswana, with an average of about 33 percent.[1] In Sri Lanka, the setting for this research, households headed by women constitute 18 percent of all families.

Our research focused on differences in factors associated with use and evaluation of health services in male- and female-headed households in villages in rural Sri Lanka. A number of dimensions that may influence health and subsequent use of services differentiate households headed by men and women.

COMPARISON OF MALE- AND FEMALE-HEADED HOUSEHOLDS

"The head of the household is generally the person who is responsible for the upkeep and maintenance of the household."[2] Households headed and managed by women irrespective of marital status are considered as female-headed households and may include widows, the divorced, the separated, and also wives living with children and perhaps other family members when their husbands are away much of the time. In rural areas, households run by women most often result from the death of the husband or from his temporary or permanent migration.[3]

Households managed by women are more vulnerable to poverty than those headed by men. These women retain primary responsibility for childcare and sometimes caregiving to other adults, for house maintenance, and for earning income to be used by other household members. The women who head households are concentrated in low-paid, low-status occupations, are more likely than men to be unemployed and untrained for any occupation, and have few prospects for self-impovement.[4] With increasing numbers of female-headed households the disparity between incomes of men and women has become an important factor in accounting for inequalities among families.[5]

Focusing specifically on the income levels of these households, Boatright observed that the major determinant of higher poverty rates of women seemed to be household status.[6] Women who head their own households are nearly five times as likely as their male counterparts to be poor; they have the highest poverty rates of any group of household heads, and they comprise an increasing proportion of those in poverty. The percentage of poor people living in female-headed families has risen more rapidly than the percentage of the poor in the total population.

Although male-headed households often can count on the supplementary earnings of a wife, female households have fewer supplementary workers or they have seasonal workers who are also female with comparable occupational and income constraints as the household head. These difficulties have implications for health and subsequent demands for healthcare. Female-headed households, for example, are more likely to be located in areas with substandard housing, unsafe drinking water, and inadequate services and to have insufficient income for a nutritionally balanced diet.[7]

Women who are responsible for families experience more acute and chronic morbidity than their counterparts who reside in intact households with husbands, children, and other family members. Yet, the health of women is not always directly reflected in the health of their children; for example, in Africa and India, despite the economic disadvantages of female households, there were fewer than average underweight children. A partial explanation for this seeming anomaly may be that the nutritional status of children is possibly less dependent on total household income than on the income of the mother. Even in male-headed households, women are more likely to use discretionary economic resources to secure food for their families or for other basic needs, whereas men more often direct their resources toward investments, goods, entertainment, or leisure activities.[8]

But the poverty of female-headed households affects the health of the children and their intake of calories and nutrients, clothing and shelter, sanitary facilities, the availability of adult supervision, and the use of medical care.[9] Also, income is purchased by women through extra work hours that reduce the time they spend in childcare. The mortality of children of unmarried mothers was found to be higher than that of the currently married. Moreover, children of currently married persons tended to have lower mortality rates than children of women in any other marital category.[10] Differences in the well-being of children of married and nonmarried heads of households were attributed partially to the higher educational attainment of the more advantaged mothers. It is also possible that widowhood and divorce are associated with substantial stress, which in turn affects child health. Circumstances of employment are salient to the health of adults. Hibberd observed that women of all ages employed in jobs with a higher degree of social support and integration had better health than women in jobs with little social support and integration through work.[11]

HOUSEHOLDS OF OLDER WOMEN

Whereas female-headed families with children may have different needs from those with both parents present, older women in developing areas also have greater needs for medical, social, and economic assistance in old age than do men. Generally, households headed by older women in developing regions have less favorable life circumstances in terms of poverty and health than do those headed by men or younger women. In many areas of the world, older women have received poorer healthcare, experienced malnutrition, and have had lower social status throughout their lives, in part, because of their gender. Yet, adapting to social change, including adoption of new health programs, can be difficult for those whose lives have been confined to domestic roles and who have had little contact with the outside world.[12]

Undernutrition is a primary factor affecting the health of the aged in developing regions. Elderly poor in Sri Lanka are most influenced by shortages of food during times of crisis. During a recent famine, for example, 45 percent of the increase in deaths were among those aged 65 or over compared to a 20 percent increase in deaths among infants.[13] In some areas the nutritional circumstances of older women and widows leave them especially at risk of poor health. For example, a study in Bangladesh found that older men consumed almost as much protein as younger men of working age, but older women received much less, especially if they were widowed.[14] Demands of women, particularly the unmarried, for health and social services are greater than those of men, in part because women live longer than men and because they have more chronic illnesses than men of the same age.[15] The very poor who do not reach old age contend with the most unfavorable circumstances.[16]

In developing societies, the primary and often only source of support for a widow is her children, usually her sons. But there are substantial numbers of older widows in developing countries who do not have sons, or any children who will assist them in later life. On the other hand, as younger women become more educated, join the labor force, and become more equal to men, they also may achieve more companionship and equality in their marital relationship. With more egalitarian marriages and increased prevalence of the nuclear family, sons and daughters-in-law may feel less obligation to provide assistance to their aged parents. Some research suggests that where these transitions in female employment and marital relationships are beginning to occur, elderly widows are increasingly worried that they will not be cared for by their sons.[17] Older men are much more likely than women to receive social and personal support in traditional families owing to their high status as males, their economic independence, and the likelihood of their being married and having a spouse to provide needed care. Older widows, however, are disadvantaged in comparison to married men but fare better than widows.

HOUSEHOLD STRUCTURE, DEMOGRAPHIC CHARACTERISTICS, AND HEALTH BEHAVIOR

Pratt observed that a family's ability to function effectively, including seeking and using healthcare when needed, depends on its structure.[18] In households supported by females without spouses, there may be different health behaviors, less time spent on the family in attending to its needs, and poorer health status than in households having both husbands and wives present.[19] The household structure not only may affect the health of women but also may be a determinant of health of the whole family as well as an influence on the ability of its members to identify problems and use appropriate healthcare services. Yet, despite a need in rural areas for additional health services, they are often underused by persons who could benefit from them. Furthermore, the effects of household structure on health may extend beyond physical health

to mental health as well. Both widows and widowers have poorer psychological well-being than their married counterparts.[20]

All of this is not to say that most women do not possess significant specialized knowledge concerning healthcare. Their knowledge extends beyond simply knowing how to provide their families with adequate food, water, fuel, and disposal of household waste, although such tasks may be extraordinarily difficult and complex. Women are expected to address the needs of the chronically ill and of the elderly or disabled household members for diet, exercise, and rest.

> They also manage acute illness episodes by determining when family members are ill and deciding what kind of care they will receive. It is usually women who prescribe remedies, decide at what point in an illness to seek outside attention and what type of practitioner to consult.[21]

The role of women in implementing primary healthcare programs is always vital, but in female-headed households application of health skills may assume even greater importance. The home is the critical focus of primary healthcare; it is where "families live in ways that are either healthy or burdened with risk, where behavior is influenced by neighbors, and where decisions that affect health are made."[22]

Women must have both knowledge and autonomy to promote and protect the health of their families. Educated women are able to interpret health messages, are easier to educate further about health matters, and have fewer cultural values that are barriers to learning new health practices. The lower literacy rates of women compared with those of men, however, are likely to make informal education of women more difficult. Literacy rates are lower among female heads of families, especially among the aged.

In previous tests of models of use of services, formal education has not been reflected consistently in demands for care.[23] Education may have an independent positive impact on health status or it may influence health through its effect on practices such as the boiling of water, securing of immunizations, knowledge of disease, and recognition of symptoms. In turn, knowledge and attitudes reflected in these behaviors may figure indirectly in the use of services. One view is that those with more education are also likely to earn higher wages and salaries and therefore stand to gain more economic benefit from maintaining better health than those with less education who are in lower-level occupations.[24] Higher levels of education may be related to securing preventive healthcare, whereas less education may be associated with greater needs for curative treatment.

Education generally is linked with household income, which in turn is associated with obtaining medical care even when it is free and publicly available. Low income remains a barrier to use of healthcare services in settings where care is free.[25] Values regarding care are influenced by income, and they affect subsequent decisions to avail oneself or family members of care. Income is related to marital status, which also seems to be linked with use of services.

Generally the literature, based largely on research conducted in Western societies, suggests that the unmarried will make greater demands than the married for healthcare.[26] Insofar as health status is a primary factor in determining use of services[27] and the unmarried, especially older widows, tend to have poorer health,[28] then we might expect that the aged and the unmarried would require more healthcare.

In the absence of data on health status, Chernichovsky and Meesook argued that age could be used to represent current health.[29] From an economic perspective they suggested that with increasing age the desire to invest in health may decline because the amount of time that benefits obtained from healthcare could be enjoyed would be less. Consequently, younger persons with a longer period of life remaining may be more eager to incur health expenditures than the aged. At the same time, however, increased medical care may be required to offset deteriorating physical conditions of the aged, and the costs of maintaining health will increase with age. Even so, Chernichovsky and Meesook concluded that as a proxy for health status, the effect of age on demand for medical care was ambiguous.

In developing countries a number of variables (i.e., age, gender, widowhood) may be proxies for poverty as well as for health. Because in households headed by women, members experience more chronic illness, poorer nutrition, lower income, and greater dependence on kin, we anticipated that these families would make greater use of health services. In our research, comparisons were made between the use and evaluation of healthcare services in male- and female-headed households.

Demographic characteristics (age, marital status, education, and occupation of head of household), amount of land used, and health and nutritional practices (e.g., protein, fruit, and vegetable consumption; immunization; toilet facilities; use of boiled water) of the male and female households were considered as determinants of use of and satisfaction with health services in two villages in Sri Lanka. Because the number of female-headed households, both young and old, is increasing, and because they tend to be poorer, older, and located more often in rural areas with fewer healthcare services, our research raises some important issues about determinants of their use of healthcare compared to factors influencing the families of men.

METHODOLOGY

Sample. Data were collected from interviews with 643 heads of households from two villages in Hambantota, Sri Lanka—295 from Horawinna and 348 from Karametiya. There were 69 female- and 226 male-headed households in Horawinna and 67 female- and 281 male-headed households in Karametiya.

The two villages were selected to maximize heterogeneity in geography, economic activities, and social conditions. Karametiya is bordered by a main, public road on one side and small mountain range on the other. Owing to the road and transportation facilities, services are more accessible in Karametiya, which is located in a wetter zone with more dense settlements than in Horawinna. In both villages, similar agricultural patterns prevail with citronella cultivation being dominant in each. Small tile factories and brick-making units use available clay deposits in Karametiya. Although land is scarcer in Karametiya, there is less disparity in the size of the plots, whereas there is more variation in land holdings in Horawinna, which has some large landowners. The very poorest people with little access to land and temporary homes comprise 31 percent in Karametiya compared with 63 percent in Horawinna. There was little difference in the distance to water; one-fifth (Karametiya) to one-quarter (Horawinna) of the families walked more than one-half mile for drinking water.

The Interview.   The interviews requested information on family composition, marital status, age, education, occupational status, number of dependents, housing condition, water supply, toilet facilities, and health and nutritional practices. A team of trained interviewers consisting of local officers, village organization leaders, and members of educational rural youth groups conducted the interviews.

Measures

Demographic Characteristics.   Age was coded into five categories ranging from 16 (coded 1) to 65 years or over (coded 5). There were 69 percent of the women and 79 percent of men under age 65. Marital status was assessed and coded as unmarried (0) and married (1). Of female heads of households, 62 percent were widowed in contrast to 23 percent widowered for male heads of households. Education was coded into three categories: no education, illiterate (0), literate, no formal education (1), and education, literate (2). Occupational categories were coded from lowest to highest, and they were based, in part, on income and the social status accorded the occupation. Occupations included laborers, cultivators, skilled jobs (e.g., carpenters,

blacksmiths, potters), teachers, clerks, and merchants. Amount of land owned, leased, and/or encroached was used as a measure of socioeconomic status. All parcels of land used by the household, regardless of tenure, were summed to obtain the total number of acres.

Preventive Health Practices and Diet.   Preventive health practices were assessed by determining the availability of a toilet, use of immunizations, and use of boiled water (1, no; 2, yes). In three separate questions, respondents indicated whether they and their families consumed protein, vegetables, and fruits (1, no; 2, yes).

Use and Evaluation of Health Services.   Use of health services (medical–curative) was assessed by summing responses to the questions concerning how often persons used three types of service—a dispensary, a hospital, and an ayurvedic (a traditional practitioner who also has formal medical training). Response categories were rarely (1), regularly (2), and frequently (3). Higher scores indicated greater use of services.

Evaluation of healthcare was assessed by summing responses to the questions about satisfaction of families with services provided by the dispensary, the hospital, and the ayurvedic. Response categories were poor (1), satisfied (2), and good (3). Higher scores indicated more satisfaction with services.

RESULTS

Comparisons of Male and Female Heads of Households.   About one-fifth of the households in Karametiya and Horawinna (23 percent) were headed by women. In the two villages female heads of households were more often widows (64 and 54 percent in Karametiya and Horawinna, respectively) than men were widowers (4 and 3 percent). Women heads of households were significantly older than men ($t = 3.27$; $p < .001$) in Karametiya but not in Horawinna. About 34 and 27 percent of female heads of households in Karametiya and Horawinna were over 55 years of age as compared to 16.7 percent and 19.5 percent of the males, respectively.

Female heads of households in Karametiya and Horawinna, respectively, were much more likely (67 percent and 84 percent) than males (15 percent and 18 percent) to have had no formal education. Most of these women with no education were illiterate. When these figures are compared with the national illiteracy rates of 13 percent and 24 percent, for males and females, the disadvantaged situation of women who managed households is clear.

Examination of occupations of household heads indicated that most of the employed female household heads worked as casual laborers (50 percent and 30 percent of employed women and 15 percent and 12 percent of employed men in Karametiya and Horawinna respectively). The most socially and economically favored occupations, such as government employment, cultivation, and skilled labor, were held mainly by male household heads. There was a significant difference in the occupational status of jobs held by female and male heads of households in both villages ($t = 10.51, 6.90; p < .001$).

Also, unemployment was more acute among the female heads of households, who were most often the primary breadwinners in their families. For example, about two-thirds of female heads of households were not working in contrast to 22 and 29 percent of male heads of households in Karametiya and Horawinna. The total amount of land, which was the main productive asset of the family, was an indication of socioeconomic status, and the male-headed families used more land than their female counterparts ($t = 1.72, p < .09$) in Karametiya, but not in Horawinna ($t = .10$, ns).

The female-headed households used health services more frequently than the male-headed households in Karametiya ($t = 2.07, p < .05$), but about the same in Horawinna ($t = 1.12$, ns). Accordingly female heads of households tended to be more positive toward health services than the male heads of households in Karametiya ($t = 1.88, p < .06$) but not

in Horawinna ($t = .87$, ns). Evaluation of health services by female and male heads of households varied with the level of use of health services in both villages ($r = .40, .41$ for females and $r = .44, .45$ for males in Karametiya and Horawinna, respectively). Those who more frequently used services evaluated them more positively.

Multivariate Analyses of Use and Evaluation of Health Services. Initial inspection of zero-order correlations indicated that somewhat different factors were linked with use of services and satisfaction depending on gender and village (tables 1, 2). Generally more of the variables were significantly correlated with use by households of women and especially in Karametiya. Immunization was the most common correlate of use in both male and female households.

Use of Services. Separate multiple regression analyses were performed for male- and female-headed households in the two villages. The model, which included demographic characteristics (age, marital status, education, occupation), health and dietary practices (boiled water, toilet facilities, immunization, protein, vegetable, and fruit intake) and amount of land, explained 36 and 23 percent of variance in use of health services by female-headed households, and 26 and 8 percent of the variance for male-headed households in Karametiya and Horawinna, respectively (table 1). Thus, the model explained more variance in the use of health services in female-headed than in male-headed households and in the village of Karametiya than in the village of Horawinna.

Households with immunized family members used health services less frequently than those with nonimmunized family members, irrespective of gender of the head of the household. This type of preventive activity was the only factor that predicted use of healthcare for households regardless of gender.

Female heads of households were both married and unmarried, and marital status was espe-

TABLE 1 Summary of Multiple Regression Analyses for Use of Health Services, for Males and Females in Karametiya and Horawinna

| | KARAMETIYA | | | | HORAWINNA | | | |
| | Male | | Female | | Male | | Female | |
	r	β	r	β	r	β	r	β
Age	−.03	−.03	−.18	−.37***	.14	.14*	.07	.01
Marital status	.03	.05	−.28	−.35***	.00	−.04	.21	−.22*
Education	−.16	−.07	−.12	−.24*	−.03	−.06	.09	.04
Occupation	−.29	−.22***	.09	.21	.07	.03	.20	.19
Boiled water	−.02	.00	−.07	−.11	−.12	−.10	.31	−.18
Protein	−.01	.01	−.08	−.09	−.10	−.10	−.18	−.14
Vegetables	−.05	.00	−.01	.22	.09	.14*	−.07	.01
Fruit	−.01	.07	−.01	.01	.09	.06	.09	−.01
Acreage	−.14	−.05	−.01	.05	.03	.04	−.05	−.05
Toilet	−.04	−.01	−.14	.00	.10	.06	.07	−.13
Immunization	−.47	−.44***	−.37	−.38***	−.12	−.14*	−.23	−.22*
R^2		.28		.36		.09		.23

*$p < .10$

**$p < .05$

***$p < .01$

cially important in determining use of services in these households. In both villages families of the unmarried made greater demands on services. And families of older women used services less frequently. Among male-headed households in Karametiya, those who practiced immunization and had higher social status as reflected by the occupation of the head of the household made fewer demands on the healthcare system. Occupation, however, affected use of health services differently for households of men and women in one village. In Karametiya, households of men employed in higher-level occupations had less demand for health services. They may have obtained more prestigious paid medical care from private practitioners rather than from the government health institutions. Families of employed women made use of services at the same level as their counterparts not involved in paid work (table 1). None of the

factors predicted demands for health services in households of men in Horawinna.

Evaluation of Services. Similar models explained 37 and 26 percent of variance in evaluations of health services by female heads of households, whereas they accounted for only 16 and 5 percent of variance in evaluations by male heads of households in Karametiya and Horawinna, respectively (table 2). In Horawinna, female heads of households who embraced positive health practices (i.e., boiling water and immunization) were less satisfied with health services. In Karametiya, demographic characteristics such as marital status, education, and occupation were important in assessments of health services by women. Older, married, and more educated women in this village, however, were less satisfied with the health services. Households of men in higher status occupations were less satisfied with

TABLE 2   Summary of Multiple Regression Analyses for Satisfaction with Health Services for Males and Females in Karametiya and Horawinna

| | KARAMETIYA | | | | HORAWINNA | | | |
| | Male | | Female | | Male | | Female | |
	r	β	r	β	r	β	r	β
Age	.00	.02	−.17	−.41***	.05	.02	.11	.24*
Marital status	−.02	.01	−.43	−.50***	.02	.00	−.23	−.15
Education	−.04	.01	.00	−.23*	−.02	−.04	.12	.16
Occupation	−.22	.20***	.19	.23*	.08	.07	.17	.13
Boiled water	.09	.07	.08	−.02	−.10	−.08	−.37	−.25**
Protein	.14	.08	.08	−.03	−.08	−.08	−.19	−.06
Vegetables	.09	.04	.11	.19	.01	.05	−.11	−.08
Fruit	.15	.16***	.21	.11	.08	.03	.15	.05
Acreage	−.10	−.06	.08	.11	.14	.11	.03	−.06
Toilet	.05	.05	.03	.05	.04	.04	.11	.05
Immunization	−.24	−.24***	−.03	−.07	−.08	−.08	−.17	−.22*
R^2		.16		.38		.05		.26

*$p < .10$

**$p < .05$

***$p < .01$

healthcare, whereas women with better jobs had more positive views of medical services (table 2).

DISCUSSION

This research provided an opportunity to compare households of males and females in their use and evaluation of services. The relative importance of demographic characteristics and of health and dietary practices for use and assessment of health services was examined.

Gender of head of household was a factor in determining income, assets, and social circumstances. It might be reasoned that their low income, lesser education, and generally disadvantaged social status would affect the use of preventive measures by members of female households and also obstruct them from seeking care when needed. Research in Western countries found that finances, for example, were a major factor in decisions to delay care.[30] In a society with free medical care, however, income should be less salient. On the other hand, need, as assessed by poor health, has been consistently correlated with greater use of services.[31] Members of female households report poorer health, perhaps, in part, as a result of their poverty.[32] Also, women heads of families experience significantly more acute and chronic health problems than those who live with husbands, parents, and children.[33] Owing to the differences in the health status of families headed by men and women, it was anticipated that female-headed households would make greater demands on health services. Our research provided at least partial support for this view, because members of households managed by females used health services more frequently than families of males in one of the villages, and there was a tendency for them to demand more care in the other setting. In their role as principal decisionmaker and healthcare provider for the family, female heads of households may attempt to diminish risk by using available healthcare more frequently. Free government healthcare as in Sri Lanka may result in greater healthcare demands in the rural areas of developing countries, where the proportion of female-headed families is increasing.

For women, especially in Karametiya, characteristics such as age, marital status, and education figured in their use and evaluation of health services. An important finding was the salience of marital status in seeking care for women and female-headed households in both villages but not for male-headed households. Most of the female heads of households in both communities were unmarried (64, 53 percent). The households of unmarried women, regardless of the age of the head, availed themselves of more services than the households of their married counterparts. This result corroborated the findings from Western countries that show the married making less use of health services[34] than the unmarried, and points to the importance of marital status for the families of women as it affects help seeking in a less-developed place. With projected increases in the number of unmarried female heads of households in developing countries, demand for healthcare at the village level will likely escalate.

Furthermore, positive evaluations of healthcare by households of the unmarried also may contribute to increased use of services. Those who use healthcare services the most and find them satisfying are likely to maintain, if not increase, their demand.

The literature suggests contradictory predictions as to the effect of education on use of services and as to which households will ultimately seek more care. Most of the female household heads in both communities were illiterate (67, 86 percent). On the other hand, it might be expected that education would increase preventive behaviors, which in turn might diminish the need for curative care. But poorer families who do not engage in positive health habits and who give less attention to prevention consequently may experience more ill health

that would prompt greater usage. In general, the healthcare services considered in this research were curative rather than preventive.

As in previous research, education in this study had an inconsistent effect on use. When education was linked to use, generally the more educated used services least. Hence, being illiterate was not a barrier to obtaining care among the households we studied. It was expected that education might be reflected in more preventive behaviors; however, in inspecting the relationship between education and boiling of water, obtaining of immunizations, and availability of a toilet, only 4 of the 12 tests (3 preventive behaviors by gender by 2 communities) were significant, and the relationships were very modest relationships, with all but 1 less than $r = .14$. It might be reasoned that households of illiterate women would generate higher demand for services as a result of the lack of preventive health practices by family members; however, immunization was the only preventive behavior consistently linked with use of services for all groups. Moreover, education was not associated with securing immunizations by the majority of families. It may be that an effect of informal education and of the primary care movement has been to diminish the salience of formal schooling in prevention, leaving care seeking by and large independent of schooling of heads of households.

Older women were less satisfied with healthcare, and they and their families used it less frequently than households of younger women in Karametiya. This may be owing to the family composition of older households; they include fewer children who tend to create more demands for healthcare in younger households. Furthermore, lack of transportation, social isolation, and traditional beliefs may have contributed also to fewer demands and less satisfaction of older female heads of households. It may be that these older women were survivors who had long contended with less formal healthcare. Other literature suggests that the needs of older women in many cultures go unmet.[35] Such a situation may well call attention to potential mismatches between the health needs of elderly women, who will be an increasingly larger group, and the availability of services that recently have been oriented toward child and maternal care.

In contrast to the households of older women, families of older men made use of health services at the same level as those of younger men although the older men tended to be less satisfied with the healthcare they received. Older males may have had younger wives with children that in part accounted for use of care comparable to that of younger families.

Perhaps it is significant that the families who sought immunization, which primarily affects children, used fewer health services regardless of the type of household. This may indicate that many of the health needs of families were generated by children and that such preventive measures were very salient in keeping costly curative healthcare demand at lower levels.

Several practices that might be expected to influence health and, perhaps, be reflected in subsequent demand for services did not affect use of healthcare. Diet, toilet facilities, and the use of boiled water, for example, generally were not associated with formal care. It may be that the impact of preventive practices is indirect through their effect on need or health status that in turn alters the demand for services.

When adoption of preventive practices was linked with evaluation of services, the relationship was usually negative. It may be that persons who are attentive to health concerns may hold greater expectations for the formal care they receive and are disappointed when it fails to attain the quality they hoped to realize.

The model investigated here was more useful in accounting for the health behavior and healthcare evaluation of households of women than of those of men. Assessments of health or impairment are usually correlates of use of services. Even though measures of health were not available, the model accounted for as much or more of the variance in use of services by women than is usually reported in research in which health status is the most important determinant of demand for services.

Some of the findings may be useful in targeting groups which warrant the most attention. The interrelationships between age, marital status, and use of services deserve consideration. Although age was linked with marital status and the latter figured prominently in demand for services by families of women, households of the old did not disproportionately use healthcare. Indeed, in one of the villages age of the head of the household was negatively related to the use of services. Families of aged widows made fewer demands than those of younger widows and the divorced, although both used healthcare more frequently than households of married women. Thus, for these households, age was not a proxy for greater demands for healthcare; rather marital status would have been more useful in identifying groups who expressed the most need for services. Future research and planning for healthcare should take into account not only the gender of the head of the household but also marital status, especially among families managed by women.

NOTES

1. John S. Akin, Charles Griffith, David Guilkey, and Barry Popkin, *The Demand for Primary Health Services in the Third World* (Totowa, NJ: Rowman and Allanheld, 1985).

2. Joycellin Massiah, *Women as Heads of Households in the Caribbean: Family Structure and Feminine Status* (United Kingdom: UNESCO, 1983), p. 15.

3. C. H. Browner, "Women, Household, and Health in Latin America," *Social Science and Medicine* 28 (1989): 463–67.

4. Massiah, *Women as Heads*, p. 15.

5. Hilary Graham, *Women, Health, and Family* (United Kingdom: Harvester Press, 1984), pp. 1–8.

6. Julie W. Boatright, "Women and Poverty," *Women and Health* 12 (1987): 21–40.

7. Browner, "Women, Household, and Health," pp. 462–67.

8. Ibid.

9. United Nations, *Socio-Economic Differentials in Child Mortality in Developing Countries* (New York: United Nations, 1985), pp. 191–227.

10. Ibid.

11. Judith H. Hibberd and Clyde R. Pope, "Employment Status, Employment Characteristics, and Women's Health," *Women and Health* 10 (1985): 59–77.

12. Marsel Heisel, "Older Women in Developing Countries," *Women and Health* 14 (1988): 253–72.

13. Ibid.

14. James E. Lubben, "Gender Differences in the Relationship of Widowhood and Psychological Well-Being among Low Income Elderly," *Women and Health* 14 (1988): 161–89.

15. Pat M. Keith, *The Unmarried in Later Life* (New York: Praeger, 1989).

16. Heisel, "Older Women," pp. 253–72.

17. Ibid.

18. Lois Pratt, *Family Structure and Effective Health Behavior* (Boston, MA: Houghton, 1976).

19. Akin et al., *Demand for Primary Health Services.*

20. Lubben, "Gender Differences," pp. 161–89.

21. Browner, "Women, Household, and Wealth," p. 465.

22. John H. Byant, "Health for All," *World Health Forum* 9 (1988): 300.

23. Dov Chernichovsky and Oey A. Meesook, "Utilization of Health Services in Indonesia," *Social Science and Medicine* 23, no. 6 (1986): 611–20; Fredric Wolinsky, Rodney Coe, and Ray Mosely, "The Use of Health Services by Elderly Americans: Implications from a Regression-Based Cohort Analysis," in *Health and Aging,* ed. Russell Ward and Sheldon Tobin (New York: Springer, 1987).

24. Chernichovsky and Meesook, "Utilization of Health Services," pp. 611–20.

25. Ibid.

26. Marie R. Haug, "Age and Medical Care Utilization Patterns," *Journal of Gerontology* 36 (January 1981): 103–111; Keith, *Unmarried in Later Life.*

27. Wolinsky, Coe, and Mosely, "Use of Health Services."

28. Heisel, "Older Women," pp. 253–72.

29. Chernichovsky and Meesook, "Utilization of Health Services," pp. 611–20.

30. Keith, *Unmarried in Later Life.*

31. Wolinsky, Coe, and Mosely, "Use of Health Services."

32. Browner, "Women, Household, and Health," pp. 462–67.

33. Ofra Anson, "Living Arrangements and Women's Health," *Social Science and Medicine* (1988): 201–8.

34. Haug, "Age and Medical Care," pp. 103–11.

35. Masako Osako, "Increase of Elderly Poor in Developing Nations—The Implications of Dependency Theory and Modernization Theory for the Aging of World Population," in *Aging and the Aged in the Third World: Part I,* ed. Vinson Sutlive, Nathan Altshuler, and Mario Zamora (Williamsburg, VA: College of William and Mary, 1982).

CHAPTER 5

ILLNESS BEHAVIOR, PART ONE

Illness behavior as a central concept in medical sociology argues that symptoms related to biomedical disorders reflect learned sociocultural expectations of behavior, that this behavior is associated with a person's social position within the larger social structure, and that a person's response to such symptoms depends on characteristics such as ethnic background, race, age, social class, and sex. To explain illness behavior, a number of theoretical models have been developed within medical sociology (see, for example, Suchman, 1965; Zola, 1973; Dingwall, 1977; Mechanic, 1978).

Suchman (1965) developed the most notable model. He identified a series of stages through which an individual travels in order to achieve recovery from the illness. Beginning with the appearance of symptoms in Stage One, the illness experience progresses to recovery and rehabilitation in Stage Five. This progression, however, has become problematic, because Suchman describes stages of *acute* illness but, increasingly, illness is *chronic*, not acute. Thus, Suchman's stages may not reflect current illness reality. Nevertheless, his model and others provide a framework within which illness experiences can be understood and explained.

The articles in this chapter illustrate the range of applications associated with the concept of illness behavior. In the first article, David Mechanic discusses not only the importance of illness behavior relative to public health but also the concept of the sick role as a starting point for any discussion of illness behavior (this point is also made in the third article). Mechanic presents findings from a study (Mechanic and Volkart, 1961) of male university

students and the factors associated with students' appearance or nonappearance for a medical opinion on a number of medical problems. A key point in this article is the relationship between stress and illness behavior. According to Mechanic, the greater the stress a person experiences, the greater is the person's utilization of medical facilities.

Mechanic also discusses four dimensions of illness. These dimensions are aspects of what he refers to as "illness recognition" and "illness danger," and they can be applied to specific illnesses. For example, a cold is recognizable and generally not dangerous, whereas hepatitis is recognizable but may be dangerous. The application of these two categories, however, is a recognition that the perception of illness differs among persons. Mechanic concludes that an understanding of illness behavior and of the attitudes and values associated with the adoption of the patient role is essential to the operation of health programs.

In the second article, Y. H. Cheng and Peter W. H. Lee examine cultural differences among Chinese medical students in Hong Kong. Building on earlier research efforts to document cultural differences in illness behavior, Cheng and Lee discuss Chinese concepts such as yin and yang in relation to health and illness.

Their research of 143 Chinese preclinical medical students involved the use of daily diaries in which the students recorded all the symptoms they experienced over a one-week period. Generally, females have been identified as experiencing greater numbers of medical symptoms than men. An important finding by Cheng and Lee was the lack of difference between males and females with regard to the number of symptoms experienced. Cheng and Lee point out, however, that female respondents in their research are not representative of women in the general population. For example, female medical students are less likely to be married and have children.

A second area that Cheng and Lee discuss is the "iceberg effect." They also discuss the "lay referral system" which gives students who are experiencing an illness the opportunity to utilize multiple health resources, including Chinese herbal medicine and Western patent medicines.

In the third article, Nicholas A. Christakis and colleagues examine illness behavior within a developing world perspective. They explore the relationship between illness behavior and the health transition—the century-long increase in life expectancy that has occurred in all countries as well as changes in the types of diseases from which people die. The authors point out that illness behavior is a dynamic concept influenced by societal changes that, in turn, influence changes within the health of the larger population. As a result, the authors contend, illness behavior is a component of the health transition.

Connecting illness behavior to medical pluralism, Christakis and colleagues offer an extensive review of the literature. They conclude that although biomedicine may be available, a host of factors (such as distance from practitioners and the cause of a problem) interact to influence a patient's choice of a healer. Utilizing maternal education, the authors also examine the influence of socioeconomic changes on illness behavior. They also address the relationship between changes in illness behavior and social changes associated with the health transition.

In essence, Christakis and colleagues conclude that to properly understand the genesis of the health transition, it is necessary to take local cultural variations into account. Illness behavior is incorporated into this argument because of its individual-level and societal-level analysis. According to the authors, "[B]ecause it illuminates the social nature of the individual, an illness behavior perspective offers a valuable alternative to large-scale epidemiological studies in tracing the social origins of changes in health status" (Christakis, Ware, and Kleinman, 1994, p. 297).

The three articles in Chapter 5 illustrate the importance of illness behavior as a central concept in medical sociology. All three identify the importance of a situational interpretation of illness behavior. They also point to the sociodemographics of respondents as an important variable.

REFERENCES

Christakis, N. A., Ware, N. C., and Kleinmen, A. 1994. Illness Behavior and the Health Transition in the Developing World. In *Health and Social Change in International Perspective*, ed. L. C. Chen, A. Kleinman, and N. C. Ware, pp. 275–302. Cambridge, MA: Harvard Center for Population and Development Studies 1994.

Dingwall, R. 1977. *Aspects of Illness*. New York: St. Martin's Press.

Mechanic, D. 1978. *Medical Sociology*. 2nd ed. New York: Free Press.

Mechanic, D., and E. H. Volkart. 1961. Stress, Illness Behavior, and the Sick Role. *American Sociological Review*, vol. 26, pp. 51–58.

Suchman, E. A. 1965. Stages of Illness and Medical Care. *Journal of Health and Human Behavior*, vol. 6, no. 3, pp. 114–128.

Zola, I. K. 1973. Pathways to the Doctor: From Person to Patient. *Social Science and Medicine*, vol. 7, pp. 677–689.

AMERICAN PERSPECTIVE

THE CONCEPT OF ILLNESS BEHAVIOR

DAVID MECHANIC

One of the principal tasks of the medical sciences is to understand and determine the conditions under which particular symptoms or disease entities arise either in individuals or among groups of individuals. Public health physicians have the further problem of effecting the arrival of "ill" persons at medical settings so that treatment can be effectively administered. Whether we concern ourselves with the necessary conditions for building adequate etiological theories or those for bringing treatment to persons most in need of such help, it is necessary that we understand the influence of a variety of norms, values, fears, and expected rewards and punishments on how a symptomatic person behaves.

Such considerations lead us to propose a concept of *illness behaviour.* By this term we refer to the ways in which given symptoms may be differentially perceived, evaluated, and acted (or not acted) upon by different kinds of persons. Whether by reason of earlier experiences with illness, differential training in respect to symptoms, or whatever, some persons will make light of symptoms, shrug them off, and avoid seeking medical care; others will respond to the slightest twinges of pain or discomfort by quickly seeking such medical care as is available. In short, the realm of illness behaviour falls logically and chronologically between two major traditional concerns of medical science: etiology and therapy. Variables affecting illness behavior come into play prior to medical scrutiny and treatment, but after etiological processes have been initiated. In this sense, illness behavior even determines whether diagnosis and treatment will begin at all.

We are here dealing with an area important for public health and medical sociology and it be-

comes a matter of both theoretical and practical concern to discover the sources and consequences of different illness behaviors. And if, in given populations, there are systematic differences in illness behavior, this fact has obvious implications for public health programs [5], estimated needs for medical care, medical economics, and our understanding of health and illness in general.

That the behavioral sciences can shed some light on such questions is indicated, for example, by the researches of Koos and Saunders. Koos [7] found that upper-class persons more often reported themselves ill than lower-class persons, and also that they were more likely to seek treatment when afflicted. Lower-class persons, on the other hand, while having more actual symptoms, reported themselves to be less often ill, and were the least likely of all persons in the community studied to visit a physician. Similarly, Saunders [8], comparing the attitudes and behavior of Spanish- and English-speaking populations in the Southwest, found many differences in the way the two populations responded to illness and used medical facilities. Whereas the "Anglos" preferred modern medical science and hospitalization for many illnesses, the Spanish-speaking people were more likely to rely on folk-medicine and family care and support.

The concept of the "social role of the sick person" as developed by Sigerist [9] and elaborated by Parsons [10], provides a convenient starting point in approaching illness behavior. According to Parsons' analysis, when a person's illness has been legitimized by medical sanction, or that of intimates and/or persons having influence over him, the person occupies a special role in society. During the time of the illness, he may be relieved of usual demands and obligations and his "sick role" takes priority over other social roles (e.g. occupational, familial, etc.). Moreover, the person is expected to seek help in restoring his full energies and to cooperate in the treatment process. Persons may be motivated to adopt the sick role to obtain release from various kinds of responsibilities; but there are also others who fear the dependence of the sick role or who are suspicious of physicians and avoid seeking medical advice even when serious symptoms appear.

Whether a person does or does not assume the sick role when ill is dependent on a variety of group and personal factors. The person's age, sex, and position in his social group as well as the importance of his role for the group must be considered [1]. If a man's failure to appear at work—even for one day—results in hardship for his family, it is likely he will avoid consulting a physician and the possibility of being encouraged to assume the sick role unless his symptoms become so serious as to prevent him from working; if time and money are available and a short departure from usual roles impose no undue hardships, the person is more likely to seek medical advice, get into bed, and release himself from his usual role demands.

Another factor of importance is the person's learned behaviors for dealing with symptoms. These behaviors may be learned for ideological reasons as with the Christian Scientist or for practical reasons as with the members of lower-income groups. What symptoms the person recognizes as important or worthy of attention and what he neglects or tends to ignore largely conditions when and for what reasons he might appear for medical diagnosis. This has often been a considerable problem for public health people as the evaluations by patient and physician of what constitutes serious symptoms and what necessitates treatment and attention may, indeed, be discrepant. One of the prime functions of public health programs is to teach populations to accept, and behave in accordance with, the definitions made by the medical profession.

In evaluating how best to bring about successful educational programs, two questions become apparent: (1) what are the factors affecting the appearance or nonappearance of persons for medical diagnosis? and (2) how can these people be reached most effectively by educational and information programs?

The latter problem is outside the scope of this paper, but Professor Volkart and I have explored the former problem to some extent in an investigation of 614 male students at a large University. These subjects were approximately of the same age, and lived and ate their meals in the same university dormitory. Because of school requirements, the academic demands made upon them were also substantially similar. Data were obtained by means of both a questionnaire and investigation of their medical records. Using a series of hypothetical questions concerning whether these students would seek advice from a physician if they had various symptoms, we were able to distinguish students with varied inclinations to seek medical attention. Our concern then became threefold: (1) what is the relationship between the inclination to seek medical attention and the actual use of medical facilities as measured by the students' health records? (2) what social and personal factors are associated with the expressed inclination to seek medical advice? and (3) what diagnostic categories are most affected by different inclinations to seek medical advice? As expected, we found that the actual frequency of visits made to a free University medical clinic was highly associated with a high inclination to seek medical help as measured by responses to a set of hypothetical medical conditions. The measure of inclination to seek medical advice, also, was significantly related to the person's religion, his social class position, his dependency on others, and the magnitude of stress he reported. More specifically, we found that approximately 71 per cent of the Jews in the sample and 70 per cent of the Episcopalians expressed a high inclination to use medical facilities in various hypothetical situations, only 32 per cent of Christian

Scientists and 42 per cent of Catholics did so. These differences persisted within social class groups indicating that class influences on religious affiliation could not explain all of the variance. Our findings suggested a theory of learned alternative channels for dealing with life stress situations, including illness. Symptoms presented to the physician by Jews and Episcopalians may be presented to priests, lay practitioners and druggists by members of other groups. The differences observed and the theory suggested are being investigated now with other populations.

These findings suggest the importance of further investigations of cultural and social responses to *dis-ease*. Zborowski's classic study [11] of reactions to pain showed that Jewish, Italian, Irish and "Old American" patients responded differently. While Jews and Italians responded emotionally tending to exaggerate their pain experience, Irish and "Old Americans," in contrast, were more stoical. Response to pain and response to disease takes place within an elaborate cultural context, in which the patient, his family, and the community respond in socially patterned ways. Zborowski reports how Jewish and Italian respondents related that their mother showed over-protective and over-concerned attitudes toward the child's health, participation in sports and the like, and that they were constantly warned of the advisability of avoiding colds, injuries, fights, and other threatening behavior. While excessive concern in clinical situations may be regarded as hypochondriasis or even malingering, it is essential for the practicing physician to recognize that these patterns are often acquired in the child's training process and that the patient's prior training affects how and when he presents himself and his symptoms to his physician.

One of the main concerns of our research was the effects of "stress" on illness behavior. We found that persons who reported high "stress" as measured by frequency of loneliness and nervousness, were significantly more likely to use medical facilities than persons with lesser "stress." While 60 per cent of our high stress respondents visited

the health service three or more times during the period studied, only 38 per cent of the low stress persons visited this service frequently. Moreover, we found that stress was associated, also, with the inclination to use medical facilities expressed in various hypothetical situations. While 60 per cent of high stress persons expressed a high inclination to use medical facilities, only 43 per cent of the low stress persons did so. In the group with a high inclination to use medical facilities as measured by hypothetical situations, 73 per cent of persons under high stress made three or more visits during the period observed, while in the same group only 46 per cent of low stress persons were such frequent visitors. In the group with low inclination to use medical facilities, 42 per cent of high stress persons visited three or more times, as compared with only 30 per cent of the low stress persons. Thus, stress was more likely to affect the act of using medical facilities among persons who already had a high inclination to use such facilities.

We suspected that the type of stress experienced by a person might be important in its effect on his illness behavior. This idea was based on the assumption that the physician's role is ideally suited to the needs of persons in interpersonal difficulty. The physician's role includes the technical skills and knowledge to deal with "illnesses"; and because it involves communication, interaction, and nurturance, it also meets the interpersonal needs of such persons. Interaction with a physician is suited, also, for persons in interpersonal difficulty in that it can be initiated with little difficulty, not requiring the complex and subtle cues and response often necessary in other types of relationships. Also, the primary function of the physician is to aid and restore health, and this serves to insure that the patient will not be rejected openly or humiliated. Nor is he likely to be condemned for his various symptoms and complaints—at least initially. In many ways, then, the doctor–patient relationship can serve as a temporary substitute for other kinds of insufficient or inadequate interpersonal relationships.

In our study, questionnaire data were obtained dealing with students' experiences, worries and difficulties during their freshman year. As expected, it was found that students having more interpersonal difficulties (worries about interpersonal matters, worries about dating, feelings of loneliness, etc.) were more likely to express a high inclination to use medical facilities than were persons with lesser interpersonal difficulties. It was further suggested that interpersonal stresses exerted greater effects on persons' expressed inclinations to use medical facilities than did noninterpersonal stresses of similar importance like worries about money, finding studies interesting, etc. These data support the interpretation that interpersonal stress is a significant factor affecting who will seek medical care and when. Aside from clear emergencies and acute illnesses, which scarcely permit alternatives, the maintenance of a doctor–patient relationship involves an interaction between certain services the physician offers and certain needs of the patient which may go beyond "traditional medicine" in its usual condition.

In evaluating how various diagnostic categories were related to the inclination to seek medical aid as measured by hypothetical situations, we proposed the following rationale; a given illness may be regarded as having certain dimensions or characteristics, more or less perceptible to the sick person and possible to others in his social environment. In the context under study, four dimensions seemed of particular importance.

1. The frequency with which the illness occurs in a given population, i.e., its commonality;
2. The relative familiarity of the symptoms to the average member of the group;
3. The relative predictability of the outcome of the illness; and
4. The amount of threat and loss that is likely to result from the illness.

The first two dimensions refer to the problem of "illness recognition"; the last two to the problem of "illness danger." When a particular symptomatology is both easily recognizable and relatively devoid of probable danger, it is a routine illness; when a given symptomatology occurs more frequently in the population, it is more difficult to identify, and when its mystery then casts the shadow of danger, there is likely to be a greater sense of concern.

The common cold, for example, as its name suggests, is both easily recognizable and relatively devoid of danger—at least initially. Hepatitis, on the other hand, is less often encountered by most persons and is more likely (and accurately) to be perceived as potentially dangerous.

The point to this approach to illness is that persons perceive symptoms differently. The definition of a symptom may greatly exaggerate its consequences as well as affect the behavior of the patient involved. We expected, therefore, that persons who expressed a high inclination to use medical facilities on our hypothetical questions would seek help under slight provocation; when their symptoms are common and familiar, or unusual and perplexing, they will probably seek medical diagnosis and treatment immediately. Persons with a low inclination to seek medical advice, on the other hand, are more likely to ignore "routine" illnesses and common aches and pains; only the more unusual or severe illnesses should bring them to medical attention.

In our analysis of diagnostic data, illnesses were classified on a matrix which permitted us to focus on illness "sites," irrespective of etiology, e.g., gastrointestinal, skin; or on a given etiological category, irrespective of site, e.g., viral, traumatic; or the possible combinations of etiologies and sites, e.g., viral respiratory or bacterial skin. Sixteen such diagnostic categories were used in the analysis of our data. These categories were classified as to whether or not they met the criteria of "routine illness" indicated (commonality, familiarity, predictability, and lack of threat). Our hypothesis concerning the relationship between inclination to seek medical attention and "routine" and "nonroutine" illness was, then, tested and confirmed.

Persons with a high tendency to seek medical aid were significantly more likely to than low tendency persons to report to the health service for diagnoses of illnesses meeting the criteria of "routine illness" for our population. These categories included respiratory, viral, viral respiratory, bacterial, and bacterial respiratory categories. Those illnesses classified as "non-routine" (those less common in the population studied, less familiar, less predictable, and threatening illnesses) did not show such large or statistically significant relationships to the inclination to seek medical care. Included among these categories were allergic conditions, poisonings, unknown skin, etc. [2].

From the public health point of view, the results must be scrutinized with some caution. For a symptom viewed by a layman as not serious, may be of great medical consequence. For example, cancer is often not detected until fairly widespread in the organism, because the layman has not learned, as yet, to view the early signs of cancer as signs sufficient to merit medical consultation. Persons, of course, also sometimes visit the physician unnecessarily, thus, wasting valuable medical time. Physicians and others working on public health information programs have the difficult task of teaching laymen that some of the symptoms, often defined as minor, are important, indeed, and that early detection might greatly reduce the future consequences of the illness, while, at the same time, discouraging tendencies toward hypochondriasis.

These findings also have important implications from the point of view of medical research.

The data demonstrate that there are differential visiting patterns for different categories of illness. Thus, clinic and hospital cases used for the study of some illnesses, especially the more "routine" ones, may represent highly select and biased cases from which generalization may not be possible to the larger group of persons in the general population having that illness. The observation, for example, that persons who are ill (with whatever diagnosis) are also under stress is inadequate for any assertion of causality. Individuals with similar medical conditions who are not under stress may not seek medical advice. For some illnesses, at least, appearance in medical statistics may be as much a result of patterns of illness behavior and situational events as it is of the symptoms experienced.

If precise understanding of medical etiology is to be developed, and if health programs are to operate at maximum effectiveness, it is essential that we have a deeper understanding of the concept of illness behavior. It is necessary that we learn a good deal more about the various attitudes, values, and social definitions applied to symptoms, and how these influence the adoption of patient roles. What is equally important is that this understanding be used constructively and effectively in medical practice; and that the person be regarded as a social being with hopes and fears and varied predispositions which are influenced by the groups within which he lives.

REFERENCES

1. Mechanic, David: Illness and social disability—some problems in analysis, *Pacif. Sociol. Rev.* **2,** 37–41, 1959.
2. Mechanic, David and Volkart, Edmund H.: Illness behavior and medical diagnosis, *J. Hlth. Hum. Behavior.* **1,** 86–94, 1960.
3. Mechanic, David and Volkart, Edmund H.: Stress, illness behavior and the sick role, *Amer. Sociol. Rev.* **26,** 51–58, 1961.
4. Mechanic, David and Volkart, Edmund H.: *Interpersonal Worry and Doctor–Patient Relationship,* Paper read at the meetings of the American Sociological Association, St. Louis, Missouri, August, 1961
5. *Health Education Monographs,* Oakland, California Society of Public Health Educators.
6. Simmons, O. G.: *Social Status and Public Health,* Social Science Research Council Pamphlet 13, New York, 1958.
7. Koos, Earl: *The Health of Regionville: What the People Thought and Did about It,* Columbia University Press: New York, 1954.

8. Saunders, Lyle: *Cultural Differences and Medical Care,* Russell Sage Foundation, New York, 1954.

9. Sigerist, Henry E. The special position of the sick, in *Henry E. Sigerist on the Sociology of Medicine*, M. I. Roemer (ed.), New York, M. D. Publications, 1960.

10. Parsons, Talcott: *The Social System,* Chapter X, The Free Press, Glencoe, 1951.

11. Zborowski, Mark. Cultural components in responses to pain, *J. Soc. Issues.* **8,** 16–30, 1952.

DEVELOPED WORLD PERSPECTIVE

ILLNESS BEHAVIOUR IN CHINESE MEDICAL STUDENTS

Y. H. CHENG AND PETER W. H. LEE

Illness and health are relative to a set of norms which varies from time to time and from society to society. People who feel ill may have different responses towards their "dis-ease." Such reactions were defined by Mechanic and Volkart (1961) as "the way in which symptoms are perceived, evaluated and acted upon by a person who recognizes some pain, discomfort or other signs of organic malfunction." Illness is a subjective feeling about health-related problems (Fitzpatrick, 1986). Perception of a bodily or psychological state as a symptom of illness involves more than the initial awareness. It includes an evaluation that there may be something wrong with the individual him/herself (Miller & Miller, 1981). This process in recognizing something as "wrong" is inevitably coloured by social definitions, as well as the individual's knowledge and fear of the potential consequences of the suspected illness (Apple, 1960).

A person's perception and subsequent action in relation to the same set of symptoms may be highly variable. One person may hardly acknowledge an illness condition such that no alterations are effected in life. A different person may tolerate the symptoms and gradually accommodate himself to the associated deterioration. Still another with a milder form of the same condition will show immense social and psychological disabilities. Suchman (1965) divided the illness experience into five stages with concomitant psychological and behavioural changes. The patient is seen to proceed from

an initial stage of symptom experience, to the assumption of the sick role, medical care contact, dependent patient role and ultimate recovery. Dingwall (1976) however, was critical of such conceptualization on the grounds of its lack of a clear empirical reference. He noted that it is too rational of someone who is sick to consult doctor, receive treatment and recover. Scambler and Scambler (1984) also reported that the majority of illnesses are either ignored or receive non-medical attention. Last (1963) used the term "illness iceberg" to refer to the fact that most symptoms are not brought to the doctor's attention. Various studies (Wadsworth et al., 1971; Dunnell & Cartwright, 1972; Scambler, Scambler, & Craig, 1981) on different subject populations have demonstrated that it is very common for individuals to experience symptoms and illnesses. However, only a very small proportion of such symptoms will be presented to doctors. The proportion of symptoms and illnesses that comes into contact with the doctor forms only the tip of the iceberg. Health statistics are therefore not representative of all the symptoms people have suffered. A simplistic "stimulus-response" model is inadequate in explaining illness behaviour.

Factors like visibility of symptoms, perceived seriousness, disruptions caused, frequency and intensity of symptoms, and tolerance threshold also influenced the extent to which an individual defines himself as sick and his subsequent illness related behaviour (Mechanic, 1978). Lay referral systems

(Freidson, 1970) also play a part in help-seeking behaviour. When an individual feels sick, he may discuss his troubles with family members, neighbours, friends and workmates. As Freidson (1970) notes, the degree of congruence between the subcultures of the potential patient and that of the doctor and the relative number of lay consultants are two important aspects of the lay referral systems that affect the seeking of medical attention. The higher the degree of congruence of the two subcultures, the higher the chance the patient would go to see the doctor; and the more lay consultants, the more likely people are to be influenced by them. Illness experience is thus complexly determined.

Not only are there vast individual differences, responses to illness and disease are markedly different across cultures. Zborowski (1952) and Zola (1966) noted different responses to pain in different ethnic groups. The Chinese also have a culturally predetermined set of behaviours in response to ill-health largely influenced by traditional Chinese thought on health and illness. Concepts of the Doa (which means "the way") and the Yin and Yang are important landmarks in Chinese medical thought (Jewel, 1983). Doa, is the way of maintaining harmony between the secular world and beyond. Doa, as the supreme regulator of the universe, also prescribes a code of conduct for guiding behaviour in maintaining health. Yin and Yang are the primogenial elements from which the universe was evolved. Health is achieved when Yin and Yang are in harmony. Disharmony or undue predominance by either would result in ill-health and death. Qi (energy), on the other hand, is the source of life (Jewel, 1983; Koo, 1984). Health is the product of the sufficient accumulation and flow of qi in the body. Because of the Yin–Yang dualism, qualitative and polarized distinctions of qi in terms of "hot" and "cold" are held by the Chinese. If the body energy is not in balance, excess "hot" or "cold" will result and ailments will develop. Thus, when ill, especially with minor ailments, various dietary adjustments (e.g., intake of herbal tea) to re-establish the balance in the flow of "hot" and "cold" energy is common (Koo, 1984).

Illness behaviour in a group of Chinese preclinical medical students is studied in the present study. Medical students are chosen because of their unique socialization in both traditional Chinese and Western thoughts on health and illness. Our research questions are: Are there any differences in illness behaviour between the general public and the medical students? What is the nature of illness behaviour in a culture influenced by both Chinese and Western concepts of illness, health and treatment?

METHOD

143 second-year medical students of the University of Hong Kong participated in this study in January, 1986. Data for analyses were based on the health diaries conducted by subjects. Participation in the study was a compulsory part of the Behavioural Sciences subcourse on illness behaviour.

Subjects were asked to complete a health diary for one week. The health diary was divided into two parts. In the first part, subjects were asked to note down what they did about the symptoms experienced, the consequences and the reasons for their actions. In the second part, daily recordings were made of every symptom, illness and feeling of discomfort experienced. Statistical analysis of data was based on Eta-square (correlation ratio) and Gamma to measure the strength of association between variables. Chi-square (χ^2) and t tests were used to the test of significance with $p < 0.05$ accepted as a satisfactory level of significance.

RESULTS

143 health diaries (31 females and 112 males) were included for analysis. In the one-week study period, the number of symptoms experienced ranged from 0 to 11. The mean number of symptoms reported was 4. 4.9% of the students reported no symptom. Female subjects experienced a slightly higher mean number of symptoms compared with male subjects (4.3 compared to 4.05 respectively), but the association between sex and no. of symp-

toms experienced is very weak and the difference did not achieve a statistically significant level (eta-square = 0.65, $p < .633$).

11.2% of the students consulted a medical practitioner for their symptoms. No sex difference was noted in consulting behaviour. The majority of respondents (80.4%) took non-medical actions such as changing their diet or taking a rest. 45.5% of the respondents took non-prescribed medicine during the study period.

A higher number of symptoms experienced predicted an increased likelihood that subjects would talk with family members and significant others about their symptoms (eta-square = .434, $p < .001$). However, symptom frequency could only reduce 14% of the error in predicting whether or not someone consulted a doctor (eta-square = .140, $p < .538$).

Among the symptoms experienced, undue tiredness, running nose and headache were most frequently reported, comprising 10.1%, 9.9% and 9.0% of the overall reported symptoms respectively. Other symptoms noted were: poor sleep (6.2%), sore throat (6.1%), skin troubles (5.9%), cough (5.5%), muscle pain (5.4%), cold/flu (4.7%), and eye problems (4.3%). Including a category for unclassified symptoms (i.e. other), a total of 26 symptoms were reported in all (Table 1). Symptoms were subsequently classified into five groups. The two most prevalent groups were "psychosomatic" symptoms such as feeling miserable or depressed, undue tiredness, poor sleep, etc. (38.4%), and the group including fever, cough, sore throat, etc. (35.6%) (Table 2).

Only a very small proportion of respondents reported being anxious about the symptoms (3.3%) or felt that their symptoms were serious (5.5%). A very strong association was noted between perceived severity of symptoms and anxiety (Gamma = .87, $p < .001$).

A weak association was noted between sex and perceived severity of symptoms and anxiety (Gamma = .13, $p < .157$; Gamma = .14, $p < .476$). Perceived severity was, however, significantly related to endorsement of items on "talked to friends

TABLE 1 Types of Symptoms Experienced by the Respondents

SYMPTOM TYPE	SYMPTOM EXPERIENCED (%)
Fever	.3
Asthma	.2
Shortage of breadth	1.0
Cough	5.5
Sore throat	6.1
Running nose	9.9
Cold/flu	4.7
Headache	9.0
Diarrhea	1.2
Constipation	1.4
Stomach upset	2.6
Pains in chest	1.4
Pains in joints/limbs	3.1
Skin troubles	5.9
Eye problems	4.3
Dental problems	.7
Feeling miserable/depressed	4.9
Undue tiredness	10.1
Poor appetite	1.4
Poor sleep	6.2
Muscle pain	5.4
General weakness	3.5
Feeling anxious	3.5
Feeling easily irritated	2.3
Accidents	1.7
Others	3.8
	100.0

Total Number of Symptoms experienced = 577

or relatives about the symptom," "took medication for it," and "consulted a medical practitioner about it" (Table 3). Anxiety level exerted a similar relationship to the above variables with the exception of "took medication for the symptom" (Table 3). When compared with the value of Gamma, anxiety level had a better predictive power to the items of "talk to friends or relatives" and "consult doctor."

In terms of degree of disruption of normal functioning, 25.6% of the symptoms experienced had no disruptive effect at all. 48.4% of the symptoms experienced were reported to be mildly

TABLE 2   Symptoms Experienced by Two Classes of Students

	MEDIC 88		MEDIC 89	
SYMPTOM GROUP	f	%	f	%
Fever, cough, sore throat, running nose, cold/flu, headache	249	37.5	205	35.6
Asthma, shortage of breath	6	.9	7	1.2
Diarrhea, constipation, stomach upset	71	10.7	30	5.2
Pains in chest, pains in joints/limbs, skin troubles, eye problems, dental problems	147	22.1	89	15.4
Feeling miserable/depressed, undue tiredness, *poor appetite, *poor sleep, *muscle pain, *general weakness, *feeling anxious, *feeling easily irritated, accidents	145	21.8	224	38.8
Others	46	7.0	22	3.8
	664[a]	100.0	557[b]	100.0

*Items included in Medic 89 Study only.

[a]Total number of symptoms experienced by another 2nd year class in the previous year

[b]Total number of symptoms experienced by the subjects of the present study

TABLE 3   Subjective Estimates of Symptom Severity, Anxiety about Symptom and Relationship with Action Taken

	ESTIMATED SEVERITY				
	Mild (N = 260)	Moderate (N = 285)	Severe (N = 32)		
ACTION TAKEN	(% of Respondents Taking Action)			Gamma	χ^2
Talk to friends or relatives	25.4	37.5	75.0	0.39	***
Take medication	20.0	28.4	43.7	0.27	**
Consult doctor	2.3	4.6	15.6	0.47	**

	ESTIMATED ANXIETY				
	Mild (N = 423)	Moderate (N = 135)	Severe (N = 19)		
ACTION TAKEN	(% of Respondents Taking Action)			Gamma	χ^2
Talk to friends or relatives	26.5	51.1	84.2	0.55	***
Take medication	24.3	28.1	31.6	0.11	NS
Consult doctor	1.4	10.4	21.1	0.77	***

***$p < .001$ **$p < .01$

disrupting. Perceived severity and subsequent anxiety experienced were significantly related to daily life disruptions experienced (Table 4). The more severe and anxious one felt about the symptoms, the greater the degree of disruption experienced.

Consultation with a doctor was significantly influenced by the respondents' social contacts. When the discomforting symptom was reported to friends or relatives and advice was sought, respondents would most likely comply when the advice was to go to see a doctor (Gamma = −.93, $p < .001$).

DISCUSSIONS

Sex Difference

No sex difference was noted in the number of symptoms experienced and the frequency of consulting a doctor. The result seemed to contradict previous findings that utilization of health services is greater for females than males. For example, Cockerham (1978) noted that due to the different physiological structures between males and females, health service utilization is especially high during the female's childbearing years. According to the General Household Survey done in Hong Kong (H. K. Census & Statistics Department, 1984), the female consultation rate was noted to be higher than the male's from age 15 onwards. The lack of such sex differences in our present data was probably due to the unique nature of our student population compared to the general public. Females in the general public with a comparable age (in their twenty or early twenties) may be married and more likely to be child-bearing. However, our female students were still pursuing their education in medicine. The chances of getting married and having a baby or related physical ailments leading to increased contact with the doctor were therefore low.

The "Illness Iceberg" Effect

An "illness iceberg" effect was noted in our group of medical students. Relatively few symptoms

TABLE 4 Relationship between Degree of Disruption Caused by Discomfort and Subjective Estimates of Symptom Severity and Anxiety

	ESTIMATED SEVERITY				
	Mild (N = 260)	Moderate (N = 285)	Severe (N = 32)		
DEGREE OF DISRUPTION	%	%	%	Gamma	χ^2
Mild	95.0	60.7	21.9		
Moderate	5.0	35.8	46.9	0.85	***
Severe	0.0	3.5	31.2		

	ESTIMATED ANXIETY				
	Mild (N = 423)	Moderate (N = 135)	Severe (N = 19)		
DEGREE OF DISRUPTION	%	%	%	Gamma	χ^2
Mild	85.6	46.7	10.5		
Moderate	14.2	47.4	31.6	0.79	***
Severe	.2	5.9	57.9		

***$p < .001$

were experienced. Of those who experienced symptoms, 80.4% took various non-medical action (e.g. self-medication, changing their life style, or diet therapy). Self-prescription of over the counter medicine was high (45.5%). This was consistent with Kleinman's (1980) observation that in any complex society, a "popular sector" of health care can be easily found. When sick, people follow a "hierarchy of resort" ranging from self-medication to consultation with others (Helman, 1985). In our study, the use of patent medicines, traditional folk remedies, and changes in diet and behaviour were most commonly employed. A heavy emphasis on rest combined with the use of a household stock of medicines of a widely varied nature was prevalent. Western patent medicine, traditional Chinese herbal medicine, tonics, and commercially available patent medicine (a combination of both herbal and Western medicinal ingredients) from Mainland China were utilized. This practice of stocking a variety of medicines at home had been reported elsewhere and locally (Dunnell & Cartwright, 1972; Lee, 1972). The uniquely "local" practice, however, seemed to be that there is a systematic and logical pattern of choice between Western medicine, Chinese herbal medicine and tonics, and/or combination of herbal and Western medicine (as in Mainland China's manufactured patent medication). Lee (1975) noted that in the initial stage for common diseases, most Chinese resorted to self-medication. If discomfort and symptoms persist, people would consult with Chinese herbalists for treatment and advice on self help instructions. Consultation with Western trained doctors seemed to be more complexly determined, often resulting from initial stages of self help and traditional help failures. The disease model is then reluctantly taken up and the patient becomes less reliant on self help, succumbing oneself rather passively to the more technologically oriented practices of the doctor "expert." This deeply entrenched background of self help practice was evident even in our subjects, despite their being trained in the Western mode of medical practice. Health restoring behav-

iour exhibited was not necessarily in line with the formal training of our subjects. The situation is attributed to Chinese medical thought and the cultural practices among the Chinese. The emphasis on re-establishing the balance of the body energy by means of changing one's behaviour, adjusting one's diet and ingestion of suitable tonics is still widely prevalent in our subjects.

About 10% of those who experienced symptoms consulted a doctor. However, no hospital admissions were reported. It might be that no one experienced any symptoms of a serious enough nature to warrant hospitalization. On the other hand, hospitalization enforces a "sick role" in patients (Parsons, 1951). A person's adoption of the sick role is not straightforward or automatic. The keen competition and heavy "academic work" in our subjects would effectively deter any such health restoring role due to its severely disruptive effect on valued activities. This role priority as a successful student over that of a patient would make self-medication or simply taking no action for the "dis-ease" more attractive as a coping response (Robinson, 1973).

Symptoms Experienced

Stress related symptoms complicated by psychological states of the individual accounted for a significant proportion of the total reported symptoms (Table 2). The second term of the second year medical curriculum was usually regarded to be much more stress provoking than the first term with the introduction of additional topics and assignments. Results from a previous group of 2nd year students who completed their Health Diary practical a year before but in the 1st term indicated some interesting differences. The duration of the previous group's Health Diary lasted two weeks. After adjusting for duration of the health diary, it was noted that psychosomatic-related ailments accounted for just over one fifth of the total symptoms experienced (Table 2). The discrepancy in actual work demands and complexity between the two groups might in fact lead to differences in experience and reports of stress related symptoms.

Degree of Severity and Anxiety About Symptoms

Research indicates that symptoms which appear in a "striking" way (such as a sharp pain in any part of the body, or intense headache) are more likely to be considered seriously and more likely to prompt medical contacts than those which present themselves less dramatically (Mechanic, 1978; Scambler, 1986). Present results were in line with this formulation. The more severe the symptom was perceived, the more likely was one to talk to friends or relatives about the symptom, to take medication, and to bring the symptom to the doctor's attention. The perceived severity of experienced symptoms was also related to the extent of disruption of the subjects' daily life. The resultant anxiety and uncertainty was likely to cause increased attention to the symptoms to the neglect of normal daily life functions. Social support and reinforcement through sympathy and common advice to take a rest or "don't work too hard" would conceivably relieve some of the anxiety but at the same time might reinforce the severity suspected to start with. With increased social concern, it was also likely that individuals would experience and report more disruptions simply to justify to himself and others this increased privilege.

The extent to which anxiety alters an individual's recognition of symptoms and help seeking behaviour is complex (Mechanic, 1978). For instance, a high level of anxiety may lead to a denial of symptoms and in turn, may delay the seeking of competent help. However, probably due to the less dramatic symptoms reported in the health diary, a strong relationship between anxiety level and help-seeking behaviour was noted. Data reveal that anxiety is more predictive than severity in this instance. Anxiety seemed to function in prompting more communication with friends or relatives about the illness, leading to the increased likelihood of consulting a doctor. Interestingly enough,

anxiety level is not significantly related to self-medication. This calls attention to the multidimensional aspects of illness behaviour, of which different determinants need to be sought.

Lay Referral

Freidson (1970) postulated a consultation network which he named the "lay referral system." Whether or not people consult a doctor, seek alternative medical care, or choose to do nothing about their symptoms seemed to be dependent on whether the health seeking subculture is congruent with the professional subculture. Our data indicated that when advice was being sought from friends or relatives, and the advice was congruent to that of seeing a doctor, nearly half of the respondents actually paid a visit to the doctor's office. On the other hand, among those who were advised to do nothing, or where no direct mention of seeing a doctor was evident, doctor consultation was negligible. Thus, when the subculture of the lay referral system was congruent with the professional one, an increased utilization of health services was evident.

SUMMARY AND CONCLUSION

The present study was carried out in the form of health surveys. Therefore its share of the limitations inherent in such research methods needs to be taken into account when results are being interpreted. The data collected with such a method may be exaggerated and the actual health situation of the subjects studied may be overlooked. Reporting bias and inaccuracy may also be present. However, the large number of subjects studied and the consistency of our present findings with the existing literature tend to add weight to the credibility of our findings. It was noted that there are both common and unique features of illness behaviour and symptom experiences in the medical students studied. Sex differences had a weak association with symptom experience and frequency of medical consultation. Psychosomatic related ailments was noted to be prevalent and closely related to academic work pressure. The iceberg effect in symptom reporting was evident. Subjective estimates of symptom severity and perceived anxiety were predictive of talking to friends, consulting a doctor and the amount of disruption of normal functioning reported. The "lay referral" effect in predicting help seeking behaviour was also clearly demonstrated. Subjects' self medication/treatment behaviour was influenced heavily by traditional Chinese medical thought despite their ongoing secondary socialization in Western medicine. Chinese lay beliefs and remedies on health and disease were highly prominent in influencing health actions and thinking. An interesting research question is whether the influence of such lay practice and conceptions would be diminished in the later years of medical training. A further longitudinal perspective tracing the changes and consistencies in health actions and thinking of this group of medical students would be particularly worthwhile especially in the light of the mix of Western and Chinese culture in the Hong Kong society.

REFERENCES

Apple, D. 1960. How laymen define illness. *Journal of Health and Human Behavior,* **1,** 219–225.

Cockerham, W. C. 1978. *Medical sociology.* New Jersey: Prentice Hall.

Dingwall, R. 1976. *Aspects of illness.* London: Martin Robertson.

Dunnell, K., & Cartwright, A. 1972. *Medicine—Takers, prescribers and hoarders.* London: Routledge & Kegan Paul.

Fitzpatrick, R. M. 1986. Social concepts of disease and illness. In D. L. Patrick & G. Scambler (Eds.), *Sociology as applied to medicine.* London: Bailliere Tindall.

Freidson, E. 1970. *Profession of medicine.* New York: Dodd, Mead & Company.

Helman, C. 1985. *Culture, health and illness.* Bristol: Wright.

Hong Kong, Census and Statistics Department. 1984. *Social data collected by the General Household Survey. Special topics report II.* Hong Kong: Government printer.

Jewel, J. A. 1983. Theoretical basis of Chinese traditional medicine. In S. M. Hiller & J. A. Jewell (Eds.), *Health care and traditional medicine in China, 1800–1982.* London: Routledge & Kegan Paul.

Kleinman, A. 1980. *Patients and healers in the context of culture.* Berkeley: University of California Press.

Koo, L. C. 1984. The use of food to treat and prevent disease in Chinese culture. *Social Science and Medicine* **18,** 757–766.

Last, J. M. 1963. The iceberg: Completing the clinical picture in general practice. *Lancet,* **2,** 28–31.

Lee, R. P. L. 1972. *Study of health systems in Kwun Tong: Preliminary research report no. 1. Health attitudes and behaviour on Chinese residents.* Hong Kong: Social Research Centre, Chinese University of Hong Kong.

Lee, R. P. L. 1975. Interaction between Chinese and Western medicine in Hong Kong: Modernization and professional inequality. In A. Kleinman et al. (Eds.), *Medicine in Chinese cultures: Comparative studies of health care in Chinese and other societies.* U.S. Department of Health, Education and Welfare, Public Health Service, National Institutes of Health.

Mechanic, D. 1978. *Medical sociology.* New York: Free Press.

Mechanic, D., & Volkart, E. H. 1961. Stress, illness behaviour and the sick role. *American Sociological Review,* **26,** 51–58.

Miller, A. E., & Miller, M. G. 1981. *Options for health and health care.* New York: Wiley.

Parsons, T. 1951. *The social system.* London: Routledge & Kegan Paul.

Robinson, D. 1973. *Patients, practitioners and medical care.* London: William Heinemann Medical Books.

Scambler, A., Scambler, G., & Craig, D. 1981. Kinship and friendship networks and women's demand for primary care. *Journal of Royal College of General Practitioners,* **31,** 746–750.

Scambler, G. 1986. Illness behaviour. In D. L. Patrick & G. Scambler (Eds.), *Sociology as applied to medicine.* London: Bailliere Tindall.

Scambler, G., & Scambler, A. 1984. The illness iceberg and aspects of consulting behaviour. In R. Fitzpatrick et al. (Eds.), *The experience of illness.* London: Tavistock.

Suchman, E. A. 1965. Social patterns of illness and medical care. *Journal of Health and Human Behavior,* **6,** 114–128.

Wadsworth, M. E. J., Butterifield, W. J. H., & Blaney, R. 1971. *Health and sickness: The choice of treatment.* London: Tavistock.

Zborowski, M. 1952. Cultural components in response to pain. *Journal of Social Issues,* **8,** 16–30.

Zola, I. K. 1966. Culture and symptoms: An analysis of patient's presenting complaints. *American Sociological Review,* **31,** 615–630.

DEVELOPING WORLD PERSPECTIVE

ILLNESS BEHAVIOR AND THE HEALTH TRANSITION IN THE DEVELOPING WORLD

NICHOLAS A. CHRISTAKIS, NORMA C. WARE, AND ARTHUR KLEINMAN

INTRODUCTION

The "health transition" refers to the ongoing, worldwide increase in life expectancy that has occurred since the beginning of the twentieth century, more especially since the 1960s. In the 25 years from 1960 to 1985, global life expectancy at birth increased from approximately 48 to 59 years. Since this increase occurred in all regions of the world, the mortality differential between the developed and developing world has persisted (United Nations 1985).

The health transition also encompasses the changing configuration of causes of death and the changing character of morbidity. Acute infectious disease now accounts for less of the morbidity burden in some countries (although it remains a serious problem in sub-Saharan Africa, India, and the Middle East), while chronic disease (e.g., heart disease, stroke, and cancer) and behavioral problems (e.g., substance abuse, child abuse, depression, anxiety disorders, and suicide) account for more. This has resulted in a so-called "triple burden" of acute illness, chronic illness, and behavioral pathology in the Third World. Medically speaking, then, the health transition has three essential aspects: a decline in mortality, a change in morbidity, and an increase in behavioral pathology.[1]

John Caldwell has cogently argued that the positive aspects of the health transition have resulted from the complex and synergistic interplay of modernizing social forces (e.g., urbanization, economic development, mass communication, and improved education) and direct biomedical interventions, such as childhood immunization, oral rehydration therapy, and village health systems (1986). This proposition is based on the premise that as a result of modernization, people in the developing world are somehow increasing their use of available biomedical health resources in ways that result in prolonged life and improved health. Generally, the argument is that in the developing world—under the pressures of modernization and socioeconomic change—people consider biomedicine to be more effective than traditional medicine, that they avail themselves of biomedicine whenever possible, that biomedicine is increasingly accessible, that biomedicine is indeed more effective than traditional medicine, and that, as a result of all these, health improves.

Recognizing the value of this theoretical contribution to our understanding of the health transition, this chapter seeks to build upon Caldwell's formulation by probing some of the complexities it subsumes. The analysis is intended to show how these two types of factors—modernizing social forces and biomedical interventions—might result in the changes that characterize the health transition, and also how they are actually placed out in local cultural settings in the developing world. A review of cross-cultural studies reveals that "biomedicine" assumes different forms in different contexts, and that it is not always either the preferred mode of healing or the most effective one.

By focusing on one aspect of modernizing socioeconomic change—maternal education—and by documenting cultural differences in the perception and use of biomedicine in situations of medical pluralism, we hope to demonstrate convincingly that any adequate explanation of the health transition must take local cultural variation into account. To organize and concretize the discussion of local differences, we will draw upon the notion of illness behavior—the constellation of meanings and activities exhibited by an individual and his or her social circle in response to bodily indications perceived as symptoms (Mechanic 1978).

Our primary aim here, then, is to advance the theoretical proposition that the effects of both modernizing social change and biomedical interventions upon health status in the developing world are mediated by local-level processes, in particular, illness behavior.

The available cross-cultural data suggest not only that illness behavior is a mediating variable in the health transition, but also that it is undergoing change. Worldwide transformations in health status are leading to rapid changes in illness behavior, at the same time that illness behavior—often motivated by large-scale socioeconomic changes—is producing changes in health. In short, illness behavior is dynamic. Thus, our second aim is to argue that illness behavior should be considered part of the health transition.

ILLNESS BEHAVIOR

In a given individual or social network, illness behavior involves monitoring the body, recognizing and interpreting symptoms, and taking remedial action (e.g., seeking lay or professional help) to rectify the perceived abnormality. Help may be sought from a number of sources in the patient's social network, including friends, family, folk heal-

ers, and professionals. To focus on illness behavior is to emphasize the response of human beings to morbidity—to sickness and suffering—rather than to mortality *per se.*

Illness behavior also encompasses the ongoing response of the sick individual and those around him or her to the course of the illness. Examples here include attention to symptoms, compliance with therapeutic advice, changes in treatment regimens, and evaluation of therapeutic efficacy and outcome.

The notion of illness behavior should be distinguished from that of health behavior. The latter includes advertent and inadvertent behaviors that maintain health, or, conversely, place persons and groups at risk for ill health. Thus, behavioral risk factors for acute infectious diseases (e.g., hygienic practices, sexual behaviors) and for chronic conditions (e.g., cigarette smoking, alcohol and drug abuse, dietary practices) can be thought of as health behaviors, as can practices that are health enhancing (e.g., exercise, proper diet).

Thus, we see that illness behavior is one component of the larger category of health behavior. Although illness behavior is the primary focus of this discussion, we will also consider health enhancing behaviors (e.g., maintenance of adequate nutrition or use of vaccination services) that are initiated in the absence of illness. Health behavior and illness behavior are inextricably linked.

Included under the rubric of illness behavior is what is termed the health- or help-seeking process—a series of activities aimed at rectifying the perceived aberration in the individual's state of health (Chrisman 1977). Help-seeking begins with symptom definition or an evaluation of the bodily problem. A strategy for responding to the symptoms, the treatment action plan, is then devised. Treatment action may involve any combination of self care, family care, and care from folk and professional healers. The degree to which this plan is carried out by the ill person and his/her family is termed adherence (or compliance). Adherence is in turn strongly influenced by an ongoing evaluation of outcome. Both symptom definition and treatment action are affected by lay consultation and referral and by the social networks in which the individual participates.

HEALER CHOICE IN MEDICALLY PLURALISTIC CULTURAL SETTINGS: A PREFERENCE FOR BIOMEDICINE?

Cross-cultural data on illness behavior from situations of medical pluralism in the developing world indicate that both the perceived efficacy of biomedicine and the decision to use biomedical services are highly variable and subject to influence by a number of intervening factors.

Medical pluralism, or the existence of several distinct therapeutic systems in a single cultural setting, is an especially important feature of medical care in the developing world (Leslie 1978). Patients may feel uncertain as to what type of care provider can cure their illness, leading them to consult both traditional and biomedical practitioners. Or they may decide that treatment of certain illnesses requires more than one type of assistance. Generally, care is sought from several types of providers concurrently or sequentially, and the various types of care are often seen as complementary rather than conflicting.

Biomedicine is often highly regarded in the developing world—but not unequivocally so. Many studies, in fact, have shown that from the point of view of the patient, modern health services are often seen as no more effective than traditional medicine. For example, a study of illness behavior in Ethiopia found that traditional medicine was felt to be as effective as modern medicine in curing a variety of complaints (Kloos et al. 1987). Even in industrial East Asia, traditional medicine is often viewed as more effective than biomedicine for certain conditions, usually chronic disease (Locke 1980). Similarly, research in Singapore revealed that nearly 60 percent of patients visiting a traditional Chinese doctor reported effectiveness as their major reason for choosing such treatment (Ho, Lun

and Ng 1984). Only a small minority gave "traditional beliefs" (7 percent) or cost (10 percent) as their major reasons for consulting a traditional practitioner. Indeed, patients in this setting had a well-articulated set of expectations regarding which type of healer—"Western" or "traditional Chinese"—was preferable for various conditions.[2] Finally, Sargent (1982) describes a setting in Benin where traditional birth attendants are perceived as more effective—and may actually be more effective—than biomedical services.[3] Indeed, perceived efficacy may accurately reflect actual efficacy. But the critical point is that it is perceived efficacy that guides healer choice.[4] In a study of the efficacy of traditional and modern healers in Taiwan, Kleinman and Gale (1982) compared matched sets of patients treated by shamans and physicians for similar illnesses. Overall, the two groups showed similar patterns of improvement across illness types. Efficacy was examined using both subjective measures (e.g., patient assessment of the effect of practitioner on outcome) and objective measures (evaluation of outcome by the research team).

Patient and community preferences for indigenous healing systems often reflect the realities of how biomedicine is practiced in much of the developing world. In fact, biomedical practice in third world settings is inadequate in a number of ways. A typical encounter between patient and health care provider may last less than two minutes (Reid 1984). Descriptions of symptoms may be limited to a single sentence. Physical or laboratory examinations may be cursory or even nonexistent. Potentially toxic medication may be prescribed without either a full course of treatment or follow-up to determine subsequent effects (Weisberg and Long 1984). Iatrogenesis, inappropriate and inadequate treatment, and failure to properly inform patients and families of potential toxicity or alternative treatment options are commonplace. Primary health care units are often staffed by practitioners who are absent while performing more lucrative private services or by medical students and junior nurses whose training is inadequate. Care may even be delivered by staff who lack the most basic medical knowledge, as has been reported in Nepal (Justice 1986).

The existence of biomedical services in the vicinity of ill people does not mean that these services will be utilized, even if they are perceived as efficacious. In an Ecuadorian Indian community, for example, the home is regarded as a refuge from illness, while the outside world is considered to be disease-promoting. Thus, one study of a Saraguro community demonstrated that Indian mothers chose to avoid therapeutic care, whether professional or traditional, that was delivered outside the home (Finerman 1987). In other research, Guatemalan peasants were shown to avoid government facilities that provided biomedical care because they lacked drugs and equipment (Annis 1981).

Young (1981a, 1981b) found that in one Mexican village the critical considerations in the decision not to use a physician were of three types: (1) preexisting preference for folk treatment, which was considered to offer a higher likelihood of cure (21 percent), (2) access problems, such as lack of money or transportation (58 percent), and (3) recent experience of failure in attempting to achieve a cure through consulting a physician (21 percent). Thus, while nearly half of the choices not to consult a physician in this Mexican village were based on perceived or proven lack of efficacy, slightly more than half were based on logistic concerns.

The results of an epidemiological study following a major outbreak of polio in Taiwan in 1982 further demonstrate that the availability of effective biomedical interventions does not *ipso facto* ensure that they will be used (Kim-Farley et al. 1984). Surveys in two counties, Yun Lin and Chia Yi, indicated that despite community-wide vaccination programs, the spread of the disease reached epidemic proportions. The most important risk factor for developing polio in this case was clearly the failure to vaccinate. An unvaccinated child was found to be 80 times more likely to contract polio than a child who had received three or more doses of vaccine. Less significant

risk factors included, in decreasing order of importance, non-municipal water supply (making a child five times more likely to develop the disease), sharing of toilets by more than one family, fathers who were unemployed or in unskilled jobs, and fathers with little education. The investigators were unable to determine, however, whether these other factors contributed independently to polio incidence or simply correlated with failure to vaccinate (Morbidity and Mortality Weekly Report 1983). Clearly, an appropriate biomedical resource, namely polio vaccination, was available in this case. However, noncompliance with the recommendation to vaccinate prevented the biomedical intervention from averting the epidemic.

The distance that must often be traveled to reach a biomedical practitioner in contrast to various types of traditional healers also represents a significant constraint on the use of biomedicine.[5] A study of physician use in northern Nigeria found that per capita utilization of local government health dispensaries declined at a rate of 25% per kilometer (Stock 1983; Ayeni, Rushton and McNulty 1987). Distance has also been shown to reduce pharmacy use in Ethiopia (Kloos et al. 1986).

Research in Bangladesh has revealed a strong correlation between distance to a diarrhea clinic and visits to the clinic when an episode of diarrhea occurs. While about 95 percent of all episodes occurring in patients who lived within one mile resulted in visits to the clinic, only about 35 percent (for females) and 70 percent (for males) of episodes occurring to patients who lived between two and three miles from the clinic were treated there (Rahaman et al. 1982).

Annis (1981) provides further evidence of the limiting effect of distance on the use of biomedical services. Citing data from the highland provinces of Guatemala, Annis observed that while only 16 percent of the local population lived within one kilometer of the health post, more than 50 percent of patient visits were made by persons living within this immediate area. Conversely, patients living more than 3.5 kilometers from the health post accounted for only 15 percent of post visits, even though more than half the population of the area lived at this distance.

The difficulty in reaching biomedical practitioners may be contrasted with the availability of the more popular varieties of traditional healers. For example, in several rural and urban Brazilian communities studied by Nations and Rebhun (1988), the population ratio of traditional healers was 1:150 in the rural communities and about 1:75 in the urban shantytown. The corresponding ratio for biomedical physicians was 1:2,000. Data from Bangladesh yield ratios for traditional healers and allopathic practitioners of 1:240 and 1:400 respectively (Sarder and Chen 1981). Finally, Ahern's (1978) research in Taipei suggests that "symbolic distance" can influence the use of biomedical practitioners, who are perceived as symbolically "more distant" from the experiential world of patients than are traditional healers.

Other sociocultural differences may also work against the use of biomedicine. Welch (1980) explains that a health post set up for the Ningerum of Papua New Guinea was at one point not widely used because the clinic staff, being from another region, were regarded by the local population as a potential source of sorcery. In rural Nepal, Justice (1986) has shown that primary health care workers are perceived as unreceptive and inaccessible to local peasants, who have therefore turned to the health center's "peon"—an uneducated handyman and member of the local community—for assistance with health problems.

In his study of disease classification and health behavior in rural Ghana, Fosu (1981) concludes that the perceived cause of a disease determines the choice between traditional healers and local biomedical clinics. The inhabitants of Bereduso, Ghana, classify diseases as being caused by natural agents, supernatural agents, or both. Fosu found that for diseases considered to have a natural cause, 3 percent of patients consulted a traditional healer, while 53 percent sought help at a local clinic. However, for diseases considered to have a supernatural cause, 31 percent consulted a traditional healer while only 15 percent turned to the clinic. A mixed pattern of consultation emerged for diseases seen as having both kinds of causes. Significantly, diseases such as tuberculosis, insanity, epilepsy, pneumonia, asthma, and leprosy were all felt to have supernatural causes. In other words, those diseases perceived to be appropriately treated by biomedicine are sometimes not the ones for which effective therapy exists; alternatively, those diseases perceived to be appropriately treated by local healers are sometimes those for which biomedicine is effective.

A final set of variables that influence the choice of a healer are the patient's personal attributes, such as age, sex, education, residence, and occupation. Visits to a diarrhea clinic in rural Bangladesh, for example, were shown to be significantly associated with the patient's age and sex; older females and younger males tended to make fewer visits when ill (Rahaman et al. 1982).

The use of medical services for sick infants is profoundly influenced by the child's sex, with utilization rates often being considerably lower for females (McCormack 1988). Das Gupta (1989) demonstrates that in rural Punjab, the second and third female children, in particular, receive less expert attention for illness episodes. Citing research in South Indian villages, Caldwell (personal communication) has observed that when seeking treatment for sick children meant traveling outside the village to the nearest health center, boys were more likely to be brought to the clinic than girls. Since traveling to the health center meant taking time off from work, fathers brought children to the clinic on the weekly market day. They were more likely to bring sons than daughters because of concerns about leaving small girls in the marketplace all day.

The point here is that treatment decisions in the medically pluralistic settings typical of the developing world are complex. In reviewing selected cross-cultural research on illness behavior, we see that the choice of a healer is shaped by a wide range of factors, among them perceptions of efficacy, practice considerations (such as distance), symbolic considerations (such as the experiential distance between patient and practitioner), the perceived cause of the ailment and whether it is viewed as life threatening, and personal attributes of the patient. This body of research shows that the existence of biomedicine as a treatment option does not mean that it will be the preferred choice.

SOCIOECONOMIC CHANGE MODIFIES ILLNESS BEHAVIOR: THE CASE OF MATERNAL EDUCATION

Maternal education provides a good tool with which to examine the issue of primary interest here: the relationship between the health transition, biomedical health interventions, and macrolevel socioeconomic change.

It has been repeatedly observed that societies with the highest levels of maternal education (which also tend to be those with the greatest female autonomy) are likely to show the highest rates of infant survival and to appear "healthier" according to other indexes. This is true of both developing and developed countries.[6] The reduction of illness and death among infants has a more profound impact on the overall health status of a country than do corresponding decreases in mortality and morbidity in adults. Indeed, some of the greatest gains of the health transition may have resulted from changes in the care of infants, that is, adult illness behavior directed toward the very young.

Analyzing data from the 1973 Nigerian segment of the Changing African Family Project, Caldwell (1979) points to maternal education as the single most significant determinant of observed differences in child mortality. His subsequent discussion of the possible explanations for this phenomenon posits two intervening factors in this relationship: increased use of Western biomedical services and changes in the "traditional balance of familial relationships." The latter is seen as acting through both a redistribution of family resources in the direction of child care (at the instigation of the mother) and an increase in maternal assertiveness.

This, in turn, leads to increased use of medical care, particularly biomedical care, for children.

This is in some ways a valid argument. However, increased use of modern medical alternatives available to traditional women may not be the most important way in which maternal education works to improve health status. The significance of illness behavior as an intervening variable seems to be far greater.

The following is intended to broaden existing conceptualizations of the impact of educated mothers upon child health by reviewing the cross-cultural literature on illness behavior in relation to maternal education and the health status of children. Again, building on previous thinking in this area, we aim to document the complexity of this relationship by (1) reflecting on the nature of education for women in the developing world, (2) suggesting that maternal education works through a variety of mechanisms to affect child health, and (3) proposing that seeking biomedical care may be only part of a larger phenomenon that is influenced not only by maternal education, but by other key social changes as well. We emphasize that our theoretical model is one that is partially supported by the literature. In short, while illness behavior helps to explain some of the effect of maternal education, it cannot explain all of it.

In much of the developing world, education for women often means one-to-six years of primary education. Any putative effect of maternal education upon child health must therefore somehow be realized on the basis of as little as one or two years in school. This simple observation strongly suggests that it is not the content of what is taught in school that is important, since health education *per se* is unlikely to be part of such limited schooling.

Since education seems to teach young girls something besides content, it is critical to disentangle the other strands of this social intervention in order to understand its impact on health status. One of these strands might be the ancillary benefits that accrue from the very "experience" of going to school. Another is the fact that education may make a woman more desirable as a spouse, thereby leading to marriage to a wealthier man, greater economic resources, and, as a result, improved health status for her children. Attending school may keep a young girl out of a dangerous work environment, thereby preserving her health for future pregnancies and increasing the birth weight (and consequent health) of her children.[7] Data from Malaysia suggest that education for women may result in postponed marriage, meaning that a mother will be older when her children are delivered. This also promotes child survival (DeVanzo 1984).

In their review of maternal education and child survival in developing countries, Cleland and van Ginneken conclude that "health beliefs and domestic practices" are essential to an explanation of the relationship between maternal education and child mortality (1988). Citing data from the United Nations and the World Bank, they show that, on average, each one-year increment in women's education corresponds to a 7 to 9 percent decline in deaths of children under five years of age. The effect is more pronounced in childhood than in infancy. After considering a number of mediating factors that might account for this effect, the authors conclude that increased education has little impact on such changes in reproductive behavior as birth spacing or nutritional practices during pregnancy. Rather, they argue that about half of the gross effect of maternal education actually reflects the economic advantages associated with education, such as clothing, housing quality, and other ancillary benefits.

Overall, however, Cleland and van Ginneken seem to agree with other authors that exposure to Western medicine necessarily results in improved health, the implication being that maternal education enhances health by increasing the use of biomedical health services. For example, the authors assume that substitution of modern drugs sold in pharmacies for traditional herbal remedies results in improved self-care.

At the same time, Cleland and van Ginneken conclude that the effect of maternal education "transcends access to modern health services" and that "it appears probable that domestic behavior is the key to the enhanced survivorship of children born to educated mothers" (1988: 1365). They postulate a number of effects of maternal education upon attitudes, including two that are not supported by the anthropological literature. These are, first, that compared to the uneducated, educated mothers "attach a higher value to the welfare and health of children," and second, that they are "less fatalistic about disease and death."

In fact, considerable empirical evidence supports the contention that maternal education has a broad range of effects upon illness behavior aside from fostering the use of biomedical services. Moreover, these effects may themselves work to improve health status.

Maternal education influences each of the following aspects of the help-seeking process: symptom definition, treatment action, adherence to treatment, evaluation of outcome, and social networks and lay consultation.[8] Maternal education influences symptom definition in a number of ways, some of which have been documented in developing world settings. Spending some time in school, even if what is taught there is not immediately relevant to health and disease, can help to develop certain cognitive abilities in ways that facilitate the identification of bodily symptoms. Learning new modes of categorization, for example, can mean that symptoms will be more readily classified as indications of illness or not, and that categories of illness will tend to be distinguished from one another (Tsui, DeClerque and Mangani 1988).

The ability to recognize the presence of illness may also be enhanced by education, as research by Das Gupta (1989) in rural Punjab, Levine et al. (1987) in urban Mexico, and McClain (1977) in Mexico suggests. Often, the content of education is ineffective in changing beliefs about disease causation and health maintenance. In some situations, however, the content of education has been shown to have a meaningful impact in such diverse areas as nutrition, sanitation, and family planning (Das Gupta 1989).

Maternal education is also related to treatment action. Changes in this aspect of illness behavior, influenced by maternal education, have been claimed to result in the increased use of biomedical services (Caldwell 1979; Cleland and van Ginneken 1988).

Most examinations of the impact of maternal education on health practices have focused upon only a small part of treatment action. The education of mothers may contribute to a change from the more person-oriented view associated with peasant and working classes to an institution-oriented view found in professional and managerial circles. As a result, maternal education can bring about an increased ability to negotiate with medical institutions.

Schooling may increase a woman's ability to procure health care in a number of ways. For example, it may foster an appreciation of institutional time, which in turn may increase access to knowledge and assistance (Lindenbaum 1990). Educated women may also be more familiar with, and therefore better skilled in handling, the interrogatory style of health care providers, especially biomedical practitioners. And education may function as a form of assertiveness training, making women more likely to leave the local area in search of health care for their dependents (Caldwell 1986).

On a practical level, maternal education influences treatment action insofar as it makes educated women better financial managers. Good financial management expands options for therapy in times of sickness (Cominsky 1987). The content of what is taught may also help mothers to choose appropriate healers and therapy (e.g., oral rehydration for diarrhea, spiritual healers for possession) and to understand disease causation (which might lead to better hygiene).

Maternal education affects adherence to treatment. Education may increase mothers' abilities to comprehend medical recommendations and to remember them or write them down accurately. With respect to cognitive development, education may modify a patient's construction of reality so that it is easier for her to assimilate and accept medical recommendations (McClain 1977). A woman's experience in school may make her more comfortable with outsiders, thereby increasing her trust in health care workers and her willingness to follow potentially efficacious medical advice.

Evaluation of treatment outcomes may vary with mothers' educational levels. A mother with little education may mistakenly decide a child is no longer ill, seriously ill, or in need of further therapy. Such decisions may result in inappropriate termination of certain potentially effective forms of care. Chronic diarrhea, for example, may be accepted as normal and therapy may be arrested.[9]

Education also has a number of predictable and documented effects upon a mother's social networks and practices of lay consultation. In many developing countries, women marry and have children when they are still very young, often by age 16. In such settings, providing even two years of primary schooling for girls is a relatively recent innovation. For these women, being in school may increase the size and sophistication of the social network, giving them access to more resourceful lay consultants.

Borrowing the terms of social network theory, school experience may increase the range and decrease the insularity of a woman's network by improving her marriage prospects and taking her into the outside world (Lindenbaum 1990). Through its effect on social networks, school experience may increase the size of the therapy management group (Janzen 1978). A women's rhetorical competence (based on a sense of self-efficacy) at communicating her concerns regarding her own illness or those of her dependents to members of her social network or family may benefit from education. For example, in Bangladesh, educated women have higher status within the family and are better able to marshal resources for the care of the ill (Lindenbaum 1990).

Maternal education has a number of predictable and demonstrated effects upon the home environment. Educated women have been shown to maintain cleaner households (Bertrand and Walmus

1988), to be better financial providers, and to provide better nutrition for their children, all of which potentially decrease disease incidence. Literacy may also facilitate the use of sanitary facilities, such as piped water, in a way that reduces the onset of disease (Esrey and Habicht 1988). Das Gupta (1989) found that better educated mothers provide more hygienic conditions for their children.

Evidence that maternal education may lead to increased illness should also be noted here. For example, educated mothers have been shown to breastfeed less (Caldwell and McDonald 1982; Goldberg et al. 1984). They are also more likely to seek employment outside the home (Farah and Preston 1982; Hobcraft, McDonald and Rustein 1984), which might adversely affect child health if there were less direct supervision of children as a result.

Our intention here has been to lay out some of the ways in which maternal education, one of many possible examples of large-scale socioeconomic change in modernizing societies, can be expected to modify health and illness behavior. All of these behavioral changes may in turn work to improve health status. Quicker identification of symptoms and more accurate recognition of disease, recourse to more appropriate or effective healers, improved compliance with recommendations that increase efficacy and reduce iatrogenesis, more appropriate evaluation of outcome, and favorable modifications of risk factors, such as diet, hygiene, and parenting practices, may all exert a positive influence on health. We now look at ways in which Western biomedicine, as it becomes an integral part of indigenous cultures, is itself modifying illness behavior.

CHANGING PATTERNS OF ILLNESS BEHAVIOR ARE PART OF THE HEALTH TRANSITION

An integral part of the health transition is an ongoing evolution in illness behavior. The health transition involves not only change in the patterning of health indicators, but also a transition in the use of health services. This is often best appreciated at the local level.

The transition in illness behavior is driven by particular aspects of traditional and cosmopolitan medical practice in the modern world. These include the proliferation of Western pharmaceuticals and convergence in the content of traditional and cosmopolitan medicine in many developing societies. Stated in general terms, illness behavior is changing under the pressure of the same social changes and health inputs that have given rise to the health transition.

Pharmaceuticals

The widespread distribution of Western pharmaceuticals, the proliferation of pharmacies throughout the developing world, the growth of indigenous pharmaceutical companies, and the fact that these companies often conduct their own research have all had a dramatic impact upon illness behavior in developing countries.

For many of the rural and urban poor in the developing world, the pharmacy is the only contact with the Western health care system. In El Salvador, for example, 55 percent of poor families and 23 percent of upper-class families in one study were shown to rely on commercial pharmaceutical practitioners as their primary source of health care (Ferguson 1988). The implications of this are clear. The easy availability of "prescription" drugs in the developing world and the ordinarily poor training of pharmacists who stand to benefit financially from the sale of their wares can lead to significant iatrogenesis and inappropriate drug use. This has been documented both in the highly urban setting of Seoul, Korea (Kim 1989), and in a more rural setting in Taiwan (Kahane 1987).

Pharmacists in the developing world dispense more than drugs. They also offer medical advice and function as comprehensive health care providers. As a result, pharmacists are perceived as being very similar to doctors. For example, Logan reports that in urban Mexico, "many people routinely consulted the local pharmacist 'almost like a doctor' [*casi como doctor*]. They presented their physical complaints and described their symptoms, expecting the pharmacists to diagnose their illnesses and to prescribe treatment. The pharmacists obliged their clients by labelling their illnesses and by selling them the pharmaceutical preparations they recommended.... [Moreover], many people self-diagnosed their illness and medicated themselves..." (Logan 1988).

Pharmacists are often preferred as care providers for some of the same reasons folk healers are preferred over physicians: they treat patients more politely, offer faster service, are more convenient, and have adequate supplies on hand. Both the care and the medications provided by pharmacists are often regarded as superior. Lay pharmacists in Guatemala, for example, are highly regarded as care providers; they are popular because of their easy accessibility, familiarity with the local people, and the fact that they extend credit (Cominsky and Scrimshaw 1980). In El Salvador, Ferguson argues, village pharmacy personnel "serve as interpreters between different medical care traditions, gleaning what they can from information they receive regarding Western medications and relying to a large extent on shared cultural understandings of the nature and treatment of illness" (Ferguson 1988: 31). The information pharmacists rely on, in general, is provided by sales representatives of local distributors.

The rampant misuse of pharmaceuticals in the developing world takes many forms. A recent study of self-medication practices in Brazil and the Philippines reveals that in both countries, antibiotics are applied as crushed powder to wounds and skin lesions, as well as taken internally (Haak and Hardon 1988). Ferguson (1988) reports having observed mothers giving babies a teaspoon of tetracycline daily "as a preventive measure," despite the fact that the drug is contraindicated for use in small children. Pills are often packaged individually in the developing world. Patients may buy no more than four pills, regardless of their complaint or the medicine's effect. Injections tend to be highly regarded in developing societies; they are felt to be intrinsically stronger and preferable, especially for

serious illness. In fact, the last few decades have seen the emergence of a wholly new type of health care provider: the itinerant injectionist. Patients demand injections (Cunningham 1970; Kleinman 1980; Good 1987).

Western medicines are available not only through biomedical practitioners and pharmacists. Traditional healers throughout the world are increasingly using Western drugs. In one study in Bangladesh, for example, 30 percent of homeopaths and 5 percent of traditional healers were found to be using allopathic drugs; 44 percent and 3 percent, respectively, were giving injections (Sarder and Chen 1981). Ninety percent of Indian traditional healers in another study made some use of Western drugs (Bhatia et al. 1975). Wolffers (1988, 1989) found that 50 percent of traditional practitioners in a rural community in Sri Lanka used Western drugs such as narcotics, antibiotics, and steroids. These practices are rationalized as being a response to the growing demand for pharmaceuticals from patients who are increasingly familiar with the procedures of biomedicine, and who expect comparable interventions from traditional healers.

Finally, we should note those instances in which the distribution of pharmaceuticals has moved beyond the domain of biomedical practitioners, pharmacists, and even traditional healers, into the hands of local entrepreneurs. For example, Whyte (1991) reports that in Uganda, hospital workers (not only doctors, but also nurses, aides, drivers, and janitorial staff) supplement their income by setting up small businesses, or "private clinics," for dispensing Western medicines that they may have appropriated from the government clinics where they work. Those who manage to procure a steady supply of drugs develop a reputation as informal medical practitioners in the community. Untrained and eager to make a profit, these practitioners tend to furnish medicines indiscriminately, invoking local cultural knowledge, if not actual misinformation, in distributing their goods.

A well-developed network for the distribution of Western drugs makes them easily and widely available for self-treatment, even in remote areas (Hardon 1987; Abosede 1984). Self-medication is the most common way of using medicines in most developing societies; this is the main impact, the most prominent inroad, that biomedicine has made in traditional communities throughout the world. For example, Whyte (1990) has also reported that in Uganda, residents prefer to purchase medicines in the marketplace rather than in a professional setting, in part because they already know what medicines they wish to use and are therefore interested neither in diagnosis nor prescription.

Studies of pharmaceutical use in Ethiopia (Kloos et al. 1988) and Mauritius (Sussman 1988) suggest that the proportion of patients who practice self-medication in a sophisticated way with Western drugs varies according to type of illness. A pharmacist in Sri Lanka described the situation thus: "The patient knows what he wants, I know what it costs, and I don't see the need for any additional information" (Wolffers 1988).

Thus, in the developing world, biomedicine is yielding control of one of its most powerful and distinctive features—its pharmacopoeia—to local pharmacists, traditional healers, and patients themselves. Owing to international and local commercial practices, the proliferation of pharmaceuticals is responsible for the commodification of stress and distress, as well as the practice of taking medicines for every problem. It is certainly responsible for a considerable amount of pharmacogenic illness in developing societies.

Convergence of Traditional and Biomedical Practice

The use of Western drugs by traditional healers is one major way in which the spread of biomedicine is changing traditional medical practice. It is just as important to realize, however, that traditional and biomedical practice are now part of a system of mutual influence in which each is being shaped by the other. Evidence suggests that in medically pluralistic settings, the differences in the therapies recommended by different types of healers are steadily decreasing. It is not unrealistic to expect, in fact, that these two systems of healing may eventually converge.

For example, in a study of Ayurvedic vaidyas and their biomedical colleagues in Sri Lanka, Waxler (1984) found that doctor–patient interaction styles, physical diagnostic techniques, and prescribing patterns were all remarkably similar. The efficacy of their work was also perceived to be comparable. Waxler argues that the persistence of distinctions between Ayurveda and biomedicine, despite this convergence of practice, is attributable to the fact that the two systems provide opportunities for social mobility to different segments of the population. Nevertheless, she considers the futures of these medical practices to be interdependent.

Similarly, Ladinsky and colleagues (1987) show that contemporary Vietnamese medicine is a "harmonious merging of Chinese, Vietnamese, and Western medical systems." For example, traditional medicines are often taken together with antibiotics to protect the patients from the possible side effects of Western medicines. A similar situation has been observed in Northern Thailand (Weisberg 1982, 1984).

The changing patterns of illness behavior documented in these examples further corroborate the argument being advanced in this chapter. Pharmacists' role as caregivers as well as drug dispensers in the developing world, the adoption of Western pharmaceuticals by traditional practitioners, the increasing reliance on Western medicines for self-treatment, and the convergence of traditional and biomedical systems of healing are all indications of the variety of ways in which Western biomedicine is being integrated into indigenous cultures. This variety is additional evidence of the complexity of the relationship between biomedical interventions and changes in health status and underscores the importance of attending to local cultural differences. In any given case, one cannot simply assume that biomedicine is effective, while traditional care or self-care is ineffective.

IMPLICATIONS FOR RESEARCH
AND HEALTH POLICY

A number of significant gaps in our knowledge of illness behavior in the developing world remain to be filled by additional research. These may be divided into the following categories: (1) the nature and efficacy of biomedical services in developing countries, (2) the precise impact of social change, such as improved maternal education, on health and illness behavior, (3) the problem of suffering, (4) illness behavior in chronic illness in Third World settings, and (5) the ways in which particular types of illness behavior work to influence health status.

An illness behavior perspective directs our attention away from abstract, idealized representations of health and health services, toward a concern with people's actual experiences as they seek, receive, and deliver health care within the give-and-take of real-life contexts. To fully understand how biomedicine is practiced in developing societies and to ascertain how effective it is, we should adopt not only the bureaucratic gaze of the public health official, but also the ethnographic gaze of the anthropologist. The anthropologist's perspective takes us well beyond formal systems of biomedical care, to the realms of traditional healing, lay practice, and self-treatment. Because most of these have not been well studied, they should figure prominently on the agenda for future research on the health transition.

The effect of specific socioeconomic changes, such as increased education of mothers, upon illness behavior also requires further study. Needed are basic descriptive and analytic studies of the actual content of education for children. The existence of parallel systems of schooling (e.g., secular and religious schools) may help to reveal the relative contributions of content and process to the effect of education upon health. How does schooling affect the illness behavior of the students themselves? Do children with more or less education vary in the kinds of health behaviors they exhibit?

Under what circumstances does education change illness beliefs?

While we tend to associate traditional healing with the developing societies of the Third World, it is important to recognize that nonbiomedical approaches to health care survive and even flourish in highly industrialized nations (McGuire 1988; Sonoda 1988). Why might this be? One reason is that unlike biomedicine, whose focus is narrowly biological, traditional healing seeks to relieve not only bodily distress, but also suffering, the psychic pain that ensues from an assault on the social, psychological, and moral worlds of the self. In ascribing meaning to the seeming pointlessness of illness, or symbolically reconnecting a sick person to his or her social world, or simply witnessing, and therefore validating, the existence of pain, the traditional healer confronts illness as human experience, not just as organic pathology. The survival of traditional healing in "developed" countries, and of "traditional" functions of the healer within biomedicine itself, testifies to the value and importance of this orientation toward the provision of care.

Like illness and death, suffering is universal to the human condition. Yet research on the health transition in developing countries has focused almost exclusively on morbidity and mortality. A responsible and humane approach to the study of health problems in the Third World requires that suffering be included as an object of analysis. An illness behavior perspective allows us to incorporate this other fundamental aspect of human experience into our evolving program of research.

As we have seen, the changing composition of morbidity in the direction of increased chronic illness is one of the defining characteristics of the health transition. Yet very little is known of the nature of illness behavior in chronic disease in the Third World or of the social factors that affect it. The wide variety of choices and practices we have described suggests that the outcome of chronic illness reflects a "social" course more than a "natural" one.

Additional research should illuminate the burden of disability in developing societies. The role of traditional healers in attending to the suffering of chronically ill individuals is of particular significance here, but so is the way in which social supports at the family and community levels amplify or dampen disablement.

Finally, we need to know more about the mechanisms and processes through which illness behavior influences health status. What are the implications for the health transition of the widespread misuse of oral antibiotics and parenteral drugs? Evidence has accumulated that in optimal circumstances, preventive services, such as vaccination and water purification, can improve the health of people in the developing world. But do curative biomedical services also make a difference in mortality at the local level? In settings of medical pluralism, do families that choose different healers for a given disease differ on objective measures of health status? Does adherence to recommend biomedical treatment affect the ultimate outcome?

The major implications of illness behavior for health policy can be indicated in a series of questions: How can health programs promote lay recognition of disease states so that appropriate action is taken quickly? How can they foster social networks instrumental in supporting and referring patients to appropriate health care providers? How can they eliminate obstacles to help seeking? How can they foster compliance with medical regimens?

Government officials, public health experts, and health care workers in international health all tend to define their policy concerns too narrowly, focusing almost exclusively on how the quality and frequency of interactions between biomedical professionals and patients might be improved. But, as we have seen, illness behavior encompasses much more than those aspects of help-seeking that result in patients' interactions with biomedical practitioners. The components of help-seeking in relation to other aspects of illness behavior are represented diagrammatically in the illustration above.

Pharmaceutical policy is an especially important area where illness behavior has implications. More attention must be devoted to the ways in

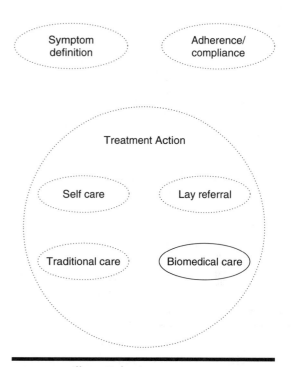

FIGURE 1   Illness Behavior

Illness behavior encompasses many purposeful actions by people confronting illness. Most attention to date has been devoted to the study of the interaction of patients with biomedical practitioners (solid line). But, as we have seen, such a focus is too narrow; many other aspects of illness behavior are relevant to the health transition, especially in the developing world (dotted lines).

which pharmaceuticals are used (and misused) in developing societies. As we have seen, the use of Western drugs bought from local pharmacies or drug peddlers is the principal contact most people throughout the developing world have with biomedicine. Too many assumptions are made, however, about drug-use behavior. For example, it is sometimes wrongly assumed that the replacement of traditional pharmacies by their biomedical counterparts is partly responsible for the health transition. From a policy perspective, much should be done to foster more appropriate use of drugs, to educate drug users and prescribers, and, where it is shown to be dangerous, to constrain drug availability (e.g., through government sponsored essential drug lists or through more stringent regulation of international pharmaceutical firms). Attempts must be made to tame the craving for injections and to foster more patience in those who expect an immediate response from Western drugs (and who stop taking them if they do not get one). Finally, communities must be empowered with the knowledge necessary for appropriate use of the technology that is already in place. How can families and communities, in other words, be encouraged to use pharmaceuticals in ways that constitute a more effective mode of self-care?

The near-veterinary quality of much biomedical care in developing societies, coupled with the pharmaceutical abuses that place populations at high risk for iatrogenesis, require responses at different levels. Control of the commercial abuse of caregiving in clinics, pharmacies, and mass media advertisements is essential. But also essential are efforts to increase lay and professional appreciation of the value of core cognitive tasks, such as careful elicitation of a history (responsible in and of itself for 80 percent of accurate diagnoses in primary care), explanation of the reasons for treatment (a cost-effective way to increase compliance and participation in preventive programs), and communication aimed at improving health education for health maintenance.

CONCLUSION

The basic point we have established is that any attempt to explain the social and behavioral roots of the health transition is incomplete unless it takes local cultural variation into account. To advance this argument, we have isolated a particular theoretical formulation—the notion that the health transition is the product of the combined forces of biomedical intervention and modernizing social change—and illustrated some of the different meanings and impacts these forces have when they are introduced into indigenous cultural settings around the world. The conceptual medium for carrying out this exercise has been illness behavior.

The decision to adopt an illness behavior perspective brings with it a number of advantages, such as the reorientation of attention away from mortality, toward the less-studied problem of morbidity. A focus on illness behavior can also be misleading for our purposes, however, unless the scope of the concept is made clear.

Because it highlights processes such as symptom identification and help-seeking, illness behavior may be mistakenly interpreted as a purely individual-level phenomenon. In fact, illness behavior is social as well as individual, because economic and political forces, socially defined relationships, and cultural meanings are all reflected in the ways individuals respond to the perception and experience of illness.

It is this capacity to span macro- and micro-levels of analysis that makes illness behavior particularly useful as an organizing framework for social science research on the health transition. Because it illuminates the social nature of the individual, an illness behavior perspective offers a valuable alternative to large-scale epidemiological studies in tracing the social origins of changes in health status. Research that approaches the social through the individual—that defines as the object of analysis particular people within a particular cultural setting—offers a valid, empirically grounded, and comparatively inexpensive approach to understanding the social and behavioral determinants of health change.

NOTES

1. The first two of these three aspects will be taken up in this chapter. For a discussion of behavioral pathologies in relation to the health transition, see Sugar, Kleinman and Heggenhougen, in this volume.

2. In fact, the classification of conditions as more appropriate for treatment by indigenous healers or biomedical practitioners varies considerably across cultures. In the case from Singapore cited above, for example, traditional Chinese

medicine was strongly preferred for rheumatism, fractures, menstrual irregularities, and anemia, and significantly preferred for diarrhea, measles, worm infestations, influenza, and constipation. In Nigeria, traditional healers have been found to be strongly preferred for psychiatric disease, fractures, snake bites, and convulsions. Nnadi and Kabat, 1984.

3. See also Sokoloff, "The Proud Midwives of Huchitan," Honors Thesis, Harvard Medical School, 1986.

4. There is further the troubling problem of the meaning of "efficacy." Is this phenomenon to be understood in terms of subjective or objective improvements—or both?

5. We recognize that important distinctions among the many different types of traditional healers found around the world are glossed over in this report. These distinctions have been subsumed under the larger category of "traditional" healer in the interest of focusing attention on the issues of primary interest for this discussion.

6. McCormack (1988) has argued, however, that maternal education in the absence of other favorable societal features, such as female autonomy and control of wealth, may not have the desired effect upon health.

7. For a more extensive discussion of the mechanisms which may link women's education to child's health, see Levine et al., in this volume.

8. Virtually all of the following discussion could apply equally well to fathers. However, mother's education has repeatedly outweighed father's education as a predictor of child health status, presumably because of mother's greater role in health care and child-rearing.

9. It is worth noting that termination of treatment may paradoxically result in better health care. For example, mothers might accept the persistence of low-grade symptoms after a course of otherwise effective therapy, thereby avoiding exposure to a new and potentially dangerous drug. Nations and Rebhun, 1988.

REFERENCES

Abosede, O. A. 1984. "Self-medication: An important aspect of primary health care." *Social Science and Medicine,* 19(7): 699–703.

Ahern, E. 1978. "Sacred and secular medicine in a Taiwan village: A study of cosmological disorders." In A. Kleinman, P. Kunstader, E. R. Alexander, and J. L. Gale, eds. *Culture and Healing in Asian Societies: Anthropological, Psychiatric, and Public Health Studies.* Cambridge, MA: Schenkman Publishing Company.

Annis, S. 1981. "Physical access and utilization of health services in rural Guatemala." *Social Science and Medicine,* 15D: 515–523.

Ayeni, B., G. Rushton, and M. L. McNulty. 1987. "Improving the geographical accessibility of health care in rural areas: A Nigerian case study." *Social Science and Medicine,* 25(10): 1083–1094.

Bertrand, W. E., and B. F. Walmus. 1988. "Maternal knowledge, attitudes and practice as predictors of diarrheal disease in young children." *International Journal of Epidemiology,* 127: 1079–1087.

Bhatia, J. C., et al. 1975. "Traditional healers and modern medicine." *Social Science and Medicine,* 9: 15–21.

Caldwell, J. C. 1979. "Education as a factor in mortality decline: An examination of Nigerian data." *Population Studies,* 33: 395–413.

Caldwell, J. C. 1986. "Routes to low mortality in poor countries." *Population and Development Review,* 12(2): 171–220.

Caldwell, J. C., and P. McDonald. 1982. "Influence of maternal education on infant and child mortality: Levels and causes." *Health Policy and Education,* 2: 251–267.

Chrisman, N. 1977. "The health seeking process." *Culture, Medicine and Psychiatry,* 1(4): 351–372.

Cleland, J. G., and J. K. van Ginneken. 1988. "Maternal education and child survival in developing countries: The search for pathways of influence." *Social Science and Medicine,* 27(12): 1357–1368.

Cominsky, S. 1987. "Women and health care on a Guatemalan plantation." *Social Science and Medicine,* 25(10): 1163–1173.

Cominsky, S., and M. Scrimshaw. 1980. "Medical pluralism on a Guatemalan plantation." *Social Science and Medicine,* 14B: 267–278.

Cunningham, C. E. 1970. "Thai injection doctors: Antibiotic mediators." *Social Science and Medicine,* 4: 1–24.

Das Gupta, M. 1989. "Death clustering, maternal education and the determinants of child mortality in rural Punjab, India." Discussion Paper Series, Center for Population Studies, Harvard University, Cambridge, MA.

DeVanzo, J. 1984. "A household survey of child mortality determinants in Malaysia." In W. H. Mosley and L. C. Chen, eds. *Child Survival.* New York: Cambridge University Press.

Esrey, S. A., and J. Habicht. 1988. "Maternal literacy modifies the effect of toilets and piped water in infant survival in Malaysia." *American Journal of Epidemiology,* 127: 1079–1087.

Farah, A. A., and S. Preston. 1982. "Child mortality differentials in Sudan." *Population and Development Review,* 8: 365.

Ferguson, A. 1988. "Commercial pharmaceutical medicine and medicalization: A case study from El Salvador." In S. van der Geest and S. R. Whyte, eds. *The Context of Medicines in Developing Countries, Studies in Pharmaceutical Anthropology.* Boston: Kluwer.

Finerman, R. 1987. "Inside out: Women's world view and family health in an Ecuadorian Indian community." *Social Science and Medicine,* 25(10): 1157–1162.

Fosu, G. B. 1981. "Disease classification in rural Ghana: Framework and implications for health behavior." *Social Science and Medicine,* 15B: 471–482.

Goldberg, H. I., et al. 1984. "Infant mortality and breastfeeding in north-eastern Brazil." *Population Studies,* 38: 105.

Good, C. 1987. *Ethnomedical Systems in Africa.* New York: Guilford Press.

Haak, H. and A. P. Hardon. 1988. "Indigenised pharmaceuticals in developing countries: Widely used, widely neglected." *The Lancet,* 8611: 620–621.

Hardon, A. 1987. "The use of modern pharmaceuticals in a Filipino village: Doctor's prescriptions and self-medication." *Social Science and Medicine,* 25, 277–292.

Ho, S. C., K. C. Lun, and W. K. Ng. 1984. "The role of Chinese traditional medical practice as a form of health care in Singapore—III. Conditions, illness behavior, and medical preferences of patients of institutional clinics." *Social Science and Medicine,* 18(9): 745–752.

Hobcraft, J. N., J. W. McDonald, and S. O. Rustein. 1984. "Socio-economic factors in infant and child mortality, a cross-national comparison." *Population Studies,* 38: 193.

Janzen, J. 1978. *The Quest for Therapy in Lower Zaire.* Berkeley: University of California Press.

Justice, J. 1986. *Policies, Plans and People—Culture and Health Development in Nepal.* Berkeley: University of California Press.

Kahane, J. D. 1987. "The Role of the Western Pharmacist in Rural Taiwanese Medical Culture." Ph.D. Dissertation. Department of Anthropology, University of Hawaii.

Kim, J. 1989. "Pharmaceutical industry in Korea." Presentation delivered to the Harvard Seminar on Medical Anthropology. Harvard University, Cambridge, MA.

Kim-Farley, R. J., et al. 1984. "Outbreak of paralytic poliomyelitis, Taiwan." *Lancet,* (2): 1322–1324.

Kleinman, A. 1980. *Patients and Healers in the Context of Culture.* Berkeley: University of California Press.

Kleinman, A., and J. L. Gale. 1982. "Patients treated by physicians and folk healers: A comparative outcome study in Taiwan." *Culture, Medicine and Psychiatry,* 6: 405–423.

Kloos, H., et al. 1986. "Utilization of pharmacies and pharmaceutical drugs in Addis Ababa, Ethiopia." *Social Science and Medicine,* 22(6): 653–672.

Kloos, H., et al. 1987. "Illness and health behaviour in Addis Ababa and rural Central Ethiopia." *Social Science and Medicine,* 25(9): 1003–1019.

Kloos, H., et al. 1988. "Buying drugs in Addis Ababa: A quantitative analysis." In S. van der Geest and S. R. Whyte, eds. *The Context of Medicines in Developing Countries, Studies in Pharmaceutical Anthropology.* Boston: Kluwer.

Ladinsky, J. L., N. D. Volk, and M. Robinson. 1987. " The influence of traditional medicine in shaping medical care practices in Vietnam today." *Social Science and Medicine,* 25(10): 1105–1110.

Leslie, C. 1978. "Pluralism and integration in the Chinese medical systems." In A. Kleinman, P. Kunstadter, E. R. Alexander, and J. L. Gale, eds. *Culture and Healing in Asian Societies.* Cambridge, MA: Schenkman Publishing Company.

LaVine, R., et al. 1987. "Schooling and maternal behavior in a Mexican city." The Population Council Fertility Determinants Research Notes, No. 16.

Lindenbaum, S. 1990. "The education of women and the mortality of children in Bangladesh." In A. Swedlund and G. Armelagos, eds. *The Health and Disease of Populations in Transition.* South Hadley, MA: Bergin and Garvey.

Locke, M. 1980. *East Asian Medicine in Urban Japan.* Berkeley: University of California Press.

Logan, K. 1988. "*Casi Como Doctor:* Pharmacists and their clients in a Mexican urban context." In S. van der Geest and S. R. Whyte, eds. *The Context of Medicines in Developing Countries, Studies in Pharmaceutical Anthropology.* Boston: Kluwer.

McClain, C. 1977. "Adaption in health behavior: Modern and traditional medicine in a west Mexican community." *Social Science and Medicine,* 11: 341–347.

McCormack, C. P. 1988. "Health and social power of women." *Social Science and Medicine,* 26(7): 677–683.

McGuire, M. 1988. *Ritual Healing in Suburban America.* New Brunswick, NJ: Rutgers University Press.

Mechanic, D. 1978. "Illness." In D. Mechanic, ed. *Medical Sociology.* New York: Free Press.

Nations, M. K., and L. A. Rebhun. 1988. "Angels with wet wings won't fly: Maternal sentiment in Brazil and the image of neglect." *Culture, Medicine and Psychiatry,* 12(2): 141–200.

Nnadi, E. E., and H. F. Kabat. 1984. "Choosing health care services in Nigeria: A developing nation." *Journal of Tropical Medicine and Hygiene,* 87: 47–51.

Rahaman, M. M., et al. 1982. "A diarrhea clinic in rural Bangladesh: Influence of distance, age, and sex on attendance and diarrheal mortality." *American Journal of Public Health,* 72: 1124–1128.

Reid, J. 1984. "The role of maternal and child health clinics in education and prevention: A case study from Papua New Guinea." *Social Science and Medicine,* 19(3): 291–303.

Sarder, A. M., and L. C. Chen. 1981. "Distribution and characteristics of non-government health practitioners in a rural area of Bangladesh." *Social Science and Medicine,* 15A: 543–550.

Sargent, C. 1982. *The Cultural Context of Therapeutic Choice: Obstetrical Case Decisions among the Bariba of Benin.* Hingham, MA: Kluwer.

Sonoda, K. 1988. *Health and Illness in Changing Japanese Society.* Tokyo: University of Tokyo Press.

Stock, R. 1983. "Distance and the utilization of health facilities in rural Nigeria." *Social Science and Medicine,* 17: 563–570.

Sussman, L. K. 1988. "The use of herbal and biomedical pharmaceuticals on Mauritius." In S. van der Geest and S. R. Whyte, eds. *The Context of Medicines in Developing Countries, Studies in Pharmaceutical Anthropology.* Boston: Kluwer.

Tsui, A. O., J. DeClerque, and N. Mangani. 1988. "Maternal and sociodemographic correlates of child morbidity in Bas Zaire: The effects of maternal reporting." *Social Science and Medicine,* 26(7): 701–713.

United Nations. 1985. *World Population Prospects: Estimates and Projections as Assessed in 1982,* Population Studies. No. 86. Department of International Economic and Social Affairs, ST/ESA/SER. A/86. New York.

Waxler, N. E. 1984. "Behavioral convergence and institutional separation: An analysis of plural medicine in Sri Lanka." *Culture, Medicine and Psychiatry,* 8(2): 187–205.

Weisberg, D. H. 1984. "Physicians' private clinics in a northern town—Patient–healer collaboration and the shape of biomedical practice." *Culture, Medicine and Psychiatry,* 8(2): 165–186.

Weisberg, D. H. 1982. "Northern Thai health care alternatives: Patient control and the structure of medical pluralism." *Social Science and Medicine,* 16: 1507–1517.

Weisberg, D., and S. L. Long. 1984. "Biomedicine in Asia." *Culture, Medicine and Psychiatry,* 8(2): 117–205.

Welsh, R. 1980. "Illness and Sorcery among the Ningerum of Papua New Guinea." Unpublished Ph.D. Dissertation, Department of Anthropology, University of Washington.

Whyte, S. 1990. Presentation to the Department of Anthropology, Harvard University, Cambridge, MA, October 30.

Whyte, S. 1991. "Medicines and self-help: The privatization of health care in eastern Uganda." In H. B. Hansen and M. Twaddle, eds. *Structural Adjustment and the State of Uganda.* London: James Curry.

Wolffers, I. 1988. "Traditional practitioners and western pharmaceuticals in Sri Lanka." In S. van der Geest and S. R. Whyte, eds. *The Context of Medicines in Developing Countries, Studies in Pharmaceutical Anthropology.* Boston: Kluwer.

Wolffers, I. 1989. "Traditional practitioners' behavioural adaptations to changing patients' demands in Sri Lanka." *Social Science and Medicine,* 29(9): 1111–1119.

Young, J. C. 1981a *Medical Choice in a Mexican Village.* New Brunswick, NJ: Rutgers University Press.

Young, J. C. 1981b. "Non-use of physicians: Methodological approaches, policy implications, and the utility of decision models." *Social Science and Medicine,* 15B: 499–506.

———. 1983. *Morbidity and Mortality Weekly Report,* 32(29): 385.

CHAPTER 6

ILLNESS BEHAVIOR, PART TWO
THE SICK ROLE

The three articles in this chapter address the concept of the sick role. One of the classic concepts in medical sociology, the sick role has had its proponents and opponents. The purpose of this introduction is to briefly address some of the concerns raised by the opponents (see, for example, Twaddle, 1979), such as whether the sick role is a cultural universal. But the introduction also examines the success of research into issues such as the influence of sociodemographic characteristics.

The sick role was originally developed by Parsons (1951) and consists of two rights and two obligations: the right to be exempt from normal role obligations and the right not to be held responsible for one's condition; the obligation to get well and the obligation to seek competent technical help for one's condition. Initially, the sick role engendered considerable research activity. Research interest, however, declined significantly in the recent past. Furthermore, as interest in cross-cultural research in medical sociology has grown, questions about the universality of concepts such as the sick role have increased. According to the three articles in this chapter, the sick role, at least without some qualifying statements regarding interpretation of the concept, is *not* a universal concept. A second but related issue is the influence of sociodemographic characteristics on sick role attitudes. These articles address the influence of a variety of characteristics on the willingness/ability of respondents to adopt the sick role.

The first article, by Frank A. Petroni, is based on research conducted in the mid-1960s in Minnesota. According to the research, sociodemographic characteristics such as socioeconomic status and age are related to sick role attitudes. Petroni, however, did not find any significant differences between males and females—regardless of their ages—in attitudes toward rights and obligations associated with the sick role. But he did find other age-based differences. For example, the right to the sick role was most legitimate for respondents in the grandparent generation, followed by those in the parent generation and finally the child generation. Petroni notes that the right to see a doctor was considered the most legitimate by the respondents, and the right to the sick role was more legitimate for those with chronic rather than acute conditions. Petroni concludes that, although evidence was not presented, the sick role may actually consist of multiple roles rather than a single role. This conclusion, held not only by Petroni but also by many other researchers, offers a possible direction for future research.

In the second article, Alexander Segall addresses sociocultural differences and the sick role. Conducting research in two Toronto hospitals, Segall examines response differences to the adoption of the sick role between Jewish and Anglo-Saxon Protestant married female housewife patients between the ages of 18 and 70. Segall reports that, on the one hand, respondents were generally in agreement with Parsons about the sick role. But on the other hand, many respondents were also "uncertain" because of contradictory responses. Although the findings do not indicate any statistically significant differences between women in these two ethnic groups, Segall argues that more research is necessary to fully understand the importance of sociocultural factors on a person's willingness to adopt the sick role.

In the third article, Eugene B. Gallagher and Janardan Subedi initially discuss the ramifications of the developed countries' relinquishing of their colonial power over indigenous populations around the world. The authors' discussion of the role of social scientists in studying third world countries is particularly useful because it raises serious questions about the role of the researcher. Their argument is also cogent as medical sociology and other areas

promote the necessity of researching and analyzing cultures of the developing world.

Gallagher and Subedi maintain that the sick role, when examined within developing countries, must be understood within the specific context of each country. They suggest that such an approach would address the issue of the universality of the sick role. Their argument brings us back to the point made at the beginning of this introduction regarding the application of the sick role outside the United States and the Western industrialized nations.

REFERENCES

Parsons, T. 1951. *The Social System.* New York: Free Press.

Twaddle, A. C. 1979. *Sickness Behavior and the Sick Role.* Boston: G. K. Hall.

THE INFLUENCE OF AGE, SEX, AND CHRONICITY IN PERCEIVED LEGITIMACY TO THE SICK ROLE

FRANK A. PETRONI

Since Parsons' seminal discussion, the concept of the sick role has received wide acceptance among social scientists.[1] Surprisingly, few researchers have questioned the validity of Parsons' unimodal conceptualization of the sick role. A notable exception is Gordon's recent study,[2] from which he suggests that, rather than one sick role, there are at least two: one in which the prognosis is critical, and the actor is given full support by others in taking the illness role; and the second, in which the prognosis is not severe and the actor is given little support. Gordon's work seriously questions the adequacy of Parsons' conceptualization of the illness role, for the latter implies that there is but one sick role. As Gordon aptly put it, "The effect of this unimodal conception has been to draw investigators' attention away from sociocultural variations in illness behavior."[3] That such variations exist has been well documented by Saunders, Zborowski,

Opler, Koos, Suchman, Rosenblatt, and Zola, to name only a few.[4]

Parsons' paradigm is also inadequate in that it neglects a number of contingencies, which Mechanic and others have indicated mediate between the recognition of symptoms and a person's willingness, or reluctance, to enter the sick role.[5] Principal among these are education, occupation, social class, cost of care, and the ability to pay for it, "other" role responsibilities, fear of discovering a serious illness, the place of health within the family's hierarchy of needs and values, and inclination to adopt the sick role.

In addition, a number of writers have implied that legitimacy to the sick role varies with age, sex, and chronicity. In general, however, empirical support for these as mediating variables has been lacking. For example, in one of his early papers, Mechanic suggested that legitimacy to assume the illness role was conditional upon the age of the potential role player.[6] He stated that in comparing a situation involving an illness of equal severity between a young child and an adult, the former is more readily permitted the sick role, and is also released from such obligations as attending school. He presents no data, however, to support this statement.

There is disagreement in the literature about which sex has a greater right to the sick role. Parsons, for example, suggested that the illness of the mother–housekeeper is more disrupting in family life than is an illness affecting any of the other family members, implying that women have less right to the sick role.[7] Such an orientation is congruent with his position that the mother is the primary agent of supportive strength for the entire family unit. Conversely, Mechanic has suggested that women have more right to assume the sick role; for they have fewer "other" role responsibilities than men, requiring time outside of the home.[8] Into the controversy, Vincent has added a provocative essay, in which he explored some neglected aspects of the family and illness.[9] Pertinent to the current discussion is Vincent's question concerning the effect that the absence of sick pay has on the mother–housekeeper's assuming the illness role; the inference is that in the absence of sick pay, she would probably take the sick role less often than her husband—providing he is entitled to such pay. On the other hand, Anderson and Feldman report that women have higher admission rates to general hospitals, a higher percentage of surgical procedures, and more physician visits per year.[10] Finally, Barker has written, "Particularly among men, illness is looked upon as a feminine characteristic to be shunned. The man who publicly announces that he does not know what it means to be sick thereby improves his masculine status."[11]

The relationship of chronicity to the sick role has not received as much attention as the relationship of either age or sex. Kassenbaum and Baumann, in a study of hospitalized patients, noted that varying chronic illnesses were accompanied by differential response patterns to the sick role, rang-

ing from dependence to denial.[12] Consequently, they concluded that illness behavior is not only a function of the expectations of one's social groups, but is also partly determined by the attributes of the illness. Because of this, the authors favored a situational approach to the study of illness behavior. And, in a more recent article, one of Freidson's major criticisms of Parsons' conceptualization of the sick role is its inability to account for chronic cases.[13] In neither of the above works, however, can it be said that chronicity was empirically validated as a sick role contingency.

HYPOTHESES

The study reported in this paper will examine three hypotheses:

> Hypothesis 1: *Perceived legitimacy to the sick role for identical symptoms varies directly with age.*
> Hypothesis 2: *Sick role legitimacy for the same symptoms varies by sex.*
> Hypothesis 3: *There is a greater perceived legitimacy to the sick role for chronic illnesses than for acute conditions.*

METHODS

The data for the current study were collected as part of a larger project of health-care patterns among three-generation families, conducted by the Family Health Care Study Center at the University of Minnesota during 1966 and 1967. This design allowed us to look at age by comparing perceptions of legitimacy to the sick role between generations, and by sex, by looking at differences between spouses.

The sample consisted of sixty-seven families, with a grandparent generation, a parent generation, and a married child of the latter, residing within a fifty-mile radius of the Minneapolis–St. Paul metropolitan area. In all, there were 201 nuclear family units drawn by area-probability sampling techniques. Because of the geographical locations of the study, the sample was largely urban, Caucasian, and culturally and religiously homogeneous. It was found that these families experienced less geographical mobility than non-three-generation families in the same area; and in socioeconomic status, the majority of respondents fell into Hollingshead's classes IV and V. In short, it was found that the sample was atypical of families from this area, but not atypical of three-generation families.[14]

In households where both spouses were available, each husband and wife was asked a series of questions—to determine his or her perceived legitimacy of the sick role—for seven hypothetical illnesses: heart trouble, diabetes, arthritis–rheumatism, an allergy, sore throat–running nose, vomiting with aches and pains, and nervousness–depression.[15] The respondents were asked four questions for each of the seven illnesses. Each question presented a choice of four possible and reflected one of the following behavioral expectations of the sick role, as discussed either by Parsons or Gordon: (1) the right to expect others to tend to one's needs, (2) the right to see a doctor, (3) the right to relinquish other role responsibilities, (4) the right to assume a dependency role vis-à-vis one's spouse. The answer choices were intended to connote varying degrees of legitimacy to these behavioral patterns, and were assigned weights from one to four. A score of one indicated little legitimacy to the sick role. Since four questions were asked in relation to each illness, the respondents could receive a sick role legitimacy score, for each of the seven conditions, ranging from four to sixteen. By adding the summed scores for the separate illnesses, we were able to as-sign an overall Perceived Sick Role Index score to each respondent, which could range from 28 to 112. Our observed range was from 32 to 103.

The answer choices for each examined component of the sick role were assumed to have face validity, since they contained phrases, as, he or she would: "treat me like everyone else," "encourage me to take care of my own needs," "see to it that I am comfortable and care for my needs," and "give me a great deal of extra care."[16]

Reliability of the items was tested by item-total correlations for each component of the sick role with the summed score for each of the individual conditions. With the exception of one sick role component—the right to relinquish other role responsibilities—the item-total correlations for the remaining three were always in excess of .73.

FINDINGS

Discovery that the item-total correlations between the right to relinquish other responsibilities and the summed score for each of the seven conditions did not yield rs of an equal magnitude, as those for the other three components of the sick role, led to a further examination of these data to determine if the right to this pattern of behavior was perceived as less legitimate than the other three. The findings, shown in Table 1, suggest that this is indeed the case.

Although the observed differences were not always large, for each of the hypothetical illnesses, the respondents perceived the right to relinquish

TABLE 1   Mean Legitimacy Score for Four Components of the Sick Role, by Condition

	HEART TROUBLE	DIABETES	ARTHRITIS	ALLERGY	SORE THROAT	VOMITING	NERVOUSNESS
Physical care	2.91	2.50	2.54	2.06	2.10	2.86	2.09
Physician usage	3.18	3.07	2.81	2.51	2.32	2.81	2.36
Role obligations	2.29	1.93	1.96	1.59	1.81	2.35	2.00
Dependency	2.74	2.62	2.46	2.25	2.31	2.62	2.35

Note: Ratings are from "1" (minimum legitimacy) to "4" (maximum legitimacy).

their other duties and obligations as the least legitimate expectation of the sick role. Conversely, the right to see a doctor was perceived as the most legitimate pattern. This finding is of interest for at least two reasons: first, it suggests that the emphasis given to the right to abandon other role responsibilities as an aspect of the illness role is not warranted—in fact, if any aspect of the sick role is to be weighted, it appears to be the right to see a doctor;[17] second, while there was consensus that seeing a doctor is an appropriate behavioral pattern if sick, this was not accompanied by the attitude that it is also all right to cut down on one's usual activities. The significance of this contradiction is apparent in cases in which the major part of the medical prescription is to "stay home and rest."

TEST OF HYPOTHESES

Sex. In testing for a sex difference in sick role legitimacy, a *t*-test for matched pairs was used. The decision to use the *t*-test for dependent samples was based on the fact that the males and females in our sample were related through marriage; also correlational analysis of between-spouse Perceived Sick Role Index scores yielded an *r* significant at better than .05 for husbands and wives in the parent generation, which indicates that the scores were not independent. On the other hand, the between-spouse scores in the grandparent and child generations were not significantly correlated.

For the entire sample, the difference in means in perceived sick role scores between males and females was significant at better than .10 (mean for males = 69.62; females = 67.04; $t = 1.83$; d.f. = 127). However, when the data was grouped by age cohorts (generation), there was no significant sex difference among respondents in either the grandparent or child generations. Conversely, among respondents in the parent generation, the difference was significant at better than .02 (mean for males = 72.75; females = 65.66; $t = 2.63$; d.f. = 57). Males in the latter group perceived more support for assuming the sick role from their wives than vice versa.

From the analysis of sex differences by subsamples, it appears that the observed overall sample variation was a function of the difference in perceived sick role scores between men and women in the parent generation. Thus the hypothesis that perceived sick role legitimacy for identical symptoms varies by sex was rejected.

The findings that males perceived more right to the sick role than females in the parent generation appears to be in conflict with a number of writers, cited earlier, who suggest that illness is a feminine quality. While we cannot be certain, the observed sex difference in the parent generation may be partly attributed to age. For example, of the fifty-seven usable, parent generation questionnaires, 72 percent of the (57) male respondents were over 50 years old, compared to 46 percent of the (57) female respondents. This difference in percentages was significant beyond .005 ($t = 3.052$; d.f. = 112).

Age. Confidence in the above explanation is buttressed by the fact that we accepted the hypothesis that perceived legitimacy to the sick role for identical symptoms varies directly with age. Age was measured indirectly by comparing perceived sick role legitimacy scores between generations. First, however, we examined the data for between-generation correlations. Perceived Sick Role Index scores between generations yielded *r*s of .02 between grandparents and parents, .08 between parents and children, and .14 between grandparents and grandchildren; none of which were significant. On the basis of these findings, a one-way analysis of variance, to test for age variations in sick role definitions, was used; for there was some indication that between generations the scores were independent. The observed *F* of 5.45 was significant beyond .05. Furthermore, the relationship was in the expected direction, with grandparents perceiving the most right to the sick role, followed by respondents in the parent and child generations.

The above, however, should not be misconstrued to mean that the younger a person is, the less right he has to the illness role. It should be remembered that in the present study we compared three age cohorts of *adults*. Dependent children were completely omitted from the analysis. If children had been included, the distribution would probably have been U shaped. That is, we would expect others to be more tolerant if the sick role is assumed either by the very young or very old.

CHRONIC VERSUS ACUTE ILLNESS

The findings in Table 2 suggest support for accepting the hypothesis that there is more legitimacy to the sick role for chronic conditions than for acute illnesses. These findings indicate that, for each of the six subsamples, the relationship between sick role legitimacy and chronicity was in the expected direction. If we look at each subsample as an independent test of the hypothesis, in six out of six tests the data reveal that, in taking the sick role, chronic, rather than acute, conditions were perceived as more legitimate illnesses.

Even though we are not completely justified in assuming that each test of the hypothesis was an independent event (because the sample was matched through marriage), a signs-test of significance indicated that the probability of obtaining the results reported here—that is, that the direction of the relationship would be the same in six tests of the hypothesis—was significant beyond .01.

The magnitude of the relationship between chronicity and sick role legitimacy was strengthened when vomiting was removed from the list of acute illnesses. It was learned that of the seven illnesses in the index, vomiting was perceived as the second most legitimate condition for taking the sick role. It was preceded in legitimacy only by heart trouble. This finding was contrary to our expectations, since vomiting, as used in this paper, is an acute illness. This fact prompted a re-examination of the data as shown in column five of Table 2.

It is suspected that vomiting receives high legitimacy because it is manifested by visible and urgent symptoms, making it more difficult to deny that something is wrong. The reasonableness of such an explanation is reinforced by the finding that the respondents' conception of the severity of a condition did not seem to influence their perceived legitimacy to the sick role for the same condition (rho = .40; N.S.). Each respondent was asked to rank the seven illnesses in terms of their severity, starting with the

TABLE 2 Mean Scores for Chronic, Acute, Organic, Functional, and Selected Acute Illnesses, by Sex and Generation

	CHRONIC[1]	ACUTE[2]	ORGANIC[3]	FUNCTIONAL[4]	SELECTED ACUTE ILLNESSES[5]
GP-Males	10.62	9.91	10.27	9.37	9.62
GP-Females	10.46	9.81	10.14	9.54	9.37
P-Males	10.99	9.87	10.43	9.72	9.16
P-Females	10.08	9.02	9.55	8.55	8.33
CH-Males	10.02	8.78	9.40	8.16	8.00
CH-Females	10.18	8.71	9.45	8.42	7.95

[1]Includes: Heart trouble, diabetes, and arthritis–rheumatism

[2]Includes: Sore throat, vomiting, and an allergy

[3]Includes: Heart trouble, diabetes, arthritis–rheumatism, allergy, sore throat, and vomiting

[4]Includes: Nervousness–depression

[5]Does not include vomiting in the list of acute conditions

most severe, which was to be ranked one, the next most severe, which was to be ranked two, etc. The results of this analysis revealed that heart trouble was the only illness for which there was a one-to-one relationship; both in perceived sick role legitimacy and severity it was ranked number one. Conversely, vomiting was given more legitimacy than diabetes, arthritis and nervousness; yet, in severity, it was ranked below each of these.

ORGANIC VERSUS FUNCTIONAL ILLNESS

The data from the current investigation also do not verify the inference that nonorganic conditions *per se,* as legitimate symptoms for taking the sick role, receive less support from others. For example, the findings in columns three and four of Table 2 indicate that there is more perceived right to the sick role for organic illnesses; however, when vomiting was removed from the list of acute conditions, the respondents perceived more support from others for taking the illness role for nervousness and depression than they did for illnesses such as a sore throat or an allergy (see columns four and five, Table 2).

Since this trend was observed in five of the six subsamples, it appears that the rejection of mental illness as a legitimate disability may not be as complete as is often reported or assumed.

Finally, in addition to severity, it may be argued that perception of legitimacy to the sick role is influenced by the respondent's personal experience with the seven conditions in the index. Since it could be argued that individuals who experienced a number of the seven illnesses would receive more support from their spouses for taking the sick role, or that if illness is commonplace, the reaction of the spouse may be more blasé and less supportive; we made no predictions about the direction of the relationship between "illness experience" and sick role legitimacy.

To examine this relationship, each respondent was assigned a crude illness-experience score based on the number of illnesses in the index with which he had some personal experience. Analysis

of the data by generations revealed that the relationship was inverse for each of the three subsamples. Among grandparents the observed r of −.303, although weak, was statistically significant at the .05 level. Among respondents in the parent and child generations, the rs were −.094 and −.148 respectively, neither of which was significant.

Of interest, however, was the finding that, in each of the generational subsamples, the relationship between perceived right to take the sick role and illness experience was negative. This finding indicates that perhaps one familial adjustment to illness when it occurs frequently, is to deny the person afflicted a special status and set of role expectations.

DISCUSSION

The data from the current study should be examined in relationship to the earlier findings reported by Apple[18] and Phillips.[19] In a study of sixty middle class Americans, Apple reported that the meaning of illness for the layman is to have an ailment of recent origin which interferes with one's usual activities. However, Apple's findings also imply that chronic illnesses are less apt to be viewed as sick role conditions than are acute illnesses since some chronic illnesses, such as heart trouble and cancer, in the early stages, may not interfere with one's usual activities. On the other hand, the findings from the current study indicate that our respondents perceived chronic illnesses as more legitimate reasons for taking the sick role than acute illnesses. The one exception was vomiting; a condition marked by high visibility.

These findings, concerning the dimension of chronicity, seem to be in conflict, but the exact nature of the conflict is not clear-cut. We cannot be certain that the observed differences reflect real differences. It is possible that part of these differences may be due to what Campbell and Fiske[20] refer to as "method variance." For example, in most of the eight descriptions of persons with "illness" symptoms used by Apple, the descriptions did not name a specific illness condition. In the study reported here, the subjects were asked to respond to seven concrete illnesses. Furthermore, in Apple's study the referent in the descriptions was impersonal: each description was prefaced by "Here's a man…" or "Here's a woman…," followed by symptoms varied for duration, changes in usual activities, and degree of ambiguity. In the current study, the referent (the person with the hypothetical illness) was the respondent himself.

Another factor which may account for part of the observed differences from the two studies is the fact that Apple's sample was largely middle class, while ours was largely lower class. Also, given our knowledge of the inability of lower class people to respond competently to abstract messages, there is some doubt that our respondents would have been able to answer the questions if we had replicated Apple's procedure. For example, in our experience with respondents who were widowed, for the most part, we found they were not able to focus on how their spouse would have reacted had they been afflicted with any of the illnesses in the index. Yet the same respondents did not have difficulties in answering most of the questions of the larger study.

Of equal interest, in comparing the results of these two studies, is Apple's finding that in the layman's mind interference with one's usual activities is the single most important condition associated with illness.[21] Our findings indicate that the layman perceives this component of the sick role as the one for which he has the least support.

Phillips, in his study of rejection of the mentally ill, reported a direct association between rejection and the visibility of deviant behavior. Furthermore, this relationship was independent of clinical assessments of the severity of the symptomatology. Although Phillips focused on emotional illnesses, his finding that visibility influenced the labeling process provides insight into our data. For example, our finding that vomiting was the second most legitimate condition for assuming the sick role might reflect the influence of visibility on the spouse's willingness to label the person with the symptoms "ill," and support him in the sick role.

However, the data reported here do not support Phillips' observation that men have less legitimacy to the illness role than women, even when controlling for age.[22] On the contrary, our findings strongly suggest that age cuts across the sex factor as a sick role contingency. In our sample, females perceived more right to the sick role than males only among respondents from the child generation. Conversely, among respondents in the grandparent and parent generations, it was the males who perceived more right to the sick role. However, this difference was only significant among respondents in the parent generation. It was also noted that in the two oldest generations the males were appreciatively older than their female counterparts. At the same time, these differences cannot be explained as an artifact of a direct relationship between illness frequency and age, because there were no significant differences in the frequency of reported illnesses among males and females in either the grandparent or parent generation.

In the absence then of a more plausible explanation, it seems reasonable to conclude that sex may be overshadowed by age in influencing a person's right to assume the sick role.

SUMMARY

The findings presented in this paper in part support the hypotheses that sick role definitions vary by age, sex, and chronicity. First, it was noted that legitimacy to take the sick role for the same symptoms was contingent upon the age of the potential incumbent. In general the relationship was direct; however, because the sample included adults only, caution should be exercised in over generalizing this finding. Second, it was seen that the respondents perceived more right to take the illness role if afflicted with a chronic condition, e.g., heart trouble, diabetes, or arthritis, than for acute illnesses. Third, it appears that the visibility and urgency of an illness, such as vomiting, cuts across the variables of age, sex, and chronicity in determining the imputed legitimacy of an illness as a sick role condition. This finding suggests that it might be fruitful in a future study to examine visibility in its own right as a sick role contingency. Fourth, there was no empirical support for the hypothesis that sick role legitimacy varies by sex. In fact, the sex difference noted among respondents in the parent generation may be more a function of age than sex *per se.*

The findings also indicated that of the four aspects of the sick role examined, the right to relinquish other role responsibilities was viewed as a pattern of behavior for which the incumbent of the illness role has the least support. Finally, it was learned that illness experience, rather than enhancing one's right to the sick role, seems to have the opposite effect. It would be interesting to examine this factor in relationship to delay in seeking medical attention.

In short, the results of this study seem to confirm Mechanic's suggestion that legitimacy to the sick role is contingent upon the age of the potential role player. There is also some support for Kassenbaum and Baumann's observation that commitment to the sick role and sick role performance is influenced by chronicity.

These findings, joined to those of Gordon's cited earlier, point in the general direction that rather than one sick role, there may be many sick roles. To be sure this is not definitive in the current study, but is only implied.

Future investigations in this area may be more fruitful if at least three classes of variables impinging on legitimacy to the sick role are controlled. First, specific situational factors surrounding the illness need to be examined. For example, a male from the lower class may feel more compelled to reject the sick role if confronted with cold symptoms just prior to Christmas, than if the same symptoms appeared shortly after receipt of an income tax refund. Second, as we have seen in this paper, the characteristics of the illness itself seem to influence legitimacy to the sick role, and need to be controlled. Specifically, is the illness chronic or acute, organic or functional, visible or hidden? And third, the characteristics of the role player himself need to be examined; his age, socioeconomic status, ethnicity, religious orientation, education, etc.

Rigorous investigations with the above model as a framework might eventually lead to the delineation of a sick role typology.

FOOTNOTES

*The author is Research Sociologist at the Menninger Foundation, Topeka, Kansas. The paper was originally read at the annual meeting of the Midwest Sociological Association, April, 1968. The research was supported, in part, by a grant from the Division of Community Health Services and Medical Care Administration, USPHS Grant CH 00167-02. The author wishes to acknowledge Theodor J. Litman for his assistance in carrying out this research.

1. For a discussion of the sick role see Talcott Parsons, *The Social System* (New York: The Free Press, a Division of The Macmillan Co., 1951), Chapter 10, 428–79.

2. Gerald Gordon, *Role Theory and Illness: A Sociological Perspective* (New Haven, Connecticut: College and University Press, 1966).

3. See David Mechanic, "Illness and Social Disability: Some Problems in Analysis," *Pacific Sociological Review,* 2 (Spring, 1959); Gerald Gordon, *op. cit.,* and Earl Koos, *The Health of Regionville* (New York: Columbia University Press, 1954).

4. Gerald Gordon, *op. cit.,* 97.

5. See Lyle Saunders, *Cultural Differences and Medical Care* (New York: Russell Sage Foundation, 1954); Mark Zborowski, "Cultural Components in Response to Pain," *Journal of Social Issues,* 8 (Fall, 1952), 16–30; Marvin K. Opler (ed.), *Culture and Mental Illness* (New York: The Macmillan Co., 1959); Earl Koos, *The Health of Regionville, op. cit.;* Daniel Rosenblatt and Edward A. Suchman, "Blue Collar Attitudes and Information Toward Health and Illness," in Arthur B. Shostak and William Gomberg (eds.), *Blue Collar World: Studies of the American Worker* (Englewood Cliffs, New Jersey: Prentice Hall, Inc., 1965); and Irving Kenneth Zola, "Culture and Symptoms: An Analysis of Patients' Presenting Symptoms," *American Sociological Review,* 31 (October, 1966), 615–30.

6. David Mechanic, *op. cit.,* 40.

7. Talcott Parsons and Renee Fox, "Illness, Therapy, and the Modern Urban Family," in E. Gartly Jaco (ed.), *Patients, Physicians and Illness* (New York: The Free Press, A Division of The Macmillan Co., 1958), 250.

8. See David Mechanic, "Perceptions of Parental Response to Illness: A Research Note," *Journal of Health and Human Behavior,* 6 (Winter, 1965), 253–56.

9. Clark E. Vincent, "The Family in Health and Illness: Some Neglected Areas," *Annals of Political and Social Science,* (March, 1963), 109–16.

10. Odin W. Anderson and Jacob W. Feldman, "*Family Medical Costs and Voluntary Health Insurance: A Nationwide Survey* (New York: McGraw-Hill Book Co., 1956).

11. Roger G. Barker et al., *Adjustment to Physical Handicap and Illness* (New York: Social Science Research Council, 1953), 317.

12. Gene G. Kassenbaum and Barbara O. Baumann, "Dimensions of the Sick Role in Chronic Illness," *Journal of Health and Human Behavior,* 6 (Spring, 1966), 16–27.

13. Eliot Freidson, "Disability as Social Deviance," in Marvin Sussman (ed.), *Sociology and Rehabilitation* (Published by the American Sociological Association, 1966), 71–99.

14. In comparing our sample with that of a study of three-generation families done nine years earlier by Reuben Hill and Associates at the Family Studies Center, University of Minnesota, it was learned that the two samples only differed in religious composition. Our sample showed a lack of religious stability over the three generations. For example, 34 percent of the grandparents were Catholic as compared to 42 percent and 51 percent of the parents and children, respectively.

15. The writer wishes to acknowledge Dr. Theodor Litman of the University of Minnesota, for his assistance in the selection of illnesses included in the index. Our criteria were to select conditions which would be well known and which covered a wide range of chronic and acute illnesses.

16. The answer choices presented here are those for the component the right to have others tend to one's physical needs and comfort. They are shown in ascending order of legitimacy. Since the same answer choices were presented for this component under each illness, the order was varied as a guard against response set.

17. Such an emphasis is implied in Edward A. Suchman, "Stages of Illness and Medical Care," *Journal of Health and Human Behavior,* 6 (Fall, 1965), 114–28; and Barbara L. Blackwell, "Upper-Middle-Class Adult Expectations About Entering the Sick Role for Physical and Psychiatric Dysfunctions," *Journal of Health and Social Behavior,* 8 (June, 1967), 83–95.

18. Dorien Apple, "How Laymen Define Illness," *Journal of Health and Human Behavior,* 1 (Summer, 1960), 219–25.

19. Derek L. Phillips, "Rejection of the Mentally Ill: The Influence of Behavior and Sex," *American Sociological Review,* 29 (October, 1964), 679–87.

20. Donald T. Campbell and Donald W. Fiske, "Convergent and Discriminant Validation by the Multitrait–Multimethod Matrix," *Psychological Bulletin,* 56 (March, 1959), 81–105.

21. Dorien Apple, *op. cit.,* 223.

22. Derek Phillips, *op. cit.,* 685.

DEVELOPED WORLD PERSPECTIVE

SOCIOCULTURAL VARIATION IN SICK ROLE BEHAVIOURAL EXPECTATIONS

ALEXANDER SEGALL

SOCIOCULTURAL FACTORS AND ILLNESS BEHAVIOUR

The cultural approach to the analysis of health and illness involves the study of "the relationship between cultural content and cultural life styles on the one hand, and definitions of health and responses to illness on the other"[7]. The distinctive way of life which characterizes a particular group or subgroup of a society may influence illness behaviour in a variety of ways. For example subcultural groups vary in the extent to which bodily conditions are perceived, evaluated and expressed as symptomatic of a state of illness. In other words, what is recognized as health or illness is largely a matter of cultural prescription. Furthermore, the cultural context also influences beliefs in regard to the cause of illness and the alternative forms of treatment considered.

There have been a number of empirical studies of the relationship between sociocultural factors and selected aspects of illness behaviour, including the following: (1) the meaning attached to the sensation of pain and the style of pain expression [20]; (2) the perception and reporting of symptoms [21]; (3) knowledge about the causes of various diseases and preventive medical behaviour [3,17]; and (4) willingness to consult a physician and to utilize health care facilities [8]. These studies all stress the importance of the influence exerted by sociocultural factors, such as dimensions of the sick role model (as originally acknowledged by Parsons [11]). However, this body of research provides very limited information regarding sociocultural variations in an extremely important aspect of the social process of "being sick," i.e. the perception of and willingness to adopt the sick role.

SOCIOCULTURAL DIFFERENCES AND THE SICK ROLE

A review of the literature reveals a lack of studies which have attempted, in a systematic and comprehensive fashion, to determine whether sociocultural differences exist in sick role behavioural expectations. The general tendency has been to accept uncritically the assumption that the pattern of expected behaviour described by Parsons is the same for all members of society. In fact, Gordon has argued that one effect of Parsons' original conceptualization "has been to draw investigators' attention away from sociocultural variations in illness behaviour" [4].

The role of the sick person was described by Parsons [11] in terms of two major rights and two major duties. Briefly, these four closely interrelated dimensions of the sick role are: (right one) the occupant of the sick role is exempt from responsibility for the incapacity, as it is beyond his control; (right two) he is also exempt from normal social role responsibilities; (duty one) the sick person is expected to recognize that illness is inherently undesirable and that he has an obligation to get well; and (duty two) he also has an obligation to seek technically competent help and to cooperate in the process of trying to get well.

The sick role concept has been widely utilized in the study of many different types of conditions. The Parsonian model (which is best typified by temporary, acute physical illness episodes) has been employed in the study of: chronic illness and physical disability [5,2]; aging [6]; pregnancy [15]; and alcoholism [14]. All of these studies demonstrate that the dimensions of the sick role model (as originally acknowledged by Parsons) are relative to the nature and severity of the illness.

However, the sick role is not only affected by the nature of the illness, but also by social and cultural factors. "Consequently, it is necessary to determine the extent to which Parsons' description of sick role expectations is valid. Equally important is whether these expectations are affected by sociocultural variations" [4]. Indeed, one must ask to what extent the set of expectations described by Parsons is actually representative of different sociocultural groups. In view of the evidence provided by Mechanic, Suchman, Zola and others regarding the sociocultural patterning of conceptions of illness and help-seeking behaviour, it is also reasonable to anticipate the existence of a variety of subcultural beliefs regarding behaviour appropriate to the sick role.

In general terms, then, the objectives of the present study were to determine: (1) how closely actual perception of the rights and duties of the sick role correspond to the Parsonian model; and (2) whether systematic sociocultural differences exist in the behavioural expectations held regarding the rights and duties of the sick role; and (3) whether systematic sociocultural differences exist in willingness to adopt the sick role.

RESEARCH DESIGN

Population Studied.   The most frequently studied groups, in this area of research, have been Jewish, Italian Catholics, Irish Catholics and Anglo-Saxon Protestants. For the sake of comparison, this study focused upon the members of two of these groups i.e., Jewish and Anglo-Saxon Protestants. Ethnic group affiliation was determined initially by the respondents' stated religious preference. Once the respondents had been categorized in terms of ethnic group affiliation they were chosen on the basis of the similarity of their illness and hospitalization experience. This step was necessary, in order for the study to be able to contribute to an increased understanding of how ethnic background may lead to different sick role behavioural expectations. The respondents who were included in this study were drawn from a population of hospitalized patients who had undergone the same surgical procedure at either of two major Toronto hospitals.

In an effort to isolate the effects of ethnicity further, a number of restrictions were placed on the type of patients included in this study, i.e. only Anglo-Saxon Protestant or Jewish married housewives between 18 and 70 years of age were interviewed. The interviewing of patients began March, 1970, and concluded February, 1971. The present paper is based upon the information provided by 70 of these patients.

Data Collection.   The interviews were conducted in the patients' hospital room and lasted on the average, approximately 45 min. Data were gathered regarding medical–hospital and personal–social factors, as well as the patients' sick role expectations and behaviour. Two Likert-type attitude scales were designed to get at the patients' perception of the kind of behaviour which would be ap-

propriate for a person who was sick and their willingness to enter the role of the sick person.[I]

Perception of the Sick Role Scale consisted of eight items (one positive and one negative statement pertaining to each of the rights and duties of the sick role as outlined by Parsons). The four positive statements were presented first, followed by the four negative statements, so that the two complementary items for each right and duty would be evenly distributed. The patients responded to each of the eight attitudinal statements in the scale by indicating whether or not they agreed.[II] The Willingness to Adopt the Sick Role Scale consisted of ten items, all negatively stated. Again, the respondents were asked to agree or disagree, and a high score on this scale was interpreted as a high willingness to adopt the sick role.[III]

Method of Analysis.   The SPSS integrated system of computer programmes was used for the analysis of the data [10]. A two-way analysis was conducted to determine the nature of the relationship between ethnic group affiliation and the various indicators employed to gauge sick role expectations and behaviour.

PRESENTATION OF RESULTS
AND RELATED DISCUSSION

The Hospitalized Patient: Some Characteristics. The Anglo-Saxon Protestant and Jewish female patients included in this study were found to be essentially similar in a number of respects, i.e. age, size of family, level of education and family income. Almost all of the patients reported that they have children, although very few reported having over four children. In addition, the majority of the patients had attended high school and reported a total family income for the preceding year in approximately the same range. All of the patients had been in a hospital before. The majority had been hospitalized four to six times and for most of the patients their last stay was within the past ten years.

Both groups of patients, then, were quite similar in a variety of ways.

Variation in Perception of the Rights and Duties of the Sick Role.   Few of the respondents interviewed in this study disagreed completely with Parsons' conceptualization of the sick role. At the same time, the respondents' perception of the sick role did not overwhelmingly support the Parsonian model as many of the respondents were classified as "uncertain" due to their rather indefinite (or sometimes contradictory) responses. In fact, only one clear-cut area of agreement was found between Parsons' description of "ideal" sick role expectations and the respondents' perception of how a person should behave when sick, i.e. 84% of the respondents felt that a sick person has an obligation to try to get well. In other words, these patients would agree with Parsons that "to be ill is inherently undesirable" [11] and that the occupant of the sick role should strive to achieve a state of "good health."

To understand why so many of the respondents fell into the "uncertain" category, the attitudinal statements included in this scale must be considered individually.[IV] In investigating the first right of the sick role, it was found that the majority of the women felt that a sick person cannot be "held responsible" for his condition. At the same time, only 31% of the patients agreed that "no matter how careful a person is, he can expect a good deal of illness in his lifetime." Many of the women said that

an individual can take certain steps to minimize the occurrence of illness. What the patients seemed to be suggesting was that when a person becomes sick it is generally not "his own fault," although by being "careful" illness may be prevented.

Turning to the second right of the sick role, the majority of the women (69%) agreed that "when a person is sick, it is alright to have others do things for you," but were divided in regard to whether "one should try to keep up with the routine housework even when not feeling well." The respondents often qualified their answers by adding that it would "depend on how sick you are." Thus actual exemption from normal role responsibilities (e.g. child care, housework) depends upon the nature and severity of the illness.

The patients' perception of the sick person's obligation to try to get well and to seek technically competent help was much more consistent than their perception of the other aspects of the sick role. As previously mentioned, the majority of the patients felt that "a person should try to get well as quickly as possible," and were very eager to terminate their dependency on others. Although the consensus was not as great, many of the respondents (65%) also believed that a sick person should seek technically competent help and cooperate in the process of trying to get well.

Although the present research evidence is somewhat limited and unclear, it offers little support for Parsons' general formulation of the rights and duties of the sick role (with the possible excep-

TABLE 1   Respondents' perception of the rights and duties of the sick role

| | PERCEPTUAL PATTERN | | | | | |
| | Negative | | Uncertain | | Positive | |
RIGHTS AND DUTIES	No.	%	No.	%	No.	%
Right 1—Exempt from responsibility for incapacity	6	8	48	69	16	23
Right 2—Exempt from normal role responsibilities	11	16	32	45	27	39
Duty 1—Obligation to try to get well	0	0	11	16	59	84
Duty 2—Obligation to seek competent help	4	6	37	53	29	41

tion of the sick person's obligation to try to get better). These findings are consistent with the results of other recent attempts to examine empirically the validity of the sick role conceptualization. For example, Twaddle [19] found that many of the respondents he interviewed did not perceive the rights and duties of the sick role in a manner consistent with Parsons' formulation. In a similar fashion, Berkanovic [1] interpreted his findings as evidence that the sick role is an inadequate conceptual tool.

Is the Parsonian model applicable to the members of different ethnic groups? In what way were the perceptual patterns described in the preceding section affected by the respondents' ethnic affiliation? In an attempt to answer these questions, the responses of the Anglo-Saxon Protestant and Jewish women were compared on each of the attitudinal items as well as the scale scores.

The two groups of patients were found to share basically the same expectations in regard to the sick role. Although the Anglo-Saxon Protestant patients generally perceived the sick role more in terms of the Parsonian ideal model than the Jewish patients, the differences between the two groups were not statistically different (i.e. $P > 0.05$). In one case (i.e. exemption from responsibility for the incapacity) the pattern was reversed. The Anglo-Saxon Protestant patients expressed the view that a

person can do many things for him/herself to maintain a state of "good health." For these patients, the individual was viewed as capable of exercising a good deal of control over the state of his/her bodily condition.

Variation in Willingness to Adopt the Sick Role. In contrast to the very limited number of studies that have focused upon variation in the behavioural expectations associated with the sick role, a great many research efforts have explored willingness to adopt the sick role [4,13,12]. Some studies have concentrated upon the relationship between ethnic and religious background and individual medical orientation, including factors such as acceptance of the sick role [8,17]. Generally, willingness to adopt the sick role has been operationalized as willingness to consult a doctor. A typical finding reported by these studies is that Jewish respondents display a greater willingness to consult a physician and more frequently utilize treatment facilities, than either Protestant or Catholic respondents.

A major weakness of this type of study is that only one dimension of the individual's willingness to adopt the sick role has been investigated. In addition to exploring "tendency" or "inclination" to visit a doctor, it is equally important to know if the person is actually ready to stop performing "normal" social roles and at the same time become

TABLE 2 Relationship between the Respondents' Ethnic Group Affiliation and a Positive or "Ideal" Perception of the Rights and Duties of the Sick Role

| RIGHTS AND DUTIES | ETHNIC AFFILIATION | | | |
| | Anglo-Saxon Protestant | | Jewish | |
	No.	%	No.	%
Right 1	6	15.0	10	33.3
Right 2	17	42.5	10	33.3
Right 3	34	85.0	25	83.3
Right 4	19	47.5	10	33.3

TABLE 3 Relationship between the Respondents' Ethnic Group Affiliation and Willingness to Adopt the Sick Role

| WILLINGNESS TO ADOPT | ETHNIC AFFILIATION | | | |
| | Anglo-Saxon Protestant | | Jewish | |
	No.	%	No.	%
High	20	50	23	77
Uncertain	12	30	3	10
Low	8	20	4	13
Total	40	100	30	100

dependent upon others for his well-being. Another limitation of research in this field is that attempts have been made to measure willingness to adopt the sick role, without first specifying the nature of the role expectations held by the respondents. Just what type of behavioural pattern is the individual willing to adopt when sick? The respondents' expectations in regard to the kind of behaviour perceived as appropriate for a sick person must first be understood if expressions of willingness to adopt the sick role are to be meaningfully interpreted.

In the present study, the respondents' willingness to adopt the sick role was measured by a Likert-type attitude scale. The patients' responses have been summarized in Table 3.

Jewish patients displayed a greater willingness to adopt the sick role, while Protestant patients were more likely to be uncertain about their feelings rather than completely opposed to accepting the role of the sick person. Although the difference between the two groups of patients on their attitude scale scores was not statistically significant (i.e. $P > 0.05$) there was a clearly discernible trend in the way in which they responded to the scale items.

For instance, Protestant patients more frequently stated that they find it hard to give in and go to bed when sick, and hate to admit that they are not feeling well. To support her answer, one Anglo-Saxon Protestant patient emphatically stated, "I like to be known as a healthy person." (A reference once again to the belief that the individual should be able to exert some influence or control over his "state of health".) In addition, Protestant patients agreed more readily than Jewish patients with the statement "If you ignore and don't worry about them, many physical symptoms will go away."

The reluctance of the Anglo-Saxon Protestant respondents to adopt the sick role was further illustrated by the fact that 55% (in contrast to only 27% of the Jewish respondents) agreed that when they think they are getting sick, they find it difficult to talk to others about their condition ($P < 0.05$). Based upon these findings, it may be concluded that what the Anglo-Saxon Protestant respondents

were basically objecting to was the dependency upon others which accompanies the adoption of the sick role. They were, however, as willing as the Jewish respondents to accept the other dimensions of the sick role. For example an equal proportion of the two groups of women expressed similar views about consulting a doctor and going to the hospital for medical care.

SUMMARY AND CONCLUSIONS

The fact that statistically significant differences were not found between these two groups in the present study does not necessarily indicate that there are no differences between Anglo-Saxon Protestant and Jewish respondents in their perception of and willingness to adopt the sick role. To understand the influence of sociocultural factors upon the sick role, more attention must be devoted to defining operationally the sick role concept and developing precise means of measurement.[V] The evidence seems to indicate that the sick role (as perceived by Parsons) is not a unitary concept and "empirically, the ideal model of the sick role is often not fully realized" [9].

Furthermore, ethnicity is a diffuse variable, which has been measured by a variety of indicators. For example, Mechanic [8] relied upon stated religious preference and Suchman [17] utilized three characteristics (race, religion and country of birth). To what extent can variations in illness behaviour be explained in terms of these indicators of ethnicity? It is clear that the concept of ethnicity also requires further theoretical and methodological refinement if the nature of the relationship between ethnicity and illness behaviour is to be adequately understood.

Before the willingness of the members of different ethnic groups to adopt the sick role can be compared, their perception of the sick role must be understood. The range of behaviour perceived as appropriate for the sick person must be specified. Future attempts to measure willingness to adopt the sick role must also specify which dimensions of the role are being considered. All of these steps must be taken if the sick role concept is to have a meaningful relation to social reality, and the influence of ethnic group membership is to be understood as a determinant of whether a person will adopt the sick role, and if he/she does, in what manner.

I. The statements included in these scales were adapted from the indices developed by Zola [21]; Mechanic [8]; and Suchman [17,18].

II. The response categories for the positively stated items were scored 3 (agree), 2 (uncertain) and 1 (disagree), while the scoring for the four items stated in a negative sense was reversed. Those respondents who displayed an "ideal" perceptual pattern (according to the Parsonian model) agreed with the first statement and disagreed with the second statement for each of the four dimensions of the sick role. These respondents were assigned a score of six and were categorized as "positive" in Table 1; the opposite response pattern resulted in a score of two, which was interpreted as an indication of a "negative" perceptual pattern. All other combinations of responses (i.e., scores of 3, 4, and 5) were categorized as "uncertain."

III. Since all ten of the items were negatively stated, they were scored 1 (agree), 2 (uncertain) and 3 (disagree). The scores on this scale ranged from 10 to 30 and were categorized as: "low" willingness (10–18); "uncertain" (19–21); and "high" willingness (22–30).

IV. The patients' responses to each of the eight items were analyzed separately, as well as their combined responses to the complementary items pertaining to the four dimensions of the sick role. The findings have been summarized in the tables presented in an effort to make the paper more readable. For more detailed information about the results of the statistical analysis see Segall [16].

It should be acknowledged that the results may be partially explained in terms of the scaling procedure employed. In Likert's method of summated ratings, differences may be masked by adding together the individual's scores on the items to arrive at a scale score.

V. For a more detailed assessment of the present status of this conceptual model and implications for future research see A. Segall, "The Sick Role Concept: Understanding Illness Behaviour," forthcoming in the *Journal of Health and Social Behavior* 1976.

REFERENCES

1. Berkanovic E. Lay conceptions of the sick role. *Soc. Forces* **51,** 53, 1972.
2. Callahan E. M. *et al.* The sick role in chronic illness: some reactions. *J. Chron. Dis.* **19,** 883, 1966.
3. Croog S. H. Ethnic origins and responses to health questionnaires. *Hum. Org.* **20,** 65, 1961.
4. Gordon G. *Role Theory and Illness: A Sociological Perspective.* College and University Press, New Haven, CT, 1966.
5. Kassenbaum G. G. and Baumann B. O. Dimensions of the sick role in chronic illness. *J. Hlth & Hum. Behav.* **6,** 16, 1965.
6. Lipman A. and Sterne R. S. Aging in the United States: ascription of a terminal sick role. *Social & Soc. Res.* **53,** 194, 1969.
7. Mechanic D. *Medical Sociology.* Free Press, New York, 1968.
8. Mechanic D. Religion, religiosity, and illness behaviour. *Hum. Org.* **22,** 202, 1963.
9. Mechanic D. and Volkart E. H. Stress illness behaviour and the sick role. *Am. Sociol. Rev.* **26,** 51, 1961.
10. Nie N., Bent D. H. and Hull C. H. *Statistical Package for the Social Sciences.* McGraw-Hill, New York, 1970.
11. Parsons T. *The Social System.* The Free Press, New York, 1951.

12. Petroni F. A. Social class, family size and the sick role. *J. Marriage & Fam.* **31,** 728, 1969.
13. Phillips D. L. Self-reliance and the inclination to adopt the sick role. *Soc. Forces* **43,** 555, 1965.
14. Roman P. M. and Trice H. M. The sick role, labelling theory and the deviant drinker. *Int. J. Soc. Psychiat.* **14,** 245, 1968.
15. Rosengren W. R. The sick role during pregnancy: a note on research in progress. *J. Hlth & Hum. Behav.* **3,** 213, 1962.
16. Segall A. Sociocultural Variations in Illness Behaviour. Unpublished Ph.D. dissertation. Department of Sociology, University of Toronto, 1972.
17. Suchman E. A. Sociomedical variations among ethnic groups. *Am. J. Sociol.* **70,** 319, 1964.
18. Suchman E. A. Social patterns of illness and medical care. *J. Hlth & Hum. Behav.* **6,** 2, 1965.
19. Twaddle A. C. Health decisions and sick role variations: an exploration. *J. Hlth & Hum. Behav.* **10,** 105, 1969.
20. Zborowski M. *People in Pain.* Jossey-Bass, San Francisco, 1969.
21. Zola I. K. Culture and symptoms—an analysis of patients presenting complaints. *Am. Sociol. Rev.* **31,** 615, 1966.

DEVELOPING WORLD PERSPECTIVE

STUDYING HEALTH IN DEVELOPING SOCIETIES: A CONCEPTUALLY INFORMED RESEARCH AGENDA

EUGENE B. GALLAGHER AND JANARDAN SUBEDI

INTRODUCTION

Although health and health care have become leading topics on the research agenda of the social sciences, not much attention has been directed to the health situation of developing societies. Academic course offerings, as mirrored in university catalogues, and professional meetings of social science organizations reflect this lack. It stands out all the more as an area of neglect given the intensity of popular interest in health in Western societies (Cockerham 1983).

Scholarly journals also reflect this lack. Academic publishing expanded enormously from the mid-1960's to the mid-1980's, with the appearance of many journals dedicated to minutely specialized topics. Despite this expansion, only two journals—*Social Science and Medicine* and *Culture Medicine and Psychiatry*—demonstrate a consistent interest in publishing material on Third World health and illness. The former holds the wider focus, taking manuscripts from many social science disciplines, and dealing with broadly medical, as well as psychiatric conditions. The latter deals especially with psychiatric materials, interpreting them through anthropological paradigms. Among major sociological journals in the United States, the only one devoted to health—*Journal of Health and Social Behavior*—publishes little material on Third World health, save for a special issue in 1989 devoted entirely to that subject.

How is this lack to be accounted for? Najman (1989) sees it as part of a reluctance of Western nations to become involved in latter-day consequences, most of them adverse, of their earlier colonial domination of much of the developing world. Following the Second World War, "[w]hen the Western nations handed power back to indigenous administrations, they left behind the diseases they had introduced, but little else" (p. 343). Najman's explanation amounts to an invocation of bad conscience; social scientists, located mainly in Western societies, shrink from studying societies that have been damaged, in health status as in other respects, by Western exploitation. While we see merit in Najman's view, we would add to it other explanations, more specific to the social sciences.

First, as between sociologists and anthropologists, the former have a marked tendency to focus their research on health–medical processes in their own country. In the United States, for example, collegial encouragement and funding opportunities are much greater for medical sociology research conducted inside its borders than for research conducted outside. Anthropologists are less bound by national affinities; medical anthropologists have devoted a great deal of effort to understanding the meaning of non-Western conceptions of health and illness within larger cultural belief systems. Medical anthropology has in the main remained true to this intellectual goal. However, it has not wholeheartedly embraced the study of change in the health-care systems of developing societies as Western, cosmopolitan medicine takes hold.

Second, it is difficult to apply the investigative tools of social science in many developing societies. Authoritarian political regimes do not easily accommodate disinterested social inquiry. They may attempt to manipulate the social scientist into producing information that shores up the status quo. All social relationships are more context-laden and personalized; an investigator is not as free as in the more open Western societies to draw up a random list of households in a geographic area and then to set about interviewing persons who are complete strangers to him or her.

Third, the conceptual paradigms that guide much social science research may hold little relevance for Third World health, given the pressing problems of infectious disease, infant and other premature mortality, and widespread lack of health resources. Take, for example the stress model, which has motivated many studies in the United States (Pearlin et al., 1981). It links mental health problems such as depression or psychosomatic complaints to the combination of stressful life events and lack of social support. Despite its seeming attention to circumstances in people's lives, the stress paradigm disregards the cultural, political, and social milieu in which people live. This paradigm rises out of, and is ideologically resonant with, individualistic American values (Young 1980). It is not likely to find straightforward application in Third World societies that have less detached, more socially grounded notions of interpersonal tension and malaise.

The foregoing should be regarded as a caveat, not an absolute prohibition against applying paradigms generated in the West to Third World settings. There is obvious scientific value in cumulative replicated research. A research finding that holds up in different settings—including different societies—is more robust and valid if the investigator can satisfy himself or herself that the social dynamics underlying the replicated findings are similar in the two societies. Lacking that replication may amount to a specious or random confirmation. The danger of mechanical replication is particularly great in regard to survey research methods. Cross-national investigators can become so absorbed in the translation of questionnaires and the training of interviewers that they lose sight of the basic fact that the underlying modes of thought and premises of social action are so different in different societies that replication is not a reasonable endeavor. Unfortunately nothing in the ongoing

conduct of the survey will signal the folly of the endeavor.

RESEARCH TOPICS IN THIRD WORLD HEALTH: THE SICK ROLE

The strategy of "testing the limits" is familiar to clinical psychologists who engage in projective testing. From long experience with such tests, psychologists know that certain responses—projections (in the psychological sense)—are common responses to a given ambiguous stimuli. It then becomes a matter of importance in personality dynamics and possible psychopathology whether a subject gives such common responses; and, if not, whether he or she under prompting from the tester can "see," or recognize the response in the stimulus that he or she failed to offer spontaneously. One of the cards in the standard Rorschach set is, for example, commonly interpreted to be a butterfly. Under "testing the limits," the tester will ask the subject who does not volunteer butterfly whether he or she can see a butterfly "in there." Testing the limits provides further valuable inference about the subject's personality. The subject who cannot "see the butterfly" may have a perceptual vacuum, possible suggestive of organic deficit, or perhaps the subject resists social suggestion and compliance.

A similar approach applied to Third World health will, we believe, yield naturalistic, enforced data that will provide insights into the societies under investigation and also will further increase our understanding of existing basic medical–health concepts.

Such a strategy would be fruitful, we believe, for examining the sick role in Third World societies. Social scientists studying health–medical processes in Western societies recognize the sick role, as formulated by Parsons (1951) as one of the key concepts for studying illness. Parsons delineates four social expectations that define the sick role. First, the sick-role occupant is to regard the condition of illness as lying outside his/her personal control and volition (e.g. even if a lung cancer sufferer was a lifetime cigarette smoker, his illness is not something he or she wanted). Second, the sick individual is relieved of social responsibilities in proportion to the disability imposed by the illness and/or the requirements of treatment. Third, the sick-role occupant is expected to get well (i.e. not to prolong the role-occupancy, which might occur because the exemptions and entitlement of the role are seen as attractive). Finally, the sick-role occupant is expected to seek competent help—in Western society, most often a doctor—and to heed the advice and directives of the competent helper.

Few concepts current in medical anthropology and medical sociology have been so thoroughly anatomized and critiqued as the sick role (see: Arluke 1988; Gallagher 1976; Levine and Kozloff 1978; Meile 1986; Segall 1976). Many sick-role analysts have attempted to determine whether, among the general public and among selected types of patients, the four components of the sick role actually correspond to the ways that people ordinarily think about illness and about being a patient. Using different research instruments and study populations, many studies find that the sick-role paradigm stands up to scrutiny; yet a suspicion persists that it is rooted in American values especially American middle-class values. Despite the allegation of culture-boundedness, virtually no attempts have been made to assess its status in non-Western cultures and developing societies. Does the sick role exist in them? Is it close to the sick role as propounded by Parsons? Can the sick role be regarded as a transcultural universal, or does the assertion of universality strain the Parsonian conception in some cultures?

IS THE SICK ROLE A CULTURAL UNIVERSAL?

The dearth of research endeavor on this issue is another example of the point made at the outset of this paper, namely that the social sciences, even their medically-focused subfields, have addressed Third World health and illness topics only to a slight degree.

We believe that grappling with the sick role in Third World contexts would be important for settling the issue of universality—primarily a theoretical question. A second question, one with theoretical overtones but also practical implications, concerns whether or how frequently the sick role is stretched by the role occupant into a self-indulgent claim for attention and for exemption from responsibility—beyond what the illness and the treatment require. This question lies in the domain of thinking about the secondary gains to be had through illness and the Parsonian idea that only mechanisms of social control—which may sometimes be inadequate—keep the sick role from sliding into a deviant escape from social obligations.

Exploration of this second question in developing societies will clarify the part that the family plays in assigning and maintaining the sick role for its ill member. As noted above, the patient may resist his or her path toward recovery. It does not follow, however, that the patient's family is consistently in the opposite camp—pushing the patient, that is, toward health and away from illness. The family may harbor and overprotect, blocking the path toward recovery. Given the strength of family ties and the viability of the extended family as a daily social reality in developing societies (and, in contrast, its attenuation in industrialized societies), we may ask whether the Third World family reinforces or subverts the sick-role component that requires the sick person to want to get well, and to behave accordingly.

It would be too broad a statement, and one for which we have no evidence, to say that families in developing societies interfere with treatment or retard patients' recovery. Short of that, however, it has been our observation in Third World hospitals that extended families often visit patients en bloc, becoming far more visible and "space-dominating" than in developed-society hospitals. Moreover, in Third World hospitals, families take an active role in the ongoing care of the patient, cooking meals for him or her, cleaning the patient's room, sometimes staying in it overnight (Schneider in press). At the very least, the extended family is characteristically a factor to be reckoned with, by professional medical personnel as well as the patient, whether its overall effect is toward or away from the recovery component of the sick role.

Family influence is stronger in chronic illness than in acute illness. In the long haul of chronicity, the level of medical intervention usually recedes, leaving the patient to his or her own devices and those of the family. Patient independence becomes—or potentially can become—an important goal. Despite the waning of medical involvement, other professional skills sometimes assume critical importance for helping the patient to walk again, speak again, resume the so-called activities of daily living, and carry out other accustomed lines of behavior.

ASSESSING REHABILITATION GOALS IN DEVELOPING SOCIETIES

In this phase of illness, the complex, elusive concept of rehabilitation comes into play, whether or not it is specifically identified as such, and regardless of how it is actually implemented. The mobilization of rehabilitation resources in the face of chronic illness, long-term disability, and diffuse aging-related impairment has proved difficult in industrialized societies. We believe that, for many reasons, rehabilitation is even more difficult to achieve in Third World societies. Chief among these reasons are the rural, hard-to-reach dispersion of the population and the limited supply of professional resources as well as their metropolitan concentration. Here we wish to deal, however, not with the distribution of resources but with the strength of rehabilitation as a cultural value.

The position of persons with chronic illnesses and disabilities in developing societies has been less studied than other aspects of health and medical care. In part this lack may be due to the rough correlation of chronic illness and disability with older age; in societies where the average age for the entire national population may be 15 or 16, social scientists along with government planners and health personnel do not squarely address problems

of the older disabled; improving infant and child health status seems a more urgent priority than rehabilitation (Tout 1989).

Acknowledging the latter point, we nevertheless believe that chronic illness and disability form a topic ripe for study in developing societies—from the standpoint of public policy and human welfare as well, as closer to our own focus, the understanding of health and health care. We advance two specific questions for research that fall within the general domain of this topic. (1) First, can the disposition of Third World societies toward rehabilitation goals be characterized in general value terms and compared with the corresponding values in the industrialized societies?

This is a difficult question not only because of the geographic and cultural scope of the Third World but more intrinsically, because rehabilitation is difficult to define, even for professionals who are steadily engaged in rehabilitation activities. Let us offer a formal definition, taken from a medical dictionary (Roper 1978). This source defines rehabilitation as "[a] planned program in which the convalescent or disabled person progresses towards, or maintains, the maximum degree of physical and psychological independence of which he is capable."

This definition accents the status of the patient as a freely acting, independent individual. This is what DeCraemer (1983) sees as the essential quality of "personhood" in Western culture, in contrast to the more socially-framed concepts of the person found in non-Western societies. The patient or disabled person who becomes a rehabilitation client has imputed to him or her a desire for physically and socially unfettered autonomy (similar parameters lie in the Parsonian formulation of the sick role, though less explicitly). It is on the basis of such an image of rehabilitation that professionalized rehabilitation personnel engage the patient. The questions we pose for Third World health researchers to investigate are the following. What is the cultural strength of the rehabilitation concept in developing societies compared with industrialized societies? To what extent is rehabilitation a projection of individualistic Western values? Can "proto-rehabilitation" concepts pertaining to recovery, social functionality, restoration of function, autonomous dignity, and personhood be found in the culture of daily life in Third World societies?

(2) What is the impact of extended family systems on the setting and accomplishment of rehabilitation goals in Third World societies? Viable extended families are full of interpersonal resources nuclear families lack. For example, grandparents can engage in extensive child care that enables mothers and fathers of small children to work, study, and pursue career lines. In intergenerational terms, the parents then pay back—not literally to their own parents, who provided the original service, but to their own children when those children become working parents and they become grandparents. In regard to child care, the extended family can substitute for, and perhaps qualitatively surpass, formally-organized community child-care services that are increasingly abundant in the urban areas of industrialized societies. The potential of extended families for rehabilitation activity is no doubt equally great but questions arise, requiring study in Third World contexts, whether family resources in balance operate to promote the patient's recovery and autonomy or to prolong chronicity.

Without prejudging what the results of careful investigation might disclose, we wish to sketch here both sides of the issue. Nagi, one of the few American sociologists who has closely examined disability in developing societies, has an optimistic view of the family and community there as a ready but unrecognized repertoire of skills and services for helping the disabled (1981): "...the strength of family ties and the primary relations in the community remain, in developing societies, a strong resource upon which plans for the delivery of services and benefits must be founded" (p. 272).

The other side of the perspective sees in the family a force that, through its affectionate desire to help and to protect the disabled person, maintains him or her in a state of dependency. A telling

example of this comes from a research report on Bedouin clients of Soroka Hospital in the Negev desert of southern Israel (Lewando-Hundt et al. 1980):

> One's family is expected to adjust to one's limited functioning.... The blind are assumed to be unable to undertake any physical activity without guidance. The deaf are not expected to know how to lip-read. Their relatives and friends learn how to communicate with them by gesture. In the case of the dialysis patients, there is a readiness to care for them, even unnecessarily. For example, [Patient] D has a prosthesis and crutches. He barely uses either, for his sons and grandsons push him in his wheelchair or carry him when necessary. (pp. 10–11)

Overprotective, contra-rehabilitative family behavior such as the foregoing is by no means confined to developing societies; similar examples of over protectiveness occur in the West (Strauss 1975), but our hypothesis is that it is less common there. We wish to insert this cautionary note to remind the reader that, in our view, all differences to be found between Third World and industrialized societies are a matter of degree, not of absolutes. This is why we earlier put forth the conceptual strategy of testing the limits for a norm or value characteristic of one type of society to see how well it fits in another type. The same approach can be applied to the notion of rehabilitation. We believe that it fits in well with, indeed exemplifies, an individualistic conception of the person found in Western societies. This idea does not mean, however, that such thinking is completely absent in Third World societies. We suppose that it exists there but it is overshadowed by strong familial conceptions of the services and respect due to a disabled family member.

HEALTH CARE AS A VEHICLE OF MODERNITY?

The preceding research agenda dealt with the sick role, both in its usual medical mode and in chronic illness—asking whether its social basis and interpersonal framework are the same in developing societies as in the industrialized societies. The questions we raised dealt in one way or another with patients, their families, and professionals.

The last area of research that we propose deals with the symbolic meaning of health/medical care (for purposes of mapping this agenda, we do not distinguish medical from health care) in modern society.

We start with the non-controversial premise that health is universally desired; disease and disability are avoided when possible and resented or despaired over when unavoidable. This generalization does not mean however that the health care system has historically been a prominent part of society, comparable in weight and distinctness to social structures for religion, law, and the production of material goods. In recent decades, however, it has achieved such distinctness. The "health care system" is now recognized as an integral, non-adventitious component of modern society as much as industrial production and networks of transportation and communication (Field, 1989).

A strong and intriguing implication of this is that health care carries with it, beyond its direct utility for dealing with disease, the symbolic, "value-added" signification of modernity (Gallagher 1988). Popular symbols of modernity often accent technology, which is a tangible, dramatic medium for depicting progress. Thus, in a developing society (and the situation is not entirely different in developed societies), icons of progress might include, for example, a dazzling equipped teaching hospital or a demonstration of advanced combat aircraft. The symbolic valence would be increased in the developing society if, in both cases, native-born sons (or daughters) of the nation were shown to be using the technology—a surgeon, perhaps, or a fighter pilot.

These considerations allow us to formulate guiding questions about medical resources in developing societies. If health care, considered categorically, has symbolic meaning, then does the advancement of health services in developing societies become freighted with symbolic modernity? How does the role and the figure of the medical doctor—a pivotal actor in health care systems everywhere—become identified with societal progress? In another direction, how does the medical role connect with the society's conceptions of authority, compassion, wisdom and skill? Can symbolic medical display, e.g. a teaching hospital in the capital city, be contrasted with—even opposed to—real medical services; or is there a seamless integration between the tangible delivery of medical services and the ways in which they are socially represented? If there is a gap, then to what extent does symbolic action, e.g. to demonstrate technological advancement, to show the solicitude of a perhaps authoritarian regime for the well-being of the populace—take precedence over widespread needs for health services, perhaps even as a token gesture toward meeting them?

Apart from the glamour of advanced medical technology, everyday medicine makes deep inroads into the soma and psyche of patients. This leads to the proposition: there is no area of modern life where the degree of intimate application of scientific knowledge to individual human well-being exceeds that found in modern medicine. We wish to qualify the foregoing proposition and, in so doing clarify its meaning and bearing on health in the context of societal development.

Whatever the state of bioscience, the doctor's eye, and hand, and knowledge may falter in bringing it to bear upon the patient. Uncertainty exists in all branches of medical practice. At some point it crosses over into frank ignorance, as with the long, yet unrequited quest for the cures of cancer and schizophrenia. Uncertainty even hangs over known and tested techniques, such as renal transplantation; they work with some patients but not all. The individual practitioner faces his/her own limitations of skill and knowledge and hopes for the best, perhaps with a boost from luck or providence. Uncertainty can on occasion move from being a marginal parameter running throughout all of medicine into a central, dramatic force shaping the attitudes and expectations of patients and providers, as with new experimental treatments for lethal diseases and in much of surgery. Despite this, modern medicine is carried out on benefit of a much broader base of empirical knowledge than prescientific modes of coping with disease.

In further reference to the foregoing proposition, we note that although some other fields of technical application may draw upon a higher quantum of rigorous science, they are not as closely tied to the individual, phenotypic human being as medicine. It takes a great deal of precision, in physics, chemistry, and astronomy, to place a human on the moon—but this feat entails nothing like the reach of medicine over and into the human body. Similarly, all the scientific knowledge brought to bear upon the construction of an automobile or an office building is pointed toward an object that people can use or consume in a standard, impersonal fashion. It is not "intimate" in the sense of medicine.

These aspects of medicine give it a unique position in the broad spectrum of changes and challenges that confront persons in developing societies as their societies move toward industrialization, urbanization, bureaucratization, mass education, and all the other channels of modernity. Many of these other channels draw the person as an individual into impersonal, contractual activities and relationships that detach him from familial roots, communal support, and cultural traditions. Modern medicine also ignores, or regards with indifference, traditional beliefs about the human body. These traditions vary across societies and culture areas. No society has been without them but they have greater viability in pre-industrial and rural societies. Obvious examples include the Greek humoral theory, still strong in Latin America and the Middle East, the Chinese doctrine of "chi" or vital force, and various cultural conceptions about physiological differences between male and

female, and between the various racial groups of mankind.

Modern medicine subverts, through its failure to reinforce, a culture's traditional resources for interpreting and coping with malaise in everyday life. We are not here referring to the specific rubric of traditional medicine as a set of techniques and roles, but rather to the complex of beliefs concerning health, of which traditional medicine is only the most conspicuous segment. The total complex forms a "home"—an intelligible, emotionally secure position—that in the view of the sociologist Berger (Berger et al., 1973) and other interpreters of modernity, is lost during modernization.

In industrialized societies, the "home" of traditional beliefs about the human body and illness has been eroding for many decades. Patients may wish for doctors who were more supportive and communicative but they expect to be dealt with by medical personnel in the detached cognitive framework of modern medicine. In developing societies with strong indigenous medical systems, there is a co-existence, sometimes colored by competition, between the indigenous systems and the offerings of modern medicine. This co-existence has been studied by anthropologists and sociologists under the rubric of "medical pluralism" (Leslie, 1980).

Modern medicine draws intellectually upon biomedical science but, as a form of practice, it characteristically holds a tolerant attitude toward indigenous medical traditions. It is not a fierce, uncompromising religious or political ideology intent on domination. Toleration is also the typical stance of the indigenous traditions. Gradually they are losing out, for lack of—one might say—zealous partisans. There are, however, counter-movements that arise not from pure defense of tradition but from other powerfully persisting sources of social power that compete with the dynamism of modern medicine. The dogged survival of midwifery in developing societies illustrates the values of neighborhood attachment and the cohesion of female culture, which may be particularly strong in developing societies where not many women have emerged into more impersonal, public modes of social participation (Colfer and Gallagher, 1992; Sukkary, 1981). In contemporary Western industrialized societies, the feminist movement is also trying to wrest back control of prenatal care and delivery from medical obstetrics—through greater use of midwives, home birthing, and natural childbirth.

We proposed earlier that the adoption of modern medicine and its penetration into the health care apparatus of a developing society stands as a symbolic index of its modernity. This admittedly very broad proposition requires a finer specifi-

cation of how modern medicine becomes institutionalized in society. In addition to translating biomedical knowledge into practical techniques physicians also enhance their collective prerogatives and professional power vis-à-vis patients. Fundamental values and traditions in a society regarding modes of helping and modes of social influence come into play in the delivery of medical services, as distinct from their technical content and the efficacy in promoting health. These trends must be dissected and given their due weight in a composite analysis of the expansion of modern medicine into developing societies.

REFERENCES CITED

Arluke, Arnold
1988. "The Sick Role Concept." In: *Health Behavior: Emerging Research Perspectives*, David S. Gochman (ed.) pp. 169–180. New York: Plenum Press.

Berger, Peter, Brigitte Berger, and Hansfried Kellner.
1973. *The Homeless Mind: Modernization and Consciousness*. New York: Random House.

Cockerham, William C.
1983. "The State of Medical Sociology in the United States, Great Britain, West Germany and Austria: Applied vs Pure Theory." *Social Science and Medicine,* 17(20) 1513–1527.

Colfer, Carol J. Pierce, and Eugene B. Gallagher
In press. "Home and Hospital Birthing in Oman: An Observational Study with Recommendations for Hospital Practice." In: *Health and Health Care in Developing Societies: Sociological Perspectives*, Peter Conrad and Eugene B. Gallagher (eds.). Philadelphia: Temple University Press.

DeCraemer, Willie
1983. "A Cross-Cultural Perspective on Personhood." *Milbank Memorial Quarterly*, 61(1) 19–34.

Field, Mark G.
1989. "Introduction." In: *Success and Crisis in National Health Care Systems—A Comparative Approach,* Mark G. Field (ed.) pp. 1–2. New York: Routledge.

Gallagher, Eugene B.
1976. "Lines of Reconstruction and Extension in the Parsonian Sociology of Illness." *Social Science and Medicine,* 10 207–218.

1988. "Modernization and Medical Care." *Sociological Perspectives,* 31(1) 59–87.

Leslie, Charles
1980. "Medical Pluralism in World Perspective." *Social Science and Medicine,* 14B 191–175.

Levine, Sol, and Martin A. Kozloff
1978. "The Sick Role: Assessment and Overview." In: *Annual Review of Sociology,* Ralph H. Turner, James Coleman and Renee C. Fox (eds.). Palo Alto CA: Annual Reviews, Inc.

Lewando-Hundt, Gillian, Stanley Rabinowitz, Naomi Shohat, and Gabriel M. Danovitch
"The Influence of Socio-Cultural Factors on Adaptation to Dialysis Treatment." Unpublished manuscript. Beersheba Israel: Ben Gurion University of the Negev.

Meile, Richard L.
1986. "Pathways to Patienthood: Sick Role and Labeling Perspectives." *Social Science and Medicine,* 22 35–40.

Nagi, Said Z.
1981. "The Disabled in Developing Societies." *International Social Security Review,* 34(3) 59–273.

Najman, Jakob M.
1989. "Health Care in Developing Countries." In: *Handbook of Medical Sociology* (Fourth Edition), Howard E. Freeman and Sol Levine (eds.) pp. 332–346. New York: Prentice Hall.

Parsons, Talcott
1951. *The Social System.* New York: The Free Press.

Pearlin, Leonard I., Morton A. Lieberman, Elizabeth G. Menaghan, and Joseph T. Mullan
1981. "The Stress Process." *Journal of Health and Social Behavior,* 22 337–356.

Roper, Nancy
1978. *New American Pocket Dictionary.* New York: Churchill Livingstone.

Schneider, Joseph W.
In press. "Family Care Work in a 'Modern' Chinese Hospital." In: *Health and Health Care in Developing Countries: Sociological Perspectives.* Peter Conrad and Eugene B. Gallagher (eds.). Philadelphia: Temple University Press.

Segall, A.
1976. "The Sick Role Concept: Understanding Illness Behavior." *Journal of Health and Social Behavior* 17 162–169.

Strauss, Anselm L.
1975. *Chronic Illness and Quality of Life.* Saint Louis: C. V. Mosby Company.

Sukkary, Soileir
1981. "She Is No Stranger: The Traditional Midwife in Egypt." *Medical Anthropology,* 5 (Winter) 26–34.

Tout, Kenneth
1989. *Ageing in Developing Countries.* New York: Oxford University Press.

Young, Allen
1980. "The Discourse on Stress and the Reproduction of Conventional Knowledge." *Social Science and Medicine,* 14B 133–146.

CHAPTER 7

MENTAL ILLNESS

If you were asked to define mental illness, what criteria would you employ? Would your definition focus on individual-level behavior? Would you label behaviors that are at odds with the norms of society as possibly exhibitions of mental illness? Such criteria of mental illness may be the domain of psychiatry. Sociology is interested in mental illness from a very different perspective.

Consider the following quotation from Brenner (1973, p. 226), who points out that "economic change has a substantial impact on psychiatry as an institution and on the lives of persons who eventually become mentally hospitalized…[and] that historically, the role of psychiatry as an institution has been intimately tied to dislocations in the economic system." In this quotation, Brenner illustrates the impact of the larger social structure on individual behavior that becomes labeled as mental illness. Historically, the sociological approach dates to the work of Durkheim and the relationship of suicide rates to a variety of sociodemographic factors. More specifically, the sociology of mental illness argues "that the ways in which societies are organized, not just biological and psychological characteristics of individuals, must be considered as causal factors in mental illness" (Tausig, Michello, and Subedi, 1999, p. 4).

The articles in this chapter address mental illness from a sociological perspective. In the first article, Virginia Aldige Hiday examines the social context of mental illness and violence. She offers an extensive literature review to document previous efforts to examine the relationship between violence and mental illness. Essentially, Hiday argues that the relationship between violence and mental illness must take into account a broader range of conditions and experiences that impact on the individual. Based on previous research, Hiday identifies four areas for examination: (1) defining the variables and their association, (2) identifying the circumstances within which violence occurs, (3) the impact of alcohol and drug abuse, and (4) the co-occurrence of violence and persons with antisocial personality disorder. Utilizing those four areas as well as a number of additional variables, Hiday constructs a causal model in which mental illness and violence are connected to social stratification. Thus, she argues that conditions such as poverty and social disorganization are key to the emergence of mental disorders and ultimately to violence.

In the second article, Hugh L. Freeman offers a historical overview of mental health care in Great Britain. His starting point is the building of a "lunatic house" adjacent to Guy's Hospital in London in the early 1700s. By the mid-nineteenth century, such additions to general hospitals had ceased. In their place emerged hospitals that specialized in treating mental illness. The only other facility available for the mentally ill was the Poor Law workhouse. Thus, throughout the nineteenth and into the twentieth century, general hospitals provided few services related to mental illness, and confinement in mental hospitals was, for many, the only available means of treatment.

Hospitals for the mentally ill and general hospitals continued to differentiate services until the middle of the twentieth century. In 1948, with the advent of the National Health Service (NHS), all hospitals in Great Britain, including mental hospitals, came under the purview of a central, unified system. In 1959, the Mental Health Act eliminated the designation of "mental hospitals," allowing patients to be admitted and provided care in general hospitals. Shortly thereafter, the NHS created a new type of hospital, the District General Hospital (DGH). The DGH was able to provide a range of specialty areas for persons with psychiatric disorders. Also at this time, in the early 1960s, came a push for "community care" for the mentally ill. Given all of these changes, the number of patients housed in mental hospitals in Great Britain dropped.

Freeman points out that the application of psychiatric knowledge in Great Britain remained very atheoretical and grounded in mental health policy that utilized conventional models of patient treatment. By the 1970s and 1980s, however, he argues, the rise of "antipsychiatry" brought about a new theoretical interpretation of mental illness. Proponents of this approach argued for increased levels of diagnosis and for treatment at the community level in respite houses, mental health centers, and so forth (the emergence of such facilities is similar to experiences in the United States). The Community Care Act of 1990 mandated local social services to attend to the needs of the mentally ill within the community. The devolution of services (and monies) from the large mental hospitals of the nineteenth century to community-based services for the mentally ill reflects changing beliefs about the mentally ill within the larger social system.

The third article, by Ilona Blue, relates social and economic inequalities among residents of São Paulo, Brazil, to their mental health. Blue outlines a number of specific points about persons experiencing mental ill-health in countries of the Southern Hemisphere. For example, the range of individuals with common mental disorders has been estimated to be between 12 and 46 percent. Another disturbing statistic is that most who experience common mental disorders will not have any contact with health service personnel. Blue offers explanations for differences in the mental health status of respondents in three different locations in São Paulo. Examining the stress of respondents in these locations, she argues that socioenvironmental factors are related to the levels of stress.

Although the three articles in Chapter 7 examine different aspects of mental illness (violence, hospitals, social stratification, and the urban environment), a common thread links them. This thread is the impact of social structure on mental illness. The relationship is clearly identified in the first and third articles. The second article addresses the issue tangentially. Although differences between populations were perhaps more evident in earlier years of the hospitalization of mental health services, the institutionalization of the National Health Service was an effort to ensure equality of access to medical as well as mental health services.

REFERENCES

Brenner, M. Harvey. 1973. *Mental Illness and the Economy.* Cambridge, MA: Harvard University Press.
Tausig, Mark, Janet Michello, and Sree Subedi. 1999. *A Sociology of Mental Illness.* Upper Saddle River, NJ: Prentice Hall.

THE SOCIAL CONTEXT OF MENTAL ILLNESS AND VIOLENCE

VIRGINIA ALDIGÉ HIDAY

The public tends to hold a stereotypical image of mentally ill persons as dangerous and unpredictable. More specifically, the image is of persons who unexpectedly lash out violently towards others (Gerbner et al. 1981; Link et al. 1987; Monahan 1992; Nunnally 1961; Rabkin 1972, 1974; Steadman and Cocozza 1978; Weiss 1986). Some early empirical studies gave support to this stereotype (Lagos, Perlmutter, and Suefinger 1977; Rofman, Askinazi, and Fant 1980; Sosowsky 1980). Among social scientists, however, a strong intellectual tradition developed which held that the stereotype was false and that mentally ill persons were no more dangerous than others (Link and Cullen 1986; Miller 1976; Monahan 1981; Monahan and Steadman 1983; Morse 1978, 1982; Rabkin 1979; Shah 1974, 1978; Warren 1977, 1982).

Recently some social scientists of this tradition have reversed their position on the basis of new, more sophisticated studies (Monahan 1992; Hodgins 1993). These studies have found a modest association between major mental illness and violence which cannot be explained away as spurious with demographic and historical controls. This paper discusses their findings and further examines social factors framing the relationship between the two variables. It suggests that, to understand the relationship, socializing conditions and intervening experiences must be taken into account more fully. It examines unanswered questions about those conditions and experiences, and proposes a causal model which suggests only indirect and contingent paths between mental illness and violence. But first, this paper briefly reviews earlier studies supporting the stereotype and the social science critique of their weaknesses, and describes in greater detail the two recent research projects which have underpinned the social scientists' reversal.

EARLIER STUDIES

Research supporting the stereotype of violent mentally ill persons offered three types of evidence: (1) reports of dangerous behavior among mental patients prior to, during, and after hospitalization (Hiday 1988; Lagos et al. 1977; McNiel and Binder 1986; Rofman et al. 1980; Tardiff and Sweillam 1980; Yesavage et al. 1982); (2) high rates of mental illness among jail inmates (Lamb and Grant 1982, 1983; Swank and Winer 1976; Valdiserri, Carroll, and Hartl 1986; Washington and Diamond 1985); and (3) higher rates of arrest among mental health patients than among the general population (Durbin, Pasework, and Albers 1977; Giovannoni and Gurel 1967; Schuerman and Kobrin 1984; Sosowsky 1980).

A number of social scientists challenged this evidence, pointing out that the data were not valid to answer the question of the relative violence of the mentally ill because of major methodological flaws in the sampling of mentally ill persons and comparison groups, and in the measurement of violence and mental illness. More specifically, they contended that mental patients were far from representative of all mentally-disordered persons; that the general population was not an appropriate comparison group, especially not for mental patients discharged from state hospitals, who typically constituted the mentally-disordered samples; that dangerousness measures, often derived from legal and medical documents, were unreliable, poorly defined, and frequently too broad; that there was no control group with which to compare levels of dangerousness; and that arrests and the condition of being an inmate were inadequate measures of violence (Hiday 1992, 1988; Mulvey and Lidz 1993; Monahan 1981; Monahan and Steadman 1983; Rabkin 1979; Shah 1974; Steadman, Cocozza, and Melick 1978).

With similar data but improved methodology, some social scientists demonstrated that arrest rate differences between mentally ill patients and the general population disappeared when age, gender, socioeconomic status, and arrest history were controlled (Melick, Steadman, and Cocozza 1979; Steadman et al. 1978; Steadman and Felson 1984; Steadman and Ribner 1982). Nonetheless, these studies as well were unable to evaluate fully the question of the relative violence of the mentally ill since the researchers did not have large, random surveys of communities to identify reliably both treated and untreated cases of mental illness, and to assess violence reliably among both non–mentally ill and mentally ill persons.

THE NEW EVIDENCE

Recently, two separate teams of social science researchers creatively adapted large psychiatric epidemiological surveys, which were designed for other purposes but which had reliable measures of treated and untreated mental illness, to address the question of the relative violence of the mentally ill. Although their violence measures indicate only the presence or absence of a few major violent behaviors, these studies represent an important advance, for they provide the first estimates of violence levels in the community among both non–mentally ill and mentally ill persons.

One team, led by Jeffrey Swanson (1994, 1993; Swanson et al. 1990), analyzed the Epidemiologic Catchment Area (ECA) data which reliably identified in the general population persons meeting psychiatric diagnostic criteria for the major psychoses and a number of other mental disorders (Robins et al. 1981; Robins and Regier 1991).

Swanson and his colleagues generated a measure of violence from items embedded in the symptom criteria of antisocial personality and alcohol abuse/dependence disorders.[1] They found that most mentally ill people were not violent; only a small minority with major mental illness (7%) committed any violent acts in the previous year. This rate of violence, however, is higher than for those who do not meet any of the diagnostic criteria (2%). They also found that substance abuse/dependence carried much higher prevalence rates of violence than major mental illness (alcohol, 25%; drug, 35%), and that the comorbidity of major mental illness with substance abuse raised the rate of violence (29%) above mental illness alone. These results held with controls for age, gender, marital status, and SES. In terms of relative risks for violence, major mental illness was not as important as being young, male, single, lower class, and substance abusing or substance dependent.

The other team led by Bruce Link (Link and Stueve 1994; Link, Andrews, and Cullen 1992) used data from a survey of psychiatric patients and community residents, designed as a methods study to compare one-month and one-year versions of the Psychiatric Epidemiology Research Interview (PERI, Dohrenwend et al. 1980). The survey contained five items measuring recent and past self-reported violence.[2] To these they added official lifetime total arrests and arrests for violent offenses. To the survey's controls for individual sociodemographic characteristics and need for approval, they added controls for community violence and community social context. Their data indicated that new, ongoing, and former patients had substantially higher rates of violence than never-treated community members. Narrowing their analysis to recent violence and to recent psychotic symptomatology as measured by the PERI scale, all differences between patient groups and the never-treated community sample disappeared. In other words, psychotic symptoms, not patient status, predicted violence. Furthermore, they found that psychotic symptoms significantly predicted violence in the never-treated group. Swanson (1994) has since supported the importance of active psychotic symptoms in finding that ECA ex-patients with no arrest history and no psychopathological symptoms for one year were no more violent than those in the general population.

Carrying their analysis further, Link and Stueve (1994) tested the hypothesis that it is the nature and content of the psychotic episode which is important. They reasoned that it is not psychotic symptoms in general, such as odd delusions or hallucinations or disorganization, which are the connection to violent behavior, but rather that it is those psychotic symptoms which produce feelings of personal threat or involve intrusion of thoughts that can override self-control. When the disordered person believes s/he is gravely threatened by others who intend harm, and believes that others are dominating her/his mind, constraints on behavior are more likely to be overridden, and violence becomes more likely. Using the same data set with the same controls, but only three-symptom items indicative of threat/control-override, their hypothesis was supported: differences between patient and never-treated groups with regard to recent violence disappeared when the threat/control-override symptoms were controlled; and threat/control-override symptoms were significant predictors of recent violence even when other psychotic symptoms and the individual and community controls were held constant. Swanson et al. (1995) have since tested and supported this hypothesis with the ECA data.

Two points need to be emphasized about these recent epidemiological studies: (1) not all mentally ill persons have higher rates of violence, but only those who have major mental illness and recent psychotic symptomatology; and (2) the contribution to violence of major mental illness, current psychotic symptoms, or threat/control-override symptoms is only modest. Other variables are much more strongly predictive: being a young, adult, single, male, of lower socioeconomic status, and being a substance abuser hold far greater risks of violence.

THE NATURE OF THE RELATIONSHIP

These studies have established that there is a relationship between major mental illness and violence that cannot be explained by inadequate sampling or inappropriate comparison groups, but we still have much to decipher before we can understand the nature of the relationship. Most important to examine closely are four substantive areas[3]: (1) the direction of the association; (2) the situation in which violence occurs; (3) the role of alcohol and drug abuse; and (4) the role of cooccurring psychopathy or antisocial personality disorder.

The Direction of the Association between Major Mental Illness and Violence. Swanson and Link have shown the relationship to be between recent active symptomatology and recent violence, but without information on the timing or sequencing of events, we cannot know the direction of causality. Many have assumed it is from the illness or symptoms to violence (Bloom 1989; Hodgins 1993; Krakowski, Volavka, and Brizer 1986). Indeed, Link and Stueve (1994) hypothesize that the threat/control-override psychotic symptoms induce fear and disrupt internal controls to produce violence. A recent unpublished study with sequential data by Mulvey et al. (1994) gives some support to this view. They found that psychiatric symptomatology in mental patients at the time of evaluation in an emergency room was moderately predictive of violence in the ensuing six months, even when the patient's prior violence was controlled for. However, not all members of their sample carried a diagnosis of major mental illness, and not all symptoms were indicative of psychosis.

It may be that causality runs from violence to major mental illness. Violence may lead to fear, suspicion, and distrust as well as to head injuries, which may lead to mental illness. A number of studies have reported the high rates of victimization experienced by mentally ill persons, especially abuse as children and from spouses as adults (Bryer et al. 1987; Carmen, Rieker, and Mills 1984; Estroff and Zimmer 1994; Kessler and

Magee 1994; Rose, Peabody, and Stratigeas 1991; Winfield et al. 1990). On the other hand, there may be a more complex, interactive relationship between violence and major mental disorder which produces future violence.

Mirowsky and Ross (1983) hypothesize and support with community survey data a link between victimization and paranoid beliefs which is embedded in the stratification system. They argue that persons in low socioeconomic positions are characterized by powerlessness, exploitation, and threat of victimization. Although Mirowsky and Ross were not addressing violence directly, much victimization is violent, especially among the poor (Drake et al. 1990; Dodge, Bates, and Pettit et al. 1990; Seltzer and Kalmuss 1988). These conditions of lower-class life produce a belief in external control which, with fear, leads to mistrust and suspicion of others (Mirowsky and Ross 1983). Persons with thought problems or delusions and hallucinations are particularly vulnerable, and their mistrust is likely to turn into paranoid beliefs (Mirowsky 1985). While Mirowsky did not tie these paranoid beliefs to violent physical assaults by mentally-disordered persons, the work of Link and his colleagues points to that connection. Furthermore, the prevalence of violence in the environment at the bottom of the stratification system makes it more likely that lower class persons with paranoid beliefs will choose violence as a solution to their perceived threats. Mental illness thus produces the delusions and hallucinations, but location in the stratification system produces the attendant distrust, suspicion, and socialization to physical aggression. The interaction between mental illness and underclass life (including the violence therein) results later in higher rates of violence among those with severe mental disorder.

The Situation in Which Violence Occurs. Although some scholars have pointed for more than a decade to the need for research on the situations surrounding violent incidents, few studies have been directed to situational variables (Felson and

Steadman 1983; Steadman 1982; Steadman and Ribner 1982). Violence associated with mentally ill persons is generally described apart from any social or interpersonal interaction, and apart from the interpersonal history of those involved. Persons with major mental illness may often be provoked, or their symptomatology may lead to tense situations as nerves fray and as others try to persuade them to desist in the annoying behavior or to comply with treatment. These situations may then result in pushing, hitting, and fighting (Edwards and Reid 1983; Sheridan et al. 1990; Straznickas, McNiel, and Binder 1993), especially in environments where physical aggression is commonly used in disputes (Steadman 1982; Yesavage et al. 1983). Alternatively, the vulnerability of persons with major disorders may make them attractive objects for bullying which provokes them to defensive violent acts. A history of such bullying may make the mentally ill person more reactive, especially towards long-time perpetrators. In these situations, major mental illness and its symptomatology would be an indirect cause, rather than a direct cause of violence. (Link et al. [1992] and Monahan [1992] also make this point).

Estroff and Zimmer (1994) emphasize the context of violent incidents and point out that "violence seldom happens unilaterally." Through in-depth interviews with severely ill mental patients and their significant others, they found that mentally ill persons were often victims of violence by members of their close social networks. Estroff and Zimmer thus interpret many of their subjects' high scores on perception of hostility (the PERI paranoia subscale) to be based in reality—that is, on the violence and threatening relations actually experienced. They warn that aggressive behavior is too often blamed on mentally ill persons, and that the legitimate fears of the mentally disordered are too often considered symptoms of psychotic diagnosis because situations and interpersonal histories are not taken into account.

One can expect that mentally-disordered persons will react in the same manner and for the same reasons as non–mentally disordered persons in situations of unfairness, which by definition bullying and victimization meet. Thus, one can predict that persons with a major mental illness who suffer a history of being bullied and victimized will become predisposed to anticipating mistreatment, will appraise situations antagonistically, and will become angry more frequently than others not so provoked (Dodge et al. 1990; Novaco 1994). While anger is neither necessary nor sufficient for physical aggression, it is significantly related to violence among both mental patients and nonpatients (Dodge et al. 1990; Kay, Wolkenfeld, and Murrill 1988; Novaco 1994; Segal et al. 1988).

The Role of Alcohol and Drug Intoxication. In the studies of Swanson, Link, and their colleagues, we do not know whether alcohol or drug abuse was involved in the violent incidents, except in the case of one item in Swanson's study. However, we know that substance abuse—especially long term abuse—is associated with violence (Collins and Schlenger 1988; Drake et al. 1990; Hodgins 1992; Lindqvist and Allebeck 1989; Pihl and Peterson 1993), and we know from Swanson and his colleagues (1990, 1993) that substance abuse/dependence increases the risk of violence among persons with major mental illness by a fourfold factor. Recent studies of jail and prison inmates which have used standardized, reliable diagnostic instruments and have reported higher prevalence rates of major mental disorders than in the general population (Coté and Hodgins 1990; Teplin 1990), have found on closer inspection that these mentally-disordered inmates tend to be substance abusers (Abram 1989; Abram and Teplin 1991; Coté and Hodgins 1990). For instance, city jail detainees with severe psychotic illness (schizophrenia or major affective disorder) in Teplin's sample (1990) were highly likely to be substance abusers or substance-dependent (84.8% with alcohol and 57.9% with drugs), and they were likely to have been using drugs or alcohol at the time of their arrests (56.5% drinking and 47.5% using drugs, according to Abram and Teplin 1991). Danish male homicide offenders with a major psychosis showed an even greater propensity to be intoxicated at the time of the homicide (89%; Gottlieb, Gabrielson, and Kramp 1987). Since some persons with severe mental illness become intoxicated on alcohol in amounts less that that required for meeting diagnostic criteria for substance abuse (Drake et al. 1990), intoxication at the time of violent incidents needs to be examined as well as substance abuse/dependence, or we may miss an important explanation of the association between severe mental illness and violence.

The Role of Psychopathy/Antisocial Personality Disorder (ASP).[4] Link did not measure ASP, and Swanson could not control for ASP since his primary measures of violence were symptoms of that disorder. It may be, however, that ASP co-occurs in the case of mentally-disordered persons who are violent, and that ASP rather than major mental illness or active psychosis propels the assaultive behavior. Four studies suggest that this may be the case although the first two do not separate violent from nonviolent offenders. Among their jail detainee sample, Abram and Teplin (1991) reported that just over two-thirds (68.7%) of those with a major mental illness also met criteria for a diagnosis of ASP. (Only 6% of those with major mental illness had neither substance abuse/dependence nor ASP.) Furthermore, Abram (1990) found among those with major depression that ASP was the primary syndrome in that it preceded both the substance abuse/dependence and the depression in terms of its appearance in their lives. Robins' (1993) analysis of ECA data also found ASP to be primary. They reported that the association between crime and major mental illness completely disappeared when controls were placed for ASP adult symptoms, childhood conduct disorder symptoms (generally considered integral to ASP diagnosis), and substance abuse. They concluded that the association of major mental illness with crime is not direct, but occurs when these disorders are secondary to ASP and substance abuse.

More directly, two studies linked psychopathy with violence among offenders with major mental disorders. Rice and Harris (1992) found ASP, as measured by the Hare Psychopathy Checklist (Revised Hare and Hart 1993), to predict violent recidivism among schizophrenic patients who were evaluated in a forensic psychiatric hospital. Hafner and Boker (1982) found persons with major mental illness who committed a violent crime over a 10-year period to be basically different from nonoffending mentally-disordered persons in having a history of antisocial traits which preceded the onset of their psychosis. These mentally ill offenders also tended to have delusions and fears, which suggests that it is only a certain type of psychotic individual who also is ASP who becomes violent.

It is not unlikely that both ASP and substance abuse are involved in the violent behavior of the severely mentally ill, given that almost 90 percent of active psychotic episodes occur among persons with three or more lifetime disorders (Kessler et al. 1994), and given that ASP and substance abuse are very closely associated (Boyd et al. 1984; Gorton and Akhtar 1990; Robins, Tipp, and Przybeck 1991).

We need to examine these variables and their relation to mental illness and violence in the larger social context to be able to understand the association between mental illness and violence. Consideration of the larger social context is important not only to control the confounding potential of socio-economic status, neighborhood stability, and community crime, as Swanson, Link, and their colleagues did, but also to ascertain on the individual level how position in the social stratification system affects the conditions of life such that individuals with severe mental illness become involved in violent incidents. Violence and some manifestations of mental illness largely grow from the structural arrangements in which individuals are embedded. These arrangements determine to a great extent the experiences, people, and situations

to which individuals are exposed and from which they learn, as well as the resources and opportunities from which individuals are able to draw (Pearlin 1992).

MODELING THE RELATIONSHIP

As a first step in examining variables important to the relationship between mental illness and violence in the larger social context, we propose a causal model[5] (Figure 1). Our causal model links social stratification with both major mental illness and violence through the structured types of strains, events, situations, and persons an individual experiences as an integral part of life. It posits that the social context is responsible for violence committed by persons with severe mental illness because it shapes both their nonpsychotic behavior and their manifestations of active psychosis.

The model concentrates on explicating violence-inducing social forces, and neglects mediators such as compliance with appropriate medication and supportive instrumental and emotional relationships. Obviously, a complete model would have to include such mediators along with the demographic variables of age and gender, which have well-established relationships to violence. Figure 1 depicts them only as moderating factors which need to be considered in the production of violence. The model also focuses on severe mental illness or psychosis, separating it from other psychiatric Axis I and Axis II disorders, and from substance abuse/dependence and antisocial personality disorder, which both play important parts in the model.

The model begins with two exogenous variables: *social disorganization/poverty,* and *neurobiological pathology.* Neurobiological pathology, involving abnormalities in both brain function and structure, is causative in substance abuse/dependence and in severe mental illness. Several lines of research support these causal links. Behavioral genetics with family, twin, and adoption studies has provided strong evidence that genetic factors are

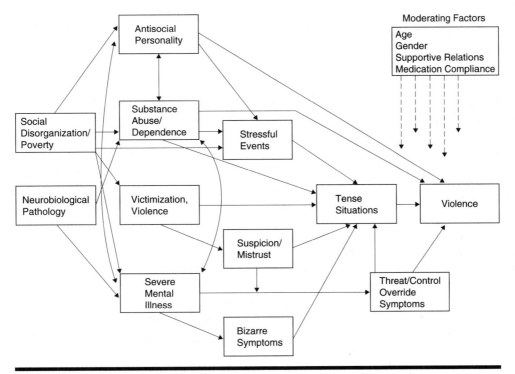

FIGURE 1   Causal Model Linking Social Stratification with Mental Illness and Violence

operative in schizophrenia, affective disorders, and alcoholism (Cannon et al. 1994; Kelty et al. 1994; Kendler and Silverman 1991; Moldin 1994), and epidemiological studies have found prenatal infections and specific insults such as anoxia to be risk factors in the development of schizophrenia (Green, Satz, and Christenson 1994; Mednick et al. 1988; Mednick, Huttunen, and Machon 1994; Torrey et al. 1994). However, the exact mechanisms producing the disorders have been difficult to characterize. Indirect pharmacologic evidence suggests neurochemical explanations, but even their research has been unable to identify the specific defects responsible for behavioral manifestations of psychoses (Csernansky and Newcomer 1994; Martin, Owen, and Morihisa 1987). A newer line of research is pursuing theories that structural brain abnormalities play a part in vulnerability to schizophrenia (Cannon and Marco 1994; Csernansky and

Newcomer 1994). While the available evidence shows that neurobiological pathology is causative, it also indicates that neurobiological pathology alone cannot account for the disorders. Our model suggests that social disorganization is another causative agent in severe mental illness and substance abuse/dependence, affecting the development and course of these disorders (Cohen 1993; Dohrenwend et al. 1992).

Social disorganization is found in conditions of poverty, but it is not merely a matter of low income or loss of income. Rather, it is the condition of having extremely low income for a large percentage of one's life and of what that means in today's society; living with constant deprivation, lacking hope of having anything better, and believing in an inexplicable world where external forces arbitrarily determine what outcomes occur, outcomes that are too often negative and painful. More importantly, social disorganization is the breakdown of family and other micro-institutions which give meaning and sustain the individual. Thus, individuals living in these conditions lose their moorings, live in a state of anomie, and have increasingly fewer chances to overcome their current poverty and deprivation, especially by legal means. These individuals have little sense of control, and few constructive ways of expressing anger and fear. Families in social disorganization tend to be fatherless, and to offer little shelter from a hostile world and little guidance to overcoming environmental deprivations. Communities in social disorganization are characterized by persistent poverty, inability to exert social control over their members, and few opportunities beyond menial or illegal jobs.

Since the early days of social science research, empirical studies have found mental illness, substance abuse, and other forms of deviance to be more frequent in conditions of poverty and social disorganization (Barker et al. 1992; Catalano 1991; Faris and Dunham 1939; Holzer et al. 1986; Leighton et al. 1963; Srole et al. 1962). And, since the early days of sociology, cultural norms and socioeconomic deprivation have been major explanations of the relationship (see Kohn [1972] and Wheaton [1980] for links to mental illness through distrust, fatalism, coping ability, and effort). More recently, stress theorists have pointed to the chronic strain of social disorganization and poverty as principal causes of stress. They have shown how long-term economic and social deprivation may lead directly and indirectly through life events to greater symptomatology (including substance abuse) and psychotic episodes in adults (Bruce, Takeuchi, and Leaf 1991; Catalano 1991; Catalano et al. 1993a,b; Cohen 1993; Dohrenwend 1990; Dohrenwend et al. 1992; Kessler 1982; Pearlin 1989; Pearlin et al. 1981). Even more recently, researchers have posited that both current and persistent poverty affect children as well as adults, demonstrating their impact on children's manifestations of mental disorder symptomatology (depression, anxiety, dependency, and antisocial behavior) through their detrimental effect on parental behavior (Avison 1993; McLeod and Shanahan 1993). Such childhood symptoms, though not indicative of major mental disorder and not set for life (Garmezy 1991), place these children at a disadvantage, as they go through life, in coping with adverse conditions, including the likely continuing strain of social disorganization and poverty and any major neurobiological pathology which may become active (Cohen 1993).

Severe mental illness, ASP, and substance abuse/dependence could each be predisposing, precipitating, or perpetuating factors in the other two (Gorton and Akhtar 1990); thus, there are no causal arrows from one of the three to any of the others. Since the model attempts to predict later violence, we need only note the interrelationships among the three (curved lines), and not tease out their complex associations.

The model indicates that social disorganization and the accompanying poverty lead to victimization and violence. Although there is debate in the literature as to whether absolute or relative poverty affects violence, both official records and survey data find violence higher in lower socioeconomic groups and in poverty areas (Barker et al. 1992; Dodge et al. 1990; Land, McCall, and Cohen 1990; Link et al. 1992; National Research Council 1993; Patterson 1991; Rosenberg and Fenley 1991; Seltzer and Kalmuss 1988; Swanson et al. 1990; Widom 1989). The violence occurs both inside the family in the form of spouse, child, and elder abuse, and outside the family from acquaintances and strangers, and among others the individual observes. Evidence from ECA data also points to recent economic hardship in the form of job loss as causing violence and being more predictive of violence than psychiatric disorder (Catalano et al. 1993a). Similarly, victimization, which incorporates not only violence but also other types of harm and exploitation, is more likely to occur among those living in poverty areas (Mirowsky 1985; Mirowsky and Ross 1983; National Research Council 1993; Rosenberg and Fenley 1991).

The model indicates that substance abuse/dependence and ASP lead directly to violence.

Indeed, the criteria for each of these diagnoses include violent behaviors as well as other behaviors which are likely to lead to violence such as irritability, aggressiveness, and impulsivity (American Psychiatric Association 1987; Helzer, Burnam, and McEvoy 1991; Robins et al. 1991). They also lead to stressful events (negative life events) through the results of their respective behaviors. For instance, through intoxication, persons with substance abuse/dependence or ASP are more likely to be arrested, lose their jobs, experience divorce, and the like (Catalano et al. 1993b; Collins and Schlenger 1988).

In the model, social disorganization and poverty, because of the chronic strain they produce, lead to stressful events such as job loss and separation (Pearlin 1989, 1992; Wheaton 1980). Stressful events, in turn, lead directly to tense or conflictive situations which can result in violent outcomes (Catalano et al. 1993a; Levinson and Ramsey 1979; National Research Council 1993; Steadman and Ribner 1982). Tense or conflictive situations in the model are similar to Novaco's "provocation categories" (1994). They include situations in which recurrent problems emerge. Examples of these are when chronically scarce resources such as food, space, and spending money must be divided among members of a chaotic and congested household, and when goal-directed behavior is blocked and is seen to be inconsiderate, arbitrary, and unfair, as in the case of a family's attempts to thwart an alcoholic from meeting his buddies at a bar. Additional examples of problem-enhancing situations are a group demeaning, bullying, manipulating, or falsely accusing one of its members; group members becoming annoyed and irritated at bizarre symptoms of mentally ill persons; and others reacting with fear or coercive measures to the words and actions of a mentally-disordered person. These tense situations are more likely to erupt in violence under conditions where physical attack is an acceptable, if not a preferable, alternative in conflicts (National Research Council 1993; Rosenberg and Fenley 1991; Oliver 1994; Toch 1992; Yesavage et al. 1983).

Following Mirowsky and Ross (1983), the model posits that victimization and violence lead to a psychological belief system of suspicion/mistrust. The model shows that the belief system of suspicion/mistrust interacts with severe mental illness to produce the threat/control-override symptoms which lead to violence. Since most command hallucinations and threating delusions do not lead to violence (Hellerstein, Frosch, and Koenigsberg 1987), more than these symptoms is required. One path from threat/control-override symptoms to violence is direct, but another goes through tense situations. The model also posits a third path from severe mental illness to violence—through bizarre symptoms which lead to tense situations as others try to check the individual in his behavior, or become annoyed by the behavior. The link from severe mental illness to violence in any case is only through active psychotic symptoms.

SUMMARY AND CONCLUSIONS

The model presented in this paper of the association between mental illness and violence posits that severe mental illness, even active psychosis, is not a sufficient cause of violence. Rather, for severe mental illness to lead to violence, social factors must intervene. The model postulates that social disorganization and poverty is a basic cause, that it is the conditions of social disorganization and poverty which affect the course of major mental illness and produce the cooccurring antisocial personality and substance disorders, and the environment of victimization and violence. The model posits that it is when severe mental illness is combined with antisocial personality and substance disorders, and is shaped by an environment of violence, that the behavior of the severely mentally disordered is likely to become violent. The severely mentally ill become physically assaultive for one of three reasons: (1) they abuse substances and/or have an antisocial personality disorder, which lead to violence directly or indirectly through stressful events and tense situations (in any case it is the substance abuse and/or ASP, not the mental illness, propelling the violence); (2) they have active psychosis, which causes bizarre symptoms that lead to tense situations and ultimately to violence; (3) they have active psychosis which, in interaction with suspicion/mistrust, causes threat/control-override symptoms that lead to violence either directly or indirectly through tense situations. The tense situations are likely to turn into violent interactions because of the environment of violence/victimization in which they occur, an environment created by social disorganization and poverty.

Placing mental illness and violence in this social context gives a more balanced view than the dominant medical model's focus on the individual in etiology, prognosis and treatment. The model incorporates neurobiological causes of severe mental illness, but emphasizes the social nature of its course, manifestations, and links with violence. Where violence by severely mentally ill persons is not propelled by substance abuse/dependence or ASP, it arises in most cases out of tense social situations in which severely mentally ill persons and others interact. While a tense situation may be brought about because of the symptomatology of the mentally-disordered person, the interaction becomes violent because one or both parties learned from earlier experiences that pushing, shoving, hitting, and so on were acceptable methods of settling disputes, and failed to learn alternative conflict resolution techniques.

By developing this model of the association between mental illness and violence, we hope to direct research away from an overemphasis on intrapsychic forces with direct links to violence, and towards social forces which link severe mental illness and violence indirectly through multiple pathways. Such research requires longitudinal data with relatively frequent observations and reports from more than one source in order to capture the timing and sequencing of episodes of psychotic symptomatology, stressful events, tense situations, and incidences of violence, relevant characteristics of the imminent tense situation (including emotion, disagreement, provocation, and participants' conflict history), immediate and historical alcohol and drug abuse/dependence, and early and current experience of social disorganization and poverty in the family and neighborhood.

We also hope that the model and ensuing research can be used to guide clinicians to look for substance abuse/dependence, ASP, and violence/victimization in patients' early and present environments, especially among family and friends. Besides giving appropriate medication and seeking compliance, clinicians may do well to work with patients and their families on coping strategies, particularly conflict resolution and avoidance of tense situations. However, according to the model, preventive measures that reach beyond the clinic will need to be employed if the link between major mental disorder and violence is to be severed. Such measures could include programs to teach conflict coping and prosocial skills to at-risk children and their parents as those developed by the Oregon Social Learning Center (Dishion, Patterson, and Kavanagh 1992; Tremblay et al. 1992) or more general programs aimed at strengthening families and integrating communities. More basic alleviation of social disorganization and poverty will require larger-scale political and economic action.

Finally, we hope that the model and ensuing research can be used to allay the public's fears of mentally ill persons by locating the cause of violence among the mentally ill in social forces. Reassurance of the public is particularly important now that an epidemiological association between violence and active symptoms of severe mental illness has been established.

NOTES

1. A respondent was rated violent for having done any of the following in the previous year: having used a weapon such as stick, knife, or gun in a fight (except in the occupational line of duty); having been in more than one fight that came to blows other than with spouse or partner; having spanked or hit a child hard enough so that s/he had bruises, having had to

stay in bed, or see a doctor; having hit or thrown things at spouse/partner, and having hit or thrown things first on more than one occasion, regardless of who started the argument; and having gotten into physical fights while drinking.

2. The items were: hitting in past month/year, fighting in past five years, weapon use in past five years, ever hurting someone badly in a fight, and ever being arrested.

3. A fifth area needing investigation is the frequency and severity of violence. Our measurement has not allowed us to know how often the violence occurs or how much harm is perpetrated by the violence. It may be that, although more mentally ill people are violent, the violent non–mentally ill are more *frequently* violent and/or their violence does more physical harm. Data concerning these aspects of violent behavior would give us more information and a better understanding of the relationship between violence and mental illness. Current research studies (Lidz, Mulvey, and Gardner 1993; Monahan and Steadman 1994) should provide such data.

4. Antisocial personality disorder (ASP) is a recognized Axis II diagnosis of the American Psychiatric Association, characterized by violation of social norms across many areas, including irresponsibility and aggressiveness towards others beginning in childhood and continuing into adulthood (Robins et al. 1991). As with other personality disorders, there is much comorbidity with Axis I disorders (Gorton and Akhtar 1990). The diagnosis is faulted for being no more than a medicalization of bad behavior. Furthermore, there have been major problems with both validity and reliability in its diagnosis (Hart, Hare, and Forth 1994);

and attempts to link ASP with crime and violence can easily fall into a tautology: being an offender or engaging in violence leads to a diagnosis of ASP; then ASP is said to predict crime and violence. Ongoing empirical work by Hare and Hart and their associates (1993, 1994) has shown an association between psychopathy (their preferred term) and violence while avoiding the tautology. They measure two stable factors underlying psychopathy/ASP, only one of which includes violent and/or criminal behavior. The two factors are: (1) interpersonal and affective characteristics (e.g., superficiality, grandiosity, manipulativeness, irresponsibility, and lack of remorse and empathy); and (2) impulsive, antisocial and unstable lifestyle (including violent and criminal behavior). They have found that the affective-interpersonal factor is as predictive of violence as is the social deviance factor (Hart et al. 1994).

5. Causal modeling is a formal methodology employed to test for theorized causal inference in situations where experimentation is impossible. We use a causal model because it best explicates our theory of the network of causal relations between important variables linked with each other in producing the association between severe mental illness and violence. Causal modeling forces specification of assumptions and develops implications that are not obvious which, in verbal theorizing, are often hidden. It is an important step in guiding research because it directs attention to variables needing measurement and can be translated into mathematical equations to test the theory's predictions with statistical procedures (Blalock 1961, 1969; Heise 1975).

REFERENCES

Abram, Karen M. 1989. "The Effect of Coocurring Disorders on Criminal Careers: Interaction of Antisocial Personality, Alcohol, and Drug Disorders." *International Journal of Law and Psychiatry* 12:133–48.

———. 1990. "The Problem of Coocurring Disorders among Jail Detainees: Antisocial Disorder, Alcoholism, Drug Abuse, and Depression." *Law and Human Behavior* 14:333–46.

Abram, Karen M., and Linda A. Teplin. 1991. "Coocurring Disorders among Mentally Ill Jail Detainees: Implications for Public Policy." *American Psychologist* 46:1036–45.

American Psychiatric Association. 1987. *Diagnostic and Statistical Manual of Mental Disorders.* 3d ed. rev. Washington, DC: American Psychiatric Association.

Avison, William R. 1993. "Families in Poverty: A Stress Process Analysis of the Psychosocial Consequences." Paper presented to the Society for the Study of Social Problems, Miami Beach, FL.

Barker, Peggy R., Ronald W. Manderscheid, Gerry E. Hendershot, Susan S. Jack, Charlotte A. Schoenborn, and Ingrid Goldstrom. 1992. "Serious Mental Illness and Disability in the Adult Household Population: United States, 1989." *Advance Data from Vital and Health Statistics,* no. 218. Hyattsville, MD: National Center for Health Statistics.

Blalock, Hubert M. Jr. 1961. *Causal Inferences in Nonexperimental Research.* Chapel Hill, NC: University of North Carolina Press.

———. 1969. *Theory Construction: From Verbal to Mathematical Formulations.* Englewood Cliffs, NJ: Prentice Hall.

Bloom, Joseph. 1989. "The Character of Danger in Psychiatric Practice: Are the Mentally Ill Dangerous?" *Bulletin of the American Academy of Psychiatry and Law* 17:241–54.

Boyd, Jeffrey H., Jack D. Burke, Ernest Gruenberg, Charles E. Holzer, Donald S. Rae, Linda K. George,

Marvin Karno, Roger Stoltzman, Larry McEvoy, and Gerald Nestadt. 1984. "Exclusion Criteria of DSM-III: A Study of Cooccurrence of Hierarchy-Free Syndromes." *Archives of General Psychiatry* 41:983–89.

Bruce, Martha L., David T. Takeuchi, and Philip J. Leaf. 1991. "Poverty and Psychiatric Status: Longitudinal Evidence from the New Haven Epidemiologic Catchment Area Study." *Archives of General Psychiatry* 48:470–74.

Bryer, Jeffrey B., Bernadette A. Nelson, Jean B. Miller, and Pamela A. Krol. 1987. "Childhood Sexual and Physical Abuse as Factors in Adult Psychiatric Illness." *American Journal of Psychiatry* 144:1423–30.

Cannon, Tyrone D., and Elysa Marco. 1994. "Structural Brain Abnormalities as Indicators of Vulnerability to Schizophrenia." *Schizophrenia Bulletin* 20:89–102.

Cannon, Tyrone D., Lisa E. Zorrilla, Derri Shtasel, Raquel E. Gur, Ruben C. Gur, Elysa J. Marco, Paul Moberg, and R. Arlen Price. 1994. "Neuropsychological Functioning in Siblings Discordant for Schizophrenia and Healthy Volunteers." *Archives of General Psychiatry* 51:651–61.

Carmen, Elaine, Patricia Rieker, and Trudy Mills. 1984. "Victims of Violence and Psychiatric Illness." *American Journal of Psychiatry* 141:378–83.

Catalano, Ralph. 1991. "The Health Effects of Economic Insecurity: An Analytic Review." *American Journal of Public Health* 81:1148–52.

Catalano, Ralph, David Dooley, Raymond W. Novaco, Georjeanna Wilson, and Richard Hough. 1993a. "Using ECA Survey Data to Examine the Effect of Job Layoffs on Violent Behavior." *Hospital and Community Psychiatry* 44:874–79.

Catalano, Ralph, David Dooley, Georjeanna Wilson, and Richard Hough. 1993b. "Job Loss and Alcohol Abuse: A Test Using Data from the Epidemiologic Catchment Area Project." *Journal of Health and Social Behavior* 34:215–25.

Cohen, Carl I. 1993. "Poverty and the Course of Schizophrenia: Implications for Research and Policy." *Hospital and Community Psychiatry* 44:951–58.

Collins, James J., and William E. Schlenger. 1988. "Acute and Chronic Effects of Alcohol Use on Violence." *Journal of Studies on Alcohol* 49:516–21.

Coté, Gilles and Sheilagh Hodgins. 1990. "Cooccurring Mental Disorders among Criminal Offenders." *Bulletin of the American Academy of Psychiatry and Law* 18:271–81.

———. 1992. "The Prevalence of Major Mental Disorders among Homicide Offenders." *International Journal of Law and Psychiatry* 15:89–99.

Csernansky, John G., and John W. Newcomer. 1994. "Are There Neurochemical Indicators of Risk for Schizophrenia?" *Schizophrenia Bulletin* 20:75–88.

Dishion, Thomas J., Gerald R. Patterson, and Kathryn A. Kavanagh. 1992. "An Experimental Test of the Coercion Model: Linking Theory, Measurement, and Intervention." Pp. 253–82 in *Preventing Antisocial Behavior: Interventions from Birth Through Adolescent,* edited by J. McCord and R. E. Tremblay. New York: Guilford.

Dodge, Kenneth A., John E. Bates, and Gregory S. Pettit. 1990. "Mechanisms in the Cycle of Violence." *Science* 250:1678–83.

Dohrenwend, Bruce P. 1990. "Socioeconomic Status and Psychiatry Disorders: Are the Issues Still Compelling?" *Social Psychiatry and Psychiatric Epidemiology* 25:41–47.

Dohrenwend, Bruce P., Itzhak Levav, Patrick E. Shrout, Sharon Schwartz, Guedalia Naveh, Bruce G. Link, Andrew E. Skodol, and Ann Stueve. 1992. "Socioeconomic Status and Psychiatric Disorders: The Causation-Selection Issue." *Science* 255:946–52.

Dohrenwend, Bruce P., Patrick E. Shrout, Gladys Ergi, and Frederick S. Mendelsohn. 1980. "Nonspecific Psychological Distress and Other Dimensions of Psychopathology: Measures for Use in the General Population." *Archives of General Psychiatry* 37:1229–36.

Drake, Robert E., Fred C. Osher, Douglas L. Noordsy, Stephanie C. Hurlbut, Gregory B. Teague, and Malcolm S. Beaudett. 1990. "Diagnosis of Alcohol Use Disorders in Schizophrenia." *Schizophrenia Bulletin* 16:57–67.

Durbin, Jeffrey, Richard Pasework, and Dale Albers. 1977. "Criminality and Mental Illness: A Study of Arrest Rates in a Rural State." *American Journal of Psychiatry* 134:80–83.

Edwards, J. Guy, and William H. Reid. 1983. "Violence in Psychiatric Facilities in Europe and the United States." Pp. 131–42 in *Assaults within Psychiatric Facilities,* edited by V. R. Lion and W. H. Reid. New York: Grune and Stratton.

Estroff, Sue E., and Catherine Zimmer. 1994. "Social Networks, Social Support, and Violence among Persons with Severe, Persistent Mental Illness." Pp. 269–95 in *Violence and Mental Disorder,* edited by J. Monahan and H. J. Steadman. Chicago, IL: University of Chicago Press.

Faris, Robert, and Warren Dunham. 1939. *Mental Disorders in Urban Areas.* Chicago, IL: University of Chicago Press.

Felson, Richard B., and Henry J. Steadman. 1983. "Situational Factors in Disputes Leading to Criminal Violence." *Criminology* 21:59–74.

Garmezy, Norman. 1991. "Resilience in Children's Adaptation to Negative Life Events and Stressed Environments." *Pediatric Annals* 20:1–6.

Gerbner, George, Larry Gross, Michael Morgan, and Nancy Signorielli. 1981. "Health and Medicine on Television." *New England Journal of Medicine* 305:901–904.

Giovannoni, Jeanne, and Lee Gurel. 1967. "Socially Disruptive Behavior of Ex-Mental Patients." *Archives of General Psychiatry* 17:146–53.

Gorton, Gregg, and Salman Akhtar. 1990. "The Literature on Personality Disorders, 1985–88: Trends, Issues, and Controversies." *Hospital and Community Psychiatry* 41:39–51.

Gottlieb, Peter, Gorm Gabrielsen, and Peter Kramp. 1987. "Psychotic Homicides in Copenhagen from 1959 to 1988." *Acta Psychiatrica Scandinavica* 76:285–92.

Green, Michael F., Paul Satz, and Cynthia Christenson. 1994. "Minor Physical Anomalies in Schizophrenic Patients, Bipolar Patients, and Their Siblings." *Schizophrenia Bulletin* 20:433–40.

Hafner, Heinz, and Wolfgang Boker. 1982. *Crimes of Violence by Mentally Abnormal Offenders.* Translated by H. Marshall. New York: Cambridge Unversity Press.

Hare, Robert D., and Stephen D. Hart. 1993. "Psychopathy, Mental Disorder, and Crime." Pp. 104–15 in *Mental Disorder and Crime,* edited by S. Hodgins. Newbury Park, CA: Sage.

Hart, Stephen D., Robert D. Hare, and Adelle E. Forth. 1994. "Psychopathy as a Risk Marker for Violence: Development and Validation of a Screening Version of the Revised Psychopathy Checklist." Pp. 81–98 in *Violence and Mental Disorder,* edited by J. Monahan and H. J. Steadman. Chicago: University of Chicago Press.

Heise, David R. 1975. *Causal Analysis.* New York: Wiley.

Hellerstein, David, William Frosch, and Harold W. Koenigsberg. 1987. "The Clinical Significance of Command Hallucinations." *American Journal of Psychiatry* 144:219–21.

Helzer, John E., Audry Burnam, and Lawrence T. McEvoy. 1991. "Alcohol Abuse and Dependence." Pp. 81–115 in *Psychiatric Disorders in America: The Epidemiologic Catchment Area Study,* edited by L. N. Robins and D. A. Regier. New York: Free Press.

Hiday, Virginia A. 1988. "Civil Commitment: A Review of Empirical Research." *Behavioral Sciences and the Law* 6:15–44.

———. 1992. "Civil Commitment and Arrests: An Investigation of the Criminalization Thesis." *Journal of Nervous and Mental Disease* 180:184–91.

Hodgins, Sheilagh. 1992. "Mental Disorder, Intellectual Deficiency, and Crime: Evidence from a Birth Cohort." *Archives of General Psychiatry* 49:476–83.

———. 1993. *Mental Disorder and Crime.* London, England: Sage.

Holzer, Charles E., Brent M. Shea, Jeffrey W. Swanson, Phillip Leaf, Jerome Myers, Linda George, Myrna Weissman, and Phillip Bednarski. 1986. "The Increased Risk for Specific Psychiatric Disorders among Persons of Low Socioeconomic Status." *American Journal of Social Psychiatry* 4:259–71.

Kay, Stanley R., Fred Wolkenfeld, and Lisa M. Murrill. 1988. "Profiles of Aggression among Psychiatric Inpatients II: Covariates and Predictors." *Journal of Nervous and Mental Disease* 176:547–57.

Kelty, Seymour, Paul S. Wender, Bjorn Jacobson, Loring J. Ingraham, Lennart Jansson, Britta Faber, and Dennis K. Kinney. 1994. "Mental Illness in the Biological and Adoptive Relatives of Schizophrenic Adoptees: Replication of the Copenhagen Study in the Rest of Denmark." *Archives of General Psychiatry* 51:442–55.

Kendler, Kenneth S., and Jeremy M. Silverman. 1991. "Behavior Genetics." Pp. 19–31 in *Foundations of Psychiatry,* edited by K. Davis, H. Klar, and J. T. Coyle. Philadelphia, PA: W. B. Saunders.

Kessler, Ronald C. 1982. "A Disaggregation of the Relationship between Socioeconomic Status and Psychological Distress." *American Sociological Review* 47:752–64.

Kessler, Ronald C., and William J. Magee. 1994. "Childhood Family Violence and Adult Recurrent Depression." *Journal of Health and Social Behavior* 35:13–27.

Kessler, Ronald C., Katherine A. McGonagle, Shanyang Zhao, Christopher B. Nelson, Michael Hughes, Suzann Eshleman, Hans-Ulrich Wittchen, and Kenneth S. Kendler. 1994. "Lifetime and 12-month Prevalence of DSM-III-R Psychiatric Disorders in the United States: Results from the National Comorbidity Survey." *Archives of General Psychiatry* 51:8–19.

Kohn, Melvin. 1972. "Class, Family, and Schizophrenia." *Social Forces* 50:295–302.

Krakowski, Menachem, Jan Volavka, and David Brizer. 1986. "Psychopathology and Violence: A Review of the Literature." *Comprehensive Psychiatry* 27:131–48.

Lagos, John M., Kenneth Perlmutter, and Herbert Suefinger. 1977. "Fear of the Mentally Ill: Empirical Support for the Common Man's Response." *American Journal of Psychiatry* 134:1134–37.

Lamb, H. Richard and Robert W. Grant. 1982. "The Mentally Ill in an Urban County Jail." *Archives of General Psychiatry* 39:17–22.

———. 1983. "Mentally Ill Women in a County Jail." *Archives of General Psychiatry* 40:363–68.

Land, Kenneth C., Patricia L. McCall, and Lawrence E. Cohen. 1990. "Structural Covariates of Homicide Rates: Are There Any Invariances across Time and Social Space?" *American Journal of Sociology* 95:922–63.

Leighton, Dorthea C., John S. Harding, David B. Macklin, Allister M. MacMillan, and Alexander H. Leighton. 1963. *The Character of Danger: Psychiatric Symptoms in Selected Communities.* New York: Basic Books.

Levinson, Richard M., and Georgeann Ramsey. 1979. "Dangerousness, Stress, and Mental Health Evaluations." *Journal of Health and Social Behavior* 20:178–87.

Lidz, Charles W., Edward P. Mulvey, and William P. Gardner. 1993. "The Accuracy of Predictions of Violence to Others." *Journal of the American Medical Association* 269:1007–11.

Lindqvist, P., and P. Allebeck. 1989. "Schizophrenia and Assaultive Behavior: The Role of Alcohol and Drug Abuse." *Acta Psychiatrica Scandinavica* 82:191–95.

Link, Bruce G., and Frank T. Cullen. 1986. "Contact with the Mentally Ill and Perceptions of How Dangerous They Are." *Journal of Health and Social Behavior* 27:289–303.

Link, Bruce G., and Ann Stueve. 1994. "Psychotic Symptoms and the Violent/Illegal Behavior of Mental Patients Compared to Community Controls." Pp. 137–60 in *Violence and Mental Disorder,* edited by J. Monahan and H. J. Steadman. Chicago, IL: University of Chicago Press.

Link, Bruce G., Howard Andrews, and Frank T. Cullen. 1992. "The Violent and Illegal Behavior of Mental Patients Reconsidered." *American Sociological Review* 57:275–92.

Link, Bruce G., Frank T. Cullen, James Frank, and John F. Wozniak. 1987. "The Social Rejection of Ex–Mental Patients: Understanding Why Labels Matter." *American Journal of Sociology* 92:1461–500.

Martin, Martha B., Cynthia M. Owen, and John M. Morihisa. 1987. "An Overview of Neurotransmitters and Neuroreceptors." Pp. 55–85 in *Textbook of Neuropsychiatry,* edited by R. E. Hales and S. C. Yudofsky. Washington, DC: American Psychiatric Press.

McLeod, Jane D., and Michael J. Shanahan. 1993. "Poverty, Parenting, and Children's Mental Health." *American Sociological Review* 58:351–66.

McNiel, Dale E., and Renee L. Binder. 1986. "Violence, Civil Commitment, and Hospitalization." *Journal of Nervous and Mental Disease* 174:107–11.

Mednick, Sarnoff A., Matti O. Huttunen, and Ricardo A. Machon. 1994. "Prenatal Influenza Infections and Adult Schizophrenia." *Schizophrenia Bulletin* 20:263–67.

Mednick, Sarnoff A., Ricardo A. Machon, Matti O. Huttunen, and Douglas Bonett. 1988. "Adult Schizophrenia: Following Prenatal Exposure to an Influenza Epidemic." *Archives of General Psychiatry* 45:189–92.

Melick, Mary E., Henry J. Steadman, and Joseph J. Cocozza. 1979. "The Medicalization of Criminal Behavior among Mental Patients." *Journal of Health and Social Behavior* 20:228–37.

Miller, Kent. 1976. *Managing Madness: The Case against Civil Commitment.* New York: Free Press.

Mirowsky, John. 1985. "Disorder and Its Context: Paranoid Beliefs as Thematic Elements of Thought Problems, Hallucinations, and Delusions under Threatening Social Conditions." Pp. 139–84 in *Research in Community and Mental Health,* Vol. 5, edited by J. R. Greenley. Greenwich, CT: JAI Press.

Mirowsky, John, and Catherine E. Ross. 1983. "Paranoia and the Structure of Powerlessness." *American Sociological Review* 48:228–39.

Moldin, Steven O. 1994. "Indicators of Liability to Schizophrenia: Perspectives from Genetic Epidemiology." *Schizophrenia Bulletin* 20:169–84.

Monahan, John. 1981. *The Clinical Prediction of Violent Behavior.* Washington, DC: U.S. Government Printing Office.

———. 1992. "Mental Disorder and Violent Behavior: Perceptions and Evidence." *American Psychologist* 47:511–21.

Monahan, John, and Henry J. Steadman. 1983. "Crime and Mental Disorder: An Epidemiological Approach." Pp. 145–89 in *Crime and Justice: An Annual Review of Research,* edited by M. Tonry and N. Morris. Chicago, IL: University of Chicago Press.

———. 1994. "Toward a Rejuvenation of Risk Assessment Research." Pp. 1–17 in *Violence and Mental Disorder: Developments in Risk Assessment,* edited by J. Monahan and H. J. Steadman. Chicago, IL: University of Chicago Press.

Morse, Stephen. 1978. "Crazy Behavior, Morals, and Science: An Analysis of Mental Health Law." *Southern California Law Review* 51:527–89.

———. 1982. "A Preference for Liberty: The Case against Involuntary Commitment of the Mentally Disordered." *California Law Review* 70:54–106.

Mulvey, Edward P., and Charles W. Lidz. 1993. "Measuring Patient Violence in Dangerousness Research." *Law and Human Behavior* 17:277–88.

Mulvey, Edward P., William Gardner, Charles W. Lidz, Jessica Graus, and Ester C. Shaw. 1994. "Symptomatology and Violence among Mental Patients." Unpublished Manuscript.

National Research Council. 1993. *Understanding and Preventing Violence,* edited by A. J. Reiss, Jr., and J. A. Roth. Washington, DC: National Academy Press.

Novaco, Raymond W. 1994. "Anger as a Risk Factor for Violence among the Mentally Disordered." Pp. 21–59 in *Violence and Mental Disorder,* edited by J. Monahan and H. J. Steadman. Chicago, IL: University of Chicago Press.

Nunnally, Jum C. 1961. *Popular Conceptions of Mental Health.* New York: Holt, Rinehart, and Winston.

Oliver, William. 1994. *The Violent Social World of Black Men.* New York: Lexington Books.

Patterson, E. Britt. 1991. "Poverty, Income, Inequality, and Community Crime Rates." *Criminology* 29:755–76.

Pearlin, Leonard I. 1989. "The Sociological Study of Stress." *Journal of Health and Social Behavior* 30:241–56.

———. 1992. "Structure and Meaning in Medical Sociology." *Journal of Health and Social Behavior* 33:1–9.

Pearlin, Leonard I., Morton A. Leiberman, Elizabeth G. Menaghan, and Joseph T. Mullan. 1981. "The Stress Process." *Journal of Health and Social Behavior* 22:337–56.

Pihl, Robert O., and Jordan B. Peterson. 1993. "Alcohol/Drug Use and Aggressive Behavior." Pp. 263–83 in *Mental Disorder and Crime,* edited by S. Hodgins. London, England: Sage.

Rabkin, Judith G. 1972. "Opinions about Mental Illness: A Review of the Literature." *Psychological Bulletin* 77:153–71.

———. 1974. "Public Attitudes toward Mental Illness: A Review of the Literature." *Schizophrenia Bulletin* 10:9–33.

———. 1979. "Criminal Behavior of Discharged Mental Patients: A Critical Appraisal of the Research." *Psychological Bulletin* 86a:1–27.

Rice, Marnie, and Grant T. Harris. 1992. "A Comparison of Criminal Recidivism among Schizophrenic and Nonschizophrenic Offenders." *International Journal of Law and Psychiatry* 15:397–408.

Robins, Lee. 1993. "Childhood Conduct Problems, Adult Psychopathology, and Crime." Pp. 173–93 in *Mental Disorder and Crime,* edited by S. Hodgins. London, England: Sage.

Robins, Lee, Jayson Tipp, and Thomas Przybeck. 1991. "Antisocial Personality." Pp. 258–90 in *Psychiatric Disorders in America: The Epidemiologic Catchment Area Study,* edited by L. N. Robins and D. A. Regier. New York: Free Press.

Robins, Lee, John E. Helzer, Jack Croughan, and Kathryn Ratcliff. 1981. "National Institute of Mental Health Diagnostic Interview Schedule: Its History, Characteristics, and Validity." *Archives of General Psychiatry* 38:381–89.

Robins, Lee, and Darrel A. Regier, eds. 1991. *Psychiatric Disorders in America: The Epidemiologic Catchment Area Study.* New York: Free Press.

Rofman, Ethan S., Clifford E. Askinazi, and Emily Fant. 1980. "The Prediction of Dangerous Behavior in Emergency Civil Commitment." *American Journal of Psychiatry* 137:1061–64.

Rose, Stephan M., Carolyn G. Peabody, and Barbara Stratigeas. 1991. "Undetected Abuse among Intensive Case Management Clients." *Hospital and Community Psychiatry* 42:499–503.

Rosenberg, Mark L., and Mary Ann Fenley. 1991. *Violence in America: A Public Health Approach.* New York: Oxford University Press.

Schuerman, Leo A., and Solomon Kobrin. 1984. "Exposure of Community Mental Health Clients to the Criminal Justice System: Client/Criminal or Patient/Prisoner." Pp. 87–118 in *Mental Health and Criminal Justice,* edited by L. A. Teplin. Beverly Hills, CA: Sage.

Segal, Steven P., Margaret A. Watson, Stephen M. Goldfinger, and David S. Averbuck. 1988. "Civil Commitment in the Psychiatric Emergency Room II: Mental Disorder Indicators and Three Dangerousness Criteria." *Archives of General Psychiatry* 45:753–58.

Seltzer, Judith A., and Debra Kalmuss. 1988. "Socialization and Stress Explanations for Spouse Abuse." *Social Forces* 67:473–91.

Shah, Saleem A. 1974. "Some Interactions of Law and Mental Health in the Handling of Social Deviance." *Catholic University Law Review* 23:674–719.

———. 1978. "Dangerousness and Mental Illness: Some Conceptual, Prediction, and Policy Dilemmas." Pp. 153–91 in *Dangerous Behavior: A Problem in Law and Mental Health,* edited by D. J. Fredericks. Rockville, MD: DHEW Publication No. (ADM) 78–563.

Sheridan, Miriam, Rosemary Henrion, Linda Robinson, and Virginia Baxter. 1990. "Precipitants of Violence in a Psychiatric Inpatient Setting." *Hospital and Community Psychiatry* 41:776–80.

Sosowsky, Larry. 1980. "Explaining the Increased Arrest Rate among Mental Patients: A Cautionary Note." *American Journal of Psychiatry* 137:1602–605.

Srole, Leo, Thomas Langer, Stanley Michael, Marvin Opler, and Thomas Rennie. 1962. *Mental Health in the Metropolis: The Midtown Manhattan Study.* New York: McGraw-Hill.

Steadman, Henry J. 1982. "A Situational Approach to Violence." *International Journal of Law and Psychiatry* 5:171–86.

Steadman, Henry J., and Joseph J. Cocozza. 1978. "Selective Reporting and the Public's Misconceptions of the Criminally Insane." *Public Opinion Quarterly* 42:523–33.

Steadman, Henry J., Joseph J. Cocozza, and Mary E. Melick. 1978. "Explaining the Increased Arrest Rate among Mental Patients: The Changing Clientele of State Hospitals." *American Journal of Psychiatry* 135:816–20.

Steadman, Henry J., and Richard B. Felson. 1984. "Self-Reports of Violence: Ex–Mental Patients, Ex-Offenders and the General Population." *Criminology* 22:321–42.

Steadman, Henry J., and Stephen A. Ribner. 1982. "Life Stress and Violence among Ex–Mental Patients." *Social Science and Medicine* 16:1641–47.

Straznickas, Katherine A., Dale E. McNiel, and Renee L. Binder. 1993. "Violence toward Family Care Givers by Mentally Ill Relatives." *Hospital and Community Psychiatry* 44:385–87.

Swank, Glenn E., and Darryl Winer. 1976. "Occurrence of Psychiatric Disorder in a County Jail Population." *American Journal of Psychiatry* 133:1331–33.

Swanson, Jeffrey W. 1993. "Alcohol Abuse, Mental Disorder, and Assaultive Behavior: An Epidemiologic Inquiry." *Alcohol Health and Research World* 17:123–32.

———. 1994. "Mental Disorder, Substance Abuse, and Community Violence: An Epidemiological Approach." Pp. 101–36 in *Violence and Mental Disorder,* edited by J. Monahan and H. J. Steadman. Chicago, IL: University of Chicago Press.

Swanson, Jeffrey W., Charles E. Holzer, Vijay K. Ganju, and Robert T. Jono. 1990. "Violence and Psychiatric Disorder in the Community: Evidence from the Epidemiologic Catchment Area Surveys." *Hospital and Community Psychiatry* 41:761–70.

Swanson, Jeffrey W., Randy Borum, John Monahan, and Marvin Swartz. 1995. "Psychotic Symptoms and the Risk of Violent Behavior: Evidence from the Epidemiologic Catchment Area Surveys." Unpublished manuscript.

Tardiff, Kenneth, and Attia Sweillam. 1980. "Assault, Suicide, and Mental Illness." *Archives of General Psychiatry* 37:164–69.

Teplin, Linda. 1990. "The Prevalence of Severe Mental Disorder among Male Urban Jail Detainees: Comparison with the Epidemiologic Catchment Area Program." *American Journal of Public Health* 80:663–69.

Toch, Hans. 1992. *Violent Men: An Inquiry into the Psychology of Violence,* rev. ed. Washington, DC: American Psychological Association.

Torrey, E. Fuller, Edward H. Taylor, H. Stefan Bracha, Ann E. Bowler, Thomas F. McNeil, Robert R. Rawlings, Patricia O. Quinn, Llewellyn B. Bigelow, Kenneth Rickler, Karin Sjostrom, Edmund S. Higgins, and Irving I. Gottesman. 1994. "Prenatal Origins of Schizophrenia in a Subgroup of Discordant Monozygotic Twins." *Schizophrenia Bulletin* 20:423–32.

Tremblay, Richard E., Frank Vitaro, Lucie Bertrand, Marc LeBlanc, Helene Beauchesne, Helene Boileau, and Lucille David. 1992. "Parent and Child Training to Prevent Early Onset of Delinquency: The Montreal Longitudinal–Experimental Study." Pp. 117–38 in *Preventing Antisocial Behavior: Interventions from Birth through Adolescence,* edited by J. McCord and R. E. Tremblay. New York: Guilford.

Valdiserri, Edwin V., Kenneth R. Carroll, and Alan J. Hartl. 1986. "A Study of Offenses Committed by Psychotic Inmates in a County Jail." *Hospital and Community Psychiatry* 37:163–66.

Warren, Carol A. B. 1977. "Involuntary Commitment for Mental Disorder: The Application of California's Lanterman–Petris–Short Act." *Law and Society Review* 11:629–50.

———. 1982. *Court of Last Resort.* Chicago, IL: University of Chicago Press.

Washington, Pat, and Ronald J. Diamond. 1985. "Prevalence of Mental Illness among Women Incarcerated in Five California County Jails." *Research in Community Mental Health* 5:33–41.

Weiss, Marc F. 1986. "Children's Attitudes toward the Mentally Ill: A Developmental Analysis." *Psychological Reports* 58:11–20.

Wheaton, Blair. 1980. "The Sociogenesis of Psychological Disorder: An Attributional Theory." *Journal of Health and Social Behavior* 21:100–124.

Widom, Cathy S. 1989. "Does Violence Beget Violence? A Critical Examination of the Literature." *Psychological Bulletin* 106:3–28.

Winfield, Idee, Linda K. George, Marvin Swartz, and Dan G. Blazer. 1990. "Sexual Assault and Psychiatric Disorders among a Community Sample of Women." *American Journal of Psychiatry* 147:335–41.

Yesavage, Jerome A., Jacqueline M. T. Becker, Paul D. Werner, Michael J. Patton, Kenneth Seeman, David W. Brunsting, and Mark J. Mills. 1983. "Family Conflict, Psychopathology, and Dangerous Behavior by Schizophrenic Inpatients." *Psychiatry Research* 8:271–80.

Yesavage, Jerome A., Paul D. Werner, Jacqueline M. T. Becker, and Mark J. Mills. 1982. "The Context of Involuntary Commitment on the Basis of Danger to Others." *Journal of Nervous and Mental Disease* 170:622–27.

DEVELOPED WORLD PERSPECTIVE

THE GENERAL HOSPITAL AND MENTAL HEALTH CARE: A BRITISH PERSPECTIVE

HUGH L. FREEMAN

Treatment of psychiatric patients in British general hospitals, which began in the eighteenth century, came to a premature end in the mid-nineteenth century. The mental hospital was then left largely unchallenged for more than a century; when general hospitals started to make a significant contribution once again, they did so within the unified orbit of the National Health Service (NHS). In the 1960s, British hospital planning was founded on the district general hospital (DGH), incorporating psychiatry as a major specialty. These units were to form the hub of a district mental health service, where most chronic disorders would be assigned to "community care," which was primarily the responsibility of local social services. The mental hospital, therefore, appeared to be obsolete, but the questions of whether its range of functions could be entirely reproduced in small units and of how many of these functions could be assumed by the general hospital still remain unanswered, particularly in the uncertain climate of a much diminished welfare state.

THE EARLY PERIOD

Guy's Hospital, London, opened an adjacent "lunatic house" for 20 patients in 1728, representing for first formal provision for the mentally ill in a British general hospital. In most provincial cities, voluntary general hospitals were being established at that time, and several included a section for the mentally ill. A parallel development was the growth of private madhouses, comprising anything from a few cases taken into the home of a doctor or clergyman to a substantial institution that might accept pauper cases as well (Parry-Jones 1972). By the second half of the eighteenth century, there were several specialist hospitals for the mentally ill in England, and one was established in Dublin. The private madhouses, however, often ill-treated and wrongfully confined those in their charge, and general hospitals eventually found it convenient to unburden themselves of a problem that was not consistent with the acute medicosurgical model that characterized their main activities. For reasons that are far from clear, the psychiatric annexes of general hospitals had ceased to exist by the mid-nineteenth century (Mayou 1989). Had this not happened, the subsequent history of managing psychiatric disorder in Britain would have been entirely different.

The specialized mental hospital, then, became by far the most important location for full-time institutional care of the mentally ill, as it did in the United States and Western Europe. Around the time that a national system of mental hospitals was being established, therefore, in the 1840s, the contribution of general hospitals came to an end—and did not resume for a century. The only other institution to contain many cases of mental disorder was the Poor Law workhouse, whose mentally disordered were supposed to be transferred to asylums. Because this would have been more expensive, such a move was often resisted by the Poor Law Guardians. Nevertheless the asylum population grew remorselessly, and, in the words used by Rumbaut (1994) to describe Dorothea Dix's crusade for humane care of the mentally ill in the United States: "[It] was too effective, [ending] in the long run by flooding the mental hospitals."

The relentless accumulation of morbidity in workhouses, however, led to the development in them of "infirmary annexes," and, in a largely unplanned way, their rudimentary medical and nursing care increasingly came to resemble that practiced in general hospitals. In the early part of this century, "mental observation wards" were developed in many of these annexes, where cases were admitted initially and then transferred to an asylum if they did not recover quickly. In 1948, the workhouse infirmaries were to provide, first, many of the hospital resources for the new National Health Service (NHS) and, somewhat later, the sites for most general hospital psychiatry.

During the late nineteenth and early twentieth centuries, voluntary general hospitals, like their counterparts in the United States, dealt with some less severe psychiatric disorders, but these cases were treated by general physicians or neurologists; their psychological aspects were not always recognized (Bynum 1985). A very small number of psychiatric outpatient clinics were established at general hospitals, but even by the late 1930s, only one teaching hospital had a psychiatric ward. Although disorders like "shell shock" (Merskey 1991) and "soldier's heart" were very common in World War I, only one of the facilities set up to deal with such cases outside of mental hospitals survived long after 1918. During the 1930s, the workhouse infirmaries became "municipal hospitals,"

often with a great improvement in standards, while some observation wards began to treat acute patients. Outpatient clinics also increased in number and were mostly staffed by doctors from mental hospitals, although some independent psychiatrists also saw outpatients at voluntary hospitals. That general hospitals could play a bigger role became clear when they temporarily accepted mental hospital patients for the treatment of tertiary syphilis with malarial mosquitoes and encountered virtually no major problems of management (Freeman and Bennett 1991).

By 1939, however, scarcely any modern development had occurred in the mental health care system; indeed, most hospitals had hardly changed since the late nineteenth century. Those in Britain who were dissatisfied with the contribution of general hospitals pointed to the example of the United States, where several large teaching departments had been endowed by the Rockefeller Foundation and 40 general hospital psychiatric units were operating in 1940 (Greenhill 1979). Nevertheless, a process of medicalization had begun in Britain, whereby mental illness would no longer be treated primarily under the auspices of the Poor Law, which had applied to all except a small minority who were wealthy enough to make private arrangements. In the planning for an NHS during World War II, mental illness services were excluded on the grounds that their administrative and legal arrangements were so different from those of general hospitals that they could not be combined in a single structure. This proposed separation, however, was eventually dropped, and British mental health care would from then on primarily reflect the structure of a comprehensive NHS.

This service, which began in mid-1948, was a mixture of radical and conservative aspects. It was radical in nationalizing all hospitals—mental and general, municipal and voluntary—and giving them all the same administrative pattern; only some small private hospitals (a few of them psychiatric) were left out. At the same time, national salary scales were established for all hospital staff—medical, nursing, and ancillary. Its conservative aspect lay in the preservation of the primacy of general practice (GP), which meant that specialists would normally only see patients on referral from GPs, who would thus remain as independent practitioners under contract with the NHS to care for the people registered on their lists—totaling well over 90 percent of the population. The new service also left city and county local authorities responsible for community health, including the mental welfare officers who undertook compulsory psychiatric admissions. Administratively, therefore, the NHS was split into three compartments, integrated only at the national level and cooperating locally to widely varying degrees. This division created significant problems in the evolution of psychiatric services, which care for many long-term disorders. In other areas of the welfare state, social services and social security diffused into the general community—away from the previous institutional basis of the Poor law. In child care, for instance, orphanages and other institutions were replaced by small homes or foster care, and the same process emerged in the care of the elderly; this noninstitutional ideology may well have influenced views about the management of psychiatric disorder.

GENERAL HOSPITAL PSYCHIATRY IN THE NHS

At the inception of the NHS, 44 percent of all hospital beds nationally were in mental or mental deficiency (retardation) hospitals, whereas general hospitals contained only a miniscule number of psychiatric beds. The new doctors recruited in large numbers into psychiatry to fulfill the needs of the armed forces would have been unlikely, in any case, to accept the authoritarian, hierarchical culture of prewar mental hospitals; the general hospital offered them a more congenial working situation. Under the comprehensive structure of the NHS, a new psychiatric service could now be de-

veloped anywhere, if the resources could be found, and the administrative autonomy of consultants was particularly useful in this connection. Because the NHS staffing system was unified, psychiatrists (and later nurses) could divide their work between mental and general hospitals or transfer from one to the other. Also, because all hospital services were centrally financed, the monetary aspects of any changes were very simple. The biggest obstacles to improvement were the lack of trained specialists and the almost total absence of capital for new building. Because of the NHS, however, British psychiatry remained unified, and almost all specialists devoted the greatest part of their time to hospital-based clinical work, rather than to private practice.

Like the older, established specialties, psychiatry participated in the diffusion of services from the largest centers. However, the fact that many mental hospitals were in rural areas, a situation that succeeded in the United States, made it difficult for them to provide a readily accessible service; the problem was worst in London, where nearly all these hospitals were on the distant periphery of the metropolitan area. This geographic factor was a significant spur to the development of psychiatry in general hospitals.

An event of great importance for general hospital psychiatry in Britain was the passage in 1959 of the Mental Health Act—a comprehensive reorganization of all law pertaining to mental illness and mental retardation. As far as possible, it removed legal formalities from the hospital care of psychiatric disorders, and it abolished the special designation of mental hospitals. A psychiatric patient could now be admitted to any hospital, either informally (on the same basis as medical or surgical patients) or under legal compulsion. In practice, the proportion of patients admitted compulsorily dropped to a new low, and, even in these cases, the required stay was usually brief. The legal and administrative flexibility achieved by this reform was undoubtedly a very favorable factor in the development of British mental health services. It was both an embodiment of ideological changes in society since World War II and a stimulus to further developments in the services themselves. The act embodied the recommendations of a Royal Commission that, in many ways, resembled the Joint Commission in the United States, although Britain did not adopt the American model of community mental health centers, which became entirely independent of mental hospitals.

In 1961, the minister of health announced that he expected to see a 50 percent reduction in mental hospital beds in England and Wales over the next 15 years (Powell 1961). This prediction was based on a study showing a steady fall in occupied beds between 1954 and 1959, after a previous constant rise, despite the fact that admissions were still increasing (Tooth and Brooke 1961). The following year, a national hospital plan embodied the concept of the district general hospital (DGH), containing about 700 beds, which would provide all major specialist services—including acute psychiatry—for populations averaging 200,000. If alternative care had to be provided for chronic patients, "the community" now emerged as the solution to this problem, and it followed that there would eventually be no further role for the great majority of existing mental hospitals. This was a bold objective, however, considering that, in 1960, there were then only about 4,000 psychiatric beds in DGHs, compared with the almost 150,000 located in mental hospitals (Rehin and Martin 1963). Nevertheless, the detailed planning proposals were in fact generally modest, and, particularly in Scotland, a generally conservative policy was maintained, even though the level of bed provision there was much higher than that in England and Wales.

While the activities of outpatient clinics and day hospitals were growing steadily—the number of new outpatients per annum increased by 50 percent between 1949 and 1959 (Ministry of Health 1959)—local authorities were mostly very slow to increase their community services. Titmuss (1961) warned against the assumption that "community care" could provide an alternative to long-stay hos-

pitals, when it was little more than an aspiration in many places. Also, studies of outpatient psychiatry during the 1960s (Martin 1984) showed that there was "no serious question…of [it] replacing the hospital wards"; mostly, it "complemented the in-patient service by providing pre-admission screening and post-discharge follow-up." Day hospitals, which began in the same year as the NHS, were important because they introduced a new element of flexibility (Farndale 1961); they were to have an increasingly important role in the evolution of mental health services, and some day units were established in or near general hospitals.

The reasons for this major switch of inpatient care (at least for acute cases) primarily to general hospitals are far from clear, particularly in light of the fact that the influential expert committee of the World Health Organization (1953), although advocating a more community-oriented mental health system, saw its hospital base remaining as a specialized institution. Indeed, the committee stated that "the more the psychiatric hospital imitates the general hospital…the less successful it will be in creating the atmosphere it needs." Rehin and Martin (1963) could find "no solid foundation" of evaluation on which the new policy had been founded. It has often been said (see, for example, Jones 1993) that the main motivation was a wish to avoid the enormous cost of bringing the run-down mental hospitals up to an acceptable standard. However, my own examination of government records from the period has failed to reveal any evidence for this view, and it is arguable that the creation of an almost entirely new system of hospital units could be at least as expensive as renovation, particularly because most mental hospitals would have to continue operating for many years, if at a reduced level.

Electroconvulsive therapy had come into general use in Britain around the end of World War II, chlorpromazine became available in 1954, and antidepressants began to be used in 1959; these innovations made it possible for effective treatment to be given to large numbers of patients outside of mental hospitals—as outpatients, day patients, or inpatients in general hospitals. Psychotherapy, however, had little place in mainstream British psychiatry—partly for ideological reasons related to the structure of the NHS and partly because of the extreme shortage of professional staff.

Echoing the American view voiced by Hamburg (1957) that, in a general hospital unit, "there is a strong tendency to adopt methods of policy-making which are very similar to those used previously in the hospital," critics like Barton (1963) claimed that the general hospital was an unsuitable setting for most psychiatric patients. Similarly, Jones (1963) said that, of the four functions of the mental hospital (custody, protection, clinical treatment, and socialization), only the third could be adequately performed in a general hospital. In her view, the new policy implied that the NHS would confine itself to the care of acute patients, leaving everything else to community services, which seemed poorly equipped to accept such a responsibility. It would in fact have required an enormous increase in local authority finances for them to have done this, but successive governments refused to make a specific grant for community mental health services. The only other possible ways of ensuring effective community services—creating a new, nationally funded agency for them, or amalgamating them with the NHS—have always been regarded as politically impossible, although the latter was accomplished in Northern Ireland in 1974 (Prior 1993).

A forerunner of later national developments occurred in the Northwest of England beginning in the early 1950s. The region's mental hospitals, which were of a poor standard, were each responsible for nearly a million people, living mainly in old industrial areas. Effectively, the hospital board decided to bypass them by appointing new consultants to the former municipal hospitals in its larger towns; each of these had a mental observation ward, together with some long-stay wards occupied by patients with chronic mental disorders (Pickstone 1989). They did, however, all have

some nurses with psychiatric training—specialized nursing had become one of the greatest assets of British mental hospitals. Fifteen general hospital units were eventually developed; the larger ones, with up to 220 beds, provided a comprehensive psychiatric service for anywhere from 200,000 to 250,000 people, while the smaller ones accommodated their medium- and long-stay patients in the nearest mental hospital. In every case, however, collaboration was emphasized, both with GPs in the districts served and with the local authority, which (to varying degrees) provided community services. Because the psychiatric unit was in the center of its population, patients could be treated flexibly as inpatients, outpatients, or day patients, according to their needs; they could also be visited by doctors, nurses, or social workers (Freeman 1960). The other services of the general hospital, including geriatric medicine, were readily accessible. The underlying principles were service to a geographically defined population, continuous and final responsibility for psychiatric disorders in that population, and the integration of all local resources, with the dissolution of administrative barriers (Freeman 1963). Thus, it was the hub of a district (or community-based) psychiatric service.

For some years, similar developments elsewhere in Britain occurred in isolated pockets and on a much more limited scale (see, e.g., Dunckley and Lewis 1963). Jones (1993) argued that this model was not generalizable because the circumstances were unusual, and, from the viewpoint of the 1990s, they appear to have been relatively easy: the units were mostly in medium-sized towns that constituted coherent communities. But the only alternative available at the time was the old-style mental hospital. These institutions usually had some advantages, like spacious grounds, but in all other respects—particularly lack of stigma—doctors and patients increasingly felt that the comprehensive district service based in the general hospital was to be preferred (Kessel 1973). At the national level, this development was noticed by the Ministry of Health, which had decided, in the mid-1950s, that no further mental hospitals should be built. Tuberculosis (TB), a disease for which a shortage of hospital beds had been chronic, quickly resolved this difficulty after effective drugs became available; the ministry considered the experience with TB a relevant example (Godber 1988).

Ironically, the 20 years after their demise was proclaimed in 1961 turned into probably the most active period ever for British mental hospitals. Very large sums were in fact spent on modernizing them, and patients' living conditions were improved out of all recognition, in conjunction with the development of treatment and occupational facilities. The large buildings and grounds also provided space for new, specialized units—forensic, addiction, child and adolescent, psychogeriatric— which would have been very difficult to accommodate elsewhere. Both the psychiatry of old age and the rehabilitation of chronically handicapped patients evolved as separate medical subspecialties, in ways that were unique internationally; these developments began in the mental hospitals, and spread later to general hospitals and other sites. During this time, the psychiatric profession was evolving into a fairly large and well-trained specialty, symbolized by the establishment in 1971 of the Royal College of Psychiatrists, which aspired to equality with the older specialties.

At one time, it seemed that mental and general hospitals might evolve jointly, through nonpsychiatric specialties moving into mental hospital accommodation. However, apart from Lancaster, where the mental hospital was on the edge of a small city (Smith 1963), this imaginative proposal—which would have embodied McKeown's (1958) idea of the "balanced hospital community"—never gained much acceptance. In fact, changes in British mental health services during the 1960s were very slow; a "demonstration project" in Worcester to show how a traditional county mental hospital could be replaced by a network of smaller facilities took 20 years to complete (Hall and Brockington 1990). A very optimistic report, however, from the first district psychiatric unit to be established in central London (Baker 1969) seems to have influenced government thinking, because it was quoted in *Hospital Services for the Mentally Ill* published by the Ministry of Health (1971) as the first official statement of that policy. The Ministry recommended that, in each district, a comprehensive, integrated mental health service should be based on a psychiatric department in a DGH, supported by a geriatric department and by local-authority community services. This constituted what was often described as a "dispersed institution." Referral of chronically ill patients to mental hospitals was discouraged, and the mental hospitals were expected to run down toward closure, although no time-scale was given. Yet by 1970, DGH units in England still accounted for only 15.5 percent of all psychiatric admissions. In 1971, all social workers were brought into comprehensive "generic" departments of the local authorities, so that hospital psychiatric units then had to negotiate with them for their social work service.

The official view of the hospital's function (Brothwood 1973) was one of providing medical and nursing care for those people with psychiatric disorders for whom such care was the primary need, and it was increasingly to be found at DGHs. On the other hand, the chronically handicapped should not become long-term hospital residents. The basic provision of psychiatric beds (0.5 per thousand population) was to be supplemented by beds and day places for the elderly with severe dementia, as well as by some medium-security beds for seriously disturbed cases (on a regional basis). The definitive national policy emerged two years later (Department of Health and Social Services 1975), stating that the DGH psychiatric unit was to be seen, "not simply as an inpatient department but as a centre providing facilities for treatment on both a day and inpatient basis and as the base from which the Specialist Therapeutic Team provides advice and consultation." Although one of the main objectives of the program was to be the relocation of specialists services from mental hospitals into DGH units, the government's aim was "not to close or run down the mental illness hospitals but to replace them with a local and better range of facilities." By this time, however, government expenditure had been jeopardized by the oil crisis, rendering the timetable of development for mental health services much more uncertain.

The 1975 document has been much criticized as viewing mental health primarily in terms of service structures and types of staff, rather than in the context of individual needs that are provided for in more normal settings. It had a well-formulated, coherent, and in some respects sophisticated approach, but carried neither a credible time-scale for making capital available to build the new DGH units and other facilities, nor any reasonable possibility that the necessary community services would actually be provided. Yet, if any part of the network was missing, the service could not function effectively. This was a time when managerialism was thought to provide the answer to most contemporary problems in Britain, but the generic "integration" of social work had resulted in the disintegration of the better and more coordinated mental health services (Jones 1979). Ideally, each district was to have one DGH, but circumstances rarely provided such a neat solution; hospitals were often in the wrong place for the present-day population, while the perenial shortage of capital prevented small or obsolete facilities from being combined and rationalized. However, with the NHS reorganization of 1974, planning of "health" services began for the first time; up to then, regional and local NHS authorities had only been responsible for hospitals.

THE PRESENT ERA

For 30 years, general hospital psychiatry in Britain proceeded on a slow but steady course of development, hardly affected by political upheavals. Except in marginal respects, the NHS—and to some extent the welfare state—had risen above politics. Below the national level, it was a professionally administered service, in which medical opinion was highly influential. If there was still a major un-resolved problem in mental health care—other than overall lack of resources—it was the split in responsibility between the NHS and local authority community services. The concept of the DGH psychiatric unit became largely absorbed into that of the comprehensive district mental health service. Following the usual course of events in British social history, this policy had evolved inductively from a combination of trends and initiatives, rather than being deduced from any general political or economic principle. One of these trends was the continuous drop, between 1955 and 1975, in occupied mental hospital beds—a loss over those 20 years that totaled 60,000. Compared with the United States, deinstitutionalization proceeded slowly and was less influenced by financial considerations; reprovision of the mental hospital's facilities was more strongly emphasized in Britain. The comprehensive structure of the NHS allowed this process to take place on a planned basis, although the establishment of community services had to be negotiated with the local authorities. However, the argument that psychiatric hospitals were absorbing a disproportionate amount of the total mental health budget was increasingly heard.

No reductionistic explanation of this process is credible, however; a series of largely unconnected innovations gradually changed the way in which mental health care was delivered. The most important of these developments were DGH psychiatric units, therapeutic communities, day hospitals, sheltered workshops, social clubs, hostels, home visits, hospital open doors, and physical treatments. Almost all were pragmatic, not dependent on any particular theoretical basis, and not part (until much later) of any comprehensive policy. They were reinforced both by a more egalitarian culture following World War II, which was less accepting of hierarchical institutions, and by the philosophy of the emergent welfare state (Bennett 1978).

Unlike American policy at that time, particularly the community mental health center program, British developments were not greatly concerned with "preventive" activities, with "consultation" theory, or with the active participation of communities (except through voluntary organizations). British psychiatry had a firm biological basis, much influenced by European phenomenology, but it drew little from psychoanalysis, which was then all-powerful in American teaching and practice. Mental health policy remained firmly rooted in the conventional models of medicine, nursing, social work, clinical psychology, and occupational therapy. It was an atheoretical, pragmatic amalgam, which could incorporate elements of psychodynamic theory, learning theory, social theory, and the concept of a "therapeutic community," to the extent that these had proved their clinical usefulness. The activities of the DGH unit were governed by this nonideological culture.

In the 1970s and 1980s, however, cultural and ideological shifts that affected the care of the mentally ill were of two opposed tendencies. The first was "antipsychiatry"—one of the offshoots of the European and American "cultural revolution" that began with the students' revolt of 1968 and that was heavily colored by Marxism (Sedgwick 1982). In practical terms, the teaching of psychology, social work, and nursing in Europe became strongly influenced by such concepts, with the result that many of the practitioners of these disciplines saw it as a primary task to undermine "psychiatric hegemony," not only by agitating for change within existing institutions, but also by developing alternatives. As a consequence, the DGH unit, which had first appeared to be in the vanguard, became somehow transmuted into a "reactionary" organization, with the same unfavorable characteristics that had been attributed to the mental hospital in the 1950s. The alternatives to it that began to be proposed were mental health centers, crisis intervention in the home, and noninstitutional care of various forms like "respite houses," with varying degrees of professional involvement, but no psychiatric direction. Thus, the pragmatic question of *where* mentally ill patients could best be treated was converted into an ideological issue.

The second tendency was radical, right-wing monetarism. Capturing both the British Conservative Party and the Republican Party in the United States, it was profoundly opposed to the "liberal consensus" that had created the welfare state in Britain. For some years after the Conservative victory in 1979, the Thatcher administration made only limited changes to the NHS, but, after 1988, it instituted major "reforms," which have had a profound influence on mental health care, including the services provided in DGHs.

Shortly before this, an officially sponsored symposium in 1985 on mental health services (Wilkinson and Freeman 1986) included current government guidance on DGH units. Experience was said to have shown—although no data were given—that adult psychiatric beds should be at a level of 0.3–0.5 per thousand population; more would be needed, however, if there was no access to staffed hostels in the community. A separate ward for the assessment and short-term treatment of elderly psychiatric patients was advised, but these beds would be deducted from the basic provision. It was admitted that "new long-stay" patients—as opposed to those remaining from before about 1970—might begin to accumulate, thereby threatening the viability of the DGH unit, but the only solution offered was the well-staffed "hospital hostel," as developed in only three places in Britain (see, e.g., Goldberg et al. 1985). Where a DGH was not centrally located for the community it served, some of the day hospital places were to be removed from it, and relocated in a more convenient situation.

At that time, there were still 56,000 patients in the old mental hospitals in England; the total was dwindling by about 2,000 per annum. DGH units accounted for 13,000 beds; nationally 38 percent of psychiatric admissions were going to DGH units, but in the Manchester region—where the policy had begun—the figure was 82 percent (Goldberg 1986). The usage of mental hospital beds in that region was then less than half the national average, but Goldberg felt that a service centered in the DGH, rather than in a mental hospital, was more vulnerable to budgetary reductions, which were then beginning to affect both the NHS and social services. On the one hand, it was being suggested (Simpson, Hyde, and Faragher 1989) that many DGH units were, in fact, unsuitable for patients with long-term problems because they might suffer from the proximity of acutely disturbed cases, absence of privacy, deflections of staff attention to short-stay cases, and lack of appropriate facilities for rehabilitation.

Although government policy on mental hospitals remained overtly unchanged—that is, they were not to close until an adequate alternative service for the local population was in place—it became clear that there were few financial savings from having a reduced, as opposed to a closed, institution. It was argued that the fixed assets of mental hospitals were underexploited, even though the real needs of patients were often not being met there. Therefore, both financial constraints and ideological pressure hastened the rate of closure. This process was further accelerated by an administrative reorganization of the NHS in 1984, in which consensus management (where health professionals were influential) was replaced by executive general managers. To some extent, there was a parallel with the two distinct phases described in the U.S. deinstitutionalization process: a "benign" phase (lasting from 1956 to 1965), in which new admissions were discharged earlier and better-functioning, long-stay patients were resettled; and a "radical" phase, when occupancy was drastically reduced in response to financial pressures (Morrissey 1982). In Britain, as a result of the major changes in 1989, the resources of DGH units began to be steadily reduced, a trend that gathered momentum during the early 1990s.

By the end of 1993, 89 out of the 130 mental hospitals that existed in England in 1953 had already been closed and the total number of psychiatric beds was a little over 50,000 (Kingdon and Freeman 1995). However, because one of the

changes of recent years has been the dismantling of many information systems relating to mental health services, data describing the current situation are difficult to obtain. Davidge et al. (1993) claim that "the actual number of places available for the mentally ill has remained little changed" over the past decade, with "some 80,000 beds of one type or another" in England. This is because "the 'loss' of beds in large hospitals has been matched by the provision of alternative places in smaller NHS hospitals, local authority accommodation and private hospitals and homes [plus] an unquantified level of provision in various housing schemes which do not appear in official statistics." However, a place in a "bed and breakfast" hostel, operated for profit by an unqualified person, can in no way be equivalent to a bed in a fully staffed hospital with a wide range of facilities. Yet, to a significant extent, the first had replaced the second. The closure of Friern—a large mental hospital in North London—has been intensively studied (Leff et al. 1994); over 80 percent of the inpatients were resettled in the community; the remainder were transferred to another hospital. So far, this community reprovision has been generally successful, but its cost has been very high, and the extent to which these conclusions from a demonstration project could apply elsewhere remains uncertain. In fact, no general statement can be made about the condition of mentally ill patients placed in noninstitutional settings because the relevant information is unobtainable. A survey in one coastal town, however, produced disquieting results (Barnes and Thornicroft 1993).

The NHS and Community Care Act of 1990 requires local social service and health authorities jointly to agree on needs-based individual care plans for long-term and severely ill psychiatric patients. For each person, a case manager (later renamed "care manager") is to be nominated in order to ensure that patients' needs are met as fully as possible. This change had been largely provoked by the unplanned rise in social security payments for care of the elderly (often with dementia) in private nursing homes. From 1993, the responsibility for payment was transferred from the national social security budget to local social services; the local authorities were given some money to provide for the elderly, but then had to balance this task against all their other responsibilities, including care of the nonelderly mentally ill. Whereas social services had previously owned and operated their own residential facilities (including those for the mentally ill), they were now expected to change their function steadily to that of a purchasing agent. The consequences of this change will not be fully known for some time; it seems to be—like many policies—one that would work reasonably well if adequately funded, but that will likely fail because it is being introduced without these resources (Thornicroft 1994). In one mixed industrial–rural area in the Midlands, however, the combination of DGH and community services was said to be coping well and was not under serious strain (Groves 1994).

The rate of change in British health services during the past ten years has been dizzying, as it has been in social services, education, and many other aspects of national life. Yet, as seen in the United States rather earlier, organizational changes appear to have been "hurriedly put into place… poorly conceived, improperly implemented, and ineffectively administered, without any systematic attempt to assess their impact" (Rossi and Freeman 1993). NHS services are now mostly provided by self-governing "trusts," with fixed budgets, in which provision is altered for financial reasons, irrespective of patients' needs. District health authorities have become the purchasers, but no longer the providers, of services for their populations—the same purchaser–provider split that has been imposed on social services. Similarly, groups of GPs ("fund-holders") are now purchasing all specialist care for the patients on their lists; they can make a choice in the kinds they buy, which will not necessarily be to the benefit of patients with more serious psychiatric disorders. The long-term effects of this "internal market" are almost impossi-

ble to predict, but its commercial ideology seems inappropriate to either health or social care. The results of 40 years of progress toward developing an integrated mental health system for each population have been jeopardized by a fragmentation into independent units, each of which is negotiating and bargaining with all the others, theoretically on a basis of "competition." Sir Douglas Black (1994) describes the intrusion of an internal market and the split between purchasers and providers as "unnecessary threats to the cooperation towards a worthwhile common purpose which was a hallmark of the NHS."

Mental health services have been affected both by the overall changes in the NHS and social services and by specific measures affecting psychiatry; these two pressures have not always been consistent (Davies and Peck 1994). In the first place, while district health authorities have to purchase services for population-based needs, fundholding GPs (who are to become the majority) have a strong incentive to obtain the cheapest care for individual patients. One way of doing this is to employ psychiatric nurses or counselors themselves, rather than refer patients to the district mental health service. This runs directly counter to the government's declared policy for mental health services: to concentrate on the severely mentally ill and work through multidisciplinary teams. A similar discrepancy occurs between health authorities (with their community responsibilities) and social services, which are obligated to purchase residential or day care on an individual basis. Furthermore, the whole philosophy of this contracting process was predicated on the model of single episodes of inpatient care, like elective surgery, whereas in psychiatry, the episodes are often impossible to define, the outcome is complex, and treatment methods are controversial. The "reforms" have been responsible for a massive inflation of management costs (which in the unreformed NHS were the lowest in the world) without real evidence up to now of clinical benefits or increased productivity (Light 1994). When all purchasing authorities in one health region were asked about the plans for child and adolescent mental health, they were found to have very limited knowledge of those services and to have made little or no attempt to set standards of quality or to monitor what was provided (Vanstraelen and Cottrell 1994).

Can all the functions that were served by the mental hospital be reproduced outside of it? The House of Commons Health Committee (1994) identified 15 functions of old psychiatric institutions; some of these (food, clothing, basic income) have become the responsibility of social security, while others (assessment and treatment, outpatient care) have mostly been transferred to the DGH. Long-term care for the mentally retarded and the management of forensic cases have been absorbed by specialized services, although the latter are very inadequate. However, functions such as respite care, asylum, shelter, recreation, "a social world," and occupational rehabilitation, while notionally the responsibility of local social services, have ceased to exist in many places. In the committee's view, the mental hospital achieved real economics of scale, "offset by the lack of independence, choice, privacy, and individualised care for patients." The committee could have added that the stigma of an identifiably psychiatric institution was a strongly negative feature for many patients and their relatives. They concluded that an acceptable mental health service should provide functions similar to those of the old institutions—with some new ones added—but it should do so in a different location and style.

Bachrach (1984) warned Britain against underestimating the diversity of services needed to replace psychiatric institutions because "the problems of using the same community facilities for new and old long-term patients came as a disruptive and expensive surprise in the U.S." The fall in mental hospital beds in the United States was matched by a considerable growth in psychiatric care in general hospitals, although some of this increase may have been only apparent, a result of changing diagnostic practices. More recently, associated with the rise of managed care arrangements, the use of inpatient beds has been much reduced, "but this shift of patients has occurred because of cost-containment objectives and outcome or effectiveness [has] been poorly considered" (Sharfstein 1994).

CONCLUSION

This account leads to the conclusion that general hospital psychiatry has only a limited meaning in isolation, not least because psychiatric disorders have a strong tendency to chronicity. It is increasingly recognized that the treatment of major depression, for instance, may not be a matter of weeks or months, but, rather, possibly of several years (Kupfer 1993). Within this period, only a fairly short time may be spent as a hospital inpatient, but if the management is to be effective, the episode of full-time care must be integrated with outpatient care, possibly with day-hospital attendance and/or home supervision, and certainly with long-term oversight by the GP. Furthermore, unless the DGH unit has alternative placements (hospital–hostels, staffed hostels, medium-secure units) for those patients whose chronic disabilities or disturbance prevent them from going out without risk, it will often be impossible to admit people with acute illnesses because beds will be permanently blocked. In those circumstances, no one will gain admission unless he or she is in such a state of disturbance as to constitute an immediate danger to themselves or others, and, afterwards, the person may well be discharged before it is clinically advisable. A survey by the Royal College of Psychiatrists (1994) of inner-city London psychiatric units revealed this to be the situation now; they were running at an average capacity of 111 percent. Even if the nondisturbed, such as patients with severe depression, should actually gain admission, the ward environment is likely to be very unsuitable for them. One of the main underlying problems has been the national failure to provide beds in medium-secure units on the scale advocated by expert reports over many years; patients with "challenging behavior" therefore occupy acute beds inappropriately for very long periods,

Just as the growth of private madhouses was beyond the monitoring capacity of eighteenth-century governments, so the recent housing of mentally ill people in thousands of settings throughout the country presents an impossible problem of supervising standards. In the 1960s and 1970s, "scandals in mental hospitals" were influential in discrediting large institutions in Britain, notwithstanding that almost all of these cases involved mentally retarded or psychogeriatric, rather than psychiatric, patients. What was generally overlooked in this connection, however, was that such situations were discovered and remedied because there was a manageable number of hospitals and a functioning system of inspection. Yet the more the system fragments, the more difficult this task becomes, and it is now clear that health and social service authorities mostly lack the resources to do it (Royal College of Nursing 1994). As Turner-Crowson (1993) points out, "Noninstitutional systems tend to be poorly defined, fragmented, and vulnerable to adverse change."

Perhaps general hospital psychiatry has always contained an inherent flaw, in that it was designed essentially for the management of acute illnesses. If it includes the resources to cope also with the most severe chronic disorders from a sizable population, its capacity might approach that of a small mental hospital—as some of the Manchester region units did in the 1960s, and as many now do in Germany (Bauer 1994). But is this simply a reinvention of the mental hospital, sharing a common site with the rest of medical care—as proposed in McKeown's "balanced hospital community"? Thornicroft and Strathdee (1994) propose that "the debate on numbers of hospital beds should now be widened to include the contributions of agencies other than health providers, such as social services, housing, and voluntary agencies, which substantially reduce the need for inpatient care." How far that need can safely be reduced, however, remains undetermined. The latest government document on mental health policy (Department of Health 1993) recommends adding "user-friendly" alternative sites to the DGH

(mental health centers, hostels, ordinary housing) for much of acute psychiatric care and long-term residential care arrangements. This represents a fundamental change from the predominant national assumption of the last 30 years that the DGH unit would serve as the base from which other mental health provision would take place, yet the evaluation of nonhospital acute care has so far reached only a preliminary stage. Analysis of the work of psychiatric services is hampered by the fact that most data "are based largely on paradigms derived from analysis of medical and surgical services that do not reflect the nature of mental health care (Flannigan et al. 1994).

Two further problems in this reorientation away from hospitals do not seem to have received adequate attention. When an institution-based service is changed to a locally based one, it has been recognized that resources seem to drift away from the care of people with the most severe and chronic disorders and toward services for those who are neurotic and plagued by personality and relationship problems. Avoiding such a tendency requires the "clear setting of goals and monitoring of the extent to which they are reached" (Turner-Crowson 1993), and it is not clear that this is being done in Britain. Secondly, this policy also seems to overlook the enormous progress made recently in biological psychiatry; investigation or treatment along these lines can only take place in a setting closely allied to general medicine, that is, the DGH. Because the DGH, with its high levels of technology, almost always has the first claim to resources, moving psychiatry to "community settings" would seem very likely to give the mentally ill a worse deal. At the very least, they deserve as much access to the facilities of the general hospital as other patients.

It seems unlikely that many mental hospitals will still exist in England by the end of this decade, except in vestigial form. Therefore, anyone needing acute treatment and care for psychiatric disorder of at least moderate severity should have immediate access to a general hospital unit that is equipped with appropriate facilities. The extent to which cases previously thought to need admission (Leff 1985) can be satisfactorily managed in other settings should be fully investigated before beds are further reduced. Relatively small numbers of people with severe, chronic psychoses will need to be under the full-time care of professional staff, but in units that do not need to be on a hospital site; an American estimate of these numbers was 15 per 100,000 population (Gudeman and Shore 1984). Those with less severe chronic disorders can be ac-

commodated in settings with varying degrees of support, from staffed hostels to their own homes. For every district population, there needs to be an integrated management and information system to ensure that patients are not neglected, their families do not have to carry unreasonable burdens, and the community is not exposed to unnecessary risks. The extent to which this scenario can be achieved in Britain remains very uncertain at present.

REFERENCES

Bachrach, L. 1984. An American Warning. *Open Mind* 11:16.

Baker, A. A. 1969. Psychiatric Unit in a District General Hospital. *Lancet* 1:1090–2.

Barnes, J. S., and G. Thornicroft. 1993. The Last Resort? Bed and Breakfast Accommodations for Mentally Ill People in a Seaside Town. *Health Trends* 25:87–90.

Barton, R. 1963. The Psychiatric Hospital. In *Trends in the Mental Health Services,* eds. H. L. Freeman, and J. Farndale. Oxford: Pergamon.

Bauer, M. 1994. Psychiatry in Former East and West Germany since Reunification. *Psychiatric Bulletin* 18:637–9.

Bennett, D. H. 1978. Community Psychiatry. *British Journal of Psychiatry* 132:209–20.

Black, D. 1994. *A Doctor Looks at Health Economics.* London: Office of Health Economics.

Brothwood, J. 1973. The Development of National Policy. In *Policy for Action,* eds. R. Cawley and G. McLachlan. London: Oxford University Press.

Bynum, W. F. 1985. The Nervous Patient in 18th and 19th Century Britain. In *The Anatomy of Madness* (vol. 1), eds. W. F. Bynum, R. Porter, and M. Shepherd. London: Tavistock.

Davidge, M., S. Elias, B. Jayes, K. Wood, and J. Yates. 1993. *Survey of English Mental Illness Hospitals, March 1993.* Birmingham: Health Services Management Center.

Davies, S., and E. Peck. 1994. Recent Government Policy and Legislation: An Overview. *Psychiatric Bulletin* 18:662–5.

Department of Health. 1993. *The Health of the Nation. Key Area Handbook. Mental Illness.* London.

Department of Health and Social Services. 1975. *Better Services for the Mentally Ill* (cmnd. 6233). London: Her Majesty's Stationery Office.

Dunckley, E. W., and E. Lewis. 1963. North Wing: A Psychiatric Unit in a General Hospital. *Lancet* 1:156–9.

Farndale, J. 1961. *The Day Hospital Movement in Great Britain.* Oxford: Pergamon.

Flannigan, C. B., G. R. Glover, J. K. Wing, S. W. Lewis, P. E. Bebbington, and S. T. Feeney. 1994. Inner London Collaborative Audit of Admissions in Two Health Districts. III: Reasons for Acute Admissions to Psychiatric Wards. *British Journal of Psychiatry* 165:750–9.

Freeman, H. L. 1960. Oldham and District Psychiatric Service. *Lancet* 1:218–21.

———. 1963. Community Mental Health Services: Some General and Practical Considerations. *Comprehensive Psychiatry* 4:417–25.

Freeman, H. L., and D. H. Bennett. 1991. Origins and Development. In *Community Psychiatry: The Principles,* eds. D. H. Bennett and H. L. Freeman. London: Churchill Livingstone.

Godber, G. E. 1988. Interview with Hugh Freeman. *Psychiatric Bulletin* 12:513–19.

Goldberg, D. 1986. Implementation of Mental Health Policies in the North-West of England. In *The Provision of Mental Health Services in Britain: The Way Ahead,* eds. G. Wilkinson and H. L. Freeman. London: Gaskell.

Goldberg, D., K. Bridges, W. Cooper, C. Hyde, C. Sterling, and R. Wyatt. 1985. Douglas House: A New Type of Hostel Ward for Chronic Psychotic Patients. *British Journal of Psychiatry* 147:383–8.

Greenhill, M. 1979. Psychiatric Units in General Hospitals. *Hospital and Community Psychiatry* 30:169–82.

Groves, T. 1994. Community Care: The First Year. *British Medical Journal* 308:1044–6.

Gudeman, J., and M. Shore. 1984. Beyond Deinstitutionalisation. *New England Journal of Medicine* 311:832–6.

Hall, P., and I. Brockington. 1990. *The Closure of Mental Hospitals.* London: Gaskell.

Hamburg, D. A. 1957. Therapeutic Aspects of Communication and Administrative Policy in the Psychiatric Section of a General Hospital. In *The Patient and the Mental Hospital,* eds. M. Greenblatt, S. Leavens, and R. Williams. Glencoe, Ill.: Free Press.

House of Commons Health Committee. 1994. *Final Report.* London: Her Majesty's Stationery Office.

Jones, K. 1963. The Role and Function of the Mental Hospital. In *Trends in the Mental Health Services,* eds. H. L. Freeman and J. Farndale. Oxford: Pergamon.

———. 1979. Integration or Disintegration in the Mental Health Services. *Journal of the Royal Society of Medicine* 72:640–8.

———. 1993. *Asylums and After.* London: Athlone.

Kessel, N. 1973. The District General Hospital Is Where the Action Is. In *Policy for Action,* eds. R. H. Cawley and G. McLachlan. London: Oxford University Press.

Kingdon, D., and H. L. Freeman. 1995. Personnel Options in the Treatment of Schizophrenia. In *The Economics of Schizophrenia,* eds. M. Moscarelli and N. Sartorius. Chichester, U.K.: Wiley.

Kupfer, D. 1993. Management of Recurrent Depression. *Journal of Clinical Psychiatry* 54 (suppl.):29–33.

Leff, J. P. 1985. The Need for Hospital Care. In *The Provision of Mental Health Services in Britain: The Way Ahead,* eds. G. Wilkinson and H. L. Freeman. London: Gaskell.

Leff, J. P., G. Thornicroft, N. Coxhead, and C. Crawford. 1994. The TAPS Project: A Five-Year Follow-Up of Long-Stay Psychiatric Patients Discharged to the Community. *British Journal of Psychiatry* 165 (suppl. 25):13–17.

Ligth, D. W. 1994. Managed Care: False and Real Solutions. *Lancet* 344:1197–9.

Martin, F. M. 1984. *Between the Acts: Community Mental Health Services 1959–1983.* London: Nuffield Provincial Hospitals Trust.

Mayou, R. 1989. The History of General Hospital Psychiatry. *British Journal of Medicine* 155: 764–76.

McKeown, T. 1958. The Concept of a Balanced Hospital Community. *Lancet* 1:682–5.

Merskey, H. 1991. Shell-Shock: In *150 Years of British Psychiatry.* eds. G. E. Berrios and H. L. Freeman. London: Gaskell.

Ministry of Health. 1959. *Report for the Year 1959.* London: Her Majesty's Stationery Office.

———. 1971. *Hospital Services for the Mentally Ill.* London: Her Majesty's Stationery Office.

Morrissey, J. 1982. Deinstitutionalising the Mentally Ill: Process, Outcomes and New Directions. In *Deviance and Mental Illness,* ed. W. Grove. Beverly Hills: Sage.

Parry-Jones, W. 1972. *The Trade in Lunacy.* London: Routledge and Kegan Paul.

Pickstone, J. V. 1989. Psychiatry in District General Hospitals. In *Medical Innovations in Historical Perspectives.* London: Macmillan.

Powell, J. E. 1961. Opening Address. In *Emerging Patterns for Medical Health Services and the Public.* London: National Association for Mental Health.

Prior, P. 1993. Mental Health Services in Northern Ireland. PhD thesis, Queen's University, Belfast, Ireland.

Rehin, G., and F. M. Martin. 1963. Some Problems for Research in Community Care. In *Trends in the Mental Health Services,* eds. H. L. Freeman and J. Farndale. Oxford: Pergamon.

Rossi, P. H., and H. L. Freeman. 1993. *Evaluation: A Systematic Approach,* 5th ed. London: Sage.

Royal College of Nursing. 1994. *An Inspector Calls.* London.

Royal College of Psychiatrists. 1994. *Monitoring Inner London Services.* London.

Rumbaut, R. B. 1994. Book Review. *New England Journal of Medicine* 330:1547.

Sedgwick, P. 1982. *Psycho-Politics.* London: Pluto Press.

Sharfstein, S. S. 1994. Book Review. *American Journal of Psychiatry* 151:1518.

Simpson, C. J., C. E. Hyde, and E. B. Faragher. 1989. The Chronically Mentally Ill in Community Facilities: A Study of Quality of Life. *British Journal of Psychiatry* 154:77–82.

Smith, S. 1963. The Future of Mental Hospitals. In *Trends in the Mental Health Services,* eds. H. L. Freeman and J. Farndale. Oxford: Pergamon.

Thornicroft, G. 1994. The NHS and Community Care Act 1990. *Psychiatric Bulletin* 18:13–17.

Thornicroft, G., and G. Strathdee. 1994. How Many Psychiatric Beds? *British Medical Journal* 309:970–1.

Titmuss, R. 1961. Community Care, Faction or Fiction? In *Emerging Patterns for the Mental Health Services and the Public.* London: National Association for Mental Health.

Tooth, G., and E. M. Brooke. 1961. Trends in the Mental Hospital Population and Their Effect on Future Planning. *Lancet* 1:710–13.

Turner-Crowson, J. 1993. *Reshaping Mental Illness Services: Implications for Britain of US Experience.* London: King's Fund Institute.

Vanstraelen, M., and D. Cottrell. 1994. Child and Adolescent Mental Health Services: Purchaser's Knowledge and Plans. *British Medical Journal* 309:259–61.

Wilkinson, G., and H. L. Freeman. 1986. *The Provision of Mental Health Services in Britain: The Way Ahead.* London: Gaskell.

World Health Organization. 1953. *The Community Mental Hospital* (WHO technical report series, 73). Geneva.

DEVELOPING WORLD PERSPECTIVE

URBAN INEQUALITIES IN MENTAL HEALTH: THE CASE OF SÃO PAULO, BRAZIL

ILONA BLUE

I. INTRODUCTION

For cities to prosper, it is argued, urban populations as a whole should have the opportunity to enjoy good health. In the background paper on "Creating Healthy Cities in the 21st Century" presented at the recent United Nations Conference on Human Settlements, it was stated that in healthy cities "...promoting health and preventing disease and injury was recognized as being in everyone's interest and as everyone's responsibility."[1] Allowing large proportions of an urban population to experience significantly inferior living conditions is unjust and has implications for the health and well-being of all the occupants of a city. Maintaining human health is vital not only from a humane standpoint but also from an economic one—healthy workers are productive workers.

Despite this, urban inequalities in health exist and, in the cities of the South,[2] the scale of such differentials is often large and the range of health problems faced by the urban poor extensive. Stephens *et al* undertook a study of health differentials in Accra, Ghana and São Paulo, Brazil.[3] They found, as expected, that the urban poor suffered disproportionately from the infectious and parasitic diseases associated with inadequate provision for water supply, sanitation, drainage and garbage collection. But they also found that the urban poor suffered disproportionately from non-communicable diseases (e.g. heart disease) which had been considered primarily as diseases suffered by wealthier groups and associated with their diets and lifestyles. It was concluded that inequalities in physical, social and environmental conditions were largely responsible for such differentials and that there was a lack of understanding of the implications of social disadvantage and a tendency for the material disadvantages of urban poverty to be considered in isolation of the broader context in which poverty occurs.[4]

Although the World Health Organization's popular definition of health gives physical and mental health equal emphasis, mental health has never enjoyed the attention devoted to physical health problems on international public health agendas. In spite of this, work done on mental health issues has recognized poverty as a risk factor for mental ill-health.[5] This paper aims to describe why a consideration of mental ill-health in cities in the South is important. It will also discuss urban inequalities in mental health status, using São Paulo as an example, and possible explanations for this inequality will be examined.

II. MENTAL HEALTH IN THE SOUTH

Despite the relatively low status accorded to mental ill-health on international public health agendas, it is gradually being recognized as a serious problem in the South. It is a problem that affects a large number of people, creates a great deal of suffering and produces a considerable burden on health services and society as a whole. What follows is a list of some of the main points pertinent to any consideration of mental ill-health in the South.

- Around 90 per cent of all mental disorders can be classified as common mental disorders.[6] "The clinical features of such morbidity include a mixture of anxiety, depression, insomnia, fatigue, irritability, poor memory/concentration, somatic symptoms, and somatic concern."[7] Those suffering from common mental disorders are often unable to work, may have difficulties bringing up their children and can suffer from related physical health problems.

- The prevalence of common mental disorders has been estimated at between 12 and 46 per cent in countries in the South depending on how mental ill-health is measured and on the samples used.[8] In terms of the burden such disorders place on society, the publication of the "World Development Report 1993: Investing in Health" provided the first estimate of the impact of mental disorders on the global burden of disease.[9] It was found, for example, that, among young adult (15–44 year old) women in "demographically developing countries," depression was the fifth largest cause of the disease burden, coming after maternal causes, sexually transmitted diseases, tuberculosis and HIV.[10] The methods employed in the calculation of the global burden of disease are not ideal and much of the data used in the World Development Report were of poor quality or based on the estimates of expert committees. However, the global burden of disease analysis does provide a starting point. Informed estimates leading to explicit valuation are preferable to no formal estimates (and ultimately implicit valuation forming the basis of decision-making).

- The majority of people suffering from common mental disorders are not in touch with health services. But those who are tend to present with a variety of superficial physical complaints (for example headaches, general aches and pains) that are caused by their underlying mental ill-health. The failure on the part of medical professionals to recognize cases of mental ill-health due to patients presenting with physical symptoms results in low detection rates of common mental disorders. This, in turn, results in inappropriate treatment being given and the misallocation of, frequently scarce, resources. It also obscures the true levels of mental ill-health in a community.

- The burden of common mental disorders falls predominantly on young adults (15–49 years old). Given that this is the most economically productive group in any society, the implications of this preponderance of mental ill-health are grave. Within the adult population, women appear to suffer around twice the rates of common mental disorders as men. Explanations for this highly consistent finding vary but Paykel[11] identifies four possibilities: the different help-seeking behaviour of the sexes; biological causes; social causes; and the differential acknowledgment and direction of distress. Paykel concludes that it is most probably a combination of all the above factors, particularly the last two, that has led to women suffering predominantly from common mental disorders. All the explanations work in the same direction, that is, to increase the prevalence in women as compared to men.

- Literature exploring the possible causes of common mental disorders emphasizes the importance of social and environmental factors and the relatively minor role played by biological factors.[12] Risk factors for common mental disorders vary and include those related to long-term difficulty due to a poor social and physical environment, for example over-crowded housing, unemployment, and inse-cure tenure. Negative life events, for example, the death of a spouse, loss of employment, separation from partner and migration have also been shown to be related to mental ill-health.[13] However, it is important to bear in mind that some life events, although consid-ered negative, can, in certain circumstances, have beneficial impacts on health, for example migration might involve a move from a deprived area to one with relatively greater opportunities and facilities. In addition to long-term difficulties and life events, a lack of positive social support has been found to be detrimental to mental health. Thoits describes social support as "…'a social fund' from which people may draw when handling stres-sors…(it) usually refers to the functions per-formed for the individual by significant others, such as family members, friends, and co-workers." She goes on to state that "We al-ready know from amassed epidemiological and survey based evidence that social support, a sense of control and self-esteem, and certain coping skills make a significant difference in preventing or reducing physical and mental health problems."[14]

• There are problems associated with definitions of mental ill-health. This is because the exist-ence of a universal state of mental *health* on which definitions of mental *ill-health* could be based was counter-intuitive to many. However, a study using data from 15 countries stressed the existence of similar forms of psychological disorder across cultures.[15]

The preceding list has presented, among other things, a justification for the consideration of men-tal health problems in the South where the empha-sis has traditionally rested on health problems of a physical nature. In addition to the focus on coun-tries in the South, urban areas have attracted the at-tention of various researchers investigating mental health. To date, studies comparing rates of mental ill-health in urban and rural areas have not pro-duced any consistent findings and it would appear that the question of whether or not urban areas pro-duce higher rates of mental ill-health than rural ar-eas is likely to remain in dispute.[16] It is now widely accepted that it is poverty, rather than rural or ur-ban residence, that plays a crucial role in creating high levels of stress and subsequent mental ill-health.[17] However, focusing on urban areas makes sense for the following reasons: this is where the majority of the world's population will live in the future; the problems of urban and rural health are different in nature (although not necessarily in ex-tent or severity) and this needs to be taken into ac-count in research; and urbanization has resulted in changes in social structure which have an impact on mental health.

III. INEQUALITIES IN MENTAL HEALTH IN THE CITY OF SÃO PAULO

Urbanization can provide opportunities for positive growth but those able to enjoy the beneficial im-pacts of urbanization are often in the minority—the majority of urban dwellers face various threats to their livelihoods. "Increasingly, cities are becom-ing the world's starkest symbol of the maldistribu-tion of resources, both physical and societal. These inequalities have serious impacts on the health of urban dwellers everywhere but especially in the fast-growing towns and cities in the developing world.[18]

Recent work exploring inequalities in health in large urban centres of the South has stressed the dynamic nature of the health profiles of such cities. Stephens, considering the case of São Paulo, elab-orates on the complexity of health inequalities in the city: infectious and parasitic diseases (predom-inantly related to a poor physical environment) still play a relatively important role in childhood ill-health but it is the non-communicable diseases (including mental ill-health), more explicitly related to socio-economic factors, that now feature prominently in adult life and which require an altogether different public health perspective if efforts for their reduction are to succeed.[19]

Between 1991 and 1992, the "Brazilian Multicentric Study of Psychiatric Morbidity" was carried out in three urban centres: Brasilia, Porto Alegre and São Paulo.[20] Within the city of São Paulo, data were collected in three sub-districts, Brasilândia, Vila Guilherme and Aclimacão, chosen for their contrasting socio-economic characteristics. A cluster sampling technique was used and each respondent (the sample numbered 1,742) was screened for the presence of a mental disorder using a questionnaire developed in Brazil, the "Questionnaire for Adult Psychiatric Morbidity."[21] In addition to the information collected related to mental health, questions were also asked about socio-demographic variables. The data revealed a highly significant ($p < 0.001$) variation in the prevalence of probable cases of mental disorder across the three sub-districts: 21 per cent in Brasilândia (the lowest socio-economic subdistrict); 16 per cent in Vila Guilherme (the middle socio-economic sub-district); and 12 per cent in Aclimacão (the highest socio-economic subdistrict). These differences in prevalence are even more striking when it is considered that the majority of the population in São Paulo resides in subdistricts similar in nature to Brasilândia and only a minority are able to enjoy the prosperous conditions found in Aclimacão. The next section will seek to shed some light on reasons why this inequality in mental ill-health occurs.

IV. POSSIBLE EXPLANATIONS FOR THE INEQUALITY IN MENTAL HEALTH STATUS

That people living in low-income urban environments suffer disproportionately from mental health problems as compared to their richer urban neighbours will come as no surprise to many readers.

Marsella states that as development progressed, "…material wealth, political power and social status emerged as the only apparent safeguards against the pressing tides of uncertainty that accompanied urbanization." He goes on to state that "…poverty, as a composite index of deprivation and disorganization, will most likely emerge as the single greatest predictor of urban mortality and physical and mental morbidity. This fact must be acknowledged, for poverty is not an uncontrollable virus but rather the outcome of specific social, political and economic circumstances which can be prevented.[22] Despite Marsella's broad view of the impact of poverty on mental health, research attempting to explain the link between poverty and mental ill-health has tended to have a narrow focus on individual level risk factors (for example, migration status, unemployment, low income and lack of education).

In the case of São Paulo, data from the Brazilian Multicentric Study revealed significant differences between the percentage of migrants in the three subdistricts, with Brasilândia containing the highest percentage of migrants and Aclimacão the lowest. The pattern was similar for those whose family income fell into the lowest category. Further analysis of these data is currently being undertaken by the author. However, previous research relating to the link between migration and mental health has stressed that migration alone cannot be considered as a risk factor for mental health. It is only when recent migration is combined with low-income status that any significant increase in the risk of becoming mentally ill is observed.[23]

Such analysis is typical of mainstream epidemiology and other disciplines espousing quantitative methods and is useful in highlighting at-risk groups. However, the focus on individual risk factors as causes of mental ill-health has been at the expense of a consideration of the wider impact of poverty as suggested by Marsella. This imbalance is understandable when it is considered that public health professionals traditionally seek out specific cause–effect relationships that can then be the fo-

cus of relatively simple interventions but it is now understood that the full complexity of urban health problems must not only be recognized but explicitly taken into account when actions for their amelioration are devised.[24]

In the case of common mental disorders, with their vast array of associated social and environmental determinants, following an individual exposure–disease model is particularly problematic. Lacking the basic goods and facilities for quality of life to be maintained is only one aspect of poverty—how people relate to the deprived circumstances in which they find themselves and the social meanings attached to those circumstances is another, less well-analyzed, aspect. Wilkinson suggests that the link between inequalities in wealth and inequalities in health (both mental and physical) revolves around psycho-social factors.[25]

> First, psycho-social processes emanating from a perception of one's status, economic insecurity or relative deprivation may impact directly on health. Second, psycho-social stress may affect smoking and other health related behaviour. Third, attempts by people on low incomes to maintain socially acceptable standards in more visible areas of consumption are likely to involve saving on food and other necessities which could damage health.[26]

In urban areas, where inequalities in wealth are both vast and visible, Wilkinson's hypothesis that a reaction to "how the other half live" can have an impact on health seems particularly appropriate. Notions of inequality imply strong links between people and their surroundings (including the environment and other people). The effects of place or community on health are increasingly being acknowledged and it is clear that many of the factors related to mental ill-health operate at a level beyond the direct influence of any one individual.[27] The importance of considering such contextual factors is summarized in the following citation:

> Lack of amenities and opportunities to lead healthy or health-promoting lives may be as important for assessing the health needs of the population as knowledge of their personal characteristics, and policies designed to improve local environments may be as effective as individually targeted health promotion activities...We therefore advocate research which focuses directly on the health-promoting or health-threatening features of local social and physical environments, and local and national health promotion policies which take into account features of places as well as features of people.[28]

In addition to recent work emphasizing the links between place, context or environment and health, some work has attempted to link contextual issues with mental health in particular. Ekblad refers to the pioneering work of Selye on the subject of stress.[29] Selye defined stress as an incongruence between individuals and their environments. He used the term environment in a broad sense to include both physical aspects (e.g. overcrowding, pollution) and social aspects (e.g. lifestyle factors). Ekblad et al emphasize the way in which urbanization has produced social and environmental changes that impact on stress levels and, therefore, mental health. They divide the built environment into three levels: housing characteristics, the wider neighbourhood and the urban area as a whole. Good quality housing is that which provides sufficient space, easy access to services and friends and few personal hazards. A health-promoting neighbourhood would be one where there is good physical infrastructure (roads, drains, etc.) and services (health, educational, etc.).[30] In terms of the urban area as a whole, Satterthwaite mentions the importance of residents' level of satisfaction with the housing and neighbourhood as compared to other parts of the urban area.[31]

In seeking to elucidate the kinds of stress-inducing factors that operate at a contextual level and analyze how these vary between sub-districts with (usually) inhabitants of contrasting socio-economic status, focus group discussions were held with women living in the three previously mentioned sub-districts in São Paulo.

The discussions revolved around the following themes:

- a description of the women's daily lives;
- background information on the sub-district;

- information on recent changes in the sub-district;
- negative aspects of living in the sub-district;
- positive aspects of living in the sub-district;
- a comparison of the sub-district with the rest of the city; and
- information on the well-being of residents.

The questions were ordered in such a way as to allow the participants to respond to relatively simple queries at the start of the discussion before proceeding to the more complex issues that made up the bulk of the discussion. It was decided to exclude any mention of mental health as this often gives rise to notions of severe mental disorder (for example schizophrenia) and could have detracted from the aim of the discussions. Four focus groups were conducted in each sub-district and each focus group consisted of between four and six women. The participants were from low-income households, varied in age from 19 to 86 years old and were of different migratory and educational status. Some initial findings from the focus group discussions are presented here, briefly.

Concentrating on the factors that the women considered stressful, some differences between the three sub-districts emerged and what follows is a brief glimpse at some of the findings. In the case of Brasilândia, women mentioned a multitude of problems ranging from deficiencies in the physical infrastructure in the sub-district to security issues and the threat of violence:

I don't like where I live, there are a lot of shacks. The roads aren't paved. We made the drains ourselves. There are people who live right on top of sewage. There's flooding…there's a place near where I live where the water runs down the road—I don't want my son to get ill. —Carla, Brasilândia

There is a lack of safety at night. We listen to gunshots, there's violence. The traffic is violent, cars don't stop at traffic lights. They don't look out for children going to school. —Denise, Brasilândia

Where I live there are gunshots, even during the day. If we are outside when it happens, we run in because we are frightened. This happens at any time, not just at night. People grab their kids and run away.
—Maria, Brasilândia.

In the case of Vila Guilherme, specific problems related to frequent flooding and heavy traffic were discussed. Violence was also mentioned as a problem, mainly in terms of burglaries and car theft but, in general, the women did not feel that the situation was as bad as in the other parts of the city.

The flooding needs to be stopped. Last week my furniture got ruined…my son was ill, his cold didn't get better because of the damp. We had three floods in one week. —Ana, Vila Guilherme

There's the problem of the lorries. They've already broken my wall twice…they destroy the pavements…when they switch on their engines at five in the morning no one sleeps…if you open the window, you get that strong smell of fumes and burning oil…it makes me feel ill, I have to keep the windows closed all day.
—Susie, Vila Guilherme

A boy was run over and died on the road. Various children have been run over. There are a lot of cars. Everyone here would like there to be road bumps…the people drive quickly, carelessly. There are no traffic signs. —Rosa, Vila Guilherme

They robbed my house twice. The house can't be left empty. I'm scared of leaving the house to go and look for a job. —Joana, Vila Guilherme

In Aclimacão, after mentioning various problems related to the physical facilities and appearance of the sub-district (rubbish in the street, pollution), the women talked mainly of the fear of violence.

What really worries people is safety. All the houses on my road have bars (at the windows) and even so thieves got into my neighbour's house. People worry. I live close to the park and worry when the children go out to play.

—Alice, Aclimacão

The general complaint of the women in the neighbourhood is of fear. They are afraid to go out and sweep the pavement because a burglar might get into the house.
—Freda, Aclimacão

The preceding quotations provide an idea of the range of socio-environmental factors perceived as stressors by the women themselves. Clearly, women living in all three sub-districts find their and their families' well-being threatened by a variety of socio-environmental factors. They worry about the effects of factors that operate largely beyond their immediate control. From the above quotations, it can be seen that the severity and type of environmental threats varies between the sub-districts with the women in Brasilândia facing a greater number of more extreme stressors than those living in Vila Guilherme and Aclimacão.

IV. CONCLUSION

In an editorial on urban health issues in *The Lancet* it was stated that "...to keep cities profitable into the 21st century more attention will need to be paid to aspects of health other than the purely physical."[32] Mental ill-health is a growing problem and one that urgently requires attention. This paper has attempted to highlight the significant public health impact of mental ill-health in cities of the South and advocates increasing resources being directed towards tackling this problem.

The inequalities in mental ill-health in São Paulo were demonstrated and possible reasons for this variation provided. It is suggested that for the problem of mental ill-health to be successfully confronted, a broad understanding of poverty, taking into account both individual and contextual factors, is required. Such an approach is in line with current thinking in urban health research which suggests that an integrated approach, and one that acknowledges the complexity of urban health problems, is the way forward.[33]

REFERENCES

1. WHO (1996), "Creating healthy cities in the 21st century," dialogue on health in human settlements, background paper, United Nations Conference on Human Settlements, 3–14 June 1996, page 1.
2. In this paper, the term "the South" is used to denote countries in Africa, Latin America and Asia (except Japan). The author is aware of the unsatisfactory nature of this term.
3. Stephens, C., I. Timaeus, M. Akerman, et al. (1994), *Environment and Health in Developing Countries: An Analysis of Intraurban Differentials Using Existing Data,* London School of Hygiene and Tropical Medicine, UK; SEADE, Brazil; and Republic of Ghana.
4. Stephens, C. (1995), "The urban environment, poverty and health in developing countries" in *Health Policy and Planning* Vol. 10, No. 2, pages 109–121.
5. Harpham, T. (1994), "Urbanization and mental health in developing countries: a research role for social scientists, public health professionals and social psychiatrists" in *Social Science and Medicine* Vol. 39, No. 2, pages 233–245.
6. Goldberg, D., and P. Huxley (1992), *Common Mental Disorders,* Routledge, London.
7. Cheng, T. A. (1989), "Urbanization and minor psychiatric morbidity: a community study in Taiwan" in *Social Psychiatry and Psychiatric Epidemiology* Vol. 24, pages 309–316.
8. See reference 5.

9. World Bank (1993), *World Development Report 1993: Investing in Health,* Oxford University Press.
10. Blue, I., and T. Harpham (1994), "The World Bank *World Development Report 1993: Investing in Health* reveals the burden of common mental disorders but ignores its implications" in *British Journal of Psychiatry* Vol. 165, pages 9–12.
11. Paykel, E. S. (1991), "Depression in women" in *British Journal of Psychiatry* Vol. 158 (Supplement 10), pages 22–29.
12. See reference 7.
13. See reference 5.
14. Thoits, P. A. (1995), "Stress, coping, and social support processes: Where are we? What next?" in *Journal of Health and Social Behaviour* (extra issue) pages 64 and 70.
15. Ormel, J., B. VonKroff, S. Ustun, *et al.* (1994), "Common mental disorders and disability across cultures" in *JAMA* Vol. 272, pages 1741–1748; see also Pretorius, W. (1995), "Mental disorders and disability across cultures: a view from South Africa" in *The Lancet* Vol. 345, page 534.
16. Webb, L. (1984), "Rural–urban difference in mental disorder" in Freeman, H. L. (editor), *Mental Health and the Environment,* Churchill Livingstone, London.
17. Harpham, T., and I. Blue (editors) (1995), *Urbanization and Mental Health in Developing Countries,* Avebury, Aldershot, UK; see also Desjarlais, R., L. Eisenberg, B. Good,

and A. Kleinman (1995), *World Mental Health: Problems and Priorities in Low-Income Countries.* Oxford University Press, New York.

18. Stephens, C., G. McGranahan, *et al.* (1996), "Urban environment and health" in World Resources Institute, *World Resources: A Guide to the Global Environment 1996–97,* Oxford University Press, page 31.

19. See note 4

20. Almeida-Filho, N., J. J. Mari, E. Coutinho, *et al.* (1991), *The Brazilian Multicentric Study of Psychiatric Morbidity: Methodological Features and Prevalence Estimates,* unpublished manuscript; see also Mari, J. J., N. Almeido-Filho, E. Coutinho, *et al.* (1993), "The epidemiology of psychotropic drug use in the city of São Paulo" in *Psychological Medicine* Vol. 23, pages 467–474.

21. Santana, V. (1982), "Estudo epidemiologico das doencas mentais em um bairro de Salvador" in *Serie de Estudos em Saude (Secretaris de Saude de Bahia)* Vol. 3, pages 1–122 (supplement).

22. Marsella, A. (1990), "Urbanization and mental disorders: an overview of theory and research, and recommendations for interventions and research," paper prepared for the World Health Organization's Commission on Health and the Environment, pages 2 and 4.

23. Reichenheim, M., and T. Harpham (1991), "Maternal mental health in a squatter settlement in Rio de Janeiro" *British Journal of Psychiatry* Vol. 159, pages 683–690.

24. See reference 4.

25. Wilkinson, R. (1994), "The epidemiological transition: from material scarcity to social disadvantage?" in *Daedalus* Vol. 123, No. 4, pages 61–78; see also Wilkinson, R. (in press), "How can secular improvements in life expectancy be explained?" in Blaub, D., *et al* (editors), *Health and Society,* Routledge, UK.

26. See Wilkinson (1994) in reference 25.

27. Ekblad, S. (1993), "Stressful environments and their effects on quality of life in Third World Cities" in *Environment and Urbanization* Vol. 5(2), pages 125–134; see also Satterthwaite, D. (1993), "The impact on health of urban environments" in *Environment and Urbanization* Vol. 5, No. 2, pages 87–111; also Jones, K., C. Duncan, and G. Moon (1994), "Individuals and their ecologies: analyzing the geography of chronic illness within a multilevel modeling framework," paper presented at the 6th international Medical Geography Symposium, July 1994, University of British Columbia, Vancouver; and Macintyre, S., S. Maciver, and A. Sooman, (1994), "Area, class and health; should we be focusing on places or people?" in *Journal of Social Policy* Vol. 22, No. 2, pages 213–234.

28. See Macintyre, Maciver, and Sooman (1994), page 232, in reference 27.

29. See Ekblad (1993) in reference 27; see also Selye, H. (1956), *The Stress of Life,* McGraw-Hill, New York; and Selye, H. (1974), *Stress without Distress,* Lippincott, Philadelphia.

30. Ekblad, S., *et al.* (1991), *Stressors, Chinese City Dwellings and Quality of Life,* Swedish Council for Building Research, D12.

31. See Satterthwaite (1993) in reference 27.

32. Anon (1994), "Editorial: city limits" in *The Lancet* Vol. 343, pages 1303–1304, May 28.

33. See reference 1; see also Werna, E., I. Blue, and T. Harpham (1996), "The changing agenda for urban health" in Cohen, M., *et al.* (editors), *Preparing for the Urban Future: Global Pressures and Local Forces,* Woodrow Wilson Center Press, Washington, DC, and reference 4.

PART THREE

HEALTH CARE PROVIDERS

CHAPTER 8

PHYSICIANS

The future of the medical profession is one of change. As Hafferty and McKinlay (1993:3) point out, some of these changes include

> the evolving nature of physician autonomy, changes in the structure and dynamics of the physician–patient relationship, the transformation of collegial relations, and an ongoing debate about what constitutes quality in health care—how it should be assessed and the role medicine can and should play in its delivery.

These issues are not unique to the medical profession in the United States, but they do not constitute a listing of experiences associated with the medical profession worldwide (Hafferty and McKinlay, 1993). In addition, the medical profession is also experiencing change in the demographic characteristics of its members. What do these changes mean? For physicians, these changes may signal an alteration of their location within the larger society. The changes also indicate a shift in how physicians do their work. It is within this context that the articles for this chapter are located.

In the first article, Timothy J. Hoff addresses a number of changes occurring in the medical profession. He points out that the increasing number of women entering the profession is the most important demographic change to occur in the last two decades. Within the growth of women as physicians however, Hoff is really interested in the employment choices of women in medicine. In addition to an increase in the number of women in medicine, greater numbers of people from minority racial and ethnic groups as well as members of the lower and middle classes have also entered medicine in the recent past. Hoff points out that physicians who are female, minority, and from the lower or middle class are more likely to be practicing medicine as a salaried employee. He argues that factors such as managed care and corporate medicine, and the opportunities associated with potential self-employment, influence physicians' employment choices.

In the second article, Randolph K. Quaye examines how physician status is changing in Sweden. Given that Sweden has one of the healthiest populations in the world because of a carefully planned and publicly run health care system, the research examines the impact of a number of structural changes (the Stockholm model, the implementation of DRGs, the Family Doctor's Act) on physicians. Although the purpose of these changes was to reduce health care costs by increasing competition among providers, not all physicians agreed that this approach was effective. Most of the doctors interviewed expressed concern that these changes negatively impacted care for the elderly. Quaye also found that the majority of physicians interviewed did not believe that patients received less medical treatment than was necessary as a result of the structural changes, but 20 percent believed that economics was related to treatment. The majority of physicians also believed that the environment within which they worked had deteriorated as a result of these structural changes within the health care system. For example, a majority of those interviewed responded that the autonomy of the physician had diminished. Finally, Quaye notes that in Sweden, the role of family doctors as gate-keepers needs to be enhanced.

In the final article, Sydney D. White chronicles the experiences of health care practitioners in a Chinese village from the 1950s to the present. Throughout the period under study, White identifies the influence of the state in determining what type (Chinese or Western or both) of medicine would be provided at the village (or brigade) level. The consequences of this change at the village level are addressed. White also examines the financial arrangements imposed on the local health care centers and the consequences of these arrangements. For example, the brigade initially absorbed many of the costs associated with health care, but many of these costs were later passed on to individuals living within the brigade (village). As health care moved into the decollectivization period, co-operative clinics were closed and physicians went into private practice. Although efforts to "professionalize" physicians have occurred throughout the period, other factors (such as location of practice, fees, or connections to family) are more important to village residents. The result is that the next generation of physicians in the village will come from the children of current physicians.

The common theme of the articles in Chapter 8 is the changing status of the medical profession. The three articles illustrate the changing relationship between the state and physicians—in other words, how the actions of the state influence physician autonomy and even physician/patient relationships. It appears that the status of the physician is changing in vastly different ways in many countries of the world.

REFERENCE

Hafferty, F. W., and J. B. McKinlay. 1993. *The Changing Medical Profession: An International Perspective.* New York: Oxford University Press.

SAME PROFESSION, DIFFERENT PEOPLE: STRATIFICATION, STRUCTURE, AND PHYSICIANS' EMPLOYMENT CHOICES[1]

TIMOTHY J. HOFF[2]

INTRODUCTION

This study looks at a major trend occurring within the medical profession over the past 15 years: the movement of large numbers of physicians into salaried employment. Theoretical models of professions debate the outcome of the shift in work status from self-employed practice to employment within an organization (Freidson, 1985, 1986; Hall, 1968; McKinlay, 1982; McKinlay and Stoeckle, 1988).

The debate focuses primarily on how professional autonomy is affected by salaried employment. Less examined are how both stratifying forces within medicine and external changes occurring in health care simultaneously affect physicians' employment choices.

The primary perspective taken in this analysis is that professions such as medicine are increasingly composed of a number of demographic groups with different values, interests, and job opportunities. This diversity in turn influences the employment structure within these professions (Abbott, 1991; Brint, 1994; Heinz and Laumann, 1982). In this paper, a sample of young physicians was examined to identify and compare the relative effects of stratification (in this case demographic) and structure on the likelihood of physicians working in salaried as opposed to self-employment. A general aim of the study is to encourage researchers to consider more carefully how changes occurring within professions may be linked to large-scale structural developments such as the one focused upon here. The sociology of professions has traditionally focused more on the implications of these developments for professional status and autonomy instead of how they may disproportionately affect various intraprofessional segments. This focus threatens to reduce professions to monolithic entities and oversimplify our understanding of the total personal and situational context within which structural change affecting professionals occurs.

BACKGROUND AND HYPOTHESES

Professions such as medicine currently are subject to major internal and external changes. Externally, economic and organizational developments in health care have had a dramatic effect on physicians' work. This change manifests itself in two related trends: (a) the increasing use of new financing mechanisms to pay for health care services, and (b) the proliferation of large, vertically integrated organizations. Both trends are important components of the new "managed care" system. Physicians now get paid primarily on a prospective (i.e., before the service is delivered) rather than retrospective basis. This shifts their focus from the revenue to the expense side of the balance sheet. Prospective reimbursement has facilitated the growth of rationalized corporate structures such as health maintenance organizations (HMOs), which can achieve the economies of scale necessary to

stay profitable within a fixed budget. As a result, traditional opportunities and incentives for physicians to pursue self-employment are less commonly found, and the economic viability of the solo or small-group, self-employed practice has eroded over time. HMOs will provide care to approximately 25% of the U.S. population by the end of 1997, doubling their membership in less than 10 years. This growth is expected to continue at a double-digit rate for at least the next five years (Interstudy Publications, 1995).

The major sociological perspectives on professions focus upon whether or not these types of changes erode professional status and autonomy. Specifically, the trend toward salaried employment among physicians is cited as evidence for the waning of their collective dominance. The proletarianization perspective states that salaried employment in bureaucratic organizations is indicative of physician "deskilling" and increased nonphysician control over all aspects of medical "production," including professional work (McKinlay, 1982; McKinlay and Arches, 1985). Physicians lose control over their work as they are forced to sell their labor power to capitalist interests. The corporatization view assesses physicians' salaried status in a similar way, although concentrating more on how management (as owners' agent) sets up structures within the organization to control and regulate physicians and their work tasks (McKinlay and Stoeckle, 1988). However, Freidson (1985, 1986) challenges these assertions. He states that salaried status does not by itself mean that professionals as a group have less control over their work. Instead, it is physicians' relationship to the health care market, that is, how in demand and readily available their services are in the community, that determines their level of autonomy.

These perspectives share one important characteristic. Since they focus on structural relations between professions (as organized entities) and their environments, they understate the differentiated nature of professions such as medicine (Hafferty and

Wolinsky, 1991). An implicit assumption is made that where a number of diverse strata do exist within a profession, their differences (for example, in terms of values and beliefs) are secondary to a desire for autonomy and self-regulation over their work. Even when researchers do emphasize the medical profession's diversity, it is often cast in traditional ways based upon skill level or the type of work involved (for example, generalists vs. specialists) and for the purpose of determining which group has more or less control in a given work situation (see Prechel and Gupman, 1995; also Starr, 1982). This is no doubt partially due to the fact that much of the literature asserts that it is professionals' knowledge or skill level that is the key factor in determining the level of autonomy they are granted over their work by the state and general public (Abbott, 1988). Arguably, the focus on autonomy in professional studies encourages thinking about stratification within medicine in limited ways, primarily in terms of a knowledge-based or functional division of labor.

Emphasis on "traditional" professional values such as autonomy have also made self-employment the ideal-type employment status for professionals. The congruence between autonomy and self-employment may have fit better with the demographic makeup of the medical profession up to the 1970s when over 90% of physicians were white males, usually from upper class backgrounds (Starr, 1982). It made sense to consider medicine a homogeneous profession during this time, composed of individuals sharing similar views about their work. It was also logical to assume that salaried employment impinged negatively upon physicians' autonomy, given their presumed entrepreneurial values. Yet, these assumptions can no longer be taken for granted in an increasingly diversified profession without examination of the employment choices made by new groups becoming doctors and how they compare to more traditional groups' choices.

The past two decades have witnessed important new forms of stratification within medicine

due to the rising number of females, minority groups, and lower and middle class individuals entering medical school. Currently, there are few data addressing the interplay of stratification *and* structural forces in relation to the salaried employment trend. Questions such as the following are relatively unexplored: (a) which groups of physicians are more likely to find themselves in salaried jobs, (b) what are some of the reasons these groups find themselves there, and (c) how are physicians' employment choices constrained or enhanced as a result of recent structural developments (like the advent of health maintenance organizations) in the health care industry? These are questions that receive greater attention in the study of other fields of work and industries and even in other professions (cf. Heinz and Laumann, 1982, for a detailed study on stratification in the legal profession). However, in medicine we must no longer assume "that a name represents a coherent group of people" (Abbott, 1991: 42). Therefore, it is important to begin to explore these questions in greater detail as they pertain to physicians.

New Demographic Groups Becoming Physicians

The most important demographic change occurring within medicine over the past two decades has been the increasing number of women becoming physicians. Since 1970, the number of male physicians has grown 79%, while the number of female physicians has increased 425% (American Medical Association, 1995). Over 20% of current doctors are women, compared to 10% in 1985. This percentage will grow much higher, since over 45% of current medical school students are women, up from 13% in 1970 (Nickens *et al.,* 1994). This dramatic increase is the result of two factors: (a) a parallel increase in the percentage of women in the general labor force, and (b) greater opportunity for women to enroll in medical school due to a breakdown in the traditional stereotype that professional work is "men's work." These factors stem from larger social trends occurring during the 1960s and 1970s, particularly the civil rights and later women's movement (Kosa, 1971; Starr, 1982).

Women are often assumed a priori to be less able to pursue self-employment in a field of work for one or two reasons: (a) preemployment socialization influences that stress family and marital over work roles (Becker, 1985; Pleck, 1977), or (b) job and workplace barriers that make it more difficult for women to pursue anything but salaried employment (Kanter, 1977). Yet there has been little research looking directly at female physicians' employment choices. Most research has instead examined personal characteristics related to the number of hours worked and work-related values as compared to male physicians. For instance, women doctors have been found to prefer working fewer hours than male physicians and are more likely to work part-time (Shye, 1991; Uhlenberg and Cooney, 1990). They tend to emphasize marital and family roles over professional roles, while men do the opposite (Ducker, 1980; Ehrensing, 1986; Hertz, 1986).

In addition, women doctors have been found to experience stress related to things such as the number of hours worked and the lack of free time, whereas men worry most about maintaining a certain income level (Richardson and Burke, 1991; Weisman and Teitlebaum, 1987). Male and female physicians' views on medical work also have been found to differ substantially. Men have been shown to be more instrumental in their values: focusing on income, owning their own practice, and specific career goals. This same research shows that women physicians emphasize these things much less, believing that they can be successful doctors without owning a practice or being completely dedicated to all aspects of the medical profession (Betz and O'Connell, 1988; Clavan and Robak, 1980; Lemkau *et al.,* 1987).

While some might claim that these data offer partial support for the preemployment socialization perspective, others dispute the tenuous connections made between such findings and women's choice of salaried employment. Instead, they assert that women physicians face the same structural barriers in the workplace as other female workers (see Acker and Van Houten, 1974; also, Kanter, 1977). These barriers limit their employment opportunities (Lorber, 1991). For example, in medicine successful self-employment relies upon a steady stream of patient referrals, access to appropriate office space, back-up coverage for patients from other physicians, and hospital privileges (Freidson, 1970). These are things that are largely contingent upon informal associations built up over time with other colleagues. Lorber (1984), in her detailed study of women physicians, found that compared to young male doctors, young female doctors faced greater obstacles in developing these associations and in becoming accepted in physician communities dominated by "old boy networks." As a result, they did not have the same opportunities as men to obtain the necessary ingredients for a financially stable, self-employed practice. Thus, they were more likely to end up working as salaried employees.

There is evidence that the large majority of female physicians work as salaried employees (American Medical Association, 1995). However, what is less well known is how much more likely they are than men to choose salaried employment and how this hypothesized difference compares to differences that may exist between other newly important physician strata. These questions are useful to address before moving to explanations of why female physicians might end up in salaried rather than self-employment. Hypothesis 1 tests for the presence of a gender difference in employment status, while each interaction hypothesis attempts to get at an aspect of the gender socialization and job model explanation of why any such difference may exist.

Hypothesis 1. Female physicians will be more likely than male physicians to work as salaried employees, even after controlling for other structural and stratification variables.

Hypothesis 1a. This gender difference is moderated by marital status, that is, married female physicians are more likely to work as salaried employees than unmarried female physicians, compared to men of the same marital status.

Hypothesis 1b. This gender difference becomes significantly smaller for male and female physicians who did not live in their current practice environment during residency or medical school, compared to male and female physicians who did previously live in their current practice environment.[3]

New racial and ethnic groups are also entering medicine in greater numbers. The percentage of medical degrees awarded annually to members of minority groups such as Blacks and Hispanics has increased from 3% in 1965 to 30% today (Nickens *et al.*, 1994). Their professional values and employment opportunities may be different from those associated with white physicians and also with female physicians. There are few data on this, although earlier studies of black physicians showed that they entered medicine at least partially to provide a service to members of their communities (see Curtis, 1971). In addition, recent empirical evidence shows that minority physicians are over four times more likely than non-Hispanic white physicians to care for minority patients (Moy and Bartman, 1995).

How do these new physician groups relate to the overall trend toward salaried employment among physicians? One possibility is that nonwhite physicians face greater barriers to self-employment than white physicians and therefore are more likely to be salaried employees. These barriers are the same as for would-be minority entrepreneurs in other fields of work and include: (a) obtaining the necessary capital and financing to open a self-

employed practice, (b) developing a reliable customer base to support the practice, (c) lacking community support, and (d) insufficient available management training (Boyd, 1990; Fratoe, 1984).

An alternative possibility is that if many minority physicians end up practicing in minority communities, they may have greater opportunities and incentives for self-employment in these areas. From an ecological perspective, these opportunities and incentives might arise from the fact that large-scale, organized medicine is more likely to develop in areas where there are already high levels of competition for patients, greater numbers of insured individuals, high per capita incomes, a number of large businesses, and the presence of established health care corporate interests (see Wholey *et al.*, 1993; also Christianson *et al.*, 1991; Morrisey and Ashby, 1982). For minority communities that do not meet these criteria, an "enclave-like" environment could exist for minority physicians, offering increased financial opportunity and fewer barriers to entry for them to pursue self-employment (Boyd, 1990; Carroll, 1993). Thus, the ecological perspective suggests that there might be little or no racial or ethnic difference related to employment status, while a labor market segmentation perspective suggests that minority physicians will be disproportionately represented in salaried employment.

Hypothesis 2. Black and Hispanic physicians are more likely than white physicians to work as salaried employees, even after controlling for other structural and stratification variables.

More physicians from the lower and middle classes are also becoming physicians, due mainly to a number of federally sponsored programs enacted in the 1970s and 1980s that provide financial support for individuals from lower socioeconomic backgrounds to attend medical school. This was in response to a dramatic increase in the demand for health services resulting from new programs such

as Medicaid and Medicare (Mechanic, 1986; Starr, 1982). This increase in demand threatened to create a shortage of physicians, so medical schools began to recruit more widely than ever before. Similar to minority physicians, physicians from lower socioeconomic backgrounds also may not possess the same values or professional expectations as those from upper class backgrounds who become physicians. The desire for a steady job, a decent paycheck, and a 9-to-5 lifestyle can be more important than being a business owner or entrepreneur (Hoff and McCaffrey, 1996). As a result, these individuals may tend to view salaried employment as an acceptable and even desirable career choice. This is an important point, because it posits a value shift (in the form of new professional values) underlying increased salaried employment, rather than salaried employment impinging negatively upon physicians' value systems.

However, while socioeconomic background may be an important factor influencing the employment choices of physicians, medicine's internal division of labor with respect to function is a structural feature that should play a moderating role on this overall effect. That is, the type of work physicians perform plays an influential role in determining their employment setting, regardless of certain demographic characteristics such as class background. Abbott's (1988) model of jurisdictional competition between intraprofessional groups provides a theoretical rationale for the link between specialty and employment status. Historically, within medicine certain specialties such as radiology, anesthesiology, and pathology became organization bound as hospitals provided the expensive technology and insulation from the economic environment needed to help them establish their own work jurisdictions and compete effectively with other medical specialties.

These other specialties relying less on technology and more on claims of expert knowledge in securing control over their work jurisdictions used public prestige and an existing clientele for their services to gain market power without becoming economically dependent upon hospitals (Starr, 1982). As a result, they enjoyed greater self-employment opportunities. Yet, as these specialties grew more reliant upon services that only the hospital could provide (such as x-ray imaging, laboratory tests, anesthesia for operations, etc.), the groups providing those services were able to achieve legitimacy within the medical profession. Even today, it can be argued the type of work physicians perform continues to shape their employment choices in this manner.

> *Hypothesis 3.* Physicians from upper class backgrounds will be less likely than physicians from lower and middle class backgrounds to work as salaried employees, even after controlling for other structural and stratification variables.
> *Hypothesis 3a.* The effect of socioeconomic background on employment status is moderated by medical specialty, generally becoming less meaningful for physicians whose work has traditionally been conducted within organizationally based settings.

The rising cost of medical education has increased the level of financial debt young physicians incur, regardless of class. Over 80% of a sample of medical students in 1987 reported owing money for their medical training. The average debt in this same study was $35,621, up from $26,496 only three years earlier (Clare *et al.,* 1987). Among 1994 medical school graduates, this figure was $63,855 (Johnsson, 1996). Long residency programs of three years or more for most specialties force young physicians to incur additional financial obligations. This makes self-employment in physicians' early careers problematic, as the eagerness and ability to take on additional financial risk in becoming self-employed are severely limited. Self-employment right out of residency becomes possible only for a chosen few, that is, those lucky enough to have little or no debt.

Hypothesis 4. Higher levels of financial debt increase the likelihood of salaried employment for physicians, even after controlling for socioeconomic background.

Structural Factors Influencing Physicians' Employment Choices

The influence of medicine's internal diversity on physicians' employment choices has already been discussed for hospital- vs. office-based specialties. However, the organizational and financing changes discussed at the outset of the paper are creating a second major intraprofessional struggle between different specialties. This is seen in the shift in emphasis from specialty to primary care services. Specialists have always enjoyed higher prestige among the public, due to the perception that they possess the most sophisticated medical knowledge (Freidson, 1970). They earn higher incomes relative to primary care physicians, with specialists making more than double the median income for primary care doctors. Their level of autonomy also has traditionally exceeded that of generalist physicians. This greater autonomy is a direct result of the perceived complexity of their knowledge and the uncertainty associated with the diagnostic and treatment processes that comprise their work (Abbott, 1988).

However, the rise of managed care and corporate medicine places disproportionate emphasis on primary care physicians at the expense of specialists, threatening to narrow the differentials noted above. In achieving the economies of scale needed to remain profitable and to compete with other providers, managed care organizations rely heavily on primary care physicians as "gatekeepers" to coordinate patient care and control referrals of patients to more expensive specialists. For example, HMOs employ many more primary care physicians than specialists, as shown by several studies done of staffing and health services' utilization in HMOs (see Gamliel *et al.,* 1995; Weiner, 1994). As a result of their gatekeeper role, primary care physicians may find increased autonomy in these work

settings relative to specialists (Schulz *et al.,* 1990). In addition, the increased demand for generalists in the marketplace is resulting in a slow but steady narrowing of income differentials between the two groups (Mitka, 1996; Page, 1995). The trade-off, however, is that primary care physicians increasingly have to perform their work as salaried employees rather than self-employed practitioners.

There is another important advantage of salaried employment for primary care physicians. In a prospective reimbursement system, self-employment for primary care physicians means assuming direct financial risk for being inefficient in controlling patients' utilization of services and their own referrals to specialists. As salaried employees, however, they can transfer this risk to the organization while receiving a stable wage reflective of their increased value as gatekeepers. Specialists are likely to find these work settings less desirable precisely because of the lower income and utilization associated with their services (Baker and Cantor, 1993). This notion, combined with the prestige still accorded by the *general population* to specialty medicine, means that specialists will be more likely to gravitate towards self-employed practice by themselves or, increasingly, with other specialists in large multispecialty practices.

Hypothesis 5. Primary care physicians (family practitioners, internists, and pediatricians) will be more likely than specialist physicians to work as salaried employees, even after controlling for other structural and stratification variables.

As stated earlier, physicians' ability to enter into self-employed practice early in their medical careers is enhanced by associations built up with other colleagues in their practice area over a period of several years (Lorber, 1984; Starr, 1982). The ingredients necessary for a successful self-employed practice depend upon this informal network of relationships between physicians and other physicians. For young physicians, the crucial time

to build these relationships is during medical school and residency. Therefore, it is plausible to suggest that young physicians who live in their current practice environment during this time period would have a greater opportunity to become self-employed than physicians who do not end up practicing in their medical school or residency location. Greater opportunity does not automatically translate into increased self-employment. However, it should have a meaningful effect on young physicians' employment choices.

> *Hypothesis 6.* Physicians who did not live in their current practice environment during medical school and residency will be more likely than physicians who did previously live in their current practice environment to work as salaried employees, even after controlling for other structural and stratification variables.

ANALYSIS

The sample for the logistic regression analysis consisted of 5215 young physicians responding to a 1987 survey asking them about their current job and practice patterns. This survey was sponsored by the American Medical Association Education and Research Foundation. Young was defined as less than 40 years of age and being out of residency for at least one year but less than six complete years. The survey asked questions relating to the respondent's work setting, current practice arrangements, career choice, family background, patient care activities, and current income and expenses. Personal and demographic characteristics such as marital status, race, number and ages of children, educational debt, parents' education and income, and work location also were gathered for each doctor.

Dependent Variable

The dependent variable reflected whether the physician was in salaried (1 = salaried) or self (0 = self)

employment at the time of the survey. If physicians were not solo or part owners of their practices, they were instructed to respond as salaried employees. A total of 2647 physicians responded as self-employed, while 2546 responded as salaried employees (22 respondents did not provide an answer).

Predictor Variables

Structural, stratification, family status, and several control variables were included in a logistic regression analysis testing hypotheses one through six. The interaction terms were entered last in the overall model.

Structural Variables. *Type of work* (whether physicians performed primary care, specialty, or other type of work) was represented by two dummy-coded variables, with specialist being the omitted category of reference (specialist = 0). Primary care physicians included family or general practitioners, internists, and pediatricians. Other type of work included those specialties such as radiology and anesthesiology that traditionally are found within organizational settings such as hospitals. *Whether or not physicians had lived in their current work location while in medical school or residency* was included as a dummy-coded variable, with physicians who had previously lived in their current location the omitted category of reference.

Stratification Variables. The demographic variables of interest for analyzing the effects of internal stratification on employment status were physicians' gender, race, socioeconomic background, and current level of educational debt. Gender and race were represented by single-coded dummy variable. *Gender* was measured by the number of physicians answering either male (= 0) or female (= 1), while *race* was originally divided on the survey into five distinct categories of black-Hispanic, black-non-Hispanic, other, white-Hispanic, and white, non-Hispanic. However, because of the limited

number of cases for several of the categories, these five categories were collapsed into only two: white, non-Hispanic (= 0) and nonwhite (= 1). Age was not included in the analysis because the frequency distribution in the sample was not large enough to create theoretically meaningful comparisons among different age groups. All physicians in the sample were considered in their early career stages as opposed to middle career or late career (groups that would make excellent comparisons). Thus, the sample consists of one distinct age cohort of physicians. *Current level of educational debt* was recorded in absolute dollar terms (in 000s), while *socioeconomic background* was measured through a 5-point ordinal scale indicating physicians' opinion of their parents' class background while growing up, with 1 indicating lower class and 5 upper class.

Family Status Variables.   Variables measuring the family status of the physician included *marital status* and *number of children*. Marital status was represented by a single dummy-coded variable (0 = not currently married, 1 = currently married) since over 95% of the cases fell into either the currently married or never married category. Those who were widowed, divorced, or separated (combined n = 273/5215 or 5%) were included in the currently not married category. The number of children was coded as the actual number of children ranging from 0 to highest number.

Control Variables.   Several control variables were included in the logistic regression model to partial out potentially significant geographic location effects on physicians' employment status. The *geographic region of the country the physician worked in* was included as a series of three dummy-coded variables, with the western region of the U.S. the omitted category of reference. *Urban* or *rural location* was also used as a control variable. Physicians in rural areas are more likely to own practices, while urban areas in general

should have a higher concentration of physician–employees because of the greater overall number of physicians and the presence of institutional health providers. This factor was represented by a single dummy-coded variable (0 = non-MSA, 1 = MSA) indicating if the physician worked in a Metropolitan Statistical Area (MSA; i.e., urban location) or not.

Method of Analysis

The primary statistical technique used in testing the hypotheses is logistic regression using the SPSS–Windows program. This technique is recommended when the dependent variable is categorical. The dependent variable for this study was dichotomous. Its predicted value was expressed as a logarithmic odds ratio (i.e., predicted logit), in this case the log odds of a physician working as a salaried employee. The coefficient of the predictor variable(s) is not a beta, but represents the effect (+ or –) in additive terms of a one-unit increase in that variable on the log odds of the dependent variable. This effect can also be expressed in a multiplicative form, by taking the antilog transformation of the logit coefficient, and in terms of the increase or decrease in the probability of working as a salaried employee, compared with some reference probability. All three interpretations are used in this analysis.

RESULTS

Descriptive statistics and results are displayed in Tables 1 and 2. The control variables were entered first into the equation, followed by the sets of predictor variables, and finally individual interaction terms. Two models are presented in Table 2; Model 1 presents main effects only for all the variables, and does not include any interaction terms. Model 2 includes all predictor variables contained in Model 1, in addition to a set of interaction terms. With the exception of the main effect logit coefficients in Model 2 for variables included in the interaction

TABLE 1   Means and Standard Deviations of Predictor Variables

PREDICTED VARIABLES (ALL RANGES 0–1 UNLESS OTHERWISE NOTED)	TOTAL SAMPLE	SALARIED PHYSICIANS
Controls		
Geographic region (0 = West)		
Northeast	.22	.23
	(.41)	(.42)
Midwest	.21	.21
	(.41)	(.41)
South	.36	.36
	(.48)	(.48)
Urban or rural location (0 = rural)	.84	.88
	(.36)	(.32)
Lived in current work location previously (0 = yes)	.58	.58
	(.49)	(.49)
Demographic factors		
Gender (0 = male)	.22	.28
	(.42)	(.45)
Race/ethnicity (0 = white, non-Hispanic) Nonwhite	.33	.33
Type of work (0 = specialist)	(.47)	(.47)
Primary care physician[a]	.52	.53
	(.50)	(.50)
Other[b]	.21	.24
	(.40)	(.43)
Economic factors		
Socioeconomic background (range: 1–5)	2.97	2.92
	(1.13)	(1.11)
Level of educational debt at present (in 000s: 0–325)	14.51	14.55
	(19.75)	(16.47)
Family status factors		
Marital status (0 = not currently married)	.81	.77
	(.39)	(.42)
Number of children (range: 0–14)	1.96	1.88
	(.98)	(.91)
Number of cases	5215	2546

[a]Primary care physician includes internists, family practitioners, and pediatricians.
[b]Other includes radiologists, psychiatrists, anesthesiologists, pathologists, and emergency medicine physicians.

terms, the results are almost identical across models. Due to uncertainty surrounding the interpretation of main effects for variables that are part of interaction terms in the same equation, Model 1 (the main effects only model) is used to discuss the results in relationship to the stated hypothesis.[4] The main effects only model had a –2 log likelihood value of 6835.74 with 14 degrees of freedom

TABLE 2 Logistic Regression Coefficients—Analysis of Current Employment Status

PREDICTOR VARIABLES	MODEL 1 COEFFICIENT	MODEL 2 COEFFICIENT	ODDS[c] MULTIPLIERS
Controls			
Geographic region (0 = West)			
Northeast	.237[a]	.237[a]	1.27
Midwest	.176	.175	
South	.132	.137	
Urban or rural location (0 = rural)	.624[b]	.629[b]	1.87
Structural factors			
Lived in current work location previously (0 = yes)	.157[a]	.160[a]	1.17
Type of work (0 = specialist)			
Primary care physician	.429[b]	.332	1.54
Other	.660[b]	.140	1.94
Stratification factors			
Gender (0 = male)	.597[b]	.596[b]	1.82
Race/ethnicity (0 = white, non-Hispanic)			
Nonwhite	−.038	−.047	
Socioeconomic background (range: 1–5)	−.072[a]	−.128[a]	.93
Level of educational debt at present (in 000s: 0–325)	−.003	−.003	
Family status factors			
Marital status (0 = not currently married)	−.152	−.160	
Number of children (range: 0–14)	−.038[b]	−.037[b]	.96
Interaction terms			
Socioeconomic Background × Type of Work			
Socioeconomic Background × Primary Care			.032
Socioeconomic Background × Other			.174[a]
Intercept	−.979[b]	−.807[b]	
−2 Log Likelihood X^2	6835.74[b]	6827.98[b,d]	
Unlogged mean of dependent variable	.493 (number of cases = 5167)		

[a]$p < .01$.

[b]$p < .001$.

[c]Antilog transformations of Model 1 logit coefficients.

[d]X^2 test for overall significance of two interaction terms: 7.76 with $2df$ ($p < .05$).

($p < .001$). This represented an χ^2 (chi-square) difference of 325 with 13 degrees of freedom ($p < .001$) compared to the baseline model containing only the intercept term. Several individual predictor variables found not significant were included in this model, due to meaningfulness of the nonsignificant finding(s).

Two of the control variables had significant effects on employment status, indicating that geographic location does influence physicians' em-

ployment status. First, young physicians practicing in the northeast region of the United States were more likely to be working as salaried employees than physicians in the west ($p < .01$). This is slightly surprising, given the longer history of managed care and organized medicine in the western part of the country (see Christianson *et al.,* 1991). In addition, the effect of urban or rural location ($p < .001$) was controlled for, so the reason for this positive coefficient was not due to the presence of larger urban areas within the northeast.

As the size of the urban or rural location coefficient indicates, urban physicians were much more likely to work as salaried employees than rural physicians, holding constant demographic and other structural variables. This effect meant that urban physicians had a predicted probability of working as salaried employees that was 15.2% greater than the probability for rural physicians. This finding is not unexpected, since most rural settings do not have the large, concentrated patient base necessary for justifying the existence of large-scale forms of health care organization. These organizations employ large numbers of physicians on a salaried basis. In addition, many teaching hospitals and academic medical centers (where both residents and faculty are usually paid on a salaried basis) are located in urban areas.

Several of the predictor variables were also significant. Hypothesis 1 suggested that female physicians were more likely than male physicians to be working as salaried employees, even after controlling for other stratification and structural variables. This hypothesis was supported in that female physicians in the sample had an odds of working as salaried employees 1.82 times greater (e^{597}) than the odds for male physicians ($p < .001$). This meant that being female increased a physician's probability of working as a salaried employee from 49.3% (the observed sample probability used in this example for male physicians) to 63.9%, an increase of 14.6%. The explanation for this relatively large (in comparison to other effects

in the model) gender difference is open to speculation, and it is an important topic for future empirical research. The difference could be partially explained by the gender socialization literature (i.e., that female physicians emphasize different preferences than male physicians, and that these preferences fit better with salaried employment (Clavan and Robak, 1980; Uhlenberg and Cooney, 1990). Or, the difference may also be related to a larger number of structural barriers (of the type discussed) faced by female physicians who wish to open their own practice.

Hypothesis 1a attempted to get at the idea of gender socialization playing a part in female physicians' preference for salaried employment. Yet, a test for interaction between gender and marital status was not significant (and not included in the model), indicating that at least in this study, the spousal role did not influence to any great degree the original gender difference in the model. This difference (.597) was consistent for both married and unmarried physicians. The argument could be made that this finding does not disprove the effects of preemployment socialization based on gender, since single female physicians might choose salaried employment to the same extent as married female physicians because of the *expectation* they will eventually take on marital and family responsibilities.

Hypothesis 1b attempted to get at the notion that female physicians may face greater barriers than male physicians in developing relationships with other doctors in the community that are important for successful self-employment. It was hypothesized that the gender difference related to employment status would be smaller for male and female physicians who had not lived in their current practice setting during medical school or residency, compared to physicians who had lived there. The idea is that women who had previously lived in their work setting would have a more difficult time than similar male physicians in building the informal network and associations needed to

stay self-employed (whether because of the exist-ence of "old boy networks" or other forms of dis-crimination). This would be reflected in the larger gender difference for this group relative to women and men who had not previously lived in their work setting. However, a test for interaction between gender and previous residence in the current work setting was not statistically significant at the .05 level, although the interaction coefficient was bor-derline ($p < .06$) and negative (indicating a de-crease in the gender difference for physicians who had not previously lived in their practice setting vs. those who had prior residency). Nonetheless, while a clear difference with respect to employment choice was demonstrated between male and female physicians, no statistical support was provided for either the gender socialization or workplace barrier perspectives.

Hypothesis 2, stating that minority physicians such as blacks and Hispanics would be more likely than white, non-Hispanic physicians to work as sal-aried employees was not supported by the data. White physicians were just as likely as black or His-panic physicians to work in salaried employment. This nonsignificant finding is meaningful because it suggests that greater examination of minority phy-sicians' employment opportunities is warranted. It could be that much of the racial difference we might expect to be related to employment status was cap-tured in the effects of several other variables also in-cluded in the analysis. However, excluding several of these variables (such as gender, socioeconomic background, and urban or rural location) from the analysis did not make the mean difference between white and nonwhite physicians significant. One ex-planation mentioned earlier and worth exploring in future studies is that if it is true that black and His-panic physicians practice in communities where they can treat similar patient populations, then it may be easier for them to become self-employed in these areas given potentially stronger demand for services, less organized interests, and fewer barriers to entry. This finding is in need of greater study be-cause it suggests that race or ethnicity *by itself* plays no significant role in influencing chosen employ-ment status among young physicians.

Socioeconomic background was supported as having an influence upon the type of employment status chosen by a physician. Those doctors coming from upper class backgrounds were less likely to be found working as salaried employees compared to those from lower and middle-class backgrounds ($p < .01$). The variable's negative effect ($-.072$) on the log odds of working as a salaried employee trans-lated into a decreased probability of approximately 2% for upper-class individuals vs. those from lower classes. Although a small difference, this finding supports Hypothesis 3. However, what is interesting about this finding is that the difference in predicted probabilities is so small. One would think that phy-sicians coming from a higher socioeconomic back-ground would be much more likely than physicians from lower- and middle-class backgrounds to be in self-employed practice due to differences in both professional values and financial ability. Maybe these differences are not as great or influential as is anecdotally thought.

This notion is further supported by the accep-tance of Hypothesis 3a, which proposed a moderat-ing role played by specialty on the relationship between socioeconomic background and employ-ment status. A test for interaction between socio-economic background and type of work was conducted and the logit coefficients included in the second equation. As Model 2 in Table 2 shows, in one instance a significant positive interaction effect was found. The category of "other" physicians in-cludes those specialties whose work has tradition-ally been performed in hospital-based settings such as radiology, pathology, emergency medicine, and anesthesiology. The positive coefficient for the sec-ond interaction term ($p < .01$) indicated that the effect of socioeconomic background on the likeli-hood of salaried employment (the logit coefficient in Model 1) was removed for these other physicians vs. specialists and primary care doctors. Thus, the

kind of work physicians perform influences their employment choices in a meaningful way. The significant mean difference between other physicians vs. specialists (as evidenced by the logit coefficient in Model 1) also supports this thesis. Specialists such as cardiologists, obstetricians, and neurologists, whose professional power historically has been cultivated more through knowledge exploitation and less through organizational means, still appears to have a greater likelihood of achieving self-employment status within the profession.

Hypothesis 4, stating that the higher the level of educational debt for a physician, the higher probability of salaried employment, was not supported by the data. Given all the anecdotal evidence citing the importance of educational debt in influencing physicians' employment choices, this finding is also in need of additional research, to see if debt is an important factor in choosing among employment alternatives, especially when other variables are taken into account.

Hypothesis 5 stated that primary care physicians would be more likely than specialists to work as salaried employees. As Model 1 shows, the dummy-coded variable representing the primary care/specialist mean difference was significant ($p < .001$). Primary care physicians had an odds of working as salaried employees that was 1.54 times the odds of specialists, translating into a predicted probability of salaried employment for primary care doctors approximately 11% greater that the probability for specialists (60% vs. 49%). One possible explanation already discussed for this higher probability is the increased use of primary care physicians by managed care organizations such as HMOs. HMOs are becoming the dominant organizational form in health care. It is within this type of work setting where primary care physicians may be able to achieve greater autonomy relative to specialists. Investigating the specific reasons why primary care doctors might choose salaried work settings to a greater extent than specialists (besides the demand argument) will aid our understanding

of how major changes in health care organizations (e.g., the current proliferation of HMOs) affect intraprofessional relations.

Hypothesis 6 was also supported in that physicians who had not lived in their current practice setting during medical school or residency were significantly more likely to be working as salaried employees ($p < .01$). This effect remained even after controlling for gender, race, and socioeconomic background. Those without prior residence were approximately 4% more likely than those with prior residence to be in salaried employment, using the observed sample probability for salaried physicians of 49% as the reference group probability. This finding supports the idea that there is something about having previously lived in one's practice environment that increases the chances for self-employment. This something may indeed be the greater opportunities available to build business, social, and patient relationships. As discussed earlier, these informal networks are important in helping to acquire the patient base, back-up support, hospital relationships, and office space necessary for physicians to sustain themselves economically as self-employed practitioners.

STUDY LIMITATIONS AND CONCLUSION

Several limitations of this study must be pointed out. First, the analytical approach taken was one in which a series of stratification, structural, and control variables were explored statistically for their effects on the dependent variable, employment status. The hypotheses tested covered a wide range of current developments occurring within and external to the medical profession. Each of the meaningful effects found in this analysis should be considered only in the context of what it might imply given replication. These effects should be investigated in detail through hypotheses and analytic models that offer adequate opportunity to test alternative explanations. Differences in employment status between men and women and the lack of significant difference

between white and non-white physicians are two important areas for future research.

Second, the predictors examined do not comprise a set of all possible influences on the salaried employment trend within medicine. For instance, only "young" physicians were focused upon in this analysis. The effects of age and tenure as moderating variables should be investigated to determine whether relationships between the predictors examined and employment choice vary over time or length of physicians' work careers. One would suspect that certain effects in the model would change over time, such as the influence of having lived in one's practice environment during medical school or residency. For instance, older physicians practicing in the same area for several years may be able to build the informal ties necessary to become self-employed, even if they did not live there during their training years. Also, additional organizational and ecological variables need inclusion in future research to better compare the effects of structural and internal stratifying forces on employment choice. For example, factors such as (a) the mix of health providers (i.e., physicians and organizations) and medical specialties in a geographic area; (b) types of patient populations; and (c) the historical relationships among physicians, insurers, hospitals, and others within specific localities should all be brought into analyses of employment shifts. This study addressed only a small but currently important group of structural variables. Finally, this survey was conducted in 1987; future studies should attempt to replicate one or more of these findings.

The main point of this study is that there needs to be greater appreciation for the roles played by factors *internal* to professions in relation to large-scale developments such as shifting employment trends. The sociology of professions has traditionally been focused at the organizational and ecological levels. This is mainly the result of its emphasis on issues of professional dominance and autonomy. How a profession acquires, maintains, and potentially loses control over its work is arguably tied to questions about how it resists or succumbs to challenges from other stakeholders (such as the state, other professions, the public) in its environment. Thus, attention to intraprofessional processes becomes less important, since it is the profession as actor that is central to the analysis (Freidson, 1985). Separate from this power perspective, the ecological approach to studying professions such as medicine has continued to intensify with interest in how existing economic and organizational changes occurring in health care lead to processes of variation, selection, and retention among health care organizations (see Wholey *et al.,* 1993; also Christianson *et al.,* 1991).

However, the results presented show the relevance of integrating stratification perspectives into this emerging research. Organizational forms in health care may follow an environmentally determined pattern, yet which group of individuals end up working within these structures and why are questions that have been downplayed to a large extent in the professional literature. Although exploratory in nature, the findings indicate that in addition to the effects of structure (i.e., specialty, geographic location, and informal social networks), recent stratifying forces within medicine also play a significant role in influencing the current trend toward salaried employment. For example, women physicians appear to be disproportionately represented in salaried employment compared to other groups. This implies that they may face similar issues in making their employment choices as do women in other forms of work. Although those issues could not be substantiated in this analysis, an interesting question to address is how more educated and "professionalized" women compare to unskilled and semiskilled female workers in their attempts to break out of traditional employment patterns.

In addition, the nonsignificant finding with respect to race suggests that there could be something unique about professional work or the systemwide changes occurring in medicine that affords black and Hispanic physicians equal or greater opportunity for self-employment relative to white physicians. Investigating this in detail could inform and

build upon research on minority entrepreneurs in other types of work. In general, comparative studies of professionals vs. other types of workers of the same demographic background would be useful in helping to understand how being in a "professional" occupation may or may not provide different groups with the ability to break free from traditional work stereotypes. That the significant effects in the model are distributed fairly evenly across stratification and structural variables implies that to focus only on one or the other in explaining professional change results in a less than complete understanding of modern professions.

The study of professions in the 1990s and beyond must deal with issues of gender, social class, race and ethnicity, and family life because to ignore them risks missing the opportunity to understand what it means to be a professional for various groups in our society. We know little about those individuals becoming professionals at the present time. Not all those who become physicians do so for the same reasons, and not all necessarily want the same things or have the same values, beliefs, expectations, or job opportunities. It seems obvious to make this point, until one realizes that much of the sociological literature has worked from the assumption of a single ideal type for the expert; the white, entrepreneurial, upwardly mobile male. Given increasing diversity within all professions, we can no longer build upon that foundation. We may discover that traditional values such as autonomy no longer mean the same thing or have the same importance across new professional strata (Stoeckle, 1988). We may also end up with new definitions of professionalism matching the desires and expectations of these strata. From a macro perspective, the implications of this internal diversity relate to important questions of intraprofessional cohesion and solidarity that have been posed (Abbott, 1991; Freidson, 1985). Arguably, what is currently happening *within* professions is equally as profound and important as what is going on outside of them. It is time to explore this assertion in detail, especially in rapidly changing professions such as medicine.

NOTES

1. I would like to thank Richard Alba, Sue Faerman, Richard Hall, David McCaffrey, and several anonymous reviewers for their helpful and thought-provoking suggestions. An earlier draft of this paper was presented at the Association on Employment Practices and Principles annual meeting, New Orleans, October 1995.
2. Department of Health Policy, Management, and Behavior, University at Albany, SUNY, Albany, New York 12220.
3. The logic underlying this hypothesis is that of those physicians who previously lived in their current practice environment, men would have had a greater opportunity in cultivating the informal colleague networks important to successful self-employment. Thus, prior residence would add to the original gender difference.

4. For a concise discussion of the different points of view, see Jaccard *et al.* (1990, pp. 14–15, 26–27, 34–35). In general, their position (and the one assumed in this study) is that in models including product (interaction) terms, the main effect coefficients for the variables included in those terms represent *conditional* rather than *general* relationships, that is, the specific case where all the X variables in the interaction but one equal zero. If however, these other X variables have metrics in which a zero value is not meaningful, then interpretation of the main effect coefficients is problematic since the effect described would be for a case where one or more X variables has a meaningless value.

REFERENCES

Abbott, Andrew
1988   *The System of Professions: An Essay on the Expert Division of Labor.* Chicago: University of Chicago Press.
1991   "The future of professions: Occupation and expertise in the age of organization." In Samuel Bacharach (ed.), *Research in the Sociology of Organizations: Vol. 8. Professions and Organizations:* 1–13. Greenwich, CT: JAI Press.
Acker, J. and D. R. Van Houten
1974   "Differential recruitment and control: The sex-structuring of organization." *Administrative Science Quarterly* 19:152–163.

American Medical Association
1995   *Physician Characteristics and Distribution in the U.S.* Chicago: American Medical Association.

Baker, Lawrence and Joel Cantor
1993   "Physician satisfaction under managed care." *Health Affairs* (Supplement 1993): 258–270.

Becker, G. S.
1985   "Human capital, effort, and the sexual division of labor." *Journal of Labor Economics* 3:533–558.

Betz, M. and L. O'Connell
1988   "Work orientations of males and females: Exploring the gender socialization approach." *Sociological Inquiry* 59:318–330.

Boyd, Robert L.
1990   "Black and Asian self-employment in large metropolitan areas: A comparative analysis." *Social Problems* 37:258–274.

Brint, Stephen
1994   *In an Age of Experts: The Changing Role of Professionals in Politics and Public Life.* Princeton, NJ: Princeton University Press.

Carroll, Glenn R.
1993   "A sociological view of why firms differ." *Strategic Management Journal* 14:237–249.

Christianson, J. B., Susan M. Sanchez, Douglas R. Wholey, and Maureen Shadel
1991   "The HMO industry: Evolution in population demographics and market structure." *Medical Care Review* 48:3–46.

Clare, F. L., E. Spratley, P. Schwab, and J. K. Inglehart
1987   "Trends in health personnel." *Health Affairs* 6:90–103.

Clavan, Sylvia and Nicholas Robak
1980   "Choosing to become a doctor: Contemporary men and women medical students." *Social Science Forum* 3:1–14.

Curtis, James L.
1971   *Blacks, Medical Schools, and Society.* Ann Arbor: University of Michigan Press.

Ducker, D. G.
1980   "The effects of two sources of role strain on women physicians." *Sex Roles* 6:549–559.

Ehrensing, R. H.
1986   "Attitudes towards women physicians: A multispecialty group practice perspective." *The Internist* 27:17–18.

Fratoe, Frank
1984   "Sociological perspectives on minority business ownership: A synthesis of the literature with research and policy implications." Report presented to the Research Division of the Minority Business Development Agency, U.S. Department of Commerce. Washington, DC.

Freidson, Eliot
1970   *Professional Dominance: The Social Structure of Medical Care.* New York: Atherton Press.
1985   "The reorganization of the medical profession." *Medical Care Review* 42:11–35.
1986   *Professional Powers: A Study of the Institutionalization of Formal Knowledge.* Chicago: University of Chicago Press.

Gamliel, Sandy, Robert Politzer, Marc Rivo, and Fitzhugh Mullan
1995   "Managed care on the march: Will physicians meet the challenge?" *Health Affairs* 14 (summer): 131–142.

Hafferty, Frederic and Frederic Wolinsky
1991   "Conflicting characterizations of professional dominance." In J. A. Levy (ed.), *Current Research on Occupations and Professions:* Vol. 6:225–249. Greenwich, CT: JAI Press.

Hall, Richard
1968   "Professionalization and bureaucratization." *American Sociological Review* 33:92–104.

Heinz, J. P. and E. O. Laumann
1982   *Chicago Lawyers: The Social Structure of the Bar.* New York and Chicago: Russell Sage and American Bar Foundation.

Hertz, Rosanna
1986   *More Equal than Others: Women and Men in Dual-Career Marriages.* Berkeley, CA: University of California Press.

Hoff, Timothy J. and David P. McCaffrey
1996   "Resisting, adapting, and negotiating: How physicians cope with organizational and economic change." *Work and Occupations* 23:165–189.

Interstudy Publications
1995   *The Competitive Edge Industry Report.* Minneapolis, Minnesota: Author.

Jaccard, James, Robert Turrisi, and Choi K. Wan (Series Editor: Michael Lewis-Beck)
1990   "Interaction effects in multiple regression." In *Sage University Paper Series on Quantitative Applications in the Social Sciences:* 07–072. Newbury Park, CA: Sage.

Johnsson, Julie
1996   "Solo practice: Down, not out." *American Medical News* 39:7–8.

Kanter, R. M.
1977   *Men and Women of the Corporation.* New York: Basic Books.
Kosa, John
1971   "Women and medicine in a changing world." In Athena Theodore (ed.), *The Professional Woman:* 709–719. Cambridge, MA: Schenkman Publishing Co.
Lemkau, Jeanne, James Rafferty, Richard Purdy, and John Rudisill
1987   "Sex role stress and job burnout among family practice physicians." *Journal of Vocational Behavior* 31:81–90.
Lorber, Judith
1984   *Women Physicians: Careers, Status, and Power.* New York: Tavistock Publications.
1991   "Can women physicians ever be true equals in the American medical profession?" In Helena Z. Lopata (ed.), *Current Research on Occupations and Professions:* Vol. 6:25–37, Greenwich, CT: JAI Press.
McKinlay, John B.
1982   "Toward the proletarianization of physicians." In Charles Derber (ed.), *Professionals as Workers: Mental Labor in Advanced Capitalism:* 37–62. Boston, MA: G. K. Hall and Co.
McKinlay, John B. and J. Arches
1985   "Towards the proletarianization of physicians." *International Journal of Health Services* 15:161–195.
McKinlay, John B. and J. D. Stoeckle
1988   "Corporatization and the social transformation of doctoring." *International Journal of Health Services* 18:191–205.
Mechanic, David
1986   *From Advocacy to Allocation: The Evolving American Health Care System.* New York: The Free Press.
Mitka, Mike
1996   "Doctor pay shrinks for the first time in 1994." *American Medical News* 39(4):1, 7–8.
Morrisey, Michael A. and Cynthia Ashby
1982   "An empirical analysis of HMO market share." *Inquiry* 19:136–149.
Moy, Ernest, and Barbara A. Bartman
1995   "Physician race and care of minority and medically indigent patients." *Journal of the American Medical Association* 273:1515–1520.
Nickens, H. W., T. P. Ready, and R. G. Petersdorf
1994   "Racial and ethnic diversity in U.S. medical schools." *The New England Journal of Medicine* 331:472–476.

Page, Leigh
1995   "Signs of a shifting marketplace" *American Medical News* 38(22):3, 30.
Pleck, J. H.
1977   "The work–family role system." *Social Problems* 24:417–427.
Prechel, Harland and Anne Gupman
1995   "Changing economic conditions and their effects on professional autonomy: An analysis of family practitioners and oncologists." *Sociological Forum* 10:245–271.
Richardson, A. M. and R. J. Burke
1991   "Occupational stress and job satisfaction among physicians: Sex differences." *Social Science and Medicine* 33:1179–1187.
Schulz, R., W. E. Scheckler, C. Girard, and K. Barker
1990   "Physician adaptation to health maintenance organizations and implications for management." *Health Services Research* 25:43–63.
Shye, Diana
1991   "Gender differences in Israeli physicians' career patterns, productivity, and family structure." *Social Science and Medicine* 32:1169–1181.
Starr, Paul
1982   *The Social Transformation of American Medicine.* New York: Basic Books.
Stoeckle, J.
1988   "Reflections on modern doctoring." *The Milbank Quarterly* 66 (Supplement 2): 76–91.
Uhlenberg, P. and T. M. Cooney
1990   "Male and female physicians: Family and career comparisons." *Social Science and Medicine* 30: 373–378.
Weiner, Jonathan P.
1994   Forecasting the effects of health reform on U.S. physician workforce requirement: Evidence from HMO staffing patterns." *Journal of the American Medical Association* 272:222–230.
Weisman, Carol and Martha Teitlebaum
1987   "The work–family role system and physician productivity." *Journal of Health and Social Behavior* 28:247–257.
Wholey, Douglas R., Jon B. Christianson, and Susan M. Sanchez
1993   "The effect of physician and corporate interests on the formation of health maintenance organizations." *American Journal of Sociology* 98:164–200.

<u>DEVELOPED WORLD PERSPECTIVE</u>

STRUGGLE FOR CONTROL: GENERAL PRACTITIONERS IN THE SWEDISH HEALTH CARE SYSTEM

RANDOLPH K. QUAYE

This paper introduces an international perspective into existing research and scholarship on the changing status of the medical profession in Sweden and investigates the dominant (sometimes explicit and usually implicit) question that "medicine is undergoing significant change with serious implications for the practice of medicine."[1] In the preface to *The Changing Medical Professions: An International Perspective,* McKinlay and Hafferty[2] stated that "As nations across the globe face the rising tide of health care costs and the prospect of massive changes in the organization and financing of health care, issues of the structure of physician autonomy, shifts in the status of state–professional relations and ultimately the reconceptualization of medicine and its place in society will shape the debate in medicine" (p. 1). Duran-Arenas and Kennedy[3] suggested that "state power is central in the analysis of professional power and that the relationship between the state and the medical profession mediated by community or societal concerns may play a major role in predicting the future role of doctors" (p. 37).

This paper reports findings on the perspectives of general practitioners (GPs) in Sweden since the introduction of the Stockholm model. While previous research has concluded that, by and large, in the decade of cost control and retrenchment, doctors have suffered because of loss of autonomy and increased deskilling, the experience in Sweden in particular as it relates to GPs might be different at least in relation to their economic and social status with the other medical specialties. There is no doubt that in Sweden there is the "potential" for a deep split within the ranks of the "profession" as a result of the legislation on family doctors.

The empirical work carried out as a part of this study was undertaken in summer 1994. At that time, there were relatively few studies examining the impact of the Stockholm model on physicians' behaviour. Preliminary studies conducted by Forsberg and Calltorp[4] generally focused on the impact of economic incentives on physician behaviour, but not directly on the impact of the Stockholm model.

METHOD AND DATA COLLECTION

The introduction of market reforms, such as competition among hospitals and doctors and the use of diagnostic related groups (DRGs) (the DRG developed at Yale University uses a case mix to classify hospital in-patients into patient care categories according to the patient's primary and secondary diagnosis, procedure performed, age, discharge status and whether the patient has certain complications), have brought the issues of economic incentives and physician's behaviour into the emerging health care structure in Sweden.[5]

The research design was exploratory with the intention of discovering the perspectives of general practitioners on several aspects of the Stockholm model and the introduction of the legislation on family doctors. The aim was

- to discuss why the Stockholm model was introduced and to examine the positive and negative aspects of the model,
- to examine the result of the family doctor's legislation on the practice of medicine by GPs and
- to explore if physicians' behaviour was a result of reimbursement incentives or merely a reflection of their professional training or socialization.[6]

A focus interview guide was constructed. Twenty-two physicians were interviewed. Eleven were general practitioners, 7 chief of clinics and 2 deputy chief. Of the 22 physicians interviewed, 15 (71%) of them were male and 7 (29%) were female. A large percentage of the physicians (78%) had worked in the medical field for more than 10 years. Questions asked was derived from both analysis and simulation of the likely results of the health care changes in Sweden. For example, since doctors are capitated, we expect to see patterns of under-utilization since the gatekeeping role has come to imply simply the medically limited and bureaucratic function of opening or closing the gate to the high cost of medical service.[6]

The subjects were asked to describe how long they had been working and how much they knew about the Stockholm model. Questions also focused on professional autonomy, use of DRGs and their impact on clinical decisions, issues of overwork, isolation and "dumping" of patients, in particular, the elderly.

Interviews were tape-recorded and transcribed. A content analysis was performed on major themes on the interview transcripts. *Table 1* represents a selected sociodemographic profile of the respondents. This paper reports on the results of that study.

BACKGROUND TO THE PROBLEM

Health care of the highest quality is what one would expect to receive in Sweden. The evolution of the Swedish thinking on health was infused with the concept of social justice. This meant that all individuals have an equal right to live a rich and full life, with rights to security, freedom, happiness, the right to cultural opportunities, employment and influence in the community.[7]

In terms of morbidity and mortality, as well as other measures of health, Sweden continues to have one of the world's healthiest populations.[8] Its infant mortality rate of 4.8 per 1,000 live births, like its average life expectancy of 75.5 years for

TABLE 1 Demographic Profile of Respondents (N = 22)

	N	%
Sex		
Male	15	71
Female	7	29
Age (years)		
20–29	1	5
30–39	9	47
40–49	6	32
50–59	3	16
Specialty		
Chief of clinic	7	33
Deputy chief	2	9
General practitioner	11	52
Job tenure		
<10 years	4	22
>10 years	14	78

The total number of respondents varies due to missing values.

men and 80.8 for women, places Sweden near the top of international comparative statistics.[9]

The relative success enjoyed by Swedes in the area of health care delivery is based on public and rational planning of health care. As is well documented, health care is regarded in Sweden as a task for the public sector.[10] The public sector share in total health expenditure is 89.5% compared with 42.4% in the US.[11] Private health care exists on a limited basis. Only 5% of physicians work full time in private practice. The responsibility for health services and medical care rests with 23 autonomous county councils and 3 large municipalities (Göteborg, Malmö and Gotland). Health care delivery accounts for about 75–80% of the total expenditures of the county councils.

Among the industrialized countries of the world, Sweden has succeeded in controlling cost, reducing its total health expenditure as a percentage of GNP from 9.4% in 1980 to 7.5% in 1992.[12] The decline is presented in *Table 2*.

It is tempting to argue that expenditures on health care can be reduced without increasing the

TABLE 2 Total Health Care Expenditure as a Percentage of GNP

COUNTRY	1970	1980	1990	1992
Sweden	7.2	9.4	8.6	7.5
Norway	5.0	6.6	7.4	7.9
Denmark	6.1	6.8	6.3	6.4
Finland	5.7	6.5	7.8	8.5
USA	7.4	9.2	12.1	13.5
OECD average	5.5	7.0	7.6	8.2

Source: From OECD.[12] *Internal Markets in the Making: Health Systems in Canada, Iceland, and the United Kingdom.* Health Policy Studies No. 6. Copyright © OECD, 1995.

length of queues or decreasing the quality of and access to care. However, in the last few years discussions on the necessity of rationing care for cancer patients in Stockholm hospitals, the long waiting lists for hip replacement, cataract and coronary surgery and lack of incentives for efficiency for both providers and consumers and the uncoordinated financing structure, have led many Swedish county councils to initiate new ways of financing and organizing health care in Sweden. These initiatives culminated in the establishment of several health care models such as the Stockholm and the Dala models.

Background on the Stockholm Model

In January 1992, the Stockholm county council (with approximately 1.7 million people) embarked on a new way of financing and organizing health care. The Stockholm model was introduced to strengthen the position of patients and to provide more effective health care or, in other words, "more and better health care for the money" (p. 112).[13] Within this model, an internal market system was created for hospital services and the roles of purchasers and producers were kept separate. The producing organizations (primarily acute care hospitals, family doctor services and psychiat-

ric and geriatric care) were paid for results in accordance with the relevant reimbursement system. Prices were determined through an elaborate points system based on DRGs that result in a standard maximum price list.[14]

Another feature of the model is that patients will be free to choose a provider as long as the choice is between providers on the same level. Money is patient linked when the patient exercises freedom of choice. Competition is to be encouraged and the procurement of services is to be done competitively.[10] It is also anticipated that the number of beds in surgical wards will be reduced by 30%. At the same time, more emphasis will be placed on day and pre-planned surgeries.[10]

Another provision is the Family Doctor's Act. Under this act, a family doctor may be publicly or privately employed or be an active independent entrepreneur. The county council is responsible for all persons living within the county council and patients have the right to choose a family doctor. Section 5 of the Act allows family doctors to keep a special list of the persons whose family doctor he or she is. The family doctor is required to notify the county council about the identity of those persons. Not more than a year after commencing activities, a family doctor shall have at least a minimum of 1,000 listed patients and a maximum of 3,000 persons.[15]

The remuneration paid to a family doctor shall consist predominantly of a fixed amount for every person listed (capitation payment). The local area health boards, however, have the right to pay extra reimbursement to family doctors who are active in thinly populated areas or in areas with an exceptionally heavy care load.[16] Over and above the per capita reimbursement rate, there is a special visit reimbursement for all patients. The visit reimbursement is the same as the patient charge paid by the patient. At the moment, costs for premises and for medical services are not included in the basis of the per capita reimbursement. It is anticipated that these costs will gradually be transferred to the fam-

ily doctor. From 1996, costs for premises will be calculated based on a fixed standard area and rent.

These charges make the role of a physician in Sweden similar to the role of physicians in the health maintenance organizations in the United States. Studies conducted by Dietrich et al.[17] suggested that 75% of medical care (fees for service) are managed by primary care physicians. In the British health care system, 75% of the population's contact with doctors is handled by GPs. Individuals are free to choose their GPs, but there is little choice in rural areas. As in the Swedish system, GPs enjoy greater clinical freedom and their remuneration is paid through capitation, fees for services and practice allowances.

The following 4 principles behind the Family Doctor's Act have emerged from the above discussion:

- to reduce greater use of hospital resources by strengthening the primary health care sector;
- to ensure continuity of care for patients;
- to encourage competition among health care providers;
- to achieve greater productivity and efficiency as well as increasing patient choice of access to health care.

RESULTS

Perspectives on the Stockholm Model

Respondents were asked to (i) discuss why the Stockholm model was introduced and how informed they are about the Stockholm model and (ii) to examine the positive and negative aspects of the model. More than half of the respondents replied that they were well informed. Only 11% replied that they had little knowledge about the Stockholm model. Almost all respondents reported that the Stockholm model was introduced to reduce queues for elective surgery, to focus on the treatment of patients and to create a producer–purchaser relationship which was greatly influenced by

changes in the British health care system. One GP argued that "the Stockholm model was created simply because the politicians could not make the financial cutbacks in health care as needed, so they thought that by creating an internal market system, they would be able to solve the problem." Overwhelmingly, the respondents, all the GPs (52%) and 7 (33%) chiefs of clinics, reported that the Stockholm model had the benefit of increasing productivity, decreasing lists of those waiting for elective surgery and increasing access to care. They also pointed out that attitudes from care providers have become more polite and more service minded. They also mentioned that the Stockholm model had instilled in the minds of doctors and administrators the important need for cost control. As one doctor put it, "the climate for the discussion of these cost controls has also changed. Before, we never talked about priority-setting. This is a big change." As another GP put it, "the ideal situation is to have 2,500 healthy patients on your list. There is a greater danger of reducing or rationing care, if the cost exceeds what was budgeted for per patient."

When respondents were asked to evaluate the major shortcomings of the Stockholm model, answers differed according to specialty. GPs criticized the use of DRGs as cost control strategy. They reasoned that "there is always a risk that when you pay doctors with this (DRGs) that things that are well-paid will increase and other things that are very important, but have low reimbursement rates, may suffer."

Among clinic chiefs (while they think the DRG is a good system), all complained that the current weight/reimbursement rates are not right. One respondent stated that the "so called Stockholm model does not work today and cannot work in the future because the politicians have reduced the reimbursement rate so much that I think the volume and quality of care is not sufficient to meet the demands of the patients." One respondent stated that "the DRG system is not based on calculations of real cost or time; it is arbitrarily selected." Another

respondent argued that the "DRG is a good system provided that it is regarded by the professionals as a sound and fair one. Many of us feel that it does not cover true cost and therefore must be looked at carefully." When respondents were asked whether DRGs is a good system for care payment as currently utilized in the Swedish system, only 11% responded that the system was good. Overwhelming, the respondents reported that the Stockholm model had led to a reduction in hospital stays. Before the implementation of the model, the average stay was 13 days, while today, it has decreased to 11 days. Between 1990 and 1992, the number of hospital beds in the Stockholm county council was reduced from 6,000 to 4,500.[18]

Competition between Providers

Some respondents (60%) reported that the Stockholm model had introduced competition between providers. This was seen in the closure of some hospitals as well as in increases in referrals by doctors. As to whether the referral to hospitals were made because of the efficiency of the hospitals, one respondent suggested that it was because they did not have any choice since 2 of the hospitals had closed down. Competition did not exist in those hospitals where they had a monopoly (paediatric hospitals, for example).

While chiefs of clinics (42%) agreed that competition between providers was strong at the beginning (1990–1991), in particular between medical and surgical departments, the interventions by politicians have prevented hospitals from effective competition. One respondent stated "Nacka should not have survived and I am not sure we can afford it, but opinion in Nacka suggested that we keep it open so they closed the emergency department in the evening and now other hospitals have to refer some of their patients to Nacka so that they have something to do. This is ineffective. Politicians should have kept out of it and allowed the market to decide the outcome."

Patient Choice

All the respondents answered that patients have more choice than before but the ability to make these choices may be limited by geographical boundaries. Patients continue to go to the nearest hospital and therefore may not be willing to use a wide range of services if other services are considered to be too far away. Regarding the impact of these changes on the quality of care, some of the respondents indicated that it was too early to tell. Some suggested that there are preliminary indications that the quality of care may be suffering, but they could not prove it.

Impact on the Elderly

Regarding the impact of the Stockholm model on elderly care, all the GPs and 5 chiefs of clinics felt that the Ädel reform had contributed negatively to the care for the elderly. A chief of clinic stated that "one might suspect that some patients are being sent home early since it reduces cost and saves money." This observation is consistent with a study conducted by Svensson and Garelius.[19] In their study, they discovered that patients had been admitted to hospitals more frequently and had been discharged earlier than before the introduction of the Stockholm model.[19] A possible reason for the reduction in the length of stay could be the fact that the municipalities during the same period under the Ädel reform, had similar incentives.[20] The Ädel reform of 1992 created clear lines of accountability and transferred the overall responsibility for care of the elderly to the municipalities, making them liable for the costs of continued hospitalization of patients who have completed medical treatment and are awaiting transfer to community care.[21] The reform included a transfer of approximately 500 long-term somatic medical care institutions with approximately 3,000 beds from the county councils to the municipalities. The municipalities also incur financial responsibility for acute medical care and geriatric care. As a result of these

changes, there is pressure on the municipalities to offer suitable housing alternatives against a constrained budget. It is this arrangement more than the use of DRGs that some of the respondents attributed to the possible "dumping" of elderly patients. As one respondent stated, "We have less clinical freedom now than before because we have less resources and more patients. You are expected to carry out more consultations at a faster pace than before. There is always the pressure to send the patient out because you are not paid until the patient is discharged. Admitted patients do not bring money, but discharged patients do."

Impact of DRGs on Patient Care

When respondents were asked whether the introduction of the Stockholm model had led to changes in their clinic with regard to the profitability of patients and whether patients were treated less than was medically necessary, 64% said seldom and 7% said never. Only 7% said often and 14% said very often. *Table 3* illustrates the results. This is suggestive that while overall (70%) the respondents did not draw a connection between economic incentives and treatment choice, the fact that 20% linked economic incentives to treatment procedures suggests that there is a need for caution. When the doctors were asked if the clinical economic performance (result) would influence/affect their future work situation, 75% said yes. Only 6% of the respondents said no. *Table 4* illustrates this conclusion. Their responses lead one to speculate that while they may not make medical decisions on the profitability of patients, it does appear that they at least think about cost control

TABLE 3 Profitable Patients

VALUE LABEL	VALUE	FREQUENCY	%	VALID%	CUMULATIVE%
Often	1	1	4.5	7.1	7.1
Very often	2	2	9.1	14.3	21.4
Seldom	3	9	40.9	64.3	85.7
Never	4	1	4.5	7.1	92.9
Don't know	5	1	4.5	7.1	100.0
Missing	9	8	36.4		
Total		22	100.0	100.0	

Valid cases: 14; missing cases: 8

TABLE 4 Clinical Economic Performance Affects Future Work?

VALUE LABEL	VALUE	FREQUENCY	%	VALID%	CUMULATIVE %
Yes much	1	12	54.5	75.0	75.0
Yes very much	2	2	9.1	12.5	87.5
Yes	3	1	4.5	6.3	93.8
Not at all	4	1	4.5	6.3	100.0
Missing	9	6	27.3		
Total		22	100.0	100.0	

Valid cases: 16; missing cases: 6

when ordering treatment procedures. When respondents were asked to evaluate the impact of cost containment policies on various hospital resources and treatment procedures, 31% reported that they had made changes as a result of the introduction of the Stockholm model.

Patient Autonomy

The respondents reported that the introduction of market reforms in the Swedish health care system had limited their clinical freedom. Only 6% of the doctors interviewed agreed with the statement that the Stockholm model had improved their work situation. Fifty-two percent reported that their work situation had become progressively worse. *Table 5* illustrates this conclusion. They also reported that they had been spending too much time on paperwork. When physicians were asked whether they

would be satisfied working in their various departments 5 years from now, 28% disagreed with the statement. *Tables 6 and 7* illustrate this conclusion. Fifty-eight percent of the physicians interviewed agreed that professional autonomy is diminishing. This view is shared unanimously by GPs and chiefs of clinics. A chief of clinic stated that "I have been working for 16 years and this is the first time I have heard my head of department telling me to organize my work so that we can treat the patient quickly and in a reasonable manner. Earlier, it was said that we had to have a number of patients waiting for surgery so that we could get more money." Almost all the GPs reported that the Stockholm model had enhanced their social and economic status in relationship to other doctors, in particular, those in hospitals. One respondent stated, "our status has improved. In a way we have more power and hospitals are more responsive to us. Earlier,

TABLE 5   Work Environment

VALUE LABEL	VALUE	FREQUENCY	%	VALID %	CUMULATIVE %
Better	2	1	4.5	6.7	6.7
Unchanged	3	6	27.3	40.0	46.7
Worse	4	4	18.2	26.7	73.3
Much worse	5	4	18.2	26.7	100.0
Missing	9	7	31.8		
Total		22	100.0	100.0	

Valid cases: 15; missing cases: 7

TABLE 6   Diminishing Autonomy

VALUE LABEL	VALUE	FREQUENCY	%	VALID %	CUMULATIVE %
Strongly Agree	1	4	18.2	23.5	23.5
Agree	2	6	27.3	35.3	58.8
Disagree	4	6	27.3	35.3	94.1
Strongly Disagree	5	1	4.5	5.9	100.0
Missing	9	5	22.7		
Total		22	100.0	100.0	

Valid cases: 17; missing cases: 5

TABLE 7   Satisfied with Job

VALUE LABEL	VALUE	FREQUENCY	%	VALID %	CUMULATIVE %
Strongly Agree	1	7	31.8	41.2	41.2
Agree	2	5	22.7	29.4	70.6
Disagree	4	2	9.1	11.8	82.4
Strongly Disagree	5	3	13.6	17.6	100.0
Missing	9	5	22.7		
Total		22	100.0	100.0	

Valid cases: 17; missing cases: 5

they thought we were all jerks." One hospital surgeon echoed the same sentiment when he stated that "now you have to be more polite to the general practitioner than before."

The new change has no doubt led to hospital doctors and administrators depending on GPs for referral. As one hospital administrator noted, "we have now to define GPs as our customers; so they are as important as the patient. That is a big change." Another respondent stated, "politicians love them" (GPs) and they have a very strong support for increasing the number of general practitioners. This has led to the general practitioners being better salaried than the hospital doctors.

Overwhelmingly, family doctors see the current legislation on family doctors as having the potential for making them "gatekeepers," similar to the British system. As one GP noted, "I have been praying for this day for almost 12 years now."

DISCUSSION

This paper has reported on the perspectives of Swedish doctors (GPs) concerning the introduction of the Stockholm model and its likely impact on their work, quality of care and treatment of the elderly. The majority of doctors interviewed rejected the use of the DRG as a mode of payment simply because they felt the weights do not measure the true cost.

On the question of the changing role of family doctors as a result of the legislation on family doctors, there was a great deal of support across all segments of the medical profession that such a move is timely and necessary for reducing the cost of health care in Sweden. There are other preliminary studies which were conducted by Svensson and Garelius[19] which noted that these findings reflect the social circumstances of the physicians studied.

There is no doubt that health care financing in Sweden is changing and that the whole debate about rationing care may take centre-stage as politicians and the medical profession grapple with the impact of such changes on the quality and delivery of care resources. As in the United States and the United Kingdom, the gatekeeping role of family doctors is not only important, but it is deemed imperative in each country's attempt to reduce cost.

Contrary to other published studies about the dangers of GPs holding down costs through risks of under-treatment, some studies do show that primary care physicians may be superior in providing continuity and comprehensiveness in care.[6] Care, however, must be taken that their role as "fund holders" does not lead to compromise and a decrease in the quality of care.

Another area of concern in the Ädel reform is its likely impact on elderly care. While there is no concrete evidence that patients are being "dumped," there are enough questions and concerns raised

about early discharge to require further examination and discussion. DRGs, if they are going to be an effective cost control strategy, should be based on proper weights and should reflect the work done.

Above all, the gatekeeping role of family doctors needs to be strengthened. This requires that more GPs be trained and there should exist the political will on the part of all those concerned to attract more doctors into this field. While doctors (Swedish) did not enter the medical profession to make money, the time has come for a critical reevaluation of these issues. Perhaps, cooperation rather than competition between hospitals with little political influence would ensure greater equity, efficiency and productivity of health care resources. This is the Swedish challenge and the evidence presented here suggests that it can be successfully met.

REFERENCES

1. McKinlay J, Stoeckle J. Corporatization and the social transformation of doctoring. *Int J Hlth Services* 1988; 18(2): 191–205.

2. McKinlay J, Hafferty F. *The changing medical profession: an international perspective.* New York: Oxford University Press, 1993.

3. Duran-Arenas L, Kennedy M. The constitution of physicians' power: a theoretical framework for comparative analysis. *Soc Sci Med* 1991; 32(6):643–8.

4. Forsberg E, Calltorp J. *Ekonomiska incitament och medicinskt handlande första aret av Stockholmsmodellen (Economic incentives on physician's behaviour).* Huddinge, Sweden: Huddinge sjukhus, Samhàllsmedicinska enheten, 1993.

5. Davis K, Anderson G, Rowland D, Steinberg E. *Health care cost containment.* Baltimore: The Johns Hopkins University Press, 1990.

6. Franks P, Nutting P, Clancy C. Gatekeeping revisited: protecting patients from overtreatment. *New Engl J Med* 1991; 6:425–9.

7. Aker S. *The right to health.* Ann Arbor, Michigan: University Microfilms International, 1980.

8. Saltman RB, Von Otter C. Revitalizing public health care systems: a proposal for public competition in Sweden. *Hlth Policy* 1987; 7(1):21–40.

9. Swedish Institute. *The health care system in Sweden.* Stockholm: Swedish Institute, 1995.

10. Hakansson S. New ways of financing and organizing health care in Sweden. *Int J Hlth Management* 1994; 9(1):103–24.

11. OECD. *US health care at the crossroads.* Paris: OECD, 1992.

12. OECD. *Internal markets in the making.* Paris: OECD, 1994.

13. Medical and health care board. *Regulations in the Stockholm model.* Stockholm: Medical and Health Care Board, 1994.

14. Glennerster H, Matsaganis M. The English and Swedish health reforms. *Int J Hlth Services* 1994; 24(2):231–51.

15. Ministry of Health and Social Affairs. *Health and medical services legislation and family doctor's legislation.* Stockholm: Ministry of Health and Social Affairs, 1994.

16. National Board of Health and Welfare. *Welfare and public health in Sweden.* Stockholm: Socialstyrelsen, 1995.

17. Dietrich AJ, Nelson EC, Kirk JW, Zubikoff M, O'Connor GT. Do primary physicians actually manage their patients' fee for service care? *J Am Med Assoc* 1990.

18. Federation of Swedish County Councils. *Monitoring the European health for all strategy 1993–1994.* Stockholm: Federation of Swedish County Councils, 1994.

19. Svensson H, Garelius L. *Har ekonomiska incitament paverkat läkarnas beslutsfattande? Utvärdering av Stockholmsmodellen (Have economic incentives affected the physicians' decision-making? An evaluation of the Stockholm model).* Spri report 392. Stockholm: Spri, 1994.

20. Faffel M, editor. *Comparative health systems: descripted analysis of fourteen national health systems.* University Park, Pennsylvania: Pennsylvania State University Press, 1995.

21. Federation of Swedish County Councils. *Health care utilization and resources in Sweden 1980–1992.* Stockholm: Modin Tryck, 1993.

FROM "BAREFOOT DOCTOR" TO "VILLAGE DOCTOR" IN TIGER SPRINGS VILLAGE: A CASE STUDY OF RURAL HEALTH CARE TRANSFORMATIONS IN SOCIALIST CHINA

SYDNEY D. WHITE

During the 1970s, a flurry of publications emerged in "the West" on the dramatic Cultural Revolution developments which were taking place in rural health care in the People's Republic of China.[1] These reports, for the most part, lauded the implementation of the new system of "cooperative medicine" in general, and the innovative approach to training "barefoot doctors" in particular. Both cooperative medicine and the barefoot doctors, it was believed, reflected an approach to health care which was focussed on rural areas, and which was decentralized, deprofessionalized, grassroots-based, egalitarian, "low-tech," economically feasible, and culturally appropriate. The PRC model became internationally renowned in public health and health development circles, and in fact served as the inspiration for the World Health Organization's Primary Health Care initiative which was formulated at the now legendary 1978 Alma Ata conference.

In the early to mid-1980s, however, with the advent of post-Mao political and economic changes in the PRC, specifically rural decollectivization, a second flurry of publications emerged in Western countries.[2] Many of these articles were as cautionary as the previous spate of articles were exuberant. The fate of rural health care in China, it was feared, was seriously threatened given that the structure of cooperative medicine was premised on the structure of the rural collective. It was believed that the changes signaled a tendency towards an urban-biased, recentralized, re-professionalized, hierarchical, "high-tech" focussed, increasingly inegalitarian and expensive health care system which was inaccessible to many rural residents, and

which de-emphasized and consequently lowered the status of Chinese medicine.

Since the late 1980s, a number of additional scholarly publications—many of them resulting from collaborations between scholars based in "the West" with PRC scholars—have addressed the changes in rural health in the post-Mao PRC very much in terms of issues framed by the earlier scholarly dialogue.[3]

The nature of the data upon which the assessments of rural health care policy have been based has certainly shifted over time. The assessments of the earliest wave of publications in particular (with a few exceptions) were made on the basis of relatively brief, government-arranged visits by the authors to carefully circumscribed locations in the PRC. Consequently, from the very beginning, assessments tended to focus on the health care policies and their implications rather than on how the policies were experienced and negotiated at the local level. This was certainly understandable given the nature of the times. While the quality of the "on-the-ground" data which serve as the basis for assessments in many of the "second wave" and especially "third wave" publications has improved, and has expanded to include both interviews and large-scale surveys, there is still very limited long-term, fieldwork-based ethnographic research on rural health in the PRC.[4]

I present this article in the spirit of providing an ethnographically-based case study from a distinctive geographical and historical context of the PRC—the relatively remote reaches of Tiger Springs Village (a pseudonym) in the Lijiang basin

of southwest China's Yunnan Province in 1989–1990. One of the extremely important observations which has emerged from the "second-wave" and "third-wave" literatures, however, is the tremendous degree of regional and even village-to-village (formerly brigade-to-brigade) variation in the experience of rural health care throughout the PRC during both the collective and post-collective eras. Thus, while I am presenting a case study as a potential foil, as it were, to the representation of rural health care practices in the scholarly literature, I would like to make it very clear that Tiger Springs' experience can in no way be taken to be singularly representative of the experiences of the vast remainder of rural China, nor even of the rural Lijiang basin.

Nonetheless, in providing a village-based case study of how Maoist and post-Mao policy changes with respect to rural health care were played out in one corner of the PRC, my intention is, in fact, to re-examine some of the assumptions made and concerns raised by scholars during all three phases of the discussion outlined above. If China's innovative experiences with respect to rural health are to continue to serve as a potential model for international health policy, it is critical that they are first better understood in historical and cultural context.

This article presents several key points about the practice of rural healthcare in Tiger Springs and the Lijiang basin both during and after collectivization. It raises issues with respect to the financing of rural health care, with respect to its relative emphasis on preventive and primary care versus curing and secondary and tertiary care, with respect to issues of villagers' access to health services, with respect to issues of training and/or professionalization of village health practitioners, and with respect to issues of relative emphasis on Chinese versus Western medicine.

The article begins with a brief introduction to Tiger Springs Village and the nature of the data upon which my findings are based. The next section focuses primarily on the implementation of cooperative medicine in Tiger Springs during the

Cultural Revolution (officially designated as the period from 1965–1975), but first provides a brief history of the post-1949 health care infrastructure which was established in the basin prior to the beginning of cooperative medicine. The subsequent section examines the impact of decollectivization and post-Mao changes in general on health care in Tiger Springs starting in the early 1980s; in the process of outlining the actual changes, however, it also addresses some of the discrepancies between policy and actual practice both prior to and since decollectivization, and consequently some of the misconceptions often reflected in the scholarly literature. In order to illustrate even more specifically how policies were played out in practice, the backgrounds and experiences of Tiger Springs health practitioners during both periods will be addressed in the final section. The conclusion presents a summary of my central arguments and analysis, as well as some reflections on both the scholarly representations of the cooperative medicine saga in the PRC and the very real issues for PRC rural health care that are at stake.

BACKGROUND

Tiger Springs "administrative village" consists of approximately 2000 residents and roughly 500 households, and is located in the northwestern part of the Lijiang basin. It is approximately five kilometers from Dayanzhen, the town (population approximately 60,000 in 1990) which serves as the government seat for both Lijiang County and Lijiang Prefecture. Tiger Springs is one of the villages which makes up White Sands Township (Bai Sha Xiang); this township directly abuts the Jade Dragon Snow Mountain, which towers more than 19,000 feet over the approximately 7400 foot basin floor.

The Lijiang basin is historically the symbolic and political/administrative heartland of the Naxi people, who have been officially designated as a "minority nationality" since the 1949 Chinese Communist Revolution (as opposed to being mem-

bers of the Han Chinese majority). However, not only has basin Naxi identity been significantly influenced by Han culture for centuries, but the majority of basin Naxi participated in the Underground Communist Party prior to the revolution, and have been zealous participants both in the Party and virtually every political movement since 1949. Thus while clearly Tiger Springs and the Lijiang basin cannot be taken to be completely representative of all China (as is the case for any one village or region, for that matter), it can be safely assumed that the villagers, village practitioners, and public health bureaus of the basin adhered to central government policies as much as (and, in many instances, more so than) other parts of the PRC.

It is also important to note that while the villages in the Lijiang basin are by no means the wealthiest in the economic continuum of the rural PRC, neither are they by any means the poorest. Most villagers in the basin enjoy a hard-working but comfortable existence unlike the much more impoverished existence of villagers in the more remote "mountainous villages" adjacent to the basin. Within the basin, of course, there is socio-economic variation between villages as well as within villages.

My analysis in this article is primarily focussed on the experiences of the villagers and village health practitioners of Tiger Springs, with whom I carried out the rural component of my Lijiang basin research. The analysis is, however, also informed by intensive interviews with and observations of a number of heath practitioners from other villages in the basin (interviews with a total of 23 village health practitioners were conducted), and interviews with the ten county and prefectural branches of the public health system which were based in Dayanzhen.[5]

COOPERATIVE MEDICINE AND TIGER SPRINGS BRIGADE

In the early 1950s, various bureaus of what is now the public health infrastructure were established in

the town of Dayanzhen, and the beginnings of a corresponding public health infrastructure were established in the villages of the basin and throughout the other villages of Lijiang County. Basic health care centers were first set up at the *qu* level (an administrative level from 1949–1958 between the current township and county levels), and smaller clinics were gradually set up at what was to become the brigade level with collectivization in 1958 (and which in turn would become the "administrative village" after decollectivization in the early 1980s). These health care centers were set up both to serve as rural based liaisons with the Hygiene and Preventive Health Bureau and the Women's and Children's Health Protection Bureau, as well as to serve other basic health care needs.

In Tiger Springs, a clinic was set up in 1956 (during the period of "advanced level cooperatives") staffed by one of the Chinese medicine practitioners from the village, He Zhi-ming (a pseudonym). He was joined in 1957 by another villager, Yang Ru-Jin (also a pseudonym), who had studied Western medicine in the military. Prior to the formulation of "integrated Chinese and Western medicine" during the Cultural Revolution, the general principle informing medical practice in these rural clinics from their inception was "Chinese and Western medicine united," which operated on the assumption of a division of labor between the two systems. By the time of collectivization in 1958, the whole county apparently had Health Protection Clinics at the brigade level.

Most brigades implemented cooperative medicine in 1968 or 1969; this system of brigade-sponsored health care persisted in most rural areas until it was dismantled along with the brigades in the early 1980s (this occurred in some areas of the basin as early as 1981, and in other areas as late as 1984).

One Lijiang basin brigade in what is now Gold Mountain Township, which was known for its particularly "revolutionary" spirit, actually started up their cooperative medicine station in 1965, based

on an article about Mao's now-famous directive which the two founding doctors read in the *People's Daily*. They considered themselves to be following Mao's advice to "seize the revolution," and were particularly proud of the recognition banners awarded them by the provincial Revolutionary Working Committee which still hang in their now half-abandoned health station.

Tiger Springs did not have a reputation for being as "revolutionary" as some other brigades in the basin, perhaps because most of the families in the brigade had been engaged in family-based handicrafts businesses and trade before the revolution. However, like virtually everywhere else in the basin, both villagers and practitioners quickly responded to Mao's call for cooperative medicine. In 1969 the Tiger Springs Brigade cooperative medicine clinic was set up in the village temple, which prior to 1949 had been the domain of the village gods.

According to the official vision of cooperative medicine, each member of the brigade would pay only one yuan per year and five fen (0.05 yuan) for each visit to the clinic, theoretically providing the financial basis for collective health insurance. This policy was in fact followed initially in many of the brigades throughout the basin, although most brigades ultimately ended up subsidizing up to 50% of the cooperative health care costs. The workpoint system which supported both the staff and the extensive herbal medicine collecting expeditions in essence also subsidized the cooperative medicine system. In Tiger Springs Brigade, however, true cooperative medicine lasted only three years. Villagers as well as practitioners stated that too many people took advantage of the system (an accusation often leveled at those who have state supported health care in contemporary China) and bankrupted the brigade's finances.[6] After the first couple of years, the one yuan per year, five fen (0.05 yuan) per visit system was discontinued in Tiger Springs in favor of higher pay-per-visit fee, though in other respects the cooperative medicine clinic

persisted (i.e., in terms of the workpoint system and to a more limited degree subsidies from the brigade).

Generally speaking, the practitioners who made up the brigade cooperative medicine staffs in the basin (as seems to have been the case in other parts of the PRC) consisted of one or two older Chinese medicine doctors (or at least practitioners who had a store of family-transmitted healing knowledge), one or two younger to middle-aged practitioners trained in Western medicine (usually having acquired it while in the People's Liberation Army—PLA—medical corps), and two or more younger practitioners who inevitably had "good" (i.e., ideologically-correct) family backgrounds and were selected by their collectives to study to be bonafide "barefoot doctors," midwives, or nurses. The key operating concepts in the practice of cooperative medicine were to "serve the people," to "learn through experience,"[7] and to continually strive towards the practice of "integrated Chinese and Western medicine" (hereafter to be referred to as "integrated medicine"). Chinese medicine doctors were to learn from practitioners of Western medicine, and vice versa.

The first cohorts of barefoot doctor trainees (in the first few years of cooperative medicine) on average received only a month and a half to two months of training at the Number 65 army hospital in Nankou (just south of Dayanzhen), although some trainees received up to six months of training. Later cohorts (e.g., in the mid-1970s) were provided with six-month training courses, and, as the Cultural Revolution began to wane, intensive "update" training courses in Dayanzhen hospitals and at the prefectural Hygiene School were arranged. In any case, most of the (Western medicine) doctors from the hospitals were "sent down" from the towns and cities to work in brigade clinics, and so barefoot doctors were actually more likely to encounter these hospital doctors in the brigade clinics than in the town-based hospitals. While each cooperative medicine practitioner nominally special-

ized in either Chinese or Western medicine, as stated above, their mission was to help each other and study from each other. *The Barefoot Doctor's Manual,* which they used as their reference book, and the periodic training sessions during the Cultural Revolution reinforced the model of integrated medicine, which was the medical practice sanctioned by the cooperative medicine initiative.[8]

The public health hygiene campaigns also made their way from the central government's Ministry of Public Health through the town-based public health bureaus to the villages. Every year, each brigade would carry out their three "patriotic health movements," and practitioners were responsible for evaluating households according to their conformity to state standards of hygiene.

Another important hallmark of cooperative medicine was the strong emphasis placed on the use of herbal medicine. This was the response of practitioners and patients alike to another of Mao's calls, and he invoked both nationalist and pragmatic criteria for pursuing the use of herbal medicine. Large bi-annual herbal medicine collecting expeditions set off to spend two weeks to a month on the slopes of the Jade Dragon Snow Mountain or other mountains in the vicinity. Practitioners estimate that 40–80% of the prescriptions made during the Cultural Revolution were based on herbal medicine, and that the brigade cooperative medicine clinics on average kept from 200–500 kinds of herbal medicine in stock.[9] Town-based hospitals and clinics were also encouraged to practice integrated medicine, and to place a strong priority on herbal medicine treatments.

COOPERATIVE MEDICINE AS A MODEL FOR PRIMARY HEALTH CARE, THE PROFESSIONALIZATION CONTROVERSY, AND POST-MAO CHANGES IN TIGER SPRINGS

It was perhaps precisely because cooperative medicine and the barefoot doctors served as a model for rural health care in general and the World Health

Organization (WHO) 1978 formulated Primary Health Care (PHC) initiative in particular that the policy changes in rural PRC health were regarded with such alarm by Western public health and health development scholars in the 1980s. In keeping with WHO's PHC directive, in "third world" countries throughout the world rural health care practitioners who, like the barefoot doctors, were themselves from villages, were to be selected and trained in basic biomedical health care techniques, including emergency care medicine and preventive medicine. Following China's three tiered health care system, health stations were to be set up to offer increasingly complex levels of health care treatment at increasingly more centralized facilities (on a rural–urban continuum). In the spirit of appropriate technology (i.e., using low-cost, locally available resources), indigenous medical practices were to be incorporated (where "appropriate") along with biomedical practices by indigenous rural health practitioners, following the model of integrated Chinese and Western medicine. It is understandable that it came as a bit of a shock that the rural health care system which served as the model for this policy was seen as being about to undergo a major transformation.

Many of the second wave of publications referred to earlier made some somber predictions about the likely demise of cooperative medicine with decollectivization, and the impact of this on peasant access to and standards of rural health care. A shift was predicted from revolutionary egalitarianism towards professionalization, and all that this implies in terms of unequal access to quality health care between rural and urban sectors of the Chinese population. Also predicted was a shift of emphasis from "low-tech," grassroots-based care to "high-tech," centralized care, and a decline in the status of Chinese medicine with respect to Western medicine.

It is important to note here that the particular framing of these and other issues was reflective of the Western scholarly literature rather than the way

the issues were framed among public health officials and village practitioners in the PRC. This is not to say that there were not concerned public health officials, disgruntled village practitioners, or concerned villagers, but rather that the changes were interpreted as just one consequence of a lot of other major changes which were happening simultaneously. The Lijiang basin experience of cooperative medicine can perhaps serve as one case which might clarify why the issues were framed differently by Western scholars than they were on the ground in the PRC.

First and foremost, the financing and political-economics of cooperative medicine during the Maoist period was not as seamless a solution as it might seem to have been from reading much of the Western scholarly literature. "Self-reliance" was the mantra for "peasants" (following the PRC term of reference for village residents) during the Maoist period, just as it has continued to be during the post-Maoist period. Brigades (in the Lijiang basin and elsewhere) had to subsidize the cooperative medicine health care system beyond the relatively low fees which each member of the brigade initially paid. The peasants were thus also in essence subsidizing the system through their collective labor. The predominantly full-time staff of the clinic was paid in workpoints, and the extensive bi-annual herbal medicine collecting expeditions (which provided 40–80% of the treatments in the clinics) and the on-average twenty individuals which they required were also subsidized by the workpoint system. In addition, the Western medicine pharmaceuticals and equipment, as well as other costs of running the clinic, all were subsidized by the brigade's (i.e., the peasants') finances. The central government covered the costs of the (initially six-week and later six-month) training programs for barefoot doctors and midwives, as well as provided certain vaccines and treatments (such as for the prolapsed uterus and cystitis conditions which were the targets of one particular campaign) without charge. Major illnesses which required treatment at mid-level healthcare clinics or at the hospitals in Dayanzhen were in theory supposed to be reimbursed by the brigades as well (though Dayanzhen hospitals claimed that if the brigades did not pay there was nothing the hospitals could do).

The decision about how to absorb these costs came down to the brigade. In the case of Tiger Springs Brigade, after the first few years of cooperative medicine, it was decided that the brigade could not absorb all the costs, and the costs were passed back to the individual members of the brigade. While this meant that brigade members were individually charged fees for medicine and for clinic visits, these costs were still in essence subsidized by the brigade, since the brigade absorbed the workpoint costs of the members of the cooperative medicine team and the herbal medicine expeditions. For the most common illnesses, such as colds, stomach problems, influenza, and dysentery, the per-visit costs to the clinic in Tiger Springs were somewhat more than the 0.05 yuan paid by members of brigades who continued to fully participate in cooperative medicine. It was the major medical conditions (e.g., surgery, problem pregnancies or Caesarian sections, etc.) which would deplete the meager savings of individual peasant households in Tiger Springs Brigade. For other brigades, however, such as the more "revolutionary" East Wind Brigade mentioned above, the cooperative medicine system fully alleviated peasant concerns about medical costs (though of course they, not the central government, were essentially paying for it themselves).

The transition to the post-collectivization dissolution of cooperative medicine consequently did not have as great an economic impact on Tiger Springs Brigade as it did on East Wind Brigade (both of which became "administrative villages"). With decollectivization, cooperative medicine clinics were for the most part disbanded. The Tiger Springs Brigade clinic was formally closed and most of the practitioners took up private practices in the contexts of their own homes. The govern-

ment instituted set prices for various services which the practitioners could not exceed. An average visit in 1990 was 0.50 yuan, a percentage increase (approximately fivefold) in keeping with the percentage increase in Tiger Springs income since decollectivization. Village residents certainly complain about the cost of health care, particularly the potential threat of catastrophic illness, but when asked whether they would like a return to cooperative medicine, they see it as integrally linked to the collectivization era and not possible now. Tiger Springs village practitioners adopt much the same "that was then and this is now" sort of attitude when asked to comparatively evaluate cooperative medicine with the contemporary private practice/responsibility system of operating medical practice. In contrast, practitioners of formerly more revolutionary villages such as East Wind are much more vocal in their disapproval of the substitution of private practice and the responsibility system for cooperative medicine and collectivization.

However, the state public health infrastructure by no means vanished from the villages with decollectivization. With decollectivization, the public health bureau also implemented stipends for three designated practitioners in each administrative village to carry out the work of the Hygiene and Preventive Health Bureau, the Woman's and Children's Health Protection Bureau, and the Birth Planning Bureau. A stipend of 20 yuan was attached to the performance of the duties for each bureau.

In Tiger Springs, three village practitioners (two of whom were formally part of cooperative medicine and one who was not) shared the administering and recording responsibilities for the vaccinations as well as the stipend set aside for this up until 1989. In 1989, county public health policy dictated that just one person be placed in charge of these responsibilities, and the practitioner who was chosen was selected because he was the only practitioner among the three of them to have passed the Western medicine certification examination.

A female health practitioner from Tiger Springs (who was also formerly a part of cooperative medicine) has carried out midwifery responsibilities (including the keeping of childbirth statistical records) for the village and received the 20 yuan stipend from the Women's and Children's Health Protection Bureau since decollectivization.

With the implementation of the shifting policies of the Birth Planning program in the late 1970s and early 1980s, a public health stipend of 20 yuan was given to another Tiger Springs woman placed in charge of these responsibilities. She also happened to be in charge of the Women's Association (for which there is a 20 yuan stipend from the state as well). Although she had no formal training as a health practitioner, she was in charge of birth control as well as of enforcing the policy.

Despite the fact that these village stipends were relatively minimal stipends by town standards, they are supplemented by other modest fees which practitioners charge their village clients (and which are also regulated by the government). Most importantly, however, they reflect that the Public Health Bureau has consistently maintained a presence in the village context in the post-Mao era.

Concerns were also expressed by Western scholars that the "professionalization" of rural health care would lead to the large scale reduction of rural health practitioners. Although a number of articles cite statistics which reflect a national post-decollectivization drop in numbers of village doctors, it is not clear whether these statistics include village practitioners who have not successfully passed the exams but who may still be practicing. Certainly all practitioners in Lijiang county were required to take an examination in either Western medicine or Chinese medicine in the early 1980s. Professional licensing tests became available as early as 1978, and village practitioners who had not taken the tests by 1982 or 1983 were required to do so then. In the basin, however, whether or not one passed the test did not dictate whether or not one could continue to practice. It unquestionably

added to the "face" and "fame" of a practitioner if he or she was successful in passing the test, and the particular practitioner would lose no time in posting the certificate in his or her respective home-based clinic. The completion of in-person or correspondence training courses, and the accompanying certificate, could also enhance one's reputation and was encouraged by the state. Passing the certification test also did make a difference in whether or not one became a designated village representative or a specific public health bureau (assuming any of the practitioners in a given village passed the examination). Tiger Springs village practitioner reputations, however, depend on much more than certificates from state examinations, and whether or not one has passed the exam does not necessarily count for a tremendous amount among the villagers in their therapeutic decisions. More significant factors in therapeutic resort include the reputation of a particular practitioner in treating a particular illness, their relative skill with either the Western medicine or Chinese medicine cure which the patient determines is appropriate to a particular illness, the convenience of their location, the history of personal or family connections with the practitioner, and their fees.

An additional concern of the Western public health scholarly literature was the fear that the status of Chinese medicine might decline vis-à-vis Western medicine. Tracing the relationship between Chinese medicine and Western medicine in the contemporary rural Lijiang basin is a complicated epistemological and practical undertaking.[10] With respect to national policy as it has been played out at the local level, integrated medicine is in theory no longer officially promoted in either training or clinical contexts. With decollectivization in the early 1980s, the study of integrated medicine became redivided into its pre–Cultural Revolution/pre–cooperative medicine incarnation of "separate but equal" fields of Chinese medicine and Western medicine. This division of labor has also been reinstituted in the Lijiang County Hospi-

tal and the Lijiang Prefectural Hospital (both located in Dayanzhen). Most village doctors in the basin who began their study of medicine after 1949, however, continue to refer to their own practices as integrated medicine, regardless of their own particular specializations in either Chinese or Western medicine.

Since decollectivization, there has unquestionably also been a shift (borne out by my clinical observations as well as the Lijiang Prefectural Pharmaceutical Company's statistics) from a relatively strong reliance on Chinese medicine pharmaceuticals (40–80%) during cooperative medicine, to a predominant reliance (at least in the clinical context) on Western medicine pharmaceuticals (approximately 80%) in contemporary rural health clinics. An overwhelming majority of the afflictions treated by village practitioners are treated with injections of antibiotics, as well as some other Western medicine pharmaceuticals such as antihelminthic medications for worms. If one has the money, "going to get an injection" is considered to be the thing to do for most illnesses. Starting with the implementation of cooperative medicine, getting an injection of antibiotics became as much a part of a visit to a clinic in the rural areas as it was in the urban areas prior to Mao's Cultural Revolution emphasis on rural health care.

Village practitioners all agree that a major reason why there is much less Chinese herbal medicine used now than during cooperative medicine is that it is neither economically viable nor physically possible for them as individual practitioners to organize extensive herbal medicine collecting expeditions of the same scale as those undertaken during collectivization. The purchase of many types of Chinese medicine from the Pharmaceutical Company is not cost-effective for village practitioners either, since they cannot expect to recover the costs from village clients. Most village practitioners acknowledge that Western medicine is the treatment of primary resort these days because it is convenient, quick, and not prohibitively expensive

(depending on the economic status of the client). In part, it is the case that if a villager decides to treat an affliction with Chinese medicine (or at least herbal medicine), they usually do it themselves, either through gathering the herbal medicine or purchasing it at the pharmacy, rather than going to see the village practitioner. And it is critical to note that most village practitioners and patients alike continue to speak of the superiority of Chinese medicine over Western medicine.

One might be tempted to interpret this shift from heavy reliance on Chinese medicine pharmaceuticals to Western medicine pharmaceuticals as an indication of an emerging primacy of Western medical epistemology in rural China. While injections of antibiotics are clearly categorized by practitioners and patients alike as a technique of Western medicine, however, I have argued in detail elsewhere (White 1993) that the way in which they are used is closely linked to health bolstering techniques from Chinese medical epistemology. In general, I argue that it is Chinese medical epistemology which came to play the prevailing role in the Mao inspired "integrated Chinese and Western medicine," and that this continues to be the case in terms of how the legacy of this system of medicine is practiced in the post-Mao era rural context of the basin.

TIGER SPRINGS HEALTH PRACTITIONERS DURING AND AFTER COOPERATIVE MEDICINE

Most of the practitioners who were incorporated into the brigade-level cooperative medicine clinic are still practicing today in Tiger Springs, albeit as private practitioners. The Tiger Springs Brigade cooperative medicine clinic itself consisted of five to six main practitioners throughout its more than ten year history (Table 1). (All of the names used for these practitioners are, of course, pseudonyms.) All of these cooperative medicine era practitioners, with the exception of Dr. Ming (see below) were nominated by the leaders of the brigade primarily

on the basis of their family backgrounds (i.e., they all came from families with "good" class backgrounds), and on the basis of how "capable" they were. Only two additional health practitioners have joined the ranks of these original practitioners in the post-Mao era.

Doctor Shi was officially designated by the Brigade Party leadership to serve as a barefoot doctor; it was he who was put in charge of founding the cooperative medicine clinic in Tiger Springs in 1969, at age 22, and he served as its head in the ensuing years. Originally from one of the poorest families in the village, he had completed three years of primary school education. He had received his basic medical training through serving as a health aide for the military doctors in the PLA, and had then completed an additional six months of training at the above-mentioned Number 65 (military) hospital in the Lijiang basin. Later on, in the 1970s he underwent another six months of training in integrated medicine at the prefectural Hygiene School in the Basin. Following Mao's dictum to "learn through experience," he studied Chinese medicine with his uncle, Dr. He (see below), and Western medicine while working at the clinic with Dr. Ming. Although he was primarily designated as a Western medicine practitioner in the clinic, he represents his previous and current form of medical practice as "integrated medicine." He did not pass the certification examination which he took in Western medicine in 1982, his very basic literacy no doubt presenting a significant obstacle; nonetheless, he is the second most popular practitioner in contemporary Tiger Springs.

In 1969, he was joined by Dr. Ming, then in his 40s, who was a doctor trained in Western medicine from the Lijiang County Hospital. Dr. Ming was "sent down" to Tiger Springs Brigade to "learn from the peasants" for the duration of the Cultural Revolution since he had a (family) "history problem" (i.e., his family had a bad class label), and since Tiger Springs was, in fact, his "native village." He is no longer in Tiger Springs, since he

TABLE 1 _____

Tiger Springs Medical Practitioners prior to, during, and after Cooperative Medicine

PRE-COOPERATIVE MEDICINE

The first Tiger Springs clinic was set up in 1956 by He Zhi-ming (a Chinese medicine practitioner). He was joined by Yang Ru-jin in 1957 (who studied Western medicine in the PLA). Together they practiced "Chinese medicine and Western medicine united." In 1958, the clinic was redesignated as a "Health Protection Office."

TIGER SPRINGS BRIGADE COOPERATIVE MEDICINE CLINIC (1969–1983)

"True" cooperative medicine (i.e., 1.5 yuan per year/ 0.05 yuan per visit per brigade member) lasted only for the first three years; cooperative medicine persisted through 1983, supplemented by the brigade workpoint system, but at a higher fee per visit cost.

There were six main practitioners:

Dr. Shi: Brigade-designated barefoot doctor from Tiger Springs who had previous PLA training in Western medicine, but consistently refers to himself as a practitioner of integrated Chinese and Western medicine; he was 22 in 1969, and was responsible for organizing cooperative medicine for the brigade.

Dr. Ming: Doctor trained in Western medicine from Lijiang County Hospital, "sent down" to Tiger Springs for the duration of the Cultural Revolution; Naxi, originally from Tiger Springs; he was in his early 40's in 1969.

Dr. He: Chinese medicine practitioner, with specialties in bone setting and gynecological problems; Naxi from Tiger Springs; he was 48 in 1969.

Li Hong: Trained as a barefoot doctor to practice integrated medicine; began as a clinic accountant in 1972; Naxi from Tiger Springs; he was in his early 20's in 1969.

Mu Ru-yi: Originally head midwife, but left Tiger Springs in the mid-1970's; Naxi from Tiger Springs; she was in her early 30's in 1969.

Lu Xiao-yan: Studied midwifery with Mu Ru-yi in the early 1970's; Han originally from Tenchong (she married into Tiger Springs); in her early 20's when she began to study/practice.

A variety of other midwives and "hygiene workers" who also practiced in the clinic on a periodic and temporary basis.

TIGER SPRINGS INDEPENDENT PRACTITIONERS IN THE POST-MAO ERA (SINCE 1983)

Cooperative medicine was officially dismantled in 1983 in Tiger Springs, at the same time as decollectivization occurred. All practitioners have been designated as "village doctors," and all now practice medicine out of their own homes. Testing for professional licensing in either Western medicine or Chinese medicine began to be encouraged in 1978, and was required by 1982/83. Not passing the exam did not disallow practitioners from continuing to practice, but village level public health bureau representatives were selected from among those practitioners who have passed the certification exams.

There are currently six main practitioners:

Dr. Shi: Integrated medicine; did not pass certification exam in Western medicine in 1983; is the second most popular practitioner in Tiger Springs; he was 43 in 1990.

Dr. He: Chinese medicine; did not pass certification exam in Chinese medicine in 1983; is still popular as a practitioner and is teaching his secret remedies to his nephew, Dr. Shi; he was 69 in 1990.

Li Hong: Hygiene and Preventative Health Station representative for Tiger Springs, and responsible for all vaccines for the administrative village since 1989; receives 20 yuan per month as a stipend for this service; shared Prevention Station work and stipend with Dr. Shi and Dr. Wang from 1984–1989; passed Western medicine certification exam in 1982, but does not treat patients; in his mid-40's in 1990.

Dr. Wang: Integrated medicine; passed certification exam in Chinese medicine in 1978; began to practice openly in 1986 (formerly banned from participation in cooperative medicine due to bad family background); most popular

practitioner in Tiger Springs; Naxi from Tiger Springs; he was 51 in 1990.

Lu Xiao-yan: Tiger Springs midwife and Women's and Children's Health Protection Station representative; receives a stipend of 20 yuan per month for these services; passed the certification exam in Western medicine in 1983; she was age 43 in 1990.

Mu Xiang-hua: Birth planning representative since 1979/80 and Women's Association representative since 1970; receives 20 yuan per month from each bureau; Naxi from Tiger Springs; she was 41 in 1990.

---

returned to the hospital as soon as the Cultural Revolution began to wind down, but he was very much respected and regarded as a valuable resource by the other members of the cooperative medicine team.

Dr. Shi was also able, in 1969, to persuade his maternal uncle, Dr. He, who was then 48, to come back to serve in Tiger Springs from a neighboring brigade's cooperative medicine clinic. Dr. He was an "old Chinese medicine doctor," who actually had been "too naughty" in his youth to complete an apprenticeship with a bonafide Chinese medicine doctor, but, after a multifaceted career, he later studied Chinese medicine on his own, and also brought a number of family-inherited (from his mother and maternal grandfather) secret herbal remedies with him to the clinic. His particular specialties were in bone setting and gynecological problems. By his account, he "only studied a little bit of Western medicine." Although he took the certification examination in Chinese medicine in 1983, he did not pass it (as in the case of his nephew, Dr. He's very basic literacy was an obstacle); nonetheless he is still popular as a practitioner and is passing on his secret remedies to his nephew, Dr. Shi. He was 69 in 1990.

Li Hong was a young man in his early 20s from Tiger Springs who became the "accountant" for the clinic in 1972, gradually studied medicine on his own, and later was officially "chosen by the people" as a barefoot doctor. He describes the medicine that he practices as integrated medicine. Although he passed the Western medicine certifi-

cation exam in 1983, he no longer treats patients; rather, he has become the Hygiene and Preventive Health Station representative for Tiger Springs, a service for which he receives 20 yuan per month as a stipend. While he shared the Hygiene and Preventive Health Station work and stipend with Dr. Shi and Dr. Wang (see below) from 1984–1989, he has been designated as the sole practitioner responsible for all vaccines for the village since 1989. He was in his mid-40s in 1990.

Mu Ru-yi, a woman who was in her early 30s in 1969, initially was the only woman on the team. She took on the midwifery work for several years, though she eventually left the Lijiang basin in the mid-1970s. Lu Xiao-yan, who is still practicing in the village, was in her early 20s when she began to study midwifery skills with Mu Ru-yi as a health aide in the early 1970s. She eventually took over Mu Ru-yi's duties, and is currently in charge of midwifery for Tiger Springs. She is actually Han and not Naxi, since she is from Tenchong (in southwestern Yunnan) and married into the village. She had a fifth-grade primary school education, having had to quit school because of "family difficulties." She passed the Western medicine examination in 1983, and is the designated Women's and Children's Health Protection Station representative for Tiger Springs; she receives a stipend of 20 yuan per month for these services. She was age 43 in 1990.

Additionally, during cooperative medicine, there were eighteen health aides, one nominated by each of the production teams which made up

the brigade. Seventeen of these were female, and their task was to study both midwifery (with the staff midwife), and to help around the clinic with giving injections and filling medical prescriptions. Two of these health aides would serve at the clinic during any given month. Essentially all of the young women who had been trained as health aides had married out of the village (with the exception of Lu Xiao-yan, who had of course married into the village).

During the first three years of cooperative medicine (1969–1972) in Tiger Springs, classes for all members of the clinic staff were set up on Monday and Saturday evenings. All doctors aimed to practice integrated medicine, whatever their respective specializations. There were always two doctors on staff during each of the morning and afternoon shifts. All three of the male doctors (Shi, He, and Ming—later replaced by Li) would carry out the vaccination work in the brigade school, and set up times for each production team to come in. On average, there were more than one hundred patients per day during the first three years of the clinic, while "true" cooperative medicine lasted.

While the brigade-based organizational structure of cooperative medicine essentially dissolved with post-Mao era decollectivization, as mentioned above, the practitioners for the most part remain the same, as does the epistemology of the integrated medicine which they practice. The only contemporary Tiger Springs health practitioner who did not practice as part of cooperative medicine is Dr. Wang, who is not the most popular practitioner in the village. He had completed his lower middle school education (equivalent to ninth-grade level) with high scores at the best school in the prefecture, but had been barred from continuing on to senior middle school by his "bad" family background (i.e., his father was labeled as a "rich peasant"). His bad class label had also prevented him from practicing medicine during collectivization, but he had studied both Chinese and Western medicine on his own since he was 17 (i.e., since 1975). He began

formal study of medicine in the late 1970s through correspondence courses, passed the certification examination in Chinese medicine in 1978, and began to practice medicine openly in 1986. Although he only officially began to practice after the dismantling of cooperative medicine, he very much considers the form of medicine he practices to be integrated medicine. He also includes as part of his repertoire a number of "secret herbal remedies" passed down through his family from his great-grandfather. He was 51 in 1990.

Mu Xiang-hua is not exactly a health practitioner in contemporary Tiger Springs, but she has been the Birth Planning representative since 1979–1980 and the Women's Association representative since 1970. She receives 20 yuan per month from each bureau. She has garnered quite a reputation for enforcing a two-child policy in the village, and also for setting up a kindergarten for village children in her home. She was 41 in 1990.

There was clearly a gendered division of labor in the Tiger Springs cooperative medicine clinic which was reflected throughout the other clinics in the basin. With a few exceptions, women took on the tasks of midwifery, gynecological problems, and being nurses; primarily men took on the healing tasks and inevitably became the "doctors" (as reflected in terms of address). This division of labor reflected both the pre-1949 pattern of male Chinese medicine doctors and female midwives, and is reflected in the post-Mao public health division of labor in the villages between the male Hygiene and Preventive Health Station representatives and female Women's and Children's Health Protection Station representatives (see White 1993 for more details).

Regardless of how "revolutionary" the particular village, the situation since the decollectivization in most of the basin villages with respect to cooperative medicine parallels that of Tiger Springs. Village practitioners may get together once or twice a year to help out with vaccinations for their village. The former brigade clinic may be main-

tained for these functions or in order for one or two practitioners to use the facility. Nevertheless, virtually all practitioners are practicing privately, and most of them are practicing out of their own homes. Aside from the meager stipends from the county public health bureau, and the vaccination program, there is no outside financial support.

CONCLUSIONS

This article addresses several key issues. The first is regarding the financing of rural health care, which will continue to be a critical issue for the residents of the rural PRC. Clearly, cooperative medicine, which was a solution for some peasants but not for others, is not a feasible option in the post-Mao era. Despite decollectivization, the preventive and primary care aspects of rural health remain more or less in place, and are, to a degree, subsidized and maintained by the state; they are, however, no longer subsidized by the collectives. With respect to secondary and tertiary care interventions, villagers unquestionably bear the brunt of medical costs (unlike their usually urban compatriots who have state work unit positions), but this was also true, albeit to varying degrees and in some cases on a more indirect basis, for most brigades during collectivization. The forte of rural health care since the Maoist period has always been preventive and primary care medicine. For access to secondary and tertiary interventions, villagers must rely primarily on themselves, their relatives, and other friends for support.

Moves towards collective, prepaid health insurance schemes have been documented in the recent scholarly literature for some rural areas of the PRC. As has also been documented, however, these are primarily in more prosperous rather than poorer villages. It is clear that the central government needs to play a role in supporting a national health care "safety net," and that the doctrine of "self-reliance" which has always been preached to village residents in the PRC is not going to be sufficient to protect the access of poorer and even mid-level income peasants from the ever-increasing costs of secondary and tertiary care in the contemporary PRC.

With respect to the professionalization issue, despite Public Health Bureau moves towards professionalization of "village doctors," whether or not they are certified has a minimal effect on the village doctors who are still practicing in the Lijiang basin; additionally, the epistemological foundation of their therapeutic practice continues to be the Cultural Revolution formulated integrated Chinese and Western medicine. The vast majority of current practitioners in the Lijiang basin were part of cooperative medicine clinics and were trained under the legacy of integrated medicine. It is likely that most future village practitioners will be the sons and sometimes daughters of current practitioners, who will have studied with their parents and perhaps been exposed to six months or more of an outside training course (probably in Western medicine) at the prefectural Hygiene School or at a Dayanzhen hospital. It is also likely that the practices of these family inheritors will be informed by the legacy of integrated medicine.

In seeking to understand why cooperative medicine and the barefoot doctors so captured the imagination of Western scholars, it is critical to acknowledge the profound significance and relative success of rural health care in socialist China. Establishing a rural health care infrastructure in the PRC was clearly one of the great achievements of the Maoist leadership. It is also important to acknowledge the efforts of the post-Mao leadership to keep that infrastructure in place, at least with respect to preventive and primary care aspects of health care. The key issue confronting the contemporary leadership is how to resolve the dilemma of rural residents being denied access to secondary and tertiary health care in urban clinics and hospitals unless they can pay for it up front. What scholars of this issue need to realize is that cooperative medicine did not completely resolve this issue for many villagers either.

Finally, it is critical to examine the relationship between a public health approach and a health care approach to addressing the long-term issues of villager well-being in the rural PRC.[11] The PRC government has kept a clear priority on vaccination programs (which at least in the Lijiang basin were vigilantly maintained), but has not, to my mind, continued to sufficiently prioritize other preventive care priorities, such as sanitation and other environmental health issues, maternal and child health issues, women's health issues (e.g., Wong *et al.* 1995), and health (and general) education issues. While issues of unequal access to health care loom large as a spectre which needs to be contended with in a country which is rapidly differentiating itself into classes of haves and have-nots, so do fundamental issues in public health and their integral relationship to other dimensions of the political-economy need to be attended to.

NOTES

1. Key contributors to this "first wave" include (though are not limited to) Horn, 1969, 1972, 1976; V. W. Sidel 1972a, 1972b; Sidel and Sidel 1973, 1977; Pickowicz 1973; Rifkin 1973, 1978; Wegman, Lin, and Purcell, eds. 1973; Lampton 1974, 1977; Hsu 1974; P. K.-M. New 1974a, 1974b; New and New 1975, 1977, 1978; Li 1975; Wang 1975; P. C. Chen 1976; Chabot 1976; and Mechanic and Kleinman 1978.

2. Key contributors to this "second wave" include (though, again, are not limited to) Rosenthal and Ponger 1980; Blendon 1981; Lampton 1981; P.-C. Chen 1981; Wegman 1982; Hinman *et al.* 1982; V. W. Sidel 1982; Sidel and Sidel 1982; Henderson and Cohen 1982, 1984; Rosenthal and Greiner 1982; Hsiao 1984; Jamison *et al.* 1984; New and Cheung 1984; Koplan *et al.* 1985; and New 1986.

3. Contributors to this discussion since the late 1980s include C. C. Chen 1989; Yang, Lin, and Lawson 1991; The World Bank 1992; Chen, Hu, and Lin 1993; Gu *et al.* 1993; Henderson, Akin, *et al.* 1994; Henderson, Jin *et al.* 1995; Hsiao 1995; Liu *et al.* 1995; Feng *et al.* 1995; Wong *et al.* 1995; Hsiao and Liu 1995; Bloom and Gu 1977.

4. Notable exceptions include the fieldwork-based work of Jack and Salamith Potter (1990), who wrote about cooperative medicine in Zengbu Village in Guangdong Province from 1979 through the early 1980s, and of Shu-min Huang (1988), who has written about Maoist and post-Mao transformations in rural health care based on his research in Lin Village on Xiamen island in Fujian Province in 1984–1985.

5. My data for the six Tiger Springs practitioners interviewed includes intensive half-day initial interviews, and repeated clinical observations. My data for each of the remaining seventeen Lijiang basin village practitioners are based on a full day of alternate interviewing and clinical observation. My data for county and prefectural public health bureau interviews are also based on a combination of intensive informational interviews with members of the respective units and observations where possible. I also interviewed a number of town-based practitioners as part of my research.

6. One Tiger Springs village practitioner jokingly made an analogy between the excesses of eating indulged in by villagers ("chi da guo fan," or "eating the state's rice") at the beginning of the Great Leap Forward (1959–1961), and the excesses of medicine utilization indulged in by villagers at the inception of cooperative medicine ("chi do guo yao," or "eating the state's medicine").

7. See Farquhar (1994) for a detailed discussion of this principle.

8. I have addressed the epistemology and practice of integrated medicine in extensive detail elsewhere (see White 1993).

9. Yunnan is especially renowned for its herbal medicine.

10. Again, please see White (1993) for much more detailed discussion of the rural practice of integrated medicine.

11. Thanks to one of the anonymous reviewers for pointing out the significance of this issue vis-à-vis recent developments in the PRC.

REFERENCES CITED

Blendon, Robert J.
1981. Public Health versus Personal Medical Care: The Dilemma of Post-Mao China. *New England Journal of Medicine* 304(16):981–982.

Bloom, Gerald and Gu Xingyuan
1997. Health Sector Reform: Lessons from China. *Social Science and Medicine* 45(3):351–360.

Chabot, H. T. J.
1976. The Chinese System of Health Care: An Inquiry into Public Health in the People's Republic of China. *Tropical and Geographical Medicine* (Supplement) 28:S87–S134.

Chen, C. C., in collaboration with Frederica M. Bunge
1989. *Medicine in Rural China: A Personal Account.* Berkeley: University of California Press.

Chen, Pi-Chao
1976. *Population and Health Policy in the People's Republic of China.* Washington, D.C.: Interdisciplinary Communications Program, Smithsonian Institution, Occasional Monograph Series No. 9.
1981. *Rural Health and Birth Planning in China.* International Fertility Research Program. Research Triangle Park, North Carolina.

Chen, Xiao-ming, Teh-wei Hu, and Zihua Lin
1993. The Rise and Decline of the Cooperative Medical System in Rural China. *International Journal of Health Services* 23(4):731–742.

Farquhar, Judith
1994. *Knowing Practice: The Clinical Encounter of Chinese Medicine.* Boulder: Westview Press.

Feng Xueshan, Tang Shenglan, Gerald Bloom, Malcolm Segall, and Gu Xingyuan
1995. Cooperative Medical Schemes in Contemporary Rural China. *Social Science and Medicine* 41(8): 1111–1118.

Gu Xingyuan, Gerald Bloom, Tang Shenglan, Zhu Yingya, Zhou Shouqi, and Chen Xingbao
1993. Financing Health Care in Rural China: Preliminary Report of a Nationwide Study. *Social Science and Medicine* 36(4):385–391.

Henderson, Gail, John Akin, Li Zhiming, Jin Shuigao, Ma Haijiang, and Ge Keyou
1994. Equity and the Utilization of Health Services: Report of an Eight-Province Survey in China. *Social Science and Medicine* 39(5):687–699.

Henderson, Gail, Jin Shuigao, John Akin, Li Zhiming, Wang Jianmin, Ma Haijiang, He Yunan, Zhang Xiping, Chang Ying, and Ge Keyou
1995. Distribution of Medical Insurance in China. *Social Science and Medicine* 41(8):1119–1130.

Henderson, Gail E. and Myron S. Cohen
1982. Health Care in the People's Republic of China: A View from Inside the System. *American Journal of Public Health* 72(11):1238–1245.
1984. *The Chinese Hospital: A Socialist Work Unit.* New Haven: Yale University Press.

Hinman, Alan R., Robert L. Parker, Gu Xue-qi, Gu Xingyuan, Ye Xifu, and Huang De-yu, eds.
1982. Health Services in Shanghai County. *American Journal of Public Health* (Supplement)72.

Horn, Joshua S.
1969. *Away with All Pests: An English Surgeon in People's China, 1954–1969.* London: Monthly Review Press.
1972. Building a Rural Health Service in the People's Republic of China. *International Journal of Health Services* 2(3):377–383.
1976. *Health Care in China.* Anglo-Chinese Educational Institute, Modern China Series No. 8, London.

Hsiao, William C. L.
1984. Transformation of Health Care in China. *The New England Journal of Medicine* 310(14):932–936.
1995. The Chinese Health Care System: Lessons for Other Nations: *Social Science and Medicine* 41(8):1047–1055.

Hsiao, William C. L. and Yuanli Liu
1996. Economic Reform and Health—Lessons from China. *The New England Journal of Medicine* 335(6):430–431.

Hsu, Robert C.
1974. The Barefoot Doctor of the People's Republic of China—Some Problems. *The New England Journal of Medicine* 29(3):124–127.

Huang, Shu-Min
1988. Transforming China's Collective Health Care System: A Village Study. *Social Science and Medicine* 27(9):879–888.

Jamison, Dean T., John R. Evans, Timothy King, Ian Porter, Nicholas Prescott, and Andre Prost
1984. *China: the Health Sector.* The World Bank, Washington, D.C.

Koplan, Jeffrey P., Alan R. Hinman, Robert L. Parker, Gong You-Long, and Yang Ming-Ding
1985. The Barefoot Doctor: Shanghai County Revisited. *American Journal of Public Health* 75(7): 768–770.

Lampton, David M.
1974. *Health, Conflict and the Chinese Political System.* Center for Chinese Studies, University of Michigan, Ann Arbor.
1977. *The Politics of Medicine in China: The Policy Process, 1949–1977.* Boulder: Westview Press.
1981. Changing Health Policy in the Post-Mao Era. *Yale Journal of Biology and Medicine* 54:21–26.

Li, Victor H.
1975. Politics and Health Care in China: The Barefoot Doctors. *Stanford Law Review* 27:827–840.

Liu, Yuanli, William C. L. Hsiao, Qing Li, Xingzhu Liu, and Minghui Ren
1995. Transformation of China's Rural Health Care Financing. *Social Science and Medicine* 41(8): 1085–1093.

Mechanic, David and Arthur Kleinman
1978. *The Organization, Delivery and Financing of Rural Care in the People's Republic of China.* Research and Analytic Report Series No. 10, University of Wisconsin, Madison.

New, Peter Kong-Ming
1974a. Barefoot Doctors and Health Care in the People's Republic of China. *Ekistics* 38(226):220–224.

1974b. Barefoot Doctors and Health Care in China. *Eastern Horizon* 13(3):7–19.

1986. Primary Health Care in the People's Republic of China: A March Backward? *Human Organization* 45(2):147–153.

New, Peter Kong-Ming and Yuet Wah Cheung
1984. The Evolution of Health Care in China: A Backward Look into the Future. *Medical Anthropology* 18:170–179.

New, Peter Kong-Ming and Mary Louie New
1975. The Links between Health and the Political Structure in New China. *Human Organization* 34(3): 237–251.

1977. Barefoot Doctors in China: Healers for All Seasons. In *Culture, Disease and Healing: Studies in Medical Anthropology,* David Landy, ed. Pp. 503–510. New York: Macmillan Co.

1978. Reflections on Health Care in China: Lessons for the West. *Comparative Medicine East and West* VI(I):15–22.

Pickowicz, Paul G.
1973. Barefoot Doctors in China: People, politics, and paramedicine. In *Modern China and Traditional Chinese Medicine,* G. B. Risse, ed. Springfield, IL: Charles C. Thomas.

Potter, Salamith Heins and Jack M. Potter
1990. *China's Peasants: The Anthropology of a Revolution.* Cambridge: Cambridge University Press.

Rifkin, Susan B.
1973. Health Care for Rural Areas. In *Medicine and Public Health in the People's Republic of China,* J. R. Quinn, ed. Pp. 137–150. U.S. Department of Health, Education, and Welfare Publ. No. (NIH) 72-67, John E. Fogerty International Center for Advanced Study in the Health Sciences, National Institutes of Health, Bethesda, MD.

1978. Politics of Barefoot Medicine. *The Lancet,* January 7, 1978:34.

Rosenthal, Marilyn M. and Jay R. Greiner
1982. The Barefoot Doctors of China: From Political Creation to Professionalism. *Human Organization* 41(4):330–341.

Rosenthal, Marilyn M. and Paul Ponger
1980. *Rural Health Care Delivery in the People's Republic of China: An Update.* Unpublished manuscript. University of Michigan, Dearborn.

Sidel, Victor W.
1972a. The Barefoot Doctors of the People's Republic of China. *The New England Journal of Medicine* 286(24):1292–1300.

1972b. Some observations on the Organization of Health Care in the People's Republic of China. *International Journal of Health Services* 2(3):385–395.

1982. Medical Care in China: Equity vs. Modernization. *American Journal of Public Health* 72(11):1224–1226.

Sidel, Victor W. and Ruth Sidel
1973. *Serve the People: Observations on Medicine in the People's Republic of China.* New York: Josiah Macy Jr. Foundation.

1977. Primary Health Care in Relationship to Socio-Political Structure. *Social Science and Medicine* 11:415–419.

1982. *The Health of China.* Boston: Beacon.

Wang, Virginia Li
1975. Training of the Barefoot Doctor in the People's Republic of China. *International Journal of Health Services* 5(3):475–488.

Wegman, Myron E.
1982. Public Health in China. *American Journal of Public Health* 72(9):978–979.

Wegman, Myron E., Tsung-yi Lin, and Elizabeth F. Parcell, eds.
1973. *Public Health in the People's Republic of China.* New York: Josiah Macy, Jr. Foundation.

White, Sydney D.
1993. *Medical Discourses, Naxi Identities, and the State: Transformations in Socialist China.* Ph.D. dissertation. University of California, Berkeley.

Wong, Glenn C., Virginia C. Li, Mary Ann Burris, and Yueping Xiang
1995.   Seeking Women's Voices: Setting the Context for Women's Health Intervention in Two Rural Counties in Yunnan, China. *Social Science and Medicine* 41(8):1147–1157.
World Bank, The
1992.   *China: Long-Term Issues and Options in the Health Transition.* Washington, D.C.

Yang, Pei-Lin, Vivian Lin, and James Lawson
1991.   Health Policy Reform in the People's Republic of China. *International Journal of Health Services* 21(3):481–491.

CHAPTER 9

NURSING

The nursing profession worldwide continues to suffer from a identity crisis. On the one hand, nurses are considered professionals within the health care community. On the other hand, nurses' relationship with doctors resembles a paternalistic family relationship in which the male doctor dictates to the female nurse what will be done and how. Factors accounting for the existence of this dual identity are endemic to the institutional structures within which most nurses today are employed. Although many nursing programs have attempted to improve the status of nurses vis-à-vis physicians, considerable efforts remain.

The common thread running through the articles in this chapter is the topic of socialization to the profession of nursing. In the first article, Diane M. Eddy and her colleagues examine the differences in occupational values held by professionals in the field of nursing and students enrolled in nursing programs. Surveying students and nursing faculty, the authors report that value scores of faculty were higher than student value scores and that faculty and students differed in what they valued. For example, according to the authors, nursing faculty valued freedom, equality, and human dignity more than nursing students did, and nursing students valued esthetics more than nursing faculty did. The authors conclude that student values are a reflection of socialization into the profession and that further research is needed to identify factors associated with values development in nurses.

In the second article, Linda Reutter and her colleagues discuss the socialization of nursing students in Canada. They utilize the sociological theories of structural functionalism and interac-

tionism, and they relate the consequences associated with each perspective to socialization. For example, the functionalist approach addresses issues such as shared norms and values that are internalized through a process of socialization, and interactionism argues that meaning is acquired through interaction with others. The authors provide an analysis of the socialization process as students progress from year one to year four of nursing school. The findings from their research support others who argue that nursing students internalize faculty values. In addition, nursing students internalize the requirements necessary for the world of clinical practice. Thus, the authors conclude that nursing students experience two distinct processes that socialize them to the student role as well as to the nursing role.

In the third article, Patricia AbuGharbieh and Wafika Suliman discuss socialization to the nursing role in Jordan. In much the same way that nurses are socialized in the developed world (because of the emphasis on Western medicine in Jordan), nurses in Jordan face similar but increased obstacles because of traditional role expectations ascribed to women. Like nurses in other countries, nurses in Jordan are socialized through formal education as well as in the work setting. The nursing program in Jordan, however, lacks clarity, as does much of the clinical setting, although the relationship between nurse and physician is clearly defined. The socialization process is also hampered by the lack of role models and the fact that students who enter nursing in Jordan are rarely the most intellectually gifted, because nursing is a relatively low-status position within the academic

community. Given the difficulties associated with socialization to the nursing profession, efforts continue to enhance the role of nurses in Jordan. The authors offer a number of points they believe address the need for more effective enactment of the nursing role.

The articles in Chapter 9 articulate a growing dilemma for the nursing profession. On the one hand, the need for nurses grows as the medical field attempts to lessen its need for physicians and transfer an increasing amount of work to nursing staff. On the other hand, nursing itself faces the possibility of deprofessionalization, which would inhibit nurses' efforts to lobby for increased recognition and support.

AMERICAN PERSPECTIVE

IMPORTANCE OF PROFESSIONAL NURSING VALUES: A NATIONAL STUDY OF BACCALAUREATE PROGRAMS

DIANE M. EDDY, VICTORIA ELFRINK, DARLENE WEIS, AND MARY JANE SCHANK

INTRODUCTION

Professional values are standards for action that are accepted by the practitioner and/or professional group and provide a framework for evaluating beliefs and attitudes that influence behavior. According to Raths, Harmin, and Simon (1966) and Kratwohl, Bloom, and Masia (1964), values are learned; they arise from personal experiences, they form a basis for behavior, and they are evidenced in a consistent behavior pattern. Values are important in the delivery of nursing care because nurses repeatedly face the need to make decisions about value-laden practice dilemmas (Benner, 1985).

Students enter nursing programs with values that are modified and expanded through the educational process to help them make decisions consistent with professional norms (AACN, 1986). Nurse educators can facilitate this process in two ways: (a) by exhibiting their commitment to professional values through role modeling behaviors related to those values; and (b) by systematically providing other value development opportunities that serve to socialize nursing students to the profession. Faculty socialization about professional values is important to the development of the neophyte nurse because values that are operational in the bureaucratic health care system are often at variance with professional nursing values (Benner, 1985).

Little research has been done on professional nursing values; a few studies, however, suggest that values education experiences are planned informally and included randomly in nursing curricula (Aroskar, 1976; Elfrink & Lutz, 1991; Uustal, 1983). Findings from these studies also suggest that educational experiences in the baccalaureate curricula may not be sufficient to prepare students to resolve value-laden conflicts (Elfrink, 1989). Nurse educators have a responsibility to prepare students to be moral decision makers and may perceive that they are promoting professional values development when, in fact, they are not. Questions have been raised as to whether students actually acquire the values espoused by the profession by the end of their formal education. Similarly, there is concern about how students rate the importance of these values as compared to their faculty.

This study was designed to determine if there were different perceptions of the importance of professional nursing values between undergraduate baccalaureate senior nursing students and their faculty. The American Association of Colleges of Nursing (AACN, 1986) *Essentials of College and University Education for Professional Nursing* (hereafter referred to as the *Essentials Report*) identified seven essential values (altruism, equality, esthetics, truth, freedom, human dignity, and justice) as fundamental to baccalaureate nursing education. This report provided the operational framework for the study because of its seminal importance to baccalaureate education.

LITERATURE REVIEW

The research to date on professional values development in nursing has focused on (a) measuring the importance of specific values among and between various nursing populations, and (b) examining the influence of specific formal courses of study on values development. These investigations generated knowledge about whether current educational processes facilitated professional values development.

Recent studies have used the values identified in the *Essentials Report* as a basis for constructing instruments to measure beliefs about the importance of professional values. Thurston, Flood, Shupe, and Gerald (1989), for example, constructed an instrument using the attitudes and personal qualities identified for each of the seven essential values. Fifty-three faculty members from one baccalaureate program were asked to identify the importance of each attitude or quality and also to rank the three most important attitudes or qualities. Human dignity and altruism were ranked more highly than the other qualities. Thurson et al. also compared the same faculty group's rankings on Rokeach's (1973) Personal Life Values Survey with data from an earlier study of entering nursing students. Values were ranked similarly by faculty

and students, indicating that entering students are more alike in their values than different from the faculty who teach them.

The Professional Nursing Behavior Instrument (PNB) developed by Eddy (1989) used the nursing role behaviors identified in the *Essentials Report* as exemplars of the seven essential values. Junior and senior nursing students and nursing faculty from 12 baccalaureate programs in one state were asked to indicate the importance of these behaviors in professional nursing care. Significant differences were found in the value scores: male students ranked freedom, human dignity, and truth as less important than female faculty, and female students ranked freedom as less important than faculty. Value scores of junior and senior nursing students did not differ significantly.

Some research suggests that type of educational institution and/or specific courses might be associated with nursing students' values and their moral development or judgment. Bloomquist, Cruise, and Cruise (1980), for example, used Rokeach's (1973) Personal Life Value Survey to determine whether values held by nursing students in secular and nonsecular schools changed during their education. The findings indicated that some form of values development does occur in nursing programs. Senior nursing students in both secular and nonsecular schools ranked independence and imagination higher than did freshmen in both types of programs, while students in religious-based schools valued obedience more highly than did students in secular schools.

The values of senior nursing students from one public and one private baccalaureate program and graduates of these programs who had been practicing one and five years were compared by Schank and Weis (1989). Subjects identified the professional values they used most often in daily nursing practice. Students most frequently identified "respect for human dignity" (80%) while graduates of both one and five years identified "responsibility and accountability" (92%). No significant differ-

ences, however, were found in the values identified by students or graduates from the secular and nonsecular programs.

Although the subject of values is often included in ethics, theology, and philosophy courses (Earley, Mentowski, & Shafer, 1980; Uustal, 1983), no studies have examined the influence of these courses on students' development of professional values. However, several studies that looked at the influence of ethics courses on moral reasoning or moral development found that students who had such courses did not differ significantly from other students on moral judgment (Beardsley, 1983) or moral reasoning (Gaul, 1987; Kellmer, 1985).

Thus, while significant differences have been found in some professional values held by baccalaureate nursing faculty and students, affiliation with a secular or nonsecular institution does not seem to influence these professional values. Ethics courses have not been found to influence moral reasoning or moral judgment in nursing students, although no studies have examined whether specific courses influenced students' professional values.

STUDY

Method

This study was designed to answer the following questions:

1. Are there significant differences in the professional values of baccalaureate nurse educators and senior nursing students?
2. Are there significant differences in their values depending on employment or enrollment in public or private institutions?
3. Are there significant differences in the values of senior nursing students who have and have not had courses in theology, philosophy, or ethics?
4. Are there any variables or combinations of variables that account for a significant amount of variance in the total professional value scores of students or faculty?

Sample

A cluster sampling procedure was performed using successive random drawings for NLN-accredited baccalaureate programs in private and public institutions in four regions of the country (northeast, northwest, southwest, and southeast). Because each school in the region had an equal chance for inclusion in the study, the sample was determined to be representative of the population of nurse educators and senior baccalaureate nursing students in the United States, when each sample size approached 300 (Krijcie & Morgan, 1970; Polit & Hungler, 1983).

Deans or program directors from 10 public and 16 private baccalaureate nursing programs were contacted by telephone and asked for assistance in distributing the research instruments to senior nursing students and faculty members. The materials subsequently were mailed with directions for administering and returning the completed forms.

There were 1,150 instruments distributed to students, of which 656 were returned for a 57% response rate; 646 were usable. Of the 495 instruments distributed to faculty, 350 were returned for a 70% response rate, and 312 were usable.

The mean age of students was 26.4 years, and the mean age of faculty was 43.8 years. The mean number of years of nursing practice for faculty prior to teaching was 8.8, and the mean number of years of teaching experience for faculty was 10.2. The sample was divided in several other demographic categories, which are noted in Tables 1 and 2.

Instrument

The Professional Nursing Behaviors (PNB) instrument (Eddy, 1989) was used to obtain a professional values score for each subject. The PNB contains behaviors identified in the *Essentials Report* as exemplars of each value essential to professional nursing. Subjects were asked to indicate

TABLE 1 Senior Baccalaureate Student Profile

CHARACTERISTICS	N	%
Sex		
Female	590	90.4
Male	46	7.0
Ethnic Group		
Caucasian	591	91.0
African American	11	1.7
Hispanic	5	0.8
Asian	39	6.9
Marital Status		
Single	415	65.2
Married	103	16.1
Widowed	1	0.1
Divorced/Separated	27	4.2
Student Status		
Generic	463	70.9
Second Degree	73	11.2
RN	92	17.3
LPN	21	0.03
Type of Institution		
Public	308	48.4
Private	338	51.6

Note: Discrepancy in numbers is due to missing data.

TABLE 2 Faculty Profile

CHARACTERISTICS	N	%
Sex		
Female	306	95.0
Male	11	3.4
Ethnic Group		
Caucasian	308	96.0
African American	5	1.6
Hispanic	2	0.6
Asian	5	1.6
Native American	1	0.3
Marital Status		
Married	228	70.0
Single	57	17.7
Widowed	7	2.2
Divorce/Separated	27	8.4
Highest Degree		
Doctorate in Nursing	36	11.2
Nonnursing Doctorate	52	16.1
Master's in Nursing	207	64.3
Nonnursing Master's	16	5.0
Bachelor's	7	2.2
Type of Institution		
Public	175	
Private	147	

Note: Discrepancy in numbers is due to missing data.

on a 6-point Likert scale the importance of these behaviors in the roles assumed by the professional nurse (from 1 = very unimportant to 6 = very important).

In Eddy's refinement of the PNB (1990), behavioral descriptions from the *Essentials Report* were modified slightly for clarity and tested for reliability. Cronbach's alpha was .89 for the total instrument; alphas for subscales ranged from .45 to .72. The alphas for the values subscales were considered acceptable given the limited number of behaviors in each subscale (Minium, 1978).

The behaviors on the PNB instrument were also classified according to the three major roles of graduates of baccalaureate nursing programs, identified in the *Essentials Report:* provider of care, coordinator of care, and member of a profession. A panel of experts reviewed the behavioral exemplars and determined that a relationship existed between these three roles and the behavioral exemplars. Thus, these three categories served as role subscales. To test this categorization, Cronbach's alpha was calculated on the three role categories (patient = .66; system = .72; profession = .83). The instrument also requested information about participants' institutional affiliation; whether they had had courses in ethics, theology, or philosophy; and other demographic data such as age, sex, etc.

Data Analysis

Paired dependent *t* tests were used to answer the first and third research questions. Using the institution as a unit of analysis, the means of the value scores of students and faculty were compared. Dependent *t* tests were chosen to reduce standard error and minimize the possibility of extreme scores influencing the findings (Minium, 1978). Multiple regression statistics were used to answer the second and fourth research questions.

In order to understand the relationship between formal course work and students' professional value scores, a multiple regression was calculated using the value scores of students as the dependent variable and the completion of theology, philosophy, and/or ethics courses as the predictor variables. The professional value score was also used as a dependent variable in regression analyses of selected demographic variables for students and faculty. The .05 level of significance was used.

Findings

The value scores of faculty were significantly higher than those of students ($p < .045$) (Table 3). Faculty rated the values of freedom, equality, and human dignity higher than did students, while students rated the value of esthetics higher than did

TABLE 3   Significant Value Differences between Faculty and Senior Students

VALUE	GROUP VALUING MORE HIGHLY	*t* VALUE	*p* VALUE
Equality	Faculty	3.46	.002
Esthetics	Students	−3.47	.002
Freedom	Faculty	5.14	.000
Human Dignity	Faculty	2.58	.016
Total Value Score	Faculty	2.11	.045

faculty (Table 3). Compared to students, faculty valued nine behaviors more and three behaviors less (Tables 4 and 5). The professional value scores of senior students and faculty in public institutions did not differ significantly from scores of those in private institutions. Thus, school affiliation did not influence professional values development. In addition, students who had studied ethics, philosophy, and/or theology did not have significantly higher professional value scores than did students who had not taken these courses.

The variables of age, sex, attendance at a religious high school, and previous allied health experience did not account for a significant amount of variance in students' total values scores. However,

TABLE 4   Professional Behaviors Senior Students Value Significantly More Highly than Faculty

BEHAVIOR	ROLE SUBSCALE[a]	*t* VALUE	*p* VALUE
Adapts to the environment so that it is pleasing to the patient/client (Esthetics)[b]	P	3.26	.003
Creates a pleasant work environment for self and other personnel (Esthetics)[b]	S	4.44	.000
Assists other personnel in providing care (Altruism)[b]	S	5.14	.000

[a]Role Subscale: P = Patient Value (Provider of care), S = System Value (Profession/coordinator of care), PR = Professional Value (Member of profession).

[b]Value Subscale.

TABLE 5   Professional Behaviors Faculty Value More Highly than Senior Students

BEHAVIOR	ROLE SUBSCALE[a]	t VALUE	p VALUE
Expresses ideas about ways of improving nursing and health care (Equality)[b]	PR	−3.75	.001
Provides patient care based on patients'/clients' needs regardless of patient characteristics (Equality)[b]	P	−3.61	.001
Encourages open discussion of controversial issues in the nursing profession (Freedom)[b]	PR	−5.46	.000
Honors patients'/clients' right to refuse treatment (Freedom)[b]	P	−5.28	.000
Expresses concern about social trends and issues that have implications for health care (Altruism)[b]	PR	−2.90	.008
Reports incompetent, unethical, and illegal practices of health care providers objectively and factually (Justice)[b]	PR	−3.61	.001
Maintains confidentiality of patients'/clients' and staff (Human Dignity)[b]	S	−2.65	.014
Treats patients/clients, staff with respect regardless of their background (Human Dignity)[b]	PR	−3.23	.003
Obtains sufficient data to make sound judgments before reporting infractions of organizational policy (Truth)[b]	S	−2.14	.043

[a]Role Subscale: P = Patient Value (Provider of care), S = System Value (Profession/coordinator of care), PR = Professional Value (Member of profession).

[b]Value Subscale.

when examining the influence of years of clinical practice before teaching and years of teaching experience on faculty's value scores, years of teaching experience did account for a significant amount of variance. Faculty with more years of teaching experience had higher value scores ($p < .004$).

DISCUSSION

Behaviors associated with esthetics that were rated more highly by students than by faculty dealt with "adapting and creating environments that are more pleasing to patients and staff" and "assisting staff in providing care." Both behaviors correspond to common perceptions among students of the optimal work environment. Students tend to be idealistic about their employment settings and may see their ideals as more important than do faculty, who have functioned in less-than-ideal settings (Table 4).

Faculty valued freedom and the associated behaviors of "honoring patients' right to refuse treatment" and "encouraging open discussion of controversial issues in nursing" more highly than students did (Table 5). Kramer (1975) noted that even after nurses complete their basic education, they tend to focus their energies on learning basic skills and routines. Similarly, nursing students may be focusing attention primarily on the mastery of patient care skills and not considering patient advocacy issues. Some students may even consider

the patient's right to refuse treatment unethical and may not know that patients have this right.

Two behaviors associated with equality were considered more important by faculty than by students: "expressing ideas about ways to improve nursing and health care," and "providing patient care based on patients' needs regardless of patient characteristics." One possible explanation for the students' lower rating may be related to their role as learners. Students are busy learning what currently exists in nursing and may not view opinions about health care improvement as a priority. Students' lower rating of the behavior of basing care on needs regardless of patient characteristics could be explained by their limited exposure to patients with alternative lifestyles or by a lack of opportunities to learn about the unique qualities of these patients. A lack of exposure to diverse patients may also explain why behaviors associated with human dignity (for example, treats patients/clients with respect regardless of their background) were rated significantly lower by students than by faculty.

One behavior rated lower by students was "maintaining confidentiality of patients and staff." This finding may be linked to students' perception of what constitutes confidentiality. Students may think that confidentiality exists only when information about patients or staff is not shared in any context. Students often discuss patients and staff with faculty individually, in conferences, or in papers, which may seem a breach of confidentiality.

Three additional behaviors, each representing different values, were rated significantly lower by students than by faculty: "obtaining sufficient data before reporting an infraction," "expressing concern about social trends," and "reporting incompetent practices of health care providers." Students may perceive these behaviors as existing outside of their student role. Similarly, Schank and Weis (1989) found that broader social issues were not valued as highly by students or graduates as by faculty.

There were significant differences between faculty and student scores on the patient ($p < .01$)

and professional ($p < .001$) role subscales. The most significant differences were in the professional behaviors of "expressing concerns about social issues," "reporting unethical behavior," and reporting "infractions of policies." Although faculty rated all these behaviors as important parts of the professional nurse's role, students did not find these behaviors as important.

This study, like that of Schank and Weis (1989), found no significant differences in the professional values of students and graduates from public and private institutions. The study's findings differ, however, from those of Bloomquist, Cruise, and Cruise (1980), who found significant differences in the value scores of students enrolled in public (secular) and private religious schools. However, the present study examined professional values, while Bloomquist examined general life values. Differences in the findings might be explained by the fact that faculty's professional values are more similar than their personal values, and faculty teach those professional values regardless of school affiliation.

The study of theology, philosophy, or ethics had no significant effect on the professional value scores of students within this study. This finding is consistent with those of other studies (Beardsley, 1983; Gaul, 1987; Kellmer, 1985), which found that moral reasoning did not differ significantly between students who had studied ethics and those who had not. Apparently, courses outside of nursing do not significantly influence the development of professional values among nursing students.

Because students do not appear to value providing care regardless of client characteristics, the selection of patients in various clinical areas must be reconsidered. Assigning students to care for substance abusers, the chronically mentally ill homeless, and AIDS patients would expose the students to these patients' special needs. Faculty who role model sensitivity and empathy while caring for these patients can help students learn to treat them with respect regardless of their characteristics.

The lower scores on professionalism among students compared to faculty may point to a need for instructional strategies emphasizing professional role responsibilities. Nurse educators may need to consider assignments that reinforce the importance of professionalism. For example, students could be given credit for attending professional nursing meetings or be assigned to write health care legislators about their concerns regarding health care policies.

Faculty who wish to promote values development may also need to shift from the traditional teacher role of "information giver" to that of an "expert learner" (Bevis, 1988, p. 45). The expert learner promotes learning that is contextual, dialogic, and values driven. Open discussions between students and the instructor concerning value-laden issues could help students process information about values.

Faculty with less teaching experience have lower value scores. Newer faculty may stress skills and knowledge that were emphasized in their own educational programs. Values education may need more emphasis in graduate programs. Values workshops and mentoring by experienced faculty concerning teaching and evaluating the values component of professional education may be necessary for new faculty.

Further study is recommended on teaching strategies that might encourage values development. Additionally, more research is needed on instruments to measure professional nursing values. Finally, additional research must be conducted to identify other factors that might contribute to values enhancement in professional nurses.

This is the first national study of baccalaureate programs since the publication of the *Essentials Report* (AACN, 1986) that examined the beliefs held by nurse educators and their students about the importance of each of the seven essential professional values. Since significant differences were found between faculty and students on some values, nurse educators are challenged to explore activities that could enhance values development in their students. Faculty may need to consider alternatives to current teaching strategies, faculty–student role relationships, and evaluation methods as means to enhance the values component of nursing education. In this way, faculty may help to better prepare graduates to face increasingly complex value-laden situations.

REFERENCES

American Association of Colleges of Nursing. (1986). *Essentials of college and university education for professional nursing.* Washington, DC: Author.

Aroskar, M. (1976). *Attaining autonomy through curriculum planning in nursing.* Unpublished doctoral dissertation. Boston University Publications, Boston.

Beardsley, N. Q. (1983). *Survey of teaching ethics in baccalaureate programs and the investigation of the relationship between extent of ethics content and moral reasoning levels.* Unpublished doctoral dissertation. University of Colorado, Greeley.

Benner, M. P. (1985). *Value pluralism, moral competence in nursing education.* Unpublished manuscript, University of Delaware, Newark.

Bevis, E. M. (1988). New directions for a new age. In National League for Nursing, *Curriculum revolution: Mandate for change* (pp. 27–52). (NLN Publication No. 15-2224.) New York: NLN.

Bloomquist, B. L., Cruise, P. C., & Cruise, R. J. (1980). Values of baccalaureate nursing students in secular and religious schools. *Nursing Research, 29,* 379–383.

Earley, M., Mentowski, M., & Shafer, J. (1980). *Valuing at Alverno: The valuing process in liberal education.* Milwaukee, WI: Alverno Productions.

Eddy, D. M. (1989). *Men in nursing: Comparison and contrast of values and professional behaviors of male baccalaureate students and female faculty in Ohio.* Unpublished doctoral dissertation. University of Akron, Akron.

Eddy, D. M. (1990). Men in nursing: Comparison and contrast of professional values. *Journal of Midwest Nursing Research Society, 2*(1), 21–25.

Elfrink, V. L. (1989). A description of values education practices among baccalaureate nurse educators in the United States: Current and projected practices and perceptions of the AACN essential values. *Dissertation Abstracts International, 92,* 34452.

Elfrink, V. L., & Lutz, E. M. (1991). AACN essential values: National study of faculty perceptions, practices and plans. *Journal of Professional Nursing, 7,* 239–245.

Gaul, A. L. (1987). The effects of a course in nursing ethics on the relationship between ethical choice and ethical action in baccalaureate nursing students. *Journal of Nursing Education, 26,* 113–117.

Kellmer, D. M. (1985). *The teaching of ethical decision making in schools of nursing: Variables and strategies.* Unpublished doctoral dissertation. University of South Carolina, Columbia.

Kramer, M. (1975). *Reality shock: Why nurses leave nursing.* St. Louis: C. V. Mosby Co.

Kratwohl, D. R., Bloom, B. S., & Masia, B. (1964). *Taxonomy of educational objectives: Handbook II: Affective domain.* New York: David McKay Co.

Krijcie, R. V., & Morgan, D. W. (1970). Determining the sample size for research activities. *Educational and Psychological Measurement, 30,* 607–610.

Minium, E. W. (1978). *Statistical reasoning in psychology and education.* New York: John Wiley & Sons.

Polit, D. F., & Hungler, B. P. (1983). *Nursing research: Principles and methods* (pp. 411–423). Philadelphia: J. B. Lippincott.

Raths, L. E., Harmin, M., & Simon, S. (1966). *Values and teaching* (pp. 9–10). Columbus, OH: Charles E. Merrill Books, Inc.

Rokeach, M. (1973). *The nature of human values.* New York: Free Press.

Schank, M. J., & Weis, D. (1989). A study of values of baccalaureate nursing students and graduate nurses from a secular and nonsecular program. *Journal of Professional Nursing, 5,* 17–22.

Thurston, H. I., Flood, M. G., Shupe, S., & Gerald, K. B. (1989). Values held by nursing faculty and students in a university setting. *Journal of Professional Nursing, 5,* 199–207.

Uustal, D. (1983). *Values education in baccalaureate nursing curricula in the United States.* Unpublished doctoral dissertation. Boston University Publications, Boston.

DEVELOPED WORLD PERSPECTIVE

SOCIALIZATION INTO NURSING: NURSING STUDENTS AS LEARNERS

LINDA REUTTER, PEGGY ANNE FIELD, IRIS E. CAMPBELL, AND RENE DAY

The purpose of professional socialization is to develop a personally and professionally acceptable role (Cohen, 1981). This process involves acquiring knowledge and skills as well as the norms and values of the professional culture (Jacox, 1973). Two major theoretical frameworks that have been used to explain the process of professional socialization are the functionalist approach and the interactionist approach.

The functionalist approach to professional socialization reflects the functionalist approach to role acquisition and socialization in general (Linton, 1936; Parsons, 1951). Briefly, this perspective views role expectations as grounded in shared values and norms that are internalized through a process of socialization. Individual motivation to conform to these expectations is produced by a favorable self-image that results from positive feedback from others and the assumed complementary nature of roles with correspondingly dove-tailed expectations (Stryker & Statham, 1985). Generally speaking, a functionalist perspective accords less significance to individually based determinants of social behavior and to the importance of ongoing social interaction in the creation and modification of role behaviors. That is, roles are viewed as institutionalized expectations that exist prior to interaction rather than negotiated and developed through

ongoing social interaction (Stryker & Statham, 1985).

A functionalist approach to professional socialization was first described by Merton, Reader, and Kendall (1957) in their study of medical students. This approach assumes that there is a "consensual" value system among practitioners, students, and faculty, each fulfilling interrelated functions for continuance of the system. The professional school is viewed as a suborganization of the parent profession. Faculty members, professionals in the work environment, and peers are seen as the socializing agents of students (Simpson, 1979). Faculty and students are assumed to have common objectives and to act collectively toward the acquisition of the skills, norms, and values attached to the role of the professional (Simpson, 1979). In the functionalist approach to socialization, students are regarded as relatively "passive" recipients of the education and socialization experiences offered by the professional school (Merton, Reader, & Kendall, 1957), with less emphasis placed on students' perspectives and responses in role acquisition.

The interactionist approach to professional socialization is based on symbolic interactionism. The interactionist perspective assumes that a person acquires meaning through interaction with others and the environment as well as through a reflective process (Mead, 1934). Consequently, a person will act toward others and the environment according to the meaning they have for the person. An interactionist approach views role behavior as a process rather than conformity to preexisting social norms (Turner, 1962). As in the functionalist perspective, others' expectations are seen as important components in determining role behavior; however, an interactionist perspective views role behavior as the outcome of a process of social interaction in which individuals are active and creative rather than merely responsive to the cultural internalized norms. That is, role behaviors result from "role-making" in which initial expectations

from earlier definitions of the situation may be modified through subsequent social interaction that involves taking the role of others ("role-taking"), modifying expectations and then creating new role behaviors ("role-making") (Turner, 1962). Roles are therefore continually being revised during the course of interaction. Using a dramaturgical metaphor, "the scripts are not detailed directives to be played as given but are constructed in the course of the play itself and are constrained only in outline form by the culture and social organization within which the play takes place" (Stryker & Statham, 1985, p. 312).

Professional socialization using an interactionist perspective was first described by Becker, Geer, Hughes, and Strauss (1961) in a study of medical students, and later by Olesen and Whittaker (1968) in a study of nursing students. This perspective contends that student behaviors emerge from transactions between the self and the exigencies of the situation, hence, the context of the professional educational experience is viewed as a particularly important determinant of behavior. In contrast to the functionalist view, the interactionist approach to professional socialization considers the professional school as an organized social unit independent of the parent profession (Simpson, 1979) and does not assume a consensual value system among the professional school, practitioners, and students. For example, norms of the professional school may not be reflected in the social contexts where professional roles are enacted (Freidson, 1970). Moreover, students and faculty may differ in their interests and role expectations. Socialization from a symbolic interactionist perspective is an ongoing process characterized by "situational adjustment" rather than the transmission of norms, values, and behaviors that can be transferred across all situations (Stryker and Statham, 1985). Students are seen as active participants in their professional socialization (Olesen & Whittaker, 1968; Simpson, 1979). In this perspective, emphasis is placed on the students' "reactions" to their educational experiences (Simpson, 1979)

and their management of these situations (Becker, Geer, Hughes, & Strauss, 1961).

Alternative frameworks of professional socialization combining the functionalist and interactionist approaches have been proposed by Bucher and Stelling (1977) and Simpson (1979). These researchers argue that there are various dimensions to the professional socialization process and that one approach cannot adequately capture or explain how socialization occurs. While there have been several more recent studies exploring various aspects of the socialization process in nursing (e.g., Cohen, 1981; Mackenzie, 1992; Melia, 1987; Wilson & Startup, 1991), none of these studies have examined students across an educational program. Moreover, many of these studies have been conducted in other than baccalaureate programs.

In this article, we will describe how both the functionalist and interactionist approaches are exemplified in the learning experiences of nursing students in a 4-year baccalaureate program. The results reported in this article are part of a larger study exploring how students become socialized into nursing. The methodology of the study will be discussed briefly before describing more specifically the characteristics of students as learners.

METHOD

Sample and Setting

In this study, a qualitative longitudinal exploratory design was employed. The setting for the study was a 4-year baccalaureate nursing program in a faculty of nursing in a large western Canadian university. The study protocol was approved by the Ethics Review Committee of the educational institution. The primary informants, comprising 50 nursing students across all 4 years of the program, were interviewed using a semi-structured interview guide. In addition, 81 students completed open-ended questionnaires. The total sample constituted about one-third of the student population. Of the 50 students interviewed, the majority were unmarried

(80%), female (90%), less than 25 years of age (74%); 40% were admitted from high school and 42% were transferred from other programs. The demographic data of the sample revealed that students were representative of the general nursing student population in terms of age, gender, and education prior to entry.

Data Collection

Students in each year of the program were made aware of the study through class presentations by two of the researchers. Students were given an information sheet outlining the research project and were invited to telephone the research assistant if they were willing to participate. In addition, some students, who were randomly selected from class lists, received a personal letter inviting them to participate. In total, 44 primary informants volunteered to be interviewed during the first year of the study. Open-ended questionnaires were also distributed in class; those students who had volunteered to be interviewed were asked not to respond to the questionnaire.

In the second year of the study, an additional six first year students were added to obtain better representation of the group of students who had entered nursing directly from high school. As well, all the students who had been interviewed were re-interviewed; that is, first year students were re-interviewed in their second year, second year students were re-interviewed in their third year, and so on.

The semistructured, open-ended interviews were conducted by research assistants not affiliated with the educational program. The initial interview guide was based on Melia's (1987) research. Students were asked about their perceptions of the most important things that nurses do; the nursing student role, including difficulties encountered and how these were handled; others' perceptions of nurses; students' perceptions of and interactions with other nurses; influence of nursing professors

on students' beliefs about nursing; and the role of fellow students. Questions were identical for all years of the program, except first year, in which questions relating to the nursing of patients were omitted as students had not yet been in the clinical area. The guide was revised between the first and second year of the study to explore and elaborate on themes that were emerging from the data. All interviews were tape recorded and transcribed. The questionnaires contained the same open-ended questions as the interviews, without the benefit of probe questions.

Data Analysis

Data were analyzed within the framework of symbolic interactionism and professional socialization. Analysis occurred in two phases. In the first phase, content analysis was employed to group data which shared common characteristics. The grouped data were identified into six broad categories: *shaping* (factors which shaped student identities); *becoming* (movement from "student" to "nurse"); *beliefs* (global definitions of what students believe nursing to be); *doing nursing (student)* (what the student actually does); *doing nursing (hospital or community)* (what the student sees other nurses doing); and *role (instructor, student, nurse)* (the part played by the various actors in socialization). Two subcategories, which occurred across the major categories, were *student culture* and *image.*

The second phase involved team analysis of the data. The four researchers, the project director, and three graduate nursing students reanalyzed all the categories to identify the dimensions of the initial categories and to identify further categories and processes. Data were analyzed by comparing data from students within the same year for similarities and differences in their perspectives. Comparisons were also made between years, that is, comparisons between all the students in first year and all the students in second year, and so on. Finally, for those students who were interviewed twice, the

data were examined to see what changes could be observed in students as they progressed from year to year.

The data reported in this article were drawn primarily from the category of doing nursing (student), with particular emphasis on how the learning characteristics of students changed from year to year.

Findings

First Year: "Learning the Ideal." In the first year, socialization is of a more functionalist nature in which the professional culture is transmitted primarily in classroom and laboratory settings. For some students, this constitutes the internalization of "new" professional values; for others, reinforcement of values already held. Two values repeatedly articulated by students were "caring" and a "scientific knowledge base." Caring involved the dimensions of holism, which meant attending to the patient's physical, mental, and spiritual needs, and individualizing to the patient's unique situation. For some students, embracing the importance of a scientific knowledge base for nursing practice meant overcoming the perceptions of others (and even of themselves) that nursing (and being a nursing student) is not very intellectually challenging. Through their course work, students soon realize that being a nursing student requires much hard work and is intellectually demanding. Although students are able to delineate values of the profession, they are still limited in their abilities to elaborate their views in a way that indicates these values have been fully internalized. That is, they are unable to describe how the values are played out in the practice setting.

Student activities in first year are oriented toward learning theoretical concepts, observing role models (primarily instructors in classroom and laboratory settings), and practicing basic skills. In addition to learning psychomotor skills, students also place high value on becoming comfortable commu-

nicating with patients. Indeed, for some students, patient communication and interaction is seen as the "essence of nursing." Despite initial anxieties about clinical practice, students look forward to and view as crucial the opportunity to practice their skills in the clinical setting because, as one student pointed out, "Knowledge comes through practice." Another student substantiated the view that classroom learning is necessary but not sufficient in acquiring knowledge:

> All the stuff we do in class is good background, but it's kind of pointless if you're not in the hospital too. Because no matter how much you memorize and how much you read, you really don't understand it until you do it.

In short, students appear to be saying that while norms (what is expected), values, and even skills may be learned in the classroom, the internalization of knowledge takes place when the skills are practiced in the clinical setting.

In their beginning clinical practice, students tend to be fairly passive learners, meaning that they follow the rules as presented to them, with less evidence of questioning than in later years. Perhaps, because of the nature of the practice setting (that is, practicing skills in a predictable highly structured situation even in the clinical area), there is less need to "adapt" to the particularities of the situation. That is, in keeping with a more functionalist perspective, students are still able to play out a more or less "assigned" script (Stryker & Statham, 1985).

Second Year: "Confronting Reality." In contrast to the first year where students' primary focus is on learning theoretical concepts underpinning nursing practice and the values and norms of the profession, in second year, there is a greater emphasis on applying theory to practice and on the performance aspect of socialization. As students become more involved in the clinical setting, they are faced with exigencies that lead to a more interactionist approach to learning. They are now required to cope

with "real" rather than "ideal" situations. That is, the context in which care is delivered becomes more important.

Several dimensions of the "real" versus "ideal" dichotomy emerge as students become aware of the need to adapt their classroom learning to take into account a variety of factors related to both the patient and the unit environment. This "situation (or reality) negotiating" includes individualizing care to the patient's own personal situation as well as adapting to the policies and procedures of the unit. In their interaction with patients, students become aware not only of their limited knowledge base, "that there is so much to learn," but also of the responsibility attached to the performance of skills they had previously practiced in a structured laboratory setting. The awareness of limited knowledge and experience may lead to a feeling of inadequacy, which is particularly stressful given the students' perceptions of the potentially serious consequences their inadequate knowledge poses for patients. In contrast to their earlier perception of more distinct roles, students perceive a blurring of the roles of student and nurse because there is little margin for error. "Even though you're a student, you're still a nurse."

Another aspect of the ideal versus real dichotomy is students' realization that they require more than knowledge and skills from the classroom to practice nursing. They become aware of the importance of organizational skills because the nursing skills learned in first year now need to be performed in the context of time constraints, ward routines, and the patient's unique situation. Moreover, adhering to the expectations of the nursing unit may at times be discrepant with carrying out what students perceive to be "optimal care."

The ideal versus real is also reflected in students' observations that staff nurses do not always practice nursing as the students have been taught. Students perceive that the primary ideals inculcated through their nursing education—holistic caring and scientific knowledge—are not always

reflected in nursing practice. Rather than a "consensual value system" between faculty and practitioners as purported by a functionalist perspective of professional socialization, the values to which students are socialized in the faculty may be discrepant with what they observe on the unit. Moreover, students perceive that some nurses do not value them or their nursing program. Almost all commented that one of the difficult aspects of being a student is coping with the implicit and explicit negative feedback received from staff nurses about the Bachelor of Science in Nursing (BScN) program. One student said:

> As soon as they find out we're in the BScN program, you can feel the walls going up—when you ask a question, it's like how come you don't know...you guys know everything over there.

Others pointed out that the uncertainty of staff response adds to the stress: "You either [are expected to] know nothing or they expect a lot." This stress may be accentuated by the students' recognition that staff nurses on the unit have the potential to contribute very positively to the students' learning experiences. Students, therefore, do not wish to jeopardize these opportunities.

The relationship between the students and staff nurses clearly points out that the professional school, practitioners, and students do not necessarily constitute a system bound together by mutual interest and shared outlooks. From an interactionist perspective, the uncertainty of staff nurses' behaviors and expectations means that students need to "create" appropriate responses to the particularities of each situation.

Students respond to the "reality" demands by placing great value on clinical practice. As one student said, "the first year I'm learning things, now I'm learning nursing." Students' learning activities are characterized by both observation and practice. Observation in second year, however, becomes more active as students begin to "process" rather than merely "imitate" behaviors of students,

faculty, and staff nurses. That is, students begin to critically evaluate their observations and to discriminate between role models. Because of their perceived need to master skills, students are somewhat more self-centered than in later years in that patients are perceived as "opportunities" to meet students' learning needs. In later years, patients' needs take priority over students' learning needs, as students are now seen as the means to meet patients' needs.

Because of their limited knowledge and (perhaps more importantly) their limited experience, students are still very dependent on their instructors. While students are beginning to develop clinical judgment, they do not yet trust their judgments. "Seeking validation" just to "make sure" is an important aspect of their learning:

> Sometimes...you ask a question and it's thrown back at you like well you should think through it. [But] you already have of course. But you're asking a question because you're not sure...You can say I know what it is but maybe you're totally wrong because you haven't had enough experience yet. It's the lack of experience.

Because they are still developing a sense of their own competence, students are very vulnerable to feedback. Negative comments from others about their work decrease the students' professional self-esteem. This dependency on others for appraisal of their performance is further reflected in the students' comments that they are always having to "prove" themselves, particularly to instructors. "Proving oneself" often means accommodating to each instructor's different expectations as students change clinical rotations frequently. The student's reliance on the feedback of others demonstrates that the development of a self-concept or identity as a nurse occurs through ongoing interaction with others in which the responses of others help shape the self. Differing expectations among faculty means that students need to adjust their own behavioral responses based on their anticipated responses of others.

A further consequence of the students' feelings of inadequacy is their response to the "less than ideal" care that they observe on the unit. Most students, because of their inexperience, do not feel comfortable "rocking the boat" by confronting other staff members about practices that could be modified. Moreover, they realize that speaking out could jeopardize their own (and subsequent students') learning experiences. Instead, they use this "nonexemplar" care to reaffirm their own ideals about what it is they want to be and discuss with peers and instructors how they themselves would provide care. This suggests that students may "fit in" to "get through," but do not "give in" to the norms and values of the unit. Instead, students retain and perhaps reaffirm their concept of what good nursing should look like. A comment by one student that "good nurses do what we've been taught" conveys internalization of the norms and values of the professional school, rather than of the nursing unit.

Third Year: "Becoming Comfortable with Reality." In third year, interactionist learning dominates as students learn from their clinical practice. This learning is characterized by what one student termed "fine tuning," which involves developing the art of nursing by incorporating a variety of role models, critically analyzing their own and others' experiences, and developing their own formulation and style. This reflects an interactionist approach in which the self is reflective and active in "role-making." Students continue to adapt to the reality of the situation. As they are confronted with more complex, less stable situations, organizational skills become increasingly important in implementing "optimal" rather than "ideal" care.

Because they now have a greater repertoire of skills, students begin to feel more like nurses rather than "just students." Many state that they are able to give the same quality of care as does an RN; perhaps even better, because students still have the luxury of being a learner and therefore have more time

to deliver "holistic care." Students not only feel that they have much to offer patients, but also see themselves as being of value to the staff nurses by assisting them in tasks and by "bringing a fresh outlook to the unit" because of their up-to-date knowledge. In discussing her role, one student said:

> *You're there to get clinical experience…and a lot of time to bring a fresh outlook; 'cause you're going through a program which is really current and a lot of times you'll learn something new and…it might help in the care of one patient… We're quick references because we're more current…and we can look it up if we don't know.*

Another commented that because students change rotations frequently, they may act as a "liaison" between units whereby they share information about one unit with another unit. In spite of feeling that they are valuable to staff members, however, students continue to comment about the staff nurses' negative responses toward the baccalaureate program. And in spite of increased confidence in their knowledge and skills, students still do not feel comfortable confronting staff about the less than optimal care they observe. Nevertheless, when unit policies and procedures interfere with the students' capabilities to carry out what they believe to be optimal care, they are generally more assertive.

One of the difficulties of the student role is the need to adapt to a variety of nursing units. While some students view this as advantageous, most convey that continually adjusting to a "new reality" is stressful. "It's like starting a new job every 6 weeks," a continuous orientation wherein students need to learn both the formal and informal norms of the unit, and to first determine and then seek out those staff nurses who are supportive of students. Again, this clearly reflects situation "negotiating" behavior, so characteristic of an interactionist approach.

Overall, students in third year are less dependent on their instructors, looking to other students

and staff for guidance. In contrast to second year, there is less dependence on others for appraisal about the quality of one's nursing care. Students are now able to make self-judgments about their own worth. In short, students in third year are much more confident about their knowledge and skills and some are "getting ready to fly."

At the end of third year, students may be viewed as "active evaluating trainees," who have acquired a "sense of mastery," which enables them to selectively choose elements of the program and to confidently validate their own choices (Bucher & Stelling, 1977).

Fourth Year: "Extending Beyond the Reality of Student Practice." In fourth year, students take advantage of their "learner" role to prepare for their future status as graduate nurses. The student nurse status is seen as a justification for being able to admit that "I don't know." In speaking of her senior practicum, one student said:

> This is my last chance, my last year, my last term to be able to still use my student status as an excuse or justification for why I don't know certain things...I [would] much rather suffer the embarrassment and the mortification now than be on my first job and being oriented and...having to tell someone that I need to be told or shown how do such and such.

Learning now becomes focused on the skills needed for the "real" world. Even though students have incorporated a broad holistic concept of nursing, and even though instructors reassure students that psychomotor skills that they have not yet mastered can be learned quickly, students perceive that being proficient is necessary for their emergence into the graduate nursing role. One student said, "I'm trying to use [my senior practicum] as an orientation so that by the time I graduate I'll be ready to work." The fact that students use their student status to actively prepare for the work they envision as graduate nurses suggests that their main focus is not one of merely "getting through" their student days.

The need to prepare for graduate nurse status leads students to become active in seeking out experiences that will increase their confidence. "Observation" experiences, therefore, are not viewed favorably because students feel that these experiences will not prepare them for the work world and may even connote a lack of confidence in the student. Overall, in fourth year, students are less dependent on instructors and more dependent on nurse preceptors in the field.

In fourth year, there is evidence of functionalist learning as reflected in the students' perceptions about the scope of nursing. Their view of nursing broadens to incorporate issues that go beyond the reality of their particular student practice situations. For example, students see political action strategies as legitimate nursing interventions, and they comment on the need to understand (and even restructure) the health care system and to increase public awareness of nursing's expanding role. In one sense, fourth year students espouse a broader, more futuristic view of nursing that goes beyond their direct-care experiences to incorporate a broad range of knowledge and skills. On the other hand, they use their learner role to become proficient in those tasks that will enhance their credibility in the nursing roles they will occupy upon graduation.

DISCUSSION

The findings from this research support other work which suggests that student learning reflects a combination of functionalist and interactionist approaches (Bucher & Stelling, 1977; Light, 1988; Simpson, 1979). That is, there is both internalization of professional values from the faculty and situational adjustment to the requirements of the clinical practice world. This supports Bucher and Stelling's (1977) thesis that not only does the professional school influence the shaping of students, but students also actively construct their own identities. Bucher and Stelling (1977) contend that the

concepts "active evaluating trainee" and "sense of mastery" (also identified in this study) provide the theoretical link between the functionalist and interactionist approach. The relative emphasis of each approach varied over the students' 4 years in the program. In the first year, functionalist learning predominates as students learn the "ideal" norms and values of the profession. Students are characterized as passive learners. In second year, they are confronted with reality that requires a more interactionist approach as they adapt their learning to the exigencies of the situation. They are dependent learners as they require validation of their knowledge and skills. In third year, students continue to develop their own perspective of nursing. They become more confident in their knowledge and skills, which makes them more independent of their instructors. In a sense, they have shaped their own identities. Fourth year students look beyond their practice situation, in terms of both their perspective of nursing and their anticipation of a reality beyond the student world. They are active in seeking out learning experiences that will prepare them for this new reality as graduate nurses.

The differences encountered between professional nursing schools and the work of practicing nurses might lead one to expect an emphasis on "reactive behavior." Although students were required to negotiate reality and adapt their behavior to the exigencies of the situation, they did not seem to abandon the professional values inculcated by the professional school; that is, contrary to Simpson's (1979) findings, but supporting those of Olesen and Whittaker (1968), students do not assume the "bureaucratic" values of the organization. They may attempt to "fit in" (Kelly, 1991; Mackenzie, 1992; Melia, 1987) but do not "give in" to the norms and values of the nursing unit when these are discrepant with the values and norms conveyed by the faculty. Weller, Harrison, and Katz (1988) found that the longer the students were in the program, the more congruent became their view of nursing with that of the faculty. Kelly

(1991) also found that, although students valued "fitting in" and "going along," they retained their own ideals.

Davis (1975) has suggested that the "ideological affinity" between students and faculty is increased because students identify instructors as positive role models, with negative role models tending to be practicing registered nurses. The students in this study did perceive their instructors as positive role models (Campbell, Larrivee, Field, Day, & Reutter, 1994), as mentors to be "emulated" (Merton, Reader, & Kendall, 1957). Perhaps this affinity is also enhanced because, in the clinical area, faculty are with the students on a continuing basis, particularly for the first 3 years. Moreover, faculty "control" the appraisal and evaluation of student performance; that is, they have the capacity to selectively reward and sanction student behavior. That students and faculty have similar values and objectives is supportive of a functionalist perspective of professional socialization; in contrast, the interactionist perspective of Becker and colleagues (1961) contends that the faculty and students may have different objectives, resulting in a student subculture with countervailing norms and strategies to cope with faculty expectations.

Although this study provides evidence of a dual role of "learner" and "worker" (Melia, 1987), in which students must adjust to the clinical situation by trying to adapt to the expectations of both the faculty and the norms of the unit, students did not become a part of the unit nursing team to the same degree as may occur in a more apprenticeship approach to nursing education, such as that described by Melia (1987). Therefore, the role of "worker" is less evident than the role of "learner." In other words, there may be less need for the student to manage the "segmentation" (Bucher & Stelling, 1977) or "compartmentalization" between service and education (Melia, 1987). This may further assist students to "retain" the values of the professional school.

Students do not, however, accept uncritically the values of the professional school, but instead reflect on and examine how these values can be applied to the reality of nursing practice. They derive for themselves a bedside model of reality. Mackenzie (1992) suggests that students, while being aware of the differences between the "reality of practice" and the "ideal of college," do not perceive this as problematic. She maintains that the discrepancy is more of a stumbling block for teachers than it is for students. Ashworth and Morrison (1989) go so far as to say that the ambiguity of the student role brought about by differences in education and practice is essential and provides important learning opportunities for reflection and the development of experiential knowledge.

Of practical significance is the finding, supported by others (Ashworth & Morrison, 1989; Wilson & Startup, 1991), that students perceive a conflict between staff nurses and students. The rift between baccalaureate nursing students and those nurses without baccalaureate preparation may be diminished with the implementation of the baccalaureate degree as the entry into practice. Meanwhile, students who feel that they are "outsiders" may not derive the full benefits of role modeling by expert practitioners. A positive staff student relationship may be particularly important in the first years of the program when students are at a "dependency stage" (Cohen, 1981; Windsor, 1987) and, as pointed out in this study, when approval is important in validating student competence.

The students' perceptions that the staff nurses' practice does not always reflect the values they perceive as central to nursing presents an interesting aspect of the "functionalist–interactionist" debate in professional socialization. Have these staff nurses adjusted their practice (and even their val-ues) to the situational demands of the unit (Freidson, 1970), or alternatively (but probably less likely) were they socialized to different values in their professional education? Or is their behavior the result of a combination of factors?

In terms of implications for nursing education, an understanding of the process of learning may assist in the development of appropriate teaching strategies to guide student learning. In first year, students require considerable input from teachers. In the second and third years, students need to be engaged in active learning situations. In the fourth year, students require independence from their instructors in order to develop the confidence needed to enter the graduate nurse role.

In conclusion, this study suggests that nursing students' socialization involves two interrelated but different processes: socialization to the student role and socialization to the nursing role. Socialization to the professional nursing role involves a more functionalist approach, relating to professional values, norms, and behaviors. Socialization to the student role involves learning how to nurse when one has minimal knowledge and experience and includes responding to the expectations of others, gaining their approval, and finally developing one's own self-identity as a nurse. It is based on an interactionist approach that includes coming to terms with the differences between the world of academic nursing and the practical world of the clinical area (Ashworth & Morrison, 1989). The situational adjustment that students experience during their student days may prepare them to better cope with the uncertainty and structural change they will encounter with health care reform. It is reasonable to expect that this challenge will require considerable "role-negotiating" and "role-making."

REFERENCES

Ashworth, P., & Morrison, P. (1989). Some ambiguities of the student's role in undergraduate nurse training. *Journal of Advanced Nursing,* 14, 1009–1015.

Becker, H. S., Geer, B., Hughes, E. D., & Strauss, A. L. (1961). *Boys in white: Student culture in medical school.* Chicago, IL: University of Chicago Press.

Bucher, R., & Stelling, J. G. (1977). *Becoming professional.* Beverly Hills, CA: Sage Publications.

Campbell, I., Larrivee, L., Field, P. A., Day, R., & Reutter, L. (1994). Learning to nurse in the clinical setting. *Journal of Advanced Nursing, 20,* 1125–1131.

Cohen, H. A. (1981). *The nurse's quest for a professional identity.* Menlo Park, CA: Addison-Wesley.

Davis, F. (1975). Professional socialization as subjective experience: The process of doctrinal conversion among student nurses. In C. Cox & A. Mead (Eds.), *A sociology of medical practice,* pp. 116–131. London: Collier Macmillan.

Freidson, E. (1970). *Profession of medicine.* New York, NY: Dodd, Mead.

Jacox, A. (1973). Professional socialization of nurses. *The Journal of the New York Nurses Association,* 4(4): 6–15.

Kelly, B. (1991). The professional values of English nursing undergraduates. *Journal of Advanced Nursing, 16,* 867–872.

Light, D. W. (1988). Medical and nursing education: Surface behavior and deep structure. In D. Mechanic (Ed.), *Handbook of health, health care, and the health professions,* pp. 455–478. New York, NY: Free Press.

Linton, R. (1936). *The study of man.* New York, NY: Appleton-Century.

Mackenzie, A. E. (1992). Learning from experience in the community: An ethnographic study of district nurse students. *Journal of Advanced Nursing, 17,* 682–691.

Mead, G. H. (1934). *Mind, self, and society.* Chicago, IL: University of Chicago.

Melia, K. (1987). *Learning and working: The occupational socialization of nurses.* London: Tavistock.

Merton, R. K., Reader, G. G., & Kendall, P. L. (1957). *The student physician: Introductory studies in the sociology of medical education.* Cambridge, MA: Harvard University Press.

Olesen, V. L., & Whittaker, E. V. (1968). *The silent dialogue: A study in the social psychology of professional socialization.* San Francisco, CA: Jossey-Bass.

Parsons, T. (1951). *The social system.* Glencoe, IL: Free Press.

Simpson, I. H. (1979). *From student to nurse: A longitudinal study of socialization.* Cambridge, UK: Cambridge University Press.

Stryker, S., & Statham, A. (1985). Symbolic interaction and role theory. In G. Lindzey & E. Aronson (Eds.), *The handbook of social psychology* (Vol. 1, 3rd ed.), pp. 311–378. New York, NY: Random House.

Turner, R. H. (1962). Role-taking: Process versus conformity. In A. Rose (Ed.), *Human behavior and social processes,* pp. 20–40. Boston, MA: Houghton Mifflin.

Weller, L., Harrison, M., & Katz, Z. (1988). Changes in the self and professional images of student nurses. *Journal of Advanced Nursing, 13,* 179–184.

Wilson, A., & Startup, R. (1991). Nurse socialization: Issues and problems. *Journal of Advanced Nursing, 16,* 1478–1486.

Windsor, A. (1987). Nursing students' perception of clinical experience. *Journal of Nursing Education, 26,* 150–154.

DEVELOPING WORLD PERSPECTIVE

CHANGING THE IMAGE OF NURSING IN JORDAN THROUGH EFFECTIVE ROLE NEGOTIATION

PATRICIA ABUGHARBIEH AND WAFIKA SULIMAN

Jordanian nurses lament their ill-defined role. Nurse educators, noting nurses' lack of motivation and disillusionment, have called the incompatibility between nurse education and practice a crisis.[1] Yet by their acquiescence to the role ascribed to them—or by their failure to negotiate a role consistent with their education—nurses serve to reinforce the image of nursing as menial work.

How can nurses expect to be perceived as educators when they fail to teach patients how to maintain health and manage illness? How can nurses expect physicians to appreciate their "unique body of knowledge" when they fail to interact knowledgeably with physicians during medical rounds?

What factors deter Jordanian nurses from negotiating a role in conformance with their

education? An examination of professional socialization of Jordanian nurses provides insight and potential solutions.

THE SOCIALIZATION PROCESS

Nurses are socialized first through formal nursing education and then by the work setting. Through role bargaining—negotiation with role partners on acceptable role behaviours—the graduate nurse adjusts the skills and values acquired in training to the demands and constraints of the work setting.

The incomplete role enactment characterizing nurses in Jordan led us to ask:

1. Have Jordanian educational programmes failed to instill the norms, values and behaviours of the professional nurse into their graduates?
2. What factors influence the role bargaining process between Jordanian nurses and their role partners, particularly physicians?

In an effort to answer these questions, we analyzed the nursing programme at the University of Jordan and related theories about role negotiation to Jordanian nurses and Jordanian society.

NURSING EDUCATION

Multiple factors influence the process of learning to behave, feel and see the world as a nurse. An important condition is the clarity and consensus with which nurse roles are perceived by nurse faculty, nursing students, nurses and their role partners. Other factors that may facilitate or interfere with socialization include:

- Availability of role models;
- Early socialization experiences and the "fit" between the individual's self-perception and values and those of the profession; and
- The ability to select recruits.[4]

To determine to what extent these factors have influenced the socialization of students enrolled in the nursing programme at the University of Jordan, we reviewed the curriculum, philosophy and policy statements, instructional tools and evaluation criteria. The history of the programme was obtained from faculty members with long experience with the programme.

THE NURSING PROGRAMME

The University of Jordan's nursing programme resembles baccalaureate programmes in the US to a certain extent. Many faculty members earned advanced nursing degrees in the US; the faculty's (college) philosophy statement developed in 1981 reflects contemporary American nursing practice; English is the language of instruction and ideas about roles and responsibilities of the nurse are reinforced through the use of current American texts.

However, the curriculum—essentially a medical model-type with "threads" such as pharmacology and nutrition and emphasis on basic medical sciences—reveals its origins as a combination diploma nursing/medical sciences programme established by physicians and British diploma nurses in 1973.

A lack of clarity and consensus about nurse roles in relationship to those of the physician is exemplified by other inconsistencies within the programme. For example, although man was conceived as a "biologic, psychologic, socio-cultural and spiritual being,"[8] until recently students evaluated patients using a head-to-toe assessment tool. While the nurse was described as an "autonomous individual" acting in a "collegial relationship" with the physician, physicians were involved in instruction, and a physician was dean of the programme until 1983.

And despite the availability of Jordanian nurses trained at the doctoral level, such as faculty members, physicians continue to represent nursing on national committees and councils.

In the clinical setting the relationships between nursing and medicine—and nurses and

physicians—are clear. Students realize that most physicians know nothing of nursing's "unique body of knowledge" and independent professional functions; they require that nurses "know their place" and leave the interpretation of data, decision-making and disclosure of information to physicians.

Similarly patients, not recognizing nurses as knowledgeable professionals, do not seek information from or confide in nurses. Even other nurses, particularly nursing service administrators, convey that theories and idealism are best kept in the lecture hall; task completion—executing physicians' orders and housekeeping—are the priorities of hospital nursing.

Clearly, the most important condition for effective socialization—clarity and consensus about nurse roles—is not met. While the faculty espouses a professional ideological orientation, certain aspects of the programme and the students' role partners convey the paramedical role of nursing.

NO ROLE MODELS

Another major problem is that there are few clinical nurse experts capable of putting theory into practice and demonstrating the negotiation process. Although faculty members are well-prepared theoretically, they lack training and experience in clinical nursing. Many current faculty members assumed educator roles upon graduation from the faculty's nursing/medical sciences programme, a curriculum with relatively little clinical practice. Similarly, faculty members' educational experiences in the US were largely theoretical; clinical practicums were limited to observation because of licensure and practice regulations.

As a result, nurses in the practice setting regard faculty as theoreticians rather than "real nurses." And physicians sometimes restrict student nurse contact with patients (e.g. performing certain procedures) and prefer that medical students check certain assessments (e.g. blood pressure readings), citing a lack of confidence in the ability of students and their instructors. Lacking confidence and credibility, faculty avoid the clinical setting, and clinical instruction is left to teaching assistants who tend to be less likely and less capable role models.

Besides lacking staff nurse experience and the status faculty members enjoy because of their postgraduate degrees, most teaching assistants are less familiar with American nursing practice—and consequently less able to implement—the professional practice model described by the programme's philosophy.

Without the support of role models, students hesitate to initiate behaviours that may be incongruent with the expectations of role partners. For example, although students at the Faculty of Nursing receive considerable content on patient teaching, they do not instruct patients. Rather than attempt role negotiation by teaching patients and thereby making the nurse's role as an educator and an information source explicit, students conform.

Consequently, an opportunity to challenge and perhaps change physician and patient perceptions related to the nurse's role as a health educator is missed.

The early socialization experiences of Jordanian women may also interfere with socialization into nursing because of the incongruity between the traditional roles of women in Jordanian society—wife, mother, daughter—and some of the roles ascribed to the professional nurse.[7]

Women socialized to serve, obey and defer to the judgement of males may feel a distinct incongruity between their self-perception and values, and certain nurse roles.

Can a woman who is dependent upon and subordinate to male family members, and perhaps unaccustomed to communicating with unrelated males, be expected to initiate change, exercise independent judgement, and develop collegial relationships with the primarily male physicians?

Interestingly, the evaluation tool reinforced cultural values rather than those conveyed in the philosophy. Cooperation and other personality traits rather than critical thinking were evaluated. Herein lies another example of a lack of consensus about nurse roles and behaviours.

Nursing's poor image, in combination with university admission policies, influences recruitment of quality students. In accordance with university policy, students are assigned to various "faculties" (colleges) based on their General Secondary Education Certificate Examination score and occupational preference. Because nursing is rarely a "first choice" among the intellectually gifted, low-academic achievers without a vocation for nursing have traditionally been drafted into nursing.

The inability to recruit students with such characteristics as academic ability, positive attitudes towards nursing and adequate English-language skills complicates instruction and interferes with the socialization process. How can low academic achievers who would rather be pursuing another course of study become expert and committed nurses? Would such graduates be inclined to engage in role bargaining?

While nursing is generally regarded as a female occupation because of its care-giving and nurturing aspects, increasing number of men are being admitted to the programme. During the 1987–88 academic year, 28% of the undergraduate students enrolled at the Faculty of Nursing were male.[9] Job security and the prospect of a role in administration are major attractions for men. While Jordan's nursing shortage is severe and chronic, unemployment in the favoured professions of medicine, engineering and law is increasing. Nurse roles in administration are accorded some social prestige and are consistent.

THE WORK SETTING

The graduate nurse inclined to practice in accordance with a professional practice model can expect to encounter resistance. Traditionally, the division of labour in physician-dominated health organizations has dictated that nurses practice nonscientific nurturing care, help the physician with his scientific tasks and prevent knowledge concerning errors and uncertainties from reaching patients and families.[3] Although nurse educators have claimed nurse roles as autonomous practitioners and health educators, physicians control access to patients and insist upon controlling disclosure of medical information.

The aspects of the nurse's role depend upon the interplay among professional choice, power and situational constraints. Personal propensity will determine whether the nurse attempts to negotiate a role in conformance with education while the power structure of employment—the expectations of more powerful role partners—will determine the outcome of her negotiation efforts.[5]

Historically, physicians as members of a learned profession have effectively controlled the scope of practice of all other groups of health workers.[4] In Jordan, the marked sex segregation in nursing and medicine, the roles and status of women in society and the contrasting demographic characteristics of nurses and physicians further enhance the power differential between female nurses and physicians.

RELUCTANT NEGOTIATORS

Simpson and Simpson's analysis of American semi-professions in the 1960s suggests that the predominance of women in an occupation may decrease its demands for autonomy. Women's orientation to family roles, low vocational commitment, beliefs in male superiority and desire for warm, friendly work relationships make them "tractable subordinates."[7] Jordanian nurses who no doubt fit this profile—probably to the extreme because of cultural values and norms—would be expected to be reluctant negotiators. Nurses reared in a patriarchal society where senior males are authority figures and decision-makers naturally hesitate to challenge senior male physicians.

Moreover, Jordanian nurses who do defy cultural norms and attempt negotiation will probably be unsuccessful. Factors influencing the role bargaining process—the presence of reference groups, free and open communication between bargainers, and a common level of power among bargainers[2]—are not in the nurses' favor.

Reference groups provide the individual with a source of values that influence role enactment, especially when difficult choices have to be made. Because neither the Jordanian Nurses and Midwives Association nor any other nursing body performs the functions of a true professional organization (e.g. regulation and licensing, developing standards of practice, etc.),[6] nurses lack an important source of norms and values.

For bargainers to reach agreement, role partners must be readily available to one another, be able to freely communicate and actually communicate.[2] In the case of Jordanian nurses and physicians, interactions are limited and characterized by oversensitivity. Interdisciplinary conferences and committees do not exist and nurses often vacate the patient's room rather than participate in rounds.

The degree of legitimate power or rank and the personal characteristics of bargainers also affect the outcome of bargaining. Physicians as professionals revered by Jordanian society enjoy significantly greater power, prestige and income than nurses who are regarded as low-status employees.

Further, Jordanian nurses who can be profiled as relatively younger and less intelligent females (based on secondary education examination scores) than Jordanian physicians would tend to be compliant and open to exploitation in negotiations with physicians.

SUGGESTIONS FOR EFFECTIVE ROLE NEGOTIATION

The incomplete role enactment characterizing nurses in Jordan can be related to problems in both phases of the professional socialization process. As described above, socialization through formal nursing education is hindered by lack of consensus about nurse roles, the unavailability of role models, the incongruity between the traditional role of women in Jordanian society and some of the roles ascribed to the professional nurse, and the difficulty in recruiting students with both academic ability and a vocation for nursing.

Similarly, factors such as the demographic characteristics of Jordanian nurses and physicians, the status of women in Jordanian society and the lack of a true professional nursing organization interfere with role bargaining in the work setting.

These aspects of the socialization process of Jordanian nurses serve to enhance the "natural dominance" of medicine over nursing. Consequently, the physician's view of the nurse's role (which concurs with that of the public and some nursing service administrators) prevails and nurse role enactment is limited to executing the physician's orders.

Admittedly, prospects for enactment of a professional nurse role may seem dismal given nursing's lack of planners,[6] women's roles in Jordanian society, nurses' tremendous workloads and the current oversupply of physicians. However, some fairly feasible proposals for educational reform and strategies to improve nurses' negotiating ability are suggested by our analysis. Two points deserve emphasis:

1. NOW is the time to recruit students with academic ability because of high unemployment in favoured professions (medicine and engineering); and
2. Consensus about nurse roles is critical.

Nurses must decide whether the American version of nursing such as that expressed by the University of Jordan philosophy fits Jordanian culture and society. Curricula consistent with Jordanian nurse roles and tailored to Jordan's health problems must be developed.

Through effective role negotiation and visible role enactment at the bedside and in the community, nurses can increase physician and public

awareness of nurses' knowledge and training. Nurses can begin by responding to the nursing needs of individual patients as well as those of Jordanian society, for example:

- birth spacing;
- child abuse and injury related to parents' lack of knowledge about development and safety measures;

- dental decay in children;
- lack of properly prepared staff in nursing homes; and
- the psychological needs of cancer patients and their families.

Public recognition of nurses' specialized knowledge will in turn improve the status and image of nurses in Jordan.

REFERENCES

1. Carr, S. (1985). "Nurses continue their education, training on specialized courses." *Jordan Times,* 2/28–3/1.

2. Hardy, M. (1978). "Role stress and role strain." In Hardy, M. and Conway, M. eds., *Role Theory: Perspectives for Health Professionals.* New York: Appleton-Century-Crofts.

3. Katz, F. (1969). "Nurses." In Etzioni, A. ed., *The Semi-Professions and Their Organization.* New York: Free Press.

4. Lum, J. (1978). "Reference groups and professional socialization." In Hardy, M. and Conway, M. eds., *Role Theory: Perspectives for Health Professionals.* New York: Appleton-Century-Crofts.

5. Lurie, E. (1981). "Nurse practitioners: Issues in professional socialization." *Journal of Health and Social Behavior,* 22, 31–48.

6. Sati, N. (1989). "Nursing needs a helping hand." *Jordan Times,* 10/3.

7. Simpson, R. and I. Simpson (1969). "Women and bureaucracy in the semi-professions." In Etzioni, A. ed., *The Semi-Professions and Their Organization.* New York: Free Press.

8. University of Jordan (1986). Philosophy of the Baccalaureate and Graduate Programmes. Faculty of Nursing, Amman, Jordan.

9. University of Jordan (1988). Planning and Statistical Department. *Statistical Yearbook 1987–88.* Amman, Jordan.

10. Zaky-El-Deen, M. (1981). Philosophy of the Baccalaureate and Graduate Programmes. Faculty of Nursing. Amman, Jordan.

CHAPTER 10

ALTERNATIVE MEDICINE

The articles in this chapter address alternative or complementary approaches to allopathic or Western medicine, such as those of the Navajo and the Kung. "Non-Western" approaches to medicine represent a legitimate segment of the medical field too often overlooked within the study of medicine and medical sociology. This is an area generally dominated by medical anthropologists who investigate traditional health care practices of populations within developing nations. As the articles in this chapter suggest, however, medical sociologists can offer significant insight into a variety of issues such as the dynamics of the physician/patient relationship, the organizational structure of care within populations, the meaning of medical assistance to members of a given population, and the context for basic concepts such as illness behavior, health behavior, and the sick role.

In the first article, Elaine Fox describes her ethnographic study of a health care facility that functioned as a hospital and outpatient clinic on a Navajo reservation. Fox speaks of Navajo views of medicine, in which spiritual imbalance is seen as the primary causal agent of illness. Essentially, the Navajo approach to medicine is naturalistic, unlike the approach of Anglo and other Western medical practitioners.

The focus of Fox's research was to examine the dynamics at work in a health care facility in which health care providers who were predominantly Navajo utilized a Western model of medicine at odds with traditional Navajo beliefs about illness. What coping strategies did nurses, aides, and orderlies exposed to the culturally distinct Anglo and Navajo health care systems, employ? The author found that RNs with more working experience in the "white" world had higher levels of satisfaction in the Navajo hospital environment than did the nonprofessional aides and orderlies, perhaps because of the nurses' greater awareness of medical pluralism.

In the second article, Charles Vincent and Adrian Furnham begin with an overview of the use of complementary medicine in American and British society. Their research focused on patients from the British School of Osteopathy, an acupuncture centre in South London, and the Royal Homeopathic Hospital. The authors were interested in why patients chose to try complementary medicine. They found that patients were using it for a number of reasons. Patients cited the positive value of complementary medicine. They mentioned unsatisfactory experiences with allopathic or Western medicine and unpleasant side effects. They also mentioned poor communication with physicians. Vincent and Furnham found that patients' least important reason for using complementary medicine was cost.

In the third article, Richard Katz offers a different perspective on traditional medicine. Rather than focusing on the provision of health care among a population in a developing country, he examines health care among the Kung. He describes the Kung belief in the healing powers of individuals who possess *num,* or spiritual energy, and experience *kia,* an altering of consciousness, during a healing dance. Katz provides a detailed description of the Kung healing dance, which is not only a healing experience but a community affair. The size of the dance depends on the number of dancers

and singers in the community who are able to participate. As Katz points out, the dance provides an opportunity for community members to release hostility, offers an apprenticeship opportunity to potential healers, and promotes social solidarity. In other words, the dance is part of the Kung's medical, spiritual, and community life.

The three articles in Chapter 10 offer a view of alternative or complementary or traditional medicine that is generally not found in accounts focused on Western or allopathic medicine. As each one makes clear, the meaning attached to alternative medicine is significant to those who consider it within the framework of their medical regimen.

CROSSING THE BRIDGE: ADAPTIVE STRATEGIES AMONG NAVAJO HEALTH CARE WORKERS

ELAINE FOX

INTRODUCTION

Studies show that Native Americans, as much as any other minority ethnic group in the United States, maintain strong ties to the ethnic culture of origin, choosing to bond together with other Indians after migrating from the reservation to urban areas and maintaining ties with the reservation by frequent visiting (Christopherson, Dingle 1982; Henderson 1979; Margon 1977; Steele 1973). Native Americans who have left the reservation are likely to maintain a dream of returning to the reservation in later years (Fiske 1978; Graves 1970; Griffen 1984; Metcalf 1975). Native American children are often encouraged in a lifestyle of biculturalism and are not taught to see acculturation into mainstream White society as the universal goal of participating in the dominant economic structure (Christopherson, Dingle 1982; Kunitz 1981; Steele 1973). Thus, there are apparent motivations for Native Americans residing off the reservation to maintain a sense of biculturalism.

Classic studies of Native Americans residing on reservations focused on acculturation, often noting transitional patterns of behavior as evidence of biculturalism. Voget (1956), Spindler and Spindler (1971), Polgar (1960), McFee (1968) and others attempted to identify several categories of adaptation made to the consequences of divergent cultural confrontation by creating adaptive models ranging from the traditionally oriented to the Anglo oriented. More recently Spindler (1984) suggests that acculturation is not a process leading directly to assimilation but rather can be seen as an adaptive strategy used by people who have to cope with the economic, social and political disadvantages of their position as minorities. She postulates that we are less likely to see linear continuation towards assimilation and are more prone to observe a variety of coping strategies, including reaffirmation of seemingly traditional values and behaviors, biculturalism, cultural syntheses of conflicting culture elements and managed identities. This paper is a study of the cultural confrontation experienced by a group of Navajo health care workers and the coping strategies they employ as they participate in their daily work world.

Curing and healing constructions of reality are an interesting focus for observing aspects of coping strategies among Navajo health care workers.

Anglo culture adheres to a "medical model" of illness, drawing on physiological imbalance as the etiological agent in disease while Navajo culture views spiritual imbalance as the causative agent in illness. Studies have indicated that for Navajo living in urban areas and using Anglo health systems as a primary source of health care, it is not uncommon to travel to the reservation to participate in a traditional healing ceremony at some later time (Henderson 1979; Kunitz 1983). Approximately half of all Navajo living on the reservation engage in some form of health care which utilizes both the physiological "medical model" and spiritual balance themes (Kunitz 1983).

The hospital setting of this study offers a unique opportunity to study coping strategies among Navajo workers. The "medical model" Anglo view of curing and healing dominates. Navajo health care workers may need to subordinate or integrate aspects of their own cultural allegiances to that of the dominant ideology while on the job but return home to a cultural setting which reinforces opposing or differing cultural views.

THE CULTURAL MILIEU OF NAVAJO HEALTH BELIEFS

Kleinman et al. pointed out that

> *Illness is culturally shaped in the sense that how we perceive, experience and cope with disease is based on our explanations of sickness, explanations specific to the social positions we occupy and systems of meaning we employ. (1978 252)*

The Navajo people adhere to a naturalistic perspective with regard to health and illness. Illness, either physical or mental, is seen to be the result of upsetting the balance of nature. A Navajo who is living the traditional "way," that is, being in balance with all things in nature, should be healthy. Of course, the Navajo are aware that life is full of dangers that may threaten the natural harmony. Illness may be a state which happens to someone through no fault of his own. Sickness, therefore, is viewed as the

product of some imbalance or disorder between the person and the Holy People (gods), nature, or another person (Kluckhohn, Leighton 1946; Levy 1983; Witherspoon 1974).

Considering this orientation, restoring harmony is central to the nature and purpose of traditional health care practices. Restoration occurs in the form of curing rites performed by a medicine man. Referred to as "sings," these ceremonies re-enact the creation of the world through myth, song, prayer, and drama and place the patient in a recreated world, closely identifying the patient with the good and power of various deities (Witherspoon 1974). Therefore, the curing of illness falls within the realm of the religious framework of the Navajo culture.

There are several major religious health care provider roles in Navajo culture. The first of these is the diagnostician, an individual who goes into a spiritual trance and provides the patient with an etiological basis for the illness. Given the particular diagnosis derived by trance, the patient secures the services of a medicine man who is skilled at the religious curing ceremony for that particular illness. These two roles constitute the majority of traditional Navajo health care services (Kunitz 1983; Levy 1983; Nurge 1975). Playing a decreasing role today because of acculturation, herbalists and bone setters have all but disappeared from the reservation.

Several major differences exist between Navajo and Anglo treatment plans. In the Anglo system there is an implied confidentiality between the patient and physician. Navajo curing ceremonies, on the other hand, call for the full participation of all family members and friends. Thus, there is community involvement and knowledge of the illness. In addition, Anglo physicians diagnose and treat diseases (abnormalities in the structure and function of body organs and systems), whereas patients suffer illnesses (experiences of disvalued changes in status of being and social function; the human experience of sickness) (Kleinman et al 1978 251). For Navajo patients, illness problems—the difficulties in living

resulting from sickness—are usually viewed as constituting the entire disorder. Therefore, the "notion of locating the cause of a disease in physiological process is foreign to Navajo thought" (Kluckhohn, Leighton 1946 132). As Levy states:

> No Navajo disease is known by the symptoms it produces or by the part of the body it is thought to affect. Because the traditional health culture does not rely upon a knowledge of symptoms in the diagnostic process, Navajo patients often have difficulty understanding the purpose of history taking and physical examination, a circumstance that often leads to misunderstanding in the clinical setting. (1983 132)

Studies indicate that three-fourths of all Navajo presently living on the reservation participate in at least some aspect of modern medical practice (Kunitz 1983). This is an apparent discrepancy with regard to the traditional Navajo view of health and illness. However, as Levy (1983) pointed out, Navajo believe that modern medicine will remove the symptoms of illness (pain, fever, etc.) but do not consider themselves "cured" of the illness until completion of a healing ritual by a medicine man.

METHODOLOGY

I conducted fieldwork on the Navajo reservation at the Navajo Nation Health Foundation (NNHF) in Ganado, Arizona, during the summer months of 1984–1989. This health care facility provides care to some 30,000 Navajo patients a year in its combined hospital and out-patient care facilities. While an occasional Anglo visitor or staff member may be treated for a minor illness in the out-patient clinic, during the course of this field study, only Navajo patients were admitted to the hospital inpatient facility. Approximately half of these Navajo patients were not bilingual, speaking only their native tongue, indicating the high levels of traditionalism found in this geographic area of the reservation.

While the governing board of the NNHF is Navajo, the administrative structure is composed primarily of Anglo professionals whose services are contracted for by the Navajo tribe. Seven Anglo medical physicians staff both the out-patient clinic as well as the hospital facility and all are employed by the NNHF on a contractual basis. The director of nursing, the head nurse, and the majority of the nursing staff are Anglo. All non-professional staff are Navajo.

I have spent the past five summers living on the reservation and working in the health care facility as a registered nurse. While the Anglo staff is aware that I am a sociologist and a college professor, their interaction with me has primarily been as a nurse colleague and another resident of the reservation. The Navajo staff is also aware of my academic training yet interact with me as "the Anglo nurse who likes us so much she comes back every year." As a result of this long-term relationship with Navajo staff members, respondents interviewed for this paper appeared to be exceptionally open.

I conducted interviews with the Navajo health care personnel of the hospital component of the facility. Eighteen interviews in all were conducted, seven of these with registered nurses and the remainder with aides and orderlies. Two additional interviews were conducted with Navajo nurses working outside the hospital facility, one with the director of field site clinics and another with a nurse–midwife who has worked at NNHF for number of years.

Professional Navajo health care workers such as registered nurses, laboratory technicians and so forth should have more experience in coping with divergent or bicultural settings. Having been reared on the reservation, presumably with higher levels of traditionalism when compared to urban reared Indians, these people have subsequently left the reservation for extended periods of time to be educated in Anglo colleges, only to return again to live on the reservation but work within an Anglo environment. Non-professional health care staff such as aides and orderlies have typically not been exposed to extended Anglo urban influences, have

not left the reservation for any extended periods of time and thus can be assumed to experience more difficulty in traversing the Anglo dominated medical environment.

All but one of the respondents had been reared on the reservation. Excluding the one exception, all stated they had been reared in fairly traditional to very traditional families, with those citing themselves as having been traditionally reared noting they did not speak English until starting school. None of the non-professional staff had lived off the reservation for any period of time and the professional nursing staff had left only to complete educational requirements prior to returning permanently.

All but the one respondent had participated in religious healing ceremonies (either traditional, Peyote or both) as a child and adult and all those participating professed a belief in the curing and healing capability of the ceremonies. All respondents also utilized Anglo medicine. The one exception was a nurse who had been reared off the reservation in a nearby border town. She had been taken to several ceremonies as a child by her grandmother and while she did not profess a strong belief in the healing power of the ceremonies, she did acknowledge the possibility of their effectiveness.

Wagner noted that

> at least since Malinowski's time, it has been commonly assumed that religion embodies the culture's basic philosophy, mythology, and other symbol systems (the 'ideological' variables) more clearly than other institutionalized spheres. (1975 162)

These respondents profess a belief and participate in religious curing ceremonies, either in the traditional Navajo form or the syncretic Peyote variation. They also utilize Anglo medicine, giving evidence of bicultural functioning in two rather divergent frames of reference surrounding issues of curing and healing.

The purpose of this research was not to categorize the respondents with regard to a traditional,

transitional, or Anglo orientation. Rather, given the multicultural, pluralistic world inhabited by these individuals, I was interested in describing the tensions and pulls encountered in a dominant, medical model work environment as well as the coping strategies employed when two different cultural systems impinge on and affect behavior in the work setting.

Interviews were designed to elicit from the respondents some idea of specific problem areas each had encountered on the job as well as the personal coping strategies utilized. My goal was not individual biography but rather the parametering of possible generic coping strategies.

CULTURAL CONFIGURATIONS AND COPING STRATEGIES

Job Satisfaction

Berger and Luckmann (1966 140) have addressed the problems inherent in a situation of pluralistic constructions of reality by referring to the strength of primary socialization. They point out that the formal processes of secondary socialization are presupposed by a preceding primary socialization, that is, an already formed self and an already internalized world. For the Navajo respondents employed at NNHF, a bicultural approach to curing and healing has been the basic primary socialization focus, an acceptance of the efficacy of both Anglo medicine as well as traditional medicine. However, the work environment of the hospital is clearly ruled by the dominant Anglo ideology of physiological imbalance. Navajo health care workers then necessarily find themselves in a difficult position at times. Kunitz has noted:

> ...Many Navajo paraprofessionals work alongside non-Indian professionals who have well developed professional ideologies and explanations for the conditions with which they are confronted. Often these explanations are at variance with those of the Navajo themselves. (1981 186)

One might naturally expect to find the more non-traditional Navajo working within the Anglo health care structure. However, on the reservation, even if one does not believe in the Anglo health care structure and/or has difficulty navigating the work environment of dominant Anglo culture, economic pressures alone could force such involvement with Anglo establishment. With unemployment ranging as high as sixty to seventy percent for some areas of the Navajo reservation, a job of any type may be highly valued for the income it provides whatever the cultural conflicts it presents (Kunitz 1983).

Interviews with the respondents indicated that for some of them income alone was the sustaining motivation for continued employment at NNHF. Seven of the respondents, typically the most traditional and the least educated, stated that they would secure other work if it were available. Much of the dissatisfaction with work vocalized by the respondents centered around issues associated with conflicting cultural healing methods. As one aide confided,

> Sometimes I don't do what they (nurses) tell me to do (to patients) because I know it won't do any good and sometimes it will just hurt the person and still won't do any good, so I just don't do it. They think I don't do it because I am dumb or something. But I know it won't do any good.

On the other hand, professional workers such as registered nurses consistently express high levels of job satisfaction. This in itself should not be surprising given the higher wages and social prestige associated with professional nursing. However, apparently more was at work here than simple status differentiation. These women typically characterized themselves as carrying on a "medical legacy." All described themselves as descending from families that had historically produced a medicine man. As one nurse explained:

> My people see my carrying on the tradition set by my grandfather. He was a well known medicine man who did many curing ceremonies. In Navajo tradition there is a place for a number of different types of healers (bone-setters, herbalists, etc.). I think they see my role as an extension of that in a sense. Instead of a healer in only the traditional way, I am seen as a healer as part of the incorporation of the Anglo way. Of course, I will sometimes advise my patients to have a ceremony if it is needed, so I don't deny the old way either.

In a sense, it may be the ability to perceive themselves as carrying out the traditional role of healer in a bicultural performance which, at least partially, aids these nurses with greater job satisfaction. Certainly these women face culture conflicts as well as the aides. However, from the more powerful position of registered nurse, they are able to make bicultural recommendations to patients as a strategy to combat a culturally monolithic work environment, a strategy the aids feel incapable of exercising.

The Cultural Timing of Work Requirements

The conflict between cultural worlds is played out in a number of ways in the hospital setting. One such issue is concerned with temporality, often a concern which relates to job satisfaction. Anglo treatment strategies are regulated by strict time schedules. As Zerubavel notes:

> Time is very central to the definition of norms and their boundaries. That an act is considered legitimate when it takes place at one time and illegitimate when it takes place at another time implies that the legitimacy of social acts is, to a large extent, temporally situated. (1979 55)

Adherence to strict time schedules is not a part of traditional Navajo lifestyle (Reifel 1957). For the Navajo, the future and past are not particularly relevant. Focus is placed on the present. Navajo live with an exultation of 'now.'

This is best demonstrated by the Navajo concept of 'walking in beauty.' One who is in touch with nature, in harmony with all the interrelated components of the universe, spiritually balanced,

in essence, concentrated on the world as it is at the moment, is walking in beauty (Witherspoon 1974). Timing is intuitive and subjective rather than scientific and objective. While this may well be a beautiful sense of enjoying 'being,' it can create difficulties in health care. For example, given the traditional Navajo focus on 'now,' asking a Navajo patient to describe previous experience with his/her illness does not produce a good result. The patient does not understand why an episode of illness two years ago may be pertinent to the illness being experienced at the moment. Instructing a Navajo non-professional health care worker to carry out a precisely defined program regimented by a strict time schedule with a strong future orientation does not produce a particularly good outcome either. This lack of adherence to a prescribed time schedule was a continual source of frustration for Anglo staff on one hand and for the Navajo staff on the other. As one aide complained,

I don't know why they (nurses) get so upset all the time about this. I do that treatment four times a day like the doctor says he is to have it done. I don't do it exactly when they want it done, but it gets done. Sometimes it just isn't right to do it when they want it done so I wait until later or I do it earlier.

Interviews with staff indicated that a conflicting view of the importance of "time" presented ongoing problems for them on the job. Getting to work on time, leaving work on time, time for lunch, time to do patient treatments and, for nurses, time to give certain medications, all created obstacles in job enjoyment. As one aide noted,

You can sure tell that Anglos invented the clock. Everyone is clock crazy around here. They get mad if you are late for work. They get mad if you don't eat lunch on time. I guess they think everyone has a clock. I guess they don't understand that sometimes I have family problems I have to take care of before I can come to work by the clock.

An Anglo nurse who has lived and worked on the reservation for a number of years commented

on the Navajo perception of time and the problems it can create for staff.

If you want to make it on the reservation you have to get used to Indian time. You could give yourself a stroke trying to make them do things on your time schedule. It just doesn't work. After a couple of years you learn it really doesn't matter if something is done at nine o'clock or ten o'clock or even eleven o'clock. You just can't make these people change their sense of time.

Observations of the staff over a five year period indicated that, indeed, the Navajo staff were only marginally willing to adjust to Anglo imposed time schedules. Compliance with time schedules remains an ongoing source of conflict between Anglos who have not adjusted to "Indian time" and Navajo staff.

Moore has noted that:

The transition from temporally lax and variable work pattern to a tightly timed and temporally recompensed work schedule is one of the major changes in attitude required of the newly recruited worker in underdeveloped areas undergoing economic modernization. (Moore 1963 25)

Burger and Luckmann (1966) further point out that transmission of institutional meanings obviously implies control and legitimation procedures. Such procedures are lacking at NNHF. Being late may get a staff member reprimanded but it does not bring about termination or other serious consequences such as loss of wages or job probation. In fact, while Anglos may complain about the alternative temporality of the Navajo staff, the relative lack of institutional controls to regulate time, the legitimizing of acts at discrepant times and the eventual willingness on the part of Anglos to adjust to Navajo time indicates that the traditional Navajo view superseded the dominant Anglo perspective in this matter.

Circumventing Communication Conflicts about Illness

Since a large part of Navajo religion is focused on restoration of health, one would expect them to

have an elaborate vocabulary regarding disease and illness. This is not the case. While there are a lot of synonyms for *sick* and *sickness*, illness symptoms are divided into four basic categories: aches, pains, disturbing dreams, and feeling bad all over (Werner 1965).

A native patient is as likely to offer 'feeling bad all over' to the native diagnostician as he is to a medical physician. 'Feeling bad all over' is accepted by the native diagnostician, but the medical physician wants clarification as to degree, duration, specific organs involved—questions whose significance the Navajo do not understand. As noted earlier, no Navajo disease is known by the symptoms it produces or by the part of the body it is thought to affect. The notion of locating the cause of an illness in physiological processes is foreign to Navajo thought. The major problem that has faced Anglo health care workers in treating Navajo sickness and disease is that Navajo do not account for illness in biological terms. There is no precedent for treating the body or parts of the body separately. Navajo healing ceremonies are designed to cure the whole person. In addition, Native Americans simply do not like to ask questions. Respect for others is noticeable in avoidance of questioning (Martin 1981).

A Navajo patient can feel a great deal of frustration when attempting to answer all the many and varied questions put to him/her by an Anglo health care provider, particularly given that he/she may not see any point to the whole thing. Navajo health care workers who do not wholeheartedly advocate an Anglo conceptualization of illness can also encounter the situation with frustration, especially when asked to translate the interaction between the traditional patient who does not speak English and the health care provider who does not speak Navajo. As one Navajo aide complained:

> *I don't understand why the doctors have to ask all these questions. Some of them don't make any sense and it just seems rude to be asking them. And the patients don't understand them either.*

Since translating for Anglo health care workers was an ongoing source of conflict and frustration for the aides, it is precisely the type of situation which would generate innovative strategies for dealing with cultural discrepancies. The non-professional staff has developed two major coping strategies for dealing with this cultural barrier. The first method occurs when they evaluate and sift through the series of questions they are asked to put before the patient and choose to either not ask specific questions or to alter the questions to forms which they feel are more 'acceptable' in terms of Navajo etiquette or ideology. In a sense, they detour around the cultural obstacles. As one aide explained:

> *I just try to put it in terms that the patient might understand. A lot of times it isn't exactly what the doctor or nurse want to know but it's as close as you can get. Most of the time the patient doesn't even understand why the doctors want to know some of the things they ask.*

A second coping strategy for dealing with the translation issue is simply to refuse to do it. One aide explained to me that she had set up the situation so she isn't asked to translate.

> *I don't get asked to do that. I just act like I don't understand English very well so they pick on someone else.*

And yet another aide commented:

> *Sometimes I just don't ask them (the physician's questions). I just tell the doctor that the patient doesn't know.*

The aides can effectively utilize these two strategies most of the time. However, there is one exception. This exception is an Anglo physician married to a Navajo woman who has lived on the reservation for over ten years. While not fluent in Navajo, he understands the language fairly well. None of the aids like to translate for him and generally tried to avoid him when he came on the floor to visit patients. When questioned about the avoidance strategy, one aide confided,

Yes, you are right (laughing). We do all run when he comes on the floor. He knows when we are translating right and when we aren't. He makes us ask everything he wants to know. Dr. X (another physician) is easy to translate for. He believes anything you tell him. Sometimes I've just asked patients about their sheep and then tell him (Dr. X) anything I want to. The patients like him because they think he is interested in their sheep.

Registered nurses, on the other hand, trained in Anglo systems of health and illness, do recognize the importance of ascertaining a complete medical history and denied during interviews they had difficulty in completing this task when required. However, researcher observations over many months indicated clearly that the Navajo nurses would avoid these tasks whenever possible, often assigning an aide to do this work when perhaps the nurse was more fluent bilingually. Thus, a strategy utilized by Navajo nurses to avoid this task was the definition of translation as "aides" work and not the task of a professional nurse, a job assignment clearly in conflict with normative constructions of reality in non-reservation Anglo hospitals.

Again, drawing on Berger and Luckmann, examination of the translation conflicts experienced by Navajo staff can be observed as a product of language incompatibilities. As these theorists note:

Language objectivates the shared experiences and makes them available to all within the linguistic community, thus becoming both the basis and the instrument of the collective stock of knowledge. (1966 68).

Given the two competing constructions of reality at work in the hospital environment, and particularly given that the Navajo language does not lend itself well to translating physiologically based questions, it is not surprising to see issues of translation crop up as sources of conflict experienced by Navajo health care workers. Quite clearly, among most of the non-professional staff interviewed, skepticism towards the institutional definition was apparent by their manipulation of the translation interaction. Professional nurses used a different

manipulative stance, one that invoked a stratification system that removes them from the responsibility of such endeavors.

An additional interesting point is lodged in the fact that registered nurses are exposed to the translation interaction between physicians and aides on a daily basis. They were aware of the instances when an inquiry from a physician to his patient regarding his previous health history took the form of polite comments on a herd of sheep. However, they didn't "give the show away." From a Goffmanian (1967) perspective, they are good team players with primary allegiance being shown to the traditional 'world.'

Expectations of Medical Knowledge and Skill

Spindler (1984), in her discussion of diffusion models, commented on the importance of such processes as syncretization (the blending of traits from separate traditions into something new) as well as reinterpretation (the "fitting" of a borrowed trait to a sociocultural system). These processes are observed among the responsibilities at NNHF with regard to curing and healing practices and perceptions of clinical realities.

Kleinman et al. has noted that clinical realities vary by social setting and type of practitioner. The biomedical view of clinical reality assumes that

biologic concerns are more basic, real, clinically significant than psychologic or sociocultural issues. Disease, not illness, is the chief concern; curing, not healing, is the chief objective. (Kleinman et al. 1978 255)

In Navajo traditional medicine, the diagnosing and healing of sickness is a matter of spiritual, intuitive knowledge rather than scientific knowledge which is lodged in biological dysfunction. A medicine man, Anglo or Navajo, should *know* what is wrong with the patient. When Anglo physicians don't know, or subject their patients to many questions or painful physical examination in order to scientifically discover the cause and subsequent

cure of disease, non-professional Navajo staff may lose patience. As one Navajo aide explained:

> Sometimes I get mad because I tell the doctor that the patient says he just hurts all over and that is what is wrong with him. And that is what is wrong with him. But the doctors are never satisfied with that. Sometimes I get mad at the doctors because they are supposed to know what is wrong with the people without asking all those stupid questions.

In addition to consternation regarding the physician's inability to know what was wrong with the patient, aides also expressed anger at what they considered to be the Anglo staff's lack of recognition of the importance of Navajo healing procedures, particularly during episodes of illness when no clear cause of illness has been ascertained. One Navajo aide expressed her displeasure in this manner:

> Sometimes I get mad because they (doctors) don't know what is wrong with the patient but they don't understand that the medicine man can know. I think sometimes the doctors ought to tell the patient to go home and have a ceremony but they don't ever do that. They think only their medicine works. Medicine men know that Anglo medicine works sometimes. Why don't Anglos know that Navajo medicine can work too?

Several points of interest have been expressed in the preceding quotes. Clearly a sense of 'knowing' what is wrong with a patient was expected by the non-professional staff on the part of the Anglo medical staff. And just as clearly, this expectation was not always met. Aides experienced anger when physicians didn't 'know' and patients must suffer as a result of this. Aides possessed a bicultural interpretation of 'medical knowledge,' projecting the expectation of 'knowledge' from the traditional system to that of the Anglo system, or, in other words, generalizing their own 'everyday' understanding to a foreign system of thought. It is an uneasy bicultural synthesis that doesn't always fit for the aides. And yet, they try to make it fit. And when it doesn't, when physicians don't

'know,' the aides turn to medicine men and ceremonies.

Registered nurses, on the other hand, were able to articulate more succinctly the differences in 'knowing' among traditional and Anglo health care providers. One registered nurse described the differences this way:

> I define the ability on the part of Navajo medicine as "intuitive–spiritual" sources of knowledge. A medicine man, given his spiritual sense of knowledge, would simply "know" when a patient would need to seek the services of an Anglo physician. Medicine men are more attuned to a "total sense" of the patient. Anglo medicine just concentrates on a physiological basis but traditional medicine is more complete, holistic…Anglo medicine deals with the "conscious" part of the person.

Another registered nurse explained,

> Traditionalists have always known there is a connection between physical, the mind, body, and soul and the spiritual. Anglo medicine is based in physiology. The major problem I see in modern medicine is physicians seem to have some kind of mentality that they have exclusive rights to do whatever they want to this patient as this is their territory exclusively. It is almost like territorialism or something…Medicine men don't have this mentality. The main objective is to get the patient well. It is a holistic approach, not a tunnel vision approach…and the medicine man will use whatever is necessary to meet that objective, even referring to physicians if necessary. Certainly, though, physicians don't refer back to medicine men.

As mentioned previously, aides were likely to become angry with Anglo physicians and their lack of recognition of the efficacy of Navajo practices. Registered nurses did not express anger at this. Unlike the aides who project the Navajo expectation of 'knowing' to Anglo medicine, they do not expect physicians to appreciate the effectiveness of Navajo healing practices. When nurses were asked during interviews how they approached and managed the rejection of traditional practices, their responses reflected an acceptance of the limited scope and vision of the Anglo system. One nurse,

in explaining her lack of anger when confronted with the rigidity of the hospital setting, remarked:

> *Oh, I don't get upset as some do. I recognize that the Anglo is limited in some ways. The Anglo doctor can be very good at what he does—he just doesn't do everything. He isn't holistic as the traditional medicine man is. I don't expect him to be.*

Another nurse elaborated on her strategy for combating the structure of the Anglo view:

> *Sometimes I go against the institution and simply tell the patient to get a ceremony and then come back. Or I try to arrange for a patient to have a healer visit them at the hospital if the condition of the patient prohibits leaving. I've had trouble with physicians over this. I have thirty hours towards my doctorate in nursing and they (physicians) expect me to have given up all traditionalism and see my referring back to it as my "going native" or something. I just recognize the inadequacies of biomedicine at times and, in the sense of the traditional healer, use all things available to cure the patient. I don't limit myself to simply one method of health care. Not like physicians do. All they see is their way.*

In short, Navajo aides want medical physicians to 'heal' as well as cure. Professional staff, without much rancor, understand that medical physicians can only 'cure.'

CONCLUSION

As noted previously, Spindler (1984) suggests that a study of biculturalism should also include a basic formatting of coping strategies rather than a singular focus on the parametering of a continuum of assimilation. This ethnographic study of Navajo health care workers has provided for the reader a description of some of the tensions and pulls experienced by the respondents when faced with conflicting or competing constructions of reality brought about by the occasional disjunctions of cultural pluralism.

Berger and Luckmann (1966) have noted that it is important to bear in mind that most modern societies are pluralistic, that is, have a shared core universe, taken for granted as such, and different partial universes coexisting in a state of mutual accommodation. They further suggest that pluralism encourages both skepticism and innovation and is thus inherently subversive of the taken for granted reality of the traditional status quo. For the respondents in this study, the pluralism of their work environment is occasionally problematic and coping strategies emerge as a mechanism for bridging the cultural gap. Differences among the respondents emerge as a result of greater or lesser experiences with the Anglo culture.

The registered nurses, with greater experiences in an Anglo defined world, enjoy more satisfaction in the work environment. They are more adept at recognizing the dichotomies and contradictions of the pluralistic world and therefore are better able to travel through the pitfalls of biculturalism. These workers don't have expectations of physicians which won't be met, nor do they profess consternation when Navajo ceremonies are ignored by the dominant structure. When faced with conflicts of culture choices, they bridge the span by advocating pluralistic usage of both types of healing strategies. They maintain an Indian identity within an Anglo defined status and role. When faced with differing constructions of reality, they employ successful strategies for avoiding or co-opting the situation.

Non-professional staff, on the other hand, are likely to encounter the same situations with less ability to manage conflicts. They hold misconceptions of the Anglo model and generalize characteristics belonging to the traditional healer to the modern medical physician and occasionally find themselves disappointed by the inadequacy of the fit. Their biculturalism is more mosaic than that of the nurses. However, as indicated by their strategies to avoid or manipulate the translation interaction, as well as set the temporality of the work schedule to a certain degree, they have found ways to cope with their work environment.

The purpose of this article was not to describe a continuum of acculturation or to categorize Navajo health care workers into a particular orientation of accommodation. However, striking similarities to McFee's (1968) study of the "150 percent man" emerges with his description of the "interpreters." Characteristics of his "interpreters" include having received a good education in White schools, having a wide range of experiences in parts of White culture, being accepted by the Indian group and the accomplishment of the maintenance of an Indian identity. These characteristics also describe the registered nurses in this study. They too wish to combine the "best of the Indian way with the best of the White way."

Presumably, with their education and training, they could have chosen to not return to the reservation past completion of their education, yet they did elect to do so. They continue to participate in themselves and advocate for their patients Indian ceremonies. As mentioned previously, these nurses are good team players and do not give away the translation show of the aides, thereby supporting and identifying with the Navajo traditions. They are also, in a sense, one hundred and fifty percent people.

The Navajo health care workers described in the study, by their own definition, take with them to work a bicultural orientation to curing and healing. At the work place they find themselves involved in a pluralistic world. Sometimes they are able to deflect Anglo conceptions and procedures. Sometimes they must give way to them. Some are better than others at bridging the gap between their multiple worlds. But all demonstrate, more or less, the ability to cope, to accommodate, to survive.

REFERENCES

Berger P, T Luckmann 1966 *The Social Construction of Reality* NY: Anchor

Christopherson V, S Dingle 1982 Factors related to traditionalism among Navajo students *Ethnic Racial Studies* 5 213–222

Fiske S 1978 Rules of address: Navajo women in Los Angeles *J Anthropological Res* 34 72–91

Goffman E 1967 *Interaction Ritual* NY: Doubleday

Graves TD 1970 The personal adjustment of Navajo migrants to Denver, CO *Amer Anthropologist* 72 35–54

Griffen J 1984 Culture contact, women and work: the Navajo example *Soc Sci J* 21 29–39

Henderson E 1979 Skilled and unskilled blue collar Navajo workers: occupational diversity in an American Indian tribe *Soc Sci J* 16 63–80

Kleinman A, L Eisenberg, B Good 1978 Culture, illness and care: clinical lessons from anthropologic and cross-cultural research *Ann Internal Medicine* 88 251–258

Kluckhohn C, D Leighton 1946 *The Navajo* Cambridge: Harvard U Press

Kunitz S 1981 Underdevelopment, demographic change and health care on the Navajo reservation *Soc Sci Medicine* 15 175–192

——— 1983 *Disease Change and the Role of Medicine: The Navajo Experience* Berkeley: U California Press

Levy J 1983 Traditional Navajo health beliefs and practices. In S Kunitz ed *Disease Change and the Role of Medicine: The Navajo Experience* Berkeley: U California Press

Margon A 1977 Indians and immigrants: a comparison of groups new to the city *J Ethnic Studies* 4 4 17–28

Martin M 1981 Native American medicine: thoughts for post-traditional healers *J Amer Medical Ass* 245 2 141–143

McFee M 1968 The 150% man, a product of Blackfeet acculturation *Amer Anthropologist* 70 1096–1107

Metcalf A 1975 From schoolgirl to mother: the effects of education on Navajo women *Soc Prob* 23 5 535–544

Moore W 1963 *Man, Time and Society* NY: Wiley

Nurge E 1975 Anthropological perspectives for medical students *Human Organiz: J Appl Anthropology* 34 4 345–352

Polgar S 1960 Biculturation of Mesa okie teenage boys *Amer Anthropologist* 62 98–121

Reifel B 1957 Cultural factors in social adjustment *Indian Education* #298 Bureau of Indian Affairs

Spindler G, L Spindler 1971 *Dreamers without Power* Stanford: Holt, Rinehart, & Winston

Spindler LS 1984 *Culture Change and Modernization* Stanford: Waveland Press

Steele H 1973 The acculturation/assimilation model in urban Indian studies. In N Yetman ed *Majority and Minority* Boston: Allyn and Bacon

Voget FW 1956 The American Indian in transition: reformation and accommodation *Amer Anthropologist* 58 249–263

Wagner RM 1975 Pattern and process in ritual syncretism: the case of peyotism among the Navajo *J Anthropological Res* 31 162–181

Werner O 1965 Semantics of Navajo medical terms *Internat J Amer Linguistics* 31 1 1–17

Witherspoon G 1974 The central concepts of Navajo world view *Linguistics* 119 41–59

Zerubavel E 1979 Private time and public time *Soc Forces* 58 1 38–58

DEVELOPED WORLD PERSPECTIVE

WHY DO PATIENTS TURN TO COMPLEMENTARY MEDICINE? AN EMPIRICAL STUDY

CHARLES VINCENT AND ADRIAN FURNHAM

Complementary (alternative) medicine is now widely used throughout the developed world. The major complementary therapies, such as acupuncture, homeopathy, herbalism and osteopathy, are extensively used and increasingly accepted (British Medical Association, 1993). In the United Kingdom, Fulder & Munro (1985) found that in 1981 complementary consultations averaged 19500 per 100000 people, or 6.5 per cent of general practice consultations. Acupuncture, chiropractic and osteopathy were the most popular specialties with about two million consultations per year each. Overall, about 1.5 million people (2.5 per cent of the population) were receiving courses of treatment in a single year. Thomas and colleagues (1991) estimated that her more restricted group of professionally registered complementary practitioners undertook four million consultations per year, roughly one for every 55 patient consultations with an NHS general practitioner.

In Europe, studies suggest that between a third and a half of the adult population have used complementary medicine at some time. Where self-medication with homeopathic and herbal remedies is included in the definition (for studies in Belgium, Finland and France), approximately a third of people have had complementary treatment in the previous year (Lewith & Aldridge, 1991; Sharma, 1992). In the USA, Eisenberg, Kessler & Foster (1993) have recently found that more visits are made to providers of unconventional therapy (which includes the more widely known complementary therapies) than to all US primary care physicians (general practitioners). The expenditure on unconventional therapies was comparable to that spent on all hospitalizations in the US. Eisenberg's definition ("commonly used interventions neither taught widely in US medical schools nor generally available in US hospitals") included all the major complementary therapies, vitamin and mineral supplements, and other complementary remedies. Also included, however, were taking exercise and relaxation techniques—hardly unconventional techniques. The results exaggerate the use of truly unconventional therapies, but nevertheless show a widespread use and acceptance.

There is also growing interest in complementary medicine within the health professions. Questionnaire studies have examined the attitudes of orthodox medical students and practitioners

(Anderson & Anderson, 1987; Reilly, 1983; Wharton & Lewith, 1986) and found high rates of interest and knowledge, and referral of patients to complementary medicine.

The reasons for this increased interest and use of complementary medicine are not well understood, though many opinions have been offered. Some have suggested that the move towards complementary medicine represents a "flight from science" (Smith, 1983) or credulous faith in occult or paranormal phenomena (Baum, 1989; Skrabanek, 1988). The one small empirical study, a survey of 65 patients attending a clinic of complementary medicine, found that the failure of conventional medicine (for their complaints) was the main reason for attending (Moore, Phipps, Marcer & Lewith, 1985). In all studies, patients using complementary or unconventional therapies tend to be those with relatively more education and higher incomes (Sharma, 1992). These results are "not compatible with a picture of a patient unable to understand the medical possibilities or to make discriminating choices" (Fulder & Munro, 1985). Furthermore, it is becoming clear that it is relatively rare for complementary patients to abandon orthodox medicine. Complementary therapies, which are generally used for chronic, as opposed to life-threatening, conditions are generally used as an adjunct to conventional treatment, rather than as a replacement for it (Thomas, Carr, Westlake & Williams, 1991). Patients seem instead to consider a range of therapeutic options including self-medication, complementary medicine and conventional treatment and will make use of different forms of medicine on different occasions (Eisenberg *et al.,* 1993; Thomas *et al.,* 1991).

There are a number of possible reasons for turning to complementary medicine. Some patients are "pushed" because they may have become dissatisfied with the orthodox medicine, rejecting its reliance on high technology and wary of the dangers of invasive techniques and the toxicity of many drugs. Others are "pulled" because, while

they may retain a belief in the value and effectiveness of orthodox medicine, at least in certain areas they find some aspects of complementary medicine attractive. They may regard it as especially efficacious for some conditions, as dealing more with the emotional aspects of illness, or as having a spiritual dimension that is not seen as important in orthodox medicine.

This study examined the reasons people seek complementary treatment, in an effort to provide empirical data after almost a decade of speculation about patients' motives for seeking complementary treatment. Three of the main systems of complementary medicine were contrasted, as reasons may vary according to the type of treatment and problem concerned. No one hypothesis was tested. Rather all the various suggestions for the attraction of these more established and accepted complementary therapies were explored.

METHOD

Subjects

A total of 268 patients, 201 (74.9 per cent) female, took part in the study: 89 were attending the British School of Osteopathy, 92 a large acupuncture centre in South London, and 87 the Royal Homeopathic Hospital. Response rate averaged 78 per cent in the three groups. The usual reason given for not completing the questionnaire was shortage of time before their appointment. Mean age of subjects was 43.3 years (range 16–71 years); 43 per cent were married or living together; and 43.4 per cent were educated to degree level. Further information on demographic characteristics of each group is given below.

Questionnaire

The questionnaire covered three broad areas: (a) basic demographic information; (b) history of present complaint, previous treatment, and other health problems; (c) reasons for seeking comple-

mentary treatment. Reasons for seeking comple-mentary treatment (shown in Table 3) were derived from preliminary interviews with patients and from the literature on complementary medi-cine (e.g. Sharma, 1992). A broad cross-section of potential reasons was used to cover as wide a spec-trum as possible. Twenty reasons were used in the final list, each being rated on a five-point scale from 1 (not at all important) to 5 (extremely important).

Procedure

Patients were approached while waiting for treat-ment at one of the three study locations. The re-search assistant gave a short account of the nature

and purpose of the study and they were invited to take part in a study of their reasons for seeking complementary treatment. Complete anonymity and confidentiality were assured as no names were requested on the questionnaire. Questionnaires were returned just before their appointment. On occasion subjects returned their questionnaire by post, but this was not encouraged.

RESULTS

Demographic Information

Demographic information and relevant medical history for the three groups is shown in Table 1. A high proportion (74.8 per cent) of all subjects were

TABLE 1   Demographic Characteristics and Medical History

	ACUPUNCTURE	HOMEOPATHY	OSTEOPATHY	CHI OR F RATIO
Sex (% female)	84.4	81.3	60.0	Chi = 16.2 $p < .001$
Age	38.5	47.8	43.8	$F = 7.32$ $p < .001$
Marital status (% married/living together)	50.0	34.9	43.5	Chi = 4.00 n.s.
Education (% with degree)	57.8	31.2	39.3	Chi = 9.13 $p < .001$
Serious illness last 5 years (%)	23.0	32.5	12.5	Chi = 9.13 $p < .01$
Treatment for emotional problems (%)	29.9	29.1	20.0	Chi = 2.64 n.s.
Previous comp. treatment (%)	60.7	42.5	42.7	Chi = 7.51 $p < .05$
Duration current problem (years)	8.9	11.2	4.8	$F = 11.64$ $p < .001$
Consultation with doctor (%)	83.7	96.5	67.4	Chi = 25.3 $p < .001$
Previous orthodox treatment (%)	67.4	80.0	45.2	Chi = 27.8 $p < .001$
Effectiveness: moderate or good (%)	26.9	27.4	34.7	Chi = 3.74 n.s.
Satisfaction: moderate or good (%)	10.6	23.0	26.5	Chi = 8.61 n.s.

female, particularly in the acupuncture and home-opathy groups. Over 40 per cent were educated to degree level, the figure reaching 57 per cent in the acupuncture group. The groups differed on sex, marital status and education; these factors were entered as covariates in later analyses together with relevant medical history variables. That is, because the groups differed on certain demographic grounds statistical procedures were employed to take account of these differences so that it was possible to explain differences in reasons for choice purely in terms of treatment choice. It should be noted that in terms of demographic variables these samples are not atypical when compared to many London based GP clinics. But compared to patients who chose exclusively orthodox medicine, it seems these three groups were more sceptical of orthodox medicine's efficacy and less satisfied with the treatment (Furnham & Smith, 1988).

Current Complaint and Medical History

The principal complaint for which patients sought complementary treatment is shown in Table 2. The classification was based on that used by Thomas *et*

al. (1991) in their study of complementary practitioners and patients, which was in turn based on the International Classification of Diseases (ICD 9). All patients recorded a main complaint; 17.9 per cent recorded a second concurrent complaint and 4 per cent a third complaint also. Additional complaints were fairly evenly distributed between categories.

Osteopathy patients had almost invariably sought help for musculoskeletal (neck pain, back pain, injuries) or arthritic conditions. Acupuncture and homeopathy were used for a much wider range of conditions, with allergic and stress-related conditions being especially common. All conditions tended to be chronic in nature, mostly of long duration (mean 8.2 years), and not life threatening. The five homeopathy patients with cancer had all received conventional treatment, although two were not currently receiving it.

The great majority of patients (82.6 per cent) had consulted a doctor about their complaint, though this was less common with osteopathic treatment for musculoskeletal complaints. Most had also had previous orthodox treatment, though usually with limited success and less satisfaction. Over a quarter of patients admitted receiving treatment for emotional problems, though this in-

TABLE 2   Principal Complaints for Which Treatment Was Sought (figures are percentages of complaints for each group)

	ACUPUNCTURE	HOMEOPATHY	OSTEOPATHY
Musculoskeletal/rheumatic	15.2	24.1	95.5
Allergy/skin disorders	14.1	28.7	—
Stress/anxiety/depression/insomnia	21.7	1.1	1.1
Respiratory	7.6	5.7	—
Viral/M. E.	7.6	11.5	—
Gynaecological	13.0	3.4	—
Digestive disorders	4.3	4.6	—
Migraine/headache	3.3	4.6	2.2
Cancer	—	5.7	—
Smoking/addictions	2.2	1.1	—
Others	11.0	9.5	1.2
Total	100	100	100

cluded any form of counselling for relationship difficulties and other problems of day-to-day living. Subjects were not asked specifically about psychiatric problems.

Reasons for Seeking Complementary Treatment

Table 3 shows the complete list of reasons and the mean ratings on a five-point (1 to 5) scale of importance for each of the three groups. Significant differences between groups (Scheffe multiple comparisons) are shown with pairs of letters in the table.

The importance of most of the reasons is clear, with few scoring below the midpoint (3) of the scale, representing moderate importance. High scores were found in all groups for lack of effectiveness of orthodox medicine, a belief that complementary medicine would be effective, valuing the emphasis on treating the whole person and wanting to take an active part in maintaining their health. Significant differences between groups were seen on eight items; homeopathy patients felt more strongly about the naturalness of complementary therapy and were more despairing about their illness. Acupuncture patients were more sceptical and critical of orthodox medicine than osteopathy patients.

Factor Analysis of Reasons

A principal component analysis with varimax rotation was carried out to reduce the 20 reasons to a smaller number of clearly interpretable factors. Initial analyses revealed six factors with eigenvalues of greater than 1.00, but the scree test showed a break in the series of eigenvalues between factors 5 and 6. In addition the five-factor solution offered a clearer interpretation and a more parsimonious solution. The principal factor loadings are shown in Table 4, with loadings below .30 being excluded as not being relevant to the solution (Tabachnik & Fidell, 1989). In order, the factors accounted for 28, 16, 9, 7 and 4 per cent of the variance respectively.

Comparison of Factors between Groups

Factor scores were calculated by averaging the individual items scores for the relevant questions. Where an item (question) loaded on more than one factor, it was included in the highest loading factor. Missing data on individual items were replaced by the mean value for that item.

Two factors stand out as being more important than the others: the *positive value of complementary medicine* and, with slightly less importance, *previous experience of orthodox medicine as ineffective*. After these the *dangers and side-effects of orthodox medicine* and *poor communication with doctors* are still important for a proportion of the patients.

Analysis of variance between groups revealed significant differences between groups on three factors. However, as the groups differed on a number of demographic and medical factors, analysis of covariance was carried out with the following factors entered as covariates: age, sex, educational level, previous serious illness, duration of complaint and previous orthodox treatment. Results of ANCOVA were essentially the same as results for ANOVA for two factors (side-effects of orthodox medicine and availability of complementary medicine) with no covariates reaching significance. However, differences between groups on the effectiveness of orthodox medicine became non-significant when corrected for the imbalance in previous experience of orthodox treatment. The only differences remaining indicated that the side-effects and dangers of modern medicine were of significantly less concern to the osteopathy group, and the availability of osteopathy was more a factor in relation to this group of patients.

DISCUSSION

This study was concerned with why patients of recognized alternative or complementary medical therapies chose that therapy. The majority of complementary patients had been, at some time, patients of orthodox medical practitioners and had

TABLE 3 Reasons for Having Complementary Treatment

	ACUPUNCTURE	HOMEOPATHY	OSTEOPATHY	F RATIO	p
1. Because orthodox treatment was not effective for my particular problem	4.51 (1.28)	4.23 (1.33)	4.48 (1.59)	0.91	n.s.
2. Because the orthodox treatment I received was too distressing	3.94 (2.10)	3.57 (2.16)	4.42 (2.21)	2.85	n.s.
3. Because the orthodox treatment I received had unpleasant side-effects	4.29 (1.92)	3.80 (1.87)	4.60 (2.11)	3.03	.05
4. Because I believe that orthodox medicine generally has too many unpleasant side-effects	3.70 (1.61)	4.24 (1.59)	4.05 (2.08)	1.96	n.s.
5. Because I believe that orthodox medicine is generally ineffective	3.25_a (1.72)	3.30 (1.92)	4.00_a (1.87)	4.07	.01
6. Because my doctor did not understand my problem	3.80 (1.89)	3.80 (1.93)	4.44 (1.74)	3.05	.05
7. Because I found it difficult to talk to my doctor	3.48 (2.09)	3.71 (2.17)	4.23 (2.19)	2.58	n.s.
8. Because my doctor did not give me enough time	3.64_a (1.98)	4.15 (1.99)	4.42_a (1.90)	3.40	.05
9. Because I was persuaded to come by a friend or relative	3.62 (2.02)	4.34 (2.11)	4.31 (1.72)	3.48	.05
10. Because it was easier to get an appointment with a complementary practitioner	3.16_a (2.33)	3.62 (2.43)	4.33_a (1.89)	5.53	.005
11. Because I have a more equal relationship with my complementary practitioner than with my doctor	3.86 (1.55)	4.18 (1.99)	4.34 (1.89)	1.52	n.s.
12. Because I believe complementary therapy will be more effective for my problem than orthodox medicine	4.49 (0.96)	4.50 (1.04)	4.74 (0.67)	1.98	n.s.
13. Because I believe that complementary medicine enables me to take a more active part in maintaining my health	4.37 (0.92)	4.69_a (0.85)	4.28_a (1.26)	3.44	.05
14. Because I value the emphasis on treating the whole person	4.72 (0.71)	4.73 (0.87)	4.49 (1.13)	1.77	n.s.
15. Because I feel so relaxed after complementary treatment sessions	4.04 (1.37)	4.26 (1.76)	4.58 (1.48)	1.26	n.s.
16. Because the explanation of my illness that I was given by my complementary practitioner made sense to me	4.06 (1.30)	4.28 (1.37)	4.42 (1.21)	1.66	n.s.
17. Because I value a form of therapy that involves actually touching me	3.20_a (1.72)	3.97_a (2.18)	3.58 (1.82)	3.29	.05
18. Because I feel that complementary treatment is a more natural form of healing than orthodox medicine	3.81_a (1.40)	$4.45_{a,b}$ (1.03)	3.88_b (1.46)	5.44	.001
19. Because complementary treatment is less expensive than orthodox private medicine	$2.66_{a,b}$ (2.04)	3.83_a (2.19)	3.63_b (2.01)	7.04	.001
20. Because I am desperate and will try anything	3.42_a (1.97)	4.59_a (1.38)	4.01 (1.92)	8.34	.001

Note: Pairs of letters indicate significant differences (Scheffe comparisons).

TABLE 4 Reasons for Having Complementary Treatment

	FACTOR 1	FACTOR 2	FACTOR 3	FACTOR 4	FACTOR 5
1. Because orthodox treatment was not effective for my particular problem	—	—	—	—	.81
2. Because the orthodox treatment I received was too distressing	—	—	.71	—	—
3. Because the orthodox treatment I received had unpleasant side-effects	—	—	.83	—	—
4. Because I believe that orthodox medicine generally has too many unpleasant side-effects	.36	—	.69	—	—
5. Because I believe that orthodox medicine is generally ineffective	.36	.39	—	—	—
6. Because my doctor did not understand my problem	—	.77	—	—	—
7. Because I found it difficult to talk to my doctor	—	.88	—	—	—
8. Because my doctor did not give me enough time	—	.83	—	—	—
9. Because I was persuaded to come by a friend or relative	—	—	—	.67	—
10. Because it was easier to get an appointment with a complementary practitioner	—	—	—	.76	—
11. Because I have a more equal relationship with my complementary practitioner than with my doctor	.42	.37	—	—	—
12. Because I believe that complementary therapy will be more effective for my problem than orthodox medicine	.68	—	—	—	—
13. Because I believe complementary medicine enables me to take a more active part in maintaining my health	.71	—	—	—	—
14. Because I value the emphasis on treating the whole person	.68	—	—	—	—
15. Because I feel so relaxed after complementary treatment sessions	.45	—	—	—	—
16. Because the explanation of my illness that I was given by my complementary practitioner made sense to me	.51	—	—	—	—
17. Because I value a form of therapy that involves actually touching me	.53	—	—	.43	—
18. Because I feel that complementary treatment is a more natural form of healing than orthodox medicine	.68	—	—	—	—
19. Because complementary treatment is less expensive than orthodox private medicine	.34	—	—	.46	—
20. Because I am desperate and will try anything	—	—	—	.37	.49

Note: Factor loadings below .30 have been excluded.

TABLE 5   Factor Scores by Patient Group

FACTOR	ACUPUNCTURE	HOMOEOPATHY	OSTEOPATHY	MEAN	F RATIO/SIG.
Value of complementary medicine	3.92	3.88	3.98	3.90	.11, n.s.
Poor doctor communication	2.85	2.95	2.89	2.90	.19, n.s.
Side-effects of orthodox medicine	3.05_a	3.01_b	$2.67_{a,b}$	2.91	4.13, $p = .017$
Availability of complementary medicine	2.18_a	2.37_b	$2.91_{a,b}$	2.49	19.2, $p = .001$
Orthodox medicine ineffective	3.51	3.95	3.52	3.66	7.00, $p = .001$

Note: Letters indicate pairs of groups whose means are significantly different ($p < .05$) in Scheffe multiple comparisons.

come to complementary medicine after receiving orthodox treatment. Different complementary therapies attracted different kinds of complaint. Over 90 per cent of the osteopathy patients had muscular skeletal problems and over a quarter of the homeopathic patients had allergies or skin disorders. Over a fifth of acupuncture patients were seeking treatment for psychological or stress-related problems, and over a quarter of the total sample had received some help for emotional problems in the past. This does not necessarily mean a high incidence of psychological or psychiatric disorders, but may show the importance that complementary medical patients attach to the emotional aspects of their problems and to counselling aspects of treatment.

Of the 20 reasons they were presented with, the patients agreed strongly with almost a third. The reasons that were most strongly endorsed were "because I value the emphasis on treating the whole person"; "because I believe complementary therapy will be more effective for my problem than orthodox medicine"; "because I believe that complementary medicine will enable me to take a more active part in maintaining my health"; and "because orthodox treatment was not effective for my particular problem." There was little difference between the groups on their rating of the most important reasons.

The least important reasons rated by the groups included "because complementary treatment is less expensive than orthodox private medicine" and "because I value a form of therapy that involves actually touching me." Curiously there were significant differences between the groups on these reasons: the acupuncture patients rated costs as much less important than did the homeopathy patients, in spite of the fact that the homeopathy patients were attending a National Health Service hospital. The homeopathy group rated the fact that their chosen therapy allowed them a more active part in their health more highly than the osteopathy group, suggesting that a discussion of diet and life-style factors may play a stronger role in homeopathic consultations. Patients did not perceive orthodox medicine as generally ineffective, indicating that they are not suffering from a wholesale disillusion with medicine. Orthodox medicine is only seen as ineffective for their specific problems.

The factor analysis of the 20 reasons gave fairly clear results which underpinned many speculations from researchers in this field. The first, most important, factor was clearly a "pull" factor which included items that stressed that complementary treatment was more natural, effective, relaxing, sensible and that one could take an active part in it. The second, with almost equal impor-

tance, was the specific failure of orthodox medicine to bring them relief. The third factor was also a specific "push" factor and concerned the adverse side-effects of orthodox medicine. The fourth was a highly specific "push" factor which primarily concerned poor communication between patients and orthodox medicine practitioners. The fifth, relatively unimportant, factor stressed the easy, cost effective and available nature of complementary therapies. Clearly these different factors, although not strongly distinguished between the three complementary therapies, are likely to differ in importance for each individual according to their specific medical history, personal beliefs and temperament.

Three of the factors showed significant differences between the three patient groups. Acupuncture and homeopathy patients seemed "put off" by the potential side-effects of medicine more than the osteopathy group. This was probably due to the nature of the problems they presented with and possible use of drugs by orthodox doctors. A second difference between the groups indicated that the osteopathy patients rated the availability of their therapy as more important than the other two groups. The final factor which referred to the ineffective nature of orthodox medicine was rated most highly by the homeopathic group, who may have complaints that are particularly resistant to orthodox treatment. This would explain why group differences were no longer found after covariates, including severity of illness, were controlled for.

Other studies have failed to find marked differences between complementary medicine patients and general practice patients on a range of factors: health beliefs, views on the perceived efficacy of orthodox and complementary treatments and attitudes and values (Furnham & Smith, 1988; Vincent & Furnham, 1994). Complementary medicine patients do not appear to be "in flight from science" or to have generally unusual views. Certainly some aspects of complementary therapies have a strong appeal, which is as yet insufficiently understood. A belief in the efficacy of the treatment plays a part, whether gained from personal experience or, prior to beginning the treatment, from the personal recommendation of friends. This study suggests that other factors may play a part: many patients agreed that the willingness of their practitioners to discuss emotional factors, the explanations given for their illnesses, the chance to play an active part in their treatments were all important reasons for seeking complementary treatment.

This has been an exploratory study, which should provide guidance for future empirical work on treatment choice in complementary medicine. This questionnaire could be refined, by excluding questions that do not load highly on single factors, to provide a better focused instrument. Other aspects of the complementary consultation (the role of explanations, etc.) could be explored in more detail. It would have been valuable to have included more questions on the role of discussion of emotional aspects of illness in the questionnaire, in an effort to delineate more precisely those aspects of complementary therapies that patients find most important. Future studies should also separate the reasons for beginning treatment with complementary medicine from the reasons for continuing it. It is possible, for instance, that the failure of orthodox medicine is the strongest motive for seeking complementary treatment but that once treatment has been experienced other, more positive factors become more important. In one recent exploratory study, a large proportion of those who had tried complementary therapies perceived little benefit from them (Murray & Shepherd, 1993) suggesting a high level of on–off treatments. This suggests continuing users may be a particularly interesting, and possibly unusual, subgroup of those who try complementary medicine. A more detailed medical history, including information about previous orthodox treatment, might also shed light on the initial move to complementary forms of treatment.

ACKNOWLEDGMENTS

We are grateful to the Research Council for Complementary Medicine for supporting the study. We thank the following people for assisting with the study: Dr. Fisher at the Royal National Homeopathic Hospital; research staff and receptionists at the British School of Osteopathy; Kim Farley and the practitioners at the Traditional Acupuncture Centre.

REFERENCES

Anderson, E. & Anderson, P. (1987). General practitioners and alternative medicine. *Journal of the Royal College of General Practitioners,* **37,** 52–55.

Baum, M. (1989). Rationalism versus irrationalism in the care of the sick: Science versus the absurd (editorial). *Medical Journal of Australia,* **151,** 607–608.

British Medical Association (1993). *Complementary Medicine: Report of the Board of Science and Education.* Oxford: Oxford University Press.

Eisenberg, D., Kessler, R. C. & Foster, C. (1993). Unconventional medicine in the United States. *New England Journal of Medicine,* **328,** 246–252.

Fulder, S. J. & Munro, R. E. (1985). Complementary medicine in the United Kingdom: Patients, practitioners, and consultants. *Lancet,* **ii,** 542–545.

Furnham, A. & Smith, C. (1988). Choosing alternative medicine: A comparison of the beliefs of patients visiting a GP and a homeopath. *Social Science and Medicine,* **26,** 685–687.

Lewith, G. T. & Aldridge, D. A. (1991). *Complementary Medicine and the European Community.* Saffron Waldon: C. W. Daniel.

Moore, J., Phipps, K., Marcer, D. & Lewith, G. T. (1985). Why do people seek treatment by alternative medicine? *British Medical Journal,* **290,** 28–29.

Murray, J. & Shepherd, S. (1993). Alternative or additional medicine? An exploratory study in general practice. *Social Science and Medicine,* **37,** 938–988.

Reilly, D. T. (1983). Young doctors' views on alternative medicine. *British Medical Journal,* **287,** 337–339.

Sharma, U. (1992). *Complementary Medicine Today: Practitioners and Patients.* London: Routledge.

Skrabanek, P. (1988). Paranormal health claims. *Experientia,* **44,** 303–309.

Smith, T. (1983). Alternative medicine (editorial). *British Medical Journal,* **287,** 307–308.

Tabachnik, B. G. & Fidell, L. S. (1989). *Using Multivariate Statistics.* New York: Harper & Row.

Thomas, K. J., Carr, J., Westlake, L. & Williams, B. T. (1991). Use of non-orthodox and conventional health care in Great Britain. *British Medical Journal,* **302,** 207–210.

Vincent, C. A. & Furnham, A. (1994). The perceived efficacy of orthodox and complementary medicine. *Complementary Therapies in Medicine,* **2,** 128–134.

Wharton, R. & Lewith, G. (1986). Complementary medicine and the general practitioner. *British Medical Journal,* **292,** 1498–1500.

DEVELOPING WORLD PERSPECTIVE

THE KUNG APPROACH TO HEALING

RICHARD KATZ

For the Kung, healing is more than curing, more than the application of medicine. Healing seeks to establish health and growth on physical, psychological, social, and spiritual levels; it involves work on the individual, the group, and the surrounding environment and cosmos. Healing pervades Kung culture, as a fundamental integrating and enhancing force. The culture's emphasis on sharing and egalitarianism, its vital life of the spirit and strong community, are expressed in and supported by the healing tradition. The central event in this tradition is the all-night healing dance.

Four times a month on the average, night signals the start of a healing dance. The women sit around the fire, singing and rhythmically clapping. The men, sometimes joined by women, dance around the singers. As the dance intensifies, *num,* or spiritual energy is activated in the healers, both men and women, but mostly among the dancing men. As num is activated in them, they begin to *kia* or experience an enhancement of their consciousness. While experiencing kia, they heal all those at the dance. Before the sun rises fully the next morning, the dance usually ends. Those at the dance find it exciting, joyful, powerful. "Being at a dance makes our hearts happy," the Kung say.

The dance is a community event in which the entire camp participates. The people's belief in the healing power of num brings substance to the dance. All who come are given healing. In the dance, the people confront the uncertainties and contradictions of their experience, attempting to resolve issues dividing the group, reaffirming the group's spiritual cohesion. And they do so in a way which is harmonious with their own and their culture's maintenance and growth.

The Kung do not look upon their healing dances as separate from the other activities of daily life. Like hunting, gathering, and socializing, dancing is another thing they do. The dance is a point of marked intensity and significance in their daily lives.

As if to underscore the unity of the dance with their ongoing lives, the Kung make some of their spiciest jokes in the dance. A healer works himself into a state of kia, dancing energetically and sweating profusely, when someone outside the dance circle yells to him: "Hey, your large black penis is dragging around the circle." The dance lightens up for a moment. But the joke does not disrupt the dance or the healer. If there is a sudden crisis at the dance, such as an inexperienced healer losing control, the humor immediately subsides, not because it is inappropriate, but because other activities, such as physically restraining the frightened healer,

require the participants' complete attention. The earthiness of the Kung's jokes is very much a part of their contact with the supernatural.

The healing dance is open and public, a routine cultural event to which all Kung have access. To become a healer is to follow a normal pattern of socialization. Healing is not reserved for a few persons with unique characteristics or extraordinary powers. Nor is there a special class or caste or guild of healers, enjoying special privileges in the culture. By the time they reach adulthood, more than half the men and 10 percent of the women have become healers.

These characteristics of the dance establish its importance in the study of healing and consciousness. Moreover, the dance seems to be an old part of Kung hunting–gathering life. The rock paintings of South Africa include depictions of a healing dance much like the *dwa,* or Giraffe, the dominant healing dance of today (Lewis-Williams, 1980; Vinnicombe, 1975). The healing dance must therefore be at least several hundred years old, and perhaps older.

A broad range of fundamental activities are focused in the dance. Healing in the most generic sense is provided. It may take the form of curing an ill body or mind, as the healer pulls out the sickness; or of mending the social fabric, as the dance provides for a manageable release of hostility and an increased sense of social solidarity; or of protecting the village from misfortune, as the healer pleads with the gods for relief from the Kalahari's harshness. And the healing takes the form of enhancing consciousness, as the dance brings its participants into contact with the spirits and gods.

The dance provides the training ground for aspiring healers. It also provides the healers with opportunities for fulfillment and growth, where all can experience a sense of well-being, and where some may experience what Westerners would call a spiritual development. In the dance, the Kung find a vehicle for artistic expression. And from the dance, they receive profound knowledge, as the

healer reports on those extended encounters with the gods which can occur during especially difficult healing efforts.

These activities are integrated with and reinforce each other, forming a continuous source of curing, counsel, protection, and enhancement. The healing is stimulated by the atmosphere generated at the dance. As individual healers go into kia, other Kung participating in the dance in various ways and to various degrees themselves experience an alteration of their state of consciousness, even if they do not go into kia. An atmosphere develops in which one person's experience of kia has a contagious effect on others.

The dance provides the focal point for what anthropologists consider to be the central features of a culture. The dance is the Kung's primary expression of "religion," "medicine," and "cosmology." It is their primary "ritual." For the Kung, the dance is, quite simply, an orienting and integrating event of unique importance.

Certain events or happenings make a dance more likely to occur, such as a severe illness, especially if it is sudden; the killing of a big game animal; the return of absent family members; and visits from close relatives or "important" persons like the anthropologists. Most often dances are held because people want to sing and dance together, as part of their continuing effort to prevent incipient sickness, which they believe resides in everyone, from becoming severe and manifest; as part of their desire to contact the gods and seek their protection; as part of their wish to have an evening of enjoyment and companionship.

The actual frequency of dances is influenced by ecological and sociological factors, a most important one being whether the Kung are camped at a permanent water-hole or out in the bush. When they are camped around the permanent water-holes, though their hunting and gathering remain demanding, camps move infrequently and then only for short distances. This leaves more time and energy available for dances, which can occur once,

perhaps twice a week. When the Kung are out in the bush, especially as the dry season approaches, they are constantly on the move, and their hunting, gathering, and water collection can require greater effort. Less time and energy are available for dancing. Dances occur perhaps two or three times a month, and then usually to treat a specific illness.

The number of persons in the camp who can support a dance is another important factor in the number of dances. While the Kung are located at a permanent water-hole, there are usually enough strong singers and dancers to begin and maintain a dance, though sometimes persons from several camps are needed. In the bush, where the Kung move about in much smaller groups, there is a personnel shortage. A typical group may have only four adult males, and they must often be out hunting. The number needed for a dance is often missing.

The composition of a camp is also a factor in the frequency of dances. At the permanent water-hole of Xaixai, the different Kung camps have different amounts of dancing. One camp, for example, has many young and middle-aged people but few children and old persons as compared to the other camps. Because the children need supervision at a dance, they subtract from the resources available to maintain the dance. The very old are usually not active participants. So this camp has more dances than other Xaixai villages.

Finally, the prevailing social climate affects the number of dances. For a period of time at Xaixai when there is much tension between the two main camps, no healing dances take place. Persons simply do not want to spend the long intimate hours of the dance in each other's company. Yet a large dance finally brings the camps together to resolve their conflicts. As the small Kung groups move about in the bush, they may not see other groups for weeks, even months. When the groups do meet, a dance is in their hearts and quickly comes to fruition. As they sing and dance together, their sense of isolation vanishes. The dance is an organic event, its occurrence remaining sensitive to

the moods and hopes of the people at the time. When a camp is in good spirits, there may be a period of frequent and intense dancing. At other times when a mood of lethargy prevails in the camp, the dancing seems to shrivel up the same as the green bushes in the blistering heat of the desert dry season. A compelling reason for a dance may then exist, yet no dance occurs.

The size of the dances varies. A large dance, in which several camps participate, includes about fifty to eighty persons. There are infants and little ones, frisky adolescents and slow moving old people. In such a large dance, fifteen to thirty women may be singing at different times. The singers are usually adults, joined by some of the more enthusiastic adolescents. Their ages vary across the full range of adulthood, though rarely including the very old. About seven to fifteen men may be dancing at any one time, most of them young or middle-aged.

Smaller dances, usually started and maintained by a single camp, have about fifteen to twenty persons at the dance, with seven to ten women singing and four or five men dancing. At these, younger boys and girls may participate to bring the complement of singers and dancers up to a sufficient level. Perhaps one-quarter of the singers and two-thirds of the dancers may be healers at any one dance regardless of its size. The potential for healing is thus ever-present and pervasive.

Occasionally there are very large dances, usually to celebrate special events. These may go on continuously for several days, sustained through the long, hot days by a few hardy singers and dancers, accelerating during the cooler hours of the night when the crowds build. There can be up to two hundred persons at such a dance, with perhaps thirty to forty singers at any one time sitting two or three deep in a circle around the fire, and perhaps fifteen to twenty five dancers. Sometimes it becomes impossible for so many dancers to form one circle. Two dance fires are built, with the singers divided up around each one, and dancers circling both fires in a figure-eight pattern. The killing of a large animal, such as an eland, may motivate this kind of dance. When many people gather to help eat and share the enormous quantity of meat, the mood for dancing is aroused. From their black neighbors, the Kung have learned about Christian celebrations. During this season, the blacks may slaughter a cow or two, and that amount of available food, plus the festive air, invariably stimulate a very large, long dance.

No special equipment is necessary for the dance. Dance rattles (*zhorosi*) are used when available. They are made from dried cocoons with pieces of ostrich eggshell inside, strung on pieces of fiber. Preferably, a pair of rattles is used, one string being wrapped around each of the dancer's calves, though when rattles are in short supply, a dancer may use only one string. Usually several pairs are available at the average-sized dance. As the dancers move around the circle, each step elicits the distinctive staccato sound of the rattles, which accompanies and accents the rhythmic texture of the dance. Most dancers also bring their walking stick to the dance. This stick, which can also be used for digging roots and carrying objects, is carved from a piece of stripped hard wood, usually with a large gnarled knot at the top serving as a handle. They use the stick to accent their dancing steps or, especially when fatigued, to support them as they continue to dance.

In their curing efforts, healers may use plant substances which contain num (Marshall, 1969). These plants are ground to a powder, mixed with marrow or fat, and put in an empty tortoise shell, several inches long. Healers place a burning coal into the mixture, wafting the smoke, which carries num, toward the patient.

Clothing for the dance is the normal everyday wear, though a special personal touch may be added, such as a feather in the headband, an extra headband, or a hat.

Typically the healing dance moves through different stages. When there is to be a dance, a

dance fire is begun in the central open area of the camp late in the afternoon as the sun disappears from the land. The women who are to sing and clap the healing songs come together informally and gradually. They sit side by side in intimate physical contact, legs intertwined, shoulder to shoulder, forming a tight circle around the fire. The dancers, both men and women, start to circle around the singers. Other smaller fires are begun slightly away from the dance fire. Persons not singing or dancing sit in little groups conversing and joking around these peripheral "talking" fires.

At the start, there is a lot of warm-up activity. The mood is casual and jovial. Many of the dancers are adolescents trying out and showing off their new dance steps. Then, almost imperceptibly, the mood intensifies. The singing and clapping become more spirited, the dancing more focused. Most of the healers at the dance are now dancing; the adolescents have either retired to the periphery or begun dancing in a more serious manner. Joking and socializing continue. The atmosphere is earnest, but not somber.

As midnight approaches, with the flickering fire illuminating the singers and dancers, a healer or two begins to stagger, then perhaps one falls. They may shudder or shake violently, their whole body convulsing in apparent pain and anguish. The experience of kia has begun. And then, either on their own or under the guidance of those who are more steady, the healers who are in kia go to each person at the dance and begin to heal. They lay their fluttering hands on a person, one hand usually on the chest, the other on the back, pulling out the sickness, while shrieking earth-shattering screams and howls known as *kowhedili,* an expression for the pain and difficulty of this healing work. Then they shake their hands vigorously toward the empty space beyond the dance, casting the sickness they have taken from the person out into the darkness.

Such healing may go on for several hours. During this time the healers plead and argue with the gods to save the people from illness, demanding that the spirits of their dead ancestors, the *gauwasi,* not take a sick one away. They plead while they are laying on their hands; they plead as they stop dancing for a moment. They turn their heads toward the sky, yelling to the spirits to let the people alone: "What business do you have here tonight! This man is not ready to go. He wants to remain with those who love him."

Gradually a calm sets in as the dance moves into the early morning hours. Some dancers sleep for a brief period; the talk is quiet, the singing soft. The dance is resting. But the dance awakens again before dawn. The atmosphere picks up as sleeping forms rise and come toward the dance circle. The singing becomes stronger, the dancers more active. Another period of healing usually occurs as the sun begins to throw its light and warmth on the persons huddled around the dance. Before the sun becomes too warm, the kia and healing subside, and the singing gradually softens, then ends. The dance is over.

People slowly, comfortably move off to their camps. During the day after the dance most things take place as if in slow motion. Some persons rest quietly, acknowledging the fatigue of their sleepless night of physical and emotional exertion. Others visit a bit, their mood relaxed and humorous.

The Kung say that kia comes from activation of an energy that they call num. Num was originally given to the Kung by the gods. Though experiencing kia is a necessary prerequisite to healing, it is painful and feared. The cause of kia—the activated num—is said to boil fiercely within the person. Some at the dance avoid kia; others experience kia but fail to develop it so that it can be applied to healing. Even among the healers, not all heal at every dance.

Those who have learned to heal are said to "possess" num. They are called *num kausi,* "masters, or owners, of num." Num resides in the pit of the stomach and the base of the spine. As healers continue their energetic dancing, becoming warm and sweating profusely, the num in them heats up

and becomes a vapor. It rises up the spine to a point approximately at the base of the skull, at which time kia results. Kinachau, an old healer, talks about the kia experience. "You dance, dance, dance, dance. Then num lifts you up in your belly and lifts you in your back, and you start to shiver. Num makes you tremble; it's hot. Your eyes are open, but you don't look around; you hold your eyes still and look straight ahead. But when you get into kia, you're looking around because you see everything, because you see what's troubling everybody. Rapid shallow breathing draws num up. What I do in my upper body with the breathing, I also do in my legs with the dancing. You don't stomp harder, you just keep steady. Then num enters every part of your body, right to the tip of your feet and even your hair."

The action and ascent of num are described by Kau Dwa, another powerful healer: "In your backbone you feel a pointed something and it works its way up. The base of your spine is tingling, tingling, tingling, tingling. Then num makes your thoughts nothing in your head."

Num is an energy held in awe and considered very powerful and mysterious. This same energy is what the healer "puts into" people in attempting to cure them. For once heated up, num can both induce kia and combat illness.

As Kung learn to have some control over their boiling num, they can apply the num to healing. They learn to *twe,* that is, to "heal" or "pull out sickness," or simply "pull." Kau Dwa describes how one can heal while experiencing kia: "When you kia, you see things you must pull out, like the death things that god has put into people. You see people properly, just as they are. Your vision does not whirl." The purpose of kia is reached. Healing results.

During kia, the Kung experience themselves as existing beyond the ordinary level. As Kinachau puts it: "When we enter kia, we are different from when our num is not boiling and small. We can do different things."

Kia itself is an intense, emotional state. Emotions are aroused to an extraordinary level, whether they be fear or exhilaration or seriousness. The Kung also practice extraordinary activities during kia. They perform cures and, as part of their effort to heal, may handle and walk on fire, see the insides of people's bodies and scenes at great distances from their camp, or travel to god's home—activities never attempted in their ordinary state. Moreover, they experience themselves as beyond their ordinary self by becoming more essential, more themselves. Toma Zho, perhaps the strongest healer at Xaixai, speaks of this increased essentiality: "I want to have a dance soon so that I can really become myself again."

Through kia, the Kung participate in what Westerners call the "religious–spiritual" dimension. Transcending themselves, they are able to contact the realm where the gods and the spirits of dead ancestors live. Sickness is a process by which these spirits, helped by the lesser god, try to carry off the sick one into their own realm. The spirits have various ways of bringing misfortune and death, such as "allowing" a lion to maul a person or a snake to bite one, or a person to fall from a tree (Marshall, 1969). But the dance is where the spirits are most likely to bring sickness.

Sent by the great god, the spirits are strong but not invincible. A struggle takes place between two groups of loving relatives, those still living and those already dead. Each group wishes to have the sick one for themselves, and neither the realm of the living nor that of the spirits is seen as bad. In their ordinary state, the Kung do not argue with the gods, such is their respect. But in kia, healers express the wishes of the living by entering directly into a struggle with the spirits and the lesser god.

When a person is seriously ill, the struggle becomes intense. The more powerful healers sometimes travel to the great god's home in the sky, bringing the confrontation directly to the source of illness. The Kung say the healer's soul makes that journey at the greatest risk to the healer's very life.

Healers undertake such a terrifying journey because they want to rescue the soul of a sick person from the god's home and bring it back to their own camp. On their return, these powerful healers may describe the god's home, at times in great detail, as well as recounting their own struggle from the sick one's soul. If a healer's num is strong, the spirits will retreat and the sick one will live. This struggle is at the heart of the healer's art and power.

Kia can be viewed as an altered state of consciousness, enhanced to the degree and quality of transcendence. As the Kung's sense of self, time, and space are being significantly altered during kia, they experience a feeling of ascent. One healer says, "When I pick up num, it explodes and throws me up in the air, and I enter heaven, and then fall down." Others during kia feel that they are "opening up" or "bursting open, like a ripe pod."

The education of men and women healers differs, but the differences are more matters of form and structure than process and experience. Essentially, the training of both sexes is the same, especially the process of receiving num. One of the most striking things about the Kung education for healing is that it is an aspect of normal socialization. Most males and more than a third of the women try to become healers. Long before persons seriously try to become healers, they play at entering kia. A group of five- and six-year-olds may perform a small "healing dance," imitating the actual dance, with its steps and healing postures, at times falling as if in kia. Through play, the children are modeling; as they grow up, they are leaning about kia. Furthermore, education for healing occurs within the context of the family, the major vehicle for socialization. The primary source of information about kia, as well as the experiential teacher of kia, is likely to be in one's immediate family, or a close relative.

But this strongly supportive context for healing is not enough. To become a healer, a Kung must first seek num. With men, this seeking usually starts at the age of approximately twenty. The young man becomes a student and for several years expresses his search by going to as many dances as possible, perhaps two or three a week. With women, the age of seeking is more variable, the search briefer. But num is not "put into" someone who cannot accept it; students must be willing and ready to receive the num which can evoke the experience of kia. They must learn to "drink num" (*chi num*), a phrase used by the Kung to describe the process and act of learning to heal, especially the experience in which kia first develops into healing.

Socialization for kia and then seeking kia are preparatory phases in the education for kia. At the heart of this educational process is the experience of kia itself. While the Kung maintain a conceptual clarity about what happens during kia, they speak of the experiential mystery at the time of kia. This is especially the case with one's first kia experiences. At its core, the education is a process of accepting a kia experience for oneself. This is very difficult, because kia is painful as well as unknown. It is greatly feared.

Along with feelings of release and liberation, kia brings profound pain and fear. In describing the onset of kia, healers speak again and again of the searing pain in the *gebesi* and sometimes in the pit of the stomach. The word *gebesi* refers to the general area between the diaphragm and the waist, especially toward the sides. The term is also used to refer to two specific organs, the liver and the spleen. A healer recalls his first experiences with num: "Num got into my stomach. It was hot and painful in my gebesi, like fire. I was surprised and I cried."

More than physical symptoms are involved. Kau Dwa makes the further dimensions of this painful fear explicit: "As we enter kia, we fear death. We fear we may die and not come back!" This fear of death without an experience of rebirth evokes its own special terror for the Kung, as it has for persons in every culture. When potential healers can face this fact of their death and "willingly" die, the fear of num can be overcome, and there can be a

breakthrough to kia. The knowledge or conviction of being reborn or coming alive again is helpful, if not essential. Wi, an older healer at Xaixai, describes this death and rebirth in kia: "Your heart stops. You're dead. Your thoughts are nothing. You breathe with difficulty. You see things, num things; you see spirits killing people. You smell burning, rotten flesh. Then you heal, you pull sickness out. You heal, heal, heal. Then you live. Your eyeballs clear and you see people clearly."

Various aspects of the dance support this critical passage. Potential healers can receive support and encouragement from a number of people—first, their teacher, who has agreed to train them and give them num. This teacher, perhaps with one or two other healers, will probably be the one who tries to put num into the student during a dance.

Num is usually sent by means of invisible arrows which are felt as painful thorns or needles. Teachers shoot these arrows of num (*num tchisi*) into the student, sometimes by snapping their fingers, always trying to regulate the number of arrows and the intensity of the num they carry.

A younger Kung talks about these arrows and this passage into and out of death: "In kia, around your neck and around your belly you feel tiny needles and thorns which prick you. Then your front spine and your back spine are pricked with these thorns. Your gebesi tightens into a balled fist. Your breathing stops. Then someone rubs your belly and the pricking stops, and you start to breathe again."

The Kung must give up what is familiar—their familiar identity—to enter the unknown territory of kia. They must experience death before they can be reborn into kia. Kia remains an experiential mystery; it demands a truly frightening passage into the unknown.

A number of other people provide support and protection. They may give the students physical support when the onset of kia makes them shaky, or lead them to others whom they can heal. These guardians also protect the students from harming themselves or others. For example, the students may want to get closer to the fire to help their num boil up. But when they try to put their heads in the fire or throw hot coals in the air, someone at the dance usually leaps up and restrains them. Another supportive and at times inspirational group is the women singers. By singing and clapping the healing songs, they stimulate the num to boil. The intensity of their singing can help to determine and regulate the depth of kia. Finally, the entire community is present at the dance—friends, family, neighbors—all of whom participate to some degree and, by their presence, offer support.

As the students continue to dance through the night ever more seriously, their num may begin to boil, and kia becomes imminent. At this point, another critical phase in the educational process occurs. The aspiring healers try to regulate their condition. When they feel kia coming on, they involuntarily draw back from and at times actively resist this transition to an altered state. Others help them to overcome this resistance and to strike a dynamic balance between the oncoming intensity of kia and their fear of it. If their kia is coming on so fast that their fear escalates and prevents them from experiencing the kia, the teacher may make them stop dancing for a while, or drink some water, or lie down—all to "cool down" their too rapidly boiling num. The num must be hot enough to evoke kia but not so hot that it provokes debilitating fear. It is never a question of merely putting num into the student; the correct amount is critical. Experienced healers are encouraged to go as deeply into kia as they can, provided they maintain enough control over the num to use it for healing.

Throughout this work at the dance, there is extensive physical contact between the students and those who are helping them. Much of the students' sensitivity to these subtle balance considerations comes from this intimate contact. The physical, emotional, and psychological aspects of support are inseparable.

The Kung speak of "carrying" in describing their healing. Carrying can refer to the concrete

physical support offered at a dance to those seeking kia as well as to the general process of helping a student learn to heal, as in the idea that experienced healers must "carry the students." Carrying also can signify the general effects of a healer's work. Powerful healers talk of how their efforts are "carrying the camp" or keeping the camp healthy.

Drugs are not used on any regular basis to induce kia. However, an indigenous drug may be used on occasion, especially by the women. If the students are having considerable difficulty reaching kia, they may be given a drug at the dance, as a training device, to mitigate their intense fear and bring them closer to the kia state. The drug experience itself becomes a preparation for kia, since both experiences are altered states of consciousness. As with other techniques used at the dance, the dosage and timing of the drug are carefully regulated by the teacher. The drug is supposed to help the students, not catapult them into yet another unknown and potentially frightening altered state.

There are specific and sometimes idiosyncratic signs that people are approaching that threshold of fear or kia. Bodies shake. Eyes are glazed or downcast. Faces appear impassive. The signs must then be interpreted. The fear can be so intense that the students must sit down, or the fear may be such that, if they stay with it, they can overcome it and enter a kia state. These signs are used not only by the students themselves but also by those helping them. If, for example, the singers sense that someone is ready to go into kia, they may intensify their singing and clapping to give the student an extra push.

The subtlety of this balancing response is shown in the case of one young Kung who is new to kia. He has a look of tremendous fear as he dances. The singing, clapping, and dancing in general are at a high pitch of intensity. Kia is threatening to overwhelm him, and he runs away from the dance. But instead of letting him stay away from the dance, two persons go and take hold of him,

one from the front, the other from behind, and physically bring him back to the dance. The three of them then continue dancing in the circle, remaining in physical contact, as the singing reaches a new level of intensity. They bring the fearful back to what he fears, but they are now physically with him. He is able to go through his fear and into kia. The approach to each potential healer depends on his or her own history and present readiness for kia.

As kia occurs at a dance, the atmosphere becomes more electric and the dance more focused. One person going into kia is usually a stimulant for others. At one dance where there are fifteen dancers, twelve of them already know how to enter kia. I try to imagine what would happen if all of them were to go into kia at once. Certainly the process of education for kia would be severely strained. But no more than two or three are in kia at any one time. What happens is a process of kia management. The more experienced healers hold back their kia until those who need more help are either under control or able to function in kia. Rarely are there people in a state of kia who need help and cannot get it.

The teachers are Kung healers. During their non-kia state, they remain ordinary persons rather than intimates of the gods or chosen instruments. They do not demand from students either obedience or a long apprenticeship. The period of learning is focused within the dance itself. The emphasis is on experiential education. The core of teaching lies at those points when kia is about to occur. The teachers are with the students at the threshold of this experience, trying to help them over their fear and into kia, then guiding them to use that kia for healing.

Though originally issuing from the gods, num now passes regularly from person to person. Teaching is primarily by example. The teachers have been there before. They may or may not experience kia at the same time as the students, but certainly they have experienced kia many times before.

The principal dance form is the Giraffe, so named because giraffe healing or num songs now dominate in it. Gemsbok and eland songs have also enjoyed a popularity in this dance form, and at times have lent their names to it. But the Giraffe is presently the central form of healing dance among the hunting–gathering Kung and is the focus of this book.

The more experienced healers do not always need a full Giraffe dance to activate their num. Severe and especially chronic illnesses usually precipitate small healings which can hardly be called a dance. One or two healers can kia and heal, supported only by their own singing of num songs and perhaps by the singing of several women. The actual dancing may be minimal; perhaps a few steps, done mostly in place.

With some chronic conditions, small healings can occur every night of the week and over long periods of time. A wife or husband often treats an ailing spouse in such a manner. Certain experienced healers can also heal themselves while sitting alone at night and singing num songs. If the healer's spouse is present, the two may sing to and for each other, healing themselves and each other.

Richard Lee (personal communication) has described one such healing. An old woman healed her husband nightly for almost a year. Diagnosed by visiting Western doctors as having cancer, her husband lasted much longer than they had expected. She "fought the battle almost single-handed." Sometimes only her daughter would sing with her. The woman's message to her husband was clear and consistent: "Your dead father is trying to take you away. Those who are still alive have been mean to you. Your dead father is going to deprive them of you. You've been good all your life. I begged your dead father to give those who are still alive another chance to be good to you. Your dead father agreed, and spared you tonight."

There are two other dances in the Dobe area where kia and healing occur, the Trees and the Drum, of which the Drum is the more important. In the Drum dance it is the women who sing and dance and experience kia. Other than the man who plays the drum and who may also experience kia, men are not generally participants. There is much less emphasis on healing in this dance as compared to the Giraffe, and the healing that does occur is more restricted to the active participants. The experience of kia, however, is quite similar in the two dances.

Whereas the Giraffe occurs everywhere and at all times, the other kia dances are more local and infrequent in their occurrence. Whereas the Giraffe is open to the entire community, uniting the community as it unfolds, the other kia dances exclude some persons. Whereas in the Giraffe, men and women contribute equally to the activation of num through their different but overlapping roles, in the other kia dances the contributions of men and women are differentially valued, their roles more sharply divided. Whereas in the Giraffe kia is experienced in order to heal, in the other dances kia is often not transformed into healing energy. The Giraffe is the dance in which healing energy becomes most deeply a part of everyone's life.

Other important rituals involving dance are *choma,* the male initiation camp set up for boys from the ages of approximately fifteen to twenty; and the Eland dance, which marks the girls' first menstruation. Dancing at choma also brings on experiences of kia. Choma and the Eland dance may each occur only once every several years. Certain persons may on occasion enter kia while playing one of the musical instruments which are a continual source of pleasure for the Kung. In the Kung manner with such instrumental music, they are playing primarily for themselves, not performing for others. There are also numerous little dance patterns and dance-games, most including singing, which are performed by the older girls and women when mood strikes them, for their own pleasure and entertainment, and for the pleasure of any others who may be watching (England, 1968; Marshall, 1969).

Herbal medicines and a healing massage are also used by the Kung, but these are supplementary treatments, usually reserved for less serious or more localized ailments. Neither requires a healing dance or the experience of kia for its use. Only when such treatments fail to work does a small specialized kia healing or a healing dance become appropriate. Plants which contain num, or medicinal plants, number more than 15 (Lee, 1979; Marshall, 1969). They may be used by people, healers and non-healers alike, for minor curing efforts and protection. Apart from the dance, persons may rub charred bits of such plants on their skin to cure an ache or pain, or bring luck in hunting. Abrasions, cuts, and infections are routinely treated with medicinal salves.

"Aches and pains" and especially a general "tiredness" can also call for a massage. The healing massage involves forceful manipulation of large areas of the body, concentrating on the shoulders, back, and stomach. The massagers rub their sweat onto the one being healed and periodically shake their hands off into space, expelling the patient's sickness. This behavior is similar to the healing behavior in the Giraffe dance. Massage can also be a preparation for healing in the Giraffe. As the healer Kana puts it: "We massage each other to get out the sickness. We also massage to make a person ready for the healing num of Giraffe."

Knowledge of herbal medicines and skill with massage are not necessarily possessed by the same person, nor are such capabilities limited to or even possessed by all healers. Koto, for example, who has never entered kia, is considered one of the best massagers.

The traditional Kung approach to healing is integral to its context in the Kalahari. Woven into the Kung's hunting–gathering lifestyle, the dance seems to highlight it. Time is definitely available for the all-night dances. Community is at the dance, and the dance establishes community. Everyone is welcome at the dance. Parents teach children about num. In a real sense, it is the community, in its activation of num, which heals and is healed. What Westerners might call the "sacred" and the "profane" merge playfully and dramatically at the dance: the raucous sexual joking as the dancers move toward kia; the dialogue between the healer and the spirits, first pleading, then insulting. And there are no restrictions in the access to num. In egalitarian fashion, all receive healing. Num is shared throughout the community. It is not meant to be hoarded by any one person; perhaps it never can be. There is no limit to num. It expands as it boils. As one person reaches kia at the dance, others are stimulated to follow. One Kung becoming a healer does not mean another cannot become one; the reverse is true, especially when the two are closely related.

The Kung do not seek num for its own sake. They seek its protection and enhancement for the individual, the group, and the culture simultaneously. The healing approach does not undermine the execution of everyday responsibilities. The healer is a hunter or gatherer who also happens to heal. Healing remains harmonious with the different levels of Kung existence. Its effectiveness depends on this context.

The question of whether kia-healing "works" depends to a large extent on who asks it. When asked by someone with a contemporary Western scientific orientation, the question usually has a rational, materialistic emphasis. Such a person usually wants to know what specific illnesses are cured, how rapidly, and how completely. If asked by a Kung, the question would have a more holistic meaning. Num is energy, one form of which can be translated as "medicine." For the Kung, healing deals with the whole person, in all aspects and situations. Healing is directed as much toward alleviating physical illness in an individual as toward enhancing the healer's understanding; as much toward resolving conflict in the village as toward establishing a proper relationship with the gods and the cosmos. A healing may be specifically directed toward one of these focuses, but the

healing in fact affects them all. For a Kung, the question would be: Does healing "heal," rather than just "cure," and does it heal "sickness" as well as "illness"?

Although the Kung word for "heal" and "cure" is the same (*twe*), as is the word for "illness" and "sickness" (*xai*), the context of usage creates distinctions. "Illness" means a more specific or delimited disease with symptoms, usually manifest. As the Kung see it, all people have sickness in them, which on occasion flares up and is expressed in an illness. This does not mean that every Kung is an ambulatory disease-ridden patient. Rather, each Kung has the potential for illness. When the Kung offer healing to all at the dance, whether they have a manifest illness or not, they are healing sickness, providing in part what Westerners would call "preventative" treatment.

"Healing" is the generic term, including in its meaning, "to cure." The Kung criterion for a cure is that someone with an illness gets better, usually with the relief or disappearance of symptoms. A supplementary criterion is that the healer sees the cause of the illness coming out of the patient. A cure does not occur with every healing effort.

When confronted by illness, the Kung healer uses num to bring the protective powers of the universe to bear on the patient and, as one possible though not necessary outcome, relieve her symptoms. A specific illness is only a manifestation of some imbalance in the whole individual as she exists in her total environment. A healing seeks to re-establish the balance in the individual–cultural–environment gestalt. One expression of this new balance might be a cure, the relief of symptoms. But the person being healed can also die, and a new balance can still be established, a healing accomplished. A healing dance may increase group cohesion during a period of tension within a camp, even though the patient for whom the dance was held dies. As the Kung say, sometimes it is proper for the spirits to take a person away. The healers, in exhausting their resources in this struggle with the spirits, confirm the correctness of the larger relationship of the community and the gods.

The full range of what in the West would be called physical, psychological, emotional, social, and spiritual illnesses are treated at the healing dance. Nearly every Kung, and many of the neighboring blacks as well, can describe how the healing dance has cured someone. Sometimes the reported cure is dramatic. For example, someone who has been clawed by a leopard and "given up for dead" is healed and recovers miraculously. More often the cure is undramatic. Someone who complains of "chest wheezing and coughing," who is experiencing respiratory congestion from what would in the West be diagnosed as chronic emphysema, is healed and then is able to go about his day in a normal way. A woman who is described as "so weak she is dying," probably with advanced tuberculosis, receives intensive healing and has a little more strength the next day. A young woman comes to the dance for healing because her "milk is not coming properly" to her nursing baby. The next day the milk returns. Another woman receives healing at the dance because her lip has become increasingly infected and swollen. After several days, the swelling and infection subside. A healing dance is held for a young healer who complains of "tired blood" and shows signs of great physical and psychological fatigue. At the dance he regains his strength, in part through his own dancing and healing. Or a woman gets relief from the discomfort of her pregnancy. Two families from different camps are in conflict over an upcoming marriage between two of their young people. Accusations of stinginess in regard to some of the gift exchanges required before the marriage fill the air. During a healing dance attended by the two families along with the rest of the camps, the tensions subside, though the conflict is not resolved to the total satisfaction of either family. After spending the night in the intense intimacy of the healing dance, the people will speak of how good it is to be together. The Kung refer to the healing dance as *num chxi*. The sense of

chxi is "to gather together to sing and dance (Beisele, personal communication).

Although the Kung try to heal the full range of illnesses, they are not unreasonable about the limits of num's healing powers. When, for example, the Kung suspect that Goba sorcery is the cause of the illness, they do not attempt further healing. Goba refers to an unfamiliar black person, in practice someone who is not recognized to be either Herero or Tswana. The Kung believe that Goba sorcery is too strong for the num.

In certain instances, after the Kung have tried as much healing as they can, they willingly admit that their num cannot deal with the illness at hand. This is the case with a boy who breaks a food taboo and is considered "crazy" because all he can say is, "Nothing. Nothing." He becomes extremely thin. Many times he receives healings. But his condition continues to deteriorate, and finally he dies. As the healer Gau puts it: "Sometimes you get someone who is ill who wants to die, but you heal him and heal him and he lives. Other times you heal him and he still dies."

The Kung are extremely pragmatic about terminal illness and death. When a person, especially an old person, is in the final throes of a fatal disease, the healing efforts usually intensify. The immediate family works on the dying person each night. But the Kung do not see num as reversing a situation which is supposed to be. Wi, one of the older healers, expresses a common Kung understanding: "Sometimes you heal and god helps you. Sometimes you heal and heal and heal, and you lose the person."

Whereas I witnessed each of the "undramatic" cures I described here, I have no first-hand data on any dramatic cures, such as the sudden healing of profound physical damage. Also, within the period of my research in the Kalahari, I could not establish the degree of experiential control that Western science demands as validation of cures, whether dramatic or ordinary. The required outcome study would have to account for the fact that most dis-

eases are self-limiting; they heal on their own, almost regardless, and sometimes in spite of, specific treatments. Such a study would be difficult to undertake, given the small size of the Kung groups and their pattern of moving about the Kalahari. The fundamental questions of what is "healing" and what is a "cure" remain.

There is also other evidence on the effectiveness of the healing dance. A practical and pragmatic people, the Kung use things that they believe work. They have been exposed to other systems of treatment, both African and Western, yet they continue to rely on their healing dance. Antibiotics may be used in conjunction with a dance, to provide extra protection or to deal with diseases particularly amenable to Western medicine, such as gonorrhea. Antibiotics are also used sometimes in conjunction with or instead of indigenous medicinal salves. Although contact with Western medicine is still limited, the pattern of that contact is clear: the Kung integrate elements from other treatment systems into the tradition of their dance. The prevailing mode of healing remains num, though the Kung attitude remains realistic. As Gau says: "Maybe our num and European medicine are similar, because sometimes people who get European medicine die, and sometimes they live. That is the same with ours."

Moreover, the neighboring blacks turn to the Kung healing dances for help, coming to the dance with an attitude of respect uncharacteristic of their general domineering attitude toward the Kung. The Hereros in the Dobe area say that num is strong and powerful. In the Ghanzi area, where several black groups live in close proximity to the Kung, their respective healing systems are often in direct competition. The Kung approach to healing is valued and sought after by these black groups.

The younger Kung are not giving up the healing dance but continue to work toward becoming healers. Young adults speak like the older ones. They express a strong belief in num and great respect for its healing powers. Gau, now in his mid-

thirties, is an impressive figure. Though still young, his views are highly respected by his fellow Kung. His feelings about black and European intrusions into the Kalahari run deep. He wants to establish Kung rights to the land they have always hunted and gathered, in the face of the overgrazing cattle of their pastoral neighbors. Yet with all his fervent orientation to contemporary political and economic affairs, Gau is one of the most promising healers. "Num is our way," he says.

BIBLIOGRAPHY

England, N. 1968. *Music among the Zu/wasi of South Western Africa and Botswana.* Ph.D. dissertation, Harvard University, Cambridge, Mass.

Lee, R. B. 1979. *The !Kung San: Men, Women and Work in a Foraging Society.* Cambridge: Cambridge University Press.

Lewis-Williams, J. B. 1980. The economic and social determinants of southern San rock art. Paper delivered at 2nd International Conference of Hunting and Gathering Societies, Quebec.

Marshall, J. 1969. The medicine dance of the !Kung bushmen. *Africa,* 39: 347–381.

Vinnicombe, P. 1975. *The People of the Eland.* Pietermaritzburg: Natal University Press.

PART FOUR

THE ORGANIZATION AND DELIVERY OF HEALTH CARE

CHAPTER 11

HOSPITALS

Hospitals are, to a great extent, a reflection of the health care system within which they are located. Hospitals manifest not only the qualities that illustrate the best of a particular health care system, but also its worst qualities. For example, the technology available in some American hospitals is cutting-edge biotechnology that will assist physicians as they save and extend the lives of countless patients. But some hospitals in inner cities and in rural America cannot find qualified physicians to treat patients in need of even routine medical services. This scenario is not unique to the United States. Other industrialized nations also experience disparities in technology and access within their hospital systems. However, because of greater government involvement in health care systems abroad, such disparities are considerably less than in the United States (Rutten and Bonsel, 1992).

For example, Gutierrez-Fisac and Fletcher (1997) point out that hospital utilization rates differed between urban and rural areas in a recent survey in Spain. But they also point out that when the size of the community and utilization rates are examined, there is no association, suggesting that access to care is not limited by size of community. In many developing countries, hospitals are generally limited to urban communities (see, for example, Hunt, 1996). And if hospitals are available in rural communities, they are limited in terms of available services and personnel. Many countries depend on rural clinics to provide services to patients; but even they can be problematic, for staffing can be difficult.

In the first article in this chapter, Rosemary Stevens examines the emergence of the hospital as

a social institution in the United States. The second and third articles address the role of others vis-à-vis the patient. In the second article, Dag Album examines patient/patient interaction in a Norwegian hospital. In the third, Joseph W. Schneider assesses the role of family and friends in a Chinese hospital. All three selections offer insight into the image of the hospital within their respective societies.

Rosemary Stevens provides a broad historical overview of the American hospital. According to her, the science of medicine emerged because of the professionalization of physicians as well as their willingness to accept the germ theory. Thus, as hospitals developed in the United States, surgery emerged as their central function.

Throughout the article, Stevens touches on some of the central features of the hospital as a social institution. For example, she addresses the concept of community as it relates to the hospital. Given that most hospitals serve the interests of a small number of people in power on the local level, the concept of community is not particularly fitting. Also, many so-called community hospitals are fragmented on the basis of race and ethnicity, religion, and social class. As Stevens points out, however, "community" hospitals generally are not stratified by the clientele they serve, or by ownership.

Stevens also examines the following themes in the history of hospitals: (1) that they remain differentiated relative to interests; (2) that decision making is not centralized but rather encompasses a variety of interest groups such as those in the health profession as well as others in the health

care field; and (3) that American hospitals have learned to adapt to an ever-changing internal (financial) dynamic.

Dag Album notes the lack of research addressing patient-to-patient interaction within hospital settings, perhaps because such relationships are considered less significant than, for example, the physician/patient relationship. In the second article, Album examines the social world of interpatient relations in a Norwegian hospital. Examining what hospital patients do and why, he offers a unique insight into the dynamics of patient behavior within an institutional setting. In Norway, patients (for the most part) are considered equal within the hospital. Patients are willing to discuss their illnesses and many other topics, but a person's occupation, income, and level of education are generally not topics for discussion.

Examining the dynamics of patient interaction, Album identifies a number of functions served by such interaction. For example, patient/patient interaction provides information about why one has been hospitalized, hospital staff and ward life, examinations and treatment within the hospital, and so forth. In other words, patient interaction is a source of advice and information about hospital routines and expectations. According to Album, this interaction not only is functional for the hospital, but also constitutes a form of work.

The third article examines hospitals in China. For a four-and-a-half month period beginning in December 1986, Joseph W. Schneider conducted fieldwork in three hospitals located in northern China. The focus of this article is the critical care unit (CCU) in a 500-bed general hospital, where Schneider did the majority of his work.

Schneider was particularly struck by the extensive use of family labor within the hospital. Family members would sweep and mop floors, bring the patient his or her favorite food, watch the patient, and monitor the patient's condition and report it to hospital staff. Some family members would even buy the necessary pharmaceuticals for the patient. If the patient had children, the hospital usually called on the son to obtain the patient's permission for such things as surgery. In other words, the child was responsible for a parent's compliance with hospital procedures. Many of the activities performed for a patient had cultural and institutional support. For example, a son or daughter could receive extensive time off from work so he or she could take care of a hospitalized parent.

As was pointed out to Schneider, the removal of family members from the hospital would create a social problem, and children were expected to provide these services for a parent. Schneider also discovered that some doctors and nurses demanded "gifts" from family members in exchange for better patient care. But this was a topic that most in the medical field were not willing to discuss with him.

The hospital is an institution in transition in China. Though modernizing, it retains many traditional features in order to control the cost of health care. Thus although members of the hospital staff at times may become upset with family members, they recognize the financial benefits of family care.

What is the common thread associated with the three articles in Chapter 11? In a word, function. In the article by Stevens, the function of the hospital is found in its relationship with other components of the health care system. Stevens points out how, in the United States during the 1920s, hospitals marketed themselves through all available media to advertise the merits of hospital care. Given the American perference for a for-profit private-sector health care system, efforts in the private and public sectors have created health insurance schemes that virtually ensure hospitals a pool of patients to fill beds and utilize medical technology.

As Album points out, one function of Norwegian hospitals is to provide patients the opportunity to engage in patient interaction as a method of socialization to the institution. Besides helping most patients adjust to hospital protocol, this process

also saves hospitals from adding staff. Similarly, the use of family members as caregivers in hospitals is, as Schneider maintains, an effort to control costs and maintain cultural traditions.

REFERENCES

Gutierrez-Fisac, Juan L., and Astrid E. Fletcher. 1997. Regional Differences in Hospital Use by Adults in Spain. *European Journal of Public Health,* vol. 7, no. 7, pp. 254–260.

Hunt, Linda M. 1996. Inequalities in the Mexican Health Care System: Problems in Managing Cancer in Southern Mexico. In Janardan Subedi and Eugene B. Gallagher (Eds.), *Society, Health, and Disease: Transcultural Perspectives* (pp. 130–147). Upper Saddle River, NJ: Prentice Hall.

Rutten, Frans F. H., and Gouke J. Bonsel. 1992. High Cost Technology in Health Care: A Benefit or a Burden? *Social Science and Medicine,* vol. 35, no. 4, pp. 567–577.

AMERICAN PERSPECTIVE

PAST IS PROLOGUE

ROSEMARY STEVENS

Hospitals for the poor and sick have existed since ancient times; the modern hospital is a relatively recent institution. If two factors can be said to define it, they are the presence of round-the-clock skilled nurses and the ability to undertake major surgery. Neither of these was a general feature of American hospitals until at least the 1880s. The first professional nursing schools, based on the Florence Nightingale's precepts, were established in 1873 at Bellevue Hospital in New York, the New Haven Hospital, and the Massachusetts General Hospital. Others followed rapidly in the next decade. Many, if not most, of the new hospitals springing up in the burgeoning towns and cities of the late nineteenth century were predicated from the beginning on the integral development of the nursing schools. Through changes in nursing alone the hospital was transformed from the often filthy, disorganized, and terrifying older institutions of the early 1870s into a monument to hope, science, and efficiency.

Total national expenditures on hospital operations for tax-supported and voluntary hospitals in 1903 were estimated to be at least $28.2 million; of this, 43 percent came from charges made to paying patients, 8 percent from tax funds, and the remainder from charitable donations and endowments. American hospitals were already mixed institutions—only partly charitable, increasingly selling their services for a fee. By the mid-1920s middle class people were using hospitals for obstetrics, tonsillectomies, and appendectomies.

Medical science was transformed through two concurrent movements between 1880 and 1914, with effects lasting to the present. The first was the professionalization of American physicians; the second, the discovery and acceptance of the germ theory, giving medicine the confidence that its major justification as a profession was its scientific base. By the late 1880s, when aseptic techniques were replacing antisepsis in the operating rooms and in the dressings used on the wards, the idea that disease was borne by specific microscopic organisms—which could be identified, avoided, and destroyed—and, more generally, that disease could be explained, was on the way to revolutionizing the

intellectual outlook and practical applications of modern medicine. Surgeons began to wear white gowns in the 1880s. Nurses and other hospital staff wore uniforms, suggesting not only cleanliness but specialized roles and organizational rituals. Beds were lined up with military precision, sheets were folded into knife-edges. Even before World War I there were complaints that the needs of patients as individuals were being subsumed to the demands of hospital organization, a process that would later be called "depersonalization." Patients were expected to conform cooperatively and passively to the cultural expectations of the institution; they were beneficiaries and prisoners of medical expertise.

Surgery became—and has remained—the heart of the American hospital, the most obvious evidence of medicine's success and an emblem of twentieth-century American values: science, know-how, the willingness to take risks (on the part of both doctors and patients), decisiveness, organization, and invention. In the 1883 *Transactions of the American Surgical Association,* Samuel Gross, the famous Philadelphia surgeon, expressed the drama of American surgery in the 1880s in words that could be applied to any decade since:

> *Progress stares us everyday in the face. The surgical profession was never so busy as it is at the present moment; never so fruitful in great and beneficent results, or so bold and daring exploits.... Operative surgery challenges the respect and admiration of the world....*

Because American hospitals developed as modern institutions at the time they did—largely between 1870 and 1914—they assumed an unusually important function as the embodiment of cultural aspirations. The hospital served both as a modern and an ideal institution, symbolizing the wealth of the new and expanding American cities, the order and glamour of science, the happy conjunction between humanitarianism and expertise in a society rife with money making. It is not coincidental that

American hospitals have been among the most luxurious and costly structures ever built. An observer writing about the New York Hospital for *Harpers Magazine* in 1878 described its elevator, which was larger than those of a fashionable hotel, as so smooth in motion that it was like "a mechanical means of getting to heaven."

Demonstration or show, even conspicuous waste, became a lasting aspect of the American hospital as a symbol—one that has as yet received too little attention by social scientists, and one cause of increasing costs. That the modern American hospital is a monument, symbolizing in its architecture and equipment more than its basic function, is apparent not only in the historical literature, but in the lavish style of buildings erected even in times of depression (including those built by the WPA in the 1930s). Another example can be drawn from the early 1960s, when there was enormous public concern about the poor hospital care available in run-down hospitals in inner-city areas. The solutions sought were for rebuilding and major renovating, rather than for the kind of making-do in draughty basements that has been a continuing characteristic of British hospital care. Today hospitals, despite concern about the massive costs of hospital care, are among the most modern, high technology, costly structures being built in modern America. They continue to speak, subtly, to an implied link between cost and expertise.

The hospital was also to symbolize medicine as a vehicle of precision and control. Mastery of diagnosis (understanding the causes and progression of disease) gives a comforting illusion of control to both doctors and patients, even when little effective treatment is available—and for most nonsurgical conditions there was little effective treatment, except good nursing techniques, until the advent of sulfa drugs in the 1930s and antibiotics after World War II. The promise of surgery and of specific remedies against infectious diseases, inherent in major discoveries before World War I, consolidated the

image of the doctor as a hero fighting disease with twentieth-century tools. The increasing subdivision of medicine into specialties after World War I carried forward this image by placing the greatest emphasis, in terms of prestige and income, on the most heroic interventions. Thus, neurosurgery carried greater prestige than psychiatry; radiotherapy than pediatrics.

As a projection of a profession whose archetypes were control, daring, and entrepreneurship, the twentieth-century American hospital (along with the medical schools) was always ill-suited to deal with chronic diseases—of which causes were multifactorial and for which medical success was often problematic—and with the collective realms of public health. Even before World War I, hospitals could be criticized for a tendency to view the hospital merely from the inside; that is, from the self-generated perceptions of its Board of Trustees and its physicians. It followed, as S. Goldstein wrote in the 1907 *Charities and the Commons,* that the hospital did "not feel itself an intimate part of the social order; it stands forbiddingly isolated and aloof." The fact that the potential existed, in theory at least, for the hospital to provide health services to the whole population in a defined service district, to compile epidemiological statistics, offer public health education and maternal and child welfare clinics, and to deal with the patient's family as well as with the patient, was to be a source of irritation to generations of disappointed critics.

The success and visibility of the hospital in providing acute, specialized care obscured its relatively limited role in the overall picture of health and disease. Nevertheless, the hospital could be described by the 1920s, as later, as an expression of pessimism, a "negative instrument of evolution," somewhat akin to refuse and sewage disposal, in that it dealt with problems of society rather than with positive solutions. Departments of social work were started in leading hospitals, following the example of the Massachusetts General Hospital in 1905, with the belief that such facilities would help to eradicate the widely held notion that the hospital was an impersonal institution and would help to elucidate the social causes of disease. Social service failed to become the core of community health care efforts for at least three reasons: the concentration of social service work on the poor, who attended outpatient departments with socially unappealing conditions—including venereal diseases, unwed motherhood, and tuberculosis: the lack of fees for social work, making it dependent on charity and on cost shifting from the hospital's paying patients; and the lack of power and the desire by the social workers themselves to become a clinical profession on the medical model, dealing with the psychosocial symptoms of individual patients rather than with community service needs.

American hospitals became successful at marketing acute services to paying patients. Public relations became an acceptable aspect of hospital management in the 1920s, with hospital fairs, radio spots, and even movies extolling the virtues of hospital care. Even in the depths of the depression of the 1930s—with enormous pressures put on local government hospitals, as the unemployed sought free medical care, together with the closing of hundreds of small institutions—most of the income to the hospital industry came from patient fees. In not-for-profit hospitals, the standard bearers for hospital quality in the United States, 71 percent of hospital income came from patients in 1935. The development of Blue Cross insurance plans in the 1930s, commercial hospital insurance in the 1940s, and Medicare in the mid-1960s, buttressed the idea of hospital care as acute services, while increasing hospital income. None of these schemes typically included out-of-hospital diagnosis, preventive services, health education, or social services, whereby hospitals could reach out to the community as comprehensive health care centers. There were no financial incentives to override the heroic, specialized medical model for hospital care.

COMMUNITY TIES

Besides the emerging character of the American hospital as an acute care facility, thriving in a market for paying patients and oriented to a broader vision of the medical profession and a money-value nexus, the hospital acquired values whose properties were largely mythological—and no less powerful for that. One of the most potent of these values was (and is) the idea of community.

Nonfederal acute care hospitals are termed "community hospitals" by the American Hospital Association, irrespective of their location, size, or level of care. The term appears to be idiosyncratically American.

Two initial points can readily be made about the notion of the community hospital. First, since hospitals are not community health centers, the term has an ironic ambiguity. Second, the word "community," like the word "voluntary" (long applied to not-for-profit hospitals) has emotive power in a much larger social and political context than the hospital field. Community flexibility stands in contrast to state or national standard-setting; voluntary activity against the implied rigidity of government intervention. Communities suggest creative, local, private activities in America, such as volunteer fire departments, school boards, or the PTA; they are part of American cultural tradition. Part of the attachment of the word "community" to hospitals reflects vague assumptions about the public good. Yet, in three specific ways American hospitals have traditionally had strong community affiliations. First, hospitals have traditionally served communities of interest within local power structures. Second, hospitals have been an important part of the hierarchical organization of the medical profession. Third, hospitals have provided centers for training, employment, and voluntary work for community residents. The combined effect of these patterns has been to define, further, the American hospital as "American."

As major expressions of charitable, social, and economic interests, the hospitals that developed in the late nineteenth and into the twentieth century reflected the segmentation of American society into diverse ethnic, religious, and occupational groups and into defined social classes. Hospitals were both a concrete expression of solidarity and a means of providing training for nurses and doctors in groups likely to be excluded from other institutions (notably, Jewish and black physicians and black nurses). They represented both community successes and community failures. By 1920 America was dotted with hospitals run by hundreds of different private associations, including Roman Catholics, Lutherans, Methodists, Episcopalians, Southern Baptists, Jews, Blacks, Swedes, and Germans, depending on the power structures of local populations. Philadelphia, for example, had seventy-one hospitals in 1923, general and specialized; it now has seventy-two. Most were run by not-for-profit associations. Their varied social origins were apparent in names such as Hospital of the University of Pennsylvania (for teaching), Jewish Hospital of Philadelphia, St. Mary's (Roman Catholic), Methodist Episcopal, Frederick Douglass (founded by the black community), and Lankenau (originally a German hospital, the name being changed because of the German role in World War I).

In many areas local governments developed hospitals out of their poorhouses for the indigent. These hospitals, like hospitals under not-for-profit auspices, ranged from tiny units of 25 or fewer beds to enormous barracks-like institutions (Philadelphia General Hospital, run by the city, reported 2,000 beds in the early 1920s). Railroads, lumber companies, and occasionally other corporations built hospitals for their employees. For example, in the first decade of the century, the Sante Fe Railroad, which ranged from Chicago to Houston and Galveston and from Santa Fe to San Francisco, could report emergency hospitals for accidents at all its major maintenance shops. These were supported by monthly contributions from employees.

The federal government operated a string of hospitals in seaports and on the major rivers, to care for sick and injured merchant seamen, and developed veterans hospitals after World War I; army hospitals served United States camps and forts. An uncounted army of physicians opened their own small hospitals to serve their paying patients, technically on a profit-making basis. In short, American hospitals arose concurrently as diverse and multipurpose institutions, serving different clienteles, with different communities of interest, and with a distinctive set of social meanings.

Reflecting patterns of social stratification and discrimination in their local communities, the new hospitals of the early twentieth century were rarely community hospitals in the sense of serving the entire population on an equal basis, even for inpatient care. The city and county hospitals that developed from the old poorhouses, such as Philadelphia General, Bellevue and Kings County in New York, Cook County in Chicago, or San Francisco General, remained institutions primarily for the very poor. When governmental or voluntary hospitals accepted private patients, they were typically housed in separate buildings, in well-furnished private rooms rather than wards, with better food cooked in separate kitchens, and with less restricted visiting hours. Indigence continued to carry the heavy weight of social stigma, even as hospitals were medicalized around progressive scientific ideas.

Until well after World War II, major differences in the patterns of disease treated by public and not-for-profit city hospitals added to the sense of social distinctions. Cleveland City Hospital (with 785 beds) was excluded from a major survey of hospitals in Cleveland in the early 1920s because it treated large groups of patients with tuberculosis, alcoholism, venereal diseases, and contagious diseases that did not appear (because patients with them were not accepted) at any other hospital in the area. Cook County was criticized in the late 1930s, as it has been since, for its poor physical surroundings, overcrowded waiting rooms, patients lying on stretchers in corridors, machinery that does not work, and shortages of even common equipment. In short, American hospitals have never, as a group, served as egalitarian forces in the culture as a whole.

Mirroring the diversity of community structure across the United States, there have also continued to be enormous variations in the relative roles of tax-supported, voluntary, and profit-making hospitals from place to place. In a settled city such as Philadelphia, class differences could be seen even among the poor patients admitted to the Pennsylvania Hospital ("respectable," "deserving" poor), and the city hospital dumping ground for all the rest. However small, governmental hospitals in counties with only one hospital probably always behaved similarly to not-for-profit or profit-making institutions in the same circumstances—taking in all social classes, with income from paying patients representing the great majority of their budgets. Such an observation suggests that control of the hospital may be less important as a distinguishing factor of American institutions than segmentation of hospital services across diverse social groups. The important variable, for social policy purposes, is not stratification by ownership but stratification by clientele, a direct reflection of "community" in the 1980s, as in the 1950s and earlier. Relatively homogeneous communities (as in rural areas or suburbs) are likely to produce more homogeneous institutions, with less social distance between patients and between staff and patients than, for example, in a major city teaching hospital, which may attract two kinds of patients—the relatively rich (on its boards and committees and as private patients of leading physicians) and the very poor, the traditional recipients of charity care. Such differences shape differing institutional personalities for different hospital and add to the diversity across hospitals in the United States. The differences have also been sharpened recently, at least in perception, by the location of investor-owned

hospitals in relatively homogeneous, middle-class areas—suggesting that ownership and social class are necessarily correlated—and by the lack of funding for indigent patients.

The passage of Medicare (for the elderly and disabled) and Medicaid (for the indigent) in 1965, in a brief period of egalitarianism, was to indicate that, at least for a short time, everyone, rich, poor, young, and old—was to be given similar if not identical hospital treatment. The power of community patterns, as well as cutbacks in Medicaid, were to prove such optimism unrealistic and short-lived. In retrospect, the egalitarian expectations for Medicaid appear as an aberration in a long history of class discrimination in hospital care in the United States. Financially tottering city and county hospitals remain the dumping grounds for patients no one else will take.

The focus on competition and managerialism of the 1970s–80s has added a new dimension to the diversity of hospital care across different communities and classes by sanctioning, on business grounds, the refusal by hospitals to serve patients who cannot pay (either directly or through insurance, Medicare, or Medicaid). For example, in Pensacola, Florida, the city turned over the management of its hospital to a profit-making organization in the 1970s, closed its emergency room and opened a fee-paying ambulatory center instead. Hospitals can indeed be seen as community institutions, in the broadest sense, reflecting the patterns and priorities of the societies in which they are based—both at the local and national levels.

At the same time, the community of reference for many hospital purposes has expanded beyond the local area, to national and state programs and national consensus-building. Physicians, through the American College of Surgeons, launched a major movement to standardize hospitals around national norms and expectations in 1917–18: the beginnings of hospital accreditation. As Blue Cross plans developed after the 1930s into statewide programs, the definition of hospital care for

reimbursement purposes was extended beyond the town or city. Statewide planning of hospital care was initiated at the time of the Hill–Burton Act in 1946, stimulated by federal construction monies provided to the states under that program and further developed through the federal health planning programs in the 1960s and 1970s, and through state certificate-of-need legislation. Medicare provided the force of national regulation and national expectations, while allowing for substantial local service variations. The diagnosis related group (DRG) program can be seen as an extension of national standard-setting through attempts to define and standardize courses of hospital treatment across the United States, for Medicare patients at least.

The courts have also had a role to play in defining national community norms, whether through asserting hospitals' responsibility for the quality of their medical care, requiring racial desegregation, or providing definitions of life and death. In these examples, the term "community" can be seen as divisible into questions of community service, community control, and community consensus. Community still remains a vague concept at best, a cherished aim with ambiguous meanings, constantly to be sought but never to be fully achieved. Its strength may lie in its idea that something should be done at the local level. In this sense the present development of local health care coalitions (of businesses, other groups, or some combination) can be seen as a continuation of a traditional theme.

The development of competing hospital systems sets up new forms of segmentation of hospital service at the local level, threatening the idea of the hospital as part of its local community power structure, or structures. The visibility of groups other than boards of trustees, physicians, and administrators is changing the broader power structure of hospital care. Stockbrokers, fringe benefits managers, business leaders, self-help groups, and unions also have legitimate, often powerful roles to play in hospital development. A 47-day strike against 30

hospitals and 15 nursing homes in New York City in the summer of 1984 affected 18,000 patients and 52,000 workers. A single bond issue can lock a hospital into a pattern of fiscal operation for 30 years, whatever its pattern of ownership may be. The activity of major purchasers of stocks and bonds, including pension funds and insurance companies, affects the availability of capital for hospital development.

In these and other examples, there is a growing array of new communities—vested interests, with diverse purposes, in constant conflict. The idea of a hospital as the embodiment of medical expertise has given way to the exercise of monopoly power by numerous groups. Hospital management and planning become the outcome of a continuing process of bargaining, negotiation, and consensus-building among differing points of view, both inside and outside the institution.

The relationship of the community of doctors to hospitals has also been marked by ambiguity. In comparison with hospitals in most other countries, American physicians have had, and still largely have, a peculiar relationship to medicine's major institution. The typical American physician remains in private, fee-for-service practice, working independently or as a member of a physician group. When the modern hospital developed in the United States, local fee-for-service practitioners volunteered their services in the hospitals, serving charity patients without charging them a fee. The medical profession became, in effect, a volunteer attending staff, since the doctors who admitted patients (and were thus crucial to the financial viability of the hospital with respect to admitting private paying patients) were not employees of the institution. From the hospital's point of view the physician could be seen as a guest of the institution. To the physician, the hospital was an extension of his or her private practice of medicine.

American hospitals have also developed in large part as open staff institutions—that is, with the expectation that all qualified physicians in a given field ought to have appointments on the attending staff of local institutions. The great majority of all physicians had some kind of hospital attachment by the late 1920s, a pattern that has continued since then. Hospital affiliations have been necessary for many of the most specialized fields. The relationship between physicians and hospitals in America is sharply distinguished, for example, from the system in Great Britain where only salaried specialists typically have hospital affiliation. Although there has been a rapid increase in the number of salaried hospital physicians in American hospitals in the last decade, the formal separation of doctors and hospitals largely continues, requiring new readjustments as hospitals become part of competing systems.

PAST AND PRESENT

What emerges out of a review of American hospital history is a set of culture-specific characteristics that mark the hospitals as American institutions. These include the segmentation and diversity of ownership of hospitals, the division between hospitals and the medical profession (a division echoed in the separate development of hospital insurance and medical insurance in the United States), the acceptance of social stratification of the patient population both among hospitals and within different institutions, the pervasiveness of the pay or commodity ethos in American medicine, and the general expectation that the role of government is necessary but should be limited to filling in gaps in medical care (through programs such as Medicare or Medicaid) and in providing an atmosphere conducive to the development of services in the private sector.

More generally, the fundamental values attached to the hospital industry and its power structures—its communities of interest—are marked by ambiguity. Strauss and his colleagues observed in Freidson's *The Hospital in Modern Society,* of a single hospital in the 1950s, that because its overall

goals were unclear, goals were constantly being negotiated within the established order of the institution. It is useful, in the 1980s, to think of this process of goal negotiation as an intrinsic, continuing element of the national hospital system.

Over and above these general observations, three specific themes mark the continuation of hospital history from past to present. First, American hospitals remain segmented in their interests, communities, and control. Second, decision making continues to be diversified; that is, diffused over communities of interest, ranging from the health professions to individual hospital boards, corporate headquarters, government programs, and major purchasers of hospital insurance. Third, American hospitals are expert at adapting very rapidly to explicit external incentives, usually financial incentives.

Where social needs are made explicit (for example, in civil rights legislation or with the passage of Medicare) American hospitals are socially responsive institutions. Where there is ambivalence or apathy (for example, in providing medical care to the homeless, uninsured, or indigent) hospitals look to other institutions—notably to government—to meet such needs, disclaiming the responsibility of being public institutions. In this respect, too, hospitals can be seen as socially responsive; that is, as reflecting the messages from the broader culture in which they are based. Lacking a unified hospital or health system, and lacking consensus about the appropriate philosophy for an American welfare state, American health policy is marked by skittishness and change.

In the absence of consensus, decisions about hospital policy have been left to the jockeying of influence among communities of interest. Part of the uneasiness about high costs and increased profit making in hospital care derives from a perceived need to develop a national consensus about hospital policy without resorting either to a government-dominated health care system or one dominated by a few massive corporations. A high-cost system is

the trade-off for avoiding either of these two extremes. The present system allows for organizational experimentation and diversity, for avoidance of draconian management decisions (the specter of rationing) and overt limitations of care for middle-class Americans, and for accommodation of conflict among reasonable but opposing points of view. In this sense the hospital system can be described in terms of constructive ambiguity. To those struggling with their implications, rapid changes cry out for simple theories of explanation and simple solutions. DRGs became the solution to the rising cost of hospital care in the 1980s, just as Medicaid was the apparent answer, in the late 1960s, to bringing the poor into the "mainstream of medicine."

The hospital system can be seen as analogous to the development of other industries; for example, consolidation of the manufacturing industry at the beginning of the twentieth century, which again followed the consolidation of the railroads. Under this model, hospitals are small firms which will inevitably move toward industrial consolidation (and which may have been held back by the monopoly interests of the medical profession). Such analogies beg the question of whether hospitals are legitimately businesses, and, if so, what does that mean. How far hospital service may be appropriately compared to manufacturing is another question that demands elucidation: indeed, whether any service industry can be appropriately compared to any manufacturing industry is an important question. The urge for simple explanations remains. Meanwhile, there are those who claim that profit making in health services is ethically wrong and socially dangerous, while others are more concerned that medicine is rapidly being dominated by a "medical–industrial complex" in which the traditional rights of doctors and patients will be swamped by the coming of the monolithic "corporation."

The search for simple theories and the "one best way" of doing things ignores the fact that organizational life in the late twentieth century is messy

and complex. Decisions have to be taken in a climate of conflict and negotiation, whether we are speaking of hospitals, factories, government, or

schools. Hospitals, like other institutions, carry with them the burdens and potential of their history.

DEVELOPED WORLD PERSPECTIVE

PATIENTS' KNOWLEDGE AND PATIENTS' WORK: PATIENT–PATIENT INTERACTION IN GENERAL HOSPITALS

DAG ALBUM

1. INTRODUCTION

During a study of the social careers of heart-attack patients (Album 1985) I did fieldwork in a hospital. While sitting in the patients' rooms during the ward round, I was struck by the intense activity between them after the doctor and nurses had left. Each of them asked the others what the doctor had said about them. It was obviously easier for them to hear, understand, and remember information given to room-mates than information aimed at them. Together, the patients reconstructed all the conversations that had taken place. After some time, often a long time, everyone was able to describe what had happened at his or her bedside.

Another ingredient in the conversation was to find out what the doctor thought about their present conditions and about their future lives. They discussed how difficult expressions could be translated into, or defined in, their language. Some of them were more familiar with medical expressions than others and acted as experts and translators. The patients also tried to figure out the reasons behind the doctor's decisions, for example, regarding tests or a revision of the training program. Even seemingly simple statements from the doctor such as: "We have received the results from yesterday's test. Nothing wrong was found" were subject to discussion and collective interpretation.

Even when they seemed to be satisfied with their efforts to remember and interpret, the conversations went on. Without overtly protesting against the medical view, they developed a view of their past, present, and future that reflected even very non-medical experiences.

What impressed me was how much the interpretational process was a communal undertaking. Remembering, translating, and constructing pictures of their illnesses, and their former and future lives, was a project for the patient group as a whole, a project in which almost everyone took part.

I have started this research note with a lengthy example of interpatient activity. It was the observations I made during this fieldwork that led to the start of my present research project, which has as its explicit aim to study patient–patient interaction in somatic hospitals.

The present study is far from completed. I have observed and interviewed patients in two hospitals. The usual length of stay for the patients was between three and five days in one of them, two weeks in the other. In addition, I draw on observations derived from the heart infarction study already mentioned. I plan to go to two more hospitals, hoping to be able to identify and interpret some of the variety characterizing interpatient life.

The findings I present must be seen as tentative. The concepts are also provisional, but I hope

they will sensitize the reader to the life of hospital patients.

What I aim in this research note is a "thick description" (Geertz 1973) of interpatient activities common to many general hospital wards. I have organized the note in the form of a funnel, beginning with restrictions set for behavior by some of the norms of the patient community, and focusing gradually on the purposes and functions of patient–patient interaction. In order to make my main point clear, I deliberately oversee variations in patterns of interaction.

2. RULES OF MANNERS

One concrete and strongly supported rule of manners in the Norwegian hospitals is expressed by this description: "In the hospital all are equals." This seemingly value-free characterization of social differentiation in the hospital points to a very strong norm. This norm is well known from other arenas in Norwegian society (Gullestad 1984), but I have never met it so forcefully and consistently as in the hospital.

Two aspects of the norm will be mentioned here. First, the norm narrows the range of topics for conversations. Patients seldom talk about their jobs or their education. Neither do they talk about their incomes. I believe this to be one of the reasons illness and other hospital affairs are used as topics to such a large extent. Hospital matters are shared by all, and as topics they are not socially dangerous.

Second, differences in standard of treatment not justified by the medical condition of the patient are held as an extreme violation of the rules. The patients enforce these rules vigorously. On one occasion, patients were annoyed because a leading politician had been given a single room. None of them preferred a single room themselves, but they judged it as unjust and a serious deviation from the norm. To place the politician in the only single room on the ward was to favor external social rank. (The staff argued that the politician would be both-

ered by the others, and would not get the rest he needed. They gave medical arguments for the difference in quality of service.)

Some patients are better at asking doctors what is wrong and what is going to be done with them than others. This skill may be associated with length of education, a social-rank characteristic brought into the hospital from outside. The competence is nevertheless accepted. It is also exploited by the others, since the competent person can explain and translate for them what they do not understand themselves. However, it is the competence shown inside and not the imported rank that is accepted and respected.

While most characteristics used to distinguish people socially outside the hospital are neglected inside, sex is more important here than in most other organizations. Patients are assigned to rooms according to sex. Often, certain rooms are always used for women and some always for men. In this way, the hospital ward is materially divided into domains for women and domains for men. In one of the hospitals I have studied, the corridor was dominated by men. In another the smoking room was dominated by women. This means that even rooms formally open for everyone are in reality to be used by men only or women only. In other words, the most obvious dividing line in the patient community is the one between men and women.

3. PATIENT INTERACTION

Patient interaction is mostly through talking. Much of the talking is about illness, treatment, the staff, and other hospital affairs. Though illness is the reason for patients being in the hospital, and the patient role is their dominant role, staff members become irritated with talk about illness. They perceive this preoccupation with illness and treatment as a sign of narrow-mindedness and of a negative, pessimistic, and skeptical attitude towards the therapeutic process. But illness and related subjects have many aspects to be discussed. To perceive this

talk as narrow-minded comes from not observing the variety of themes and the importance these themes have for patients.

Even talk about the same aspect may have different meanings, depending on style and context. In one situation it is obvious that talk about how one particular doctor behaves has as its purpose helping to pass the time. In another situation the same theme is talked about because one of the patients is going to be examined by this particular doctor the next day and wants to be informed in order to prepare him/herself. Under still other circumstances this doctor has recently visited their room and knowledge about his usual way of behaving is relevant for the interpretation of the messages he has delivered.

Perhaps even more than in other settings, conversations in hospitals include nonverbal acts. The way they dress, how they walk through the corridor, and their facial expressions are examples of the means of communication patients employ in addition to speech.

Patients admitted to hospital seldom know other patients when they arrive in the ward. What usually happens is that they start talking. Some patients are better starters than others. They are not only able to find a harmless topic of interest, but are also able to formulate their questions or comments in a way that makes it easy for others to respond.

Some situations are easier to start in than others. I suspect one of the reasons why social life is more active in the smokers' room than elsewhere is that smokers have something in common they can start talking about. When coming into the smokers' room, they are on their way simply by asking for matches or, as is often done, commenting on the density of the smoke.

Patients in local hospitals often know some of their co-patients from earlier times, and when they meet someone they do not know, they will ask where the other person comes from and try to find out if they have any common friends or acquaintances. Even in large central hospitals, however, asking from where one comes is a much-used way of starting. Place of residence is also used for purpose of identification.

Another way of getting acquainted and identifying a fellow patient is asking what kind of illness he or she is there for. Being ill is surely something they have in common and is of interest to everyone. If not too similar to that of many other patients, illness may also be used when one patient wants to refer to another who is not present.

After a while, when they have got to know each other better, the range of topics becomes broader. In smaller groups they may even exchange information about their jobs.

Severely ill patients do not talk much. They do not become acquainted in the same way as the stronger and more mobile patients do. However, they tell afterwards that they felt contact with others in the room. They compared themselves with the others, identified with them, and in one respect saw them as their closest human contacts.

The identification patients feel with fellow patients, even if they are strangers in other ways, makes it easier to establish contact. According to patients, healthy people often do not understand what it is like to be ill, even after thorough and burdensome explanations. To other patients it is sufficient to say only a few words to be understood. The empathy may even be so good that non-verbal utterances are sufficient. That is one reason why it feels good to be in the hospital.

Patients may feel lonely if they do not have any talking contact with others. Besides, to witness the intimate life of strangers is so much of a paradox that patients feel embarrassed if they do not talk with the others. In other words, to be able to start and continue conversations is an ability of importance in hospitals.

On the other hand, there is the danger of the others overwhelming you, especially if you are immobile and cannot get away from their physical presence. To be able to keep social distance in spite

of physical presence, and to do so without offending others, is also a necessary skill. "I am tired, I think I'll take a nap," is a well-used and simple statement for those who wish to withdraw from the conversation.

To become acquainted means to form a pattern of interaction and a pattern of norms and values. Characteristics of these patterns will, of course, be reflected in the themes of conversation and the other qualities of interaction that I discuss in the following sections.

3.1 Living Together

In the hospitals I visited, between two and eight persons slept and spent much of their free time in the same room. They did not know each other's preferences, but some decisions had to be taken about matters of common interest. One example is whether to keep the window open at night. This question appeared to be very important for most patients. In individual interviews I had with them, some of them told me that it was impossible for them to sleep with the window closed, others in the same room said they would become ill if the window was open. Feelings were strong. Different types of negotiations took place, sometimes of a covert kind, the opponents opening and closing the window without mentioning verbally that they were in favor of any specific solution.

What is most obvious is their tendency to adapt, to be considerate, and, above all, to avoid open conflict.

3.2 Leaving

One standard patient saying goes thus: "A hospital is the best of places to be, when you need it." Nevertheless, another favorite theme for talking, especially among the men, is when they may leave for home. They report to fellow patients about the doctor's reaction to their wishes to leave the hospital. Male patients may even boast about the offensive

style they used when they suggested an earlier leave than the staff had planned for them. For a man to state that he does not wish to go home would be considered inappropriate. In contrast, women often show a skeptical attitude towards going home, complaining about the hard time they will have with the housework when they are still not well.

When leaving, patients say, "Best of luck" and "Get well soon" to those who are around at the time. However, they seldom wait for or search for other patients who are not present to exchange greetings, even if their contacts have been of a kind that elsewhere would have been considered very close. According to patients who have been in hospital before, it is unusual to have much contact after discharge: a telephone call or a Christmas card is typically the closest form of contact. The intimacies of the patient community belong to the social world of the hospital.

4. PURPOSES AND FUNCTIONS OF PATIENT TALK

4.1 Helping Pass the Time

Much patient talk is meant to help to pass the time and help in forgetting anxieties. In interviews and in the way they behave, most patients are very insistent when they describe hospital life as boring. Especially in the afternoon, when the day's examinations and treatments are finished, time passes slowly; and their worries about being ill augment this.

Talk about illness and treatment can be used to pass the time. Other topics are often conventional. Men talk about hunting, fishing, and cars; women talk about housework, food, knitting, children, and grandchildren. Besides illness, staff members, meals, and other hospital matters, both men and women can talk about holiday travels, TV programs, and the weather. A good storyteller or joker is always popular.

As mentioned, the range of topics tends to become wider after a while, when patients get to

know each other better. On the other hand, however, if they stay in hospital longer than a week or two, the repertoire of topics tends to be used up, as life outside becomes farther and farther away and every story becomes overused. At this stage the hospital itself is well known, too. Ward rounds, doctors, nurses, examinations, treatments, meals, everything that happens is anticipated.

4.2 Finding Out about Illness

When I was doing the "infarction study" one patient told me: "I understood what was wrong with me, when I came to that room. Everyone there had heart infarction. We told each other how it felt." Usually the patients learned their diagnoses, and much more about their illnesses, from a doctor or nurse; but with very few exceptions, patients learned about their illnesses from other patients, too.

One of the first topics to be discussed among patients is symptoms. This discussion assumes a special intensity when a fellow patient has the same diagnosis. Even among patients with widely differing medical diagnoses, however, symptoms are compared. One result of these discussions is that the language needed to express symptoms is further developed and the illness is more accurately defined as a social, and not only a personal, phenomenon.

Patients who have recently become ill are especially eager to trace their illness histories backwards. They discuss whether various symptoms they have had over the last years can be understood as early signs of the illnesses that have now become manifest. They reconstruct their personal biographies. Sometimes this is done with bitterness. Knowing what they now know, they believe they could have prevented the full blow of illness.

Patients also engage in conversation about the causes of their illnesses. The explanations they arrive at can conflict with explanations given by medical experts. In the discussions between pa-

tients the question "Why did I become ill" is not only a question of causes, but also of affective and intellectual meaning.

4.3 Finding Out How Life Is Going to Be

Patients who have been ill for some time exchange views about what they find problematic about being ill, and how they are coping. They compare and learn.

Patients who have recently contracted an unexpected disease want a detailed recipe for a new way of living. Staff members only give general advice. Their information is not concrete enough. Of course patients want to be told, and are actually told, by staff about medical prospects. However, this information is only part of the information patients seek and need. They go through the ingredients of their life-styles and ask what they can, and cannot do, and what they ought, and ought not, to do.

Other patients are better informers than doctors and nurses. If they cannot give the answers, at least they understand the questions. Patients who have been hospitalized before for the disease in question are the best informants. However, when style of life is considered as one of the causes of the illness, as is the case with myocardial infarction, their authority as advisors is weakened.

4.4 Finding Out about Staff Members and Ward Life

Newcomers among patients are often shown around by a nurse when they arrive. They are told about the ward routines, what patients are expected to do, at what time meals are served, and so on. It would seem that this introduction is inadequate, or the patients are unable to listen, or both, since newcomers will often ask fellow patients for additional information.

The introduction given by other patients may also be the first one. In one of the wards I studied,

patients were often asked to wait in a patient's lounge until a bed was ready for them. While there, they often started a conversation with other patients. Sometimes the other patients were also newcomers. They talked about why they were there and what they expected from the stay. On other occasions newcomers started to talk with someone who had been there for some time. They, too, were introduced to the hospital by a patient.

The ways of being of nurses and doctors are discussed not only because of lack of other topics in helping to pass the time. Veteran patients give newcomers advice about which staff member to talk to. Just which staff member will be recommended depends upon what patients are looking for. One of the personnel may be considered the best to calm you down if you are worried; but if you wish to be permitted to use the kitchen, you may be advised to ask another.

4.5 Finding Out about Examinations and Treatment

Being in the hospital means being ill under a therapeutic regime and acquiring a new role in an organization. The ordinary roles of everyday life are left outside when a patient enters the hospital. Patients' experiences and interpretations of illness are heavily influenced by medical conceptualizations not only directly, through verbal information, but also indirectly, through medical procedures. As indicated in my introduction, what doctors do with patients is accepted by the patients as valid communication about what the doctors really believe is the matter with them.

Finding out about illness, therefore, often means finding out about examinations and treatment. Comparisons are important. If a patient learns that the test results and the plans for his or her treatment are the same as those of one of his or her room-mates, that patient is relieved if the room-mate seems to be recovering well. In the Intensive Care Unit, a heart patient who does not get oxygen

while an adjacent patient with the same disease does several times, learns that his or her case is less serious.

When patients feel insecure about how the staff judge their conditions, or about what plans the staff have for them, many of them will, of course, often ask a staff member for information and explanations. However, some patients never ask doctors or nurses; they rely on fellow patients; and even the bravest of patients, those who feel free to ask the staff whenever they wish to, will enter into further discussions with their patient colleagues. Staff members seem to think that many misunderstandings are spread in this way from patient to patient.

Patients who are going to take a test with which they are unfamiliar will often ask experienced others about it. Normally, they will also be informed by a doctor or nurse. Patients want to be informed by both staff and fellow patients. The two types of informants give different pictures of what is going to happen. The staff are more technically oriented, telling them what is going to happen from an outside point of view. The other patients tell how it feels, what the pain is like, and how they themselves reacted to it. According to my provisional data, patient information is considered more important by patients: it prepares them for what they are going to experience. Only the best of nurses can give such information, since they must first learn from experienced patients how a particular test feels.

After having gone through larger examination or treatment procedures, patients are expected to tell their fellow patients how it was. In this way a stock of knowledge is built up. Patients also expect one another to report to the others when they have received test results, which are then discussed in the group.

5. THEY DO MORE THAN TALK

Patients help each other, not only by giving information, advice, and comfort, but also by giving help of a more material kind. When one of the pa-

tients in a room is going to buy a magazine or some chocolate at the news-stand, he or she will always ask the room-mates if they want something.

This is an example of personal service offered to everyone else in the room, regardless of their physical condition. However, most of the personal services are offered to the more ill by the less ill. If there is a patient in the room who is on his or feet, the other patients do not ask one of the staff for a glass of water. What is regarded as natural to ask a fellow patient and what is considered to be the business of a nurse or another member of the staff depends on what patients consider to constitute medical matters. Patients told me that they would do everything for other patients that is not strictly medical. Thus, helping another to fasten a supporting bandage is a task for co-patients when it has been in use for a while, but a medical task for a nurse or physiotherapist when it is new.

One type of help that is often seen is one patient acting as contact between another patient and the staff. Thus, for instance, one patient will go to ask a nurse to come and talk with a fellow patient who is anxious, and needs the type of consolation that the helping patient is not able, or unwilling, to give.

In one case a patient pointed out that his room-mate had been wrong in not turning to him for help. The room-mate got worse during the night and did not want to ring the bell for the nurse, because the sound was so loud it would wake up the other patients. He therefore got out of bed and went to the nurses' station to tell them about his pain. The patient who told me the story said he understood very well why the other did not want to use the bell. What was wrong, according to him, was that the ill patient did not ask him to find a nurse.

6. PATIENT KNOWLEDGE AND WORK IN AN INFORMAL HELP SYSTEM

If we were to remove all patient interaction, we would see a radically different hospital life from the one I have described above. For the patients it would be marked by boredom, insecurity, loneliness, emptiness, and social isolation. It would also be impractical. The greatest problem would probably be the lack of help with existential problems. This does not mean that patients in the situation that now pertains overtly raise the most profound philosophical questions; but everyday talk concerns existential questions and helps the patients in grasping them.

Looked at it in this way, patient activities are functional for the patients and also for the hospital organization as a whole. It may be dysfunctional under some circumstances, but not as often as staff members believe. More often than not, the pattern of interpatient activities can be seen as an informal help system, a parallel to the work laywomen do in caring for elderly people outside of formal caretaking organizations.

We may consider a large part of the patients' activities in the hospital as work. It is unusual to call it work, since it is performed by unpaid patients and not by paid personnel. When personnel perform the same tasks, it is defined as work. What is defined as work depends more on the formal position of the performer than on the content of the activity. This implies that patients work even when no staff members are present.

If we move to a wider concept of work, a concept which also includes what people do to develop, maintain, and change social relations (Wadel 1979), a still larger part of patient–patient interaction must be interpreted as work.

Work presupposes knowledge of one kind of another. Patients bring knowledge into the hospital. Based on this knowledge, on their experiences with illness and patient roles, and on the interpretations they hear and see from staff members, they develop a negotiated knowledge (Young 1981). This is a knowledge about illness as well as about hospital life. It is necessary to know both to be a competent patient (Måseide 1987).

In social–scientific analysis of patients, illness is the experience-near (emic) concept and disease

the experience-distant (etic) (Kleinman 1980; Geertz 1983:57). It should be emphasized that patients' frames of interpretation and their stock of concrete knowledge are elaborated through social interaction. It is part of a culture. Experience-near does not mean that the knowledge is not spelled out.

I believe that the conceptions of illness and treatment among hospital patients differ in several respects from the lay conceptions held outside hospitals. The community of hospital patients has a unique culture. It is not merely a reflection of outside lay culture. In the intense social interaction of this community the experience-near concepts are refined with more vigor than in most other settings, making them more specific and more widely shared. Besides, the knowledge of hospital patients is a knowledge of hospital life as much as a knowledge of illness in a restricted sense.

The experience-near conceptualization is partly elaborated as a necessary counterpart to the medical model which patients experience in their encounter with medical procedures and medical explanations. This model proves to give a skewed and insufficient interpretation of patient life as patients experience it. The inadequacy of the disease concept is the reason why patients construct illness (Freidson 1970) differently from staff members.

7. PATIENT INTERACTION IS UNDERESTIMATED

In my description of the multifaceted lives that hospital patients live, I have consciously put many facets aside. I have done this in order to highlight my main point: Patients are engaged in activities in common, activities that are of a broad range, and have a significant impact. I have stressed the cooperative activity among hospital patients, partly because in my view it does not get the attention and esteem it deserves. This is true for the hospital personnel, and it is also the case for the sociological and anthropological literature about hospitals.

Most personnel regard interpatient activities as insignificant. First, they tend to assume that nothing much happens when no staff members are present. Second, when acknowledged, the activities are seldom considered important, but regarded as ways of spending time. To consider anything patients do as work is not possible the way they see it. If they consider the activity as having impact, it is often considered negative. This is the third point I wish to make. Nurses tend to argue that the information patients give one another is false and frightening. Conceptualizations outside the medical paradigm are considered as potentially wrong, harmful, and unworthy.

The informal organization and culture of patients, clients, or other subordinates have been subject to investigations in a variety of organizations, such as psychiatric hospitals (Stanton & Schwartz 1954; Caudill 1958; Goffman 1961) and prisons (for example, Sykes (1958) in the USA and Mathiesen (1965) in Norway). Beginning with the Hawthorne project (Roethlisberger & Dickson 1939) many studies have focused on this phenomenon in factories and other work organizations.

However, although there are some exceptions (for example, Fox 1959; Roth 1963), the organization and culture of patients have not been in the foreground in studies of somatic hospitals. The studies that have been done are from hospitals with long-term patients, which indicates that researchers have not expected anything of importance to take place between patients who stay in hospital for a short time only.

Foster and Anderson (1978:167) support my interpretation:

> In somatic hospitals, where the average stay of patients is now about a week, only under special circumstances, such as in rehabilitation wards or wards for the chronically ill, does time permit the development of true patient cultures.

The authors take it for granted that cultures cannot develop or be transmitted from veterans to new-

comers more quickly. Even if this postulate proves to be true, however, it does not necessarily follow that nothing of interest takes place. It is worth noting that social scientists and hospital staff agree that the behavior of personnel has some impact on patients. And while the members of the staff are with the patients only briefly during the day,[1] other patients are there all the time.

In spite of this, interaction between parties in general hospitals is considered insignificant. Most hospital studies focus on staff affairs. Patients and clients are presupposed to be the objects of the work done by staff. Their status as members of the hospital organization is downplayed and under-recognized.

There is an extensive literature on staff–staff and staff–patient relations. These analyses have no parallels in analyses of interpatient relations. Patients are presented as solitary individuals, living an isolated life when not taken care of by staff members or visitors. Sometimes the patients are described as victims of a depersonalizing hospital system. Such descriptions disregard the comfort work done by other patients. Some authors point out that patients acting as groups do represent a therapeutic potential: they may be taught the proper medical understanding of their illnesses. Thus, their therapeutic potential depends solely on their ability to acquire and understand medical knowledge, not on the kind of knowledge they have themselves developed.

Strauss and his co-authors (1985) differ from others in this respect. They point to the knowledge and the large amount of work performed by patients in hospitals. However, even if they mention work done by patients in groups twice in their book, their exposition is dominated by a picture of patient work as something done by individual patients helping staff members to do expert work.

It seems to me that social scientists, with Strauss et al. as a possible exception, have taken the interpretation of the staff at face value, and given the medical conception of illness and treatment a higher esteem than that of the patients. I consider this to be an unacceptable position for a sociology of medicine (Straus 1957).[2] Although I know that patients come to hospitals for medical treatment and not to socialize with other patients, I consider the social world of patients to be as sociologically interesting as the social world of other hospital members.

NOTES

1. According to a Norwegian study of a medical ward, at least one personnel member is present in the patients' room for one-tenth of the day (between 7 A.M. and 11 A.M.) (Axelsen 1976). Nowadays, the cleaning assistants, at least in hospitals in the larger cities, are often males from a Third World country. Before they were middle-aged working-class Norwegian women. This means that the patients have lost the personnel group with whom they had closest and longest contact. They are even more than before dependent on each other.

2. It would be no less unacceptable even if the patient–patient interaction proved not to have the functions of an informal help system that I suggest it has. The usefulness of their activities judged from the point of view of others is not a necessary prerequisite for treating it as worthy of being studied in the same way as more prestigious interaction systems.

REFERENCES

Album, D. 1985. På andre kjenner man seg selv—eller hvordan man larer å bli infarkpasient. *Tidsskrift for samfunnsforskning* 26, 92–117.

Axelsen, T. 1976. *Det tause sykehuset*. Oslo: Universitetsforlaget.

Caudill, W. 1958. *The Psychiatric Hospital as a Small Society*. Cambridge, Mass.: Harvard University Press.

Foster, G. M. & Anderson, B. L. 1978. *Medical Anthropology*. New York: Alfred A. Knopf.

Fox, R. C. 1959. *Experiment Perilous*. New York: Free Press.

Freidson, E. 1970. *Profession of Medicine.* New York: Dodd, Mead & Co.

Geertz, C. 1973. *The Interpretation of Cultures.* New York: Basic Books.

Geertz, C. 1983. *Local Knowledge.* New York: Basic Books.

Goffman, E. 1961. *Asylums.* New York: Doubleday Anchor Books.

Gullestad, M. 1984. *Kitchen-Table Society.* Oslo: Norwegian University Press.

Kleinman, A. 1980. *Patients and Healers in the Context of Culture.* Berkeley & Los Angeles: University of California Press.

Måseide, P. 1987. Interactional Aspects of Patient Care. Department of Sociology, University of Bergen.

Mathiesen, T. 1965. *The Defences of the Weak.* London: Tavistock.

Roethlisberger, F. J. & Dickson, W. 1939. *Management and the Worker.* Cambridge, Mass.: Harvard University Press.

Roth, J. A. 1963. *Timetables.* New York: Bobbs-Merrill.

Stanton, A. H. & Schwartz, M. S. 1954. *The Mental Hospital.* London: Tavistock.

Straus, R. 1957. The Nature and Status of Medical Sociology. *American Sociological Review* 22, 200–204.

Strauss, A. & others 1985. *Social Organization of Medical Work.* Chicago: The University of Chicago.

Sykes, G. 1958. *The Society of Captives.* Princeton: Princeton University Press.

Wadel, C. 1979. The Hidden Work of Everyday Life in S. Wallman (ed.), *Social Anthropology at Work.* London: Academic Press.

Young, A. 1981. When Rational Man Fall Sick: An Inquiry into Some Assumptions Made by Medical Anthropologists. *Culture, Medicine & Psychiatry* 5, 317–335.

DEVELOPING WORLD PERSPECTIVE

FAMILY CARE WORK AND DUTY IN A "MODERN" CHINESE HOSPITAL

JOSEPH W. SCHNEIDER

From December 1986 through April 1987, I did fieldwork at a hospital in a north China city where I lived and taught sociology. I proposed to the Chinese authorities that I examine how Chinese family members and friends contribute to the work of caring for patients in the hospital (see Strauss et al. 1985). My own experience as a son whose father recently had died after a long illness, my research on the experience of people with chronic illness (Schneider and Conrad 1983; Schneider 1988), and the stories I had heard in China about how much care work Chinese family members do in the hospital made the question both personally and professionally interesting.[1]

Although I thought my research was politically "safe," that is, it did not seem to touch topics that the government might consider sensitive, I nevertheless anticipated difficulty in gaining access (cf. Wolf 1985). After all, I was a foreigner wanting to observe and write something about modern Chinese life. I told officials that I wanted to describe sociologically (scientifically) and not to criticize Chinese practices or people, and that perhaps we Westerners could see our own high-technology, highly professionalized, and often impersonal system of health care delivery in a critically helpful light as a result of my research; that "the Chinese" may indeed have something to teach "us" in these matters.

As I began to see the officials endorse and repeat the characterizations of my work as "scientific," I appreciated as never before the legitimating power of this discourse in the face of skepticism about motives and ends. Although subsequently I

would applaud the deconstruction of scientific realism and epistemology back home, I saw that I
was again using it uncritically to get what I
wanted—access—and to assure my audience of
my "objective" methods and "progressive" ends.
Yet I knew how easy it would be to critique what I
might see; how what I would write as nonevalua-
tive description easily could be read as (that is,
could be) highly critical. Moreover, because I had
decided to privilege the perspective of family
members, it would be easy to sympathize with
them—to "take sides"—and thus no doubt run
afoul of various official or policy perspectives in
the hospital and elsewhere. Although I could perhaps use the current renewed Chinese faith in science (see Goldman and Simon 1989; Anderson
1990) and "facts" to get in, questions of the authority and power of my own voice would have to be
managed each time I began to write (Schneider
1991; Fabian 1990; Clifford 1983a). And I could
enter only with the endorsement of those in positions of power—hospital leaders and doctors—yet
I would try to tell a story about the work and care
that family members give. What posture would I
effect (then and now)?

Obviously, these dilemmas have not kept me
from writing; and since they are so fundamental to
the practice of modern social science and, I think,
unsolvable within its confines, it seems better to
make them explicit in this writing, critiquing and
perhaps abandoning some of these conventions
rather than abandoning the writing itself. Accordingly, in what follows I use conventional practices
of ethnographic reportage to create realistic scenes
("I/eye was there and I/eye am reporting the facts";
and note the opening sentence of this chapter; see
also Kondo 1990, 7–9) about care work in the hospital, along with self-reflexive commentary that
seeks to point to my own presence both in the story
the text tells as well as in the construction of the
text as vehicle for that (still quite modern) story.

First, I describe the hospital I visited—invoking "the field"—and the kinds of work family

members and hospital staff did around their patients. I proceed then to organize segments of conversations (interviews) and observations I made—
data—into a story about how, in doing the work of
giving care, these family members took up positions in a complex web of often contradictory and
always power-saturated discourses that characterize urban China in the late twentieth century.[2]
Sometimes I saw these family members as victims
of power; at other times they seemed to be skillful
wielders of power, yet usually to defend themselves and their patients against what they saw to
be much greater forces inclined not to operate in
their interests.

AT THE HOSPITAL

Over the course of four and a half months I visited
three hospitals, but I went most often to the critical
care unit (CCU) of one five-hundred-bed general
hospital. Officials told me this CCU was "one of
the best" of its kind in all of north China and that it
had received many foreign visitors. Because only
Western medicine was practiced in this unit, I took
this to mean it was offered to foreigners, and to me,
as an example of China's progress in "modern
medical care" (see Henderson 1989).

My first visit was in the company of a doctor–
official from the public health bureau, who introduced me to the unit's leaders and displayed the
necessary certified papers showing who was responsible for the decision to give me this access.
After I explained my interests and research procedures, the leaders invited me to "come any time"
and "see whatever you like." I quoted them to myself several times during the course of my visits,
when I was unsure about whether or not to move
into certain spaces.

In my proposal, I had offered to provide an interpreter to accompany me. Bureau leaders were
hesitant to allow an "outsider" whom I would
choose, and they found it difficult to secure a bureau person who had the time and English skills.

After two visits with a bureau-supplied interpreter, I began to go the unit by myself.[3] As a result, I suffered not understanding most of the conversations overheard and was unable to converse with most of the patients and their *peiban*[4]—people, mostly family members, who accompany the patient, most of whom could not speak English. Yet, because such an interpreter–official likely would have further constrained the conversations I hoped to have, I felt the loss was also a gain of sorts. I would rely on my own observation and those conversations I could have in English, supplemented by any information I could gain by asking simple questions in Chinese. I also spoke to many English-speaking Chinese not connected to the hospital but whose experience of their own hospital caregiving was informative. (In short, I'm not making this up. Am I?)

Posted visiting hours in the unit were from 4:00 to 7:30 P.M., Monday, Wednesday, Friday, and Saturday. Doctors told me that family members and friends who wished to visit at other times were required to obtain a *peiban zheng* or visitor's card from the head nurse, who would write on the card the reason for the visit, such as to bring the patient "delicious food" or to "serve the patient." This discourse of modern medical administration to the contrary, it seemed that at almost any time of the day or night there were some *peiban* on the unit. This was perhaps the first of several contradictions between what I was told and what I thought I could see.

The CCU consisted of the first floor of a two-story wing at the hospital, a building probably dating from the early 1950s. Patient and staff rooms of various sizes opened from either side of a single, long corridor. The largest ward was called the "monitor room." It had nine beds reserved for the most critically ill patients. Moveable fabric screens separated the beds, and one end of the room had storage cabinets and several wooden desks pushed together as a place for doctors and nurses to sit and write. Two smaller rooms, one ten-bed unit for women and a six-bed unit for men, were called "convalescent wards" and often received patients from the monitor room, as well as from outside the unit. Two additional rooms housing various machines and equipment were reserved for treatment. The doctors' rooms, nurses' station, unit director's office, and washroom and toilet were on the facing side of the corridor. Often two or three additional patient beds were placed against one wall in the corridor, along with cabinets, equipment, oxygen tanks, and carts.

I spent most of my time in the monitor room, standing along the wall near the door or sitting at the desk. There I could strike up quiet conversations with doctors as they sat and wrote in charts or chatted. I also had a full view of the room, the patients, and the *peiban*. I recall fancying that I was somehow less visible in those spots (the "fly on the wall" fantasy of the powerful, unnoticed gaze), although in fact, such practices located me quite visibly "with" the doctors in that space. I was thankful for my conjured sense of the "witness" of those moments at a time when I felt quite alone (the "heroic" white man holding forth under difficult conditions in the exotic place? I/eye *was* there!).

I made a few visits to an obstetrics ward and an internal medicine ward at two other hospitals, always in the company of a public health bureau or hospital official. One of these hospitals was new and both were larger than the one containing the CCU. In neither case did I have the same freedom to move and look around as I did on the CCU.

CAREGIVING LABOR: SOMETHING *PEIBAN* "LIKE TO DO" BECAUSE "DOCTORS AND NURSES ARE FEW"

As a bourgeois Western sociologist familiar with the complex specialization and control of work common to U.S. hospitals, I was immediately struck by all of the physical labor family members were doing in the CCU. This was notable in contrast to the considerably more constrained reper-

toire of activities for their U.S. counterparts in similar circumstances. I noticed a lot of washing and cleaning, bringing and taking—work that seemed, for its ordinariness, largely unnoticed by most Chinese eyes, but that I wanted to see as a display of deeply felt duty.

Washing and Cleaning

Emblematic of this physical work was a young women I noted, perhaps a daughter, who, having served supper to an older woman in the convalescent ward, went into the hall, returned with a large steaming mop, and began cleaning the floor around the woman's bed. None of the *peiban* or patients took much notice of her, but I did. As she finished the floor near the patient's bed, she proceeded to mop under and around the bed of the patient nearby, with *peiban* for that woman helpfully moving stools and shoes out of the way. Before finishing, she had mopped all of the central floor space in the ward. I saw similar mopping by both men and women *peiban* in this ward and in the monitor room. In the two specific cases where I could take note, there seemed to have been nothing spilled on the floor to occasion the mopping. Nurses and doctors were regularly in and out of the room, and they seemed to take no note of this work. Rather, it was simply another project in the evening round of bringing food, serving it, conversing, washing the supper cups and bowls, packing these away to be taken home, changing the sheets, and ministering to the patient—all proper practice for *peiban*.

Bringing and Taking

Some of what was brought and taken included the patient's "favorite food" from home; soiled bedpans and urinals; thermoses of boiled water; supplies of medicine and materials from outside the hospital; large and heavy oxygen tanks, put next to a patient's bed; doctor-written orders for lab tests on the *peiban*'s particular patient, delivered to the

appropriate offices; and even patients themselves, taken to other departments in the hospital. An immense amount of work was done by people who were not part of official hospital work force, on tasks that in the United States usually were done by employees.[5] I was deeply impressed by what I read as "the Chinese sense of family duty." Being part of and contributing to my own family and being able to care for my father had been so important to me (and no doubt still was/is).

After noticing a patient's wife bring an X-ray film into the ward for a doctor to examine, I asked the doctor why she, rather than a hospital worker, had brought it. He said that she had gone to another department and gotten it. "Is this something that *peiban* often do?" I asked. He said, "Yes, family members like to do this kind of thing, and sometimes the doctor and nurse are too few and cannot take time to get these things."[6]

Peiban sometimes carried doctor-written requests for lab work to another part of the hospital. One night I watched as one doctor filled out such a form and gave it to a man whose young sister had just been admitted. After the man left, I asked this doctor and another sitting nearby, whose English was a bit better, "These forms. You gave that man three of them. What are they and where is he taking them?" Together they offered the following:

> *Maybe observe this at night. Two labs, one outpatient and one inpatient. All doctors use outpatient lab at night because inpatient lab closed.* Peiban *take to outpatient department and this would probably cause technician to come to patient and get samples and take back to laboratory. Sometimes* peiban *go to lab to get result back. Or, doctor may call. If doctor and* peiban *do nothing, maybe tomorrow lab will send.*

Although one senior doctor told me that *peiban* were definitely not allowed to get lab reports and bring them back to the ward—according to "modern" hospital administrative procedures—there seemed to be a good deal of energy given over to this kind of expediting work. As the doctors quoted above implied, it was not so much that the

lab would not come to do the tests or would fail to send the results. Rather, *peiban,* doctors, and nurses alike saw this kind of taking and bringing work as expeditious and sensible—as normal—for family members to do. What otherwise might take three days could be accomplished in one or two. Besides, "They like to do this kind of thing," said the doctor, something I willingly heard as confirming my sense of "the Chinese sense of duty," as well as "good sense."

Similarly, if a patient was to be taken to another hospital for a special test, the work of contacting that hospital, making an appointment, and arranging transportation by means of some work unit's car all might be taken over by a family member. I spoke to one man who had done this for his father:

> The doctor here suggest to us that you should have an exam for your patient…CT—do you know? (Yes.) But if you want to have, you must contact with that other hospital by yourself. (How?) My brother-in-law have a classmate who work at CT department there…so my father went very soon. Otherwise, you wait a long time because there are so many people need and so few hospitals—only two—that have that equipment. It is often broke down and the technicians can't repair it. Perhaps some of that machines are imported from America. (We share a laugh.)

Although not officially responsible for making these arrangements, neither this son nor the doctors could be sure just how long it otherwise might take. To rely on much slower institutional channels and the people whose job it was to activate them would be considered, I think by all parties (even by me), both foolish and lazy—falling short both of common sense and proper filial duty. Besides, "Family members like to do this kind of thing, and sometimes the doctor and nurse are too few and cannot take time" to do it, the doctor said. Yes, yes, I thought. This is precisely what it means to be a "good" family member. (I liked to think of myself as a good family member.)

One man in his early thirties described how he got the peritoneal dialysis used in his father's care. We had been discussing the intravenous (IV) drip into his father's stomach as we stood near the bed. Because I had heard other *peiban* describe how they went outside the hospital to get scarce medicines, I asked him how he got this fluid. Our conversation went on like this:

HE: Yes, I go to medicine box…
I: What do you mean, "medicine box," what is that?
HE: At the factory, not far from here…
I: Wait. You mean you go to a factory to get this medicine yourself?
HE: Yes, it is not far from here. This kind of medicine all people here go get themselves. The other kind of medicine the doctor has to give.
I: How much do you get at one time?
HE: Three yuan, two jiao a bag. Each time [father] must use two bags. One day, four times. He uses eight bags a day.
I: How many bags do you buy at one time?
HE: There are ten bags in a box. At one time I buy twenty boxes.
I: You buy twenty boxes?! Do you have to take a bicycle?
HE: (*Smiling*) No, my father's factory provides a vehicle…what shall I say, a simple truck.
I: And a driver?
HE: Yes, a driver, and he helps me bring the medicine here to the hospital.
I: Where do you put the medicine when you bring it here?
HE: Outside…I am going to use a long sentence now. When there is a flat and it is second or third floor, outside is sometimes a place (*makes motions with his hands*)…what is it called?
I: Balcony? A balcony?
HE: Balcony, yes. There is in the third building a balcony and I put the medicine there. Other people put their medicine there too.
I: So each time you need the medicine you go there, four times a day?

HE: Oh, no. I put some boxes under the bed, three boxes under the bed here. When it is time for the medicine, I give it to the nurse.

Each time I read this dialogue, I am tempted to modify it so that I don't appear so naïve, so impressed by his explanation, such a "straight man" for his account. This underlines for me both the distance between and the closeness of their and my experiences and, more generally, of the Western bourgeois social scientist in the "exotic" place. It also points to my (our) presence "there" as an occasion for such accounts and performances (cf. Clifford 1983b) and thus confounds simple notions of social scientists gaining entrée and "trust" as vehicles toward making "valid" characterizations of "the setting." And, as is now widely appreciated, this passage helps us see how data are jointly produced.

Ministering and Monitoring

Another kind of work seemed to demand greater judgment and decision-making, such as in watching the patient, noting his or her condition, and reporting same to hospital staff. It revolved mostly around (IV) drops, routine reports of fluids taken in and passed, temperature readings, foods eaten, frequency and volume of bowel movements, and the operation of various machines attached to patients.

Late one cold January afternoon as I sat in the monitor room, a sixty-five to seventy-year-old man was brought from surgery, where he had been operated on that morning for pancreatic cancer. After a few minutes I asked a doctor about his condition. He said, "He is jaundiced, in shock, has lost a lot of blood, and has respiratory failure." Over the next hour, *peiban* did a good deal of ministering and monitoring work around this patient. Here are some notes—again, here set off as data—that I made as I watched:

A middle-aged woman, not a nurse, comes in, slightly breathless, and unlatches the other swinging door and props both doors open. Slowly, a bed is wheeled to the center of the room—there is very little space here—pushed and surrounded by eight or nine people. I assume they are family members. They are accompanied by two doctors in blue surgical clothes. Two of the peiban *are carrying, and holding high, IV bottles, one with blood and another with a clear solution. As doctors and nurses begin to attach the patient to machines and put the IV bottles on stands, the relatives cluster around the bed, their attention focused on the man and the doctors and nurses. I am standing a foot or two below the end of the bed when a nurse comes in and seems to ask most of the* peiban *to go back out into the hallway, leaving three people beside the bed. I'm still there too. The middle-aged woman and a man are on either side, crouched on the floor, each with one hand on the patient's knee and the other holding down a hand. As the patient tries to move his legs, these family members—children?—push the legs back down straight. They look haggard and worried. The man lets go of the knee and hand to check the blood drip going into the patient's wrist. He flicks the IV line with his fingers. Another* peiban *comes in from the hallway and they both examine the bottle and tube. One adjusts the valve and looks closely at it. Apparently not satisfied, he says something to the nurse, who has calmly noticed him doing this. She turns, examines the valve, adjusts it and goes back to her work. I can see the other drip is connected to the man's right ankle as the woman moves the blankets to examine the place where the needle is placed. Every few minutes one or two of the other* peiban *in the hallway come in, stand for a moment at the foot of the bed, say something to the woman or man there, and then go out.*

Another patient in the monitoring room, a young man in his late twenties or early thirties who had suffered brain damage in a truck accident, was in a coma and tended to regularly by his sister. She seemed to be in the ward every time I visited, over the course of one month. The doctors told me her brother had been in the hospital three months, all together. He had had a tracheotomy and was fed through a tube inserted in his nose. Another quote from my detailed notes (these really are data):

Patient 9's sister comes in and goes to the bed. She pulls the covers back, lifts the man's left and then right

arm up, and pushes the blanket up under his armpits. She touches the back of her hand against the man's cheek and looks down at him, steps away from the bed to a small stand at the head of the bed, and appears to be pouring something that looks like honey into a cup, followed by some white liquid, mixing the two. Then dry powder goes in; more mixing. She puts this down and takes the thermos out into the hall, returning moments later. She pours some of this water into a basin, testing it with her hand and on her own face, puts in a cloth, squeezes it out and proceeds to wipe the man's face, forehead, neck, holding the tube that goes into his stomach through his nose carefully to one side. She resticks the tape against his upper lip, rearranges the gauze pad covering the opening, and then takes a large syringe from the stand and draws some of the mixture into it. She connects the end of the syringe to the tube and pushes the plunger to empty the syringe. She repeats this two or three times until the mixture is gone.

Finally, I watched one evening as a middle-aged son repeatedly reattached a ventilator connection taped over his father's mouth. Each time the son would have the tube in place, the father would pull it out. This went on for twenty minutes before I left. The son looked very tired. I, too, felt tired and wondered how long it could continue, imagining his anguish out of my own from past care enforced against a father's will.

THE BURDEN OF DUTY AND THE OPPORTUNITY OF CARE

Family members were often called upon by doctors to sign permission forms for emergency procedures, tests, or surgery—to be, in short, the "person responsible." When I asked three doctors on the unit, "What is the most important thing *peiban* do for their family members?" they all said, "To sign permission forms," especially for patients who were seriously ill.

I observed such a permission form–signing by a middle-aged man whose father had suffered a cerebral hemorrhage (I thought of my favorite uncle, who died from that) and was having trouble breath-

ing. The doctors decided the patient needed a tracheotomy. I stood at this man's shoulder, outside the closed doors of the monitor room, and watched several doctors and nurses bent over his father. Suddenly, a doctor and nurse turned toward the door and motioned for the man (us?) to come into the room. (Did they want me, too? Oh no. Of course not.) The nine doctors and nurses who had been around his father's bed gathered around him as one doctor spoke, making a downward thrusting motion with his hands. This talk at the center of the huddle of white coats went on for a few minutes, with the man and doctors talking in turn. They moved to the desk and the son was given a permission form, which, after some hesitation, he signed. He came back out into the hallway and stood near the wall, looking away from the door. He had behaved like a good son, at least in the doctor's script. It perhaps wasn't that clearly so in his own.

But family members' sense of duty was considerably more diffuse than this form-signing coerced by doctors. It seems captured succinctly by a proverb one man cited when I said he was working very hard to care for his father, who suffered from a cardiopulmonary problem. He replied: "There is a saying, if a father lay in bed for a long time, his son not care well for father" (*jiu bing chaung gian wu xiao zi*). I was immediately struck by how unreasonably demanding this seemed; what, after all, was a son expected to be able to do? Quite a great deal, apparently. I couldn't avoid thinking of my own father's long illness and time in bed and the care I gave him. He was, so often, such a long time in bed; but I felt this Chinese wisdom was unreasonable. How could *we* be held responsible?

Another, older man, when discussing the routine practice of *peiban* spending the night beside a patient's bed and the importance of being vigilant, told me the following story passed on to him by another family member on the ward:

Some peiban *told me there were two* peiban *here with a patient who was very serious and couldn't breathe. The...[he points to his throat] sput...(sputum? Yes, I*

know)…and the peiban *were sound asleep. The patient died and* the doctor said that if the peiban paid more attention, the patient would not die so soon. *If the patient is so serious, like in bed 4, the* peiban *never go to sleep. [my emphasis]*

Here are complex moral instructions indeed. They draw on the *peiban*–son's sense of duty and responsibility (felt by him and fully understood by the doctors) and the authority of the doctor in the modern hospital, and they shore up the political and economic conditions of contemporary Chinese urban life. The unasked question seems to be: Who is really responsible for the proper in-hospital care of the patient? Children—perhaps especially sons—are quite familiar with the discourse of filial duty; the proverb offered by the other son specifies the scope of this work. The "doctors" indexed in the story reaffirm the nature of this duty while eliding their own and that of the nurses. The family member's task seems impossible to fulfill; yet acceptable options seem not to exist ("*meiyou banfa*—I have no choice"). Arguing that it is, rather, the doctors, nurses, and hospital who failed the patient would have to be a private discourse, which would be foolish and shortsighted to offer publicly. To ignore the duty would seem an even less available option. Family members thus reaffirmed the traditional discourse, paradoxically shoring up a system of care delivery that they often privately criticized.

Even when a patient was not "so serious," a family member might not sleep. The man who told me this story said his father suffered a gastric ulcer but was "not so serious." A few moments later he said that he routinely spent the night awake at his father's bedside, reading English books. Having heard the prophetic and chilling tale from his fellow *peiban,* I felt I could understand why.

Moreover, there was both cultural and institutional support for sons' and daughters' in-hospital care work. *Danwei*[7]—work units in China—as a matter of policy released sons, daughters, and spouses from their duties at work, usually with full

pay for a specified period of time (such as one month), so that they could be at the hospital doing various caregiving tasks. If family caregivers were few, work units also might send fellow workers to the hospital to help care for a patient. Although this could provide needed extra hands, *danwei*-supplied caregivers could bring new burdens. One middle-aged man said he was glad he and his only sister had not accepted the offer from his father's work unit to send "a person to assist us." When I asked him why they had not, he said "Because that person is not as…serious as a family member in care." He added, "Even if some unit person comes here, it's that person's job to look after the patient. But also that person feels he does something for the family and so he thinks we should do something [for him or her…like]…like take him out to eat …in a restaurant. So, we don't like that idea."

This reflects an intersection of traditional conceptions of proper family responsibility and good everyday politics; and, from the *danwei*'s side, such policy might be cheaper than paying the additional fees for special nurses. But that these conceptions do not always fit together well is indexed by the family's refusal of help from the father's *danwei*. Here the son invokes the traditional discourse of reciprocal exchange to block what might be seen as good socialist practice. The official discourse and the policy, however, remain relatively intact.

Caregiving needs, quite in contrast to being a burden, could provide a fine opportunity to demonstrate oneself as a suitable candidate for traditional family relationships while, paradoxically, serving the official discourse of "revolutionary humanitarianism" (*geming rendao zhuyi;* see Wang 1986) in the hospital in the face of "too few doctors and nurses." One man and I had the following conversation:

I: Last night when I left I noticed that there was another man sitting here [by the bed] after you had gone. Who was that?
HE: That was the boyfriend of my sister.
I: Oh, really? Why did he come?

HE: In our society, if a young man see a young girl, if father or mother is ill, that boy must take much care. It is a good chance to express kindness (*chuckles and smiles broadly*).

Moreover, not only was this care work a "good chance" to show oneself as a proper candidate for husband, it was a good chance for anyone to do what might be called "the good person."

As I watched and was impressed by all this effort, I found myself recalling scenes from hospital waiting rooms and corridors back home, scenes that I had come to read as sometimes "contests of character," in which various degrees of sacrifice and selfless work could be displayed among relatives in what seemed almost a competition to display oneself as the son or daughter or grandchild "*closest* to," "caring *most* for," "loving and loved *best* by" the patient. I myself felt ever-so-virtuous in the various caregiving tasks I did for and around my father.

The concern for "face" and the proper display of traditional duties and responsibilities in today's urban China, coupled with the official discourse of scarcity and collective responsibility for "modernization" and the still quite alive remnants of what Gail Henderson (1989) has called the "Maoist model of health care," would seem to render this work a terrain to be sought out and, perhaps, even contested. This might be one way to see, to read, all the extraordinary work these *peiban* did.

CONNECTIONS AND CARE

As Mayfair Mei-Hui Yang (1986) has pointed out in her study of *guanxi* in Beijing, establishing, nurturing, and using relationships or connections to solve life's routine but important problems is a kind of work that today is ubiquitous in China. Similarly, problems of allocating and obtaining "scarce resources"—a theme in both official and common discourses—often bring forth discussion of "back doors," *hou men(r),* as the best way to get whatever is desired.[8] One of the most desired "ob-

jects" a family member might obtain for a sick relative is to find a back door that would open into the critical care unit I visited. It could, on the one hand, literally mean the difference between life or death. On the other hand, it could mean the difference between more or less comfortable care. In either case, opening such back doors was an important way to do one's duty as a good son, daughter, or spouse. Standing in those shoes, it seemed to me a very reasonable pursuit; one I could lament, for the effort and groveling it sometimes required, but one I sensed it would be most difficult to ignore (*"meiyou banfa!"*).

Early in my visits to the CCU, I began to understand that many, if not most, of the patients had gained admission in this way. Of course, some patients were admitted because they suffered from the critical care conditions the unit was designed to serve. *Guanxi* and backdoor admissions, however, seemed easily as common. The best—and luckiest—patient was perhaps one who both fit the protocol and had good connections, providing everyone a chance to behave properly; the official discourse of modern medical administration could be invoked, pointing to this patient as exactly the sort of case the unit could serve (good, i.e., "modern" administration and delivery); the doctors could work hard for this (special) patient, invoking the discourse of selfless, perhaps even socialist, medicine (good doctors); the family members could hope, with varying degrees of certainty, that their patient would be given good care by doctors and nurses, at the same time that they could see their own activities as successful and themselves as properly responsible family members (good son/daughter/spouse).

One way *guanxi* operated was when the patient or *peiban* and one of the doctors or nurses had some personal relationship (*pengyou guanxi*). Speaking one afternoon about a newly arrived patient, one doctor said, "He has stroke and myocardial infarction. That patient's relatives knows some doctor who work in our ward, so we receive this

patient. The patient's relative wants the patient to have better care, so he came here from…[another] hospital." Later, when I asked whether all unit doctors and nurses could provide such an avenue into the unit, this doctor said:

> *I will say yes, because* we help each other. We have to work together. *We have a rule in the CCU. The doctors' and nurses' direct relatives—father, mother, child, brother, sister—if they are ill, we receive the patient immediately, even though the patient suffers from things like advanced cancer and chronic renal failure. We accept them immediately. Why do we have this rule?* We want to make our doctors and nurses happy. We want to let them feel warm to work here. *[my emphasis]*

The connection to a doctor did not have to be quite so direct as family or *gingi guanxi*. One man I spoke to explained his father's access to the unit by saying that his sister was going to marry a young doctor who worked in another department in the hospital. When I asked him if he thought it would have been difficult to gain admission without this contact, he said, "Yes, very difficult. I think many patients are more serious than my father…[but] have to stay at the emergency room…or not even there. Just give some medicine and told to go home." And, as the prospective husband noted earlier, this doctor could demonstrate his own goodness in this way.

When I heard these stories, I thought how important it would be to make friends with a doctor in China, even to put him or her in your debt, as a kind of insurance. Speaking about one patient, a doctor said:

> *This patient was introduced by some of our doctors [as a candidate for admission] because the patient give our doctors some help. Two doctors ask me, two or three times a day, urge me to receive this patient. I thought about it.* This patient helps these doctors get new houses. *If I not receive, these doctors may not be happy…*I want to keep things peaceful and quiet, *so I admit this patient. [my emphasis]*

Doctors often explained to me that the unit's scarce renal dialysis resources, for instance, were more wisely used for patients suffering acute renal failure. But, like other displays of the medical administrative discourse, this could be juxtaposed, in a very matter of fact way, with an explanation that this patient, having suffered a cerebral vascular accident (CVA)—what one doctor called patients "waiting to die"—had connections, and the patient was therefore admitted.[9]

Another kind of back door, publicly criticized of late, opens to allow officials—"important people"—entry. A man in his early forties had suffered cardiac arrest that produced brain damage. One doctor told me, "The father of patient is the head of…[a city] district. If his father not this kind of man, this patient we not receive in our ward." Another man about sixty-five, who suffered from liver cirrhosis linked to an earlier hepatitis infection, was described to me by another doctor as a "police official" to account for why he was on the ward.

Such connections also could exist between other work units and the critical care facility (cf. Yang 1986, 136–90). Because, for cadres and workers, the *danwei* will inevitably bear some or all of the costs of hospitalization and care,[10] work unit leaders can become rather directly involved in negotiating not only admission to the unit but also continued treatment. If one were an important leader, a loyal and valued worker, or if the unit were somehow liable for the injuries or illness, such connection could be invaluable both to the *danwei* and the patient.

One afternoon I sat in the director's office and watched the head of a prospective patient's factory urge the director to admit a man in his thirties with chronic renal failure—a condition not officially treated in the CCU. Not surprisingly, however, work units were interested in striking a balance between proper care and cost. Family members and patients in such situations are often happy to stay in the hospital as long as possible. As one man said, "Because the cost is supported by my father's unit, we are in no hurry to go back home. Here my father get good care and good look after."[11]

If a work unit were responsible for a worker's injury, the expectation seemed to be that they would pay all expenses, including hotel room costs for out-of-town family members and fellow workers who came to give care. One young man had been seriously injured in his work at a factory in another town. His *danwei* leaders seemed to assume responsibility; they came to the unit to encourage the doctors to "save this patient"; otherwise, as one doctor told me, "They would be seriously criticized. They have many accidents there." Not only was the work unit paying for all the care of this patient, who had been there for more than one month, but they also continued to pay his salary; they paid for all his brother's expenses to come to the city where the hospital was located; and they paid the expenses of seven fellow workers who came to share the care work. When I asked this brother how the patient came to the unit, he said, "The…*danwei* has a connection to this hospital." And in the work unit leaders' view, that this young man's father was the party secretary of the *danwei* could only strengthen their case before the hospital's leaders.

At another hospital I visited, a man had suffered chemical poisoning at work and would never regain consciousness. His unit paid for a private room, for one shift of a private nurse, and for two eight-hour shifts of fellow workers' care at the hospital. He had been a patient there for three years. I asked if his family members—a wife and two children—came to see him often. The nurse said, "Not so much anymore."

Such situations involving work units and costs can put doctors and the hospital in a difficult position relative to the patient and family members. Two doctors said that one of the reasons there is so much trouble between doctors and nurses on the one hand and family members on the other is that whereas work units want to keep costs down, family members and patients want as much care as they can get. After invoking the supply-and-demand discourse—too few nurses and resources—

one doctor said, "The doctor have trouble with patient and with patient work unit director. For example, if patient suffer from some disease, this patient need many money. The patient unit director don't hope do, so this is controversy. If patient spend money, unit must pay this money." Here, the family members may draw fully on both the *danwei*'s responsibility—using the socialist discourse—and on strongly held notions of harmony—the traditional discourse—to try to keep the patient in the hospital. The harmonious image produced by the official discourse that the doctor, nurse, *peiban,* and *danwei* all "work toward the same goal," as one senior doctor said, seemed hard to sustain in the face of these diverse efforts and interests. I doubted that any of the *peiban* I had spoken to would take it seriously as a description of the circumstances of care.

PEIBAN AND MEDICAL STAFF: STRAINS IN MANAGING CARE

Contrary to handing over responsibility for care to the specialist or expert, a position that family members in the West might find more familiar, these Chinese sons and daughters were likely to see their relationships to medical staff as requiring complex and crucial management work. I came to see that one should not merely assume that doctors and nurses will do their jobs well and give good care. The assumption in Chinese families seemed to be that if it indeed were a "job," one could count on it not being done well. The outcome of caregiving had to be managed by a range of interactions, offers, and deferences directed toward positively influencing people with authority—doctors, nurses, unit or even hospital leaders.

This, however, is not to say that the doctors whom I met or whom these *peiban* knew had behaved badly or irresponsibly. It is rather to say that the operative assumption—under the circumstances of "scarce resources," the power-infused system of "back doors," and the importance of fil-

ial duty—was that without the requisite display of appreciation or "help" to those in power, without very concerted attempts to marshal resources to control the course of events, one's patient's care likely would go badly. This then could weigh very heavily indeed on those who had ignored or failed in this kind of work.

Next to these efforts, my assumption, nurtured in the United States, that such care work is primarily a question of professional training and responsibility, requiring little "intervention" and "connections," has since come to appear more than a little naïve. Indeed, it now seems to me ideological, pressing me to think more critically about the discourses that bring that naïve subject who still trusts modernism—"me"—into being (Althusser 1971). But I recall that at the time, in that hospital, thinking about those strange assumptions, I stood firmly and uncritically on my Western, bourgeois, modernist "truth," quietly thankful to be "an American" consumer of medical care (even after more than a little experience at seeing it up close and writing about it).

For "them," however, to ingratiate oneself to doctors and nurses was an abiding and serious question. This was explained by a doctor who himself had received such help. I had asked him to translate a question to one *peiban*, asking how he knew when he would be permitted to come into the monitor room after posted visiting hours. The doctor, answering the question himself, said:

> You must understand the psychology of the peiban. *In this ward,* peiban *are forbidden but in other wards they are more. Strictly not allowed in this ward; must stay in hall [outside the unit]. Many* peiban *try many times [to come in]. If the nurse is kindhearted, easy to talk to,* peiban *will try and maybe nurse will criticize or let go in or pretend not to see* peiban *come in. (So, the* peiban *should be sensitive to the nurse's and doctor's ideas?) Yes, to clean the floor, to ask if this or that is easy for you, can I buy something for you—if you need movie tickets? There are many ways maybe to make a doctor happy. There are many things that can help with, and different things from different people and dif-*

> *ferent occupations. For example, if I want to have heat in my house, they may help with the tube…and this kind of thing. Everything.* I am the person here who can help him. [my emphasis]

With so much emphasis on calculated help-giving and receiving, it was not surprising to hear that "some" doctors and nurses received gifts from patients—although this seemed to be a sensitive subject. It was mentioned in anger by one *peiban,* who criticized one doctor whom he and his family did not like. After saying the doctor was "cold," he added, "And he receives gifts from his patients."[12]

For their part, although doctors and nurses usually acknowledged the importance of *peiban* labor in Chinese hospitals and agreed that they themselves would want their own family members' care in the hospital (the traditional discourse), they felt *peiban* could be a nuisance to their work and even troublesome to the patient (the discourse of modern hospital administration; see Henderson 1989). If a patient were seriously ill and required constant attention, they reasoned, then perhaps it was important to have a family member available most of the time. There simply were not enough nurses and "conditions were poor" (the discourse of a developing country, struggling to "modernize").

One senior doctor at another hospital said, bluntly, "We doctors don't like *peiban* because they interfere with…work and some treatment. But patient very like to have family member stay with him." One young nurse said, "Most of the *peiban* do not understand the treatment and care in the hospital and are very worried sometimes and angry when nurses use treatments. They think that if we use a machine on the patient, the patient will die…do not want us to use the machine." Although nurses acknowledged *peiban* labor, they usually were quick to point out that today nurses themselves were able to do all the necessary care work. I asked one young nurse about this. She said that even when she was very busy, she did not like having *peiban* on the ward "Because the relative ask the nurse many questions and this take time.

Sometimes this kind of condition has a bad influence on the patient." This administrative discourse casts family members as not behaving in the best interests of the patient, necessitating the intervention by the medical staff (whose interests are, of course, with the patient) to curb these negative effects, that is, to restrict and coerce the presence of *peiban* in the hospital. This sounded quite familiar to me.

By considering a hypothetical but, I think, telling account of how doctors might effect this coercion, we can appreciate how the tensions between doctors and *peiban* easily could build. The following comes from a longer conversation about permission form–signing:

DR: The most important thing a relative can do is to sign the paper!
I: What if the relative says no, won't let you do it?
DR: We continue to work until…
I: What if the patient says yes and the son says no?
DR: We ask the son, why do you not agree? Is it because of money? We tell him it is not important to worry about the money. We may try to *bring public opinion or family opinion against him.* We may go to other members of the family to try to force him to agree, or, even tell him I will tell his father in the bed that his son won't agree to pay for the treatment we want to do. This public opinion and the opinion of other family members is very important in China. *We don't want criticism.* We might even go to the *unit where the son or daughter works* and say, *"How do you educate your workers?* This son does not want to pay money for a treatment his father needs. You should do better!" This way we try to force the son.
I: What if the patient or the father says no and the son says yes?
DR: That is no problem. We do it. [my emphasis]

"Harmony" can thus be achieved coercively, using diverse discourses in quite artful ways.

Given the above, it is not surprising that doctors and nurses sometimes saw *peiban* as people who might "make trouble" for them of a more consequential kind.[13] They did seem to consider the external resources a controlled, chastened, or disappointed *peiban* could draw on in possible retaliation. For instance, the truck driver–patient who had been injured in an accident in the countryside and suffered brain damage had become a problem for the unit. His condition was medically stable and there were no treatments available, save routine maintenance care. The doctors wanted the patient to leave, but the patient's sister and family members would not agree to a transfer. One of the doctors said:

> This patient is give me a headache. He is a driver and there was a car accident…in the countryside…During his stay there (in a small country hospital) the patient's condition became worse and worse. He had ARDS syndrome [Acute Respiratory Distress Syndrome], so we received this patient here…three months! I would like this patient to go away. He was discharged [once]…and went to…[another hospital in town] but that hospital refused to accept the patient because they have no special treatment for such a condition. He stayed only at emergency room for three days, then nowhere to go so the relative came back and met me and the head nurse. My opinion was we should receive. The head nurse said we should refuse. I was afraid the relative would have some quarrel with us if the patient died. *The patient's relative has a lot of trouble with us. The trouble is the accident occurred in the countryside and the patient stayed at [the small hospital]. Came here from there, so [that hospital] refused to receive this patient too. The other side is the [city hospital in patient's hometown]. We want to transfer [patient] to [that] hospital, but* the relative doesn't believe in that hospital…She refuses to transfer. *(Could you just send the patient there, to that city hospital even if the sister says no?) No.* The patient relative must agree with the opinion. [my emphasis]

I asked this doctor what sort of trouble this sister might be able to cause. He said, "She maybe go to the health bureau or find the hospital president and say that the patient is severely ill but Dr. [his name] refuse to receive the patient. Patient die. I will be criticized." While this doctor here considers his

own and the hospital's liability—something familiar in the West—he also gives great attention to *peiban* opinion and refuses to override directly their position (a posture less familiar in the United States).

I heard stories about family members beating doctors when something "went wrong" in their patient's care. Asking direct questions about this usually brought chuckles and asides in Chinese from doctors. During a conversation with three doctors, in which I explained something about malpractice suits and insurance in the United States, one middle-aged doctor quipped, "In our country, relatives always beat the doctor, not sue the doctor." Two doctors I spoke to actually had experienced physical assaults by relatives and patients: one was attacked when a patient died unexpectedly during a delicate cerebral vascular procedure; the other, by a patient and his wife when he worked in the emergency room. Writing in the English-language *China Daily* about a possible shortage of doctors in China, a journalist reported that one reason for a "lack of enthusiasm" for the job was the "lack of necessary legislation to protect medical workers from harassment and even physical assaults by family members all too ready to accuse them of medical malpractice" (Chen 1987).

Nurses, because they were largely responsible for managing *peiban* in the hospital, often were criticized by both *peiban* and doctors. While praising "these nurses here," critics typically connected the presence of *peiban* to "too few nurses." Some family members added that nurses didn't do their work well, that they were "lazy," and that they treated relatives and *peiban* badly. In the strongest explicit condemnation of hospital care and, especially, nurses that I heard, one *peiban* said (the following is a translation):

> The trouble is they play with you in the hospital. They do not provide adequate service, not to say good service, but they play on your anxiety for the comfort of your sick family member by telling you the patient needs a companion and giving you the I.D. card, as if they were bestowing a great favor. In the intensive care unit you're told to go home and take a rest by the head nurse because there are three nurses on duty day and night for eight or six patients, but the minute you're out of the room the nurses demand to know where the family is or tell some other companion to call you because the patient wants to urinate or something. In fact, they're always right and you're always wrong. The nurses never tell you that a seriously ill patient can do without a companion. They won't do the work! What I can't understand is why they can't do their jobs by themselves like everybody else. I believe that if the hospitals provided something like normally decent service, nobody is such a sucker as to want to stay by a sick bed day and night, going without proper meals and sleep. There may be such suckers but they certainly are not in the majority. [my emphasis]

Nurses and medical officials were sensitive to such criticism and usually countered it with the modern medical discourse that separated nurses' and *peiban*'s interests on the grounds of the former's expert knowledge and training and the latter's ignorance and emotion.

One head nurse in another hospital, whom I spoke to through an interpreter, early in the project clearly invoked this discourse. When I asked her, a woman in her fifties who said she had been a nurse for thirty years, about *peiban* on the floor and in the hospital, she said:

> There has been a directive from the public health bureau that the hospitals had to be managed according to correct managing principles. This means not so many peiban. (In the past, what did these peiban do in the hospital?) They would feed the patients, clean the wards, carry urine and blood samples to the laboratory, get food from dining hall, wash patients' hands and face, help them eliminate urine and go to the toilet. Sometimes they were also responsible for watching the solution for injection [IV] because they would tell the nurse when the bottle was empty. If patient had a high fever, they could wash the patient with alcohol to bring the fever down. This is now forbidden because this work belongs to the nurses and nurse assistants. Before there was disorder, during the Cultural Revolution, and now there are new standards for the management of the hospital. We have the responsibility system. Everybody

has his or her work to do and even if you want to, you can't ask the patient's family members to do this work. This is the work of the staff. [my emphasis]

This is the "modern" Chinese hospital. It leaves little room for the more traditional discourse on caregiving that is typically invoked by family members and patients. In fact, family members appear here only at visiting hours. Moreover, it assumes adequate numbers of well-trained ("modern") medical personnel in the hospital. That all of what she described as part of a disordered past was precisely what I would soon witness in such great variety and detail helped me understand the power of the official view and the resentment of those who actually did such a great part of this work.

MODERNIZATION AND *PEIBAN* CARE

It is wonderfully convenient that, as one doctor put it, "family members 'like' to do this kind of thing"—this caregiving work—because, as another said, "If all the *peiban* in the hospitals in China were removed, that would be a social problem." That this contradiction of "modernization" in China—relying on a traditional discourse to shore up a considerably less established, "modern" one—is in some sense recognized by the Chinese health bureaucracy is indexed in a brief article titled "View on Visiting Patients in the Hospital" which appeared in a 1986 issue of the *Chinese Journal of Hospital Administration* (see also Zhong 1985). The author, arguing that it is, of course, necessary to place certain limits on "companionship" in the hospital, writes that without more resources, such tight controls on *peiban* will "only create difficulties for the patient":

Generally speaking, the patients tend to be in low spirits, particularly the severely ill ones. Some are depressed and worried, some anxious, some in dark moods, some lonely. Most of them wish to have someone from their families at their sides. This not only assures them of better care, it also reduces the patients' tenseness. It has the effect of providing them with so-

lace and contributes to their sense of security and is helpful to medical treatment and the patients' recoveries.... Many patients feel unaccustomed to nursing care from anyone who is not a family member. Some feel embarrassed or uneasy.... Clearing the hospital of companions often gives rise to arguments that affect the relationship between the patients and the medical staff.... In order to be at the patient's bedside, family members sometimes force their way into the ward, which causes rows and fights...the hospitals have made great efforts toward reducing the number of companions and controlling visiting hours. A large number of people have been employed to guard the entrances. In addition, measures have been taken, such as sudden inspections, which involve a large amount of manpower and resources.... [All of] this means there perhaps is not such a great advantage in exercising a tight control on companions and visitors. [Wang 1986, 192; my emphasis]

Indeed, from this description one might ask what the benefits of such controls are, apart from greater consistency with the "modern hospital" discourse.

What this characterization doesn't begin to acknowledge is the complex and endless *guanxi* work the family members I met performed to get their patients into the hospital, not to mention efforts toward helping ensure what they hoped would be good care once their patients were in. The deeper tensions that define the complex relationships between hospital staff and *peiban* are also ignored. In the hospital, doctors, nurses, and officials have authority in the official discourse that they use to try to gain *peiban* conformity with stated "modern" hospital rules. At the same time, they draw on traditional discourses of filial duty and harmony to coerce cooperation and care work by *peiban,* work that then goes largely unnoticed and, most recently, has even been repudiated by official regulations. Yet the doctors themselves are subject to traditional discourses of proper conduct, as well as a kind of "negative control" that keeps them mindful of their own debts to and transgressions against both traditional and socialist codes of behavior. While invoking discourses of bureaucratic authority and "modern medicine," these doctors and nurses cannot afford to forget that

not only are they "Chinese" but also their official political line is a communist one—a line that, as has so often been the case in the past, can be invoked effectively by those below and beside them against all manner of "counterrevolutionary," bourgeois, individualist, and even "feudal" conduct. The possibilities of "making trouble" for others seem to proliferate both on these official grounds and from what could be called more traditional Chinese ways of being. Finally, to complicate the picture further, family members themselves use the traditional discourses of filial responsibility in the hospital, perhaps sometimes in spite of themselves, as a way to create and recreate themselves as proper and dutiful Chinese sons, daughters, and spouses.

You will have noticed, however, that I here have moved into a totalizing, analytic voice, one common to narratives' endings, where authors are hard put to slip off the stage unnoticed and leave a pleasurable feeling of order and understanding in the audience about the object of study—in this case, "how family members care for their relatives in urban Chinese hospitals." Yet even as I began this ending I wanted to step away from it, to leave the story open, uncertain; not a story that claims to tell you what was "really there."

Although in the beginning I justified the project using my status as an experienced U.S. social scientist, from the earliest days on the CCU my own personal experiences as an American and recollections of virtue and guilt connected to my family and to my father's long illness and death strongly influenced what I saw. After initial drafts of this paper sat quietly for some time, a colleague, Min-Zhan Lu, helped me see in the paper a sentimentality and

nostalgia for duty properly done, personal sacrifices made, and a sense of family and connectedness in social relationships that, to me, often feels quite absent in the "(post)modernized" life of the United States. Readily available to help me fall into this trap were other, dog-eared, totalizing notions of "the Chinese" and of "Chinese duty." The real risk, one greater than being critical of things Chinese, was nostalgically to valorize the dutiful and seemingly never-ending care work family members in China did, while neglecting the contexts of power and coercion in which this work was done; in effect, to affirm the doctor's assessment that the way to understand this work was to see it as the product of what "[Chinese] family members 'like' to do." It was to make them out as fools, "suckers" (*shan yao dan*), as the one *peiban* put it so shatteringly. The Western bourgeois social scientist going to urban China in the late twentieth century to find parts of a cherished but gone past at home is not a picture we should abide. It affirms, at the expense of the difficult and coerced lives of the natives, imaginary selves and lives seemingly lost by privileged outsiders not subject to these complexities.

But mine is only one small instance of the endless dilemma of speaking from a centered place, from a discourse that is not simultaneously subjected to criticism and destabilization. There is no Truth there to be "brought back" (cf. Geertz 1988; Rorty 1983); and perhaps not even a "there." A sense that the ground in "modern(izing) China" is itself full of contradictions and complexities, even as I try to make it cohere in a "scientific story," provides the nonsolution on which I might end.

NOTES

Acknowledgments: An earlier version of this paper was delivered at the annual meeting of the American Sociological Association, San Antonio, Texas. 1988. Thanks to William Liu, Min-Zhan Lu, Richard Madsen, Mark Seldon, Anselm Strauss, and Hong Zhu for helpful comments on earlier drafts of the paper. Particular appreciation goes to those Chinese officials, doctors, and common people in Tianjin who helped me gain access to the hospital and to develop an understanding of what I saw.

1. I have been influenced by the symbolic interactionist ideas of Everett Hughes (1971) and Herbert Blumer (1969) in their arguments that sociologists should provide detailed descriptions of how people do things together in natural settings (see also Becker 1986). Recent critical work in

anthropology (e.g., Marcus and Fischer 1986; Clifford and Marcus 1986) and feminist deconstructive criticisms (e.g., Clough 1992; Penley 1989) have begun to undermine this position and my own faith in it, as is reflected in this paper.

2. I use "discourse" here in a quite casual way but influenced most by some of Michel Foucault's (1972) writing and especially by the rereadings of his ideas by feminist poststructuralist writers Chris Weedon (1987) and Bronwyn Davies (1989).

3. My sense of how this unaccompanied access came about is that it was too difficult to find someone to come along each time. Also, those responsible had agreed to higher officials' requests to help me; and I would be supervised by the English-speaking doctors and nurses on the unit. I feel quite sure no formal decision was made to allow this.

4. The Chinese *Peizhu,* literally translated as "accompany stay"—people who come with the patient and stay in the hospital—is also used to refer to family members and perhaps speaks more accurately to what I here describe. It was only later in the project that I discovered this other usage, and so I decided to retain the somewhat less specific term, *peiban.*

5. While this sort of unpaid labor might be attributed to socialist or party ways of conduct, sociologists of work in the United States have noted how various private and public organizations and institutions alike seem to rely on large amounts of unpaid and unrecognized labor for their continued operation (see Bucher and Stelling 1977).

6. Throughout this paper I have tried to quote the Chinese I spoke to in English as closely as possible. Some early readers objected to this "pidgin English," suggesting it demeans the Chinese speakers. I believe it to be quite opposite. To edit their English into smooth and standard form would seem to dismiss their efforts to learn and speak English. Moreover, from the beginning of the project I was quite surprised at how much I, then having only rudimentary skills in Chinese, was able to learn from these people who, without exception, told me they "could not speak English." Finally, to the extent that these "data" are taken to be informative, they are testimony that one need not have mastered Chinese language to pursue a project such as this. Perhaps this latter point is no surprise to Sinologists. To those from other lines of work who are approaching China, it may be an encouragement.

7. My introduction to the *danwei* system came with reading Gail Henderson and Myron Cohen's 1984 book, *The Chinese Hospital: A Socialist Work Unit,* before I went to China. Although their book helped me understand the hospital I visited, my concerns were considerably narrower than

theirs. Henderson and Cohen do note the presence of family members in the hospital, but they do not discuss in detail their work or their relationships to staff.

8. Mayfair Mei-Hui Yang describes several kinds of relationships that can obtain between people based on "the degree of personal emotional and moral commitment" on the one hand and "the degree of gain-and-loss calculation and interest at stake" on the other (1986, 128–35). So-called *hou men(r)* contacts thus might easily be set off from the more general *guanxi,* which can include ties of intimacy and deep commitment. I believe such distinctions go beyond the limited scope of this paper and therefore have not made them here.

9. This is not to suggest that these decisions were made easily. The director of the unit expressed his frustration at being asked to treat a thirty-year-old man, then in the emergency room, suffering from chronic renal failure, who had come from a county hospital thirty miles away. He said to me, "What am I to do? Maybe sociologists have an answer to this. What am I to do?" Later he told me he had allowed the treatment "at least for a few days."

10. The circumstances for peasants are less supportive in that, because they have no *danwei* to support them, they have to bear the costs of medical care themselves. For rich peasants, however, this might not represent the burden it at first seems to be. Obviously, for poor peasants circumstances are quite the opposite.

11. Gail Henderson's (1989, 206–10) recent paper on modernization in Chinese medical care helps us put this remark in the context of general trends of the rising cost of hospital stays, contributed to especially by those—such as this man's father—whose *danwei* pay most or all of the costs of care. At the same time, she reports, part of the Western and modernizing model, especially found in cities, is an attempt to increase turnover of patients, reducing the average length of stay. This pressure exerted by doctors and hospital officials is especially strong for those who lack some form of subsidy.

12. Given the gift-exchange calculus that Yang (1986) has described and the present context, it was not surprising to have heard stories of surgeons receiving rather large gifts of money (*hong bao*) from family members in advance of surgeries performed. Although I did not hear any firsthand accounts of this, it was brought up often in discussions with other foreigners about medical care in China. Chinese who commented on this said that "it was more common" in the recent past but that crackdowns on corruption in the hospital had reduced occurrences of the practice. That it has disappeared seems unlikely.

13. This concern that others might try to bring "trouble" seemed a fundamental adjunct to all relationships, possibly with the exception of the most intimate family ties. I felt such concern worked like a wedge to prevent or reduce the cultivation of what we in the West, perhaps especially in the United States, call "openness" in such relationships. Of course, such openness in the United States is located in a quite different context of resource availability and management and of social exchange, not to mention the presence of differences in larger cultural themes, such as individualism and privacy.

REFERENCES

Althusser, Louis. 1971. *Lenin and Philosophy and Other Essays.* New Left Books.

Anderson, Marston. 1909. *The Limits of Realism: Chinese Fiction in the Revolutionary Period.* Berkeley: University of California Press.

Becker, Howard S. 1986. "Telling about Society." In idem, *Doing Things Together.* 121–35. Evanston, IL: Northwestern University Press.

Blumer, Herbert. 1969. *Symbolic Interactionism.* Englewood Cliffs, NJ: Prentice Hall.

Bucher, Rue, and Joan G. Stelling. 1977. *Becoming Professional.* Beverly Hills: Sage.

Chen, Guanfeng. 1987. "Top Expert Warns of Shortage of Doctors." *China Daily* (March 31):1.

Clifford, James. 1983a. "On Ethnographic Authority." *Representations* I:118–46.

———. 1983b. "Power and Dialogue in Ethnography: Marcel Griaule's Initiation." In *Observers Observed: Essays on Ethnographic Fieldwork,* ed. George W. Stocking, Jr., 121–56. Madison: University of Wisconsin Press.

Clifford, James, and George E. Marcus, eds. 1986. *Writing Culture: The Poetics and Politics of Ethnography.* Berkeley: University of California Press.

Clough, Patricia Ticineto. 1992. *The End(s) of Ethnography: From Realism to Social Criticism.* Newbury Park, Calif.: Sage.

Davies, Bronwyn. 1989. *Frogs and Snails and Feminist Tales.* Sydney: Allen & Unwin.

Fabian, Johannes. 1990. "Presence and Representation: The Other and Anthropological Writing." *Critical Inquiry* 16:753–72.

Foucault, Michel. 1972. *The Archaeology of Knowledge and the Discourse on Language.* Translated by A. M. Sheridan Smith. New York: Pantheon.

Geertz, Clifford. 1988. *Works and Lives: The Anthropologist as Author.* Stanford, Calif.: Stanford University Press.

Goldman, Merle, and Denis Fred Simon. 1989. "The Onset of China's New Technological Revolution." In *Science and Technology in Post-Mao China,* ed. Denis Fred Simon and Merle Goldman, 1–22. Cambridge: Harvard University Press.

Henderson, Gail. 1989. "Issues in the Modernization of Medicine in China. In *Science and Technology in Post-Mao China,* 199–222. *See* Goldman and Simon 1989.

Henderson, Gail, and Myron Cohen. 1984. *The Chinese Hospital: A Socialist Work Unit.* New Haven: Yale University Press.

Hughes, Everett C. 1971. *The Sociological Eye.* Chicago: Aldine–Atherton.

Kondo, Dorinne K. 1990. *Crafting Selves: Power, Gender, and Discourses of Identity in a Japanese Workplace.* Chicago: University of Chicago Press.

Marcus, George E., and Michael M. J. Fischer. 1986. *Anthropology as Cultural Critique.* Chicago: University of Chicago Press.

Penley, Constance. 1989. *The Future of an Illusion: Film, Feminism, and Psychoanalysis.* Minneapolis: University of Minnesota Press.

Rorty, Richard. 1983. "Method and Morality." In *Social Science as Moral Inquiry,* ed. Norma Haan, Robert N. Bellah, Paul Rabinow, and William M. Sullivan, 155–76. New York: Columbia University Press.

Schneider, Joseph W. 1988. "Disability as Moral Experience: Epilepsy and Self in Routine Relationships." *Journal of Social Issues* 44:63–78.

———. 1991. "Troubles with Textual Authority in Sociology." *Symbolic Interaction* 14:295–319.

Schneider, Joseph W., and Peter Conrad. 1983. *Having Epilepsy: The Experience and Control of Illness.* Philadelphia: Temple University Press.

Strauss, Anselm L., Shizuko Fagerhaugh, Barbara Suczek, and Carolyn Wiener. 1985. *Social Organization of Medical Work.* Chicago: University of Chicago Press.

Weedon, Chris. 1987. *Feminist Practice and Poststructuralist Theory.* Oxford: Basil Blackwell.

Wang, Lin Ren. 1986. "Dui yiyuan peizhu tanshi wenti zhi guanjian." ("View on Visiting Patients in the Hospital.") *Zhongguo Yiyuan Guanli Zazhi* 23:192.

Wolf, Margery. 1985. *Revolution Postponed: Women in Contemporary China.* Standford, Calif.: Stanford University Press.

Yang, Mayfair Mei-Hui. 1986. "The Art of Social Relationships and Exchange in China." Ph.D. diss., De-partment of Anthropology, University of California, Berkeley.

Zhong, Shi. 1985. "An Investigation into Irregularities in Hospitals." *Chinese Sociology and Anthropology* 27:36–48.

CHAPTER 12

HEALTH CARE FINANCING

This chapter examines health care financing schemes in the United States, selected other Western industrialized nations, and rural China. These schemes differ in a variety of ways. For example, how is health care coverage paid for? In the United States, payment used to be primarily fee-for-service. Recently, the movement toward managed care in general and health maintenance organizations (HMOs) in particular has been attempting to control the ever-rising cost of health care. Even so, the United States spends more per capita on health care than any other country, and the United States also spends a greater percentage of its GDP on health care than any other country (Inglehart, 1999, Matcha, 2000). At the same time, the United States has some 45 million citizens who are uninsured. By comparison, other Western industrialized nations generally provide health care coverage to all citizens. Developing nations, such as China, continue to experiment with a variety of health care schemes.

The cost of health care is of particular concern as the populations of industrialized nations become increasingly older and utilize a greater proportion of health care resources. Responding to rising health care costs, all nations—both developed and developing—engage in some form of health care rationing (see, for example, Conrad and Brown, 1993). Whether the limiting factor is cost (as in the United States) or need (as in the United Kingdom), rationing offers one way to control health care costs. Although it is effective, it raises ethical questions about the selection of particular segments of the population for unequal access to the system.

The three articles in Chapter 12 offer a broad perspective on national differences as well as a focused examination of health care financing within the United States, Canada and Western Europe, and rural China. This approach allows for a comparison of nations' financing structures and their implications.

In the first article, Harold S. Luft focuses on Medicare and managed care, components of the U.S. health care system that represent increased numbers of citizens; and he explores potential complications as their interests collide. He begins by defining *health maintenance organizations* and *managed care,* thus differentiating between these two seemingly overlapping concepts. Continuing, Luft examines coverage patterns within the U.S. population as a whole and among Medicare recipients. He notes that health care expenditures in the United States are skewed—that is, a small proportion of covered individuals accounts for a very large proportion of the monies spent on health care. This is true of Medicare recipients as well as the general population.

Luft reports that HMOs for Medicare recipients are less expensive than the traditional fee-for-service method of health care provision for those receiving Medicare. Patient satisfaction scores, however, indicate a split in Medicare beneficiaries' views of HMOs. They like the nonfinancial aspects of HMOs but dislike the financial aspects. Luft also notes evidence that indicates a rather neutral rating of patient satisfaction with managed care. This finding stands in contrast to the generally negative image of managed care presented in the media.

In the second article, Deborah J. Chollet targets aspects of health care financing within Canada, France, Germany, the Netherlands, and the United Kingdom. Canada's public insurance health care system covers all citizens. The cost of the system is financed primarily through general revenues from federal and provincial governments. Although physicians charge fees for service, their fee schedules are negotiated on a regular basis, as are the funds that the government makes available to hospitals. In other words, there is global budgeting.

The French health care system is also a public insurance program with voluntary supplemental private insurance for services not covered by the public program (similar to Canada). The system is financed by general revenues and payroll taxes.

In Germany, some 1,200 sickness funds provide the structure for coverage of 90 percent of the population. People in the remaining 10 percent are covered through private insurance that they purchase voluntarily. The sickness funds are administered by trade and professional groups to provide health insurance coverage to their members. Because the health of members varies, contributions by members and their employers vary. Physicians are mostly in the private sector, but, as in Canada, their fee schedules are negotiated.

The Netherlands is similar to Germany in that health insurance coverage is offered through a number of government-sponsored sickness funds. In addition, approximately one-third of the population relies on private insurance plans. When Chollet wrote this article, the government was reorganizing the health care system to expand enrollment in the sickness funds to all citizens. The system is financed through payroll taxes and general revenues distributed to the sickness funds. The Netherlands, too, utilizes global budgeting.

The National Health Service (NHS) provides health care in the United Kingdom. The NHS includes some 200 District Health Authorities located within 14 regional health authorities. The system is financed through general revenues, although some services require patients to pay a user's fee. Physicians in the United Kingdom are paid on a capitation basis: a physician receives a fixed amount per person to provide health care services.

In the third article, Gu Xingyuan and colleagues outline their efforts to document the financing of health care services in rural China, where 80 percent of the total population of China lives. They conducted their research in 20 counties in 16 provinces organized by the researchers into 3 regions. Region I consisted of the most developed counties; Region III consisted of the poorest counties; the counties in Region II were in between.

Health care in rural China has experienced a number of changes. In the 1960s, cooperative health stations were established. However, by the 1970s, many of these cooperative units had closed or become private clinics. With the movement toward fee-for-service health care, most rural residents now pay for services out-of-pocket or through township-run health insurance schemes. Those unable to pay for services can turn to the township or village welfare fund for help in defraying the cost of health care.

In contrast, public sector employees—generally located in urban areas—receive free health care. In rural areas, the only public sector employees are administrative cadres, teachers, and health care workers on salary. Also located in urban areas, state-owned enterprises provide their employees with medical insurance as a fringe benefit. Thus, one purpose of the Xingyuan research was to determine the level of contributions that local insurance schemes needed to make to cover the average cost of services in rural China.

The need for increased access to some form of health care insurance is increasingly evident in rural China. According to the researchers, there is evidence that, because of cost, more and more rural Chinese are unable to receive hospital care even when it is prescribed by a physician. Thus the effort to identify and construct some form of health insurance system within villages is of particular

importance. One approach would assess each household a yearly fixed amount per person that would cover a percentage of hospital costs. Other concerns in China include health care for the aging population and care for remote villages.

The thread that runs through the articles in Chapter 12 is that regardless of the health care financing system currently in place, the search for a better system is ongoing. Although the United States maintains that health care is not a right but a commodity to be purchased like any other service, it has begun moving toward greater regulation of the health care industry. At the same time, government-controlled systems elsewhere in the industrialized world are introducing pockets of private health insurance into their systems. Scholars believe that the long-range movement in the developed nations is toward the convergence of health care financing systems into a single model. Similarly, China is attempting to construct a workable financing system for the whole of Chinese society. Given the ongoing problems within the developed world, doing so may take a long time.

REFERENCES

Conrad, Peter, and Phil Brown. 1993. Rationing Medical Care: A Sociological Reflection. *Research in the Sociology of Health Care,* vol. 10, pp. 3–22.

Inglehart, John K. 1999. The American Health Care System. *New England Journal of Medicine,* vol. 340, no. 1, pp. 70–76.

Matcha, Duane A. 2000. *Medical Sociology.* Needham Heights, MA: Allyn & Bacon.

AMERICAN PERSPECTIVE

MEDICARE AND MANAGED CARE

HAROLD S. LUFT

INTRODUCTION

As the Medicare program enters its fourth decade, it is increasingly likely that major changes will be made in how it functions. The debates are beginning concerning its long-term restructuring to deal with the impending pressures of baby boomers in the second and third decade of the twenty-first century. Short-term changes are being made as part of the budget decisions of 1997 still under discussion as this is being written. Regardless of the details, it is clear that Medicare has moved a long way from the initial legislation that prohibited government interference with the practice of medicine (Social Security Act of 1965, Title XVIII, Section 1801).

In some ways Medicare has been a leader in the managed care revolution in the United States; in other ways it has lagged. However, because Medicare accounts for roughly 30% of all expenditures for hospital care and 20% for physician services, any changes in the Medicare program will have an enormous impact on the overall system. Moreover, as the largest single payer of medical care, the uniform nature of the program carries much more weight than, say, the Medicaid programs run individually by the states, although with some federal support.

One of the major points of this chapter, however, is that focusing just on *Medicare* and managed care is likely to give a distorted picture

because Medicare is rarely the only source of coverage for beneficiaries, and its effects on the medical care system influence and are influenced by non-Medicare "actors." Because the federal perspective is often only on the "pieces of the puzzle" for which it is responsible and for which it has data, the policy discussion is often incomplete. Due to the lack of data and comprehensive research, this chapter will also be incomplete, but it is hoped that it will lead others to pursue a more complete understanding.

This chapter first offers some brief definitions of managed care in the context of the Medicare population. It then provides an overview of enrollment trends and patterns of coverage. Risk selection is a crucial problem in the Medicare program with implications not only for cost, but also for quality of care, so it is important to have a basic understanding of the issues involved. A brief review is then given of the performance of managed care plans relative to traditional fee-for-service (FFS). The next section addresses two key policy issues from the perspective of the Medicare program. A final section offers a summary and recommendations for future work.

DEFINITIONS OF MANAGED CARE

The term *health maintenance organization* has a generally accepted definition in the research literature and in legislation with respect to the various federal and state programs that regulate HMOs. Usually, it involves a health plan that accepts responsibility for the delivery of a predetermined range of necessary medical services to an enrolled population. There is minimal reliance on financial incentives such as deductibles to constrain the use of services, although copayments, e.g., $10 per visit, are commonplace. HMOs generally have a set of providers to deliver these services, and there is often no coverage for care received by outside providers, unless referred there by the plan. In many instances, the sponsor for the enrollee, such as the employer or public agency, requires that enrollees be able to choose among various HMOs, and possibly a fee-for-service option. The HMO may use a variety of financial and other mechanisms to encourage or constrain its providers to keep medical care costs within budget.

Managed care is a much broader, and less well defined concept. It is often used to include, and sometimes primarily to mean HMOs, although it usually includes systems that may not meet the specific regulatory requirements of certain public agencies. Thus, Medicare can contract with both HMOs and competitive medical plans (CMPs) that may meet different requirements but function in much the same way as HMOs. From the perspective of the public, and many health care providers (a term I will use to include hospitals, physicians, and other health professionals), managed care often includes almost any intervention that interferes with the traditional patient–provider relationship. The idealized view of that traditional relationship assumes care can be obtained from any licensed provider and the costs reimbursed by a third-party insurer with little oversight other than for outright fraud or a refusal to pay the full amount of excessively high fees. This broader concept includes situations in which a payer might require prior approval for a proposed procedure or hospital admission, or is willing to pay fees that are markedly below "usual" rates.

In this context, one might ask whether the current fee-for-service Medicare plan is not a type of managed care. Under the Prospective Payment System implemented in 1983 using Diagnosis Related Groups, Medicare pays hospitals a fixed amount for each inpatient stay based on the patient's diagnoses, not the charges or costs incurred. The payment levels are set externally, without negotiation, and the hospital has strong incentives to constrain the use of extra tests or procedures and to encourage the patient's discharge at the earliest possible time. Since 1992 physician fees under Medicare have been based on the Resource Based

Relative Value System (RBRVS), which is designed to reflect the costs of various activities, with adjustments for input prices such as malpractice and rent costs in an area. In some instances, these fees are markedly below what certain physicians may have been charging. Furthermore, there are incentives for physicians to accept these fees as payment in full and not "balance bill." Therefore, most physicians who serve Medicare beneficiaries are participating providers under Medicare and have thus agreed to the fee schedule (17). Medicare also contracts with peer review organizations (PROs) to review the patterns of care offered by health professionals and hospitals to assure that quality standards are maintained and the services rendered are appropriate. While much of the PRO focus is on inpatient care, this is beginning to expand to outpatient services. From the provider's perspective, this amounts to a substantial degree of "management" in contrast to the "good old days." While fee-for-service (FFS) Medicare maintains the patient's individual freedom of choice of provider, the pressures to discharge patients early from the hospitals are nonetheless pervasive.

While the data presented below will typically focus on HMOs or similar entities with which Medicare may have contracts, the perceptions of patients and providers may well be colored by experiences with other types of arrangements, including some which are now considered FFS Medicare. These issues may be especially important for the more subjective aspects of managed care. Even though people may be asked about current experiences, these may be assessed through the comparative lens of "what used to be" and not necessarily "what currently is."

ENROLLMENTS AND PATTERNS OF COVERAGE

Nationally, roughly 53.5 million people are enrolled in HMOs (about 44 million in "pure" HMOs and approximately 9.5 million in point-of-service plans). Among the Medicare population, only 11%

were enrolled in HMOs in 1996, and the growth rate has been extraordinary—a 41% increase in Medicare risk contract enrollment between December 1994 and January 1996 (22, p. 89). It is important, however, to place these enrollment figures in context, especially in terms of the overall structure of the Medicare program.

Many people think of Medicare as *the* health insurance program for the elderly, but it is both more and less than that. On the one hand, Medicare provides coverage for many nonelderly disabled persons and those eligible under the End Stage Renal Disease Program (ESRD). Disabled and ESRD beneficiaries accounted for 12.6% of the Medicare population in 1996 and, because of the greater medical needs of these groups, a substantially larger fraction of total expenditures (22, p. 9). On the other hand, Medicare has important limitations in benefits for the elderly. It has substantial deductibles and copayments, and does not offer coverage for outpatient pharmaceuticals—an important issue for the elderly. Medicare also requires a monthly premium for Part B services (largely outpatient physician services) that, while heavily subsidized, would be unaffordable for the poor. Thus, low-income people may be "dually eligible" for Medicare and Medicaid coverage, which combine to cover the premiums, copayments, and deductibles. Furthermore, the Medicaid part often has more extensive coverage of services, such as for outpatient drugs. Those not eligible for Medicaid often obtain supplemental insurance either individually or through their current or past employer. In 1993, only 9% of the aged beneficiaries had Medicare FFS coverage only; 31% had employer-sponsored supplemental FFS coverage; 32%, individually purchased supplemental FFS coverage; 8%, employer and individually purchased supplemental FFS coverage; 13%, Medicaid; and 7% were in HMOs (22, p. 64). The HMO premiums might be covered in full by Medicare or might require additional payments by enrollees and/or employers.

It is also important to understand the context in which enrollment in Medicare HMOs occurs. The Medicare program has two arrangements for contracting with HMOs, cost- and risk-based contracts. The cost-based contracts allow the HMO to bill Medicare as if it were a fee-for-service plan. Risk-based contracts require the HMO to offer the full set of Medicare-covered services without additional payments from Medicare for individual services. The plan is paid a fixed premium, currently set at 95% of the Adjusted Average Per Capita Cost (AAPCC), which is supposed to approximate what FFS beneficiaries in the local area would cost Medicare. Whether this is the correct rate is a very controversial policy question that is discussed below. At this point, it is merely important to know that the premium level is set by a HCFA-determined formula developed to cover the basic Medicare benefit package. An HMO may choose to forgive all or part of the normally required Part B premiums, the deductibles, and copayments, and may even add other non-covered benefits, such as outpatient pharmaceuticals. In fact, if the HMO's costs are below the HCFA payment, extra benefits or lower beneficiary payments are required by HCFA so that the HMO's profit margin for Medicare beneficiaries does not exceed that for other enrollees.

In 1996, 95% of risk contract plans offered coverage for an annual physical (not a covered benefit under FFS Medicare). Immunizations were offered by 86%, and 60% offered outpatient prescription drug coverage. Ninety-four plans offered prescription drug benefits as part of their zero premium plan, sometimes with coverage up to $1500 (26). Overall, 63% of enrollees paid no additional monthly premium, and only 18% paid $40 a month or more for their HMO coverage (7). Thus, the vast majority of HMO enrollees receive a broader benefit package at substantially lower cost than they would with a Medicare supplemental plan, even if they could find one with as broad a set of benefits.

Even though enrollment of the Medicare population in HMOs is increasing, it is spread very un-evenly across the nation. Fifty-five percent of all risk contract enrollees are in California and Florida. The bottom 36 states, with less than 1% enrolled in HMOs, account for a total of only 6% of all enrollees (see Figure 17 in Reference 20). While to some extent this reflects the relative location of Medicare eligibles, the concentration goes well beyond that. In 1996, about a quarter of beneficiaries had no managed care plan available, and of those living in areas where plans were available, the average enrollment rate was 11% (see Figure 27 in Reference 21). In 10 states, over 15% of the Medicare populations are in risk contract plans, while in 17 states, less than 1% of the beneficiaries is in such plans (see Figure 29 in Reference 21). In some counties, the proportion of Medicare beneficiaries in HMOs exceeds 35%.

Much less is known about the nature of the HMOs that enroll the Medicare population, but again it is a picture of high concentration, with 20 plans accounting for 55% of all enrollment, and 5 plans accounting for 30% (26). Furthermore, while the classic group and staff model plans such as Kaiser and Group Health have substantial enrollments, most of the new growth (except for conversion from cost to risk contracts) has been in plans with much broader networks of physicians and hospitals. This means that, in many instances, a physician will have a mix of patients with fee-for-service and HMO coverage, and often from multiple HMO plans.

This enrollment pattern has several important implications. First, because the standard Medicare FFS package, although universal, has important gaps and financial burdens, those who do not have Medicaid dual eligibility have a strong incentive to obtain supplemental insurance. In some instances, this will be made available at no cost by one's current or former employer. (Remember that Medicare eligibility is age-related, except for the disabled and ESRD beneficiaries. For those who are actively employed, private coverage bears the first responsibility for payment and Medicare is a sec-

ondary payer; most employers design a retirement health package that merely supplements Medicare.) A substantial fraction of the Medicare population pays out-of-pocket premiums to purchase a supplemental plan. The broader coverage offered by many HMOs, often with no extra premium cost, is thus a very attractive inducement to enroll. For this reason, many Medicare HMO enrollees may have joined not because they like HMOs and their style of care, but because they offer a much less expensive way to fill the gaps in FFS Medicare coverage.

Second, the high concentration of Medicare beneficiaries in certain areas means that average performance assessments of HMOs may be reflecting just a few plans and localities. If there is reason to suspect that these plans and areas are unusual, then it may be incorrect to generalize from their performance to what might occur in other parts of the nation. Put another way, southern California and southern Florida Medicare enrollments are very high, and cannot increase by a factor of more than two or three (everyone will be enrolled at that point). In the long run, Medicare HMO growth will occur in other geographic areas, even without changes in policy, so past performance may not be a reliable guide to the future.

THE ROLE OF RISK SELECTION

The distribution of medical expenditures is highly skewed, with a small fraction of the population having very high costs and the vast majority using few or no services in a year. This is true for both Medicare and other populations. Typically, about 10% of the eligible group accounts for 75% of expenditures (see Figure 18 in Reference 21). The skewness of medical care costs is one of the principal reasons why health insurance is highly desirable—it allows risk to be spread over large numbers of persons (2). This risk spreading, however, takes place only when the pool of covered persons is not selected on the basis of health risk. The classic problem with in-

dividual insurance is that potential enrollees may know they will need medical care, so the insurer is legitimately skeptical of why they want to enroll. In large employer-based groups this is not a problem, because most people join the company for a job, not because of a particular medical care need.

The Medicare program offers essentially universal coverage for all eligible people; hence, there is ample opportunity to spread risk over large numbers of individuals. However, the decision to enroll in an HMO is made by the individual (and his or her spouse) and thus may be subject to selection. Because of the potential for adverse selection, that is, the attraction of high-risk enrollees to the plan, it is often difficult for people with pre-existing conditions to purchase Medicare supplemental coverage.

The potential for selection also occurs with people joining HMOs, but in this case the tools available to the plan to deal with selection are different. Rather than just being able to modify the co-payments and deductibles and thus needing to rely on medical underwriting, an HMO is also able to make the plan less desirable to the very ill by having a more restricted set of referral physicians and hospitals. It may be able to differentially attract low-risk people by offering benefits such as dental coverage or eyeglasses that, while valuable to all, may be of relatively greater importance for healthy enrollees than for the very ill. Plan characteristics such as these may have been developed for entirely innocent reasons such as to offer additional benefits to an enrolled population that was less costly than the AAPCC offered by Medicare. Other features might have had the opposite impact, of attracting high-risk enrollees. It is much more likely, however, that the adverse cost implications of such features would lead to their modification, or even the demise of the plan due to non-competitive costs.

Certain features of Medicare enhance the importance of potential risk selection. First, the population covered—the elderly and disabled—tends to have much higher medical care needs in general, so the choice of plan and provider is more salient than

is likely to be the case for the rest of the population. Second, substantial gaps in FFS Medicare coverage make it important for beneficiaries to consider a Medicare supplemental policy or HMO coverage. Perhaps most important, Medicare has rules that, while designed to protect the beneficiary, nonetheless encourage risk selection. Medicare beneficiaries are allowed to disenroll from an HMO with 30-days notice, whereas most employer-sponsored plans allow plan switching only once a year. Also, enrollment is not handled centrally, as is the case for employers, but with individual recruitment by the health plans. This forces plans to seek out potential enrollees, and it is not surprising that they may choose to do so at the shopping mall rather than the nursing home.

The presence of risk selection is not a problem if payments to the plans take into account differences in risk. However, Medicare pays plans based on the age, sex, disability, and institutionalization status of the beneficiaries, the components of the AAPCC, and numerous studies demonstrate that these variables account for a very small fraction of the variation in medical care use (3). More important than the low explanatory power is the evidence that many HMOs enroll people at lower risk than is predicted by the AAPCC (4,16).

The limitations of the AAPCC in adequately accounting for risk differences have several important implications. One is that instead of saving 5% relative to FFS payments for people enrolled in HMOs, Medicare may actually be paying more than it would cost for those people to be in FFS (17). The desirability of this is discussed in the section below on policy issues. The more serious implication is much more subtle. Remember that one possible method for avoiding high-risk people is to have a more limited set of subspecialists and referral centers, or to make the use of available resources more difficult in the hope that high users of care will switch back to FFS. Such strategies may result in lower quality of care for enrollees, particularly those with expensive chronic conditions

who have the opportunity to selectively switch coverage options. (Poor quality of care for people with occasional acute problems is likely to result in more obvious quality problems and higher costs because inadequate treatment of acute problems is often more expensive in the long run than appropriately given interventions.)

PERFORMANCE OF HMOs FOR MEDICARE BENEFICIARIES

A recent review summarizes the published literature on HMO performance from 1986 through 1996 (13). This section highlights those findings that are most relevant to an understanding of Medicare and HMOs. Note that due to data collection and publication lags, the most recent data included in any of the papers reviewed is from 1994, and the vast majority of the evidence predates that by several years. Furthermore, there is reason to believe that the medical care system has become more competitive and cost-conscious since 1993, so some of these results may have limited bearing on current, let alone future, performance of plans.

Given the relatively small proportion of Medicare beneficiaries in HMOs, there are a disproportionate number of studies focusing on the elderly. In part, this is because of the government's responsibility for overseeing quality and cost, which has resulted in a series of large studies undertaken by both the government and private funders. The availability of extensive, uniformly collected data on the FFS "comparison" group, as well as the higher prevalence of illness among the elderly are also likely factors.

On various measures of resource use, such as hospital admissions, days, length of stay, and overall expenditures, the evidence is somewhat mixed, but the strongest evidence supports the view that HMOs use fewer resources than FFS. Measures of enrollee satisfaction generally indicate much higher ratings for HMOs with respect to the financial aspects of the plans, and generally lower satis-

faction with the non-financial aspects such as technical and interpersonal quality of care. Interestingly, lower-income enrollees, including those with Medicare–Medicaid coverage, seemed to prefer HMOs even with respect to the non-financial aspects of coverage (9). In part, this may reflect the fact that many physicians are unwilling to accept Medicaid payments, so the broad coverage offered by HMOs is a positive aspect, even for the dually eligible.

The single most common dimension of HMO performance addressed in the recent literature was quality of care, which reflects increasing concern about this issue. In some instances, quality of care was significantly better for Medicare enrollees in HMOs than for those in FFS, for example, for patients admitted to intensive care units (1) and for early detection of various cancers (18). There were a large number of studies in which quality of care was better on some measures and worse on others. Other studies showed a preponderance of findings indicating worse quality of care in HMOs. Some of these focused only on the elderly (10,19), whereas others covered a broader population, such as the Medical Outcomes Study that included many elderly in its sample (25).

In general, a preliminary pattern is emerging in these findings. The first is that, overall, the results with respect to quality of care are surprisingly balanced, with equal numbers of findings favorable and unfavorable of HMOs. If one expected that the pressures for cost containment would jeopardize quality, then the examples of better quality in HMOs provide strong contrary evidence. On the other hand, if one hoped that HMOs would be able to coordinate care to improve outcomes, the evidence suggests that this is a goal not yet achieved.

Second, there is a suggestion that HMOs are better at handling acute problems and the detection of disease through periodic screening than they are at dealing with complicated chronic conditions. There may be many reasons for this tentative observation, if indeed it is borne out in future studies;

however, this is what one might predict given what we know about HMOs, especially in the context of the Medicare program. As discussed in the preceding section, risk selection is enhanced by the structure of the Medicare program. Even if a plan did not try to get rid of high-risk enrollees, it would be financial disaster to develop visible high-quality programs to take care of the chronically ill. Once the superior performance of such programs became known, Medicare beneficiaries would flock to them, but payments would still be based on the average costs of people in their AAPCC cell, not on the AAPCC plus the extra costs associated with people having chronic conditions. Thus, superior quality of care is "punished" by the current payment system. Likewise, the absence of good, routinely available measures of quality makes it impossible to sanction any but the most egregious examples of poor quality of care, either in FFS or HMO settings.

POLICY ISSUES

There are a wide range of policy issues concerning the role of managed care plans in the Medicare program. However, we focus on two major issues: assuring quality of care and setting appropriate payment levels for health plans. In addressing these, it is important to distinguish two quite different perspectives that might be relevant for the discussion maker. The first recognizes Medicare as a program that has high political visibility and needs to be managed in a responsible way. This perspective seeks to protect the integrity of the overall program, but does not view managed care as a major tool to either reshape the health care system or to markedly change the cost or structure of Medicare. In a sense, this more passive perspective holds to the principle of non-interference in the original Medicare legislation, but also recognizes that managed care is making rapid inroads in the employed population, as well as in Medicaid programs, and Medicare will have to adapt to that reality.

The second perspective sees managed care as a valuable tool in achieving other objectives. These might include lowering the federal cost of Medicare below what would be achieved under a more passive policy. It might even extend to using Medicare's clout to reshape the larger health care system. The first of the two goals under this more activist perspective would be in keeping with the general mandate to prudently manage Medicare expenditures. The second would be much more far reaching.

From either perspective, Medicare should be concerned about the quality of care provided to Medicare beneficiaries in managed care plans, just as it should be concerned about quality in fee-for-service. Medicare should also attempt to pay managed care plans a "fair premium" for the benefits they provide. What exactly a "fair premium" should be, and how it should be determined, is a complex issue that goes beyond the scope of this chapter, but is touched upon briefly. The different perspectives (passive vs. active) will influence how one chooses to measure the benefits of managed care.

Quality of Care

It is a political reality that the Medicare program will be held responsible for the quality of care that it purchases. In 1990, the Institute of Medicine completed an extensive study, *A Strategy for Quality Assurance in Medicare,* which offered the following definition of quality of care:

> *Quality of care is the degree to which health services for individuals and populations increase the likelihood of desired health outcomes and are consistent with current professional knowledge (6).*

A key aspect of this definition is that it focuses not just on the technical quality of the services rendered, but also on their appropriateness, both from a medical and patient perspective. It also recognizes that a population-based focus is needed, so a system that offers the very best to only a few may be less desirable than a system that might offer somewhat

less, but assures coverage of a broader population and reaches out to those who otherwise would not get services. Finally, it recognizes that not all interventions work as well as one would hope, and thus high quality care will increase the likelihood of desired health outcomes, although this may not be the observed outcome in individual cases.

Two important issues arise in assessing the quality of care in managed care settings and in FFS. The first stems from the different incentives in the two systems. The fixed budget held by managed care plans creates an incentive to provide fewer services, whereas FFS provides incentives for providers to order and deliver more. Thus, one would be tempted to focus primarily on underuse in managed care and overuse in FFS. However, the situation may be more complex than it seems. Remember that most managed care plans offer more comprehensive coverage and a broader range of benefits than standard Medicare FFS. There is ample evidence that the deductibles and copayments in "Medicare classic" help constrain medical care use. The absence of certain types of coverage, such as for outpatient prescriptions, also has an impact. This means that if one were to compare managed care enrollees with those in Medicare alone, there would be incentives within the plan to constrain use, but incentives for the beneficiary to increase use.

There are two implications of these countervailing pressures, aside from the lack of guidance as to whether use should theoretically be higher or lower. The first is that the comparison group is unclear. Remember that a mere 10% of Medicare aged beneficiaries have Medicare FFS-only coverage; the vast majority have purchased supplemental coverage, either by themselves or through an employer. Yet, half of all Medicare HMO enrollees pay nothing extra for their enhanced benefits. Should their quality be compared with that of the Medicare FFS-only people, or should it be compared with those who have purchased supplemental coverage, often at substantially higher cost? Thus, if one is concerned that managed care plans constrain medical care use, should this be in com-

parison with a Medicare plan that costs the same and has high copayments that also reduce use? The notion of context is important; when *Consumer Reports* evaluates automobiles, they typically compare cars within the same general price range, rather than Chevrolets vs Mercedes.

The second point is more subtle, but is related to the previous observation. People (other than economists) generally do not perceive price as a "rationing" device and reserve the notion of rationing to situations in which goods or services are allocated in other ways. The mere fact that managed care plans largely eliminate the financial barriers to care may make people *feel* that more things are denied them. For example, an HMO enrollee is likely to be quite angry about a plan's denial of a referral for a simple consultation even though the enrollee could go to the specialist and pay out of pocket. With FFS coverage and a $200 deductible, the same visit might also be entirely out of pocket, but there is likely to be little anger. Should the lack of the consultation result in missing an important diagnostic clue, this would be seen as a quality failure in managed care, but a patient failure in FFS. An even-handed assessment of quality will have to address these conceptual issues in a creative way.

The second important complication in assessing quality is much more mundane but nevertheless important. This arises from the different types of data collected in the two settings. FFS Medicare is claims based and therefore generates detailed bills for all the services rendered, but this information is much less complete with respect to diagnoses and the status of the patient. Some HMOs have detailed encounter and electronic medical record data, which are typically better in terms of lab test results and diagnoses but less detailed in terms of what minor procedures were performed. Some HMOs capitate their medical groups and receive very little information, and even when it is obtained, there is much less consistency in information across groups than is optimal.

Managed care plans are now routinely reporting to employers measures of their quality as de-

fined in the Health Plan Employer Data Information Set (HEDIS). While this is an important step forward, these data have been criticized for focusing on too narrow a range of quality measures that are heavily weighted toward preventive activities, such as screening for breast cancer (5). A new version of HEDIS has been developed that for the first time includes the Medicare population (in addition to those covered by commercial plans and Medicaid), and plans were required to report 1996 data by June 30, 1997. In general, these approaches will be helpful in maintaining a public health/prevention focus for plans.

Measuring other aspects of quality is likely to be more difficult, both because the science of quality assessment is less well developed and, perhaps most important, because there are financial disincentives for plans to really excel in the care of the very sick or chronically ill enrollees because of the lack of risk adjustment. Thus, while the risk adjustment question is clearly on the policy agenda for the near future (see below), the policy focus is on the cost to the program. In fact, a more compelling case for risk adjustment might be its impact on the incentives for quality of care.

If Medicare can implement systems to focus on the care of the chronically and seriously ill, which implies data systems that work not only for those in HMO but also for those in FFS, then there are likely to be beneficial effects on the overall quality of care. Recalling that 10% of the enrolled population accounts for 70% of expenditures, such a targeted approach may have a major impact on both the quality and cost of care for all, and thus meet some of the goals of those with an activist perspective who see Medicare policy as focusing on overall system change, rather than just on a more narrow set of goals.

Setting Payment Levels for Health Plans

Most observers agree that the current methodology for setting premiums to be paid to managed care plans is less than optimal. In some parts of the

nation, the payments are so low that few plans are willing to take on risk contracts. In other areas, the AAPCC is so high that plans can offer extensive benefit packages with no extra premium. Payments also may vary markedly from one county to the next, in ways that appear to be arbitrary. Some of these issues are largely technical, but the most important policy ones relate to risk adjustment and who should benefit from enrolling in a managed care plan.

The risk adjustment issues are conceptually straightforward, but technically complex. Ideally, one should pay plans an amount that reflects the risk mix of their enrollees. The AAPCC was designed to do this, but is inadequate to the task because within an AAPCC cell there may be a wide range of risk. Also, the ways in which HMOs are structured and operate allow, and sometimes foster, risk selection. There are various proposals to apply new risk assessment measures to capture the mix of illness among enrollees (3).

A mixed approach would blend fixed capitation payments with FFS reimbursement of plans (14,15). Another approach would allow plans to exclude from their risk-based payment, yet still take care of, a small fraction of their enrollees who are most likely to be high cost (23,24). Yet another approach would implement supplemental payments for very high-cost conditions, along with detailed clinical information systems to monitor quality of care (8).

Regardless of the particular approach taken, the intent would be to pay more to plans that have a high proportion of potentially high-cost people, and pay less to those plans with relatively healthy people. Unlike the current situation, in which plans have strong incentives not to attract the very ill, with appropriate risk-adjusted payments plans might actually find it beneficial to attract the very ill. Developing a method to save 10% of the cost associated with people expected to have medical costs of $40,000 a year yields much more than saving 10% on the relatively healthy who cost very little and much of what the latter need is often

unavoidable. For example, little can be done by the medical profession to reduce the costs associated with accidents.

Other issues that will have to be addressed in setting the level of risk-adjusted payments are more obscure, such as the geographic variability in payments, and how to account for the costs of graduate medical education that are currently built into the FFS Medicare payments. A larger, more philosophic issue arises from the complex relationship between Medicare and the need for supplemental benefits. Currently, if managed care plans are able to care for their enrollees at less than the AAPCC level, they must return those savings to the beneficiary in extra benefits or lower premiums or copayments. In essence, these people are able to convert a fixed amount of money into broader benefits and lower out-of-pocket costs relative to Medicare alone. Put another way, they are able to get the financial coverage of Medicare supplemental insurance without paying the going rate for such coverage. This additional benefit, however, comes at the price of a more restricted choice of providers and perhaps other constraints.

This leads one to ask whether the risk-adjusted payment, regardless of how it is determined with respect to risk, should be at the level that would only cover the cost of Medicare, without supplemental coverage, or would allow this broader set of benefits, recognizing that the patient may be giving up something of value in joining the HMO. If the lower level is chosen, then it is unlikely that many people would join HMOs, since they would cost the same as the sum of Medicare + supplemental plans, yet restrict choice. On the other hand, some may argue that allowing beneficiaries to reap those extra benefits at no extra cost adds to the federal expense. There are also geographic equity issues if not everyone has the option of a managed care plan available in their locality, and income equity issues if not everyone can equally afford supplemental premiums.

There is, however, another perspective on the role of managed care plans. The recent review by

Miller & Luft (13) identified several studies of the effects of managed care on local medical care use and costs. In many of these, resource use was lower, or costs grew less rapidly, in areas with heavy managed care presence. Thus, the competitive pressure of managed care may change the behavior of all providers, helping to contain costs. The effect of managed care on the costs of the surrounding FFS system is called an externality, or spillover effect. A plausible mechanism for this is the development of new practice protocols by managed care plans that are then applied by physicians to all of their patients, including those in FFS. This may even occur if there is little difference in performance between managed care and FFS providers. If these findings are borne out in other studies, then one may wish to encourage the growth of managed care not just because it lowers costs for its own enrollees, but because it improves the performance of the overall system. (Current evidence on this "spillover" effect concentrates on cost issues, but quality may also be affected. The challenge will be to structure the incentives and quality monitoring to ensure that the competitive effect is to lower cost *and* raise quality, rather than lower quality.) From this perspective, it may well be worthwhile to offer inducements to Medicare beneficiaries to join managed care plans because this may help transform the overall system in a desired way. While "bribes" would clearly be inappropriate, allowing plans to offer additional benefits within the basic Medicare premium level, as is the case now, may be quite reasonable and would not involve a change in underlying policy. The beneficial spillover effects, however, may help offset the arguments of those who feel that even an appropriately risk-adjusted payment to managed care plans might be too high.

SUMMARY

This chapter is intended to set the stage for further thinking about the role of managed care in the Medicare program, recognizing that this is a rapidly changing area. New policy proposals are under development while this is being written, and some may have been passed by the time this is read. This chapter does not address some policy questions that may be included in a more comprehensive discussion of managed care for Medicare beneficiaries. Such questions include: whether Medicare benefits for home care, pharmaceuticals, and other services might be expanded or modified; the impact of block grants to states for Medicaid costs, and how that will affect dually eligibles; and societal perspectives on the right to die and end-of-life care. We omitted these issues largely because so little is known, either about their current impact or how the program will change.

Instead, we have chosen to focus on some underlying issues, in particular, the importance of considering Medicare in the context of other programs for the elderly and disabled, and in the context of the larger medical care environment. It is very misleading to focus only on "Medicare classic" without recognizing that less than one tenth of the Medicare beneficiaries rely solely on this program. Thus, their utilization, cost, and quality of care will be shaped by the set of coverages they have. Likewise, the heavy concentration of managed care enrollment in a few geographic areas means that the lessons we draw from existing plan performance may have little bearing on a likely much broader future enrollment pattern.

The published evidence on the performance of managed care plans is surprisingly evenhanded in terms of satisfaction and quality. This is in contrast to the media coverage, which typically focuses on problems of managed care. The conflicting perspectives may be due to the older data on which the published studies are based, or may simply reflect the fact that the media do not find very interesting stories of "no problems." (How often does one read an article about the jet plane that took off fully loaded, had a smooth flight, and landed on schedule?) It is also the case that not all the research finds HMOs better or less costly.

Perhaps a more important message is that the current system is not well designed to encourage good performance by managed care plans. The payment to plans set by HCFA does not take into account differential risk, resulting in overpayments to plans with lower than average risk. The desire for enrollee protections led to the ability to change plans on 30-day notice, but this exacerbates the selection problem. More important than the overpayment of plans is the disincentive for plans to develop high-quality programs to care for people with expensive chronic conditions. Even without systems to encourage plans to want the sickest enrollees, the absence of sensitive measures of quality and incentives for good care means that managed care will, if only by default, focus on cost, rather than quality. Moreover, the easy ability to switch plans, and the rapidly changing policy environment favors plans with short, rather than long-term perspectives on performance.

In the debates surrounding Medicare and managed care, too much attention is often paid to looking for villains, both among policy makers and health plans. A more complete understanding of how Medicare fits in the larger environment, and of how relatively obscure issues such as risk adjustment influence plans and enrollees leads to a different perspective. Increased attention to some of these policy details may allow the creation of a more effective and efficient Medicare program.

LITERATURE CITED

1. Angus DC, Linde-Zwirble WT, Sirio CA, Rotondi AJ, Chelluri L, et al. 1996. The effect of managed care on ICU length of stay. Implications for Medicare. *JAMA* 276: 1075–82.

2. Arrow KJ. 1963. Uncertainty and the welfare economics of medical care. *Am. Econ. Rev.* 53:941–73.

3. Ash A, Porell F, Gruenberg L, Sawitz E, Beiser A. 1989. Adjusting Medicare capitation payments using prior hospitalization data. *Health Care Financ. Rev.* 10:17–29.

4. Eggers P. 1980. Risk differentials between Medicare beneficiaries enrolled and not enrolled in an HMO. *Health Care Financ Rev.* 2:91–99.

5. Epstein AE. 1995. Performance reports on quality prototypes, problems, and prospects. *N. Engl. J. Med.* 333:57–61.

6. Institute of Medicine. 1990. *Medicare: A Strategy for Quality Assurance.* 1:21. Washington, DC: Natl. Acad. Press.

7. Lamphere JA, Neuman P, Langwill K, Sherman D. 1997. The surge in Medicare managed care: an update. *Health Aff.* 16:127–33.

8. Luft HS, Dudley RA. 1997. Making managed care work through improved risk adjustment and quality measurement. Submitted.

9. Lurie N, Christianson J, Finch M, Moscovice I. 1994. The effects of capitation on health and functional status of the Medicaid elderly. *Ann. Int. Med.* 120:506–11.

10. Manton KG, Newcomer R, Lowrimore GR, Vertrees JC, Harrington C. 1993. Social/health maintenance organization and fee-for-service health outcomes over time. *Health Care Financ. Rev.* 15:173–202.

11. Miller RH, Luft HS. 1994. Managed care plan performance since 1980: a literature analysis. *JAMA* 271: 1512–19.

12. Miller RH, Luft HS. 1994. Managed care plans: characteristics, growth, and premium performance. *Annu. Rev. Public Health* 15:437–59.

13. Miller RH, Luft HS. 1997. Does managed care lead to better or worse quality of care? *Health Aff.* 16:5–25.

14. Newhouse JP. 1994. Patients at risk: health reform and risk adjustment. *Health Aff.* 13:132–46.

15. Newhouse JP, Manning WG, Keeler EB, Sloss EM. 1989. Adjusting capitation rates using objective health measures and prior utilization. *Health Care Financ. Rev.* 10:41–54.

16. Pearl R. 1997. Cut urged in Medicare money to H.M.O.'s. *New York Times,* March 29, p. 10.

17. Physician Payment Review Commission. 1997. *Annual Report to Congress.* Washington, DC.

18. Riley GF, Potosky AL, Lubitz JD, Brown ML. 1994. Stage of cancer at diagnosis for Medicare HMO and fee-for-service enrollees. *Am. J. Public Health.* 84: 1598–604.

19. Shaughnessy, PW, Schlenker RE, Hittle DF. 1994. Home health care outcomes under capitated and fee-for-service payment. *Health Care Financ. Rev.* 16:187–221.

20. The Henry J. Kaiser Family Foundation. 1995. *Medicare Chart Book.* Washington, DC. Fig. 17.

21. The Henry J. Kaiser Family Foundation. 1997. *Medicare Chart Book.* Washington, DC.

22. US Dep. Health and Human Services, Health Care Financing Administration. 1996. *Profiles of Medicare.* Washington, DC.

23. van Barneveld EM, van Vliet RCJA, van de Ven WPMM. 1996. Mandatory high-risk pooling: a means for reducing the incentives for cream skimming. *Inquiry* 33: 133–43.

24. van de Ven WPMM, van Vliet RCJA. 1992. How can we prevent cream skimming in a competitive health insurance market? The great challenge for the 90's. *Dev. Health Econ. Public Policy* 1:23–46.

25. Ware JE, Bayliss MS, Rogers WH, Kosinski M, Tarlov AR. 1996. Differences in 4-year health outcomes for elderly and poor, chronically ill patients treated in HMO and fee-for-service systems. Results from the Medical Outcomes Study. *JAMA* 276:1039–47.

26. Zarabozo C, Taylor C, Hicks J. 1996. Medicare managed care: numbers and trends. *Health Care Financ. Rev.* 17: 243–61.

DEVELOPED WORLD PERSPECTIVE

HEALTH CARE FINANCING IN SELECTED INDUSTRIALIZED NATIONS: COMPARATIVE ANALYSIS AND COMMENT

DEBORAH J. CHOLLET

INTRODUCTION

The high cost of health care and deteriorating access to care among people with modest incomes or ongoing health problems have become important public issues in the United States. These problems have sparked renewed interest in the systems that other nations use to deliver and finance health care services. Many nations that are comparable to the United States in culture and economic development have centralized, universal health care financing— that pays for all of their people at a substantially lower cost than in the United States.

In the United States, spending for health care reached nearly 12 percent of Gross Domestic Product (GDP) in 1989 (the most recent year for which internationally comparable data are available).[1] Other western industrialized nations reported rates from 9 percent (Canada, France) to less than 6 percent (the United Kingdom). Per capita in 1989, health care spending in the United States averaged $2,354–40 percent more than in Canada, and more than twice the average cost of health care in the Netherlands and the United Kingdom (Table 1). These differences in coverage and cost have led to growing speculation about whether aspects of other countries' financing and delivery systems

might be adapted to use in the United States and whether any of these systems would achieve the cost control that our present system lacks.[2]

This chapter provides overviews of the health care systems of five western industrialized nations: Canada, France, Germany,[3] the Netherlands, and the United Kingdom. Of these nations, three (Canada, France, and the United Kingdom) provide compulsory, universal coverage; that is, no resident lacks financing for health care. Two, Germany and the Netherlands, provide compulsory coverage for most residents, but do not require coverage for relatively high-wage workers. With the exception of the United Kingdom, health care spending in each of these countries is above-average among the larger set of nations that are western industrial powers. But in none of these countries is health care as expensive as in the United States.

The organization of this chapter is as follows. Section 1 addresses the question of demographic, social and economic comparability among the countries selected for discussion in this chapter and the United States. Section 2 briefly describes four aspects of each health care financing system: (1) the general financing structure and benefits covered; (2) the system's sources of funds and the distribution of cost; (3) the system's relationship

TABLE 1 Health Care Spending in Selected Countries, 1989

	PER CAPITA SPENDING (U.S. DOLLARS)	U.S. SPENDING PER FOREIGN HEALTH CARE DOLLAR (PER CAPITA)	SPENDING AS A PERCENT OF GROSS DOMESTIC PRODUCT (GDP)	PUBLIC SPENDING AS A PERCENT OF TOTAL
Canada	$1,683	$1.40	8.7	75%
France	1,274	1.85	8.7	75
Germany	1,232	1.91	8.2	72
Netherlands	1,135	2.07	8.3	73
United Kingdom	836	2.82	5.8	87
United States	2,354	1.00	11.8	42

Source: From G. J. Schieber and J. P. Poullier, "International Health Spending: Issues and Trends," *Health Affairs* 10:1 (Spring 1991), pp. 106–116, copyright © 1991 The People-To-People Health Foundation, Inc. All Rights Reserved; and "OECD Health Data," copyright © OECD, 1991.

with providers and methods of cost management; and (4) the system's financing of long-term or chronic care services. Finally, section 3 identifies some key issues in adapting these systems to the United States.

COMPARATIVE DEMOGRAPHIC, SOCIAL AND ECONOMIC INDICATORS

History and unfolding events world-wide continue to remind us that cultural differences among ostensibly similar nations can be surprisingly great. Those differences notwithstanding, the social and cultural histories of both the United States and Canada have been strongly influenced by the majority populations' European roots.

The similarities among the countries discussed in this chapter and the United States, captured in a summary fashion, are striking (Table 2). All are western industrialized nations. In each, approximately one quarter of the population is under age 20, but the proportion of the population over age 65 (strongly related to mortality in World War II) varies between 11 percent in Canada and 15 percent in

Germany. Not surprisingly, all have predominantly urban populations; the United States, Canada, and France are the least urban, with about three-quarters of their populations living in cities. While economic productivity varies considerably among these nations, all are among the most affluent in the world.

The similar affluence of these countries is perhaps best exemplified by the life expectancy of their populations. In each, life expectancy at birth is approximately 76 years. At age 65, men's life expectancy varies between 13 years in Germany and 15 years in Canada. Women's life expectancy at age 65 is in all countries greater and varies over a similarly narrow range.

AN OVERVIEW OF FIVE HEALTH CARE FINANCING SYSTEMS

The following sections describe features of the health care financing systems of these five nations. For the convenience of the reader, Table 3 summarizes these systems as well as the system of health care financing in the United States.

TABLE 2 Demographic, Social and Economic Indicators for Selected Industrialized Nations and the United States

COUNTRY	POPULATION LESS THAN AGE 20 (PERCENT)	POPULATION OLDER THAN AGE 65 (PERCENT)	GROSS DOMESTIC PRODUCT PER CAPITA[b] (U.S. DOLLARS)	POPULATION LIVING IN URBAN AREAS[e] (PERCENT)	LIFE EXPECTANCY AT BIRTH[f] (YEARS)	MALE LIFE EXPECTANCY AT AGE 65 (YEARS)[g]
Canada	28.9%[a]	10.7%[a]	$17,211	76.4%	77.3	14.6
France	28.2[c]	13.4[c]	12,803	74.1	76.6	14.0
Germany	22.1[b]	15.1[b]	13,323	85.3	75.7	13.2
Netherlands	26.7[c]	12.4[c]	12,252	87.3	77.5	14.0
United Kingdom	24.5[c]	14.2[c]	12,340	92.0	76.0	13.2
United States	28.9[c]	12.4[c]	18,337	74.1	76.3	14.5

[a]1986 [b]1987 [c]1988 [d]1989 [e]1990 [f]1985–1990 [g]1980–1983

Source: From United Nations Conference on Trade and Development, *Handbook of International Trade and Development Statistics* (New York: United Nations, 1991), Table 6.10A; Jean-Pierre Poullier, "Health data file: overview and methodology," *Health Care Systems in Transition: The Search for Efficiency* (Paris: OECD, 1990); United Nations, *Demographic Yearbook, 1984* (New York: United Nations, 1984). Copyright © OECD, 1991.

Unlike the United States, none of the systems can be characterized as private. That is, none of these systems rely on voluntary private health insurance to finance care for most of their population, as the United States does. Instead, voluntary private insurance either supplements public coverage or can be purchased as primary coverage in place of a universally available public insurance plan.[4]

In the United States, public financing for acute health care (Medicare) is available only to people over age 65 and the disabled. More comprehensive public health financing (Medicaid) is available to complex categories of people whose family incomes are well below the federal poverty income standard of (for certain sub-categories) below 175 percent of the poverty standard. In general, these categories (and sub-categories) include pregnant women, children, adults in families with children, the elderly and the disabled; and in all cases they are low-income. Residual public financing for health care occurs through federal, state, county and municipal payments to support public hospital bad debt, and through direct service provision in public clinics to individuals who are uninsured and ineligible for Medicare or Medicaid.[5]

Canada

Structure and Covered Services. Canada's health care financing system consists of primary public insurance for most health care services and voluntary, supplemental private insurance for services not covered by the public program. Canada's public insurance system covers all residents; 90 percent of residents also have supplemental private insurance for services and items not covered by the public program. As in the United States, employer plans

TABLE 3 Features of Health Care Financing and Delivery: Selected Nations and the United States, 1990

FEATURE	UNITED STATES	CANADA
Percent of population covered by:		
Public insurance		
Primary	18 percent	100 percent
Supplemental	None	None
Private Insurance		
Primary	62 percent	None
Supplemental	11 percent	90 percent
Uninsured	13 percent	None
Services covered:		
Public insurance		
Acute care	Yes	Yes
Preventive care	Means-tested	Yes: some provinces also cover optometry and dental
Prescription drugs (outpatient)	Means-tested	For enrollees over age 65 in some provinces
Long-term care (LTC)	Post-acute; otherwise means-tested	Public nursing homes and hospital-based extended care
Private insurance	As determined by the market	Must exclude any service or item covered by the public plan
Financing		
Principal source(s) of public plan revenues	Payroll taxes; enrollee premiums; federal and state general revenues	Federal and provincial general revenues
Methods of provider payment:		
Hospitals	Varies by payer: mostly charge-based or prospective (diagnosis-related) payment	*Per diem* negotiated by each province; hospitals must participate
Physicians	Varies by payer; fee-for-service, capitated or scheduled fees	Fee schedule negotiated by each province; physicians must participate
Government caps total public payments to health care provider	No	Yes, by province

[a]Data on the percent of the Netherlands population covered by public and private plans are for 1990. At this writing, the Netherlands is redesigning the relative roles of its public and private insurance systems.

FRANCE	GERMANY	NETHERLANDS[a]	UNITED KINGDOM
100 percent	90 percent (compulsory for 75 percent)	62 percent (basic coverage)	100 percent
None	None	100 percent (long-term and chronic medical expenses)	None
None	9 percent	37 percent	None
90 percent	7 percent	43 percent	10 percent
None	Negligible	Negligible	None
80 percent of hospital cost; 75 percent of physicians' scheduled fees	Comprehensive hospital and medical; nominal, limited copayment	Comprehensive hospital and medical	Comprehensive hospital and medical
75 percent of scheduled fees	Limited	Limited	Yes, with nominal charge
Variously, 40–80 percent of cost	Yes, with a nominal charge	Yes	Yes; nominal charge for people aged 17–64
Medical component of LTC only	Medically intensive LTC only	Medically intensive LTC only	Medically intensive LTC only
May not supplement public coverage for hospital care	As determined by the market	As determined by the market	As determined by the market; complements universal public coverage
National general revenues and payroll taxes	Payroll taxes	Payroll taxes and national general revenues	National general revenues
Negotiated national *per diem;* hospitals may choose not to participate	Negotiated charge-based payments to contracting hospitals	Negotiated charge-based payments to contracting hospitals	Central budget allocation
Nationally negotiated fee schedule; physicians may choose not to participate	Fee schedule negotiated by each insurance plan	Fee schedule negotiated by national government	Capitated payments (primary care) or salary (specialty)
Yes	Yes	Yes	Yes

are the most common source of private insurance coverage in Canada.

Each of Canada's ten provinces and two territories separately administers the public insurance system, subject to federal requirements. Under federal guidelines, the public insurance program must provide full coverage for medical and ward-level hospital care. Most provincial plans also cover optometry (but not eyeglasses), and some cover dental care for children and prescription drugs for participants over age 65. Cost sharing is limited to medical goods and services covered at the discretion of the provincial plans and to non-elderly participants.[6]

Also under federal law, private insurance plans may not cover services or items also covered by the public programs. Consequently, private insurance plans in Canada typically cover such services or items as private or semi-private hospital accommodations, prescription drugs, ambulance services, out-of-country expenditures and long-term care services not covered by the provincial plan.

Financing. Canada's public insurance program is financed jointly by the federal and provincial governments from general revenues. Three provinces supplement this financing with a mandatory payroll tax, and two provinces charge enrollees a nominal premium for coverage.[7]

Provider Relationships and Cost Management. As in the United States, Canadian hospitals may be publicly or privately owned; most of Canada's physicians are in private practice. Binding hospital *per diem* rates and physician fee schedules are periodically negotiated between the provincial governments and each province's hospital and medical associations. The medical associations are responsible for allocating fees between general practitioners and specialists in the province.

In five provinces (including over 80 percent of Canada's population), the provincial governments set quarterly expenditure caps or targets. In these provinces, when individual providers exceed their quarterly target, the provincial government pays only 75 percent of subsequent charges.

Long-Term Care. Canada's provincial health care programs cover all care in public nursing homes or hospital-based extended care facilities. These providers serve most of Canada's institutional long-term care population.[8] But nursing home residents and residents of other extended care facilities are also charged a percentage of their social security pensions to support the cost of their care in these institutions.

France

Structure and Covered Services. Like Canada's system, France has a mandatory public insurance program and voluntary, supplemental private insurance. France's public insurance program is federally financed, and all residents of France are eligible for coverage.

Private supplemental insurance coverage is widespread; an estimated 90 percent of the population has some type of private insurance coverage. Most of France's private insurance plans are underwritten by private insurance companies. Some are managed by independent, nonprofit *mutuelles.*

France's public insurance program covers 80 percent of most inpatient hospital costs.[9] The public program also pays 75 percent of physicians' scheduled fees. In addition to hospital and medical costs, the public program covers 40 to 100 percent of the cost of prescription drugs.

Federal law prohibits private insurance payments to supplement public payment for hospital care. Consequently, the benefits provided by private insurance plans are principally for physician charges. Private insurance plans typically cover 100 percent of the difference between scheduled fees and the public program's reimbursement, and 90 percent of charges in excess of the scheduled fee for most physician services. The coverage offered by

mutuelles typically covers only the difference between scheduled physician fees and the public program reimbursement, not excess charges.

Financing.   France's public insurance program is financed by general revenues (including an earmarked tax on auto insurance) and by a payroll tax on employers and employees paid to the National Sickness Insurance Fund. Enrollees are not charged premiums.

Provider Relationships and Cost Management. While physicians based in government hospitals are salaried government employees, most of France's physicians are in private practice. The government negotiates a hospital *per diem* rate and a schedule of physician fees with their respective representing organizations, and offers higher reimbursement to hospitals and physicians that agree to "participate," that is, accept the negotiated payment rate as payment in full. Since the public program pays only the scheduled rate and private insurance plans typically also pay a percentage of scheduled fees, most providers choose to participate. Like Canada, France uses a global budgeting system to manage public health care costs. The public insurance plan has also instituted some restrictions to control physicians' prescriptions for drugs.

Long-Term Care.   France's public insurance plan covers only the medical services associated with long-term care. Consequently, it finances only 14 percent of the total cost of long term care. For the population that qualifies, needs-based public assistance programs cover the residential costs associated with long-term care as well as the cost of community-based (non-institutional) long-term care services.

Germany

Structure.   Germany's principal health insurance system is comprised of some 1,200 individually funded and administered sickness funds, each organized around a specific trade or professional group. Approximately 90 percent of the population is enrolled in these sickness funds. For about 75 percent of the population (including all hourly, salaried, or self-employed workers who earn less than a threshold amount;[10] unemployment beneficiaries; disabled workers and pensioners), membership in a sickness fund is compulsory. While participation by other workers and their dependents is voluntary, once these individuals choose not to participate in a sickness fund they may not rejoin later.

The sickness funds cover the full cost of nearly all medical goods and services, and emphasize primary care as well as some preventive care. The funds require a nominal daily copayment for the first two weeks of a hospital stay, as well as nominal copayments for outpatient prescription drugs.

Approximately 15 percent of the population participates in a private insurance plan. Of these, just over one-half (about 9 percent of the population) is enrolled in a private insurance plan as their primary source of coverage [Reinhardt 1989]. For others (7 percent of the population), the full cost of enrollment is typically employer-financed, and the private plan supplements the coverage provided by their sickness fund.

The service coverage offered by primary private insurance plans is generally comprehensive, similar to the coverage provided by the sickness funds. Supplementary private insurance typically covers private hospital accommodations, compared to the ward accommodations covered by the sickness funds. In some cases, these plans also pay an indemnity for hospital stays.

Financing.   Germany's sickness funds are privately managed; each sets a participant contribution rate to cover annual expenses. These contribution rates are paid as taxes on payroll which are levied on both employers and employees.

To support participation by pensioners and their dependents, the national social security

pension system and private retirement pensions both make special payments to the sickness funds. Since these payments are not calculated to cover the full cost of pensioners' health care, pensioners are subsidized by other participants in the sickness fund.

Provider Relationships and Cost Management. Hospital *per diem* rates in Germany are negotiated between each sickness fund and their contracting hospitals, subject to approval by the State government.[11,12] While most physicians in Germany are private practitioners, hospital-based physicians are salaried hospital employees. The sickness funds set physician fee schedules, establish expenditure targets, and reduce scheduled physician fees for physicians whose costs exceed 140 percent of the average cost profile. Physicians who treat privately insured patients are allowed to charge those patients as much as 2.3 times their scheduled fee.

Long-Term Care.   In general, long-term care facilities in Germany are considered to be social care facilities. As such, the sickness funds do not cover care provided in these facilities. Instead, public assistance in financing long-term care is provided through the welfare system and is means-tested. Means-testing for public assistance in Germany considers the financial resources of all immediate family members, including adult children.

The Netherlands

Structure.   Like the German system, health care in the Netherlands is financed through some 35 government-approved sickness funds established under the Compulsory Health Insurance Act (ZFW). Also like Germany, participation in a sickness fund is required only for wage or salaried workers (and their dependents) who earn less than an annually indexed threshold amount. In 1989, 62 percent of the Dutch population participated in sickness funds.

The more than one-third of Dutch residents who are not eligible for coverage under ZFW rely on private insurance plans to finance their health care. These plans are commonly sponsored by employers. Many employers also sponsor supplemental private insurance plans for workers who participate in the ZFW system. In the Netherlands, some 70 percent of the population participating in the sickness funds also participate in a supplemental private insurance plan.

The Dutch sickness funds provide full coverage for most hospital and medical care and for primary and preventive care. Private insurance plans in the Netherlands typically provide comprehensive coverage for hospital care (choice of hospital accommodations affects the premium), full coverage for surgical and medical procedures (including specialists' services), and optional coverage for primary care as well as various other medical goods and services.

Finally, all Dutch residents (regardless of whether they participate in a sickness fund or a private insurance plan) are covered by the Exceptional Medical Expenses Act (AWBZ). AWBZ coverage finances catastrophic hospital expenses as well as institutional care for mental health and substance abuse.

The Dutch government is moving toward substantial revision of the country's health care financing system. In particular, the government has announced its intentions to expand compulsory enrollment in sickness funds to all residents (about three-fifths of the population are now required to enroll), to integrate AWBZ coverage into that provided by the sickness funds, and to encourage private insurance underwriting and management of the sickness funds. It is anticipated that at least some of these reforms will be implemented in 1992.

Financing.   The ZFW system is financed by payroll taxes paid into a national fund and then distributed to the sickness funds. Employees who participate in a primary or supplemental private

insurance plan typically receive about one-half of the premium as a contribution from their employer. AWBZ coverage in the Dutch system is financed from national general revenues.

Provider Relationships and Cost Control. The Dutch sickness funds contract with hospitals and physicians to provide services to their participants. Hospital *per diem* amounts are negotiated nationally by the sickness funds and are uniformly adopted by the sickness funds. The Dutch government negotiates capitation amounts for general practitioners with physician associations, as well as a binding fee schedule for specialty physicians. As in Canada and Germany, the government also sets global budget targets for both hospitals and physicians.

While private insurance plans may separately negotiate both hospital *per diem* rates and physician fee schedules, in practice most private insurance plans adopt the same nationally negotiated payment rates and schedules used by the sickness funds.

The implementation of expenditure targets in the Netherlands differs from that in Canada and Germany, and accommodates the larger proportion of the population that relies on private insurance. In the Netherlands, each specialist is required to repay to the fund at the end of the year a portion of the amount by which his or her actual revenues have exceeded target average revenues for that specialty.[13] The Dutch sickness funds also use inpatient and outpatient retrospective utilization review and information feedback programs. Voluntary peer review programs have also emerged to share practice data among physicians and hospitals [Kirkman-Liff, 1989].[14]

Long-Term Care. Only patients who require relatively intensive medical care can be admitted to long-term care institutions that provide services covered by the sickness funds. Using similar coverage rules, the AWBZ pays for care for fewer than

one-third of the elderly who live in long-term care facilities. Most institutionalized elderly live in "old people's homes" and receive income-related government assistance. Similarly, most public financing for community-based long-term care is conducted through local government programs and is means-tested.

Great Britain

Structure. Great Britain's National Health Service (NHS) is arguably the most centralized delivery and financing system of any in Western Europe. Participation in the NHS is compulsory for all residents. Private insurance is relatively unusual; as of 1988, approximately 10 percent of the population had private health insurance coverage, typically as an employee benefit paid by their employer.[15] Private insurance plans typically complement NHS coverage by financing access to and choice among specialists in NHS hospitals for non-emergency surgeries,[16] as well as private (as opposed to ward-level) hospital accommodations.[17]

The NHS is operated by approximately two hundred District Health Authorities within fourteen regional health authorities. While much health planning occurs at the regional level, the District Health Authorities oversee day-to-day health services delivery and administer NHS benefits. The NHS provides comprehensive coverage for most hospital and medical care, with nominal fees for auxiliary services.

Financing. The NHS is financed directly from general revenues. For some services (prescription drugs, dental care, and eye examinations and eyeglasses) the NHS requires patients to pay significant user fees, substantially supporting the cost of those services.[18]

Provider Relationships and Cost Control. The NHS owns and operates most hospitals in the United Kingdom. Physicians in general practice are paid a capitated (per patient) amount by the

NHS; specialty physicians are salaried employees of the NHS hospital system.

Each District Health Authority's operating budget is based on the district's population demographics as a predictor of fiscal year costs. Capital budgets are allocated to the fourteen regions based on a formula that is designed to equalize resources among regions relative to each region's estimated health care needs.

Together with central government budgeting, the centralized ownership of hospitals and the complete absence of fee-for-service payment of physicians in the NHS afford an exceptional degree of control over total health care spending. The NHS accounts for approximately 85 percent of all health care spending in the United Kingdom. However, more than a decade of governmental decisions to fund the NHS at levels insufficient to cover the growth of underlying production costs has constrained the amount of care provided within the NHS system, encouraging greater use of private insurance and fee-for-service payment for hospital and specialty care. While conservative funding of the NHS and greater private financing of health may serve one goal—reducing public spending for health care—it also diminishes system wide cost control. Although the modest rate of private insurance coverage in the United Kingdom suggests that the erosion of cost control in the NHS is not yet a significant problem, the apparently strong level of popular support for "private alternatives" to NHS care [Blendon and Donelan, 1989] suggests considerable public pressure for loosening United Kingdom's system of centralized cost control.[19]

Long-Term Care. The NHS finances institutionalized long-term care services for people who require medically intensive long-term care. However, as in the Netherlands, most institutionalized elderly live in care settings that are principally residential and qualify for income-related government assistance.

CONCLUSION

The relevance to the United States of other nations' experiences in financing health care is a matter of discussion among researchers and public policy makers. While the countries reviewed in this chapter have achieved more widespread access to health care at a lower cost than the United States, the historical differences between the United States and other nations are considerable, both with respect to popular expectations about health care and popular acceptance of centralized solutions.

The U.S. system of health care is resource-intensive. The United States has relatively few physicians per capita[20] and uses hospitals in a relatively intensive fashion.[21] Consistent with this resource-intensive mode of production, health care in the United States deemphasizes preventive care (a relatively low-resource enterprise) relative to the emphasis placed on preventive care in countries where public-sector financing (and coordination of payments to providers) predominates.

The U.S. system of health care financing—mostly private insurance with public financing only for selected poor and the elderly—is unlike that found in any other western industrialized nation. While the U.S. system readily accommodates innovation and technological change relative to more centralized and regulated systems, we pay a high price for it. The U.S. system is rightly criticized as providing truly exceptional life-saving health care for many people, but denying basic care and preventive care to a significant and growing minority.

Various scholars have noted that the health care financing systems of developed nations may ultimately converge to a single general model [Davis, 1989; Reinhardt, 1989]. While the more centralized systems in Western Europe—for example, the United Kingdom and the Netherlands—are experimenting with decentralizing decision-making to improve efficiency, the least centralized system—that in the United States—is increasingly looking to features of the European systems; specifically, ne-

gotiation and regulation of health care prices to control cost. However, the effectiveness of negotiated and regulated payments in European systems hinges on universal participation in the financing system, a politically elusive goal in the United States. Reformers wishing to traverse the shortest distance between the current, "pluralistic" system of health care financing in the United States and a more coordinated system might look to the relatively decentralized German model or the evolving Netherlands' model, both financed by payroll taxes, as perhaps most readily adaptable to the United States.

One final issue—the effect of population aging on health care costs—is worthy of mention. In each of the countries, the elderly population is growing rapidly, both absolutely and as a percentage of the population. Over the next 30 years, each anticipates accelerated growth of the elderly population and of the very old population (age 85 and older) in particular. Unlike the United States, these countries have systems that allow at least some centralized control of aggregate health care costs. Neverthe-

less, all expect the soaring demand for health care associated with population aging to place considerable strains on their systems of health care delivery and financing.

In addition to the burden of rising demand for acute care, growth in the demand for long-term care may be especially problematic. Each of the systems buys long-term care in a similar way and in a way that is roughly comparable to that in the United States; relatively intensive, medical long-term care is financed through the health care financing system, and residential care is supported by means-tested public assistance programs. As in the United States, each is likely to see increasing use of medical long-term care and accelerating cost in their principal health care financing systems, unless their community-based systems for providing long-term care are greatly expanded. Unfortunately, none of these systems may be adequate to accommodate the social and fiscal circumstances that are likely to accompany the dramatic demographic change that is projected to occur in each over the next 30 years.

NOTES

1. U.S. health care spending in 1990 reached $666.2 billion, 12.2 percent of GNP. Per capita, the United States spent $2,566 in 1990, almost 1.5 times as great as national health care expenditures ten years earlier [Levit *et al.*, 1991].

2. For example, see Meyers *et al.*, (1991).

3. All references to Germany in this chapter refer specifically to the former Federal Republic of Germany.

4. At this writing, the Netherlands is revising their system toward greater private insurer management of a publicly coordinated, tax-financed system.

5. In addition to these systems, the federal government also finances various systems of direct service provision or financing for active and retired military personnel and their families, veterans of active military service, and native Americans.

6. Under federal guidelines, participants over age 65 may not be charged cost sharing.

7. Where a premium is charged, however, nonpayment cannot exclude residents from public coverage.

8. Personal care homes, which are financed by Canada's welfare system, serve fewer than one-fourth of elderly Canadians in institutions.

9. For serious illness, the public program covers 100 percent of cost, subject to a nominal daily deductible.

10. In 1991, all workers earning less than $33,353 (US) were required to participate in a sickness fund. This amount is indexed annually.

11. Hospital charges to privately insured patients are typically lower than the negotiated *per diem* rates negotiated with the sickness funds, since they do not include the cost (or services) of hospital-based physician salaries.

12. The State governments also must approve and finance capital investments, based on statewide hospital planning.

13. Specifically, physicians must pay back one-third of the first $15,000 (US) above the target and two-thirds of any income above that.

14. The Netherlands government controls the construction of facilities and acquisition of major medical equipment by means of a licensure system. These licenses are issued on

the basis of regional and national health planning [Jonssen, 1989].

15. The purchase of private insurance was made tax-deductible in 1979.

16. Medical specialists practicing in NHS hospitals commonly hold part-time salaried appointments so as to reserve time to see private patients.

17. Anderson (1989) observes that these two resources together enable private patients to "jump the queue" for elective surgical operations for which there may be long waiting lists.

18. In 1986, user fees financed an estimated 43 percent of the cost of outpatient prescription drugs and 78 percent of average charges for dental treatment [Birch, 1989].

19. Ongoing reforms of the NHS introduced by the government to achieve an "internal" market with more disaggregated decision making are intended to improve the efficiency of the NHS and the equitable distribution of resources geographically [Enthoven, 1991]. These changes will not in themselves change the system's degree of centralized cost control, and may even enhance control if better efficiency within the NHS reduces incentives for the population also to buy private insurance.

20. In 1987, the United States had 2.3 physicians per thousand population—less than in France (2.8), Germany (2.5), or the Netherlands (2.4), but more than Canada (2.2) or the United Kingdom (1.4).

21. Of the countries discussed in this chapter, the U.S. has by far the shortest average length of hospital stay (fewer than 12 days, as compared with 13 days in Canada and 17 days in Germany). However, both the average cost per day and the total cost of hospital care in the U.S. is higher than in any other industrialized nation.

REFERENCES

Anderson, Odin W. *The Health Services Continuum in Democratic States: An Inquiry into Solvable Problems* (Ann Arbor, MI: Health Administration Press, 1989).

Birch, Stephen. "Health Care Charges: Lessons from the United Kingdom," *Health Policy* 13:2 (November 1989), pp. 145–157.

Blendon, Robert J. and Karen Donelan. "British Public Opinion on National Health Service Reform," *Health Affairs* 8:4 (Winter 1989), pp. 52–62.

Davis, Karen. "Symposium: International Comparisons of Health Care Systems," *Health Care Financing Review,* Annual Supplement (December 1989), pp. 104–107.

Enthoven, Alain C. "Internal Market Reform of the British National Health Service," *Health Affairs* 10:3 (Fall 1991), pp. 60–70.

Jonssen, Bengt. "What Can Americans Learn from Europeans?" *Health Care Financing Review,* Annual Supplement (December 1989), pp. 79–93.

Kirkmann-Liff, Bradford. "Cost Containment and Physician Payment in the Netherlands," *Inquiry* (Winter 1989), pp. 468–482.

Levit, Katherine R., Helen C. Lazenby, Cathy A. Cowan and Suzanne W. Letsch. "National Health Expenditures, 1990," *Health Care Financing Review* 13:1 (Fall 1991), pp. 29–54.

Meyers, Jack A., Sharon Silow-Carroll and Sean Sullivan. *A National Health Plan in the U.S.: The Long-Term Impact on Business and the Economy* (Washington, DC: Economic and Social Research Institute, 1991).

Organisation for Economic Cooperation and Development. *Ageing Populations: The Social Policy Implications* Paris: OECD, 1988.

———. *Health Care Systems in Transition: The Search for Efficiency.* Paris: OECD, 1990.

Poullier, Jean-Pierre. "Health Data File: Overview and Methodology," *Health Care Systems in Transition: The Search for Efficiency.* (Paris: OECD, 1990).

Reinhardt, Uwe. "Symposium: International Comparisons of Health Care Systems," *Health Care Financing Review,* Annual Supplement (December 1989), pp. 97–104.

Schieber, George J. and Jean-Pierre Poullier. "International Health Spending: Issues and Trends," *Health Affairs* 10:1 (Spring 1991), pp. 106–116; and OECD Health Data, 1991.

United Nations Conference on Trade and Development. *Handbook of International Trade and Development Statistics.* New York: United Nations, 1991, Table 6.10A.

———. *Demographic Yearbook, 1984.* New York: United Nations, 1984.

DEVELOPING WORLD PERSPECTIVE

FINANCING HEALTH CARE IN RURAL CHINA: PRELIMINARY REPORT OF A NATIONWIDE STUDY

GU XINGYUAN, GERALD BLOOM, TANG SHENGLAN, ZHU YINGYA, ZHOU SHOUQI,
AND CHEN XINGBAO

1. INTRODUCTION

Eighty percent of China's population of over one billion live in the rural areas. The provision of access to adequate preventive and curative services to all these people has been a major health priority. This has required, among other things, the establishment of a stable means of financing the rural health services.

There has been a close link in China between the system of agricultural production and the mechanism of funding the health sector. Prior to 1950, agriculture was based on private and unequal ownership of land. Health services were available on the basis of the ability to pay. Subsequent to the establishment of the People's Republic, a collective agricultural system was developed. This created the economic basis for the organization of cooperative medical care schemes. A portion of the earnings of rural collective enterprises was allocated to a health care fund. Members of the collective were entitled to receive care at a subsidized price. The first such plan began in 1955 in a township in Henan Province. Cooperative schemes spread as agriculture was collectivized during the late 1950s.

During the early 1960s, the government gave explicit encouragement to the establishment of cooperative medical schemes. Further impetus was given to this process when Mao Tze-tung urged that priority in health be given to the rural areas. The so-called "three tier" structure of health services was consolidated. Primary health care was provided by "barefoot doctors" based at brigade (now village) health stations which served 1000–

3000 people. A health centre at commune (now township) level supervised the health stations and provided a combination of preventive and curative services for a population of 15,000 to 50,000. More sophisticated care was available at the county hospital, with a catchment population of 400,000 to 1,300,000. Each level had a role in the organization of preventive and promotive activities. The rural health services were financed through a combination of government funding, cash payments by patients, and funds from cooperative medical care schemes [1,2]. Ninety percent of villages were covered by such schemes in the mid and late 1970s. This system made a substantial contribution to the improvements in health which took place in China between 1950 and 1980 [3,4].

Since the late 1970s the organization of agricultural production has once more undergone a dramatic change. Collective ownership has been largely replaced by the "household responsibility system." There is evidence of a substantial increase in food production. However, the change in the economic system has posed a threat to the financial viability of rural health services. Many of the cooperative medical care schemes have collapsed [5]. By the late 1980s only 5% of rural residents were covered, according to Ministry of Public Health (MoPH) data. The majority of rural doctors (upgraded barefoot doctors) now charge fees and earn a proportion of their income by selling drugs. Many village health stations have become private clinics.

There has been a growing recognition in China of the burden which the reversion to direct user

charges is placing on the sick. Concern has also been voiced that preventive services may be less effective in some areas [6]. Initiatives have been taken at local and national levels to address the problem of financing rural health services [7]. The MoPH has constituted an Expert Commission on Health Policy and Management to assess the current situation and develop viable policy options. This body supported a large scale study of health service utilization and expenditure, which was undertaken in 1988 by the School of Public Health of the Shanghai Medical University. This paper presents preliminary findings of that study [8].

2. METHODOLOGY

2.1. Selection of Sample Counties, Townships and Villages

The study was carried out in 20 counties in 16 different provinces. These were divided evenly among areas at different levels of development. For the purpose of this report they have been organized into three regions on the basis of their level of socio-economic development (Table 1). Seven of the more highly developed counties are in region I, 6 middle

level counties in region II, and 7 of the poorer ones in region III. The per capita income of the counties in region I was over twice those in region II and almost five times those in region III. The counties in region III show many signs of underdevelopment. The prevalence of infectious diseases is higher, the level of education is lower, and the health sector is less well developed. In region I, on the other hand, there is a considerable amount of small scale industry even in the rural areas. The health problems are increasingly those of an aging population.

The counties were selected on the basis of their willingness to participate actively in the study. Therefore all of the country health bureaux were particularly interested in finding a solution to the problem of financing rural health care services. In spite of how they were chosen there is no reason to believe that their socio-economic characteristics were atypical. However, the proportion of people covered by local health insurance schemes was much higher in the sample than in the population as a whole. Over 30% were members of prepayment schemes and in region I this applied to over half of households (Table 2). A major objective of the study was to compare access to health services under the different financing systems.

TABLE 1 Socio-Economic Characteristics of the Three Regions

	SOCIO-ECONOMIC REGIONS		
	I	II	III
Number of counties	7	6	7
Average population per county ('000)	770	640	490
Income per capita, 1987 (¥)	1756	775	375
Rural income per capita, 1987 (¥)	899	524	319
Health workers/1000 people	2.0	1.9	1.9
Hospital beds/1000 people	2.1	1.8	1.4

Source: 1988 Survey, preliminary analysis

TABLE 2 Percentage of People Covered by the Various Systems of Health Care Finance in the Sample Population

	SOCIO-ECONOMIC REGION			
SYSTEMS OF FINANCE	I (%)	II (%)	III (%)	Total (%)
Self pay	42	64	88	65
Local health insurance	51	33	10	31
State medical insurance	3	1	2	2
Other	4	2	1	2

Source: 1988 Survey, preliminary analysis

The degree of coverage with medical care insurance is higher in the more developed counties. One reason for this is that the townships and villages in the richer provinces run a larger number of (nonagricultural) enterprises. These are the major sources of revenue for local administrations now that agricultural production has been devolved to households. Some of this money is paid into village or township welfare funds which can provide support for a local health insurance scheme.

Two or three representative townships were selected in each county on the basis of their socioeconomic status and the availability of health resources. Within each township one or two villages were randomly chosen for detailed study. Both the household and facility-based surveys were carried out in these sites.

2.2. Household Survey

Households were selected randomly in each study village. There were approximately 800 households per county. Data were collected on each family member of the sample. The total sample size was 62,335 rural residents.

Each household was interviewed once. Among the items covered in the questionnaire were:

- Sex, age, occupation, education, and medical care financing system of each family member.
- Episodes of ill health (days reported to be ill, sick days and days in bed) and visits to outpatient facilities of each family member during the previous 2 weeks.
- Inpatient care (admissions and inpatient days) during the preceding year (1987) and episodes when patients were referred to hospital but did not go during the same year.

2.3. Facility-Based Medical Care for Fees Survey

Information on health care expenditure was obtained from the accounts of health facilities. A random sample of admissions and outpatient visits was selected. The size of the sample was 300 outpatient visits and 300 admissions at each county hospital, 60–80 outpatient visits and admissions at each township health centre and 30 outpatient visits at each village health station. The data collected included sex, age and diagnosis of the patient, length of stay and total fees collected (broken down into medical care, other services, examinations, operations, drugs and materials). The sample comprised 14,575 outpatient visits and 8431 hospital admissions.

The average fee per outpatient visit varied from ¥2.1 at village health stations to ¥6.4 at county hospitals (Table 3). The cost per inpatient day was approximately twice that of an outpatient contact. This reflects the fact that charges for services were low. Drugs accounted for over 60% of fees for inpatient care and over 75% for outpatient visits.

2.4. Estimation of Total Health Expenditure (Fee Payment)

Mean health expenditure per capita was estimated indirectly. The household survey provided information on the average rates of utilisation of the different kinds of facilities by the sample population. The medical care fees survey provided information on the mean unit cost of these services. Average payment per person was calculated by multiplying the mean unit cost by the utilisation rate.

The methodology provides a reasonable estimate of average health expenditure per person but

TABLE 3 Average Medical Care Fees per Visit, Admission and in Inpatient Day

AVERAGE FEE	COUNTY HOSPITAL (¥)	HEALTH CENTRE (¥)	HEALTH STATION (¥)
Outpatient visit	6.4	5.6	2.1
Inpatient admission	164.6	82.8	
Inpatient day	13.6	10.6	

Source: 1988 Survey, preliminary analysis

there are some weaknesses. In the first place, it depends on accurate recall by the informant about the number of outpatient visits during the past 2 weeks and inpatient days over the past year for each household member. Secondly, the unit cost of care is estimated on the basis of only the charges to patients. However, the MoPH estimates that they represent over 80% of total hospital expenditure and an even higher percentage of the budget of most health centres and village health stations.

This methodology may have led to a relatively greater underestimate of total health expenditure in some townships with local health insurance schemes. This is because a higher proportion of the cost of care (e.g. for the payment of salaries to rural doctors and/or grants to health centres out of the health care fund) are not derived from direct charges for services. This underlines the need for future studies to measure health expenditure and finance directly.

3. THE THREE SYSTEMS OF RURAL HEALTH CARE FINANCE

Most of the costs of the rural health services are met out of local resources. Grants from county health departments fund only a small proportion of total expenditure. They commonly cover part of salaries at county hospitals (<50%) and health centres (<30%), and the operating costs of preventive services. In addition, grants for capital projects are made by both county and provincial health bureaux. Three broad systems can be identified for meeting the remainder of the costs. These are self payment (out-of-pocket by users), local health insurance schemes, and state insurance (public service medical care, and labour insurance).

3.1. Self Payment

Most of the rural population paid for medical care on an out-of-pocket basis in 1987. These patients are entitled to seek care at any facility, including any hospital, without referral.

If someone cannot afford to pay for treatment they can apply for a subsidy from the township or village welfare fund. However, it is believed that there are financial barriers to access to care for the rural poor. There are no nationally agreed rules to define the support to which poor households are entitled. Welfare funds are administered on a local basis and their size depends on the availability of local sources of revenue (largely from non-agricultural enterprises although in some cases money is collected directly from households).

There is increasing recognition of the need to provide people with a safety net against poverty now that their income is totally dependent on household production. Poor households were supported out of the income from collective production during the period of the communes. The system of basic social security has still not fully adapted to the requirements of the "household responsibility" system [9,10].

3.2. Local Health Insurance Schemes

A number of local health insurance schemes were developed during the 1980s, particularly in the more prosperous regions. There is considerable variation in the services covered, the mechanism of revenue generation and the system of management. However these schemes share some general characteristics:

- A collective medical care fund which derives revenue from individual households and township and village non-agricultural enterprises is established.
- Primary health care is provided at village health stations. Those who are referred to a health centre or hospital may be entitled to claim reimbursement for all or part of the fees. The kind of care covered and the level of reimbursement varies. Some schemes cover only inpatient or only outpatient care. Others include all curative and preventive services. Some special plans have been developed to

cover the full course of immunization against childhood diseases or the needs of a newly married couple for family planning and maternity services.

- Most of the payments to health care providers are on a fee-for-service basis (usually by the patient who claims reimbursement from the fund). In some schemes direct payments are made in the form of salaries for rural doctors (e.g. Huarong County, Hunan Province) or grants to township health centres (e.g. Jin Tan County, Jiangsu Province [11]).
- The township is the management unit of the local health insurance scheme. A management committee, which includes senior personnel from the township administration as well as from the health bureau, is constituted to be responsible for the fund.

3.3. State Medical Insurance (Public Service and Labour Insurance)

Public sector employees are entitled to free medical care. In the rural areas these include administrative cadres at township level, teachers and salaried health workers.

State-owned enterprises provide medical care insurance as a fringe benefit for their employees. Those covered by this so-called "labour insurance"

are entitled to free care and can claim a 50% reimbursement for their dependents.

It is estimated that 180 million people were covered by state medical insurance in 1987 [11]. However, most of them lived in urban centres. Only 2% of the study sample was covered by either public service or labour insurance.

4. HEALTH SERVICE UTILIZATION AND THE SYSTEM OF FINANCE

One of the objectives of the study was to compare access to health services in local insurance and self payment systems. The findings were different for outpatient and inpatient care.

4.1. Outpatient Services

The number of outpatient contacts averaged 3.3 per person per year for the sample population (Table 4). The average rates of use indicated a reasonable level of access to services in all regions and under all systems of finance. However, the average number of outpatient contacts is a crude measure of access to care. For example, the present study did not identify poor households, so it is not possible to assess whether they had particular problems of access, as is the case in other countries [12–15]. Nor did it measure the quality of services provided or

TABLE 4 Average Number of Outpatient Visits per Person per Year in the Three Socio-Economic Regions and under Different Systems of Finance

Region	SYSTEM OF FINANCE OF RURAL HEALTH SERVICES		
	Self Pay	*Local Insurance*	*Total*
Region I	3.0	3.0	3.0
Region II	2.6	2.8	2.7
Region III	3.7	n.a.*	4.3
Total	3.1	2.9	3.3

*Insufficient numbers
Source: 1988 Survey, preliminary analysis

assess other measures of access such as coverage with preventive services.

A relatively small number of townships and villages were included in the study. The data do not provide information on the numbers of villages which have no health personnel at all in the various regions and under different systems of finance.

The average cost per visit provides a crude measure of the kinds of services provided. However, it is not possible, on the basis of the available data, to ascertain whether differences were due to price discrimination or to variation in the use of resources, such as drugs. Nonetheless it is interesting to note the differences in the cost of care under the various financing systems.

The outpatient fees for those covered by state insurance were substantially above the average at each kind of facility (Table 5). For example, the average fee per outpatient visit at a county hospital varied between ¥4.7 for those in local insurance schemes and ¥8.7 for those covered by labour insurance. It is not possible to differentiate between over-provision of services to patients covered by labour insurance and under-provision to others. However, it may be relevant that profits from drug sales (they are commonly sold at a 15% mark-up) are an important source of revenue for health facilities. The annual pay of health workers includes a bonus whose size depends upon the success with which revenue is generated.

There is some evidence that people covered by a local insurance scheme paid less per visit than people who had no such coverage (Table 5). This was particularly the case at village-level. One explanation for this finding is that these patients do not need to pay consultation and treatment fees, and the rural doctors receive some of their income in the form of lump-sum payments out of village welfare funds.

4.2. Inpatient Services

There were considerable differences in hospital utilization rates between the three regions. The number of hospital admissions per thousand was over 50 in region I and under 30 in regions II and III (Table 6). The number of inpatient days per thousand varied from 542 in region I to 195 in region III. The higher rates of utilization in the more developed regions can be attributed, in part, to the supply of hospital beds which was 50% higher in region I than in region III (Table 1). Other factors such as the different age and illness profiles, the quality of hospital services, differences in medical care practice, and varying cultural attitudes among the people also may have contributed to the higher rate of hospitalization in region I [16]. However, there is evidence that the high cost of inpatient care contributed to the lower utilization levels in the poorer regions.

The charge for inpatient treatment represented a significant expenditure for a peasant family. The cost of an admission averaged ¥82.8 at a township health centre and ¥164.6 at a county hospital (Table 3). The average income per person in the ru-

TABLE 5   Average Fees Paid per Outpatient Visit at Various Facilities

FINANCING SYSTEM	COUNTY HOSPITAL (¥)	HEALTH CENTRE (¥)	HEALTH STATION (¥)
Self pay	5.4	5.3	2.4
Local insurance	4.7	5.1	1.3
State insurance	8.7	8.4	4.4
Average	6.4	5.6	2.1

Source: 1988 Survey, preliminary analysis

TABLE 6 Average Utilization of Inpatient Services during 1987 in the Three Socio-Economic Regions and under Different Systems of Finance

	SYSTEM OF FINANCE OF RURAL HEALTH SERVICES		
	Self Pay	Local Insurance	Total
Admission/1000			
Region I	44	56	52
Region II	30	25	28
Region III	24	n.a.*	25
Inpatient days/1000			
Region I	388	674	542
Region II	228	275	247
Region III	182	n.a.*	195
Total	243	477	320
Percentage referred to hospital who did not seek care			
All regions (%)	21	7	

*Insufficient numbers
Source: 1988 Survey, preliminary analysis

ral areas was ¥671 in 1987 (¥319 in region III). Therefore a typical hospital stay was equivalent to a significant proportion of the per capita income of a peasant household in a poor province (especially for a poor household). One indication that the cost of care affected utilization was the fact that 21% of people not covered by a prepayment scheme who were referred to hospital reported not seeking hospital treatment, as compared with 7% of those covered by some form of insurance (Table 6). Almost two-thirds of those not accepting admission to hospital reported that it was because of cost.

The average number of hospital days per thousand was twice as high for members of local insurance schemes than for those who had to pay the full fee in cash (Table 6). Some of this difference was due to the fact that most of the people covered by prepayment schemes lived in the more developed regions. However, within region I itself, the hospitalization rate was higher for those who were insured.

The pattern of use of facilities for inpatient care was different for people who paid for themselves than for those who were covered by a local insurance scheme (Table 7). The former were much more likely to by-pass local facilities and go directly to one in a nearby city. One argument which has been put forward for the development of prepayment schemes is that they can be designed so that they encourage better use of the referral network.

5. ANNUAL MEDICAL CARE FEES PER PERSON

One aim of the present study was to estimate the average cost of rural health services in order to provide a rough indication of the size of contributions which would be required by a local insurance scheme. It must be borne in mind that fees were not the only source of finance. Others included grants from the county health department and direct payments from township or village health funds.

406 CHAPTER 12 HEALTH CARE FINANCING

TABLE 7 Percentage of Inpatient Days in Different Providers by People in Different Medical Care Financing Systems

	TOWNSHIP HEALTH CENTRE (%)	COUNTY OR DISTRICT HOSPITAL (%)	HIGHER LEVEL FACILITY (%)
Region I			
Self pay	30	38	32
Local insurance	36	54	11
Region II			
Self pay	48	37	16
Local insurance	55	43	3
Region III			
Self pay	40	46	14
Local insurance	n.a.*	n.a.*	n.a.*

*Insufficient numbers

Source: 1988 Survey, preliminary analysis

None the less the methodology which was employed (see Section 2) has provided a reasonable estimate of the amount of local resources which were allocated to these services, particularly in areas where the population was not covered by a local insurance scheme.

Total annual fees per capita averaged ¥15.3 (Table 8). Eighty percent was for outpatient visits and the remainder for inpatient care. There was little difference between the three regions in fees paid per capita (¥18.3, ¥11.9, and ¥15.1 in regions I, II and III respectively). Payments for medical care were less than 2% of average income per person in the rural areas in region I. They accounted for a much higher proportion of household income in region III (almost 5%).

It is reasonable to assume that some families had to pay considerably more than the average proportion of their income on caring for the sick. For example, a single hospital admission could cost al-

TABLE 8 Medical Care Fee per Person–Year in the Three Socio-Economic Regions

	SOCIO-ECONOMIC REGION			
	I	*II*	*III*	**MEAN**
Total fees for OP care (¥)	12.9	9.5	12.7	12.0
Total fees for IP care (¥)	5.4	2.4	2.4	3.3
Total fees for medical care (¥)	18.3	11.9	15.1	15.3
Rural income per capita 1987 (¥)	999	524	319	671
Percentage of rural income on medical fees (%)	1.8	2.3	4.7	2.3

Source: 1988 Survey, preliminary analysis

most as much as a year's per capita income for a poor household. There is a belief among public health workers that the loss of productivity due to sickness combined with the need to meet high health care charges has been an important factor in the genesis of poor households. The potential role of local health insurance schemes and effective public welfare funds in the prevention of poverty is a subject which requires further research.

6. CONCLUSIONS

The study, the preliminary findings of which this paper presents, was carried out in support of a process of policy development. Its findings highlight a number of ways in which the system of health care finance influences the kinds of services to which the population has access.

6.1. Access to Medical Care

There is evidence that the level of charges deterred people from seeking hospital care, even when advised to do so by a doctor. This is one reason why there has been a considerable amount of interest in so-called "risk-type" local health insurance schemes in which households pay a fixed amount of money per person per year and are entitled to claim reimbursement for a percentage of hospital costs. A number of pilot projects have started by introducing this form of coverage with the intention of expanding to include outpatient care over time.

The study did not find that those who paid on a cash basis used less outpatient services. However, a number of households reported family members who did not seek care because of its cost. There is a belief among public health workers that primary health care services, including preventive programmes, have suffered with the collapse of the co-operative medical care scheme. Future studies will have to focus on specific indicators of access to curative and preventive services under the different

financing systems. Particular attention needs to be paid to vulnerable groups such as the poor, the chronically ill, and those living in remote villages. There is also a need for research on the role of local welfare funds in providing a safety net for poor households.

6.2. Incentives and Health Care Costs

A nation-wide survey is not a good instrument for assessing the effectiveness or efficiency of services. However, some of the findings suggest areas which require further study. For example, there was some evidence that the average cost of drugs per outpatient visit and inpatient stay was influenced by the system of finance of health services.

Drug sales are an important source of revenue for health facilities, accounting for over 75% of charges for outpatient care and 60% for inpatient treatment in the 1988 study. Their price included a 15% mark-up.

The surplus earned through the sale of drugs is an important source of income for doctors. Their base pay is low. The survey found that the average salary of a rural doctor was similar to the annual earnings of a peasant. However, the pay of all employees, including health workers, includes a bonus which is linked to the financial performance of their workplace. The greater the "profit" of a hospital or health centre, the larger the bonus which is paid. This provides a financial incentive for health workers to prescribe drugs. This is particularly the case for those rural doctors who do not receive any salary.

There are anecdotal reports of high levels of drug use in China. There is substantial use of injectable antibiotics, including gentamycin and kanamycin, by front-line health workers. This survey found that many health stations had stocks of over 200 different drugs. Any efforts to moderate the current rise in health care costs must address the question of drugs and the incentives which encourage high levels of use.

Where local health insurance schemes cover outpatient care and/or preventive services, the rural doctors usually receive at least a part of their income as salary. It is argued that this encourages greater attention to preventive and promotive activities. One interesting performance-related incentive was used by a scheme in Huarong County. Families paid an annual fee for children under 7 years old. This covered a full course of immunization. Part of the salary of the rural doctor was paid out of this fund. If a child was not fully immunized and contracted a preventible disease, the health station was liable for the cost of treatment. There is need for research on the impact of this and other payment systems on the effectiveness and efficiency of services which are provided.

6.3. The Development of Local Health Insurance Schemes

A number of pilot local insurance schemes have begun during the past few years. They differ considerably in the kind of care provided and the systems of management of health services. The next stage in policy development will combine the establishment of additional pilot schemes around the country with a systematic evaluation of current experiments. The aim is to develop guidelines which can be used by county health bureaux in the establishment of insurance schemes appropriate to local conditions.

The 1988 study found that the rural population in the more developed counties was provided with health care at a cost of less than 3% of the average per capita income of peasant households. The quality of the services provided and the access which was available to the poor need to be assessed further. However, the evidence suggests that it will be feasible to develop local insurance schemes to cover health care services in the richer counties.

The situation is less clear in the poorer areas. Rural households in region III spent, on average, almost 5% of their income on medical care in 1988. In spite of this, the rate of hospitalization was low and there was evidence of financial barriers to care. Villages and townships in the less developed areas run fewer non-agricultural enterprises than in the richer provinces. This means that they are more dependent on direct contributions from households to fund local health insurance schemes and welfare funds. It will be more difficult to design prepayment schemes in this region. There is a need for research to access the feasibility of funding the full range of rural health services out of village and township resources (or the need for some degree of subsidy) and to evaluate different models for financing medical care in these areas.

The "three-tier" rural health system in China greatly influenced the development of primary health care policy internationally. In the years which have followed the Alma Ata Declaration many countries have faced serious problems in financing the health sector. Lack of resources has become one of the greatest constraints to the provision of universal access to effective services and many experiments with different methods of revenue generation are presently under way [17–19]. That is why the current attempt to develop local health insurance schemes in rural China, now that production is no longer organized on a collective basis, is of such wide international interest.

REFERENCES

1. Chao Li-min, Gong You-long and Gu Shui-jiu. Financing the cooperative medical system. *AJPH* **72**, 78–80, 1982.
2. Jamison D. T. *et al. China the Health Sector.* World Bank Country Study, World Bank, Washington, 1984.
3. Sidel R. and Sidel V. W. *The Health of China: Current Conflicts in Medical and Human Services for One Billion People.* Beacon, Boston. 1984.
4. Halstead S. B., Walsh J. A. and Warren K. S. *Good Health at Low Cost.* Rockefeller Foundation, New York, 1985.
5. Chen Pi-Chao and Tuan Chi Hsien. Primary health care in rural China: post-1978 development. *Soc. Sci. Med.* **17**, 1411–1417, 1983.
6. Young M. E. Impact of the rural reform on financing rural health services in China. *Hlth Policy* **11**, 27–42, 1989.

7. Huang Shu-min. Transforming China's collective health care system: a village study. *Soc. Sci. Med.* **27,** 879–888, 1988.

8. Chinese Rural Health Care System Research Group (Eds). *Research on the Rural Health Care System in China.* Chinese language publication by Shanghai Science and Technology Press, Shanghai, 1991.

9. Ahmed E. and Hussain A. Social security in China: a historical perspective. In *Social Security in Developing Countries* (Edited by Ahmad E., Dréze J., Hills J. and Sen A.). WIDER Studies in Development Economics, Clarendon Press, Oxford, 1991.

10. Hussain A. and Liu H. Compendium of literature on the Chinese social security system. *Programme of Research into the Reform of Pricing and Market Structure in China,* CP No. 13. STICERD, London School of Economics, London, 1989.

11. Ron A., Abel-Smith B. and Tamburi G. *Health Insurance in Developing Countries.* International Labour Office, Geneva, 1990.

12. Berman P., Ormond B. and Gani A. Treatment, use and expenditure on curative care in rural Indonesia. *Hlth Policy Planning* **2,** 289–300, 1987.

13. Chernichovsky D. and Meesook O. A. Utilisation of health services in Indonesia. *Soc. Sci. Med.* **23,** 611–620, 1986.

14. Corbett J. E. M. Poverty and sickness: the high cost of ill-health. *IDS Bull.* **20,** 58–62, 1989.

15. Bloom G. Managing health sector development: markets and institutional reform. *Imperfect Markets or Imperfect States?* (Edited by Colclough C. and Manor J.). Oxford University Press, Oxford, 1991.

16. Bridgeman R. F. *Hospital Utilisation: An International Study.* Oxford University Press, Oxford, 1979.

17. Abel-Smith B. and Dua A. Community-financing in developing countries: the potential for the health sector. *Hlth Policy Planning* **3,** 95–108, 1988.

18. World Bank. *Financing Health Services in Developing Countries: An Agenda for Reform.* World Bank Policy Studies, World Bank, Washington, 1987.

19. WHO. *Economic Support for National Health for All Strategies.* WHO, Geneva, 1988.

COMPARATIVE HEALTH CARE SYSTEMS

The study of health care systems offers an opportunity to investigate on a macro level how all of the material covered in Chapters 1 through 12 "fits" and why. A comparative analysis of health care systems allows even greater analysis of those systems' similarities and differences as well as concomitant political and economic systems (see, for example, Ertler et al., 1987; Twaddle, 1996; van Atteveld, Broeders, and Lapre, 1987). It is within this framework that Chapter 13 is constructed. The articles in this chapter address the question of whether health care reform offers a positive or negative outcome for the particular country or level of development that is being investigated. As stated in Chapter 12, the issue of health care system convergence has received considerable attention as offering an alternative to the range of systems (entrepreneurial, social welfare, universal, and state sponsored) that currently exist.

The first article, by Karen Davis and colleagues, was written in the early 1990s and reflects the thinking of the time. The authors identify universal coverage as the ultimate goal of any reform effort, and they suggest an incremental approach. They identify a series of goals for the American health care system as well as recognizing that improved health care is not the only variable affecting people's lives.

Davis and her coauthors identify three possible directions for reform of the American health care system. The first would require employers to provide coverage to all employees (this is similar to President Bill Clinton's 1993 proposal). The second would encourage individuals to purchase health insurance. The third would expand Medic-aid coverage to the uninsured, who could buy into the system on a sliding scale. Although those proposals might increase the number of Americans who are covered by some form of health insurance, they are, as the authors state, incremental and in keeping with the supposed American belief in individual responsibility for health care.

In the second article, John Church and Paul Barker examine efforts to regionalize Canada's health care system. Historically, the Canadian health care system has been administered at the provincial level with funding coming from the federal and provincial governments. However, as the cost of health care continues to rise in Canada, proponents of a regionalized approach argue that greater emphasis should be given to preventive medicine and community-based services—in other words, to bringing health care closer to the people it serves and including them in the decision-making process.

Church and Barker identify five characteristics of regionalization and discuss the challenges it poses. The characteristics are governance at the regional level, global budgeting, shifting the delivery of health care services from an institutional to a community-based system, an evaluation process of health outcomes, and the reorganization of provincial health programs. The authors are critical of regionalization efforts because research (particularly from Europe) does not suggest that they will result in significant improvement of the health care delivery system. Thus, the authors warn, regionalization will not meet proponents' expectations for it.

The third article, by Kasturi Sen and Meri Koivusalo, is a critical examination of health care reform efforts aimed at developing nations by the

World Bank. The authors address three broad areas: (1) the historical context of health care within the developing world, (2) the linkage between economic policies and health care, and (3) the ideological implications of health care reform.

Sen and Koivusalo point out that developing nations are not homogeneous and do not have identical historical backgrounds. Nevertheless, many of them have been the victims of colonialism, and in the aftermath of colonial rule, health care opportunities for majority populations have not been forthcoming. Many developing countries are experiencing efforts to dismantle welfare state programs. In particular, in many places the health care sector is becoming increasingly privatized and expected to function within a market economy. The authors argue that there has been little understanding of the political and economic factors that influence the health care field.

Sen and Kiovusalo are highly critical of World Bank efforts to limit health care reforms within developing nations. They contend that, instead of addressing broad, systemwide reform efforts, the World Bank has attempted to limit reform to the poorest sectors of the population. They warn that such efforts will return many developing nations to a neocolonialism in which only a small percentage of the population will enjoy the best health care while the majority will continue to have little if any access to a health care system. Sen and Koivusalo argue that an effective health care system is one that covers the greatest number of people through a pooling of risks and resources.

The thread that binds the three articles in Chapter 13 is the question of how current health care systems can be improved. Here we see problems ranging from those affecting the most expensive health care system in the world (the U.S. system) to developing nations' attempts at system redesign to deliver effective health care services to the largest number of persons for the least amount of money and with the best health outcomes.

REFERENCES

Ertler, Wolfgang, Hannes Schmidl, Johannes M. Treytl, and Helmut Wintersberger. 1987. The Social Dimensions of Health and Health Care: An International Comparison. *Research in the Sociology of Health Care,* vol. 5, pp. 1–62.

Twaddle, Andrew W. 1996. Health Care Reforms—Toward a Framework for International Comparisons. *Social Science and Medicine,* vol. 43, no. 5, pp. 637–654.

van Atteveld, Lettie, Corine Broeders, and Ruud Lapre. 1987. International Comparative Research in Health Care: A Study of the Literature. *Health Policy,* vol. 8, pp. 105–136.

AMERICAN PERSPECTIVE

FUTURE DIRECTIONS FOR THE U.S. HEALTH CARE SYSTEM: A LONG-RANGE POLICY PROPOSAL

KAREN DAVIS, GERARD F. ANDERSON, DIANE ROWLAND, AND EARL P. STEINBERG

With few exceptions, efforts to contain health care costs have been fragmented and their effectiveness has been limited. In large part this reflects the structure of the U.S. health care financing system, with Medicare, Medicaid, and employer-provided health insurance each independently pursuing cost containment policies developed with their own interests in mind. This approach to cost containment has not succeeded in controlling health care costs. In addition, those suffering the brunt of this uncoordinated policy have been the uninsured and the poor, who have been discriminated against by a market-oriented health system.

Cost containment by insurers must be integrated into a unified policy in order to be effective. In addition, cost containment initiatives must be considered as part of a broader array of social goals—goals related to improving and maintaining the health of the public, access to care, quality of care, and commitment to excellence in research and technology. The following section sets forth a set of goals that should guide health care policy in the future. This is followed by a long-range policy proposal aimed at meeting multiple objectives for the health care system. This plan could be phased in over time as budget resources permit and as experience with each step is gained.

The primary advantage of an incremental approach is its adaptability to changing conditions in both the public and the private sector. It is especially well suited to the federal budget process, which constantly weighs competing budget priorities. New initiatives are feasible in a tight budget framework, but only if they are relatively modest in scope. Current programs are familiar to legislators, fall within clearly defined jurisdictional boundaries, and have advocates among members of authorizing committees. New programs, particularly those that are sweeping in nature, are too filled with uncertainty to prompt action on a tight legislative calendar.

There is, of course, a down side to an incremental approach. More attractive elements of a long-term package may be enacted first, leaving no momentum for further change. Administrative systems that maintain multiple programs may be more complex than a newly designed system. Tight cost control measures may also be more difficult to coordinate among multiple programs, which can be played off against each other by providers.

GOALS FOR THE U.S. HEALTH CARE SYSTEM

In a world of constrained resources, tradeoffs must be made among multiple goals. Resources for health care could alternatively be used to improve education, clean up our harbors, invest in major scientific research endeavors, or modernize the industrial plant and equipment. Workers who are busy building hospitals or health centers could be building roads or repairing bridges. Young people could be attracted into careers in science and engineering or education rather than nursing and medicine. As a society, we need to pose questions about whether we would be better off with a higher or lower share of our nation's resources going into the health sector.

Even if improving and maintaining the population's health is viewed as a top priority and worthy of considerable resources, questions need to be

raised about whether further investment in the health care sector yields the highest payoff in terms of improved health. Alternatively, the standard of living of the poor could be improved, resources could be invested in ensuring that everyone has an adequate diet, and housing, workplaces, and communities could be made safer and healthier places in which to live, work, and play. These uses of economic resources should be weighed against spending on hospital, physician, and other health care services.

Improving performance within the health care sector to achieve greater value in terms of health outcomes for the resources devoted to health care is an important overall goal. It should be recognized, however, that the pursuit of improved efficiency may sometimes conflict with the pursuit of improved health outcomes. A desire to control costs may compromise the goal of improving access to quality of care. Acceptability and freedom to choose among alternatives may also be in conflict with goals of limiting costs. Consequently, it is necessary to explicate those goals that most Americans value most highly and to evaluate the impact of alternative policy directions on those goals. As a starting point for such a process, we propose the following seven goals.

Goal 1. Reduce Preventable Mortality and Morbidity. The World Health Organization (WHO) has urged the adoption of "Health for all by the Year 2000" as a major goal of all countries. This goal calls for achieving the maximum attainable health and social well-being of the population. The United States, along with nations around the world, has committed itself to achieving major improvements in the health of the population by the end of the century. The U.S. commitment was embodied in the report of the Surgeon General entitled *Healthy People* and renewed in presentations before the World Health Assembly. In response to the WHO initiative, the United States has established goals of reducing preventable mortality and morbidity by establishing a set of health objectives to be achieved through improvements in lifestyles, reduction in occupational and environmental hazards, and accessibility of preventive health care services to the entire population.

Goal 2. Enhance the Quality of Life of All Individuals by Maintaining Their Functional Capacity as Long as Possible and by Relieving Avoidable Pain and Discomfort. As the population of the United States ages, more attention is being given to the quality of life at the end of the life span. Some health care conditions are terminal in nature and require primarily hospice care to relieve pain and assist the individual and his or her family in making the most of the time remaining. Other chronic conditions, such as Alzheimer's disease, lead to a slow deterioration in mental or physical functioning. For such conditions the primary goal should be to maintain functioning capacity as long as possible, to provide support for the patient and family, and to guarantee the patient and family control over major decisions affecting the nature of care (e.g., whether or not the patient should be placed in a nursing home or receive high-technology care).

Goal 3. Assure That No One Is Denied Health Care because of an Inability to Pay. One of the most important social goals we should try to achieve is to assure access to adequate health care services for the entire population. This is of particular importance for the most vulnerable members of society. The poor, for example, are unable to afford costly health care without assistance. An optimal health care system would assure that no one is turned away from care because of inability to pay or complex needs.

Goal 4. Assure That the Financial Burden of Health Care Expenses Is Equitably Distributed. No one should be required to pay health care bills that are high in relation to his or her family financial

resources. Catastrophic illness can pose a hardship for nearly everyone; even minor illnesses or accidents can result in serious financial hardship to the uninsured poor.

Goal 5.   *Promote Efficiency and Effectiveness in the Provision of Health Care Services.*   Despite the high expectations that Americans have for their health sector, they are also concerned with high outlays for health care. They would like to improve productivity and efficiency in the health sector by eliminating waste or unnecessary services and assuring that health benefits are received in proportion to money spent on health care. This requires a health systems approach to health care delivery.

Goal 6.   *Preserve or Enhance the Quality of Health Care.*   Americans have come to expect and demand high-quality health care. They expect their physicians to be dedicated, well trained, and highly qualified and to recommend a course of diagnosis and treatment that is in the patient's best interest. They expect hospitals and other health care facilities to be adequately equipped and staffed with qualified trained personnel and to be committed to the delivery of appropriate care. Americans also desire continued technological progress and breakthroughs in biomedical research.

Goal 7.   *Maintain the Right of Individuals to Make Choices Individually or Collectively through a Democratic Political Process.*   Individual rights are an integral part of American culture. Americans expect to be informed about choices affecting their lives and well-being and to have a say in those decisions. They feel strongly about the right to choose their own physician or health delivery system and to vote with their feet if they are dissatisfied with the care or advice they receive. Just as individuals want the right to make individual choices, they expect the right to make some decisions on a collective basis through a democratic political process.

CHOOSING AMONG ALTERNATIVES

Clearly, it is unrealistic to expect to achieve all of these social goals. Therefore, a mechanism needs to be devised to evaluate policy alternatives with these social goals in mind and to resolve inherent conflicts between individual goals. While different individuals may weigh the importance of these goals differently, a thorough analysis of policy options should define the impact of the options on access, equity, health, quality of life, quality of care, progress, and free choice, as well as the implications for the cost of care and its distribution among alternative sources of financing. In addition, policy alternatives should be evaluated in terms of the following criteria.

Effectiveness in Containing Costs.   Any policy proposal should be evaluated with a clear understanding of its costs, including additional real economic resources that must be diverted to the health sector and the budgetary costs to different levels of government. Estimates should also be available on costs shifted from the public sector to the private sector, or the reverse, and any change in cost to different individuals. Estimates of economic and budgetary costs should be available both for the point of implementation and over time.

Acceptability.   Policy options must be acceptable to patients, health care providers, and those who pay for health care services received by others. If policy options are to be viable in the long term, they need to correspond with patient expectations. The initiatives need to be simple enough to be easily understood. Similarly, physicians and other health care providers need to find policy options that are acceptable in order to avoid mass opposition or boycotting of a program.

Administrative Feasibility.   Any policy option should be relatively easy to administer. Simplicity is desirable, both for ease of understanding and for administrative purposes.

Political Feasibility. Finally, policy options need to be able to elicit political support from major interest groups—labor, business, insurance, physicians, hospitals, and consumer groups such as senior citizens' organizations and advocacy groups. Political support from all geographical regions is important, as is support from state and local government officials. While a consensus of all parties is extraordinarily difficult to obtain, accommodation to major concerns can help mitigate opposition.

A LONG-RANGE POLICY PROPOSAL

The long-range policy proposal presented here is concerned equally with assuring health insurance coverage of the entire population and containing health care costs. It has two major components: (1) universal health insurance coverage; and (2) reform of the health care system through greater coordination and equalization of provider payment among Medicare, Medicaid, and private insurance plans and greater emphasis on incentives for efficiency through promotion of HMOs.

HEALTH CARE INSURANCE COVERAGE

The central element of the long-range policy proposal is universal health insurance coverage through expansions in coverage under existing public and private health insurance plans. This coverage may be obtained through different approaches. The first approach is to require employers to cover employees and their dependents through private group health insurance plans. The second approach involves greater incentives for the purchase of private health insurance, such as eliminating excessive mandated requirements, encouraging the establishment of insurance pools with broadly based financing, including contributions by self-insured employers, and provision of vouchers to permit the uninsured to purchase private health insurance. The third approach involves public programs that would, for example, cover all

elderly and disabled under Medicare, cover all poor under Medicaid, and give any otherwise uninsured person the option of buying Medicaid coverage or coverage from an insurance pool on a sliding-scale contributory basis. Given political and economic constraints, a mixed public–private approach with a combination of these options is probably the most viable. These options could be designed as follows.

Option 1. Employer Mandate

Coverage of all full-time workers and their dependents under employer health plans could be required by law, and minimum benefit standards would be prescribed. Standards could apply to all firms, whether they elected to self-insure or to purchase coverage through health insurers. Specific elements include the following:

Eligibility. Employers would be required to cover all their full-time employees, as well as the employees' spouses and dependents. No worker or dependent could be denied coverage, nor could preexisting conditions be excluded from coverage.

Extension of Coverage. Coverage would begin upon employment and would continue at least ninety days after termination of employment, or after the death of a worker or divorce of a worker and spouse. During this postemployment period the employer would continue to share in the premium cost. Employees and their dependents would be given the right to continue coverage at group rates after this period for as long as they chose to pay the full group premium cost plus an administrative fee.

Benefits. The minimum benefit package would include inpatient hospital services, physician services, and prenatal, delivery, and infant care. Employers could provide a broader benefit package, but not less than the minimum.

Catastrophic Coverage. Proposed employer plans could include patient deductibles and coinsurance (with the exception of maternal and infant care), but cost sharing for a family would be subject to a ceiling not exceeding a certain level. Annual deductibles and coinsurance rates would be limited.

Choice of an HMO or PPO. All qualified employer plans would be required to give employees and their dependents a choice of enrollment in any federally qualified HMO or other case-managed approaches, such as PPOs, when those are available in the community, elect to be offered, and are administratively feasible for employers to provide.

Financing. Employers would be required to pay a specific percentage of premium costs for the mandated plan. Higher employer premium shares could, of course, be provided. Today, more than 85 percent of workers with employer-financed insurance are covered by plans in which the employer pays at least 75 percent of the premium. Any employer whose premium contribution for a minimum plan exceeds 5 percent of payroll would be eligible to purchase Medicaid coverage for the minimum benefit package at a premium contribution not to exceed 5 percent of payroll.

Administration. Employer plans would be federally qualified. Penalties would be assessed for misrepresentation or nonconformance with federal standards.

Reinsurance. Employer plans, HMOs, and PPOs would be eligible to buy reinsurance protection against the costs of truly extraordinary illness (over $25,000 per covered person) through insurance companies.

Option 2. Incentives for Private Health Insurance

Individuals would be encouraged to purchase health insurance from private insurance companies. Excessive regulatory requirements, which now make private insurance too costly, would need to be eliminated, and better tax incentives or other forms of financing would be necessary to expand coverage of the uninsured. Specific elements of this approach include the following:

- Elimination of state-mandated health benefits
- Establishment of state risk pools with broadly based financing, including contributions from self-insured employers
- One hundred percent tax deductibility of health insurance premiums for the self-employed
- Vouchers for the purchase of private health insurance subsidized by state or federal tax revenues

Under the voucher plan, premiums would be subsidized for low-income persons, and changes in the tax code would be used to finance a part of the cost. Specifically, the approach would include the following provisions:

Eligibility. Participants would be expected to purchase health insurance through the private insurance sector.

Benefits. A minimum benefits package would be established by federal legislation. It would include specific benefits such as inpatient hospital services, physician services, and prenatal, delivery, and infant care or the actuarial equivalent.

Choice of an HMO or PPO. Participants would have the option of using vouchers to enroll in an HMO or PPO.

Financing. Participants would receive a tax rebate for heath insurance. Rebates for singles and families would differ but would not be tied to income or how tax deductions are calculated. Participants with an income below a certain threshold would receive a federal subsidy to purchase health insurance.

Administration. The program would be administered by the federal government. Minimum benefits would be assigned by the Department of Health and Human Services, and compliance would be monitored by the Internal Revenue Service. States would ensure that public and private insurance options were available to their residents.

Reinsurance. Insurers could reinsure.

Option 3. Medicaid

The Medicaid program would be expanded to provide acute health care benefits to the entire population falling outside employer-mandated coverage and Medicare coverage. Medicaid would be a secondary payer for individuals covered under employer plans or Medicare.

Eligibility. All individuals whose income fell below the federal poverty level could be automatically covered under Medicaid. Coverage would be independent of assets. Categorical restrictions would be removed so that single individuals and childless couples would be covered. Medicaid acute-care benefits would also be available to others not eligible for coverage under employer plans in exchange for a premium set on a sliding scale with income. The premium would range from zero for those below the federal poverty level to 100 percent of the actuarial value of the Medicaid acute-care benefit package for those with incomes more than twice the federal poverty level.

Benefits. The Medicaid program would cover the current acute-care mandatory benefits plus prescription drugs, without arbitrary limits on amount, duration, or scope of benefits. Unnecessary use of services would be discouraged through utilization review and prior authorization provisions. For individuals purchasing coverage with a sliding-scale premium, modest cost-sharing provisions could be included. Health care providers would be paid at a level comparable to that under Medicare.

Financing and Administration. The net new costs of expanded Medicaid coverage would be met through federal general revenues. States, however, could continue to contribute a uniform, but lower, matching rate for all Medicaid beneficiaries. Administration of coverage for new beneficiaries would be handled through state Medicaid administrative procedures.

HEALTH SYSTEM REFORM

The second portion of the proposed plan involves changing the methods of paying hospitals, physicians, and HMOs and implementing other measures to promote enrollment in HMOs and PPOs.

Provider Payment Reform

Major reforms in current methods of paying hospitals, physicians, and HMOs would be implemented. Medicaid payment rules would follow those of Medicare, with state waivers for states that can meet performance criteria, including comparability between levels of Medicare and Medicaid payment. Employer plans would follow Medicare payment principles or an approved alternative that meets comparability criteria.

Hospitals. The DRG PPS for hospitals under Medicare would be retained and improved. Major modifications in the current system would include:

- A formula for establishing increases in PPS rates or establishment of three-year rates of increase by statute
- Incorporating an adjustment in payment rates based on the severity of cases in order to reimburse hospitals more appropriately for very expensive patients
- Refinements to the method of financing medical education, biomedical research, and technology diffusion.

- Incorporating an additional percentage allowance in the DRG payment rate to cover the cost of capital
- Encouraging states to institute or maintain their own all-payer hospital prospective payment systems, meeting the tests of generating at least the same level of budgetary savings as the DRG PPS and assuring equity among payers
- Medicare hospital payment provisions for Medicaid, with the relative DRG prospective payment rates and levels adjusted to reflect the resource cost of caring for the nonelderly Medicaid population

Physicians. Physicians would be paid according to a fee schedule under Medicare and Medicaid. The determination of a method of establishing relative values should be postponed pending further research and analysis of alternatives. The level of the fee schedule would be set to achieve approximately the same level of public expenditure as would be achieved without the change; that is, it would generate neither budgetary savings nor costs. Annual increases in the fee schedule would be pegged to achieve increases in total physician expenditures no greater than preset targets.

HMOs. Medicare, Medicaid, and employer plans would be encouraged to offer enrollees a choice of federally qualified HMOs if they are locally available. Federal qualification standards would be strengthened and closely monitored to ensure quality of care and fiscal soundness. Specific requirements include:

- Freedom of choice between health services provided on a fee-for-service basis and HMOs for all Medicare and Medicaid beneficiaries
- Multiple capitated plans wherever possible, with no more than half of the enrollees in any plan drawn from a single payer source

- A minimum benefit package including the services required in the employer minimum health benefit plans
- That all HMOs and insurance plans offer an open enrollment period
- Clear, objective, and comprehensive information on the various options to be provided by employers, unions, government, or whoever is providing services
- That HMO capitation payment rates be derived from anticipated health expenditures based on enrollee health status, but premiums paid by enrollees must not vary with health status
- Federal certification of HMOs based on quality of care and financial soundness criteria

EVALUATION OF THE PROPOSAL

This plan has several key characteristics:

- It is designed to make major gains in the achievement of the goals set forth above.
- It is a pluralistic plan with opportunities for the federal government, states, and the private sector to design health plans meeting their own special needs.
- It is incremental in nature but presents a vision of the ultimately desired system.
- It assumes that implementation of the long-range policy proposal will be achieved in phases over time rather than through a single legislative measure.

The criteria of administrative and political feasibility, in particular, rule out the wholesale adoption of health financing systems from other countries in favor of a mixed public–private system. It assumes that health care services in the United States will continue to be provided predominantly by private nonprofit or for-profit organizations and that patients will continue to have the option of selecting from a mix of FFS and prepaid modes of practice.

This proposal primarily emphasizes reform of health care financing, including health insurance coverage for all; coordinated methods of paying physicians, hospitals, and other health care providers; and incentives to reform the organization and delivery of health care services to promote efficiency and quality of care.

The proposal would contribute to improving the health of the population by removing financial barriers to medical care and increasing funding for prevention and primary care. Maternity and infant care services would be covered without cost sharing for those covered by both employer plans and Medicaid. Improved access to acute care for the uninsured would improve health and give children a better chance for a productive life.

Universal access to health care services would be guaranteed through coverage of the entire population under employer health plans, other private health insurance plans or pools, Medicare, or Medicaid. Employer plans, HMOs, and PPOs would not be permitted to exclude high-risk individuals or to charge them higher premiums.

The proposal would lead to a more equitable distribution of the financial burden of health care expenses. Maximum out-of-pocket ceilings on health care expenses would be instituted in all plans. Incentives to control costs and improve efficiency would be provided through numerous provider payment and system reform provisions. Quality standards would be developed and monitored through Medicare, Medicaid, HMOs, and PPOs. Provider payment rates would be set to ensure continued room for technological progress and development. Individuals would be given information and choices among alternative health plans.

Precise cost estimates of the long-range proposal are not now available. Cost estimates of proposals for mandating universal health insurance coverage under all three options would depend upon the specific features of each proposal. Mandating employer health insurance coverage is likely to cost employers on the order of $25–35 billion in 1990, depending on the benefit package and employer premium share. The option of encouraging the purchase of private health insurance through the provision of vouchers could cost federal or state governments $10–20 billion, depending upon the generosity of the vouchers. Federal tax relief could be generated to offset this cost by changing the tax treatment of fringe benefits. The option of expanding Medicaid coverage to the poor and subsidizing Medicaid coverage of the near-poor could cost $10–15 billion in federal and state outlays. These new public or private outlays could be offset in part by provider payment reform and incentives for improved efficiency in the health care system.

The long-range policy proposal builds on current programs and continues current administrative mechanisms. For example, state agencies would continue to have responsibility for enrolling the poor in Medicaid. Policy regarding provider payment would be established by intermediaries under Medicare. Some new administrative mechanisms would need to be established, however, to monitor the quality of care and fiscal soundness of a greater variety of health plans. More individuals would become eligible under Medicaid, and many smaller employers would be required to provide health insurance to workers and dependents for the first time.

The long-range policy proposal can be expected to have significant political support and opposition. It would ensure new revenues for the health sector through expanded insurance coverage. This should prove attractive to the hospital sector and certain groups of physicians, especially newly trained physicians. Primary care physicians should welcome the new physician payment reform; but it could prove threatening to surgeons and other specialty physicians, depending on how relative values are established. It should receive support from consumer groups and labor. Small

businesses may be concerned by the new proposed administrative and financial burdens. The insurance industry should be supportive of those approaches that expand employer-based coverage and yet preserve a role for small group and individual health insurance coverage, while leaving primary responsibility for coverage of the poor and near-poor to an expanded Medicaid program. Recognition of the problems of the uninsured, poor children and women, and the low-income elderly is growing and should increase broad public support; however, substantial federal budget deficits limit the political feasibility of any approach that requires major increases in government outlays.

The political feasibility of the proposal could be improved by a phased implementation. Modest incremental improvements in public programs and private insurance plans could be made. Experience with these changes could be obtained before moving on to the next phase. For example, it is possible to begin by expanding Medicaid coverage for those with an income below 75 percent of the poverty level, then to expand coverage for those with an income below 100 percent of the poverty level, and

then to relax the assets test. Employer plan standards could first be applied to larger firms or modified with smaller employer premium contributions. Provider payment reform provisions could be phased in gradually, gaining experience with each successive round of legislation. It is extremely desirable, however, that such a phased-in approach move each component of the proposal forward in each phase. Otherwise politically popular elements will be enacted first and no action will be taken on the more controversial elements.

A long-range policy proposal, regardless of its ultimate shape, would greatly improve the health policy deliberation process. The current system of relying on year-to-year changes in health financing programs without any consensus on a longer-range plan leads to gimmickry and instability in the health system. It gives undue weight to the fiscal objective of cutting budgetary outlays instead of basing health policy on social goals to be achieved by the health sector. It is hoped that this long-range policy proposal will facilitate informed debate leading to such a consensus.

DEVELOPED WORLD PERSPECTIVE

REGIONALIZATION OF HEALTH SERVICES IN CANADA: A CRITICAL PERSPECTIVE

JOHN CHURCH AND PAUL BARKER

Since the introduction of universal health insurance in Canada in the late 1960s, both federal and provincial governments have been attempting to reform the Canadian health care system. Over the past 25 years, a plethora of royal commissions and task forces have recommended a range of options for achieving this objective, and most recently all provincial governments have undertaken close examinations of their health care plans. Calls for reform have been fueled by steadily rising costs and

the perceived implications of changing demographics. Concern with equitable access to care, both in geographic and cultural terms, has also played a part in the evolving health care reform agenda, and questions about the extent to which physicians and hospital care are efficacious have been asked.

Central to past and current reform proposals has been a belief that a *regional* health care system will function in a more efficient and responsive

fashion. Though somewhat ill-defined in the literature, regionalization generally means an organizational arrangement involving the creation of an intermediary administrative and governance structure to carry out functions or exercise authority previously assigned to either central or local structures. According, regionalization may entail the shifting of responsibility for public health from a series of local boards to a regional agency, or a general devolution of power from a central governing agency to regional bodies. In many cases, such as in Canada, regionalization efforts include both upward and downward movements of authority and responsibility. For its supporters, a regionalized health care system addresses most of the major problems now associated with health care. The centralization of power in regional structures, for instance, facilitates both the better coordination of services and the realization of economies of scale. It may also make possible a greater equity in the delivery of services and allow for a more coherent budgetary process and the prudent containment of health care expenditures. Alternatively, the devolution or centralization of some responsibilities increases the chances that health programs will be more sensitive to local needs and provides an avenue for citizen participation in health care decision-making (1–4).

In Canada, provincial governments are responsible for health care, and nearly all of them— Ontario is the only exception—have introduced regional structures for health services. The hope, of course, is that such action will allow provincial health care plans to realize the benefits of regionalization and thereby effect health care systems that are efficient, fair, and responsive. But it is not clear that this will necessarily occur. Notwithstanding the alleged benefits of regionalization, some challenges face this particular approach to health care reform. A number of obstacles stand in the way of any attempt to integrate and coordinate health services. Achieving economies of scale for all services included within regional arrangements may

be difficult. Regionalization arrangements also require a level of information for administrative purposes that may be difficult to achieve, and experience suggests that regionalization can fail to involve citizens in health care decision-making. Finally, regionalization may actually exacerbate— not ameliorate—the problem of high health care expenditures.

The intent of this article is to examine the regionalization efforts in the various provinces of Canada. We review the forces behind the movement toward regionalization and discuss the various approaches to this reform. More important, we assess the challenges that confront efforts at regionalization and conclude that provincial governments should reconsider their commitment to the regionalization of health care services.

ORIGINS OF REGIONALIZATION

The history of the development of health care policy in Canada is well chronicled (5,6). The system that emerged from two decades of federal–provincial negotiations altered the means by which health care services were funded, but did not significantly affect the way in which service delivery was organized. Politicians and other interests have now moved to alter this situation as the incongruity between the new financing regime and the old organizational configuration has become increasingly apparent.

Over the past decade the provinces have sponsored a series of commissions, task forces, and public forums directed at reforming the health system (7). What is significant about these provincial reports is the consistency in the message across jurisdictions and in relationship to reports of the 1970s. The reports emphasize the following themes: containing costs, increasing the efficiency and effectiveness of health care, enhancing the responsiveness and accountability of the system through decentralized decision-making, and facilitating citizen participation.

The high cost of provincial health plans has been a major concern of provincial governments. The various reports and studies sometimes play down this problem, perhaps to allay fears that any possible reforms are reduced to a cost-cutting exercise, but clearly public officials are troubled by the level of health expenditures and the rapidity with which they have risen in the past decade and a half. An Ontario report, for example, points to "the rapid escalation of health care costs" (8, pp. 85–86), and separate studies on health plans in the three prairie provinces emphasize the high level of health care spending (9–11).

A further concern of the various reports on the plans is that existing services fail to improve sufficiently the health status of health care users. The authors of a government report on health care in Saskatchewan write: "We can spend our province's health dollars more effectively by reallocating funds to a broader range of activities proven to contribute to health" (12, pp. 8–9). Similarly, in Nova Scotia a ministerial committee concludes: "Years of study have shown that Nova Scotians need a system that promotes health rather than only responds to illness" (13, pp. 12–13). To enhance the effectiveness of provincial health programs, it is contended that more emphasis needs to be placed on prevention and community-based services and, more generally, that a full range of care—from the hospital at one end to home services at the other— must be established (9; 14, pp. 36–37).

The problem of efficacy in turn is related to other failings of provincial health plans. One is the absence of a coordinated and integrated approach to the provision of health services. A British Columbia royal commission on health care captures part of this problem when it notes that ministries of health engage in "vertical line management," which involves various programs operating in isolation from one another (15, pp. B40-B41). Another obstacle to coordinated planning concerns the numerous boards, agencies, and service providers responsible for the actual delivery of services (9).

As noted in a Quebec report, this situation amounts to a "maze" which frustrates not only integration efforts but also efforts to gain access to the most efficacious care (16, p. 18).

Ineffective health care also stems from the absence of local participation in health care decision-making. "There is a need for effective community participation in the design and delivery of local health services," say observers of the Saskatchewan health system (12, p. 9). An Ontario study comes to a similar conclusion: "decisions about health and social services are usually made by relatively few people, with little chance for participation by those whom the decisions affect" (17, p. 3). Some provincial health studies have also uncovered an element of unfairness. Though Medicare seeks to equalize access to health care, it does not always succeed. Certain groups—the less well off, aboriginal peoples, visible minorities—and specific regions are not provided the kind of access to health services available to others (18,19). The reports offer few details on this issue, but it is safe to conclude that the concern revolves around the negative impact of non-price factors on the aforementioned groups and regions (e.g., opportunity costs of seeking care, language problems, level of education, cultural differences) (20,21).

A final problem, one implicit in most reports and explicit in a few, is a general failure on the part of most governments to recognize adequately that provincial plans are now entering into a new stage of development, a stage that requires significant change. In the past, provincial plans have been premised on the notion that health ministries passively fund the services offered by physicians and hospitals. Under such a system, the aim was largely to remove financial barriers to traditional health care services. But now plans must become more aggressive in their management of health care. No longer can provincial governments just finance the activities of health care suppliers; they must also become actively involved in how and what services are to be provided (12, p. 5).

While a variety of treatments have been suggested for what ails the health care system, regional decision-making structures to manage and coordinate the delivery of all or most health services have emerged as the most popular remedy. Regional structures, it is argued, offer a greater opportunity for the citizenry to play a role in health care, and they also promise a health system more sensitive to local needs because of their proximity to users. Costs, too, will purportedly come under greater control, and the overall allocation of health resources will reveal, under regionalization, a greater appreciation of the needs of the population.

CHARACTERISTICS OF REGIONALIZATION (22,23)

Regionalization as a concept is open to a broad scope of interpretation. This is reflected in the variety of approaches that have evolved in Canada during the past two decades. As might be expected, the provinces have attempted to restructure their health care systems in the light of their own specific needs and limits. Nevertheless, some common characteristics can be discerned in the various regionalization efforts. A first characteristic is the creation of regional governance and management bodies composed of either appointed officials or a combination of appointed and elected officials. The new structures also entail a significant consolidation of existing board and management structures. In Saskatchewan, the 127 hospital boards, 133 nursing home boards, 45 home care boards, and 108 ambulance boards have been folded into the regional structure, and a similar consolidation has taken place in British Columbia, Alberta, Quebec, and Nova Scotia. The general aim is to effect a centralization of governance so as to facilitate coordination and planning at the regional level.

A few provinces have decided to proceed with unique arrangements. In Quebec, for example, legislation makes provision for a regional health structure which includes an elected Regional Assembly and a Regional Health and Social Services Board. New Brunswick and Newfoundland have established regional arrangements specifically for hospital care, and Newfoundland has done the same for community-based services. In Ontario, provision was made for a regional-like arrangement for long-term care services based in the community, but this was not implemented because of a change in government (22).

A second characteristic shared by most regional structures is some form of global budgeting at the regional level. This amounts to the transfer of a conditional grant from the provinces to regional authorities, with the latter being responsible for disbursing the funds to the relevant providers and organizations. In most provinces, the conditions are to be kept to a minimum, and indeed the aim often is to provide the regional authorities with an "envelope" of money that can be used in a manner deemed most appropriate by the authorities. Here, for example, is the arrangement envisioned for British Columbia: "The Boards will receive a global budget from the Ministry of Health for health services in the region, which in turn, they will allocate to the Councils" (18, p. i). In general, infusing all provincial reports and legislation is the idea of ministries providing regional health authorities with a set amount of money to be used in a manner consistent with broad provincial standards.

In addition to consolidating the existing budgets for a variety of health care services under a single regional budget envelope, most provinces are also attempting to develop a new funding formula that applies various indices of relative need (e.g., standardized mortality ratios, prevalence of marriage) to regional allocations adjusted for age and sex (24). The intention is to gear funding toward the needs of regional populations and to achieve a more equitable distribution of resources. To date, Saskatchewan is the furthest along in this aspect, having introduced a needs-based funding formula covering programs that constitute 60 percent of the budgets of the newly created districts.

A third characteristic inherent in current reforms is the shift in emphasis from institutional settings to community-based settings for delivery of services. This shift reflects both the desire to contain costs in the institutional sector and an increased recognition that institutionally delivered services are not necessarily as cost-effective as community-based service delivery. The belief is that regional structures are best suited to effect such a shift in the orientation of the health system because they allow decision-makers to move resources from one program to another without having to deal with traditional professional and organizational barriers.

A fourth characteristic underlying the current reforms is the desire to evaluate the types of outcomes that are produced by health services—a change from the previous focus on the various inputs into the system. Once developed, regional service and human resource plans based on an assessment of community needs will serve as a basis for resource allocation decisions and evaluation of outcomes. For example, regions in Quebec are required to develop regional service plans under five key program headings: social adaptation (child abuse, violence, delinquency), public health, physical health (low birth weight, cardiovascular disease, cancer), mental health (suicide, depression), and social integration (handicapped persons, elderly). Thus far, plans for only the mental health program area have been developed (25).

A fifth and final characteristic common to most reform initiatives is the downsizing and restructuring of provincial departments. Most provincial reports envision a clear devolution of responsibility from provincial health ministries to the regional authorities. For example, Saskatchewan and Alberta are divesting responsibilities and personnel for mental health, communicable disease control, public health and home care. Prince Edward Island has gone even further by establishing an interim provincial Crown agency with an appointed board of directors to coordinate the restructuring of the system. As the new regional structures are developed, personnel from both the department and the agency will be devolved to the regional boards.

All this does not mean the end of the provincial ministries of health and their ministers. The intention behind the restructuring of provincial departments is to position the province for providing administrative support to the regional structures and to emphasize an overall quality assurance as opposed to service delivery role. Thus, in all provinces that have adopted regional structures, the ministry continues to have responsibility for developing broad health priorities and ensuring that regional health authorities comply with provincial standards.

CHALLENGES OF REGIONALIZATION

Although the majority of provinces appear committed to the implementation of some form of regional health system, decision-makers face considerable challenges. These include (a) integration and coordination of the administration and delivery of services, (b) consolidation of funding, (c) development of an information infrastructure and measurement indicators that allow for outcome-based evaluation, and (d) creation of mechanisms that provide for citizen participation while at the same time limiting the tendency toward domination by purely local and/or professional interests.

Integration of Administration and Service Delivery

To date, regionalization efforts have strongly emphasized the consolidation of decision-making concerning the planning and allocation of health resources through the creation of new intermediary government structures. This is usually accompanied by the amalgamation and/or closure of local facilities and disbanding of existing local governance structures. Most provinces also intend to con-

solidate the financing of health services through some sort of regional budget. Taken together, these changes amount to a significant centralization of decision-making authority and a consolidation of previously fragmented local resources.

According to health care reformers, a unified administrative structure enhances the ability to shift funds across service delivery sectors and instills a sense of systemwide thinking among planners and providers of health services (26, p. 11). An integrated regional approach also recognizes that local communities, because of their sensitivity to local conditions, are best suited to determine the nature and scope of the services they receive.

A fundamental issue underlying the regional integration of the planning and management of services is determining the optimal size for the most efficient service delivery. The current reforms are based in part on the belief that economies of scale can be realized by managing and providing services through larger units. This suggests that outputs of a particular service can be maintained or enhanced while inputs are decreased. The evidence for the economies of scale argument, though, is mixed and incomplete (27), as is evidence about potential cost savings. As Bish and Ostrom suggest: "economies of scale vary among the different services supplied in the public sector. Some services are more efficiently produced by large jurisdictions; others are more efficiently produced by smaller units" (28, p. 78). The point here is that size is a function of the characteristics of particular services, not the other way around. For example, a study of the effects of regionalization on local government services in Ontario indicates that hard services, such as water and sewage treatment, are more likely to achieve economies of scale when provided by larger units. However, the regionalization of soft services, such as policing and social services, which tend to be labor intensive, is less likely to produce economies of scale (29). More relevant to this article, past reviews of the system-level integration of hospital services in the United States have failed to support the contention that integration leads to economies of scale, greater efficiency in service delivery (e.g., lower cost per adjusted admission), or improved patient outcomes (30–33).

Admittedly, some evidence has surfaced to suggest that while costs may actually increase through integration, quality may improve as well (34). For instance, certain but not all procedures (e.g., open-heart surgery) have better outcomes when performed in increased volume (35). Regionalization may also have the potential to eliminate simple duplication and overlap in service provision. But the fact remains that substantial uncertainty surrounds the claim that significant benefits attend the merging of all health services. Some medical procedures have failed to demonstrate significant financial or quality improvement benefits through consolidation (36). At a minimum, regionalization arrangements have to recognize that, given the varied nature of services, it is inadvisable to assume that cost savings and improved quality will flow from consolidation efforts.

The question of size in general involves the issue of whether the regions as geographically defined units have populations of sufficient size to realize significant economies of scale. In Europe, the regions encompass densely populated, geographically defined areas serving populations of 150,000 to over a million residents. In Canada, though, only a handful of metropolitan areas fall into this population range. Quebec and Nova Scotia appear to be the only provinces to address the size issue. In Quebec, regional populations average 250,000 residents. In Nova Scotia, current plans recommend the creation of regions with a minimum of 150,000 residents. In Alberta, on the other hand, regional populations range from 15,000 to 754,000 residents, with the majority having a population base of less than 100,000 residents. Saskatchewan appears to have gone in the opposite direction to Quebec and Nova Scotia in assigning regional health authorities responsibility for planning and

managing the provision of a varying range of health services for an average of 15,000 citizens. All in all, regional populations in Canada might be too small to achieve any real economies of scale or to more generally effect a coordination of health services.

A related problem, defined in the literature (37, pp. 104–105) and becoming evident in some Canadian jurisdictions, is how to create regions that are large enough to be self-contained—that is, how to prevent the transfer of costs from one region to another through cross-boundary patient traffic or deliberate externalization of costs. One possible solution is to create very large regions based on historical trade and health utilization patterns. However, in most Canadian jurisdictions the establishment of regional boundaries has been based as much on political considerations as on any other criteria. While presumably the introduction of a population-based funding model will ensure that resources are distributed according to the needs of the identified service population (including cross-boundary traffic), this creates a further political problem—particularly in rural regions, which export large numbers of patients to major urban centers. Already in Alberta, the current boundaries appear to be unraveling as communities in some of the smaller regions outside major urban centers attempt to join the larger regions (38,39).

Underlying such difficulties is the explicit goal of better coordinating the administration and delivery of health care services. Coordination is often viewed as a means of enhancing "the efficiency and effectiveness in service delivery through changes in organizational or administrative arrangements" (40, p. 21). The ability to achieve this objective is fraught with organizational, conceptual, and administrative difficulties. For example, a variety of organizational and professional interests interact in the process of policy reform. While the various actors may reach a general consensus on the need for system reform, there may be significant differences in opinion on the exact nature of the changes. Each actor is interested in maintaining or furthering its position in the system. The natural outcome of this process is often "straightforward power struggles over control, priorities or resources" (41, p. 389). Experience in Quebec suggests that the outcomes of these power struggles usually favor institutional over community-based actors.

If cooperation is not forthcoming from these interests, the implementation of meaningful change will be difficult. It will require complex discussions on matters of remuneration, scope of practice, and role substitution in a restructured system. Ultimately, while governments may be successful in changing the organizational structures, they must also overcome the dominant way of thinking and supplant this with a new corporate culture (31). The compatibility of institutional and community-based cultures is still open to debate. Without change in these areas, a shift from institutionally based to community-based service delivery may not result in better outcomes. At present neither the federal government nor the provincial governments appear to have a clear definition of what constitutes a community-based service. They seem to be relying on individual regional authorities to define what constitutes community-based services. Hardly a promising start to shifting the emphasis in the system.

Added to the challenge of achieving a consensus among health care stakeholders are the system's size and complexity and the costs already sunk in the system. For example, what happens to excess capital (buildings and equipment) in a publicly funded health care system? If decision-makers attempt to sell the excess capacity to private sector providers, they run the risk of undermining the public ethos of the health care system. If they do nothing, authorities are left with empty and sometimes relatively new facilities.

Consolidation of Funding

The move to global budgeting at the regional level may in itself be problematic. In the past, global

budgeting has been used as a means of controlling costs, but this has been achieved in a selective fashion (i.e., for hospital services). Including all health services under some sort of regional global budget may be unrealistic for several reasons. As discussed above, differing economies of scale may make the inclusion of all health services under a single budget unworkable. Certain specialty services having boundaries coterminous with the province will likely have to remain the responsibility of some sort of provincial agency.

A second challenge to global budgeting relates to the previously discussed externality problem. To be truly efficient, global budgeting will require some means for regions to charge-back services provided to residents from other regions. Unless patients are limited to receiving basic health services within a limited geographic area, charge-back arrangements could potentially apply to all health services, implying a potential increase in transaction costs (42, p. 38). The two major urban regions in Alberta have already suggested that they may levy surcharges on residents from surrounding regions who access services within their boundaries. Recently, one of these urban regions ran into a serious budget shortfall, only two months into the fiscal year, because the province did not calculate into the region's budget allocation the costs of providing services to patients from outside the region over the past two years (43).

A further challenge is that all proposed regional budgets exclude drug and physician expenditures. Given that both areas are important sources of increasing health costs, the exclusion of these potential "cost drivers" could hinder the ability of regional decision-makers to control costs and plan for the efficient allocation of resources. If a region wanted to develop a less costly and potentially more effective network of community-based services by using nurse practitioners instead of physicians, it could not do so without control over physician numbers. Nor will a region be able to control the tendency of fee-for-service practice to influence demand unless physician payments are included in regional budgetary considerations.

Even if all health services planning, delivery, and financing are integrated at the regional level, past evidence from Canada and Europe indicates that health care expenditures are best controlled by strengthening the hand of third-party payers or central political authorities. In Canada's case, the ability of provincial governments to act as single-source financiers of health care has been instrumental in achieving any success in cost-containment, and there is a fear that the decentralization of fiscal responsibility inherent in regionalization may actually result in an increase in health care costs (44).

Proponents of regionalization efforts in Canada might argue that envelopes constitute a form of closed-budget funding and, accordingly, that costs can be controlled. But experience with envelope systems in Canada suggests that the very shifting downward of responsibility for allocating funds will eventually generate pressure either to increase the amount of funds in the envelope or to supplement envelope expenditures with special allocations (45). An envelope system, like any budgeting plan, is vulnerable to political pressure for additional funding. In the case of regional envelopes, regional authorities, supported by local constituents, might become lobbies for more funding from provincial authorities. In other words, in striving to become more responsive to local concerns, decision-makers may actually become more vulnerable to local expenditure pressures. One way to prevent such an outcome would be to instill in regional health authorities the responsibility not only for spending but also for raising revenues. This might make them less willing to spend because they have no way to externalize costs. However, with this solution, another problem arises: regional health authorities may abuse their revenue sources, leading to large increases in locally generated funding. The fact that single-source funding—at the national or provincial level—is

seemingly key to cost control in health care lends some credence to such a possibility (46).

The European experience is instructive in this regard. The reforms of the National Health Service in Britain, which represent a further empowering of regional authorities, have been followed by rises in health care costs. While health care costs increased by 13 percent in the four years before the reforms, they have risen by 26 percent in the four years since reforms were introduced. Two commentators, in looking at reforms in the United Kingdom and Sweden, believe that public authorities "may have lain the foundation for an explosion of health costs" (47, pp. 249–250). The specific experience of Sweden offers additional insight into this challenge. Among the northern European countries, Sweden historically has the highest level of health care expenditures. Interestingly, Sweden also has the highest degree of decentralization, placing greater spending and revenue-raising responsibility with a series of county councils. Though the two—levels of spending and decentralization—need not be related, researchers detect cause and effect (48,49).

It is important to understand that, given the relative newness of these European reforms, we cannot come to any definitive conclusions about their impact on cost—especially since little concerted effort has gone into measuring the effects of various reforms (50). But the preliminary evidence certainly gives cause for concern. Moreover, the fact that successful cost control in the United Kingdom and elsewhere in Europe has relied on the oversight of central authorities is a reminder that regionalization efforts everywhere threaten to undermine existing sound arrangements for limiting health care expenditures (51).

Information Requirements

Efforts to develop regional systems emphasize the importance of allocating scarce health care resources so as to maximize the effectiveness of services, and organizing those services in a coordi-

nated and integrated fashion. However, a recognized problem with the current health care system is the lack of adequate mechanisms for the gathering of information, assessment of need, evaluation of cost and effect, and timely dissemination of the results. As Angus and his colleagues note (52, p. 21):

> *In the health care field, the lack of robust and appropriate measures of health outcomes places great stress on decision-making. Whereas in most industrial sectors resource use can be related directly to outputs, in the health sector it has not been possible to examine resource consumption in relation to its real output.... Without these outcome measures, there are no well-established standards for judging the effectiveness of health care.*

In the Canadian context, the public funding of health care has been focused largely on the supply or input side of the equation. Health care decision-makers have been mainly concerned with ensuring an adequate supply of health services and remuneration of providers for services delivered. Provincial data collection systems have focused on determining such things as the number of required acute and long-term care beds or the number of services rendered by physicians.

With their focus on measurement of outcomes, the new regional health systems will require a reconstruction of current data banks and reconsideration of what data should be collected and by whom. In particular, much greater emphasis will have to be placed on determining the clinical and cost effectiveness of health services. Collection of additional data and redesign of information systems will mean additional costs to the system. The information requirements for comprehensive regional decision-making will be much greater for regional boards than for individual hospital boards. Arguably, this capacity should be present before restructuring takes place.

This problem, perhaps endemic to health care, has been recognized in a number of European countries that already have regionalized health systems. For example, in Britain, which has had some

form of regionalized health system for over 40 years, the measurement of efficiency and effectiveness has been a contentious issue. The measurement of efficiency is more readily quantified and more easily grasped by politicians and administrators. The measurement of effectiveness tends to rely more heavily on qualitative data and is less easy to interpret. Attempts to determine the effectiveness of different services and establish priorities based on these comparisons have been likened to comparing different types of fruit (53). For example, without a reliable basis for judging the relative merits of health promotion versus additional surgery to alleviate delays caused by waiting lists, priority-setting exercises have been shaped as much by preference as by evidence.

The difficulty in measuring need and inequities in resource allocation across regions is illustrated by a closer look at the approach taken in the United Kingdom. Since 1977 regional resource allocation has been based on a funding formula in which distribution of funding occurs "in proportion to an objective measure of each region's needs" (54, p. 930). The impact of this formula has been the subject of an ongoing debate. This debate centers on the issue of how best to calculate the need of a given population and distribute resources in accordance with variations in relative need across regions. At the center of the debate is a lack of common agreement among experts about the appropriate mix and weighting of variables. As Sheldon and colleagues argue (55, p. 835):

> The search for an empirically based resource allocation formula of high precision in the name of the promotion of equity is largely fruitless given the impossibility of measuring the true need for, and cost of, providing health care, especially with the limited data available.

Although health reforms are well underway in the United Kingdom, the lack of good data and evaluation persists (50).

Other problems also attend the issue of information. Providing local decision-makers with tech-nical information and the support staff necessary to interpret that information will not be a cost-neutral exercise. If policy-makers agree on what information is required and determine the best means of collecting it, they must still overcome the challenge of effectively disseminating that information so that it is used, not only by regional decision-makers, but also by individual physicians in clinical settings. The collection, analysis, and dissemination of this new form of information will require cooperation from existing interests. Professionals and organizations may not be particularly cooperative in an evaluation of outcomes that might have a detrimental effect on their incomes (25, p. 211).

At the very least, if the alleged uncoordinated nature of the Canadian health system is to be replaced by an approach that allows planners to consider all health services at one time and make the most effective allocation of resources among these services, information on the cost and effectiveness of services will have to be provided to the regions. Yet, as Hurley and his colleagues note, provinces that have adopted regional health authorities "appear to give insufficient attention to the issue of how to provide regional and local bodies with good scientific evidence" (56, p. 513).

Citizen Participation

While the potential to manage the system in a more efficient and cost-effective manner is a common theme in current health care reform efforts, increased responsiveness and accountability are equally important. Underlying this thrust in reform initiatives are the widely held perceptions that governments and health professionals have become unresponsive to the needs of citizens and are not held sufficiently accountable for the expenditure of public funds. The proposed solution is to make decision-making more participatory and democratic, and less dominated by bureaucrats and professionals. This view arises from two distinct streams of thought. The first, developed through

the writings of liberal thinkers, suggests that local governments are the natural training ground for democracy, with decentralized government providing an opportunity for more direct input from citizens and a greater responsiveness and accountability by elected representatives to their constituents (57).

The second stream of thought stems from classic economic thinking that views consumers as sovereign in the marketplace. Consumer sovereignty "implies that the proper aim of economic activity is the satisfaction of consumer wants, as interpreted by themselves" (58, p. 370). This argument for enhanced consumer sovereignty represents a growing recognition of the fallibility of professional expertise and the growing importance now placed on the value preferences of consumers. It represents an effort to give consumers an increased voice in health care decision-making in relation to health professionals and bureaucrats. In theory, interaction with health-planning staff will improve consumer expertise, and the selection of representatives will enhance accountability.

The claim that local governments, by virtue of their size and proximity to voters, are more responsive and more accountable is flawed in several respects. One problem is low voter turnout in local elections. Despite the belief in the value of local democracy, local elections in Canada have, in practice, been characterized by a lower voter turnout than for provincial elections (59, pp. 311–313). Give that health care as a service is fragmented and episodic, the prospect for instilling higher participation levels in regionalization arrangements does not seem great.

A further problem concerns what Marmor and Monrone refer to as "imbalanced political markets" (60, p. 127). This imbalance relates to the nature of health care interests and the level of resources. Professional groups such as physicians tend to be concentrated and to have more at stake than consumer groups, whose interests are usually more diffuse and who possess fewer resources. Professional associations offer a variety of incentives that motivate individuals to join (e.g., collective bargaining for wages). The net result is that certain interests have both the incentive and the resources for continuing participation in the policy process, whereas others lack either the incentive or the resources to maintain a continuing presence. The nature of health care as a service contributes to this difficulty because it tends to rely on highly specialized information and on episodic and fragmented care.

An important resource held by provider and administrative interests is a virtual monopoly on a body of knowledge that is considered central to a particular industry. In the health care field, the imbalance of information between providers, administrators, and consumers would seem to undermine the economic argument for consumer sovereignty in the health care market. Health care providers and administrators will continue to possess a strong information advantage if health care decision-making remains essentially technical in nature. Current reforms suggest that the information used in regional decision-making is likely to remain highly technical.

Experience with regionalization schemes seems to confirm fears about citizen participation. Writing of decentralization in Norway, Elstad suggests that efforts to enhance the participation of local citizenry may only lead to the creation of "many local hierarchies, dominated by professionals and bureaucrats" (61, p. 557). Byorkman offers the following observation of the efforts to enhance community participation in the United Kingdom, Sweden, and the United States: "In analysis of these three countries, one finding repeatedly emerged: no matter the organizational arrangements or modes of financing, professionals dominated decision-making in the health sector" (62, p. 417). O'Neil (63) notes a similar trend in past regionalization efforts in Quebec, and a recent survey suggests that residents of Ontario are not inclined to participate in regional health care decision-making arrangements (64).

A final difficulty with citizen participation is the dual nature of the citizen as both taxpayer and consumer of services. Even if a clear consumer constituency emerges at the local level, individual consumers may still exhibit the tendency to place their needs as consumers above their needs as taxpayers. The creation of a new source of political legitimacy at the local level establishes a mechanism through which parochial interests might advocate funding increases or policy changes that restrict access to certain types of services. In the past, hospitals were successful at this game without having any formal accountability to local communities, but often with overt support from the communities they served.

Out of either an inability to fully relinquish political control from the center or a recognition of these problems, the majority of provinces have not opted to rely entirely on local elections. The reason most often cited is the need to prevent local boards being dominated by special interests, including both the traditional professional groups associated with health care and emerging consumer groups with narrow policy agendas (e.g., "pro-life"). However, given that the position of the traditionally dominant interests appears to be strengthened by the new regional structures, how will the past experiences with citizen participation be fundamentally altered?

CONCLUSION

Compelled by ballooning deficits and debts at both the federal and provincial levels, provincial governments in Canada have embarked on ambitious efforts to reform the management and delivery of publicly funded health care. A central aspect of this reform is the introduction or strengthening of regional decision-making structures.

Regionalization has been pursued as a strategy for reform because of its potential to improve the efficiency, effectiveness, and responsiveness of health care decision-making and service delivery. It promises to contain costs, integrate and coordinate

services, improve effectiveness of health care, and give the health care consumer a greater say in the operation of the health care system. Despite these claims, research and past experience provide little supportive evidence. We have suggested in this article a number of challenges associated with the integration and coordination of health services. The comparatively small size of health care regions in Canada may make it difficult to realize certain economies of scale, and there is a great deal of uncertainty about whether economies of scale are the same for all health care services. Moreover, various efforts to better integrate and coordinate services may encounter political and organizational interests inimical to change. Another challenge relates to the employment of regional envelopes and the desire to contain costs. The absence of physician and drug expenditures from regional budgets will make cost control elusive, and the decentralization of decision-making to regional bodies will weaken the ability of provincial governments to manage health care expenditures. The budgeting arrangements also will have to confront the problem of spill-overs among regions. To do so implies either increasing transaction costs among the regions or limiting the mobility of both health professionals and consumers, but most provincial governments are not particularly interested in incurring additional costs, and neither physicians nor patients will look kindly upon having their freedom curtailed.

A further problem revolves around the capacity to generate the information necessary to base resource allocation decisions on evidence about best practices and their health outcomes. Existing health information databases are fragmented and have focused on monitoring administrative inputs and some administrative outputs, with no attention paid to systematically collecting data on the relationship of inputs to health outcomes. To gather, evaluate, and disseminate the information required to make decisions at the regional level will necessitate new methods, structures, and processes. This, in turn, will require significant cooperation from

all interests and significant methodological innovation. Most provincial governments in their reform efforts have seriously underestimated the importance and the cost of developing this essential information infrastructure.

Finally, efforts to enhance citizen participation run into problems of professional dominance and citizen apathy. Research suggests that citizen participation in regional and local governance systems is typically quite low. It further indicates that regional decision-making in health care will likely be dominated by administrators and other professional groups, who have more at stake and greater resources with which to influence decision-making. Even if consumers manage to secure a strong voice, there is no guarantee that this will lead to decision-making that provides for an efficient and effective health care system. Private concerns may prevail over the public interest.

Despite the unbridled faith in regionalization, existing research provides few clues for policy-makers who must translate concepts into policies. Even more alarming is the lack of evidence concerning the impact of regionalization on the efficiency and effectiveness of health care delivery systems. What we have attempted to show in this article is that the introduction of regionalization schemes into the Canadian health care system will likely fall well short of expectations. Regionalization, of course, may work at the level of political symbolism, for it shows government responding to widespread concerns about health care in Canada. The fact that so many provincial governments have embraced regionalization certainly suggests that authorities see some political benefit in this line of action. But politically astute action is not the same as sound public policy. If governments in Canada wish to ensure a successful health care system, they must at a minimum rethink their commitment to regionalization.

REFERENCES

1. Weller, G. From "pressure group politics" to "medical–industrial complex": The development of approaches to the politics of health care. *J. Health Polit. Policy Law* 1:444–460, 1977.
2. Aucoin, P., and Bakvis, H. *The Centralization–Decentralization Conundrum.* Institute for Research on Public Policy, Montreal, 1988.
3. Mills, A., et al. *Health System Decentralization: Concepts, Issues and Country Experience.* World Health Organization, Geneva, 1990.
4. Gosselin, R. Decentralization/regionalization in health care: The Quebec experience. *Health Care Manage. Rev.* 9:7–25, 1984.
5. Taylor, M. G. *Health Insurance and Canadian Public Policy.* McGill–Queen's University Press, Montreal, 1986.
6. Naylor, D. *Private Practice, Public Payment: Canadian Medicine and the Politics of Health Insurance 1911–1966.* McGill–Queen's University Press, Kingston, 1986.
7. Angus, D. E. *Review of Significant Health Care Commissions and Task Forces in Canada since 1983–84.* Canadian Hospital Association, Canadian Medical Association, Canadian Nurses Association, Ottawa, 1991.
8. Southwestern Ontario Comprehensive Health System Planning Commission. *Working Together to Achieve Better Health for all.* Ontario Ministry of Health, Toronto, December 1991.
9. Manitoba. *Quality Health for Manitobans: The Action Plan.* Winnipeg, May, 1992.
10. Saskatchewan, Saskatchewan Commission on Directions in Health Care. *Future Directions in Health Care.* Regina, 1991.
11. Alberta, Alberta Health Planning Secretariat. *Starting Points: Recommendations for Creating a More Accountable and Affordable Health System.* Edmonton, December 1993.
12. Saskatchewan. *Working Together Toward Wellness: A Saskatchewan Vision for Health.* Regina, August 1992.
13. Nova Scotia, The Minister's Action Committee on Health System Reform. *Nova Scotia's Blueprint for Health System Reform.* Halifax, April 1994.
14. New Brunswick, Committee on Selected Health Care Programs. *Report.* Fredericton, 1989.
15. British Columbia, Royal Commission on Health Care. *Closer to Home.* Victoria, 1990.

16. Quebec, Ministry of Health and Social Services. *A Reform Centered on the Citizen.* Quebec, December 1991.

17. Ontario, Premier's Council on Health Strategy. *Local Decision-Making for Health and Social Services.* Toronto, 1991.

18. British Columbia, Ministry of Health. *New Directions for Health in British Columbia.* Victoria, 1993.

19. British Columbia. *Planning for Core Services and Standards in British Columbia.* Victoria, November 1993.

20. Birch, S., and Abelson, J. Is reasonable access what we want? Implications of, and challenges to, current Canadian policy on equity in health care. *Int. J. Health Serv.* 23:629–653, 1993.

21. Badgely, R. F. Social and economic disparities under Canadian health care. *Int. J. Health Serv.* 21:659–671, 1991.

22. Alberta, Ministry of Health. *Regionalization of Health Services Planning and Management: A Canadian Perspective.* Edmonton, July 1993.

23. Canada, Health Canada. *Provincial Health System Reform in Canada.* Ottawa, 1995.

24. Birch, S., et al. A needs-based approach to resources allocation in health care. *Can. Public Policy* 19:68–85, 1993.

25. Pineault, R., et al. The reform of Quebec's health care system: Potential for innovation? *J. Public Health Policy* 14(2):198–219, 1993.

26. Hollander, M. J. *The Costs and Cost-effectiveness of Continuing Care Services in Canada.* Queen's–University of Ottawa Economics Projects, Working Paper No. 94–06. University of Ottawa, Ottawa, 1994.

27. Long, M. J., et al. A reconsideration of economies of scale in the health care field. *Health Policy* 5:25–44, 1985.

28. Bish, R. L., and Ostrom, V. *Understanding Urban Government.* American Enterprise Institute for Public Policy Research, Washington, D.C., 1973.

29. Krushelnicki, B. W., and Belvedere, R. Government reorganization in Ontario: A comparison of service effectiveness and efficiency of regional government. *Planning Admin.* 15:59–72, 1988.

30. Shortell, S. The evolution of hospital systems: Unfulfilled promises and self-fulfilling prophesies. *Med. Care Rev.* 45:177–214, 1988.

31. Shortell, S., et al. Creating organized delivery systems: The barriers and facilitators. *Hosp. Health Ser. Admin.* 38:447–465, 1993.

32. Dowling, W. Strategic alliances as a structure for integrated delivery systems. In *Partners for the Dance: Forming Strategic Alliances in Health Care,* edited by A. D. Kaluzny, H. S. Zuckerman, and T. C. Ricketts, pp. 139–175. Health Administration Press, Ann Arbor, Mich., 1995.

33. Gelmon, S. B., and Fried, B. J. *Multi-Institutional Arrangements and the Canadian Health System.* Canadian Public Hospital Association, Ottawa, 1987.

34. Howard, J. W., and Alidina, S. Multihospital systems: Increase costs…and quality. *Dimensions Health Serv.* 64(2): 20–24, 1987.

35. Luft, H. S., et al. Should operations be regionalized? *N. Engl. J. Med.* 301:1364–1369, 1979.

36. Finkler, S. A. Cost effectiveness of regionalization— Further results for heart surgery. *Health Ser. Res.* 16:325–333, 1981.

37. Tuohy, C. J., and Evans, R. G. Pushing on a string: The decentralization of health planning in Ontario. In *The Costs of Federalism,* edited by R. T. Gotembiewski and A. Wildavsky, pp. 89–116. Transaction Books, New Brunswick, N.J., 1986.

38. Hall, V. Towns look to dump health body. *Edmonton Journal,* June 20, 1996, p. A-1.

39. Worron, T. Country to join city health authority July 1. *Edmonton Journal,* April 19, 1996, p. B-3.

40. Weiss, J. Substance vs. symbol in administrative reform: The case of human services coordination. *Policy Anal.* 7:21–45, 1981.

41. Rondeau, K. V., and Deber, R. B. Models for integrating and coordinating community based human service delivery: An analysis of organizational and economic factors. In *Restructuring Canada's Health Services System: How Do We Get There from Here,* edited by G. Thompson and R. B. Deber, pp. 387–392. University of Toronto Press, Toronto, 1992.

42. Canadian Medical Association, Working Group on Regionalization and Decentralization. *The Language of Health System Reform.* Ottawa, 1993.

43. Gibson, W., and Hanley, G. Klein to explore bills for out-of-town care. *St. Alberta and Sturgeon Gazette,* April 17, 1996, p. A-1.

44. Organization for Economic Cooperation and Development. *The Reform of Health Care: A Comparative Analysis of Seven OECD Countries.* Paris, 1992.

45. Van Loon, R. The policy and expenditure management system in the federal government: The first three years. *Can. Public Admin.* 26:2, 1983.

46. Evans, R. G. Tension, compression and shear: Directions, stresses, and outcomes of health care cost control. *J. Health Polit. Policy Law* 15:101–127, 1990.

47. Glennerster, H., and Matsaganis, M. The English and Swedish health care reforms. *Int. J. Health Serv.* 24:231–251, 1994.

48. Hollingsworth, R., Hage, J., and Hanneman, R. A. *State Intervention in Medical Care: Consequences for Britain,*

France, Sweden, and the United States, 1890–1970. Cornell University Press, Ithaca, N.Y., 1990.

49. Rehnberg, C. The Swedish experience with internal markets. In *Health Care Reform through Internal Markets,* edited by M. Jerome-Forget, J. White, and J. M. Weiner. Institute of Research on Public Policy, Montreal, 1995.

50. Maynard, A., and Bloor, K. Introducing a market to the United Kingdom's National Health Service. *N. Engl. J. Med.* 334:4, 1996.

51. Culyer, A. J., and Meads, A. The United Kingdom: Effective, efficient, equitable. *J. Health Polit. Policy Law* 17:680, 1992.

52. Angus, D. E., et al. *Sustainable Health Care for Canada: Synthesis Report.* Queen's–University of Ottawa Economics Project, Ottawa, 1995.

53. Ham, C. Priority setting in the NHS: Reports from six districts. *BMJ* 307:435–438, 1993.

54. Winyard, G. P. A. RAWP—New injustice for old? *BMJ* 283:930–932, 1981.

55. Sheldon, T. A., Smith, G. D., and Bevan, G. Weighting in the dark: Resource allocation in the NHS. *BMJ* 306:835–839, 1993.

56. Hurley, J., Lomas, J., and Bhatia, V. When tinkering is not enough: Provincial reform to manage health care resources. *Can. Public Admin.* 37:490–514, 1994.

57. Sharpe, L. J. Theories and values of local government. *Policy Stud.* 18:153–174, 1970.

58. Evans, R. G. *Strained Mercy: The Economics of Canadian Health Care.* Butterworths, Toronto, 1984.

59. Higgins, D. J. *Local and Urban Politics in Canada.* Gage, Toronto, 1986.

60. Marmor, T. R., and Morone, J. A. Representing consumer interests: Imbalanced markets, health planning, and the HSAs. *Milbank Mem. Fund Q.* 58:125–165, 1980.

61. Elstad, J. I. Health services and decentralized government: The case of primary health services in Norway. *Int. J. Health Serv.* 20:545–559, 1990.

62. Byorkman, J. W. Who governs the health sector? Comparative European and American experiences with representation, participation, and decentralization. *Comp. Politics* 17(4): 399–420, 1985.

63. O'Neill, M. Community participation in Quebec's health system: A strategy to curtail community empowerment? *Int. J. Health Serv.* 22:287–301, 1992.

64. Abelson, J., et al. Does the community want devolved authority? Results from deliberative polling in Ontario. *Can. Med. Assoc. J.* 153:403–424, 1995.

DEVELOPING WORLD PERSPECTIVE

HEALTH CARE REFORMS AND DEVELOPING COUNTRIES— A CRITICAL OVERVIEW

KASTURI SEN AND MERI KOIVUSALO

INTRODUCTION

Health care reforms have been a major issue in health policy during the 1980s and 1990s in developed as well as developing countries. Over time, the meaning of the word "reform" has shifted radically. In the period of post-colonial independence and up until the late 1970s, "reform" suggested organizational changes in the provision of health services among other services from a generalist or populist perspective, as indicated, for example, by the push towards primary health care. However, in the 1980s and 1990s "reform" has been associated especially with activities focused upon the economic value of such services. As such, the health care reforms implemented during the past decade have tended to include structural changes in the financing and organization of health services. The World Bank has played a key role in introducing this new notion of "reform" in much of the developing world.

Our critique focuses on the meaning of the term "health care reform" as employed in key World Bank documents published in the late 1980s

and early 1990s which prescribed changes in health care policies (World Bank, 1987, 1993). These health care reforms have often changed the organization and delivery of health services in order to encompass increased cost-sharing and to facilitate a rapidly expanding role for private health care practitioners and providers (both profit and non-profit). Overall, the reforms have introduced increasing market mechanisms into health care provision and opened the way for private providers generally and in the context of public sector provision in particular.

This paper focuses on three aspects of health care reforms and the provision of public services which have largely been ignored.

- First, the historical context of health care services in developing countries has tended to be overlooked, in particular, the commitment among many post-colonial states to establish public provisions of services for all of the population. Primary health care held a strong appeal in realising this commitment. In the past decade, however, many developing countries have experienced the re-emergence of a health system reminiscent of the colonial era when services were highly segregated and targeted towards an exclusive minority.
- Second, the links between macro economic policies, such as structural adjustment and their overall effects upon the provision of health care and on public sector reforms have also been ignored. This omission has undermined critical appraisal of the reform process itself (Kanji *et al.*, 1991; Werner *et al.*, 1997).
- Third, the value and ideological underpinnings of the reforms implemented, especially the validity of the economic assumptions that have guided the reform process in many countries, have been little questioned. The extent to which such assumptions are applicable to public goods such as health care and the equity and distributional consequences of such assumptions are fundamental to a long overdue

critique of current international health policy and of health systems development (Evans, 1997a; Green, 1995).

BACKGROUND

In the literature on developing countries, many reasons are cited for health care reforms. The prevailing arguments, however, are often based on an assumed consensus that reform of public services is essential because the public sector is either unable, or cannot be allowed, to operate as an effective provider of services. The diagnosis of problems associated with the public sector may well be relevant to increasing effectiveness, but the treatment prescribed thus far is of deep concern. Such treatment includes increasing sharing of costs of services by users or employing market mechanisms in the provision of health services as in the creation of internal markets or contracting from the private sector in health service provision (Mills, 1995; Leighton, 1995; Newbrander, 1997). Greater competition in the provision of health care services in this manner is assumed to be the primary mechanism through which better quality care can be provided. A decline in the utilization of public health facilities, meanwhile, is viewed as a key indicator of poor quality services and consumer dissatisfaction (Mills, 1995).

In the past two years, World Bank prescriptions for health care reform have expressed some ambiguity with respect to the policies promoted. However, two recent publications still continue to emphasize a clear commitment to the private sector as the provider of public services (World Bank, 1997a, 1997b). The health care policies proposed in these documents lend support to a diminished role for the state in service provision with contractual arrangements as well as the public/private mix in health systems. The problem with these policies is that in practice they have not achieved the expected gains in terms of cost savings and efficiency (Creese, 1990; Chabot *et al.,* 1995). Moreover, in developed countries such as the United States,

Japan, Germany, and Great Britain, the state continues to play a major role in the organization and delivery of health services. The United States has the highest per capita public expenditure on health care, even though the largest share of the national health care financing and provision is derived from the private sector, indicating the skewed nature of distribution of resources from the latter. In 1996, meanwhile, the World Health Organization voiced growing concern at its Ljubljana meeting at the rapid pace of changes in health care provision taking place in the Eastern European region, and called for caution in employing market mechanisms in the operation of health services (WHO, 1996).

The abundant literature on the financing and reorganization of health care tends to be limited to a technocentric approach. Advocates of health care reforms tend to locate their arguments within the narrow confines of efficiency and effectiveness (World Bank, 1993; Leighton, 1995). They depend heavily upon conventional economic analysis which accepts market principles as the most rational means for achieving efficiency in the developing world. It is common for such advocates to emphasize terms such as "demand" and "supply" and the provision of consumer "choice," reinforced still further by the key words of "efficiency" and "cost containment" in the provision of health care (World Bank, 1987, 1993; Akin and Birdsall, 1991; Bennett, 1991; Bennett, 1993; Berman and Khan, 1993; Creese and Kutzin, 1995). The need to contain the escalating costs of health care provision, however, tends to obscure the nature of the services to be reorganized and the most appropriate means through which cost containments might be achieved. Although repeatedly ignored, such issues remain of critical significance to the questions of equity and the distribution of limited resources.

HISTORICAL CONTEXT

It is inappropriate to treat developing countries as a homogeneous block with identical histories. Yet,

many of them do share a common or similar colonial past when health services were geared towards serving a predominantly urban elite with the addition of charities and churches as service providers. Many developing countries also share a common history, however, in trying to respond to the health needs of the whole population by replacing the colonial structures which continue to persist by supporting an active public sector. In many countries, the post-colonial state played a fundamental role in the provision and financing of public health services. In the aftermath of independence during the 1950s and 1960s, countries such as India, Sri Lanka, Tanzania and Cuba, to name but a few, attempted to redress the imbalances in service availability and accessibility by providing basic and comprehensive health services for all. The work of the Bhore Committee reflected such efforts in India (Qadeer, 1995; Banerji, 1997).

The declaration of Alma Ata in 1978 (WHO, 1978) set out a global health strategy premised upon access and equity to underpin the structure and functioning of health services throughout the world. The Alma Ata declaration stemmed, on the one hand, from the failure of vertical disease-oriented programmes focused on specific disease or intervention in contrast to more integrated and horizontal health systems development and, on the other, from the aspirations for an approach to health and health service provision emphasizing social justice and social rights (Smith and Bryant, 1988; Newell, 1988). It was argued at the time that, instead of shifting from vertical to horizontal programmes, the provision and delivery of health services needed to be considered as part of the whole social and economic development of a nation. Any improvements in services, it was stressed, needed to take into account wider questions of national structures, priorities and goals (Rifkin and Walt, 1988).

Although the attempts made by many developing countries to provide universal access to health services could be considered as directly related to

Alma Ata, the declarations in favour of comprehensive primary health care (PHC) were to be selectively implemented. In practice, emphasis was placed on the most cost-effective types of medical intervention (Walsh and Warren, 1979). Such a selective health care approach gained substantial international support from the development agencies: the US Agency for International Development (USAID), the World Bank and UNICEF supported the initiative actively (Unger and Killingsworth, 1986; Warren, 1988). Clearly this was to have an impact upon the increasing predominance of selective and vertically oriented strategies in many countries. The historical context and problems of comprehensive versus selective provision remain in our view most pertinent to the context in which the current round of health care reforms are taking place (Qadeer, 1995; Koivusalo and Ollila, 1997; Werner *et al.,* 1997). In many respects the critical tension between comprehensiveness and selectivity in health care is still at the core of health care reform policies, although it tends to be expressed in the context of the use of DALYs (Disability Adjusted Life Years), essential packages or prioritization.

In many developing countries, public sector financing currently has a low share of the national budget compared with past investment. Such low levels of funding are reinforced by the overall strategy of structural adjustment policies in particular and to a neo-liberal emphasis in development politics in general. The World Bank's analysis of structural adjustment programmes in sub-Saharan Africa shows that the share of government budget allocated to the health sector fell during the adjustment period in many countries (Jayarah and Branson, 1995). If health has not received sufficient consideration at the national level in many countries it has not been at the core of international development efforts either. The policies in the 1980s paid little attention to the close relationship between economic policies and the health status of a population. The links between structural adjust-

ment policies, public sector reforms in general and health reforms in particular are discussed only too rarely when current health reform policies and processes come under the spotlight.

POLITICAL CONTEXT

In many developing countries, health reforms have been implemented over the past decade or so as part of structural adjustment programmes and public sector reforms. As part of this process, many nascent welfare states are being dismantled with little or no debate (Sen, 1996; Social Scientist, 1996; Qadeer and Sen, 1998). In contrast to the stated aims of improving the performance and capacities of the health sector, the reforms have in practice acted in many cases as a means of making the health sector comply with the economic measures prescribed in structural adjustment policies (Loewenson, 1993; Hutchful, 1994).

Opinions on the origins of structural adjustment lending are diverse: World Bank documents have tended to stress internal factors, while others have placed greater emphasis on external factors, or on both internal and external ones (World Bank, 1993; Werner *et al.,* 1997). World Bank viewpoints have emphasized that reforms were necessitated by worsening economic conditions caused by collapsing world prices for primary commodities which had thereby reduced export earnings and any expansion of fiscal policies, for example, to support welfare measures, would only aggravate a country's debt burden (Ferroni and Grootaert, 1993). Other commentators, however, have not considered the World Bank or the IMF merely as neutral financiers, but as part of a process, or even as part of the problem, leading to the rising debt burden in the developing world (UNDP, 1992; Griffith-Jones, 1991).

During the 1970s, the share of funding to developing countries provided by private sources grew rapidly, as did the share of international lending channeled by international banks. Such

"privatization" of a large proportion of development funding was strongly welcomed by orthodox economic analysts as being the most efficient way to finance development in Third World countries. The trend was also encouraged by the IMF as a convenient mechanism for recycling funds from the "surplus" countries to oil-importing developing countries (Griffith-Jones, 1991). The United Nations Development Programme (UNDP) provides a critical appraisal of the situation:

> The international capital markets lent developing countries an average net amount of $21 billion a year in the 1970s and early 1980s—reaching a peak of $36 billion in 1981. Unfortunately, real interest rates started to rise dramatically after 1979 as the industrial countries' governments introduced restrictive monetarist policies in response to the first oil shock. This precipitated the Latin American debt crisis in 1982, after which lending suddenly dropped. By 1988, net financial transfers to developing countries were minus $35 billion. Theoretically, this should not have happened. The IMF and the World Bank were created in the 1940s specifically to avoid the experience of the 1930s. They were supposed to intervene in order to moderate the extreme cycles of unregulated financial markets. In fact, they did try to increase their net credits to the developing countries in the early 1980s. But lacking the necessary resources, as well as the official mandate to intervene in global markets in a meaningful way, they could not sustain such policies. Far from dampening the cycles, they amplified them. (UNDP, 1992)

The World Bank's structural adjustment lending has evolved over time, with initial conditions varying between countries. While the content of structural adjustment loans has been complex and varied, the basic model underpinning IMF/World Bank orthodox lending has been similar. This could be broadly divided into three central principles: reducing the role of the state relative to that of the private sector; "getting the prices right"; and opening up the economy (Woodward, 1992). The structural adjustment policies implemented in the 1980s, however, led to growing concern over their

health and social impacts. Such concerns were predominantly focused on cuts in public spending on health and social services as well as on loan conditionalities requiring, for example, the adoption of user charges in health services.

By the late 1980s, growing concern led UNICEF to urge for a change in the implementation focus of structural adjustment programmes (Cornia et al., 1987). There was increasing evidence of hardship in the aftermath of economic austerity measures, accompanied by an apparent decline in health status among vulnerable groups. Stewart (1989) suggested, for example, that by the late 1980s malnutrition had increased in 23 countries and infant mortality was rising in a number of countries, despite steady improvement during the previous decade. In practice, a number of changes advocated by UNICEF it its publication "Adjustment with a Human Face" were adopted in the structural adjustment programmes of the 1990s (Helleneier, 1994; Gibbon, 1992). The World Bank's own analysis during the 1990s admitted that adequate public sector financing had been important in countries which had successfully implemented structural adjustment programmes (Jayarah and Branson, 1995). By the late 1980s and 1990s, neglect of health issues was transformed into an increasing World Bank involvement in the health sector with special reference to health and social sector reforms. This involvement, however, opened up a new debate concerning the basis, ideology and implications of policy prescriptions implemented as part of sectoral reform policies.

Health concerns with respect to structural adjustment programmes cannot be limited to resource allocation within the public sector. It is also important to take into account policies which have influenced the determinants of health and access to health care in practice. These policies have included, e.g. lifting of price controls, freezing wages, devaluing currencies and reducing subsidies on basic essentials such as food and transport. In many countries, the consequences of such mon-

etary measures have begun to emerge only in the last 5–6 years. They appear to have had particular effects on the health and well-being of poor women. A number of studies from countries as far apart as Zimbabwe and India show that, following the introduction of structural adjustment policies, women worked longer hours with lower wages and had access to less food and other resources (Patel, 1992; Kanji and Jazdowska, 1993; Costello *et al.*, 1994; Emeagwali, 1995). These studies have highlighted a deterioration in the social and economic circumstances of poor families, in particular, in the aftermath of structural adjustment programmes. In addition, earlier studies have drawn attention to the negative impacts on child health and nutrition, and this has been linked to falling incomes, increased prices for essential commodities, declining government expenditure on basic services and women's increased workload (Stewart, 1989). Increasing hardship on families has meant that the hard-earned struggle for access to education for girls has in practice been undermined; the largest numbers of dropouts from schools in many developing countries (notably those in Asia) occurred among girls of school age.

Poverty and socio-economic inequities are known to bear a strong relevance to health status. The economic growth which has been achieved in some regions appears to have taken place at the expense of worsening trends in terms of social development and social inequalities. It has long been established that economic growth *per se* does not automatically improve health and social well-being: unless it is effectively redistributed, growth merely increases socio-economic differences (Dreze and Sen, 1990). Structural adjustment programmes seem to have reinforced inequalities through the imposition of changes in the agricultural sector towards cash cropping and the production of crops for export; such changes have affected small farmers and the landless, and have serious implications for the food security of vulnerable groups with little cash income. Despite the

overall improvement in people's health status throughout the world since the 1950s, the gains of the early 1980s in terms of nutritional and general health status are now slowing down or being reversed because of rising inequalities in the distribution of incomes and resources, a trend documented in an increasing number of case studies (Watson, 1994; Bijlmakers *et al.*, 1994; Social Scientist, 1994; Fernandes, 1997; Bennett, 1997).

While it may be difficult to make a direct and linear causal association between structural adjustment policies and health status, it may be argued that the cumulative evidence of the past decade indicates that such policies have had an important influence upon the determinants of health by reducing employment and weakening existing safety net mechanisms, particularly subsides for the poorest groups (Kanji *et al.*, 1991; Creese and Kutzin, 1995; Sen, 1996). Reducing complex policy processes into quantifiable health outcomes in counties which lack base-line or follow-up data is not possible. Yet, a growing number of local level studies in different regions suggest that changes in the organization of health care have been compounded by wider economic measures which have increased the vulnerability of majority populations in the developing world (Bijlmakers and Sanders, 1996; Loewenson, 1991; Bennett, 1997; Fernandes, 1997).

IDEOLOGICAL CONTEXT

In developing countries, health care reforms have been implemented under the aegis of structural adjustment or sectoral reform programmes. Consequently, health care reforms adopted prescribed policies which have increased the role for private providers in health care, limited the government's role and rationed service provision according to ability to pay. The aims of these policies are invariably articulated in terms of improving efficiency, effectiveness and equity; yet, the means to achieve these goals tend to lean towards neoliberal measures. Thus, it is not surprising that part

of the criticism of health care reforms and World Bank policies on health has focused on the ideological basis of the prescription (Ugalde and Jackson, 1995; Laurell and Lopez-Arellano, 1996; Social Scientist, 1994; Ihonvbere, 1995).

In the implementation of health sector reforms, little attempt has been made to define what the "health sector" is, despite the diversity of health systems prevailing in most developing countries (Social Scientist, 1994). For example, current criticism of public sector capacities negates a historical perspective as to the reasons why public provision of health services was established and its struggle to survive throughout the world. There is also little understanding of the political and economic factors which have contributed to serious underfunding, of donor preference for selective and vertical health programmes capable of showing where the funds go and what direct outcomes of activities are, or of the power of the medical and pharmaceutical lobbies for maintaining private interests. The overall effect of ignoring this historical perspective has been to systematically erode the infrastructure and human resources within the public sector in favour of the private interests involved in health care activities (Qadeer, 1995; Sen, 1996; Yang, 1997; Evans, 1997).

Unfortunately, many studies of the malfunctioning of public sector health care provision are devoid of context. They have tended to focus on "technical" limitations such as poor performance, poor economic management, over-employment and the utilization of public and private sector health care, and these tend to be assessed by relatively crude measures (Health Policy and Planning, 1995). Such an approach is in danger of oversimplification and moves the focus away from the contribution of the private sector to the disfunctioning of the public sector and detaches it from its social and political context. One of the main conclusions reached at a recent regional meeting in South Asia on the impact of structural adjustment policies on economy, health and polity (Structural Adjust-

ment, 1997) was that public sector health services have played a major role in the eradication of common diseases and improvements in basic health indicators during the 1960s and 1970s. The rapid demise of such services in recent years was considered to be largely a result of inadequate resourcing and leakage of public funds to private sector activities (Qadeer and Sen, 1998).

It has been long argued that health care is a basic right and that access to health care should not be determined by supply and demand or the vagaries of the marketplace (Rice, 1997; Evans, 1997).

In European countries, health care reforms have been criticized for the lack of evidence of their effectiveness and for an undue emphasis on markets (Maynard and Bloor, 1995; WHO, 1993; Creese, 1990). Studies are now beginning to emerge from different regions of the world highlighting the negative distributional consequences of changes to the financing of health services, especially in the developed market economies of eastern and central Europe (Mastilica, 1996). In China, despite positive achievements in the economic sphere, many of the mechanisms promoted by health care reforms have been inequitable and indeed contributed to impoverishment, especially through higher user costs of health care (Hsiao, 1995; Bogg *et al.*, 1996; Hsiao and Liu, 1996; Creese, 1990). In a Chinese study on rural health services one-third of those who lived below the poverty line were found to have become poor because of the financial losses incurred during serious illness (Chinese Rural, 1991). The experience of reforms in Vietnam is similar (Ensor and Bich San, 1996). The impact on economic and social dimensions when implementing this type of health care changes has largely been ignored (WHO, 1993). The problem is not only that health care reforms have failed to live up to their promise of improving efficiency, effectiveness and equity, but also in many cultures, the privatization of higher levels of services has led to a situation where those

who fall seriously ill or need secondary or tertiary care may be driven into poverty due to the costs of care. Although some World Bank economists have recognized that the cost of health care in countries such as Bangladesh is a serious economic burden on poor families (Phillips *et al.,* 1993), the overall policies implemented under health care reforms tend to ignore this.

In the past 5 years, a handful of studies have acknowledged that the inelasticity of demand for health care applies only to the better off (WHO, 1993; Sauerborn et al., 1994; Ensor and Bich San, 1996). When expensive health care is unavoidable for vulnerable groups (women, children, elderly people and families living at or below the poverty level), there is usually a heavy price to pay, either in debt creation or families foregoing other basic essentials such as a minimum adequate diet or schooling for girls. The impact of high cost treatment for emerging chronic disease is also being recognized in terms of its effect upon intra-household and inter-generational relations.

Despite these studies, the potential for health care costs to add considerable hardship to the lives of vulnerable families remains largely unexplored in the literature (Sen, 1996a; Sen *et al.,* 1997). Restricting public services to either public health measures or to basic packages of selected interventions inevitably prevents the poorest groups having access to tertiary care, even though they may have access to basic services. There is little evidence, moreover, that the poorest sections of society are not affected by less complicated diseases and medical problems. In fact, evidence would suggest that the opposite is the case, particularly as rapid demographic change sets in and alters the pattern of prevailing diseases (Sen, 1994).

QUALITY OF CARE UNDER PRIVATE PROVIDERS

Under health care reforms, the process of privatization has also been seen as a means to transfer government attention towards the provision only of basic services to the poorest. This is clearly advocated in the World Bank's 1997 *World Development Report*, which suggests that the state should undertake only what it can best afford (World Bank, 1997b). In many developing countries, this implies public health measures and so-called essential packages of basic care consisting of selected interventions and services. Yet, there is little evidence as to why Sri Lanka or Kerala, for instance, have managed to provide comprehensive public health services despite relatively low per capita incomes, while other countries with higher GNP per capita have not. In addition, rapid privatization is evidently creating serious concerns about the regulations and cost-containment of care; it requires governments to exercise sophisticated administrative skills if equity and quality of services are to be addressed.

In the privatization process, there is growing concern about the difficulties of access to tertiary care. This is compounded by the escalating costs of private sector provision, linked to the use of inappropriate and unsustainable technologies (e.g. Bennett, 1991), over-prescription (e.g. VCAN, 1996; Yang, 1997) and stimulating a captive market (e.g. Bennett, 1991). Subsequently, there is little choice for people than to seek health care in a private "supplier-led health" service. Despite the growing sophistication of the private for-profit sector, the quality of care is rarely guaranteed, especially when the private sector has a monopoly over a particular health market. In India where the bulk of health care providers are private, particular concern about the quality and standards of hygiene of private provisions in one state exists. There is also considerable over-prescribing of drugs in several large states (Yesudian, 1989; Berman and Khan, 1993; VCAN, 1996). Health systems become more complex the more pluralistic they are and any use of market mechanisms or competitive contracting necessitates considerable managerial capacities. In addition, countries with weak state

functions tend to be weak in legislative and regulatory structures as well. The experience of regulation in the developed world, whether in the health sector or the social sector, suggests little confidence in the ability of regulatory mechanisms to check the excesses of privatized entities (Sen, 1996a).

In general, the evidence on different aspects of health sector reforms do not reveal the positive outcomes, either in economic terms or in terms of quality of care, projected by the reforms (Green, 1995; Bennett, 1991; Creese, 1990; Watkins, 1994; Bijlmakers *et al.*, 1994; Costello *et al.*, 1994; Kanji and Jazdowska, 1993; Sauerborn *et al.*, 1994; Yang, 1997; Sen, 1996; Bogg *et al.*, 1996). Rather, they seem to reinforce the view that, in situations of gross structural socio-economic inequalities, the application of market principles acts to reinforce poverty and inequality. There is little guarantee that the implementation of market formulas improves the quality of provision, and no guarantee that they improve the health of those in greatest need. Health care reforms in developing countries appear to have ensured better markets for private sector activities for the elite complemented by lucrative investment and market opportunities for expanding transnational health care (Smith, 1996).

Considered in the context of a more liberalized global economy, many of the policies implemented have been beneficial for multi-national organizations involved in health care, including transnational pharmaceutical companies (Werner *et al.*, 1997; Yang, 1997; Koivusalo and Ollila, 1997). The international health care industry is an emerging phenomenon in the developing world as prospects increase for private health care insurance and hospital provision directed to those able to pay. Unless redirected, this trend will encourage the transnationalization of private health care and commercial managed care options in developing countries (e.g. Ho, 1995). For example, the World Bank's private sector outreach wing, The International Finance Corporation, already maps private investment possibilities in healthcare (Private Hospital Investment Opportunities, 1997).

CONCLUSION: LEARNING FROM THE PAST

For developing countries, a reversal of their health, social and economic gains over the past half century is a serious regression. It supports a re-emergence of colonial structures of health care which encourage an affluent minority sufficiently privileged to be engaged in international exchange with separate arrangements for private care, while the majority of the population remain marginalized or suffer economic hardship if they seek any health care other than the essential packages available in the public sector. Thus, the idea of a public–private mix of health services remains very tenuous since the greatest gains are to be made by the private sector and its clientele, often at the expense of the public sector (Structural Adjustment, 1997; Qadeer and Sen, 1998). In fact, some critical voices recognized this tendency as early as 1991 (Bennett, 1991; Kanji *et al.*, 1991).

There is a growing global concern about the impact of privatization of health care. The process of privatization leaves large sections of the population and particularly the poor dependent upon an inadequately equipped and shrinking public sector, while the private sector expands rapidly and becomes more high cost and available only to those able to pay (Nittayaramphong, 1997; Yang, 1997). It is important to develop case studies from different regions of the world allowing comparison of the processes and possible impacts of changes upon vulnerable groups and health systems as a whole. In view of the evidence already emerging, there is also a need to support evaluations and descriptive studies of process rather than focusing on single measures of outcomes such as clinic attendance, drug availability or waiting

times, in order to assess the overall impact of these changes. Furthermore, the cumulative effects of these changes need to be better understood. More information is needed on the meso- and macro-level impacts of the reforms on health systems development, as well as on micro-level impacts at the household level, analysed by gender and socio-economic status over a long-term time perspective.

The current fragmentation of analysis and the focus on "effectiveness of interventions" serves to obscure the changes in the nature of the health system as a whole. While non-governmental organizations might be effective at a local level or as separate entities, their combined efforts do not necessarily form a comprehensive and efficient basis for health system development as a whole. The extent to which NGOs are accountable to the populations is also unclear and rarely addressed. In addition, they too require monitoring and regulation, an aspect which is rarely considered because NGOs are presumed to act differently from private providers (e.g. Green and Matthias, 1995; Zaidi, 1996).

Increasing the costs paid by users is arguably a limited and regressive means of financing health care. The notion that promotion of private investments in health care will bring about equity and better health is not supported by the evidence. There is growing concern that strong, private and increasingly transnational interests are altering the nature and even threaten the existence of public health care systems throughout the developing world. As the twenty-first century approaches, the issue is not one of a lack of knowledge to formulate different policies, but one of ideology. It is important that this is recognized, since old and abandoned remedies are being recycled in new guises in the international arena of health reform. Current strategies of reforming the health sector are inconsistent with economic logic and remain unproven in terms of their effectiveness beyond the promotion of the ideology of neo-liberal politics epitomised by "the market".

The Alma Ata declaration of 1978 brought to the forefront the essentially political nature of health care. The meeting received considerable international support for its promotion of the wider distributive and developmental aspects of a public health care system premised upon equity of access. But in the two decades following Alma Ata, many countries have failed to reach the basic health indicators set forth by the "Health for All" agenda. Many countries also appear to be losing the opportunity to build health services based upon the principle of universal access. In sharp contrast to the principles of re-distribution and development, the health sector in developing countries is increasingly influenced by private interests and by the principle of "willingness to pay." Health care reforms have, in effect, encouraged the growth of private providers in health care and further legitimized private services for the affluent sections of the population while limiting public provision to selective, basic services for the poor.

The lessons from history clearly indicate that in order to build an effective health system providing care according to need, it is essential to cover the largest number of people by pooling risks and resources. The current policy of allowing some people to opt out of the public health system into private services seriously hampers the continuity of public services through segmentation and inequality of access, and causes deterioration of quality by subsidizing private provision by the public sector alongside the general shrinkage of public resources. Rather than reform for "betterment," the current process resembles a return to the colonial era when elite and minority classes enjoyed access to supposedly international "quality" services, while the rest of society went without or depended on the services of charities and churches.

ACKNOWLEDGMENTS

This paper arose out of a regional meeting on the health effects of structural adjustment policies, held in New Delhi, India, in September 1997 and sponsored by the European Commission's DG XII. The authors would also like to acknowledge valuable comments from Dr. Andrew Green of the Nuffield Institute of Health on an earlier draft and especially thank Ms Sarah Sexton of *Cornerhouse* for painstaking editing work.

REFERENCES

Akin, J. N., Birdsall, D. de Ferranti (1987). *Financing Health Services in Developing Countries: An Agenda for Reform.* A World Bank Policy Study. Washington, DC.

Banerjee, D. (1997). *Structural Adjustment and Health in India—A Critique.* Discussion paper. International Meeting on Health Impacts of Structural Adjustment in South Asia. New Delhi, September 1997. Unpublished.

Bennett, S. (1991). *The Mystique of Markets: Public and Private Health Care in Developing Countries.* PHP Departmental Publication, No. 4. London School of Hygiene and Tropical Medicine, London.

Bennett, J. (1997). *Structural Adjustment and Health: An Agenda for the Poor.* Discussion paper. International Meeting on Health Impacts of Structural Adjustment in South Asia. New Delhi, September 1997. Unpublished.

Berman, P., Khan, M. (1993). *Paying for India's Health Care.* Sage, New Delhi.

Bogg, L., Hengjin, D., Kell, W., Wenwei, W., Diwan, V. (1996). The cost of coverage: Rural health insurance in China. *Health Policy and Planning* **11,** 238–252.

Bijlmakers, L., Bassett, M., Sanders, D. (1994). *Health and Structural Adjustment in Rural and Urban Settings in Zimbabwe.* Interim Research Report, mimeo. Community Medicine Department, University of Zimbabwe, Harare.

Cahn, J. (1993). Challenging the new imperial authority: The World Bank and the democratization of development. Harvard *Human Rights* **6,** 160, cited in Werner, D., and Sanders, D. (1997), *Questioning the Solution: The Politics of Primary Health Care and Child Survival.* Health Wrights, Palo Alto.

Centre for Social Medicine and Community Health (1994). *Social Scientist* **22,** 9–12.

Chabot, J., Harnmeijer, J. W., Streefland, P. H. (1995). *African Primary Health Care: The Times of Economic Turbulence.* Royal Tropical Institute, Amsterdam.

Chinese Rural Health Systems Research Group (1991). *Research on the Rural Health Care Systems in China.* Cited in Hsiao, W. (1995). The Chinese health care system: Lessons for other nations. *Social Science and Medicine* **41** (8), 1047–1055.

Cornia, G. A., Jolly, R., Stewart, F. (1987). *Adjustment with a Human Face,* Vols. I and II. Clarendon Press, Oxford.

Costello, A., Watson, F., Woodward, D. (1994). *Adjustment and the Health of Mothers and Children.* Centre for International Child Health, London.

Creese, A. L. (1990). *User Charges for Health Care: A Review of Recent Experience.* World Health Organisation, SHS Paper No. 1. WHO, Geneva.

Creese, A. L., Kutzin, J. (1995). *Lessons from Cost Recovery in Health.* Forum on Health Sector Reform, World Health Organisation Discussion Paper No. 2. WHO, Geneva.

Dreze, J. P., Sen, A. K. (1990). *The Political Economy of Hunger.* Clarendon, Oxford.

Emeagwali, G. T. (1995). *Women Pay the Price.* Africa World Press, Trenton, New Jersey.

Ensor, T., Bich San, P. (1996). Access and payment for health care: The poor of northern Vietnam. *International Journal of Health Planning and Management* **11** (1), 69–83.

Evans, R. G. (1993). *User Fees for Health Care: Why a Bad Idea Keeps Coming Back.* Programme in Population Health, Working Paper No. 26. Canadian Institute for Advanced Research, Toronto.

Evans, R. G. (1997a). Health care reform: Who's selling the market and why? *Journal of Public Health Medicine* **19** (1), 45–49.

Evans, R. G. (1997b). Going for gold: The redistributive agenda behind market-based health care reform. *Journal of Health Politics, Policy and Law* **22** (2), 427–465.

Fernandes, D. (1997). *Structural Adjustment Programmes and the Health Care Services in Sri Lanka.* An overview paper presented at the South Asian regional meeting on health effects on structural adjustment, New Delhi Centre for Social Medicine, Jawaharlal Nehru University, New Delhi, September 1997.

Ferroni, M., Grootaert, C. (1993). The social dimensions of policy reform: Concepts, data, analysis. In *Understanding the Social Effects of Policy Reform,* ed. by L. Demery, M. Ferroni and C. Grootaert. World Bank, Washington, DC.

Gibbon, P. (1992). The World Bank and African poverty 1973–1991. *Journal of Modern African Studies* **30,** 193–220.

Government of India, National Sample Survey Organisation (NSSO) (1992). *42nd Round in Utilisation of Health Services in India.* New Delhi, Government of India.

Green, A. (1995). The state of health planning in the 90s. *Health Policy and Planning* **10,** 22–29.

Green, A., Matthias, A. (1995). NGOs, a policy panacea for the next millennium? *Journal of International Development* **7** (3), 565–573.

Griffith-Jones, S. (1991). International financial Markets: A case of market failure. In *States or Markets? Neo-Liberalism and the Development Policy Debate,* ed. by C. Colclough and J. Manor. Clarendon Press, Oxford.

Health Policy and Planning (1995). *Health Policy and Planning* **10** (3).

Helleneier, G. K. (1994). From adjustment to development in sub-Saharan Africa: Consensus and continuing conflict. In *From Adjustment to Development in Africa: Conflict, Convergence, Consensus?* ed. by G. A. Cornia and G. K. Helleneier. St. Martin's Press, New York.

Ho, L. S. (1995). Market reforms and China's health care system. *Social Science and Medicine* **41** (8), 1065–1072.

Hsiao, W. (1995). The Chinese health care system: Lessons for other nations. *Social Science and Medicine* **41** (8), 1047–1055.

Hsiao, W., Liu, Y. (1996). Economic reform and health—Lessons from China. *New England Journal of Medicine* **335,** 430–431.

Hutchful, E. (1994). Smoke and mirrors: The World Bank's social dimension of adjustment (SDA) programme. *Review of African Political Economy* **2,** 569–584.

Ihonvbere, J. (1995). Economic crisis, structural adjustment and Africa's future. In *Women Pay the Price—Structural Adjustment in Africa and the Caribbean,* ed. by G. T. Emeagwali, pp. 133–154. Africa World Press, Trenton, New Jersey.

Jayarah, C., Branson, W. (1995). *Structural and Sectoral Adjustment: World Bank Experience, 1980–1992.* A World Bank Operations Evaluation Study. World Bank, Washington, DC.

Kanji, N., Kanji, N., Manji, F. (1991). From development to sustained crisis: Structural adjustment, equity and health. **33,** 985–993.

Kanji, N., Jazdowska, N. (1993). Structural adjustment and women in Zimbabwe. *Review of African Political Economy* **56,** 11–26.

Kent, G. (1991). *The Politics of Children's Survival.* Praeger, New York.

Koivusalo, M., Ollila, E. (1997). *Making a Healthy World: Agencies, Actors and Policies in International Health.* Zed Books Ltd, London and New York.

Laurell, A. K., Lorez-Arellano, O. (1996). Market commodities and poor relief: The World Bank proposal for health. *International Journal of Health Services* **26,** 1–18.

Leighton, C. (1995). Overview: Health financing reforms in Africa. *Health Policy and Planning* **10** (3), 213–222.

Loewenson, R. (1991). Harvests of disease: Women at work on Zimbabwean plantations. In *Women and Health in Africa,* ed. by M. Turshen, Africa World Press, Trenton, New Jersey.

Loewenson, R. (1993). Structural adjustment and health policy in Africa. *International Journal of Health Services* **23,** 717–730.

Marree, J. T. C., Groenewegen, P. P., van der Zee, J. (1996). Health care financing reforms in the Czech Republic, the former GDR, Hungary and Poland. *Proceedings of the European Public Health Association [EUPHA], Health Care Reforms in Central and Eastern European Countries, Budapest 1995.* Soros Foundation, Debrecen.

Mastilica, M. (1996). Health care reform in Croatia. In *Health Care Reforms in Central and Eastern European Countries.* European Public Health Association, Department of Social Medicine, University Medical School, Soros Foundation, Debrecen.

Maynard, A., Bloor, J. (1995). Health care reform: Informing difficult choices. *International Journal of Health Planning and Management* **10,** 247–264.

McPake, B. (1993). Use charges for health services in developing countries: A review of the economic literature. *Social Science and Medicine* **36** (11), 1397–1405.

McPake, B., Ngalande Banda, E. E. (1995). Contracting out health services in developing countries. *Health Policy and Planning* **9** (1), 25–31.

Mills, A. (1995). *Improving the Efficiency of Public Sector Health Services in Developing Countries: Bureaucratic versus Market Approaches.* PHP Departmental Publication No. 17. London School of Tropical Medicine and Hygiene. London.

Newbrander, W. (1997). *Private Health Sector Growth in Asia: Issues and Implications.* John Wiley, Chichester.

Newell, K. W. (1988). Selective primary health care: The counter revolutions. *Social Science and Medicine* **26,** 903–906.

Nittayaramphong, S. (Ed). (1997). *Health Care Reform: At the Frontier of Research and Policy Decisions.* Ministry of Public Health, Bangkok, Thailand.

Patel, V. (1992). Women and structural adjustment in India (unpublished). Cited in Watson, F. (1994). *Human Face or Human Façade? Adjustment and the Health of Mothers and Children.* Centre for International Child Health, London.

Phillips, M., Feachem, R., Murray, C. J. L., Over, M., Kjellstrom, T. (1993). Adult health: A legitimate concern for developing countries. *American Journal of Public Health* **83,** 1257–1270.

Private Hospital Investment Opportunities (1997). *A Global Study Conducted on Behalf of the International Finance Corporation.* Taylor Associates International, Annapolis, Maryland.

Qadeer, I. (1995). The World Development Report 1993: The Brave New World of Primary Health Care. *Social Scientist* **22** (9–12), 27–40.

Qadeer, I., Sen, K. (1998). Public health debacle in South Asia: The reflection of the crisis of welfarism. South Asian regional meeting on health effects of structural adjustment policies. New Delhi, September 1997. *Journal of Public Health Medicine* **20** (1), 93–96.

Rice, T. (1997). Can markets give us the health system that we want? *Journal of Health Politics, Policy and Law* **22** (2), 382–424.

Rifkin, S., Walt, G. (1988). Why health improves: Defining the issues concerning comprehensive primary health care and selective primary health care. *Social Science and Medicine* **23,** 559–566.

Sauerborn, R., Nougtara, A., Latimer, E. (1994). The elasticity of demand for health care in Burkina Faso: Differences across age and income groups. *Health Policy and Planning* **9** (2), 185–192.

Sen, K. (1994). *Ageing—Debates on Demographic Transition and Social Policy.* Zed Books Ltd. London and New York.

Sen, K. (1996a). Health sector reforms and the implications for later life from a comparative perspective. *Health Care in Later Life* **1** (2), 73–83.

Sen, K. (1996b). Old age security and pensions in India: A critique of the current paradigm. In *Ageing and Social Policy: Global Comparisons,* ed. by P. Lloyd-Sherlock and P. Johnson. STICERD, London.

Sen, K., Roy, S. G. (1996). Demographic and epidemiological transition in India and impact upon utilisation of health services. *Report Submitted to the European Commission in the Fourth Framework for Health Systems Research.* Unpublished.

Smith, R. (1996). Global competition in health care. *British Medical Journal* **313,** 764–765.

Smith, D., Bryant, J. H. (1988). Building the infrastructure for primary health care: An overview of vertical and integrated approaches. *Social Science and Medicine* **26,** 909–917.

Stewart, F. (1989). Structural adjustment and infant health: The need for a human face. *Transactions of the Royal Society of Tropical Medicine and Hygiene* **83,** 30–31.

Structural Adjustment (1997). Conference Statement. International Meeting on Health Impacts of Structural Adjustment in South Asia. Centre for Social Medicine, New Delhi, September 1997. Unpublished.

The Social Scientist (1994). *Social Scientist* **22,** 256–259, Tulika Print, New Delhi.

Ugalde, A., Jackson, J. T. (1995). The World Bank and international health policy: A critical review. *Journal of International Development* **7,** 525–541.

UNISON (1996). *Privatisation in Health Services in Western Europe.* Public Services Privatisation Research Unit (PSPRU), UNISON, London.

United Nations Research Institute for Social Development (UNRISD) (1995). *Adjustment, Globalization and Social Development,* Geneva, February 1995.

UNDP (1992). *Human Development Report.* Oxford University Press, New York.

Unger, J. P., Killingsworth, J. R. (1986). Selective primary health care: A critical review of methods and results. *Social Science and Medicine* **22,** 1001–1013.

VCAN (1996). *Prescription Audit Analysis in Metropolitan Cities: A Study of Drug Utilisation in Urban Community,* ed. by R. Krishnangshu *et al.* Calcutta, India. Unpublished.

Walsh, J. A., Warren, K. S. (1979). Selective primary health care: An interim strategy for disease control in developing countries. *New England Journal of Medicine* **301,** 967–974.

Warren, K. S. (1988). The evolution of selective primary health care. *Social Science and Medicine* **26,** 8491–8498.

Watkins, K. (1994). *The Oxfam Poverty Report.* Oxfam, Oxford.

Watson, F. (1994). *Human Face or Human Façade? Adjustment and the Health of Mothers and Children: Annotated Bibliography Pt 1 and Pt 2.* Centre for International Child Health, London.

Werner, D., Sanders, D., Weston, J., Babb, S., Rodriguez, B. (1997). *Questioning the Solution: The Politics of Primary Health Care and Child Survival*. Health Wrights, Palo Alto.

WHO (1978). *Alma Ata 1978. Primary Health Care*. WHO, Geneva.

World Health Organisation (1995). *Lessons from Cost Recovery in Health*. Forum on Health Sector Reform. Discussion Paper No. 2. WHO, Geneva.

WHO (1996). Ljubljana Charter. *British Medical Journal* **312**, 1664–1665.

World Bank (1987). *Financing Health Services in Developing Countries: An Agenda for Reform*. World Bank, Washington, DC.

World Bank (1993). *World Development Report*. Oxford University Press, New York.

World Bank (1997a). *Population, Health and Nutrition: Sector Strategy*. World Bank, Washington, DC.

World Bank (1997b). *World Development Report*. Oxford University Press, New York.

Woodward, D. (1992). *Debt, Adjustment and Poverty in Developing Countries*, Vol. 2, *The Impact of Debt and Adjustment at the Household Level in the Developing Countries*. Pinter Publishers in association with Save the Children Fund, London.

Yang, Bong-min (1997). The role of health insurance in the growth of the private health sector in Korea. In *Private Health Sector Growth: Issues and Implications*, ed. by W. Newbrander. John Wiley, Chichester.

Yesudian, C. A. K. (1994). Behaviour of the private sector in the health market in Bombay. *Health Policy and Planning* **9** (1).

Zaidi, A. (1996). *NGOs and International Health Policy: A Critique*. University of Karachi, Centre for Development Economics, Karachi. Unpublished.

THE FUTURE OF MEDICAL SOCIOLOGY

As in any academic discipline, intellectual differences exist within medical sociology. Though not insurmountable, these differences fragment the field. Levine (1995, p. 2), however, offers hope for the integration of the theoretical and methodological differences that shape the current intellectual exchange within the discipline. And despite the differences, medical sociology is one of the largest and most active sections within sociology. What is the future of medical sociology? The preceding chapters provide some clues about its place within the larger academic marketplace of ideas, and it is safe to say that medical sociology will survive well into the twenty-first century.

Although many issues will impact the future of medical sociology, one of the most important is the extent to which the discipline brings a cross-cultural perspective to its research and teaching. The articles in this book indicate the rich body of literature that exists not only in the United States but also in other developed nations and in developing nations as well. These articles offer an introduction to the plethora of available works addressing areas cogent to medical sociology. It is on this optimistic note that this chapter rests.

In the first article, Frederic W. Hafferty and Bernice A. Pescosolido detail the historical framework on which their "executive summary" is based. They identify some of the major contributions of medical sociology—such as the sick role, stigma, and health behaviors—and they identify various strengths of medical sociology. These strengths include the ability to examine issues across social institutions and the ability to understand the social context in which individuals and

social institutions are connected. The authors also identify weaknesses associated with medical sociology. Among these weaknesses are the lack of an identifiable direction and a fragmented view of the conceptual and methodological issues associated with medical sociology. Another weakness is that disciplines other than medical sociology—for example, health economics and health psychology—cover many of the issues once addressed by medical sociology. Also, medical sociology has not been well received by those outside the field.

Through the use of focus groups, Hafferty and Pescosolido identified three action steps that they believe will allow medical sociology to reposition itself within the academic and public communities. First is better identification of the central concepts associated with medical sociology, what medical sociology does, and its accomplishments. Second is improvement of relations between the various factions within medical sociology. Third is improvement of the training of future medical sociologists to better address the internal struggles of the discipline and the external challenges associated with health and illness in the twenty-first century.

In the second article, Lisbeth M. Claus surveys the development of medical sociology in Europe. Emerging after World War II, medical sociology is situated by Claus in the historical context of its development within the different European countries, generally between the 1960s and the 1980s. As a result of the discipline's differential temporal development in Europe, the author refers to "European medical sociologies."

Claus discusses enabling and disabling factors influencing the development of the field in Europe

and major interrelated characteristics of the field there. She identifies five types of medical sociologists that have influenced the development of medical sociology in Europe: ambassadors, professionals, researchers, activists, and transients.

Claus views the future of European medical sociologies as dependent on the availability of government funding. She suggests that, given the changing social conditions and available funding streams, European medical sociologies may be more flexible and adaptable to change than medical sociology in the United States.

In the final article, Peter Conrad and Eugene B. Gallagher address the impact of Western medicine on developing countries and the dilemma posed by medical pluralism within many of these countries. The authors point out that the range of the level of development among developing countries is wide and that the histories of developing countries today are different from the experiences of Western nations some 100 years earlier. As a result, the medical experiences of many developing countries differ from those of the industrialized nations. However, many developing nations are also experiencing an increase in mortality rates from lifestyle diseases (lung cancer, heart disease, and so forth).

As stated earlier, medical sociology has not had a particularly strong presence in research and policy efforts addressing needs of the developing nations. Instead, other academic disciplines, such as anthropology, epidemiology, and health planning, have been actively researching and writing on issues associated with the developing world. However, as Conrad and Gallagher point out, among medical sociologists there is increasing research interest in the developing world.

The future of medical sociology in the United States and other nations of the developed world does not appear to be in doubt, but medical sociology needs to expand its efforts and commitment to research in the developing world. Given increased interest in that direction (as evidenced by the articles in this book), it appears that medical sociology has begun to address this concern. Thus, medical sociology seems well positioned for the changing global research and policy expectations of the twenty-first century.

REFERENCE _____

Levine, S. 1995. Time for Creative Integration in Medical Sociology. *Journal of Health and Social Behavior* (Extra Issue), 1–4.

CHARTING A FUTURE COURSE FOR MEDICAL SOCIOLOGY: EXECUTIVE SUMMARY

FREDERIC W. HAFFERTY AND BERNICE A. PESCOSOLIDO

INTRODUCTION

Massive changes in the provision of medical care as well as the rise of new health problems challenge current knowledge, medical practice and social policy. While these large scale changes in society and the medical arena call for an understanding of the social contexts of care, there is a sense, both from inside and outside, that the field of Medical Sociology has not kept pace with the

development of social policy, that the importance and relevance of this field has diminished, and that its parent discipline of Sociology has lost its taste for addressing the most pressing social and policy problems. However, given the past history and present potential of Sociology to describe emerging issues and uncover the roots of solutions, we proposed a set of activities to reverse the current state of affairs. The aims are both ambitious and achievable: to assess the strengths, locate the obstacles, and propose the solutions to realign Medical Sociology, and the discipline as a whole, to contribute to institutional social change in health and medicine. Three activities were carried out: (1) a focus group to outline central issues, barriers and potential, (2) followed by a larger meeting which brought in policy makers from outside the discipline and (3) an even larger community-building session to inform and draw in the membership of the Medical Sociology Section of the American Sociological Association. Reports were generated and input solicited at each stage of the process from a Senior Advisory Panel, many of whom founded the field.

BACKGROUND/OPPORTUNITIES

Sociology has a strong tradition of contributing to the development of significant, and often path-breaking research, teaching, and policy efforts, including pioneering multidisciplinary programs in each of these efforts. It is responsible for crucial role-setting agendas, theories and research on topics as diverse as the rise of the modern profession of medicine, the organization of the health care system, and the basic operation of social, cultural, organization, and socioeconomic factors across a wide number of areas (e.g., the "sick role," "stigma," social class and mental illness, utilization theory, health behaviors). Beginning in the Spring of 1993 with an assessment of the role of the sociological perspective in key areas (e.g., epidemiology, stress and social support, professional

dominance, mental illness) a core group of medical sociologists inventoried past contributions, located gaps and proposed future agendas in a special issue of the *Journal of Health and Social Behavior* (August 1995), funded by the Robert Wood Johnson Foundation. The present initiative, which builds upon this evaluation, comes at a time when University administrators, state government agencies, the private sector, and key federal and private foundations are rethinking their missions and the nature of partnerships they want to build. In sum, the current period represents an era of change and opportunity across a wide range of social institutions which can foster the realignment of research and training in Medical Sociology.

THE STRENGTHS OF MEDICAL SOCIOLOGY AND ITS POTENTIAL CONTRIBUTIONS TO POLICY AND THEORY IN HEALTH AND HEALTH CARE

The relationship between society and medicine is undergoing a fundamental transformation. This process is being driven in large part by forces whose origins, dynamics, interdependencies, and ultimately consequences are poorly understood. The challenges stemming from this transformation are not addressed adequately by fine tuning our research and training methods or by tinkering with ongoing health care programs. The changes underway in health and medicine represent part of a fundamental renegotiation of the relationship between Americans and their social institutions. Public confidence in institutions is eroding, corporations are downsizing, work is being separated from benefits, including health care, employer–employee relations are being restructured, and income inequality grows. Under these conditions, understanding the evolving illness profiles and the medical system without reference to its larger context will produce only piecemeal and ultimately inefficient remediation. In order to understand and shape a new health care system, we must address the complex inter-

play of social, cultural, economic, and political factors as the linkages between societies, organizations/institutions and individuals. Sociology claims two major strengths in this regard: (1) the ability to look systematically across social institutions and (2) the ability to link individuals to the larger ongoing institutional and societal contexts in which they live.

THE CURRENT WEAKNESSES OF MEDICAL SOCIOLOGY

The field currently lacks a readily identifiable core of discrete and specifically tailored conceptual and methodological tools. Ironically, part of the reason comes from the field's past success in developing relevant concepts and methodologies later adopted by other fields or disciplines as well as the existence of a wide diversity of approaches in a discipline that celebrates its lack of a single, narrow paradigm. Regardless of the reasons, however, the absence of a common accepted set of concepts and methods has had an unfortunate influence on the field of Medical Sociology. Core areas of inquiry (e.g., health behavior change and social support, the doctor–patient relationship) have been taken up by other disciplines (e.g., health psychology, health services research, social epidemiology, clinical decision making and public health). New concepts or methodological approaches have not been brought as rapidly to the field (e.g., dynamic process models and micro–macro linkage theory and methods). To compound the problem, the discipline of Sociology has not attached a sufficiently high value in either practice or in its training programs to creating linkages between cutting-edge theory and measurement in the field (e.g., social class, ethnicity, culture and gender). In general, the structure of graduate education does not reflect the core discipline's aspirations towards synthesis and linkage building, but rather separates our enterprise into discrete pieces (e.g., qualitative/quantitative methods, different theoretical schools). Within the field of Medical Sociology,

courses often lack connection to clinical medicine as well as other relevant fields such as health economics, medical anthropology, medical history and public health. There are minimal linkages to internship experiences at the organizational, funding, and policy levels. Finally, the premier training programs in Medical Sociology, which once fulfilled these aims, have virtually disappeared, and the most effective method historically for drawing top quality sociologists into the field (i.e., strong centers and predoctoral training programs) has fallen into disfavor in private and federal funding agencies. Finally, the reward structure within Sociology—while changing—still too often favors solo authorship rather than multidisciplinary teams. Even within its ranks, medical sociologists who now work across a wide variety of settings, many of which are not directly linked to traditional academic/liberal arts settings, are cut off from new findings in the parent discipline and report a gap between their work and the concerns of academic Sociology. Given these internal difficulties, those outside the field of Medical Sociology, including many policy makers and funders, do not possess a clear view of the field's contributions and potentialities. They are unable to access the expertise of a wide range of medical sociologists; they are unlikely to read the field's major journals; and they perceive many medical sociologists as unable or uninterested in framing health care issues from a policy or funding perspective.

ACTION STEPS DESIGNED TO BUILD ON STRENGTHS, ADDRESS WEAKNESSES AND TAKE ADVANTAGE OF CURRENT OPPORTUNITIES

The discussions from the Focus Group and Conference, along with input from interested colleagues and others, evolved into a set of three core challenges, with parallel agendas developed to strengthen Medical Sociology and enhance its contribution to research and policy in health and medicine. The action steps would be facilitated by

establishing task forces and working groups. *First,* we propose to address the visibility and utility of Medical Sociology for those outside the discipline by developing and disseminating central concepts, theories, research agendas and instrumentation for socio-medical and mental health research. Here, we draw from Medical Sociology's historical strength in setting new agendas, developing concepts and instrumentation, and providing tools for the new challenges of health problems and medical care. We propose to establish 3 Core Working Groups on topics central to the new medical landscape in which Sociology is critical: (1) the concept and measurement of Social Class and Inequality; (2) the concepts of Community, Social Networks and Social Support; (3) the concept of the Doctor–Patient Relationship and the Organization of Medical Work. The charge is to develop measurement strategies, pre-tests and data collection efforts in each of these areas. We also propose to focus on the dissemination of new conceptual strategies and important theoretical and empirical research in Medical Sociology to others in medical and mental health research, to policy makers and to the public. New and different vehicles are needed to address these different audiences. A Task Force on External Dissemination would organize and lead the development of new dissemination vehicles, materials and activities. *Second,* we address the challenges of strained intragroup relations. Immediately, we can improve the dissemination of available, relevant information to the community of medical sociologists (students, faculty and researchers) from public and private organizations at the center of health and health care (e.g., American Medical News (AMA)). The Task Force on Internal Dissemination would be charged with developing a list of existing materials as well as a mechanism to link academic Sociology to policy relevant issues and other disciplinary efforts. These initiatives would include the development of an electronic site. *Third,* a number of external and internal challenges can be addressed by refocusing the goals of training future generations of medical sociologists to face this new era in health and medicine. We propose the development of National Centers of Excellence in Research and Training in Medical Sociology which would not only set a new standard for training but also would provide outreach and opportunities for students, faculty and others located elsewhere through summer institutes, occasional workshop and professional development activities. These Centers would serve in leadership positions for other proposed activities and would be responsible for forging partnerships with academic, public and private agencies.

DEVELOPED WORLD PERSPECTIVE

THE DEVELOPMENT OF MEDICAL SOCIOLOGY IN EUROPE

LISBETH M. CLAUS

Medical sociology as a sociological subdiscipline has known a tremendous growth in the last decades. Since Robert Straus published in 1957 his now famous article "The Nature and Status of Medical Sociology" in the *American Sociological Review* [1] the discipline has expanded greatly. Much is known about the development of the discipline in the United States. However, no systematic information was available about the growth and status of medical sociology in Europe. To remedy this situation, a comprehensive study was undertaken on the development of European medical sociology.

It should be kept in mind that the term *European medical sociology* might in itself be a misno-

mer. Europe is a conglomeration of different nations with varied social and political systems, nationalistic groups, ethnic traditions and languages. In addition, the origins and development of medical sociology in particular countries were initially often self-contained within national boundaries and languages. Hence, it might be more appropriate to speak about the discipline in terms of *European medical sociologies.* Despite this diversification, this article presents common denominators in the growth of medical sociology in Europe since World War II. Besides illustrating common features in the origins and development of European medical sociologies, a number of characteristics of the discipline will be highlighted. They reflect the specific styles of work being done and elements of professionalization and institutionalization of the field. Finally, these state of the field evaluations are further supplemented with some reflections as to the possibility of developing a "European" medical sociology.

The generalizations presented in this article are based on data collected in a variety of ways: (1) A survey was conducted among medical sociologists working throughout Europe. A total of 646 medical sociologists from 20 different European countries responded to a mail questionnaire and supplied information on their background and activities [2]. (2) A directory of active European medical sociologists was compiled [3] and (3) in-depth sociohistorical (post–WW II) analyses and evaluations of the development of medical sociology were undertaken in five different European countries: the United Kingdom, Belgium, Poland, the Federal Republic of Germany and France. These case studies, based on secondary sources and in-depth interviews with medical sociologists, documented the origins and development of medical sociology in a particular country and evaluated the subdisciplines in the broader national context of society, paying particular attention to the state of sociology and the formal organization of health care [4].

THE ORIGINS OF MEDICAL SOCIOLOGIES IN EUROPE

"Medical sociology," or at least what the discipline is considered to be today, is mainly a post World War II development. In that sense, the origins of modern medical sociology lie in the United States since it developed there earlier. However, a scientific discipline does not rise ahistorically but develops in a particular context. It is generally assumed that modern medical sociology was made possible as a result of changing trends in health, medicine and health care. In addition, the growth and maturation of the social sciences provided theoretical frameworks and methodological tools to be applied to the subject matter. The general predisposing climate for the origins of modern medical sociology is then considered to lie in the convergence of these trends in medicine and the social sciences. A convergence which took place around the second World War.

This study focused upon the development of "modern" medical sociology and, as such, used the post World War II era as a time frame for retrospective analysis. An extrapolation and comparison between the origins and roots of American and European medical sociology is worth mentioning at this point. Although it is generally assumed that medical sociology started after the second World War, it is possible to historically trace what could have been labeled medical sociology prior to that time. In this respect, premedical sociology and its steady progression to medical sociology are contextually totally different on both continents.

In Europe, attention to the social aspects of health and disease had been present in disciplines such as social medicine, public health, and anthropology in the late 18th, 19th and early 20th centuries. Social medicine, social hygiene and public health flourished especially in France, Germany and United Kingdom. Theoretical treatises (and often empirical studies) of physicians, anthropologists, philosophers, and social activists such as

Edwin Chadwick, Rudolf Virchow, Salomon Neu-
mann, Henry E. Sigerist, Viktor von Weizsäcker,
Alfred Grotjahn, Cabanis, Louis-René Villermé
and others, could all be labeled premedical sociology. In Europe, premodern medical sociology grew
from there through social epidemiology and public
policy.

In the United States, the roots of modern medical sociology are totally different. Early modern
medical sociology was basically theoretical, abstract and non-empirical. The Flexner Report
shifted all interests in American medicine to the
"scientific" approach. As a result, medical sociology originated from a different angle in the United
States than it did in Europe. Samuel Bloom's observations of the different developments of American versus European medical sociology could be
traced back to the different historical roots of the
discipline on both continents [5].

Another situational factor which makes the origins of medical sociology different in the United
States vs Europe is the impact of the second World
War. While in the United States, the second World
War is often seen as having been instrumental in
originating medical sociology [6], the war had a
disabling effect on the origins of the discipline in
Europe. The growth of sociology in Europe was interrupted by the first and second World Wars. Especially the second World War caused a major rift
in sociology. It took almost one generation to continue and/or rebuild the sociological research traditions after the war. Although it was beyond the
scope of this study to trace these historical roots in
medical sociology, the historical context of the origin of the discipline should be kept in mind.

The origins of modern medical sociology in
the different European countries is situated at different time frames. Specific examples from the
case study analysis show that the discipline originated in the early fifties in the United Kingdom, in
the late fifties in the Federal Republic of Germany,
in the early sixties in Poland, in the mid-sixties in
Belgium, and in the mid-to-late sixties in France.

Only a few European countries developed medical
sociology in the fifties (probably limited to the
United Kingdom, the Netherlands and the Federal
Republic of Germany). In a large number of countries, medical sociology originated in the sixties. In
the majority of European countries, however, medical sociology did only originate in the seventies
and sometimes eighties. Evidence from this study
further suggests that in almost all European countries one can find at least a few people who pursue
research and/or teaching activities in medical sociology. This does in no way imply that there is an
"institutionalized" field of medical sociology in
these countries. Rather, there are individuals, often
as lonely cavaliers, pursuing medical sociology research and/or teaching activities.

Looking at additional factors which gave birth
to modern medical sociology in Europe, one needs
to mention the role of some individuals. Although
it might appear that the individual and coincidental
level was far more important than a collective
movement in the origin of medical sociology, exemplars do not arise without a historical context.
With respect to the role played by individuals, one
can identify two types of people: (1) the ones who
entered the field, and (2) the ones who promoted
the field.

THE DEVELOPMENT OF EUROPEAN
MEDICAL SOCIOLOGIES

A number of interrelated enabling and disabling
factors influenced the development of medical sociologies in Europe. Enabling factors were: the
government's role in the funding of sociological
research, the growth of the universities, the expansion of sociological research, the student revolt
movement, recommendations and/or regulations
in medical education, and medical sociology's
own professionalization. Among the disabling factors one should mention the rigid university structure, the perception of medical sociology as a
critical discipline, the power of rival disciplines,

the lack of support of the mother discipline, and the lack of training possibilities. All these factors are interconnected and part of a broader ideological scheme.

Enabling Factors

A major enabling factor has been the role played by governments in funding medical sociology research. During the sixties, a number of European governments expanded their research funding into the social sciences. This funding interest in social science research was partly based on the rationale that policy decisions should be supported by scientific research evidence. Medical sociological research benefited from research funds because of an additional factor related to the organization of the health care system. In the late forties, most European countries established national health insurance schemes. In the sixties, costs for health care exceeded all previously anticipated budgets. In addition, concerns arose whether the quality of care matched the monetary investments of the national insurance systems. These issues regarding cost and quality of health care fit a more general debate in the sixties of quantity vs quality of life. This debate was responsible for allocating resources to medical sociological research.

A second factor which enabled the development of medical sociologists in Europe was the growth of the universities in the past decades. The democratization of higher education, a larger population group, women entering universities, and in general a broadening of the educational system were factors which were responsible for the growth of the universities and the building of new universities. Although the expansion of the humanities was not an explicit goal it was a by-product of a renewed interest in higher education.

A third enabling factor was the development and advent of modern sociology itself. The second World War had a dual impact on sociology in Europe. On the one hand it interrupted sociological

activities for almost one decade, on the other hand it made the advent of a different "modern" sociology (vs classic European sociology) easier. Post World War II sociology was partly modeled after American sociology. Attention was paid to specialized knowledge areas within sociology and there was a renewed focus on research methodology. Such an emphasis, combined with the growth of the discipline in general, facilitated the development of sociological subdisciplines.

A fourth enabling factor in the development of European medical sociologies was the political climate and student movement in the late sixties. In several European countries, the student movement can directly be linked to the expansion of medical sociology. It led to experimentation with behavioral science teaching in medical education [7]. The general political climate of the sixties further enhanced the need for a "critique" of the medical care system.

The political climate of the sixties was further responsible for several new recommendations and/ or regulations concerning medical education. These recommendations emphasized the need for medical training which was better adapted to the practice of medicine. The behavioral sciences (and in particular medical sociology) were seen as one of the answers to bring medical education closer to medical practice. The introduction of these subject matters in medical school curricula provided a worksetting for many medical sociologists.

Finally, the development of European medical sociologies was enhanced by their own emerging professionalization. Although the institutionalization of medical sociological research and teaching activities in Europe was never as important as, for example, in the United States, it still enhanced the growth of the discipline. The training of a new generation of medical sociologists (although only at a limited number of places) and the usefulness and applied nature of European medical sociologists made it possible for the discipline to create for itself a raison d'etre.

Disabling Factors

A number of countervailing forces impeded the development of medical sociologies in Europe. If again, a comparison between the development of medical sociology in Europe vs the United States would be made, none of the disabling factors mentioned for Europe seem to have been at play in the United States.

A first disabling factor in the development of European medical sociologies is the "rigid" university structure in Europe. Two particular structural barriers for the development of medical sociologies are: (1) the structural position of sociology within the European universities, and (2) the way in which a professional academic career is sustained within European universities. Sociological teaching and research activities in many European universities are not necessarily conducted within autonomous sociology departments. Often, sociology is imbedded within social sciences, social and political sciences, history, law, economic sciences, etc. This structural position makes the development of a sociological subdiscipline more difficult. It is not surprising, therefore, that in many European universities medical sociology established itself within medical schools. The second barrier for the development of medical sociology (or for that matter any other discipline) in European universities is the rigid way in which professional academic careers are made (or broken) in a guild-like university structure. Although the "patron–dauphin" system as described by Renee Fox [8] should probably not be generalized to all European universities, its impact on academic research cannot be neglected. Promising researchers who are not sponsored or generated through the university system, may very well not remain committed to the field.

A second disabling factor in the development of European medical sociologies is the perception by others of being a critical discipline. Medical sociology's sometime association with neo-Marxism, the student revolt, critical analyses of health care, and its strong involvement in the political aspects of medicine have given the discipline a critical and radical label. Although among European medical sociologists one finds the whole spectrum of people (from politically conservative to the radical left), the discipline is often perceived by the medical profession as left wing. This label impedes the development of medical sociologies, especially in countries where the discipline is still highly underdeveloped.

A third disabling factor in the development of European medical sociologies is the power of rival disciplines. Medical sociology's establishment of an autonomous (but in Europe extremely broad) professional domain often reached and/or crossed the boundaries of longer established rival disciplines. Social medicine, public health, medical demography and geography are well established disciplines in Europe. These disciplines have much stronger alliances with the medical (academic) profession than medical sociology does.

A final disabling factor in the development of European medical sociologies has been the lack of support from the mother discipline. European medical sociologies did not develop within (theoretical) sociology. In addition, the discipline often became institutionalized in medical rather than sociological settings. Medical sociology was for long not recognized as a valid subarea of sociological research attention. In general, established scholars in sociology showed little support for medical sociology, while often supporting other sociological subdisciplines (labor, organizations, family, law, religion, etc.). In this sense, they monopolized resources which could have been shared with medical sociologists.

CHARACTERISTICS OF EUROPEAN MEDICAL SOCIOLOGIES

European medical sociologies are discussed in terms of a number of paradigmatic, institutionalization and professionalization features. Three ma-

jor and interrelated characteristics of European medical sociologies are: (1) The boundaries of the discipline are ill-defined and broad; (2) European medical sociologies have an applied character; and (3) European medical sociologies are "policy" analysis oriented.

(1) The Boundaries of European Medical Sociologies

In general, there is little concern about what constitutes the discipline of medical sociology in Europe. This was most clearly expressed by Magdalena Sokolowska when she stated that "In fact, we do not worry that something does not 'really belong' to medical sociology" [9]. The broad scope of the discipline of medical sociology could partly be a result of the eclectic background of European medical sociologists. However, that eclecticism is probably rooted in a European tradition of liberal arts education. Social science training in Europe today has often a broad and multidisciplinary humanistic character. Sociology training is, in many universities, imbedded in larger departments (law, philosophy, social and political sciences, etc.). The broad scope of medical sociology was especially well illustrated in the range of research topics and interests expressed by European medical sociologists in the survey.

(2) The Applied Character of European Medical Sociologies

European medical sociologies have basically an "applied" character. The pursuit of sociological knowledge as such is subordinate to the application of that knowledge in the health sphere. The definition of "applied" is, however, not uniform in the different European countries. As a general rule, one can say that medical sociological research in Europe is not aimed at knowledge for the sake of the enhancement of sociological theory in the first place. The usefulness of that knowledge is at least

as much a priority as the refinement of sociological models and paradigms. This should not leave the impression that European medical sociologies are a-theoretical. However, the pursuit of esoteric knowledge is not the sole rationale for medical sociological research. "Applied," as mentioned before, does not necessarily mean the same in all European countries. In some countries, the emphasis is on providing descriptive and evaluative research as tools for decision-makers in health care. In other countries, it means a more utilitarian and interventionist approach in shaping government policy and social welfare. In still other countries, it means defining health priorities and implementing health policy and planning. The applied character of European medical sociologies is probably related to a number of factors such as a European social welfare tradition, the governments' role in the funding of sociological research and the relationship between sociology and policy-making research.

(3) The Policy-Making Character of European Medical Sociologies

An extension of the applied nature of European medical sociologies is its focus on policy-making. How far medical sociological research has been able to be part of the policy-making progress is harder to evaluate. True, government sponsored medical sociological research projects always contain recommendations for policy makers. In how far these recommendations are incorporated in policy decisions cannot be ascertained from this study.

Institutionalization Features

The institutionalization of medical sociology in Europe is not far advanced. There are, of course, the well established centers, which at one time had large numbers of research sociologists on staff. In the seventies, it was not unusual for these centers (Aberdeen, Leuven, Warsaw) to have a concentration of a dozen medical sociologists at one time.

Outside of these centers, medical sociologists are mainly concentrated in medical schools. There are few chairs of medical sociology in sociology departments. An extreme example is the Federal Republic of Germany where all twelve medical sociology units are located within medical schools. In these European countries where medical sociology is well developed it is, in general, not institutionalized within the mother discipline "sociology." Rather, medical schools and other applied settings are the places from which medical sociologists work. This institutional framework partly accounts for the lack of medical sociology teaching programs for sociology students.

The situation of medical sociology in these countries where the discipline numbers only a few active sociologists is of particular interest. The lack of establishment of the discipline in one of these countries was elevated by a respondent to the survey as follows:

> ...Medical sociology is still considered a hybrid category which must find a scientific recognition both from medical researchers and from social scientists. The sociologists who have engaged in medical sociology studies have found actual difficulty in getting access to resources, such as the examination of medical archives in the hospitals, and difficulty of access to funds under the label "medical sociology" [10].

Not uncommon in these countries is a confusion in the division of roles between sociologists and social medicine researchers.

Professionalization Features

From the survey on the activities of European medical sociologists, it became apparent that European medical sociology has a rather low professionalization profile. The eclectic background of its members, a neglect of the transmission of a body of knowledge, and the rather loose boundaries of the discipline of medical sociology are partly responsible for this. The lack of professionalization of medical sociology is further impeded by the absence of

formal training programs in most European countries. University level teaching of medical sociology for graduate sociology students is limited to a few centers in Europe. People who desire to become medical sociologists in Europe often have to go abroad for training (in a different language). Finally, although there are a number of regional textbooks, books translated from English, and other research publications intended for medical sociologists, there are only a limited number of publications in some European countries. This problem is compounded by the lack of publication markets for certain languages. Therefore, European medical sociologists often have to rely upon textbooks and studies in another language which show little relevance to their particular society.

Medical sociology is still a very young discipline in Europe. Therefore, instead of speaking of "generations" of medical sociologists in the true sense of the word, it seems more appropriate for medical sociologists to speak of different groups or types. The following model of grouping European medical sociologists is presented as an ideal type. It needs to be adapted to the particular European country and its state of development of medical sociology. Only in countries where the discipline is firmly established can one potentially find all of the groups discussed here-after. Although this model is basically structurally defined, individual particularities (such as personalities, career commitments and opportunities) can be accounted for here. European medical sociologists are divided into five different groups: (1) the ambassadors; (2) the professionals; (3) the researchers; (4) the activists; and (5) the transients.

(1) The Ambassadors. Only a limited number of people would fit this category of "ambassadors." They are to be found among the first individuals who entered the field of medical sociology in a particular country. They attempted to institutionalize the field in their country and gave it professional status and visibility. Often, to that purpose,

they built schools which were to become bastions of medical sociological research (and sometimes of teaching). These ambassadors did not necessarily build sociological schools, in the sense of promoting a particular sociological theory. In general, these pioneers had relatively few publications. Most did, however, initially write a medical sociology textbook in their language—textbooks which synthesized the existing literature in the field (mainly American medical sociology), and were supplemented with a morphological analysis of health care in their own country. The importance of their role is to be measured in terms of synthesizing the field, attracting funding sources for the discipline, and in general, making medical sociology a visible and viable discipline in their country and abroad. Ambassadors are "process" rather than "product" type people. It should be re-emphasized that without the commitments of these ambassadors, many medical sociologists would have found it necessary to leave the field because of lack of resources.

(2) The Professionals. The second group of medical sociologists in Europe are people who were more interested in particular concepts and theories and the testing of those ideas, rather than attempting to develop or institutionalize the field of medical sociology. The "professionals" have occupied a place in medical sociology in Europe because of the particular topic they studied, because of the particular style of sociological work they represented, or for both of these reasons. They are people who are more interested in the pursuit of knowledge and its application than in the promotion of the field as such. These "professionals" have usually a heavy publication record.

Both groups, "ambassadors" and "professionals" are institutionally almost in identical positions. Career-wise, they now occupy the established chairs and tenured positions in the universities. These two groups of medical sociologists have complemented each other in many ways, they are the two sides of the same coin. While the ambassadors were able to attract funds and give recognition for the discipline, the professionals managed to produce the professional research material and credibility needed for the institutionalization of the field. In many countries these two groups often simultaneously entered the field. One group fits more the model of the managerial cadre, the other of the professional cadre.

(3) The Researchers. The researchers usually entered the field later than the ambassadors or professionals. They often were attracted by one of these groups on research tasks or were generationally students of them. The researchers deserve this name because of the varied research experience they were able to acquire. They are, however, often not responsible for attracting funds or defining the research priorities. They are a very young group of people (in their thirties) in academically insecure positions. They have probably a sufficient professional commitment to remain in the field if opportunities were created. However, the university structure and lack of academically secure future might make them abandon the career of medical sociologist. Especially in the light of the fact that the first and second group, in most countries, can be expected to remain in the field for about two decades.

(4) The Activists. This group of medical sociologists is, generation-wise, from the same cohort as the researchers. The difference is that they went into applied, non-academic work settings. They are a relatively small, but growing, group of people who work in a variety of voluntary health agencies, sick funds, hospitals, local and municipal health authorities, self-help programs, etc. They are involved in small scale action-research, and/or health education and promotion activities. In some countries they act as clinical sociologists being involved in actual patient care. There is a large gap between these activists and the academic sociologists. The

activists have, in general, a much smaller base of professional support and interaction than the academically based sociologists.

(5) The Transients.   This group of people enters and leaves the medical sociological scene depending upon the labor market. They are attracted when contract research is available. In general, they have little ambition to remain medical sociologists, or have in fact little opportunity to do so even if they wanted.

PROSPECTS FOR EUROPEAN MEDICAL SOCIOLOGIES

What awaits European medical sociologies in the eighties? The answer to this question will depend upon the particular country under consideration. In some countries where there are already a large number of active medical sociologists, an employment saturation condition is in sight. In other European countries (where the discipline is not greatly developed), medical sociology can be expected to grow if the necessary incentives are provided. One fact is clear, however. If governments (which are the major sponsors of medical sociological research) are going to restrict their funding, medical sociological research in Europe will suffer greatly. A potential restriction in government funding would have to be compensated by other funding sources. If this were not possible, a lot of medical sociologists might be (or have already been) forced to leave the field (especially the "transients" and the "researchers").

European medical sociologies, in contrast with for example American medical sociology, have a number of extra potentialities. Some of the paradigmatic features of European medical sociologies greatly compensate for the lack of institutionalization and professionalization of the discipline. The lack of stringent boundaries of medical sociology, its applied and policy-making emphasis, and the eclectic background of its medical sociologists

make it probably more flexible and adaptable to changing times and constraints. Despite the potential for flexibility of the discipline in Europe, one has to keep in mind that restrictions are likely to be imposed on the growth of the discipline in the future. Such restrictions will necessitate a number of strategies. These will include, among others, a search for alternative funding sources, a certain amount of rationalization of medical sociological research activities, continued interest in practical relevant research issues, and planned professionalization interventions rather than haphazardous ones.

TOWARDS A EUROPEAN MEDICAL SOCIOLOGY?

The last question to be addressed in this study dealt with the possibility of developing a European medical sociology. It became clear from this research that one could hardly speak of a European medical sociology but that it is more appropriate to speak of European medical sociologies. Can a European medical sociology be developed despite the social and cultural diversity of the different European countries? Although there are noticeable trends towards Europeanization, many more factors play in favor of particular medical sociologies than against. Notwithstanding the importance and richness of such national expression, the importance of harmonization of particular European medical sociologies will be pursued.

There have been, in recent years, noticeable trends towards the harmonization of European medical sociologies. In many European countries, medical sociologists are grouping themselves in formal association and informal professional groups. Several countries now have medical sociology groups (United Kingdom, Federal Republic of Germany, Switzerland, Austria, Scandinavian countries, Poland, Italy). These national associations are giving more visibility to the discipline and are facilitating contacts among medical sociolo-

gists. Among the pioneers of European medical sociologists, there is a great deal of formal and informal professional contact. Three bastions of medical sociology research (Aberdeen, Warsaw, and Leuven) are connected by bilateral agreements calling for exchange of faculty and researchers. International and supra-national organizations such as the World Health Organization (WHO) and the European Economic Community (EEC) are more and more counting on the expertise of European medical sociologists as consultants and advisors. In 1980, the WHO, Regional Office for Europe, invited five leading European medical sociologists, to discuss the contribution of sociologists to the WHO Regional Office's program development [11]. The World Health Organization, Regional Office for Europe, in that respect has shown considerable interest and support in the task of bringing European medical sociologists in closer touch with one another and to identify experts in the area.

Despite these trends, several factors are at play which inhibit the development of European medical sociology. There is among European medical sociologists a great amount of ethnocentrism, which precludes genuine professional communication and contact. It became clear from this research that, as a general rule, medical sociologists mainly work within their "language," thereby denying valuable research work being done by neighboring sociologists. It seemed more common to look at Anglo-Saxon publications than at, often more pertinent, work in another language. This, despite the fact that these medical sociologists had often a working knowledge of the language in a neighboring country. Linguistic and cultural barriers have often as a result a duplication of research activity without the benefit of cross-fertilization of the research results. In addition, a focus on local and regional rather than national samples make cross-cultural comparisons even more difficult. Comparative European research in the area of medical sociology is further limited through the lack of standardization and coordinated research methods.

What is needed to facilitate the development of a European medical sociology? Linguistic and cultural barriers among European medical sociologists and the absence of a formally organized professional network have prevented a great deal of professional contacts and potential research collaboration in the field. One of the practical aims of this study has been to bring European medical sociologists closer together by providing systematized knowledge about the field and its active components (medical sociologists). However, further steps need to be taken with regard to the professionalization of the discipline.

At this writing the foundations are being built for a "European Society of Medical Sociology." The development of a European medical sociology in the future seems inevitable. Although the harmonization of the different European medical sociologies is a worthwhile aim, the interplay of different political, social and cultural factors on the development of the sociological discipline foremost contributes to the richness of the field. Medical sociology is "alive and well" in Europe.

REFERENCES

1. Straus R. The nature and status of medical sociology. *Am Sociol. Rev.* **22,** 200, 1957.
2. Claus L. M. *The Growth of a Sociological Discipline: On the Development of Medical Sociology in Europe.* Vol. 1: The General Study. Katholieke Universiteit Leuven, Sociological Research Institute, Leuven. 1982.
3. Claus L. M. (Ed.) *European Medical Sociologists: A Directory of People Active in the Sociology of Health, Illness and Health Care.* Katholieke Universiteit Leuven, Sociological Research Institute, Leuven, 1981.
4. Claus L. M. *The Growth of a Sociological Discipline: On the Development of Medical Sociology in Europe,* Vol. 2: Case Studies. Katholieke Universiteit Leuven, Sociological Research Institute, Leuven, 1982.
5. Bloom S. W. The profession of medical sociologist and the implications for training programs. In *Teaching Medical*

Sociology (Edited by Nuyens Y. and Vansteenkiste J.), p. 37. Martinus Nijhoff, Social Science Division, Leiden, 1978.

6. Day R. A. Toward the Development of a Sociology of Sociology: The Case of Medical Sociology. University of Missouri–Columbia. Unpublished Ph.D. Dissertation, 1981.

7. Claus L. M. Medische Opleiding in Verandering: De Plaats van de Gedragswetenschappen in het Medisch Curriculum. Katholieke Universiteit Leuven, Unpublished Master's Thesis, 1973.

8. Fox R. Medical Scientist in a Château. *Science* **136,** 476, 1962.

9. Sokolowska M. *Health and Society, Selected Research and Bibliography.* Polish Academy of Science, Institute of Philosophy, Warszawa, 1978.

10. Personal letter from Italian respondent, December 1980.

11. World Health Organization. *Contribution to Sociology Programme Development in the Regional Office for Europe.* WHO Regional Office for Europe, Copenhagen, 1981.

DEVELOPING WORLD PERSPECTIVE

INTRODUCTION TO *HEALTH AND HEALTH CARE IN DEVELOPING COUNTRIES: SOCIOLOGICAL PERSPECTIVES*

PETER CONRAD AND EUGENE B. GALLAGHER

Disease and infirmity are universal problems, and all societies have developed means by which to attempt to control or influence the health and illness of their members. Most societies have developed some type of indigenous "health system," and many have designated healing specialists.

During the era of colonization, European medicine—usually in the person of medical missionaries—was exported to the colonies in an effort to spread European culture and religion and to pacify the natives (Comaroff 1992). Because the colonials' economic and political interests far outweighed their medical ones, Western medicine had a limited impact. Although the specifics varied by society, when the former colonies emerged as independent nations in the post–World War II period, they were often left with some amalgam of very limited Western medicine alongside traditional forms of indigenous healing. In the past three decades, however, the influence of Western medicine has penetrated these developing societies, often with the help of governments and international donor organizations. In most developing societies now

we find complex systems (Kleinman 1980), often manifesting dilemmas between the Western and traditional health care systems (Zeichner 1988).

The health problems in these Third World or developing countries are enormous. Enhanced sanitation and public health measures, especially vaccination, have improved health in some developing societies in recent years; yet disease remains endemic and devastating in many others. Amplified by a lack of safe water and inadequate nutrition, infectious disease rates in many countries are very high. This is especially evident in the high infant mortality from such diseases as diarrheal diseases, measles, neonatal tetanus, whooping cough, and malaria (UNICEF, 1990, 17). Infant mortality rates range from 147 per 1,000 births in Malawi, 116 in Bangladesh, 51 in Ecuador, to 44 in Egypt, compared with 7 to 12 in most Western developed countries. The life expectancy in developing countries ranges from the mid-forties in many African countries to the mid-sixties in most Latin American countries; this is compared with the mid-seventies for most developed countries (USAID, 1990).

Western medicine is making an impact on the developing world, especially in terms of public health and the training of tens of thousands of doctors. In countries like Mexico and Pakistan, however, thousands of physicians are unemployed in the cities, largely because many do not want to work in rural areas and the urban medical system cannot economically absorb them. Many countries still relegate the majority of their medical resources to urban areas, even though the highest rates of disease occur among rural peoples. While doctor-centered Western curative medicine is often exported to developing countries, limited health dollars may be better spent training community primary health workers than doctors.

Although it is sometimes useful to lump societies together as "developing," there is a huge range in the development of these countries. On the more developed end are the newly industrialized countries, such as Korea, Taiwan, and Singapore, with per capita gross national products (GNPs) of about $8,000; on the other end are some of the poorest countries in the world, such as Ethiopia, Chad, and Bangladesh, with per capita GNPs of $150. There is also great variety in terms of size (e.g., China and Haiti), history of colonialism (e.g., India and Nepal), and type of government (e.g., Cuba, Saudi Arabia, and Costa Rica), as well as location, religion, population, age structure, and so forth. For the most part, what these developing countries have in common is that they tend to be non-Western (except for Latin American countries) and in the early 1960s had very little industry and were generally economically poor. As these countries have developed in different directions and at different rates, the range of development among them is now much greater than in 1960. But the vast majority of these countries remain poor; in 1987 over sixty of these countries still had a per capita GNP of less than one thousand dollars (World Bank 1989).

It is not clear that Western development strategies, including modern biomedicine, are always appropriate in Third World situations. Contemporary industrial societies historically shifted from agricultural to industrial production and from rural to urban settlement before modern medicine and public health had substantially reduced the burden of infectious disease and lengthened life expectancy. Illness and early death were dreaded but expected and accepted. The developing nations now face a more demanding set of conditions, expectations, and challenges. Many wrestle with poverty, overpopulation, and disrupted patterns of community life. In the face of numerous obstacles, they must modernize in health care even as they shift to factory production, expand educational opportunity, and provide services for the burgeoning urban populations. In addition to rising expectations for longevity and general health, there are rising expectations for recovery from chronic diseases and disabilities. Health care, however, like other "modern" projects such as mass communication and highway construction, cannot be introduced in isolation, apart from a so-called infrastructure that includes administrative know-how, cultural resources (e.g., literacy), and a supportive physical environment—all of which are scarce. Many Third World countries are also distracted by ethnic and religious factionalism, which retards health care's progress along with much else.

Because the administrative structures of health care are still being laid down in the developing world, the influence of rational planning on health policy—bureaucratic initiatives implemented from the center outward, such the World Health Organization's "Health for All by the Year 2000" (HFA/2000)—is critically important. Yet in sharp contrast to the ultramodern spirit of biomedical health planning, traditional medicine—its theories of illness, practitioners, and remedies—remains as much more than a vestigial element in Third World health care. The range and complexity of health phenomena in the developing world are great; but it seems clear, in countries that can afford it, that

Western medicine is becoming the ideal and standard of medical care.

DRIFT TOWARD MEDICAL DOMINANCE IN THIRD WORLD HEALTH CARE

Recent trends of thought in the Third World have considered the history of health care development in the industrialized world with ambivalence. Developing countries want to emulate the health care accomplishments of the West, yet they are also determined not to repeat mistakes made there. This new thinking has called into question both the centrality of the physician's role and the relevance that clinical medicine oriented to the individual patient has for alleviating the major health problems faced by these societies: inadequate sanitation, infectious disease, high infant–child mortality, and a lack of family planning.

Similar questions can be raised about the place of clinical medicine in developed societies. Although life expectancy is higher and the burden of chronic disease heavier in developed societies, many of their health problems cannot be addressed by clinical medicine. For example, wide-spread respiratory disease attributable to tobacco use is more a challenge to health educators and public health authorities than to doctors. Other so-called lifestyle diseases or conditions, such as obesity and hypertension, are apt targets for preventive rather than clinical medicine (Levine and Lilienfeld, 1987). But clinical medicine is so strongly entrenched and such an essential feature of modern society that searching questions about its relevance and limits are largely confined to a small band of "critics of medicine" (which includes, incidentally, a number of medical sociologists).

Medical dominance is not yet an established fact in Third World societies. The health care system is still in a formative flux. For example, many health planners, including social scientists and public health physicians, wish to curtail the production of physicians in favor of other professionals—nurse–midwives and community health workers, for example—who are trained to meet the needs of the populace with preventive resources, rather than concentrate on the curative needs of the national upper class. The goal is to democratize the health care provider labor structure, as well as to widen the distribution of health care. This is seen as a way of avoiding the mistakes of the developed societies, which allowed the medical profession to assume an inordinately important role in carrying out health care.

The foregoing health care ideology has been important in the programmatic thinking of many developing countries (Bryant 1969). It has not, however, dissuaded most of them from investing in medical care, organization, and education modeled closely on the West's. Given the limited resources of most developing societies, the investment has often been substantial.

The health policy debate discussed here can be phrased as a question of whether a health system should emphasize the role of clinical medicine and individual physicians or community and preventive medical resources—or what kind of balance to strike between the two. There are great opportunities here for social scientists to make significant contributions to understanding and even shaping health care in the developing world.

MEDICAL SOCIOLOGY AND THE DEVELOPING WORLD

Social science research has already contributed significantly to our understanding of health and health care in the developing world. A perusal of the literature, however, reveals that it is overwhelmingly anthropologists, epidemiologists, international health planners, and physicians who are researching and writing on these issues. Indeed, anthropologists have been working in the "international health" arena for decades (Foster, 1982).

Specific medical sociological work in this area can rarely be found.

Over the past three decades, medical sociologists have developed a base of concepts and research tools for looking at health and health care phenomena in industrialized societies. This base includes studies of illness behavior; the sick role; doctor–patient relationships; health professional socialization; the organization of health services; medicalization; the social production of disease; the experience of illness; the relation of stress and social support to health; the effects of race, class, and gender on health and disease; the impact of medical technology; and the health care system as part of total societies. Sociological research depends upon many sources and methods: interviews, ethnographic observation, patient biographies and diaries, official documents, survey questionnaires, health care utilization statistics, health care personnel inventories, economic reports, and clinical studies.

With very few exceptions, however, medical sociologists have neglected the study of developing societies. This is not unique to medical sociology; as Alejandro Portes notes, "A major gap…exists between theoretical perspectives chosen by modern sociology and the recurrent dilemmas and restrictions faced by the non-industrialized world" (1976, 51). Western sociology often demonstrates parochialism and ethnocentrism, with sociologists assuming that concepts derived in a Western context can be universally applied (Smith 1990). In some instances, Western sociological concepts may not be appropriate for examining developing societies (e.g., the sick role or compliance may be Western constructs); by contrast, research on developing societies would likely enrich and broaden many of our Western-based sociological conceptualizations. This would force us to reexamine our knowledge in a global sense, while simultaneously shedding a fresh light on health dilemmas in the Third World.

Over the years a few articles by sociologists on health and development have appeared in journals such as *Social Science and Medicine* and *International Journal of Health Services* or in special monographs (e.g., Zeichner 1988), but these have remained on the periphery of medical sociology. A few medical sociologists, such as Ray Elling and Howard Waitzkin, have consistently examined health problems in a Third World context, but they are obvious exceptions. In the last few years, however, there have been signs that this may be changing. The fourth edition of the *Handbook of Medical Sociology* contained a chapter on "Health Care in Developing Countries" (Najman 1989), and in 1989 a special issue of *Journal of Health and Social Behavior* was dedicated to "Sociological Studies of Third World Health and Health Care."

We believe that sociological perspectives can be useful in understanding health and health care in the developing world. It seems likely that unless medical sociologists become serious about examining health issues in comparative or Third World contexts, much of our accumulated knowledge will prove irrelevant for most of the world. It would be regrettable if medical sociology were to become an artifact limited to American or Western societies. After forty years of disciplinary development, medical sociology would seem to have a great deal to offer and productive interchange to gain.

REFERENCES

Bryant, Jack. 1969. *Health and the Developing World.* Ithaca, NY: Cornell University Press.

Comaroff, Jean. 1992. "The Diseased Heart of Africa: Medicine, Colonialism and the Black Body." In *Ethnography and the Historical Imagination,* ed. John Comaroff and Jean Comaroff. Boulder, Colo.: Westview.

Foster, George M. 1982. "Applied Anthropology and International Health." *Human Organization* 41:189–197.

Gallagher, Eugene B., ed. 1989. "Sociological Studies of Third World Health and Human Care" (special single-topic issue). *Journal of Health and Social Behavior* 30 (4).

Kleinman, Arthur. 1980. *Patients and Healers in the Context of Culture.* Berkeley: University of California Press.

Levine, Sol, and Abraham Lilienfeld, eds. 1987. *Epidemiology and Health Policy.* New York: Tavistock.

Najman, Jakob M. 1989. "Health Care in Developing Countries." In *Handbook of Medical Sociology,* 4th ed., ed. H. E. Freeman and Sol Levine, pp. 1332–46. Englewood Cliffs, NJ: Prentice-Hall.

Portes, Alejandro. 1976. "On the Sociology of National Development: Theories and Issues." *American Journal of Sociology* 82:55–85.

Smith, Harold E. 1990. "Sociology and the Study of Non-Western Societies." *American Sociologist* 21:150–163.

UNICEF. 1990. *The State of the World's Children.* New York: Oxford University Press (published for United Nations Children's Fund).

USAID. 1990. *Child Survival: A Fifth Report to Congress on the USAID Program.* Washington, DC: U.S. Agency for International Development.

World Bank. 1989. *World Bank Development Report 1989.* New York: Oxford University Press (published for the World Bank).

Zeichner, Christiane I., ed. 1988. *Modern and Traditional Health Care in Developing Societies: Conflict and Co-Operation.* Lanham, MD: University Press of America.

Credits

AbuGharbieh, Patricia, and Wafika Suliman. "Changing the Image of Nursing in Jordan Through Effective Role Negotiation" is from *International Nursing Review, 39*(5), 1992. Reprinted by permission of the International Council of Nurses.

Album, Dag. "Patients' Knowledge and Patients' Work: Patient–Patient Interaction in General Hospitals" is from *Acta Sociologica, 32*(3), 1989. Reprinted by permission of Scandinavian University Press, Oslo, Norway.

Aldigé Hiday, Virginia. "The Social Context of Mental Illness and Violence" is from *Journal of Health and Social Behavior, 36*(2), June 1995. Reprinted by permission of the American Sociological Association and the author.

Bassett, Mary T., and Marvellous Mhloyi. "Women and AIDS in Zimbabwe: The Making of an Epidemic" is from *International Journal of Health Services, 21*(1), 1991. Reprinted by permission of the Baywood Publishing Co., Inc. and the authors.

Blue, Ilona. "Urban Inequalities in Mental Health: The Case of São Paulo, Brazil" is from *Environment and Urbanization, 8*(2), 1996. Copyright © 1996 by Ilona Blue. Reprinted by permission of the author.

Bullough, Vern L. "Status and Medieval Medicine" is from *Journal of Health and Human Behavior, 2*(1), 1961–1962.

Cameron, Donald, and Ian G. Jones. "John Snow, the Broad Street Pump and Modern Epidemiology" is from *International Journal of Epidemiology, 12*(4), 1983. Reprinted by permission of Oxford University Press and Ian G. Jones.

Cheng, Y. H., and Peter W. H. Lee. "Illness Behaviour in Chinese Medical Students" is from *Psychologia, 31*(4), 1988. Reprinted by permission of the Psychologia Society and the authors.

Chollet, Deborah J. "Health Care Financing in Selected Industrialized Nations: Comparative Analysis and Comment" is from *Trends in Health Benefits,* 1993. U.S. Department of Labor, Pension and Welfare Benefits Administration.

Christakis, N. A., N. C. Ware, and A. Kleinman. "Illness Behavior and the Health Transition in the Developing World" is reprinted from *Health and Social Change in International Perspective,* by L. Chen et al., editors. Copyright © 1994 Harvard Center for Population and Development Studies, Cambridge, MA.

Church, John, and Paul Barker. "Regionalization of Health Services in Canada: A Critical Perspective" is from *The International Journal of Health Services, 28*(3), 1998. Reprinted by permission of the Baywood Publishing Co. Inc., and the authors.

Claus, Lisbeth M. "The Development of Medical Sociology in Europe" is from *Social Science and Medicine, 17*(21), 1983. Reprinted by permission of Elsevier Science.

Conrad, Peter, and Eugene B. Gallagher. "Introduction" is from *Health and Health Care in Developing Countries: Sociological Perspectives.* Reprinted by permission of Temple University Press. Copyright © 1993 by Temple University. All Rights Reserved.

Davis, Karen, Gerard F. Anderson, Diane Rowland, and Earl P. Steinberg. "Future Directions for the U.S. Health Care System: A Long-Range Policy Proposal" is from *Health Care Cost Containment.* Copyright © 1990 by The Johns Hopkins University Press. Reprinted by permission.

Duffy, John. "The Community's Health" is from *From Humors to Medical Science: A History of Medicine,* 2nd edition. Copyright © 1993 by Board of Trustees of the University of Illinois. Used with permission of the University of Illinois Press.

Eddy, Diane M., Victoria Elfrink, Darlene Weis, and Mary Jane Schank. "Importance of Professional Nursing Values: A National Study of Baccalaureate Programs" is from *Journal of Nursing Education, 33*(6), 1994. Reprinted by permission of Slack, Inc.

Fox, Elaine. "Crossing the Bridge: Adaptive Strategies Among Navajo Health Care Workers" is from *Free Inquiry in Creative Sociology, 20*(1), 1992. Reprinted by permission of the University of Oklahoma.

Freeman, Hugh L. "The General Hospital and Mental Health Care: A British Perspective" is from *The Milbank Quarterly, 73*(4), 1995. Reprinted by permission of Blackwell Publishers.

Gallagher, Eugene B. "Sociological Studies of Third World Health and Health Care: Introduction" is from *Journal of Health and Social Behavior, 30,* December 1989. Reprinted by permission of the American Sociological Association and the author.

Gallagher, Eugene B., and Janardan Subedi. "Studying Health in Developing Societies: A Conceptually Informed Research Agenda" is reproduced by permission of the Anthropological Association. From *Central Issues in Anthropology, x,* 1992. Not for further reproduction.

Hafferty, Frederic W., and Bernice A. Pesosolido. Executive Summary of "Charting a Future Course for Medical Sociology: Final Report, 1996."

Hoff, Timothy J. "Same Profession, Different People: Stratification, Structure, and Physicians' Employment Choices" is from *Sociological Forum, 13*(1), 1998. Reprinted by permission of Kluwer Academic/Plenum Publishers.